The Persistence of Reality III

Texts without Referents

The Persistence of Reality

JOSEPH MARGOLIS

The Persistence of Reality

Texts without Referents

Reconciling Science and Narrative

JOSEPH MARGOLIS

Basil Blackwell

501

m32t

Basil Blackwell Ltd
108 Cowley Road, Oxford, OX4 1JF, UK

Basil Blackwell Inc.
432 Park Avenue South, Suite 1503
New York, NY 10016, USA

British Library Cataloguing in Publication Data

Margolis, Joseph, 1924–
    Texts without referents, reconciling
    science and narrative.
    1. Science : Philosophical perspectives.
    I. title   II. Series
    501

    ISBN 0-631-16319-0

Library of Congress Catalog Card No. 88-063521

Typeset in 10 on 12 pt Garamond
by Times Graphics, Singapore
Printed in Great Britain by T.J. Press Ltd, Padstow, Cornwall

For dolphins, falcons, brothers of the Sahel,
los desaparecidos, the jailors and the jailed
    of every apartheid,
    marshes, rain forests, the very air,
lucky lucky Fool however diminished within
    all this sweet space

Contents

Preface

Now that the third volume has been finished, I take the liberty of recommending a way of reading the trilogy that need not disturb the detailed arguments at any point in any one book but presumes to organize the reader's perception in moving from argument to argument and from book to book. The trilogy is a kind of novel, a *Bildungsroman*, in which the leading character is a philosophical theory that matures – by adventure and happenstance – through the principal *rites de passage* of our contemporary intellectual world. In that novelistic order of things, theories replace the humans who happen to theorize, and the fate and fortune of particular theories are traced through the details of their dialectical encounters with other theories that move through a common conceptual space.

I have always been attracted to Balzac's sense of a densely populated world of anonymous creatures from which Balzac knew he could draw at will any number of particular stories, articulating with infinite variety the seemingly regular dynamics of the encompassing collective world they share, imperfectly understand, are formed by, and tacitly alter through their own interventions.

I have gradually come to think of the many theories I have examined, philosophical and near-philosophical, as a slowly changing throng of ardent, familiar voices from which I too could draw the particular story of a favored theory – and, in doing that, thereby reveal the collective life of an entire population of theories. I find this conceit peculiarly apt applied to current philosophies; it also affords a convenient degree of freedom in presenting the "theory" of this trilogy. One can no longer just state one's theory flatly, the theory one means to defend against all competitors, meaning by that that the world will in due course yield the confirming evidence of its timeless truth. We are more interested in the risky process of theorizing viewed as a way of actually existing, of generating scientific and philosophical claims within a flux that denies the fixities of self and world – on the easy assumption of the reliability of which our shifting theories were once thought to be straightforwardly tested. Theorizing and theorized are one: the assessment of theories is the work of the theories assessed; and, for purposes of dispute, an independent world and a neutral judge are doubtful creatures of argumentative invention.

The paradoxes that result are clear enough. But here, for the moment, we may claim the temporary protection of a deliberate fiction. In a sense, the argument or story of the trilogy is intended to accommodate those paradoxes just at the point at which they cease to be tame enough to count as fictions. But *that* is the essential puzzle of our age.

I have tried to tell the story of a fledgling theory – my own, which I hope will prove one of the convincing visions of the future – coming to full strength within a world of established, official, hard-bitten, resistant, often inapt and inept theories. Confessedly, I take it to be an emancipative story, a story suited to our own particular age. It is, of course, a story of the springs of theory – hence also, with some humor, a story of the proliferating finished theories that those apparent sources appear to generate. It exhibits all the usual longings for a measure of relevance, tact, fairness, novelty, charm, scope, and power. But no author can really benefit from loitering too long among such provocative themes: they belong exclusively to the reader.

I believe I have collected a considerable throng in these books. There are a great many characters that drift in and out of particular scenes. I should like the reader to remember their first appearance and to anticipate a more and more rounded picture of each personage as it reappears – as one reads from scene to scene and from book to book and back again to earlier passages.

I can hardly convey how pretty the device seems to me: when these familiar personages make a new appearance "unaware" of the changed world in which they now move, betraying, in doing that, weaknesses in what we may remember (but need not) of the stance they appeared to take in earlier episodes.

There are central characters that inhabit all three volumes, villains and heroes alike, whose fortunes are ineluctably entangled with those of our maturing hero; and there are a great many characters of merely transient interest in the setting of a particular episode, that could easily sustain another story drawn out in another direction. They all belong to the same coherent world. They are, also, hardly fictions. I have given them authentic dialogues, pieces of quoted conversation drawn from their own original sources. I have done so partly because very few readers are likely to remember their sources or to believe that they are accurately reported, partly because introducing them thus corresponds with the conception of philosophy that is here being recorded and invented in the very act. A professional colleague (who shall remain nameless) once chided me for not getting on with the bare argument, for having cluttered my account with too many asides, too many quotes from this or that particular philosopher – as if (he insinuated) such references really mattered! His point was that I had obviously departed from the canonical style of philosophical debate. Of course he was right to say so. For my own part, I can only say that the style of argument I introduce here and throughout the trilogy is meant to undermine just that sort of timeless, context-free, ahistorical, conceptually secure mode of argument I consider utterly fatuous – the essential provocation, in fact, for certain recent well-known denials of the very relevance of the rigor and discipline of philosophical dispute itself. In philosophy, after all, the style of argument is its proper substance. (I see that I shall be misunderstood.)

I admit that the story idea is a little purple, but I enjoy it. It is, after all, a template for thinking of theories in a narrative way – agonistically. Beyond that, I insist only on this more serious claim: that philosophical argument *is* the dialogue of historicized and contexted theories. The very style of effective dispute is a function of the shifting conceptual world in which particular claims advance. It is for that reason that genuine argument is a form of rhetoric – or, better, a form of *praxis*. It is this single theme that is the intended novelty of the entire tale. The forms of argument are the forms of argument's history. Beyond the abstract stabilities of consistency, themselves always recovered anew (if recovered at all) from an endless succession of live disputes, debate favors the exemplars of actual persuasion. Original arguments seize and order their premises and conclusions from the Babel of theorizing voices that is our common culture. Consistency is the least of *their* concerns. They map a world waiting to be mapped, and the validity of their chartings is not separable from their own influence and power – simply because it is always implicitly judged (and then retrospectively denied) to be internal to them.

Order is a historical construction saved from arbitrarinesss by its own candid transience and dialectical stamina. In our own time, which, after all, is the time of this story, such themes are convincing only if they are conceived in a planetary spirit. Our arguments, therefore, cannot but be parochial. Still, we cannot help ourselves. In the meantime, I have tried to map the mappings of our thought and serve the paradoxes of self-reference.

Once again, I must thank Grace Stuart and now, also, Adele Harrison, for making the tale a readable tale.

Acknowledgements

With much alteration and many additions, the following have formed part of the chapters indicated: "The Technological Self," in Edmund F. Bynne and Joseph C. Pitt (eds), *Technological Transformation*, vol. 5 (Dordrecht: D. Reidel, forthcoming), (chapter 2); "Entailments from 'Naturalism = Phenomenology,'" in Mark A. Notturno (ed.), *Psychologism Revisited* (Dordrecht: D. Reidel, forthcoming) (chapter 3); "Constraints on the Metaphysics of Culture," *Review of Metaphysics*, XXXIX (1986) (chapter 6); "Reference as Relational: *Pro* and *Contra*," *Grazer Philosophische Studien*, XXV/XXVI (1985/6) (chapter 7); and "Forms of Life: Wittgenstein's Template for Psychological Development," in Michael Chapman and Roger A. Dixon (eds), *Meaning and the Growth of Understanding: Wittgenstein's Significance for Developmental Psychology* (Berlin: Springer-Verlag, 1987) (chapter 9).

Prologue:
A Sense of the Issue

The decisive fact to conjure with is the sheer proliferating reality of human life. It may seem as otiose to insist on it as it is preposterous to deny it. But the stubborn difficulties of analyzing human speech, human history, human consciousness, intentionality, the complexities of culture, human action and purposes, the ubiquity of meaning and significance, the very standing of the sciences as human projects, the puzzles of face-to-face communication, the interpretation of what is deposited by those now absent, the intelligibility of the world itself – all these issues have conspired to tempt us to favor a variety of desperate measures. Three strategies in particular may be mentioned, all tinged with the same contagion but hardly the same symptoms.

The most strenuous simply proclaims that the distinctively human – that is, the mental, the culturally formed forms of thinking, intending, acting, producing manifested in the life of human societies – does not exist or obtain, is not actual or real. Call this *eliminationism*. It tolerates, as a convenient but mere *façon de parler*, the *use* of the "human" idiom (the Intentional idiom, as we shall say), though it hardly ever strains to explain what it is to "use" the idiom as a merely temporary device. Presumably, to fall back to the "use" of a disciplined physical-language idiom is to use that idiom in exactly the same sense of "use" as applies to the soon-to-be-discarded idiom. The relation between the use of language and the discernment of the real structures of the world is normally not a question the eliminationist concedes an interest in, though the obvious import of his claim drives us to wonder what he might say. In any case, the clever eliminationist is not in a hurry to repudiate the language of intentions, of purposes, of meanings, of consciousness and the like. He is committed only to the presumed adequacy of (what we may call) a *physicalist* language: that is, that whatever is actual or existent can be completely described and explained in terms of a vocabulary confined to purely physical processes (and, of course, that such an explanation is itself able to yield to the same sort of description and explanation).

"Able to yield" is a deliberately contrived expression that suggests the possibility of a choice between two quite different strategies or the slippage possible between them. The eliminationist does not mean to describe or explain the *human* – in the sense remarked; he eliminates it altogether: what the term "human" appears to affirm is ultimately not (he claims) actual or real. It, too, is to be eliminated, together with the baggage of its pretended world, and *what* is to be explained is the approximative utility of that once-convenient *idiom* with respect to what, it is hoped, we may "now" affirm to be the fact of the matter.

If the human or "folk" idiom had been taken to be genuinely a realist idiom, however defective, the corrective strategy that could then claim to share the eliminationist's intent but not his specific enterprise would have tried to show that *what* was specified in the first was nothing more or less than what (if rightly vindicated, as by the Procedures of Science) the eliminationist was eventually bound to discover. Call the second strategy *reductionism*. Elimina-tionism and reductionism, then, are two forms of *physicalism*, the thesis (broadly speaking) that, if anything is discernible as actual or existent – in par-ticular, if anything is discernible as actual or existent by means of other-than-purely-physical evidence, grounds, criteria or the like – then they are also discernible by purely physical ones. Reductionism need not deny the reality of what is discerned and described by other-than-physical distinctions; it holds only that what is thus identified is identical with what is correspondingly iden-tified by purely physical means, or that what is identified by the first is at least approximatively what is more accurately or more precisely identified by the second, or that the two idioms identify in quite different ways and for quite different purposes the same entities or phenomena, which can be satisfactorily discerned for all realist purposes in purely physical terms.

So reductionism itself comes in a variety of shades. It may subscribe to type- or token-identity, or it may concede a near- or approximative identity (by way of intent), or it may fall back to equivalences of truth-claims between the two idioms without invoking identity, or it may offer a mixture of these alter-natives. Viewed generically as physicalism, what we have called reductionism is itself more usually characterized as "reductive physicalism" (the identity theory, say) or as "nonreductive physicalism" (the avoidance of identity by way of extensional equivalences).

These terminological niceties are perhaps too baldly stated, offered too early in the airing of our topic. But they manage to capture the principal lines of speculation in the entire Anglo-American range of philosophical practices at the present time. They are pitted against one another at the moment. The reductionist strain, perhaps best represented just now in the work of Donald Davidson and somewhat less unambiguously in the work of Noam Chomsky and his partisans, appears the more concessive of the two, since the full play of the human world is there admitted to be actual at the start. The eliminationist strain, perhaps best represented (as it has been for a considerable while now) by Wilfrid Sellars, is clearly collecting vigorous new adherents among the visionaries of cognitive science and neuroscience who treat reference to information and to higher-order structures of information (as in language and thought) as the work of what (they say) cannot be more than a merely heuristic and temporary convenience.

The detailed pursuit of these alternatives was in large part the concern of *Science without Unity*, the second volume of this trilogy. We shall not chase after them here. But they need to be remembered with appropriate care because, in dismissing them (in dismissing them with cause), we are left with the enormous burden of trying to make sense of *a range of real distinctions that do not in principle belong to the actual order of the physical world or do not belong to it (reductively or nonreductively) if they cannot be managed by way of extensional equivalence or identity or approximations to either.*

There is a great deal of worthwhile work in Western philosophy that ignores or postpones the inevitable confrontation with the physicalist challenge. Even in the Anglo-American tradition, although their sympathies are clearly opposed to the physicalist's thesis, one cannot say that the arguments of the original pragmatists – Charles Sanders Peirce, William James, and John Dewey – actually came to grips in a satisfactorily frontal way with the question posed. This may explain why, for instance, the fashionable American pragmatists of our own day – W. V. Quine, Donald Davidson, and Richard Rorty – none of whom has really earned the right to champion his particular version of physicalism, nevertheless do support one form or another of the physicalist program. Continental European philosophers, on the other hand, have almost solidly opposed every strand of argument that would lead to either eliminationism or reductionism. This is the convergently insistent theme of philosophy from Kant to the present, featured particularly in Hegel, Marx, Nietzsche, Husserl, Heidegger, Wittgenstein, and the enormously varied, disputatious currents of current phenomenological, existential, heremeneutic, structuralist, Frankfurt School, deconstructive, genealogical, post-structuralist, postmodernist developments.

The essential theme of the Continental European traditions, we may dare to suggest, is conveyed by the doublet of terms *subjectivity* and *intentionality*. By the first is meant (at least) the unavoidable posit of a certain precondition for every articulated cognitive relationship, for every picture of the supposed relationship between the (or a) recognizable real world and a cognizing agent or "site" apt for discerning the features of that world. That precondition may be construed *mythically* (as in Heidegger) as the predifferentiated disclosing of Being to some suitable receptive power (*Dasein*, in Heidegger's idiom), or else *critically* (as, in different ways, in Kant, Hegel, Marx, and Husserl) as the reflexive correction of what appears to be cognitively presented.

The pathos of both lines of theory rests with the ultimate defeat of any and every presumption of privilege in discerning what the putative performational forces contribute to the prejudice or distortion or delusion or normalization or necessity of our cognitive endeavors. On that reading, Hegel and Nietzsche may prove to be in rather different ways, the supreme ironists of every form of rational or objective inquiry and commitment. In any case, the preformative focus – tacit, inexplicit, guessed at reflexively within the terms of species survival, within the terms of the viability of historical societies – is taken to be centered in an otherwise unnamed source with respect to which our cognitive and cognitively informed behavior is the uniquely important flower. The very achievement of science, therefore, argues the existence of real agents capable of science; and the precondition of that achievement obliges us to admit an enormous complex of phenomena (the site of "subjectivity") that may not yield to objectivist, physicalist, extensionalist or allied strategies already carpentered by fixing the lineaments of the real world for actual scientists (by way of reductionism) or for imagined gods (by the *façon de parler* of the elimin-ationists).

Currently, "subjectivity" is the buzzword of the Husserlian, Heideggerian, Gadamerian, and even Nietzschean enthusiasts. "Rationality" is the corre-sponding, explicitly more upbeat, term favored by latter-day Kantians, Hegelians, Marxists, Frankfurt School theorists, vestigial or redeemed Enlight-enment theorists, and self-styled Continental pragmatists. By a gymnastic feat of some considerable exertion, Jürgen Habermas manages to be the best specimen of the second group. The partisans of "subjectivity" are – much to the dismay of the Hegelians and Husserlians and hermeneuts – rapidly collecting as the spiritual progeny of a more radical Heidegger and of the mar-velously dubious Jacques Derrida. The essential point of all this ferment, however, remains unchallenged within the recognizable quarrels of the most opposed schools: that is,

1 that the intelligible structures of, or the categories of objective analysis applied to, the world are, in some ineluctable way, artifacts of the precognitive conditions of human existence itself, from which they tacitly appear to emerge, to constrain inquiry and behavior (the theme of "*subjectivity*"; and

2 that cognitive inquiry and its linkage to such preconditions exhibit an ineliminable contingency, diversity, open-endedness, non-closure, arti-factuality, proneness to discontinuity and incommensurability that cannot ensure, and may not be compatible with the presumption that any line of argument could ensure, the eventual victory of *any* science or rational inquiry restricted to the eliminationist or reductionist options (the theme of "*intentionality*").

Intentionality, therefore is, in effect, the mark at least of just what is ignored or overridden by the first two strategies mentioned: by the eliminationist (notoriously, by Quine even more assertively than by Sellars), who simply denies that, in "limning the true and ultimate structure of reality," we shall have any need for intentionality, whatever its complexities may be supposed to be; and by the reductionist (mostly ambitiously, by Davidson), who, by a sleight of hand, say by applying *a priori* a Tarskian-like model of truth to natural languages, is at once and with no sweat at all able to ensure an extensionally satisfactory regimentation of such languages – that is, a happy and splendidly convenient regimentation suited to the requirements of physicalism.

The Continental European traditions are, to say the least, not yet convinced by such revelations. Unfortunately (candidly), the most ardent and influential theorists have never brought their questions to bear on the detailed claims of their Anglo-American opponents. The latter, therefore, feel entirely justified in treating the work of these theorists as mere mouthings, as nearly utterly contemptible. They are demonstrably wrong in this: the relevant illiteracy runs in both directions. The themes anchored by the notions of "subjectivity" and "intentionality" are profound ones, almost completely neglected by the present generation of American philosophers devoted to the analytic tradition. The truth is that no one can hope to show that eliminationism or reductionism – physicalism in short – is in principle incoherent or flatly untenable. But, then, no one can hope to show that the repudiation of such programs is, in its turn, irrational or incoherent or untenable or even weaker than the other. No, the arguments required need to be more temperate and less grandiose; and the arena of pertinent contest surely centers on the peculiar complexities of intentional life, particularly those of language, communication, history, interpretation, art, traditional practice, work, survival, science that constitute the unique features of human culture – just those, in fact, that are never central (if present at all) in theorizing about the physical sciences or the physical world "limned" by those sciences.

There is, it may be admitted, a certain madcap tendency in the Continental traditions that, fearing the philistinism of the unity-of-science program, fearing virulent pockets of vestigial positivism, has sought to preserve the supposed purity of the human, the "subjectivity" (the "Other," *Autrui*) along lines often motivated by moral, spiritual, and religious concerns thought to be fatally at risk under the pressure of the kind of directives just mentioned. Perhaps the partisans of this tendency are right. But, if they are, the danger perceived hardly vindicates any third strategy that removes the human from the ken of straightforward linguistic categories of analysis. Call this strategy – by a frankly pejorative term of art – *ineffabilism*: the advocacy of the thesis that *what is most essential to the human is inaccessible to the constative or declarative devices of speech admittedly suited also to making reference to individuated objects, to reidentifying them under conditions of change, to predicating of them what may be true or false, to confirming in whatever way we do what we thus predicate of them.*

The tendency in question sometimes takes the relatively moderate form of denying that the categories suited to discourse about "mere" things could be adequate to the "subjective" or "intentional" complexities of the human world; but sometimes it pretends that every effort to ascribe general attributes to "subjects" fails in a radical sense to be pertinent at all. Heidegger seems to oscillate between these two attitudes; at times, he even inclines toward the latter, as in his more pessimistic later writings when he was greatly discouraged by the encompassing vision of modern technology.

The most extreme version of this third position, influenced by Heidegger as well as by religious speculations regarding personal encounters with the divine, surfaces in a notable way in the work of Emmanuel Levinas. Levinas's view is worth bearing in mind at least because of its willing attraction to the incoherent. For Levinas both entertains the prospect of individuation or identifying referentially "any" and every "Other" (that is, any other human "subject," *Autrui*) said to be utterly, unfathomably, different from "mere" things or objects, *and* explicitly denies that such "subjects" *are* conceptually accessible at all through standard ascriptions made of human faces and human behavior. But that is flatly incoherent, since one must both affirm the presence of the Other and deny the constative conditions under which that may be done.

Furthermore, what was informally identified as the more moderate version of ineffabilism quite often resists acknowledging the adequacy or even pertinence of any determinate constative discourse – while not actually denying that there is any suitable such discourse about human persons. The usual objection is the need to avoid "metaphysics" (Heidegger), essentialisms or conceptual fixities of every sort (as in certain uses made of Derrida and Foucault and Nietzsche, and in the ulterior fear of capitulating to the tentacular powers of physicalism and its allies). In this sense, the "moderate" position is little more than a dodge for the obviously mad one. One may find more than a touch of this tendency in, for instance, the work of Hans-Georg Gadamer, in his coyer discussions of the methodological prospects of the human sciences; and, among recent Anglo-American authors, in Thomas Nagel.

What is wanted, therefore, is a fourth strategy – that is, a family of "fourth" strategies that reject ineffabilism altogether while charging that the various programs of eliminationism and reductionism have not delivered (and seem unable to deliver) satisfactorily on the analysis of the apparently unique distinctions of the world of human culture. The theme of this fourth strategy is almost absurdly straightforward.

The correction needed proceeds in two directions that are ultimately one. For one thing, even constative discourse about the physical world requires a subject, a self or agent sufficiently complex to be the site of genuine speech acts and of other activities that the mastery of language makes possible. For another, the theory of selves or persons must accommodate the entire range of human life and history and cultural achievement. The trouble with ineffabilism is that it disqualifies itself from being capable of addressing the very phenomena it wishes to set apart; and the trouble with physicalism is that it hurries too quickly to disclaim the need for ampler conceptual resources than its own, without ever having had to demonstrate the precise contexts in which it is reasonably adequate and those in which it is not.

It is easy enough to enumerate what the decisive test would have to consider. The issues are primarily ontological and methodological: the analysis of the nature of man and his cultural world, and the prospects of a human science accommodating that analysis. What will they include? We can only give a short tally here, but its topics form the master themes of the growing inquiry of this trilogy. They come to an insistent focus in the following at least – which almost to the item, are neglected by the physicalists. Here they are: on the ontological side,

- the preformation of human thinking,
- the social construction of selves,
- the ontology of persons and things,
- the emergence of human culture,
- the historicity of human existence,
- the symbiosis of the psychological and the societal,
- the praxical nature of thought,
- the social division of cultural labor,
- the reality of the intensional features of intentional life,
- the incarnate complexity of human aptitudes,
- the absence of system in the human world,
- the causal effectiveness of human action,
- the ubiquity of consensual interpretation;

and on the methodological side,

- the relationship between the natural and the human sciences,
- the nature of history,
- the meaning of intentionality,
- the objectivity of self-description,
- the mutual intelligibility of different societies,
- the conditions of knowledge.

No theory worth its salt can fail to come to terms with this entire array – and more – coherently, comprehensively, dialectically against all opposing views. Anything less is a fake, a whistling in the academic wind with the sole object of beckoning compliant followers.

The argument that follows is an attempt to meet the requirements of the fourth strategy. No known physicalism has ever addressed the full array just tallied or addressed it in an open forum. As I write, two fine new specimens have just appeared: one incomparably more powerful than the other; the second incomparably more popular than the first.[1] Neither addresses questions of historicity, the formation of the self, *praxis*, interpretation, social institutions, the complexities of intentionality uniquely keyed to human existence, the properties of a culture, or the like. Which is to say, both are entirely characteristic of the breed. It is fair to claim, therefore, that the fortunes of the fourth strategy are hardly damaged by the achievements of either of the first two strategies. In fact, the general topic of the ontology of culture and of man as an encultured entity is almost unknown in American philosophy except for the occasional invasion by Continental European thought; and, in Europe, though it is certainly explored, the ontology of culture is almost never examined in a detailed way against the encroachments of physicalism. The history of these developments signifies that we are at a new threshold (if we choose to act). We need to match whatever rigor (*not* the specific devices – simplistic extensionalisms, for instance) the physicalists may with some justice claim to have honored; and we need to accommodate whatever the Continentaal European traditions have rightly marked as distinctly human, though without any false loyalty to their own often peculiar doctrines (ineffabilist excesses, in particular).

The ideal stages of the argument required are obvious enough. First of all, provision must be made for the continuity of constative discourse across the overlapping spaces of physical nature and human culture. In thus outflanking the third strategy, and with a mind to escaping the traps of a dualism of substance or of an even more impossible idealism, we need to install a suitable *materialism* (that is, a nonreductive materialism). Here, it will be helpful to contrast physicalisms and materialisms: the first are committed (eliminatively or otherwise) to the adequacy of a physical vocabulary for all that is actual; the second are open to the emergent appearance of entities that, though not composed of anything but physical or material substance (insofar as they are characterizable compositionally), exhibit real properties that are not amenable to physicalist strategies.

From this vantage, the original positivist objectives of the 1920s and 1930s still afford a sense of direction for the principal philosophical contests of the end of the century. Their naiveté may have been softened, but the essential issues have hardly changed as much as many would now claim.

There appears to be only one ontological option that is both promising and capable of escaping the shoals of physicalism and ineffabilism (and the minor waters of dualism and idealism). That is the option of what we may call *incarnatism,* the thesis that all properties unique to the cultural world are incarnate in physical or material respects – that is, *emergent properties indissolubly complex or monadic as emergent, from which may be abstracted but not separated their intentional import* (their representational, expressive, semantic, significative, semiotic, purposive, stylistic, historical, interpretive and similar import). In the analytic tradition, the closest (but frankly insufficient) approximation to this thesis appears in the work of P. F. Strawson. What follows may be regarded as an explicit attempt to redeem and apply the enormous power of its original insight.

The crucial conceptual adjustments that this option requires include the following:

(a) that we examine the sense in which we cannot understand ourselves and our culture at any discursive level at which what emerges distinctively in human culture is terminologically precluded from our descriptive and explanatory vocabulary;

(b) that we examine how we must characterize the nature of cultural entities and phenomena so as to match, in theorizing about them, whatever we intend to predicate of them;

(c) that we examine what constraints such adjustments impose on a reasonable analysis of the most strenous topics of the human world – namely, thinking, language, knowledge and understanding, reference, action, history, societal life, the structure of persons;

(d) that we examine whether we can, whether we need not, whether we are unable to, construe the spaces of physical nature and human culture as closed systems of any sort, and what, if the human world does not form a system (of finitely many elements formed and transformed in accord with finitely many rules or laws), must be minimally conceded regardings its structure so that it may yet escape being construed as chaotic or anarchical or incapable or supporting the regularity of our sciences at least; and

(e) that we examine these questions so that the principal philosophical currents of our time may be brought to bear dialectically on each, on the inclusive ordering of all, and on the competing conceptual visions each offers against the other.

These are the issues pursued in what follows, partly caught up from the first two volumes of this trilogy. The keywords associated with each topic suggest a conspiracy of argument loose-limbed enough not to be completely guessed at the start, but sufficiently instructive to yield a small economy. Their themes (really, their keywords) may be collected in this way:

(a) emergence, top–down sciences;
(b) embodiment, incarnation;
(c) praxism, psychologism, sociology of knowledge, critique;
(d) form of life, life-world;
(e) naturalism, phenomenology, pragmatism.

Merely to list them is to deaden the significance of invoking them. For, there is at the present time no ramified account of these matters that bridges the best of the Anglo-American and Continental European philosophical traditions, reconciles the detailed analysis of all of the assembled topics within the terms of an emergent or nonreductive materialism, and in doing that demonstrates the sense in which the principal philosophical movements of our time may be said to converge on a novel and resilient pragmatism.

Throughout the account promised, one extraordinarily difficult theme will remain tacit in every argument. That is, the theme that has so clearly annoyed the settled authorities of canonical philosophy: the theme of the flux. It has been pursued, of course, maddeningly – sometimes madly – through late

Heideggerian, late Nietzschean, deconstructive, poststructuralist, postmodernist utterances. But it does have a profound relevance that we ignore at our peril, and it is certainly not captured by any particular school of thought. It cannot be captured: it would instantly dissolve if it were.

The best way to identify it is this. Consider that Husserl formulated a supreme worry about every cognitive endeavor that is assured of its competence and objectivity. Husserl asks what the range of imaginable possibilities is, housed in ordinary inquiries, that might yield a sense of conceptual invariances – invariances that would function as an insuperable formal constraint operating *not* on the distributed claims of the first sort but on the constitutive resources by which all such claims were formed. That is, Husserl asks us to consider whether the apparent fixities of our cognitive categories are truly unalterable: phenomenology is the (Kantian-like) pursuit of that question. But Husserl himself does not do full justice to a deep possibility inhering in his own question: namely, that the apparent invariances of his own procedure may well be an artifact of the utterly contingent life-world (*Lebenswelt*) we *happen* to inhabit, being the historicized, encultured, preformed or constituted creatures that we appear to be. We cannot *say* – when we cannot say by phenomenological reflection – that the seeming conceptual invariances we confront are not true invariances. They are at least "in-variances" (in Merleau-Ponty's interesting sense), apparent fixities *in* the very flux of *our* world. Only by way of something like the *via negativa* can we signify that we respect such in-variances for what they are *in* signifying our sense of the radical, insuperable limit of the horizon in which we do so. *There* is the theme that unites Hegel and Nietzsche and James and Wittgenstein and Derrida and Foucault.

There is no short way to summarize the philosophical effect of applying this "further" theme. But, if we take it that man and his culture not only have histories but are historicized – that is, that their very nature is to acquire (to be constituted) a nature congruent with the form of life (Wittgenstein), *praxis* (Marx), life-world (Husserl), or *episteme* (Foucault) within which they flourish and are reflexively identified – then we shall have taken a first step to understanding its import. For, whatever is thus identified within the horizon of those collective contexts is open to a radical and discontinuous respecification within another "similar" ensemble that, in the nature of things, we cannot possibly guess at. Our in-variances, therefore, are never invariances in Husserl's sense and, because they are not, we cannot claim that they are approximations of such invariances either.

We cannot live with this worry alone, however. The deeper point is that we guess at those in-variances we believe to be the best candidates for genuine invariances; and we invariably settle for those that, in some limited span of the flux, manage to remain reasonably intact. It is only the slow pace of conceptual change that yields a tolerable assurance regarding the structure of our world. But it is not a principled victory. That it is not explains the sense in which our transcendental arguments are themselves correspondingly infected.

The vision is a heady one, hopefully sufficient for the volume that follows. It is, however, not meant to be confined to the bare lines of convenience we have favored. For example, the world of art and history and human conversation and personal and public committment has hardly been given its full due in these pages. The distinctions need a longer inning of their own. Also, the parochialism of the disputes collected cannot be ignored – and cannot be effectively overcome, unless by enjoining the efforts of others better placed for the global forum that is now in the offing.

Note

1   I refer, respectively, to John F. Post, *The Faces of Existence; An Essay in Nonreductive Metaphysics* (Ithaca, NY: Connell University Press, 1987); and to Daniel C. Dennett, *The Intentional Stance* (Cambridge, Mass.: MIT Press, 1987).

Introduction

1

Naturalism, Phenomenology, Deconstruction

I

To admit, in however attenuated or tacit or habituated or unreflective a spirit, the sheer aptitude of human beings to affirm this or that in a languaged way, or their ability to act effectively and improvisationally in matching their manipulation of the world and themselves for their own felt needs, argues the ineliminability of the cognitive dimension of human life – and, logically, the ineliminability of a nominalizable locus or referent for cognitive attributions. One cannot really categorize the human world below this level of imputable structures: first, because discourse (human discourse) is inherently reflexive, therefore (in that sense) conscious and self-conscious, therefore cognitive; secondly, because our reflexive powers are implicated in whatever we affirm about the world; and, thirdly, because there is no known conceptual strategy by which the cognitive can be meaningfully eliminated from science or history or biography or from any descriptive reports of the same, or can be reduced to the terms of any vocabulary that scrupulously precludes whatever we take to be the attributes of the cognitive.

The point is beyond serious controversy, though it is everywhere controverted or abused where admitted. It is, also, the sane beginning for that most preposterous and charming speculation, by Julian Jaynes, regarding the "bicameral mind":

> Just as the property of wetness [Jaynes says, sensibly introducing his own mad account] cannot be derived from the properties of hydrogen and oxygen alone, so consciousness emerged at some point in evolution in a way underivable from its constituent parts. . . . We first have to start [if our theories are to have any point] from the top, from some conception of what consciousness is, from what our own introspection is. We have to be sure of that, before we can enter the nervous system and talk about its neurology.[1]

(In according Jaynes the privilege of first reference, here, we are, it must be said, easing ourselves into a remarkable thicket of puzzles – one, in fact, that

Jaynes himself has absolutely nothing to say about. It concerns the conceptual interrelationship between theorizing about the nature of the human self and theorizing about the linkage between the philosophical programs of naturalism, phenomenology, and deconstruction. There is no familiar way to address the issue. We have to invent one; and, in doing that, it will prove extremely important to have before us the clear sense of the lack of fixity of human nature itself. Jaynes provides that sense, because the very extravagance of his specific thesis confirms the reasonableness of the generic doctrine it instantiates; and the generic doctrine is just the one that needs to be recovered through a review of the complex connections binding naturalism, phenomenology, and deconstruction to one another. Jaynes's theory, frankly, is a disposable paper plate. We are not likely to confuse its own substance with what we shall oblige it to bear.)

Jaynes is not careful enough, but he makes a very good beginning. Theorizing about consciousness and cognition cannot fail to be top–down reflections at least initially. They could be transformed via a bottom–up account if emergence (in Jaynes's sense of "underivability") proved to be untenable. The claim of emergence *might* prove untenable, but there is no evidence that it is.[2] Similarly, it is true that we "first have to start" from what we take consciousness and cognition to be and then move on to "its" neurology; but, again, in doing that, we do not "have to be sure" about these matters introspectively, except in the benign sense that we provisionally fix what we take our most salient reflexive findings to be – subject to the vagaries of the shifting history of reflection and introspection (which are not quite the same thing, subject to the untotalizable plurality of human histories and cultures in which the conscious and the cognitive are emergent (the full import of which Jaynes does not fully explicate), subject to revisions due to our systematizing sciences (which, as in the tricornered disputes of naturalism, phenomenology, and deconstruction, cannot be relied on to permit us to regard our "straightforward" reports of consciousness as straightforward enough).

What is most intriguing about Jaynes's account is his double claim (1) that "consciousness" has a historically datable beginning; and (2) that the structure of the "mind" has been essentially, culturally, altered in the interval prior to and through the emergence of consciousness. Here, Jaynes sets the problem of the "origin of consciousness";[3] announces that "consciousness is a much smaller part of our mental life than we are conscious of";[4] affirms that even in speech "consciousness functions in the decision as to what to say, how we are to say it, and when we say it," but "in speaking or writing we are not really conscious of what we are actually doing at the time . . . the orderly and accomplished succession of phonemes or of written letters is somehow done for us";[5] assures us that it is possible "to conceive of human beings who are not conscious and yet can learn and solve problems";[6] suggests the solution of the puzzle of the mind, by maintaining that "thinking . . . is not conscious. Rather, it is an automatic process following a struction [that is, an instruction and construction automatized in the mind] and the materials on which the struction is to operate [by a kind of behavioral control]";[7] insists that "in reality, consciousness has no location whatever except as we imagine it has";[8] theorizes that "subjective conscious mind [the modern mind that refers experience and behavior to an 'I'] is an analog ['the analog "I" – also, the meta-phor "me" '] of what is called the real world . . . Its relation is of the same order as mathematics . . . Like mathematics, it is an operator rather than a thing or repository. And it is intimately bound up with volition and decision."[9] "Consciousness," then, "is the invention of an analog world, on the basis of language, paralleling the behavioral world."[10] It is an invention later than the appearance of writing (not yet alphabetic), which Jaynes dates from around 3000 BC. It is later than the *Iliad*, for "there is in general no consciousness in the *Iliad*."[11] And in fact it can be dated as occurring more or less "toward the end of the second millennium BC," for a variety of reasons signifying the break-down of the "bicameral mind."[12] The important point is that "consciousness is chiefly a *cultural* introduction, learned on the basis of ✓ language and taught to others, rather than any biological necessity. But that it had and still has a survival value suggests that the change to consciousness may have been assisted by a certain amount of natural selection."[13]

Jaynes may be taken to have formulated here the most extreme contempo-rary version we have of the theory that the conscious or subjective self is a his-torical invention – in a sense, also a fiction – of the *mental* processes that actualize language, the activity and technology of societies, the achievement of civilization itself. The specific theory Jaynes advances is preposterous in part, in part surely mistaken about the historical evidence from ancient civilizations, and in part misleading because of its silence regarding patent factors that should not have been ignored. For example, the family correspondence of travelling bureaucrats of the Egyptian Old Kingdom and the study of contemporary Stone Age peoples (such as the Waorani of the upper Amazon) confirm rather convincingly that the societies Jaynes effectively takes as his par-adigms of bicameral man do not actually support his thesis. His specific thesis is probably coherent though vague on essential details; and he pays no heed at all to the possibility that the "bicameral" mode may itself be no more than an institutionalized altered state or something of the sort functioning intermit-tently within a larger mode in which fully "conscious" states are also implicated. In any case, the generic speculation is much more interesting and more plausible than the details of Jaynes's own theory. It may be just plain false to claim that, in the age of the "bicameral mind," "human nature was split in two, an executive part called a god, and follower part called a man. Neither part was conscious";[14] and it may be a conceptual blunder to have assigned these different parts to the left brain and the right brain just like that.[15] There is no plausible reason why the *categories* by the use of which ascriptions made of the neurophysiological processes of the left and right brains should be the same (or of the same gauge) as those used in making ascriptions of molar cognitive agents (on any of a wide variety of theories). On the contrary, the terms of the first are understandably addressed to the *sub*-functions of the second.

But there are more important considerations that need to be mentioned in taking Jaynes's account seriously – not so much for its own particular claims as for what it cannot avoid or ignore in making its claims and for what it should not have avoided or ignored in putting them forward. (In saying this, we must remind ourselves that we are treating Jaynes as a convenient spokesman for an entire collection of diverging views that regard human nature – human persons and human selves – as historically contingent manifestations.)

The considerations in question are of two sorts: first, Jaynes is obliged to identify two "parts" of the mental life of human nature for the interval he has in mind – two distinct sites of *something* like agency, sensory perception, executive initiative and subordinate compliance, memory, linguistic ability, practical and artisanal skills; and, secondly, Jaynes is obliged to make *some* provision for the *cognitive* processing of sensory perception consistent with his denial of the consciousness of the supposed two "parts" of the bicameral mind. What he says in both cases helps immensely in leading us to appreciate what appear to be the conceptual minima without the use of which we have no idea of how to make pertinent sense of the familiar data of ancient Egyptian, Mesopotamian, Greek, and Hebrew civilizations – even if we remain all the while loyal to Jaynes's own theory. In this sense, Jaynes's theory, though it hardly ventures a conceptual analysis of the viability of the distinctions involving mind, consciousness, persons, and selves that he introduces, does manage – largely because of its *outré* presumption – to bring us closer to certain essential issues than we are otherwise likely to be able to approach in as economical or direct a manner.

Here is what he says:

> The gods [Jaynes here theorizes about the *Iliad*] take the place of consciousness. The beginnings of action are not in conscious plans, reasons, and motives; they are in the actions and speeches of gods. . . . The gods were organizations of the central nervous system and can be regarded as personae in the sense of poignant consistencies through time, amalgams of parental or admonitory images. The god is a part of the man, and quite consistent with this conception is the fact that the gods never step outside of natural laws.[16]

In effect, men are robots, automata; and the gods are similarly automatized though they function executively rather in the form of internal but separate voices, internal "hallucinations" capable of inventive and improvisational maneuvers within fairly narrow limits; their directive function is essentially "behavioral" (hence, interpretable entirely in terms of law-like bodily functions); and the man-"part" quite simply and automatically obeys what it hears (schizophrenically) as its interior orders.[17] What this means is that, for conceptual reasons, Jaynes is obliged to construe *both* parts of the bicameral mind as distinct persons or personae, "poignant consistencies through time," functional centers of command and acquiescence of a linguistically informed sort – not yet "subjective selves" in the post-bicameral sense. Jaynes is obliged to introduce *persons* to collect the relatively unitary locus from which issue the declared orders as well as to collect the relatively unitary locus from which issues the appropriately compliant behavior. These "persons" are functional sites, not substantive entities of any deeper sort (not souls, for instance), provisionally linked to "organizations of the central nervous system" but identified, theoretically, *by* their mode of functioning. They are not (yet) *selves*, in whatever sense suits the modern description of the unified, subjective, self-referential "I" – through which may be collected all the mental functions distributed through our familiar subjective life (the "metaphorical 'me' "). On this view, the personae of the god-"part" and the man-"part" of the mental life of humans are historical developments as much as are modern subjective selves; they are alterable personae *only* on the concession of some more generic functioning of persons (at the human level at which language truly functions as language – when, say, "the first sentences with a noun subject and a predicative modifier . . . may have occurred somewhere between 25,000 and 15,000 BC"[18]) in virtue of which the bicameral "parts" *are* able to confunction efficciently in the performance of any *"enduring* tasks."[19]

On this fanciful but sill coherent account, we are very close to admitting an essential functional site of articulate speech and culturally significant work that is the generic form of the human person, of which the "parts" posited in the bicameral theory are (perhaps) no more than historically transient manifestations (personae).

To this we may now add Jaynes's speculation (also conceptually obligatory for him) of the internal processing of perceptual cognition on the part of schizophrenics – who (in effect) are vestigial exemplars of the bicameral mind: "Of immense importance is the fact that the nervous system of a [schizophrenic] patient *makes* simple perceptual judgments of which the patient's "self" is not aware. And these . . . may then be transposed into voices that seem prophetic."[20] What we must remember is that, once discursive language is introduced, a language of constatives and imperatives, humans – *persons*, in the sense just drawn from Jaynes's account of the personae of the bicameral age – *must be assigned cognitive powers in some degree congruent with the accomplishments of their particular culture.* In this sense, Jaynes is obliged to improvise *some* idiom for accommodating "perceptual judgments." He treats them as cognitively pertinent – they are judgments, after all – but he assigns them to "the nervous system" and not to the (subjective) selves that (among schizophrenics) are said to be unaware of them. They are assigned, therefore, to personae that are not yet selves, and they confirm the ineliminability of some such functional site for such collected powers. Selves and personae may be historically variable ways of organizing such powers as those of stating and ordering; but those powers are, functionally (if they are, indeed, close to the

ineliminable minima of distinctly human functioning), the powers of suitably
"poignant consistencies through time, amalgams of parental or admonitory
images" or the like. They are, effectively, *the powers of persons*.

Jaynes's treatment of them as predicative continuities of some sort obscures
the fact that they must be ascribed to some suitable referent and obscures the
fact that "the nervous system" is not (or is not demonstrably) a referent to
which the functional (mental) attributes in question *can* be suitably adequated.
The confusion or conflating of the predicative and substantive treatment of
persons or person-like referents is a standard tendency in contemporary analytic
theories of mind – nowhere more explicit perhaps then in the theory advanced
by Derek Parfit.[21] Jaynes obviously means to hold to a fashionably
neurophysiological account of the mental, while permitting himself the
advantage of certain functionalized liberties of description he may require; but
he never addresses the essential question of the relationship between a purely
neurophysiological idiom and a richly intentionalized idiom. If, however, the
great civilizations he scans are real, then it is quite impossible to view the functional idiom as a mere *façon de parler*. There are, in fact, two quite distinct considerations that Jaynes overlooks – and that are characteristically overlooked in
the reductionist literature: (1) that the mental attributions in question
(whatever they are and however changeable they may be) must be ascribed to
stable referents of some sort; and (2) that the ascriptions thus made must be
conceptually adequate to the referents in question, in terms of a theory of the
nature of the latter suited to receiving the former.[22]

Persons, then, are the numerically unitary (functional) site of whatever
constative, imperative, active, perceptual, compliant functions are collected
within the mental life of humans. The theory of bicameral persons remains a
theory of persons. Human persons cannot but exhibit a certain *unicity*, a
numerically individuatable locus of functions minimally sufficient to count as
the linguistically apt creature the human being is; and, in exhibiting that unicity, it must also exhibit a certain minimal *unity* of cofunctioning functions
that, through whatever transient phases it may historically manifest, permits us
to assign, distributively, any and all the cofunctioning functions we do assign as
the "poignant consistencies through time" of this or that culture.

It is entirely possible to deny the invariance or essentialist standing of this or
that theory of the personae of this or that historical age or, in the decisive case,
the invariance or essentialist standing of reflexively and introspectively subjective *selves* ("egos," "I's"). But, if the foregoing holds, it is impossible to
challenge either prevalent views of the peculiar unity of modern selves or the
species-wide fixity of such unified selves without first acknowledging both the
unicity and the minimal unity of generic, species-wide persons. Paradigmatically, man is a cogniscent or cognizing being distinguished by his linguistic
aptitude and by his aptitude for perception and action indissolubly joined to,
and informed by, that linguistic ability. To admit such abilities *is* to admit
both the historically contingent personae of different civilizations and different

ages and the projection, within the limits of our familiarity with these, of a universalized or provisionally invariant notion of what it is, generically, to be a
human person.

There are, also, further conceptual benefits that may conveniently be
extracted from Jaynes's undertaking. First of all, in speculating (rather
skillfully) about "the stages of language development," Jaynes remarks that
"*Each new stage of words literally created new perceptions and attentions, and
such new perceptions and attentions resulted in important cultural changes which
are reflected in the archaeological record.*"[23] Generalized, this means that the
stages of true language as well as the variability of natural languages and
natural cultures (once true language has been achieved) causally entail the
emergence of (a) new personae *and* (b) new ways in which such personae perceive and attend to the world they share. In effect, Jaynes provides a
compendious schema for understanding what we should mean by construing
the nature of human persons historically. They are individually what they are
symbiotically – in virtue of sharing a common language and a common culture;
and their nature is no more fixed than are their language and culture.

Secondly, they *are* conscious and self-conscious (conscious of the functional
role they occupy and fulfill) *in whatever sense they can be assigned cognizing
functions* (distinctive "perceptions and attentions"). They may well lack the
conscious and self-conscious functions of modern "subjective" selves (which
depend on a certain history); but they must possess discriminative powers
congruent with the exercise of whatever cognitive aptitudes are attributed to
them in accounting for their having achieved the culture or civilization that
they have. Jaynes, of course, may be quite mistaken about the details of any
such civilization. For example, there is evidence that the Old Kingdom
Egyptians produced quite naturalistic sculptures of ordinary people at the same
time and in the same place as they produced their remarkable hieratic figures.
This means that they must have made a stylistic decision in shifting from the
one to the other; and that very strongly suggests that they must have already
possessed the rudiments of reflexive, deliberative selves not too distant from
the marks of the modern self.[24] They had to have observed very carefully and
deliberately the actual musculature and features of the face and body. Similarly,
but much more argumentatively, *if* the Old Testament materials surrounding
the role of Moses may be fairly construed as marking (at least) the dawning of
the novel imagination of the Hebrews of about the thirteenth centure BC – of
"history as the present under God" – centred for instance in Exodus 3 and 4
and remembered in Psalm 136, then the very tendency to recover the meaning
of the events of their society's ongoing existence in terms of that theme appears
to entail the beginning of a form of critical reflection and interpretation on the
part of the Hebrews that, once again, cannot have been altogether distant from
certain marks of the modern self.[25] To have possessed a genuine sense of historical distinction and to have addressed the secular events of their collective
career as embodying a temporally deployed revelation joining divine myth and

changing history cannot be completely reconciled with the absence of a developed and critical consciousness. (We may anticipate, here, that Jaynes is addressing, in effect, parts of the puzzle of the praxical conception of the constructed self.)

But, apart from such considerations, Jaynes simply ignores the normal sense in which being able to make perceptual judgments (in linguistically informed ways – not necessarily spoken) just *is* a form of consciousness; also, the sense in which being able to remember, to note down, to refer back again to what one did thus perceive just *is* a form of reflexive consciousness – "self-consciousness" if you will, even if not a consciousness of "self" (in the modern sense). The vagaries of avoiding the anachronism of attributing modern selves to ancient peoples (if that is what it is) should not blind us to the conceptual connection between attributions of consciousness and attributions of cognition *via* sensory perception or *per* deliberate activity. (The only setting in which cognition and consciousness can be conceptually segregated occurs, obviously, in speaking of the cognition or intelligence of machines, which may be argued to lack sensory, volitional, emotional, and deliberative powers, though the argument is not ineluctable.)

Thirdly, essential changes among (cognizing) persons or personae entail cognate changes in the cognizable world they inhabit. Here, again, Jaynes is instructive but only by way of error. For he says, "subjective conscious mind is an analog of what is called the real world . . . it is an operator rather than a thing or repository." This is mistaken in at least two decisive respects. For one thing, there is no determinate "real world" independent of the way the cognizing mind cognizes the world: mind and world are symbiotically linked – the structure of the cognizing mind corresponds to the imputed structure of the cognized world.[26] For a second, the inventions of the cognizing personae of this or that cultural age are not fictions merely because of their transience or cultural emergence or historical artifactuality: the fixity of persons or personae or selves is only the fixity of their prevailing cultural histories; *and* there *is* no real, determinately cognized world that can be specified unless there are real cognizing agents of some sort. This does not mean, of course, that cognition somehow determines the *un*cognized world (whatever we may suppose that to be).[27] But the world we posit (in Thomas Kuhn's useful phrasing) as mind-independent but (necessarily) cognized in a mind-dependent way *is* itself essentially encumbered by the very process of human inquiry. That is the simple consequence of admitting the symbiosis of realism and idealism in any serious attempt to ensure the obvious achievement of the empirical sciences.[28]

Persons, personae, or selves *are* entitative at least to the extent that we insist on the realism of the *determinate* structures we assign the world. Once we grant this, of course, it is clear that Jaynes has impoverished the account of such entities insofar as he treats them only in functionalist as opposed to "incarnatist" terms and insofar as he has somehow privileged (illicitly) his own characterization of "the real world."[29] The latter issue also affects the validity of Edmund

Husserl's phenomenological method, for there is and can be no operative disjunction (unless it is entirely derivative) between the discrimination of meanings or *noemata* assigned to the world and the discrimination of the distributed structures of the world itself.[30] There is no way of demonstrating that the "world" is merely an artifact of cognition or of denying that the historicized imputations of structure to the world are artifacts of such imputation.

Fourthly and finally, if the mental life of humans – the evolution of persons, personae, selves – is essentially historical, if the cultural development of the languaged aptitudes of humans divergently and open-endedly incorporates what we postulate as the relatively stable biological sources of the mental potentialities of the species (which may well change with such history and which may not be conveniently abstractable from such history – as far as the genetics of the mind is concerned), then *we cannot assume that history itself has an assignably regular structure*, a narratizable form, for instance, relatively invariant over the whole of cultural history.[31] Narratization is, on Jaynes's view of things, one of the causes of the beginning of "consciousness" (of the subjective self); but Jaynes himself remains obscure about whether its nature is the very structure of history and what the nature of history actually is.[32] Since he regards the appearance of the first epics of the period of early Dynastic II, in Southern Mesopotamia, as the beginning of historical narrative, even though he treats that achievement as falling within the period of bicameral mind, Jaynes cannot preclude a measure of consciousness and self-consciousness – and even the development of some sort of "self" – during the period in question, in which the modern subjective self is admittedly absent.[33] Alternatively put, persons, personae, selves are merely functional distinctions introduced for one purpose or another, that conveniently serve to map mental functions that cannot be construed in a merely functionalist manner and that cannot preclude some functional range of consciousness and "self"-consciousness through the great civilizations of the ancient world.

II

Viewed in a somewhat oblique way, the theoretical importance of admitting persons or selves as actual entities – sufficiently robust referents, at least for the ascription of mental powers – rests with the fact that a plausible theory of the empirical sciences must account (1) for the body of *distributed* truths that constitute the relatively stable core of those sciences; and (2) for a form of agental aptitude *adequated* to their admission as a human achievement. Historicize the achievement and you provide for the historicizing of the agents' nature. There is no privileging of science here: only the prudent recognition that no other part of human culture can be expected to yield a stronger sense of regularity or invariance with regard to either the cognized world or cognizing humans. So the repudiation of timeless fixities – *or*, the recovery of invariance as a first-order idealization of some sort ensuring no prior, independent, second-order or transcendentally reflexive invariances – is simply a posit adjusted to the human capacity to glean an actual science from the flux of things. The first-order fixities of human nature are no more privileged than those of the physical world, but they must be as determinate, distributively, as the other. Also, the plainly transcendental thesis of the essentially cognitive function of human beings is benign enough: it is merely holistic, formal, *en bloc*, and pretends to arrest no particular real structure against the tides of historical change.

There is, however, a most strategic consequence that can be drawn from this single, unguarded reflection: there is no conceptual strategy that could, convincingly, eliminate or demean in a cognitively dependent respect the functional, first-order *independence* of cognizing agents from the world they would and do examine (including, of course, the world that includes themselves). The charge will seem paradoxical or false. Nevertheless, it is actually its denial that proves paradoxical or false. The reason, which we shall have to elaborate with some care, is a double one: first, because the denial, taken as cognitively pertinent in a first-order sense, entails the claim it would deny; second, because the intended denial, insofar as it *is* defensible (and it is) as a second-order claim, has no function apart from first-order claims of the kind it would threaten, and has the function there only of proposing a certain *holist* constraint on any and all of the distributed claims of any first-order cognitive power.

There is no need to be mysterious about this complication. But it is a peculiarly neglected one; and, as it happens, it is of the greatest importance in accounting for the conceptual relationship among the largest philosophical programs favored at the present time – namely, what (following Husserl's terminology to some extent, as well as post-Husserlian Continental European philosophies) have come to be called *naturalism, phenomenology,* and *deconstruction* (or post-structuralism).

These are not entirely transparent terms. On the contrary, they must be somewhat deformed or attenuated as terms of art if we are to employ them to advantage in surveying the entire span of current Western philosophy. Before fixing their sense, however, it needs to be emphasized that we shall be joining a number of unlikely topics through their use: in particular, a theory of persons of selves, the vexed issue of the linkage between that theory and the interrelationship between naturalistic and phenomenological notions of science and inquiry, and the placement of that entire complex within the most comprehensive visions of the symbiosis of man and world that contemporary speculation seems able to produce. There is, therefore, a great deal being promised by the maneuver intended. Surprisingly, it may be collected in a very simple schematic way.

Let us treat *naturalism,* by conceptual fiat, as that doctrine that postulates cognitive powers adequated to the achievement of any first-order science – a realist science; a science that, for descriptive, predictive, and explanatory purposes, systematically orders a sizably large, important array of distributed truths; a science that is inventive enough to be able to alter and enlarge such a body of putative truths without putting at intolerable risk (in terms of cognitive confidence regarding the achievements of earlier phases of that science) its later, ongoing accretions and occasional reorganisations; a science that claims no privilege of any principled kind regarding the real structures of the world, truth, certainty, the assured sources of genuine knowledge, conceivability, or the like.

We may be as informal as we please here, because our sole concern is to construe what we are calling naturalism as an entirely *internalist* thesis fitted to what we acknowledge as the body of our science: in saying that, we say only that all second-order, transcendental, legitimative, pragmatist or similarly characterized speculations about the source of that cognitive achievement (in terms of reality, the correspondence of world and word, truth, certitude, validity, conceivability, and the like) are reflexively generated within and only within the conceptual space of that achievement itself.[34] (In saying that, we are of course not saying that we have any privileged assurance that there *are* no other sources of knowledge or science than those of our first-order sciences; only that we have no assurance that any would-be cognitive source we pretend to be able to tap is *not* affected in whatever way those first-order sources are.)

To define naturalism in this way is clearly to depart from the pejorative sense Husserl himself intended in identifying his own phenomenological correction of the classical philosophical tradition running chiefly from Galileo to Kant.[35] But it is, also, both to accept Husserl's legitimate criticism of what *he* means by naturalism and to avoid his own rather heady and baffling unwillingness to liberate the discipline of phenomenology from his own counterpart pretensions of cognitive privilege. If we deprive naturalism of such privilege, then we can hardly fail to do so for phenomenology; for, on the definition favored, phenomenology is itself a "kind" of naturalism – it seeks to fix apodictically a system of distributed truths, no longer (it is true) of the "particular objective sciences" or the "sciences of naive positivity" (as Husserl says) but of an even higher science addressed to all "the *forms* of conceivable worlds and . . . conceivable worlds themselves, [constructed] 'originarily' – that is: in correlation with the constitutional Apriori, the Apriori of the intentional performances that constitute them."[36] "Our meditations," says Husserl, concluding his *Cartesian Meditations*, "have in the main fulfilled their purpose, namely to show the concrete possibility of the Cartesian idea of a philosophy as an all-embracing science grounded on an absolute foundation . . . though of course in the form of an endless program."[37] Even though the cognizing "self" of the would-be higher science is not the same as that of the objective sciences, Husserl treats it as a "naturalism" in the sense (our sense, a sense deliberately distorting his own) in which it yields *distributed truths* of (even) more than what merely pertains to the "real" world of those sciences: it seeks nothing less than "the systematic unfolding of the *universal logos of all conceivable being.*"[38] It is a naturalism in the sense that it posits a cognitive power natively embedded in whatever cognitive powers we posit for the objective sciences, and in the sense that it yields, when exercised, an actual array of distributed truths that bear on the real-world achievement of those other sciences.

Thus construed, *phenomenology* (distorted, again as a term of art, from Husserl's usage) is that form of naturalism that explores the cultural or historical or technological or ideological or psychological or conceptual or critical or preformational *context* within which the positive work of our first-order sciences proceeds. Phenomenology is, therefore, a second-order legitimative undertaking – like naturalism itself – but one confined (again, in an internalist manner) to unearthing and explicating the *holist, contextual, preformative* conditions under which the distributed claims of every first-order science labor. To be "internalist" signifies having abandoned all pretense of apodicticity, "originary" cognitive sources, hierarchies of cognitive privilege, totalizing, and the like.

Our sense of phenomenology, then, is clearly not Husserl's. But it is "Husserlian" in the sense that it generalizes what Husserl himself advances as the conception of the preformational *Lebenswelt* by which the horizon of every would-be naturalist or objectivist science is constrained. If, now, phenomenological sciences *are* naturalist sciences, then even the analysis and specification of the preformative context of first-order science are subject to the preformational influences of the same postulated *Lebenswelt*.

Husserl correctly criticizes Galileo (therefore, Descartes) for having illictly substituted an idealized mathematical world for "the only real world" and, therefore, for having insinuated a source of cognitive certainty favoring the objective sciences that, assuming the precondition mentioned, *could not ever there obtain* (regardless of whether it could obtain anywhere else):

> we must note something of the highest important that occurred even as early as Galileo: the surreptitious substitution of the mathematically substracted world of idealities for the only real world, the one that is actually given through perception, that is ever experienced and experienceable – our every day life-world. This substitution was promptly passed on to his successors, the physicists of all succeeding centuries.[39]

The preformational *Lebenswelt* is itself projected, by an internalist reflection that (thereby) cannot fail to be construed as "infected," preformed, by that very same influence. It is projected as a global precondition – holistically, contextually: in whatever way it is itself distributively specified, the inquiry thereupon pursued will, once again, have to be construed as subject to a similar contextual, cognitively inexhaustible, constraint. Abandoning cognitive privilege, therefore, there is (a) no hope of contrasting in a principled way naturalism and phenomenology or first-order sciences of one or the other sort; (b) no hope of specifying distributed first-order truths except internally within a holist context that may itself yield similarly contexted, distributed truths; and

(c) no hope of arresting or exhausting the infinite play of any first-order inquiries – with respect to cognitive first sources ("the originary"), unconditional certitude ("the apodictic"), approximation to either of these within the flux of inquiry ("the verisimilitudinous"[40]), or closure or approximation to closure with respect to "all" conceptual possibilities however presumably grounded in "the only real world" ("the totalized"[41]).

Once we have these distinctions in hand, we may define _deconstruction_ – again, by way of distorting its usual usage (in Derrida, of course, since it is Derrida's term). But even in Derrida, it is transparently taken and adjusted from Heidegger's _"Destruktion"_ and, more subtly, from Husserl's own critique of naturalism and objectivism and, in the most profound sense, from Nietzsche's doctrine of the Eternal Return. In any case, in Derrida, deconstruction is not an explicit philosophical thesis. It is, so to say, the anti-philosophically insinuated _effect_ of "playing" with the usual philosophical pretensions to affirm either the doctrine of the originary or the doctrine of totalization, or both. The first is essentially the Husserlian assurance we have already noted, or whatever among naturalistic disciplines may aspire to it. The second is more difficult to fix. It is, of course, clearly associated with the structuralist presumption of Claude Lévi-Strauss's view of anthropology and related sciences. Lévi-Strauss explicitly says, "The . . . aim of anthropology is _totality._ It regards social life as a system of which all the aspects are organically connected."[42] But it is perhaps also related – by virtue of a kind of inversion of its original use in Jean-Paul Sartre's _Critique of Dialectical Reason_, where it was intended in a certain ongoing, progressive, and incompletable way – to be opposed to "totality" (In Lévi-Strauss's sense, among others). "A totality," Sartre says, "is defined as a being which, while radically distinct from the sum of its parts, is present in its entirety, in one form or another, in each of these parts, and which relates to itself either through its relation to one or more of its parts or through its relation to the relations between all or some of them." But "the dialectic [which, of course, Sartre favors] is a totalizing activity." Sartre permits himself, therefore, to speak of "the developing totalization": "If dialectical Reason exists, then, from the ontological point of view, it can only be a developing totalization, occurring where the totalization occurs, and, from the epistemological point of view, it can only be the accessibility of that totalization to a knowledge which is itself, in principle, totalizing in its procedures."[43] Totalizing is intentional, in Sartre's sense, precisely because it cannot ever fix a totality. Derrida seems to use the expression (when he does), or to intend what comes to "totalizing," in that sense (different from Sartre's) in which the philosopher or theorist pretends to have actually thereby designated a totality, a total system.

It may not unfairly be claimed that Derrida intends the "deconstruction" of totalizing and the originary largely in a negative, anti-philosophical, perhaps ineffable and inexpressible sense rather than in the philosophically explicit sense of _affirming_ (again, in an internalist manner) the impossibility of ever specifying the "system" or "totality" or (_per_ Husserl) "the universal _logos_ of all conceivable being" (or, for that matter, Wittgenstein's project in the *Tractatus*). This is surely the sense in which Derrida remarks that *"Différance* is neither a *word* nor a *concept*"[44] and draws out the insinuated lesson in all of its maddening, endless variety.

In Derrida's hands, the pejorative lable "logocentrism" or "philosophy of presence" (fatally pinned to Heidegger every bit as fittingly as to Husserl[45]) is "dangerously" implicated in *every* constative discourse. Hence, only the Nietzschean-like insinuation of the "radical alterity" of what, *per impossibile*, could have ensured the cognitive reliability and regularity of discourse – that is, its linkage to the originary or the totalized – counts, for Derrida, as deconstruction proper. Its work cannot be named, on pain of discrediting "itself." But *we* perhaps, less fastidious than Derrida – or better, *not committed to the antecedent thesis that all constative discourse is, necessarily, infected with the presumption of the originary or the totalized* – can, now, simply affirm that all such discourse lacks any privileged or principled assurance regarding either or both of those two cognitive resources. We may take the term "deconstruction" in *that* sense. So the deconstructive exercise, in one respect, is merely an extension of phenomenology and, in another, it is utterly different from it. For the phenomenological always supplies a *limited*, holist sense of context for some *particular* array of distributed claims that are inseparable from it; and the deconstructive always indicates the impossibility of supplying the context of all contexts within which the dialectical play of naturalistic and phenomenological discourse obtains. Furthermore, once thus characterized, "deconstruction" may be unceremoniously assigned a public sense detached from Derrida's invention (like "aspirin," say) and may then be found to have been ubiquitous in the philosophical tradition: in Anaximander and Nietzsche, of course, but also, in a tamer form, in Dewey, William James, Quine, Goodman, Husserl, Heidegger, Gadamer, Levinas, Foucault, Lyotard, Kuhn, Feyerabend, and others, including (even) Richard Rorty. Thus Derrida himself says that *différance*

> governs nothing, reigns over nothing, and nowhere exercises any authority. It s not announced by any capital letter. Not only is there no kingdom of *différance*, but *différance* instigates the subversion of every kingdom. Which makes it obviously threatening and infallibly dreaded by everything within us that desires a kingdom. And it is always in the name of a kingdom that one may reproach *différance* with wishing to reign, believing that one sees it aggrandize itself with a capital letter.[46]

We may now reach, at one stroke, the full finding we seek. To admit the sciences to their usual status as exemplars of man's cognitive achievement (without, of course, ignoring history, fiction, art, politics, religion, technology, law) is to admit, as fully eligible cognitively, the claims of naturalism (in our adjusted sense). To admit naturalism is to admit phenomenology; and to admit phenomenology is to admit deconstruction. The division of labor may be arranged, to be sure, in other ways. But the charm of having arranged it in the way we have is just that it deliberately trades on the prevailing intellectual winds and suffers no obvious inadequacy because of it. It is as comprehensive a vision as we seem able to supply. Of course, each ingredient may be explored in an endless variety of ways. For example, it would take no trouble to expand the deconstructive theme along lines that could favorably link Nietzsche's will to power, the Boundless of Anaximander, and the "Devoidness" of Nagarjuna.[47] But, what we cannot fail to grasp is

1 the indissoluble unity and mutual entailment of naturalism, phenomenology, and deconstruction;
2 their cognitive parity or lack of privilege *vis-à-vis* one another and *vis-à-vis* first-order science;
3 the symbiosis, because of conditions 1 and 2, of distributed and holist claims;
4 the ineliminability, therefore, of a realist or naturalistic science;
5 the validity, because of and consistent with condition 4, of affirming the independence of cognizing subjects or agents and cognized world;
6 the ineliminability, therefore, of a phenomenological interpretation of naturalistic science, inextricably linking realist and idealist elements in a union that makes no provision as such for the cognizing subjects and cognized objects of that naturalistic science;
7 the validity, because of and consistent with condition 6, of positing a preformative condition within which, relationally, cognizing subjects or agents and cognized world may be dependently posited;
8 the deconstructive presumption against any cognitive privilege of origin or conceptual totality; and
9 the cognitive viability of every form of science or human inquiry seemingly threatened by condition 8.

There you have a version of the lean *summa* of contemporary philosophy.

III

It is not merely accidental that deconstruction singles out the originary and the totalized; but it is entirely possible that other versions of that strategy would feature other insuperabilities. Deconstruction (by the cavalier adjustment we have imposed) cannot fail to proceed by a *via negativa* and by an explicit constatation. The negative route signifies the fine perception that *every* schema of categories fails to overtake the ultimate surd to which it is said to be fitted; the positive route signifies the equally fine perception that the exposé of that failure must be expressed through the self-subverting use of that very schema. Anaximander's *Apeiron* is (or may be) a botched guess combining the corporeal with the undifferentiable "source" of all systematic distinction – the pupil's dawning grasp of Thale's failure and the pupil's failure to escape as well.[48] But, if that is true, then Heraclitus's Fire cannot serve the intended purpose even if it is a metaphor for an originary flux; though it is not for that reason a failure. It is simply not a deconstructive doctrine at all: first, because the flux of world and worlds is subject to a higher *Logos*; second, because the *Logos* is not itself an artifact of deconstructively construing the Fire as a metaphor for the ultimate surd. "The wise is one," says Heraclitus, "knowing the plan by which it steers all things through all."[48] Apparently, there is no breach between the cognizable source of the cosmos identified as Fire and the alterity of what, only as thus cognized, is construed as a cosmos. It is for this reason that one finds an affinity between Heraclitus and the Stoics. Heraclitus provides a paradigm for the canonical tradition that, through endless variation, runs from Parmenides and Plato and Aristotle down through the phase of modern philosophy from Galileo to Kant that Husserl so aptly criticizes and that (most ironically) claims Husserl himself as an active spokesman (and victim). And Anaximander is distinctly equivocal, as perhaps anticipating Heraclitus in some respect (*if* the *Apeiron* "circumscribes all things and steers them all"[50]) or as anticipating a deconstructive reading of all such order (*if* the Boundless is the unutterable "origin" of cosmic orders that begin and end as do what emerges within them, and if "steering" them does not signify an ultimate *Logos*).

Once we see matters this way, it becomes possible to identify different sorts and different strengths of deconstruction, some naturalistic, some phenomenological, some more narrowly restricted to what Derrida himself seems to have had in mind in opposing those others. For example, William James's "worlds of pure experience" strains toward a deconstructive formula of a naturalistic cast, as does also John Dewey's "primary experience."[51] That is, they collapse the naturalistic order of "experience" into a phenomenologized order in which the polar subject and object are first thus related – as the structural condition operative at the *beginning* of any naturalism. Every such naturalism, then, is open – but only in a *holist*, inexplicit sense – to whatever may revise what is already determinately conceded *and* to "whatever" signifies the "distant," the inexperienceable, side of explicit "experience." To be radical, says James,

> an empiricism must neither admit into its constructions any element that is not directly experienced, nor exclude from them any element that is directly experienced. For such a philosophy, *the relations that connect experiences must themselves be experienced relations, and any kind of relation experienced must be accounted as "real" as anything else in the system.* Elements may indeed be redistributed, the original placing of things getting corrected, but a real place must be found for every kind of thing experienced, whether term or relation in the final philosophic arrangement.[52]

And yet, at the same time, speculating about the comparison in "empirical" terms between the "percepts" of two "minds," James adds (what we may call his deconstructive theme),

In point of fact the ultimate common barrier can always be pushed, by both minds, farther than any actual percept of either, until at last it resolves itself into the mere notion of imperceptibles like atoms or ether, so that, where we do terminate in percepts, *our knowledge is only* speciously completed, being, in theoretic strictness, only a virtual aknowledge of those remoter objects which conception carries out.[53]

We cannot suppose this to be very far from Derrida's double objection to Husserl's apodictic fixities – that is, from the objection based on the inaccessibility of a totalized order of conceptual distinctions within which any particular distinction remains reliably self-identical (in terms of its differences from all other such distinctions), and from the objection based on the temporalized uncertainties affecting the supposed reidentification of the same conceptual distinction used under different circumstances.[54]

There is a certain characteristic thinness in the (American) naturalized deconstructions, which, it may be reasonably argued, reach a classic and most precise form in W. V. Quine's "Two Dogmas." If we bear in mind that, on Quine's view, intra- and interlinguistic communication exhibit the same puzzles and that the fit between language and world is taken as internal to the conditions of such communication (internalist, in our sense), then, when Quine affirms in his familiar way that "the linguist's finished jungle-to-English manual has as its net yield an infinite *semantic correlation* of sentences," we may read, as deconstructive, the intent of his own explanation:

> Most of the semantic correlation is supported only by analytical hypotheses [that is, by the result of distributively specifying the presuppositions of the linguist's practice from the "phenomenologically" preformative context of that practice – or, from its *Lebenswelt*], in their extension beyond the zone where independent evidence for translation is posible. That those unverifiable translations proceed without mishap must not be taken as pragmatic evidence of good lexicography, for mishap is impossible.[55]

Quine's deconstruction, if we allow the term,[56] falters of course at the point of weakness of his entire philosophical effort – that is, at the point at which he allows the expression "most" in his explicative sentence; for it is there that we realize that his own timelessly secure extensionalism, which could not otherwise be vindicated merely by "analytical hypotheses" drawn from tacitly preformative practices, must presume a suitably congenial, firmer fit between world and word. Still, to identify Quine's wobbling use of "most" as a deconstructive nod is also to mark its naturalistic and phenomenological import as well; for Quine means by it to proceed with his extensionalism *and* to do so in the face of the unknown, preformative prejudices of natural language and natural practice which it is confidently intended to "regiment."[57] By an opposed maneuver, Nelson Goodman (who, it is rumored, believes that there is a quite close affinity between his own later work and that of Derrida[58]) unintentionally demonstrates how deconstruction can go entirely haywire when, having admitted man's cognitive aptitude in a global way, he refuses to provide a sufficiently articulate naturalism.[59]

The explicitly phenomenologized form of deconstruction is, of course, classically formulated in Heidegger's *Being and Time*. The whole purpose of the myth of *Sein* and *Dasein* is to fix the deconstructively provisional nature of all systems of categories and to construe the relationship between naturalistic subject and object as distinctions internal to the indissolubly relational characterization of *Sein* and *Dasein* – that sets the diachronically distributed, historicized, preformational contexts within which any naturalistic science or inquiry proceeds. Once that is granted, the fatal idealism of Husserl's Transcendental Ego becomes painfully plain.[60] Also, one sees at once how little is left for Derrida to do, except to rehearse his own variations regarding the ultimate surd, without ever providing a sufficiently robust recovery of the cognizing powers of man under the protection of his terribly nimble exposés. Heidegger himself is claimed, by Derrida, as a victim of the logocentric drive – and there is some justice in the charge (which Heidegger himself anticipates.)[61]

The truth is that it is really only in Nietzsche that the distinction between the naturalistic, the phenomenological, and the deconstructive is (*avant la lettre*) rendered in a sufficiently balanced and coherent way. For Nietzsche provides a sense of how we can withdraw, *by heuristically articulated stages*, from the seeming fixities of fit between world and word: so that,

(i)   negatively, we approach the unutterable surd that Derrida's *différance* attempts to "indicate"; and,

(ii)   affirmatively, we continue to use the categories of natural language while remaining true to the lesson of (i)

The implications of Nietzsche's grasp of this double theme are most extraordinary. For our present purpose, what we may collect as its most powerful instruction is this:

(a)   that the holism of the *deconstructive* thrust of thought *has absolutely no distributive import on any first-order inquiry or on any (second-order) naturalistic or phenomenological legitimation of such inquiry*;

(b)   that the symbiosis of cognized world and cognizing self *permits no privileging of the structures of self or world vis-à-vis one another, either negatively or affirmatively, with respect to either (i) or (ii)*; and

(c)   that no articulation of the structures of self and world dialectically favored over any other *can be said, on comparative grounds, to be more or less supported, confirmed, validated, or strengthened by deconstructive considerations.*

Alternatively put, first- and second-order discourse and, within second-order discourse, naturalism and phenomenology, are continuously, commensurably, dialectically, and equitably concerned *with the distributed claims of one another*;

but the discourse of deconstruction (in the sense here supplied) is radically discontinuous with these other forms of discourse – in terms of its own logical function. It is *not* incompatible with such discourse, in the sense in which pyrrhonian skepticism may be said to be incompatible with truth-claims; but there is no continuous, coherent discourse in which what is affirmed within the space of the one can be said to have a logical bearing on the distributed claims in the other: first, because there are no distributed claims of a deconstructive sort; and, second, because there are no distributed differential consequences that the holist "claims" of deconstruction can yield in the space of the other. Michel Foucault's "genealogies" may be said to form that remarkable, hybrid, paradoxical thought in which the Nietzschean lessons (a)–(c) are actually coherently combined in a single, continuous discourse.

It may well be that *Discipline and Punish* (*Surveiller et punir*) is the most compendious exhibit of Foucault's genealogical practice; for there Foucault actually unites a historical analysis of the evolution of a distinctive form of discipline arising in the seventheenth and eighteenth centuries; identifies the forms of "normalization" under which it becomes automatic and invisible to those affected and to those who would understand how it arose and how it works; and *then* moves on to link its functioning thus (and our understanding of its functioning thus) as a manifestation of an underlying generative process that has no assignable structure of its own except as (dialectically) we read back into it a reactive force subverting the subterranean structured and structuring processes of an earlier epoch. " 'Discipline'," says Foucault, "may be identified neither with an institution nor with an apparatus; it is a type of power, a modality for its exercise, comprising a whole set of instruments, techniques, procedures, levels of application, targets; it is a 'physics' or an 'anatomy' of power, a technology."[62]

This is already a union of naturalistic and phenomenological history (employing our own terms of art) anticipating a deconstructive reading of that union. It also demonstrates at a stroke, of course, both how a Marxist and a Marxist-like account of human history – in fact, any "critical" history – cannot fail to involve the same sort of union (however skewed or attenuated, however unlike the largely formal phenomenologies of Husserl and Heidegger they may be, and however different a Marxist and a Nietzschean conception of generative process must be).[63] The Marxist risks solving the phenomenological puzzle, once and for all, altogether too simply (as does Husserl also, for another reason): if he succeeds, he is entitled (he believes) to offer a "critical" history of the originary power of the economic processes of every society. The Nietzschean, on the other hand, construes all *such* inclinations toward structuralism[64] as merely self-deceptive – the internal captives of the normalizing process of "a type of power" within the space of which, reflexively, its own creatures believe and trust the claims of their radically contingent epoch.

Thus, within the historical account of torture and prisons, Foucault inserts his own Nietzschean conviction:

We should admit . . . that power produces knowledge (and not simply by encouraging it because it serves power or by applying it because it is useful); that power and knowledge directly imply one another; that there is no power relation without the correlative consitution of a field of knowledge, nor any knowledge that does not presuppose and constitute at the same time power relations. These "power-knowledge relations" are to be analyzed, therefore, not on the basis of a subject of knowledge who is or is not free in relation to the power system, but, on the contrary, the subject who knows, the objects to be known, and the modalities of knowledge must be regarded as so many effects of these fundamental implications of power–knowledge and their historical transformations. In short, it is not the activity of the subject of knowledge that produces a corpus of knowledge, useful or resistant to power, but power–knowledge, the processes and struggles that traverse it and of which it is made up, that determines the forms and possible domains of knowledge.[65]

Foucault's explicit analysis of Nietzsche confirms his deconstructive motive:

The genealogist needs history to dispel the chimeras of the origin . . . if the genealogist refuses to extend his faith in metaphysics, if he listens to history, he finds that there is "something altogether different" behind things: not a timeless and essential secret, but the secret that they have no essence, or that their essence was fabricated in a piecemeal fashion from alien forms. . . . What is found at the historical beginning of things is not the inviolable identity of their origins; it is the dissension of other things. It is disparity.[66]

But, if (as is true) Foucault *uses* the *products* of his genealogical strategy (*Discipline and Punish*, for instance) as "effective history" (*wirkliche Historie*), to achieve a certain rhetorical advantage in terms of political commitment in the present, it would be entirely wrong to dismiss the validity (yes: the validity) of first-order inquiry and of naturalism and phenomenology in promoting (as Foucault clearly intends) a certain form of (Nietzscheanized) political activism.[67]

Deconstruction cannot be collapsed into naturalism and/or phenomenology; but neither can it be convincingly represented as a mere skepticism. The rejection of "essences" (in Foucault's idiom) – which, after all, is ultimately indistinguishable from the relevant critical maneuvers of James and Dewey and Heidegger and Derrida – is *not* a rejection of science or philosophy once freed from an adherence to such essences, and it is *not* a denial that they could be thus freed. But Foucault's *caveat* is itself equivocally (though defensibly) linked to the actual recovery of science and history and philosophy *and* to the affirmation of the ultimate Nietzschean (or deconstructive) exposé. To collapse the two *is* to advocate skepticism; but it is also to make nonsense of "effective history" and the serious political commitment of humans who "have to promote new forms of subjectivity through the refusal of [modern, liberal] individuality which has been imposed on us for several centuries.''[68] However thin, desperate, pathetic or heroic we take Foucault's political ethic to be, it must be able at least to present itself as coherent and informed; and, to do that, it cannot actually privilege deconstruction in a cognitive way or reduce it to utter skepticism. There is no other possibility than to admit the full symbiosis of naturalism, phenomenology, and deconstruction.

In effect, this is what Nietzsche accomplishes. Derrida forever rushes to remind us of the inexpressible surd. He *ignores* the recovery of science and philosophy and political engagement and art for the sake of that ultimate leap: he always tempts us with its air of the sublime and the ridiculous, but he never *dismisses* those ordinary endeavors as pointless or impossible. So he offers his characteristic *jeu*:

> What am I to do in order to speak of the *a* of *différance*? It goes without saying that it cannot be *exposed*. One can expose only that which at a certain moment can become *present*, manifest, that which can be shown, presented as something present, a being-present in its truth, in the truth of a present or the presence of the present. Now if *différance* ⨉ (and I also cross out the "⨉") what makes possible the presentation of the being-present, it is never presented as such. It is never offered to the present. Or to anyone.[69]

The remark actually shows the dependence of the deconstructive moment on the ordinary first- and second-order practices that, in the hands of some, had been thought to have been abolished altogether. For his part, Foucault pursues *both* his histories (managed in the spirit of deconstruction) *and* his instruction about their deconstructive intent; hence, once again, some have wrongly supposed that Foucault dismissed the first in advancing the second. The trouble is that Foucault never quite says how they are to be linked if they are not to veer off into skepticism or some sort of nihilism.

It would not be entirely proper to pursue, here, Nietzsche's own doctrine in all its full detail. But it can be compendiously displayed; and we need to understand how easily it may be deformed by pop deconstructionists:

> A "thing-in-itself" [is] just as perverse as a "sense-in-itself," a "meaning-in-itself." There are no "facts-in-themselves," for a sense must always be projected into them before there can be "facts." . . . "Essence," the "essential nature," is something perspective and already presupposes a multiplicity. One may not ask: "who then interprets?" for the interpretation itself is a form of the will to power, exists (but not as a "being" but as a process, a becoming) as an effect.[70]

There are endless passages in Nietzsche that point to the same lesson – namely, that, in speaking of the will to power (only roughly the same as what Foucault means by power/knowledge, what Derrida means by *différance*, what

Heidegger appears to mean by *Ursprung*[71]), *the very symbiosis of cognizing self and cognized world indicates that the "chaos" underlying the will to power spontaneously bifurcates as subject and object, interprets "itself" as a world of appearances presented to apparent subjects.* There is no world, except as one is interpreted; but there is no interpreter except as there appears a world to interpret.

Jean Granier may have put the point in its most precise and compelling form:

> The primitive text of nature is thus the *chaotic being that manifests itself as a significant process.* Its figures delineate not a system or a cosmos, but, precisely, a *mask. Nature and mask determine phenomenal being, the phenomenon in its being, as chaos.* In their very being, therefore, nature and mask are the same, and the worst possible mistake would be to oppose these terms. In reality, they are strictly bound up with one another, and it is this interdependence that the sameness of their being expresses: at the Same, and not a logical or ontological identity. *The Same* – the being that comes back in eternal recurrence, that renders nature and mask copresent in the equivocal unity of the *text.*[72]

The "Eternal Return" is itself a textual representation – addressed to the cognizing subjects of cognized worlds – of the perpetual task of representing thus to themselves their involvement with their own world as the "self-bifurcating" power of the Same, the Chaos.

"Thought," Granier explains "is never external to Being. . . . What we view as Being is already a *cultural* product, a monument of human civilization."[73] The "Eternal Return" is, therefore, *not* confined within the space of naturalistic and phenomenological legitimation: on the contrary, it is the inexplicable irruption into that space (and so described within it) of what (from "its" vantage) is postualated as the unstructurable Flux or Chaos from which whatever structured Being appears, "originates." The "Eternal Return" is the endlessness of *that* spectacle, not any particular essentialism. Nietzsche deploys his lesson (his new nihilism) as a series of heuristic retreats moving (we may suggest, again heuristically) in the direction of an unutterable Boundlessness beyond the Greek and the Buddhist. Anachronistically defined, it traces the normalizations of Foucault, to and through the life-giving illusions of Heidegger's *alētheia*, to and through Derrida's surd of *différance*, to and through Nietzsche's own bifurcation of the will to power, to the postulated Void – and, asymptotically, "beyond."

It is madness, of course, to remain fixed at that point of speculation, for *to speculate* is to function within the first- and second-order conceptual space in which just this impossible "relationship" attracts our attention. To admit the charge is to admit the radical disconnection of *arguments* that pretend to move, *distributively*, between the questions of naturalism and phenomenology and the "questions" of (Nietzschean) deconstruction. But the discontinuities of determinate argument need not affect the holist continuities by which man mythologizes the impenetrable link between his cognized world and "worlded" cognition and between "them" and "that," beyond such appearances, from which they endlessly spring.

We may perhaps add here an exotic specimen of the deconstructive mentality, since we have already mentioned Anadimander's *Apeiron*, Nagarjuna's "Devoidness," Heraclitus's Fire, and now Derrida's *"différance"* and Nietzsche's "Chaos." For the Japanese Buddhists of the Kyoto School apparently criticize the "logic of identity" in the context in which the "nonidentical" refers to the amplitude of the indeterminable alterity or formlessness of the power to form any distinctions that do ("rightly") submit to the logic of identity.[74]

IV

There is an air of unreality about deconstruction, particularly in its full Nietzscheanized form; for it is, after all, addressed to *us*. To affirm it is to defeat it. It can only be insinuated as a limit toward which our conceptual imagination is drawn but cannot reach. But the *strain* of making the attempt confirms certain legitimative ("transcendental") constraints on, and within, the normal work of first- and second-order discourse.

Two findings in particular suggest themselves: first, that we can claim no structural fixity of world and self beyond what is sufficient to preserve the bare notion (the holist notion) of the conceptual legibility of cognized world to cognizing self and the conceptual adequacy of a cognizing aptitude addressed to a cognized object; and, second, that intentionality invades the whole of the space of first- and second-order discourse and is, therefore, nothing but the effect of (what we may now call, by an invented term) *cognificence,* the symbiosis of world and self within every naturalistic and phenomenological reflection. Cognificence is, so to say, the mythic bifurcation reported as Nietzsche's will to power, Foucault's power/knowledge, Derrida's *différences* as the pluralized manifestations of *différance*, Heidegger's *alētheia*. The naturalism that Husserl aptly criticized is, then, the pretension of an intelligible world unstructured by any linkage with the mind's cognizing structures and yet cognizable to that same mind (realism), or the *a priori* constitution of our intelligible world via the intersection of noumenal minds and noumenal world, cognitively penetrable to minds within the world thus formed (objectivism). But then, contrary to its own intent, Husserl's phenomenology favors an idealist, a privileged, formula for the constituted symbiosis of the intentional or intelligible world, in order to ensure a source of apodictic certainty regarding whatever may be conceived at all – *a fortiori*, what affects however we may conceive whatever is in the actual world. It is certainly possible to read Husserl more sympathetically as favoring only the exercise of eidetic variation striving for the apodictic *within* the flux of preformed experience and reflection.[75] But, then, either an approximative, progressive, asymptotic, or verisimilitudinous confidence must prove illicit, or else it can represent only a heuristic, purely formal, regulative notion that would never attempt (because it could never legitimate) a principled distinction between the apodictic and the empirically salient. It is possible to read Husserl thus, but it is difficult to support it as entirely canonical.

The deconstructive theme disallows the naturalisms and phenomenologies indicated. Their contingency is radical, and they cannot be privileged with respect to one another. In our own time, the thesis, shorn of any explicitly deconstructive sense, characteristically takes the form of *historicizing cognificence* – on the assumption that distributed claims of a historicist nature are themselves the radically contingent artifacts of such cognificence. Deconstruction, therefore, is implicit in every viable naturalism and phenomenology – but it is silent there. It is in this sense – perhaps only in this sense – that Julian Jaynes's preposterous speculation about the radical variability of the cognizing self of ancient times may be assigned a useful role. The referential unicity of a cognizing pole at every stage of man's distinctive history entails nothing regarding the essential and detailed unity of the nature of such selves; and what we require – regarding the unity of such selves adequated to the distributed acts of constative discourse (or to behavior informed by such an aptitude) – is either only formal and holist or else contingently linked to the special features ascribed to this or that historical epoch.

This is the point of analyses such as that of Foucault's *Discipline and Punish*. Thus, tracing in the greatest detail the seventeenth- and eighteenth century formation of a new sense and practice of personal discipline, Foucault is led to the following characteristic resumé:

> Through this technique [just specified], a new object was being formed; slowly, it superseded the mechanical body – the body composed of solids and assigned movements, the image of which had for so long haunted those who dreamt of disciplinary perfection. This new object is the natural body, the bearer of forces and the seat of duration; it is the body, susceptible to specified operations, which have their order, their stages, their conditions, their constituent elements. In becoming the target for new mechanisms of power, the body is offered up to new forms of knowledge. It is the body of exercise, rather than of speculative physics; a body manipulated by authority, rather than imbued with animal spirits; a body of useful training and not of rational mechanics, but one in which, by virtue of that very fact, a number of natural requirements and functional constraints are beginning to emerge.[76]

His is *not* the summary of a new discipline imposed on man; it is the summary of a new kind of man produced by a new discipline generated by the mythic force of "power/knowledge" – which is itself a reflexively formulated *text* offered by those (ultimately) formed by that same discipline, who speculate that they have been thus formed from "materials" they can only characterize in terms of what they (now) recall "must" have preceded the present forms of normalization. In admitting the historicized structures of cognizing selves, therefore, we disallow the bifurcation of mind and body, of selves and society, of thought and behavior, of theory and practice, of knowledge and world, of essence and history; and in doing that we acknowledge the ubiquity of all the intensionalized puzzles of intentionality for the whole of the intelligible world.[77] *Intentionality is cognificence viewed in its distributed variety.* It is, in a fair sense, the benefit of the rationale of deconstruction deployed through the second-order speculations of naturalism and phenomenology.

This also supplies the reason for the somewhat tamer, but entirely pertinent, insistence of Hans-Georg Gadamer on "the universal linguisticality of man's relation to the world" – which, as Gadamer rightly claims, entails that "this phenomenon ['the universality of the hermeneutical problem'] is not secondary in human existence, [so that] hermeneutics is not to be viewed as a mere subordinate discipline within the arena of the *Geisteswissenschaften.*"[78] Gadamer sees *within* the limits of a naturalized and phenomenologized world what Derrida (again, in a *non-idealist* sense) deconstructively intends in affirming: "*There is nothing outside of the text* [there is no outside-text; *il n'y a pas de hors-texte*]."[79] Gadamer's intention, of course, is to expose the invalid naturalism or objectivism (in Husserl's sense) of Jürgen Habermas's conception of "the emancipatory power of reflection" – which, true to its own Enlightenment origins, would safeguard the fixed, essential rationality of the human self from the vagaries of historical contingency it somehow pretends to have already admitted as universally (or praxically) operative. (The details do not concern us here.[80])

The import of Gadamer's occasioned complaint lies, more instructively, with his own grasp of the inseparability of advancing the hermeneutic thesis he favors and of admitting the impossibility (in doing that) of fixing (however contingently) the nature of the cognizing self unless within the assigned scope of that same thesis. If one admits the hermeneutic nature of science and ordinary speech, then, says Gadamer, "one sees that the discussion of the hermeneutic circle is in fact directed toward the structure of Being-in-the-world itself, that is toward the overcoming of the subject–object bifurcation that was the primary thrust of Heidegger's transcendental analysis of Dasein."[81] Gadamer specifically sides with Heidegger against Husserl's "ultimate transcendental justification" (and, therefore, also against Derrida's identification of his own undertaking with that of "phenomenology" in Husserl's sense).[82]

Nevertheless, Gadamer's hermeneutics *is* phenomenological (in a non-pejorative sense); and Gadamer *is*, ultimately, only a little more willing than is Habermas to concede the bearing of radically historicizing forces on the formation of the self. Thus, on the one hand, advancing a historicized and historicizing hermeneutics, Gadamer holds,

We say, for instance, that understanding and misunderstanding take place between I and thou. But the formulation "I and thou" already betrays an enormous alienation. There is nothing like an "I and thou" at all – there is neither the I nor the thou as isolated, substantial realities. I may say "thou" and I may refer to myself over against a thou, but a common understanding [*Verständigung*] always precedes these situations. We all know that to say "thou" to someone presupposes a deep common accord [*tiefes Einverständnis*]. Something enduring is already present when this word is spoken. [Against the theses of "the science of hermeneutics," the achievement of understanding presupposes] a comprehensive life-phenomenon that constitutes the "we" that we all are. Our task, it seems to me, is to transcend the prejudices that underlie the aesthetic consciousness, the historical consciousness, and the hermeneutical consciousness that has been restricted to a [mere] technique for avoiding misunderstandings and to overcome the alienations present in them all.[83]

And, on the other hand, even within the scope of this remark (and elsewhere), Gadamer ingenuously supposes that there is a determinate "we" assignable to every tradition – in which a provisional "I" and "thou" may be recovered. He also apparently believes that that determinate "we" is the very universal "we" of every human tradition. Both views are quite unnecessary, evidentially unconfirmed and unconfirmable, entirely arbitrary. Gadamer's claim is also not seriously different from Habermas's, which he rightly opposes. Gadamer merely recovers hermeneutically (or phenomenologically) what Habermas affirms naturalistically: to deny any cognitively ordered privilege between the two *is* to concede their equivalence. This, then, is the small but quite important consequence of Gadamer's hermeneutic recovery of the classical tradition.[84] There *is* no common tradition that mankind shares. There is no unique norm of civility or understanding to be recovered. There is no universal convergence of human prejudice or communication. There is only the diachronic viability of the race – and what, quite variably, it theorizes its cognizing capacities must have contributed to its own viability. Gadamer's "we" – which is the "we" of Hegel[85] – merely ensures the symbiosis of individual cognizing referents (of some sort) and the collective (and aggregatively shared) tradition that makes such referents possible. In terms of Gadamer's own dialectic, there cannot be a "we" without an I and thou, just as there cannot be an I and thou without a "we." But that admission cannot but be holist or *en bloc*, cannot favor any particular formation of an I and thou of any epoch over that of any other. It hardly fixed the nature of any I and thou within *any* history – not in Habermas's manner of privileging the essential rationality of man nor in Gadamer's manner of privileging the classical tradition within the endless play of traditions. In a word, the formations suggested by Jaynes and Foucault, if they could be independently confirmed, would have to be alternative instantiations of the hermeneutic agency Gadamer postulates for every epoch.

But to say that is simply to say ecentrically that there is no science or philosophy or history or art without a community of cognizing selves. What the tolerance of that function may be can only he guessed at – retrospectively, reflexively, prejudicially – within the narrowly formed horizons of particular such selves. And to admit that is to disabuse us of the temptations of universalism without disallowing the pursuit of candidate universals.[86] That is, it is to disabuse us of the notion that the contingent ("indicative," first-order) universals entail, implicate, or reveal *any* second-order legitimative, truly invariant universals regarding man's cognitive powers. It is only the latter that are philosophically important to dispute; it is only the latter that deconstruction is intended to undermine and that the union of naturalism and phenomenology precludes. The former are unavoidable but not conceptually troublesome.

Notes

1   Julian Jaynes, *The Origin of Consciousness in the Breakdown of the Bicameral Mind* (Boston, Mass.: Houghton Mifflin, 1976), pp. 12, 18.
2   See Joseph Margolis, *Science without Unity: Reconciling the Natural and Human Sciences* (Oxford: Basil Blackwell, 1987), ch. 10.
3   Jaynes, *The Origin of Consciousness*, p. 21.
4   Ibid., p. 23.
5   Ibid., p. 27.
6   Ibid., p. 36.
7   Ibid., p. 39; see also p. 70.
8   Ibid., p. 46; also p. 54.
9   Ibid., p. 55.
10 Ibid., p. 66
11 Ibid., pp. 68–9.
12 Ibid., p. 221.
13 Ibid., p. 220 (italics added).
14 Ibid., p. 84.
15 Ibid., ch. 5. See also Joseph Margolis, *Culture and Cultural Entities* (Dordrecht: D. Reidel, 1984), ch. 3.
16 Jaynes, *The Origin of Consciousness*, pp. 72, 74.
17 Ibid., pp. 70–5.
18 Ibid., p. 133.
19 Ibid., p. 135.
20 Ibid., p. 90 (italics added); see also pt III ch. 5.
21 See Derek Parfit, *Reasons and Persons* (Oxford: Clarendon Press, 1984), pt III; also Margolis, *Science without Unity*, ch. 3.
22 See Margolis, *Science without Unity*, ch. 3. We return to the matter of adequation below, in ch. 8.
23 Jaynes, *The Origin of Consciousness*, p. 132.
24 See for instance Wilheilm Worringer, *Abstraction and Empathy*, tr. Michael Bullock (New York: International Universities Press, 1953).

25 The argument is carefully appraised – perhaps too sanguinely – in Eric Voegelin, *Order and History*, vol. 1: *Israel and Revelation* (Baton Rouge: Louisiana State University Press, 1956), pp. 380, 124. See particularly, pt II and ch. 12.

26 See Margolis, *Science without Unity*, ch. 4.

27 This is the allegedly essential error erroneously exposed – to which we shall return in ch. 2 – in Roy Bhaskar's *Scientific Realism and Human Emancipation* (London: Verso Books, 1986)

28 See Joseph Margolis, *Pragmatism without Foundations: Reconciling Realism and Relativism* (Oxford: Basil Blackwell), 1986, ch. 11.

29 See Margolis, *Science without Unity*, chs 4, 9.

30 See for instance Ludwig Landgrede, 'The World as a Phenomenological Problem,' tr. Dorion Cairns and Donn Welton, in *The Phenomenology of Edmund Husserl*, ed. Donn Welton (Ithaca, NY: Cornell University Press, 1981); and Robert Sokolowski, *Husserlian Meditations* (Evanston, Ill.: Northwestern University Press, 1974), ch. 7.

31 This is the fatal weakness of Paul Ricoeur's theory of the narrative structure of human history. See Paul Ricoeur, *Time and Narrative*, vols 1–2, tr. Kathleen McLaughlin and David Pellauer (Chicago: University of Chicago Press, 1984, 1985).

32 Jaynes, *The Origin of Consciousness*, pp. 216–22. We return to the nature of history below, in ch. 8.

33 Jaynes, *The Origins of Consciousness*, p. 218.

34 The full account on which these remarks rest is provided in *Pragmatism without Foundations*, ch. 11.

35 Edmund Husserl, *Phenomenology and the Crisis of Philosophy*, tr. Quentin Lauer (New York: Harper and Row, 1965).

36 Edmund Husserl, *Cartesian Meditations*, tr. Dorion Cairns (The Hague: Martinus Nijhoff, 1960), Conclusion, section 64 (p. 154).

37 Ibid., p. 152.

38 Ibid., p. 155.

39 Edmund Husserl, *The Crisis of European Sciences and Transcendental Phenomenology*, tr. David Carr (Evanston, Ill.: Northwestern University Press, 1970), section 9, pp. 48–9.

40 The term is intended here in Karl Popper's sense – which is meant somehow to secure a cognitively pertinent assurance about the realist direction of inquiry, without privileged cognitive sources. See Karl R. Popper, "Two Faces of Common Sense," *Conjectures and Refutations: The Growth of Scientific Knowledge*, 2nd, rev. edn. (New York: Harper Torchbooks, 1968). Popper has had misgivings about this notion throughout the latter part of his career.

41 The term is intended in Jacques Derrida's sense, actually directed against Husserl. Husserl, as we have already noted (in having cited his *caveat* "though of course in the form of an endless program"), may be taken to have favored a version of the doctrine of verisimilitude, though one altogether different from Popper's. See Jacques Derrida: *Speech and Phenomen and Other Essays on Husserl's Theory of Signs*, tr. David B. Allison (Evanston, Ill.: Northwestern University Press, 1973), especially ch. 7; and "Différance," *Margins of Philosophy*, tr. Alan Bass (Chicago: University of Chicago Press, 1982). Derrida tends to favor the expression "the transcendentally signified" when criticizing Husserl's reliance on

the "originary" (or a similar reliance by others), and tends to favor expressions opposed to "totalizing" ("an indefinitely multiplied structure," for instance) when criticizing Lévi-Strauss and Rousseau (and other "structuralist" thinkers). See for instance Jacques Derrida, *Of Grammatology*, tr. Gayatri Chakravorty Spivak (Baltimore: John Hopkins University Press, 1976), pp. 20, 163. But the two notions are ultimately inseparable – as Derrida effectively indicates again and again.

42 Claude Lévi-Strauss, *Structural Anthropology*, tr. Claire Jacobson and Brooke Grundfest Schoepf (New York: Anchor Books, 1967), p. 362. This is the sense in which Derrida pursues Lévi-Strauss in *Of Grammatology*.

43 Jean-Paul Sartre, *Critique of Dialectical Reason, I.*, tr. Alan Sheridan-Smith, ed. Jonathan Rée (London: New Left Books, 1976), pp. 45–7.

44 Derrida, "Différance," *Margins of Philosophy*, p. 130. In another piece, "The Double Session," on reading Mallarmé's *"Livre"*, i.e. *Le "livre" de Mallarmé*, ed. Jacques Scherer (Paris: Gallimard, 1957), and commentaries on the text, Derrida offers some tantalizing remarks which Rodolphe Gasché has construed as offering a clue to Derrida's notion of a deconstructive "method" that is "both the grounds of possibilities of the canonical philosophical gestures and themes and their ungrounds, that is, that which makes them impossible." The passage from "The Double Session" goes as follows: "Its steps [said of 'dissemination,' which Gasché glosses as justifying application to deconstruction] allow for (no) *method:* no path leads around in a circle toward a first step, nor proceeds from the simple to the complex, nor leads from a beginning to an end. . . . We here note a point/ lack of method [*point de méthode*]: This does not rule out a marching order" – "The Double Session," *Dissemination*, tr. Barbara Johnson (Chicago: University of Chicago Press, 1981), p. 271. See Rodolphe Gasché, *The Tain of the Mirror: Derrida and the Philosophy of Reflection* (Cambridge, Mass.: Harvard University Press, 1986), particularly ch. 8, "Deconstructive Methodology." Gasché's remark appears on pp. 174–5, and is clearly a plausible reading of Derrida's remark. In fact, Gasché's is the only sustained account I know that seriously entertains the "methodological" import of Derrida's way of working. There are "others," to be sure; but they invariably naturalize or de-construct Derrida.

45 See for instance Derrida, *Of Grammatology*, p. 10f.

46 Derrida, "Différance," *Margins of Philosophy*, p. 22.

47 See, for example, Robert Magliola, *Derrida on the Mend* (West Lafayette, Ind.: Purdue University Press, 1984), particularly pt 3.

48 See Kathleen Freeman, *Companion to the Pre-Socratic Philosophers* (Oxford: Basil Blackwell, 1953), pp. 56–7.

49 The translation is given by Charles H. Kahn, *The Art and Thought of Heraclitus* (Cambridge: Cambridge University Press, 1979), p. 55 (Fragment LIV). See also Kahn's discussion of Fragments XXXVI, XXXVII and LIV in his Commentary.

50 Ibid., p. 19.

51 See William James, *Essays in Radical Empiricism* (New York: Longmans, Green, 1912), Lecture II; and John Dewey, *Experience and Nature*, 2nd edn., (New York: Dover, 1958) See also Sandra B. Rosenthal, *Speculative Pragmatism* (Amherst: University of Massachussetts Press, 1986), ch. 4; and Richard Rorty's essay "Overcoming the Tradition: Heidegger and Dewey," in his *Consequences of Pragmatism (Essays: 1972–1980)* (Minneapolis: University of Minnesota Press,

1982), which pursues the deconstructive theme with regard to both naturalistic and phenomenological texts.

52   James, *Essays in Radical Empiricism*, p. 42.

53   Ibid., p. 83 (italics added).

54   See Derrida, *Speech and Phenomena*, ch. 5.

55   W. V. Quine, *Word and Object* (Cambridge, Mass.: MIT Press, 1960), p. 71; see also the whole of sections 15–16.

56   See Christopher Norris, *The Deconstructive Turn* (London: Methuen, 1983), ch. 7, and *Contest of Faculties* (London: Methuen, 1985), ch. 2.

57   See Quine, *Word and Object*, section 33. "Opportunistic departure from ordinary language in a narrow sense," Quine observes, "is part of ordinary linguistic behavior. . . . [Other departures] are reserved for use as needed. . . . The quest of a simplest clearest overall pattern of canonical notation is not to be distinguished from a quest of ultimate catgeories, a limning of the most general traits of reality. Nor let it be retorted that such constructions are conventional affairs not dictated by reality; for may not the same be said of a physical theory? True, such is the nature of reality that one physical theory will get us around better than another; but similarly for canonical notation" (pp. 157–8, 161).

58   See Margolis, *Science without Unity*, ch. 4.

59   See Nelson Goodman, *Ways of Worldmaking* (Cambridge, Mass.: Harvard University Press, 1978).

60   See Husserl, *The Crisis of European Sciences and Transcendental Phenomenology*, pt IIIA.

61   See Charles B. Guignon, *Heidegger and the Problem of Knowledge* (Indianapolis: Hackett, 1983), ch. 5.

62   Michael Foucault, *Discipline and Punish: The Birth of the Prison*, tr. Alan Sheridan (New York: Vintage Books, 1979), p. 215.

63   See for instance Mark Poster, *Foucault, Marxism and History: Mode of Production versus Mode of Information* (Cambridge: Polity Press, 1984), ch. 4. Poster grasps very well what we are identifying as the naturalistic–phenomenological contrast between Foucault and Marxism, but he has nothing to say about the specifically deconstructive – or, the deconstructively read Nietzschean – aspect of Foucault. To preserve the one without the other is, however, to deform Foucault's notion of genealogy, which plays no role in Poster's account. Cf. ch. 6, below.

64   In the Marxist world, of course, the ultimate insistence of such a historicized and totalized structuralism is to be found in Louis Althusser. See Louis Althusser and Étienne Balibar, *Reading Capital*, tr. Ben Brewster (London: New Left Books, 1970); and Louis Althusser, *For Marx*, tr. Ben Brewster (London: New Left Books, 1969). See also Fredric Jameson, *The Political Unconsious* (Ithaca, NY: Cornell University Press, 1981). Jameson's book is undoubtedly the most sustained (somewhat relaxed) application of Althusser's model to literary and social criticism. It confirms by its characteristic vigor the clear sense in which the phenomenological "moment" is straightforwardly achieved by a critical Marxism that then moves on to its naturalistic objective (thus adjusted). It has no confidence at all in philosophical deconstruction, however much of it may be attracted to literature, films, architecture influenced by "postmodernist" social forces that are themselves uneasily (but not altogether accurately) linked with either post-structuralism or, within post-structuralism, deconstruction proper.

See Fredric Jameson, "Postmodernism, or the Cultural Logic of Late Capitalism," *New Left Review*, no. 146 (1984).

65 Foucault, *Discipline and Punish*, pp. 27–8.

66 Michel Foucault, "Nietzsche, Genealogy, History," in *Language, Counter-Memory, Practice:Selected Essays and Interviews*, tr. Donald F. Bouchard and Sherry Simon, ed. Donald F. Bouchard, (Ithaca, NY.: Cornell University Press, 1977).

67 See Michel Foucault, "The Subject and Power," Afterword to Hubert L. Dreyfus and Paul Rabinow, *Michel Foucault: Beyond Structuralism and Hermeneutics* (Chicago: University of Chicago Press, 1982). Dreyfus and Rabinow do actually run the serious risk, opposed to Poster's (noted above), of transforming Foucault's account into a profound skepticism – *in* favoring his own brand of political activism. This is also an excessive reading that violates the subtle balance of the genealogical approach. By far the ablest appraisal of Foucault is to be found in J. G. Merquior, *Foucault* (Berkeley, Calif.: University of California Press, 1985), particularly the summary assessment of Foucault's conceptual dilemma, ch. 10.

68 Ibid., p. 216.

69 Derrida, "Différance," *Margins of Philosophy*, p. 6.

70 Friedrich Nietzsche, *The Will of Power*, tr. Walter Kaufmann and R. J. Hollingdale, ed. Walter Kaufmann (New York: Vintage Books, 1968), section 556.

71 See for instance Reiner Schürmann, *Heidegger on Being and Acting: From Principles to Anarchy*, tr. Christine-Marie Gros in collaboration with the author (Bloomingtom: Indiana University Press, 1987), ch. 8.

72 Jean Granier, "Nietzsche's Conception of Chaos," tr. David B. Allison, in David B. Allison (ed.), *The New Nietzsche* (Cambridge, Mass.: MIT Press, 1985), p. 137. This powerful reading, which seems to capture the deepest stratum of Nietzsche's intention, is essentially absent from many standard readings of Nietzsche, however attractive they may be. See for instance Alexander Nehamas, *Nietzsche: Life as Literature* (Cambridge, Mass.: Harvard University Press, 1985); Ofelia Schutte, *Beyond Nihilism: Nietzsche without Masks* (Chicago: University of Chicago Press, 1984); Gilles Deleuze, *Nietzsche and Philosophy*, tr. Hugh Tomlinson (New York: Columbia University Press, 1983).

73 Jean Granier, "Perspectivism and Interpretation," David B. Allison, in Allsion (ed.), *The New Niezsche*, p. 190; from Jean Granier, *Le Problème de la verité dans la philosophie de Nietzsche* (Paris: Editions du Seuil, 1966).

74 See Keijo Nishitani, *Religion and Nothingness*, tr. Jan Von Bragt (Berkeley, Calif.: University of California Press, 1982). Thanks to the suggestion of J. N. Mohanty, I have had the opportunity of sampling, also, the views of Nagarjuna through a collection of careful commentaries on his contributions to the Madhyamika philosophy – particularly regarding Śunyātā ("Voidity") – which have obviously influenced the Kyoto School. See Satkari Mookerjee (ed.), *The Nava-Nalanda-Mahavihana Research Publication*, vol. 1 (Nalanda: Navanalandamahavihara, 1957).

75 See for instance J. N. Mohanty, *The Possibility of Transcendental Philosophy* (The Hague: Martinus Nijhoff, 1986).

76 Foucault, *Discipline and Punish*, p. 155; see further the whole of pt III.

77 This summarizes, succinctly, the essential unity of the sprawling variety of the

forms of intentionality. It demonstrates, therefore, the peculiar narrowness of Brentano's and Husserl's speculations on the *referents* of intentionality. See Margolis, *Science without Unity*, chs 7, 9.

78 Hans-Georg Gadamer, "On the Scope and Function of Hermeneutical Reflection," tr. G. B. Hess and R. E. Palmer, in Hans-George Gadamer, *Philosophical Hermeneutics*, ed. and tr. David E. Linge (Berkeley: University of California Press, 1976), p. 19.

79 Derrida, *Of Grammatology*, p. 158.

80 See chs 2, 8, below.

81 Hans-Georg Gadamer, "Text and Interpretation," tr. Dennis J. Schmidt in Brice R. Wachterhauser (ed.), *Hermeneutics and Modern Philosophy* (Albany, NY.: State University of New York Press, 1986), p. 379.

82 Ibid., p. 383.

83 Hans-Georg Gadamer, "The Universality of the Hermeneutical Problem," *Philosophical Hermeneutics*, pp. 7–8.

84 See Margolis, *Pragmatism without Foundations*, ch. 3.

85 Cf. Margolis, *Science without Unity*, p. 98 n. 95.

86 See Margolis, *Pragmatism without Foundations*, ch. 2.

Part One

The Context of the Human

2

The Technological Self

If we think of such practical matters as the transfer of high technology to third-world countries, we are at once forced to address the question of the moral, technical, habitual, institutional, historical, even cognitional differences between the members of "donor" and "recipient" communities. The relocation, for instance, of asbestos plants from the United States to Mexico (to elude the monitoring of health hazards, say, or to gain the advantage of cheap labor) exemplifies the natural problem of fitting an initially alien practice (at home in its own *Lebenswelt* and *Lebensform*) to the dense complexities of another viable form of life that cannot possibly accommodate, without reciprocally adjusting, the new technology and its own societal practices.[1] Confrontations of these sorts are fairly common; the inflexibilities they expose are usually construed as manifesting the divergent values and beliefs and habits of different societies. They are, in other words, taken straightforwardly as first-order or "indicative" differences – which some appropriate managerial skills may be expected to soften or offset. If, however, we view such differences in the spirit of larger phenomenological, hermeneutic, Frankfurt School, Marxist, or pragmatist reflections on the formation and preformation of the cogniscent and active powers of the very agents who play the donor and recipient roles in the transfer of technology, we are bound to consider that those differences also manifest potentially quite disparate conceptions of the nature of the world cognized and of the capacities of those who inquire – within the space of which the transfer intended is itself perceived and pursued.

The idea that *that* relationship between knower and known is, in some sense, an artifact of an incompletely fathomable symbiosis of effective life from which it is reflexively drawn, and that it is a fair guess that the relationship and our conception of it are profoundly affected and constrained by what, in the local culture of different human societies, makes their particular viability possible, is a *second-order* reflection on what we mean by objective world and cognitive competence. Cognition or science or inquiry is not a mere natural phenomenon or matter of fact, although there are of course "facts" about the knowledge of particular groups. There is no first-order science that does not implicate its own second-order legitimation; there is no legitimation that is not fitted to the practices of an actual science or inquiry; and the difference between first- and second-order matters is itself a second-order distinction. The "facts" about the science, technology, institutional life, norms and values and the like of particular societies count as facts only on the sufferance of second-order conceptions under which they are so identified – either reflexively within one's own society or at a distance with regard to another. It is easy to see, therefore, the radical import of conceding that the very formulation of a reasonable second-order conception of how we and others think, perceive, understand, act, judge, make, and appraise is itself an artifact of the tacit, preformational, horizonally limited, historically contingent, partially fathomable technology or *praxis* in accord with which our own society has proved viable.

That thesis *is* the thesis of the technological self: that the cogniscent, active agent of human societies is, in some profound sanse, historically constituted by the technological aptitudes of that society. The problem of technological transfer, therefore, is really an important exemplar of and a convenient metonym for the general puzzles of conceptual and cognitional incommensurability within the space of which we try to form, and must form, our best proposals about the nature of truth and validity, rightness and objectivity, science and rational inquiry. To admit the logical entailment of second-order convictions about the regularities of cognitive aptitude in the acknowledged accomplishment of any first-order science or activity is to pose an essential question about the epistemic standing of such science or activity. But to admit (as a second-order conjecture) that our first- and second-order powers are themselves preformed by – therefore intransparent to – the tacit technological and praxical activities by which we are first oriented in a cognitively relational way to what we regard as the objective world is *to deny any conceivable ground for ensuring that there are cogniscent invariants or essential attributes that can be assigned human persons or selves.* This is what is meant by the shorthand expression – accommodating Hegel, Marx, Nietzsche, Heidegger, Dewey, Gadamer, Foucault with equal facility – that man *is* a history and *has* no other nature. The most plausible reading of that expression is the reading supplied by the doctrine of the technological self. It has its own complexities, however, which need to be laid bare.

I

There is a double puzzle that Thomas Kuhn collects in certain well-known remarks in his *The Structure of Scientific Revolutions* that compellingly links the theory of science and the theory of human inquiry – in effect, it invites a theory of cognizing agents, of selves, of persons. One may doubt that Kuhn has formed an entirely coherent picture of the sciences, but there can be no question that he has completely neglected the analysis of what a human being must be like in order to live and work in the world he posits. Kuhn's linking these two issues remains instructive, nevertheless. For he grasps the paradox that that linkage implies – in a way that is free of his own account; and what he does say about the sciences is quite compatible with (indeed, it memorably instantiates) a number of very large doctrines that the entire sweep of Western philosophy may fairly now be said to be converging upon. These include at least

(a)   the rejection of all forms of cognitive transparency and privilege;
(b)   the indissoluble unity of realist and idealist elements in any plausible theory of the sciences;
(c)   the conceptual symbiosis of cognizing self and cognized world;
(d)   the matched historicity of self, science, and world.[2]

Doctrines (a)–(d) dissolve any hierarchical advantage that might otherwise be assigned so-called naturalistic and phenomenological theories *vis-à-vis* one another and fix at the same time the sense in which theories of either sort could incorporate so-called deconstructive or post-structuralist exposés of their own pretensions regarding any form of cognitive transparency. By a term of art – a fair term – contemporary views incorporating (a)–(d) may be dubbed *pragmatist*.[3]

Kuhn's remarks are these: first of all, that "Lavoisier . . . saw oxygen where Priestley had seen dephlogisticated air and where others had seen nothing at all. . . . Lavoisier saw nature differently . . . Lavoisier worked in a different world";[4] secondly, speaking of that phase of post-fourteenth-century physics (affecting Galileo's work) in which Buridan and Oresme's impetus theory replaces Aristotle's, that "I [that is, Kuhn] am . . . acutely aware of the difficulties created by saying that when Aristotle and Galileo looked at swinging stones, the first saw constrained fall, the second a pendulum."[5] Kuhn, of course favors the thesis that these paired scientists "pursued their research in different worlds": "Until [for example] that scholastic paradigm was invented," Kuhn says "there were no pendulums, but only swinging stones, for the scientist to see. Pendulums were brought into existence by something very like a paradigm-induced gestalt switch."[6]

We are not interested here in the bafflements of Kuhn's own conception of the sciences except as they may help us to understand what is required of a theory of the cognitively apt selves that pursue particular inquiries under the conditions Kuhn advances or, more generally, under constraints (a)–(d) that Kuhn's own views instantiate. Kuhn gladly abandons all talk of " 'the given' of experience," "immediate experience," "a pure observation-language," "mere neutral and objective reports on 'the given' "[7] But he effectively reneges on this proviso – however unwittingly – in his explanation of the viability of the contingently different "worlds" of different societies: "An appropriately programmed perceptual mechanism," he explains, "has survival value. To say that the members of different groups may have different perceptions *when confronted with the same stimuli* is not to imply that they may have just any perceptions at all."[8] The remark is fair enough. But on what grounds (accessible to Kuhn) can we speak of the operations of "the same stimuli" across different paradigms, differently "programmed perceptual mechanisms"? Kuhn maintains that

> Two groups, the members of which have systematically different sensations on receipt of the same stimuli, do *in some sense* live in different worlds. We posit the existence of stimuli to explain our perceptions of the world, and we posit their immutability to avoid both individual and social solipsism. About neither posit have I the slightest reservation. But our world is populated in the first instance not by stimuli but by the objects of our sensations, and these need not be the same, individual to individual or group to group. To the extent, of course, that individuals belong to the same group and thus share education, language, experience, and culture, we have good reason to suppose that their sensations are the same. . . . They must see things, process stimuli, in much the same ways. But where the differentiation and specialization of groups begins, we have no similar evidence for the immutability of sensations.[9]

These are very curious remarks: first, because "invariance" or "immutability" of "stimuli" (neurophysiological connections, even physical laws) are merely *posited* to forestall solipsism (skepticism, radical incommensurability, intellectual nihilism, anarchy, relativism); second, because such invariances are themselves validly relativized to the shared "form of life" of a given society *and only there*; and, third, because, apparently both intra- and intersocietally, the division of labor and historical variation *threaten our confirming any genuine, context-free invariances.*

Kuhn is not content with this kind of tenuousness. "We try," he says,

> to interpret sensations already at hand, to analyze what is for us the given. However we do that, the processes involved must ultimately be neural, and they are therefore governed by the same *physico-chemical* laws that govern perception on the one hand and the beating of our hearts on the other. But the fact that the system obeys the same laws [in all perceptual cases, presumably in all societies] provides no reason to suppose that our neural apparatus is programmed to operate the same way in interpretation as in perception or in either as in the beating of our hearts.

It is in this same context that Kuhn concludes that "An appropriately programmed perceptual mechanism has survival value."[10] This means that those who live in "different worlds" also live in "one world," that the provisional invariances internal to the different worlds of socially shared practices are also good guesses of some sort regarding the actual invariances that hold across such different worlds, that the "incommensurable viewpoints"[11] of these separate worlds are also collected within the range of commensurability (or, at least within the range of intelligibility) of the one overarching world. Incommensurability is not – or at least should not be – construed as equivalent to incommunicability or unintelligibility or untranslatability; on the contrary, moderate incommensurabilities, as much of conceptual categories as of metrical instruments, must, on pain of incoherence, be intelligible, even comparable, to the same inquirer or inquirers.[12] And yet, of course, *to be able to affirm invariances across moderate incommensurabilities signifies cognitive sources that cannot be confined within the bounds of such incommensurabilities.* Kuhn never explains that ability.

There is no question that Kuhn has put his finger on the essential puzzle of a historicized conception of science still bent on formulating the law-like invariances of the entire order of physical nature. But it is equally clear that Kuhn's solution is threatened with an ineliminable measure of incoherence. For our present purpose, it is more important to emphasize what may be called the "constructive" or "constitutive" theme in Kuhn's theories, the notion that the world we live in – we ordinary percipients as well as Aristotle and Galileo as more disciplined scientists – is in some way *constituted* by the socially shared paradigms or practices that form or preform (tacitly rather than by explicit conjecture) the way we perceive and think. Kuhn sees the matter more in terms of the general nature and psychology of human investigators than in terms of the merely formal features of potential truth-claims advanced within the relevant space; and yet, he nowhere directly considers *what* a human person must be like – constituted and reconstituted *by* such cultural forces in the same instant in which the "world" is constituted and reconstituted *by* our changing inquiries and interventions. In this sense, Kuhn offers the barest glimpse of the interesting notion – which his own theory requires and which is required by any generic theory that subscribes to (a)–(d) – that *the human self is itself technologically and praxically constituted.* The potentially radical implications of this notion normally escape our notice, in spite of the fact that constraints (a)–(d) – perhaps, now, only marginally clarified by Kuhn's own favored theories – must surely be among the most salient conceded in our own age. The point may be taken as embedded at least in Kuhn's challenging distinction between a swinging stone and a pendulum.

We are marking off a strategy of argument, possibly a map of an argument, not an actual argument. The approach enjoys a considerable economy. For, there are a surprising number of quite powerful consequences that follow from admitting (a)–(d) together with the cognate finding that, if "worlds" are constituted by the inquiries and practices of human selves, then selves are correspondingly constituted by processes internal to the formed worlds in which they contingently mature. The question of whether selves and persons may be eliminated by some ontological maneuver may be safely set aside: there is no known argument that actually effects that economy once we concede the reality of psychological experience (in however narrow or broad a sense we favor) or once we concede cognizing activities or actions informed by experience;[13] and, in any case, the eliminative maneuver can hardly pretend to have come to grips with the kind of puzzle Kuhn's examination of our historicized sciences imposes upon us.

Merely to concede the point of what may now be called

(e)   the thesis of the technological or technologized self

leads directly to a number of important findings – in a remarkably painless way. It affords a very simple conceptual lever by which to topple a large number of fashionable theories. For example, it follows instantly from the theory of the praxical or technic constitution of the self that _all_ would-be findings of invariances, natural necessities, nomic universals, essences, closed systems, indubitability, self-evidence, and the like _must be no more than idealized posits made within the indefinable limits of the competence and horizon of contingently formed and focused selves._ This is not to deny that it is entirely plausible to posit candidate regularities of such sorts. Indeed, we cannot avoid doing so if we are to accommodate (as we must) the achievement of science. First of all, mere empirical or Humean regularities – human mortality, for instance, or the fixity of the genetic code of the human species, or the ubiquity of certain anthropological constants[14] – hold only within the scope of those benign invariances Kuhn posits; and, secondly, logical necessities, as Quine has shown,[15] can always be treated as open to being denied for reasons of systematic advantage (even if, characteristically, they do not actually require that we seize the advantage).

Alternatively put, it is not the indicative invariances of empirical science or of general human practice or of the (empirical) work of logic and mathematics that count as conceptually troublesome; it is only such invariances construed as entailing or presupposing some more profoundly fixed, universal, necessary, or apodictic invariances of _cogniscence._ The theory of the technologized self is primarily a theory of the contingently constituted, societally formed, historicized, diachronically alterable practices of actual human communities. Hence, the provisionality of any would-be universals – tendered in the spirit of Kuhn himself – may readily be allowed to stand. But there remains an endless number of imposing claims of considerable influence that either utterly fail to come to grips with the flat challenge of that thesis or else, more paradoxically, appear to embrace a version of it even as they insist on invariances that the thesis would clearly disallow. Thus, at a stroke, _if_ the validity of induction and the analysis of the structure of a natural language in extensional terms were relativized to some "corpus of knowledge" (if they were treated as "epistemological" notions in that sense[16]), then inductivism and extensionalism would at best be no more than idealized presumptions that would never ensure their own preferability on logical or conceptual grounds – they could never be more than useful empirical projects.

In that sense, Peircean assurances about the long run, Popperian verisimilitude, Reichenbach's inductivism, Quine's repudiation of intentionality,

Chomsky's nativism, Davidson's apriorism extending a Tarskian conception of truth to natural languages must all be abandoned at a stroke – which is hardly to deny that, *for limited runs of cases under the control of factors outside their own scope, such projects may indeed achieve a measure of success.*[17] To risk a term of opprobrium well beyond its usual application, all such views may be fairly tagged as *logocentric.*[18] Some, for instance Quine's, are actually (or ambivalently) sympathetic to minimizing innate invariances among human "subjects" (or selves): where Quine posits such fixities, he does so always *en bloc*, never distributively; and in doing that he deliberately draws attention to no more than a principled continuity between the features of diverse cultures emerging from and embedded in a relatively uniform biology and the presumed fixities of that biology itself.[19] Quine's own attack on the analytic/synthetic distinction forbids specifying (as he himself explicitly observes) particular such fixities (in what we are calling the logocentric sense). Where such fixities are deliberately posited for the cognizing subject (the self or ego or whatnot), as in the transcendental gymnastics of Edmund Husserl's Ego or in the foundationalist presumptions of Roderick Chisholm's "first person," or where deliberate provision is made for such detailed disclosures, the thesis of the technologized self is instantly devastating – not, of course, in denying the contingent certainty of particular self-referential discoveries, only in subverting the presumption of their timeless inviolability or apodictic standing.[20]

The argument, then, may be put in a word: the world is a flux, reconstituted again and again through powers internal to its own contingent order, centered in local interventions at particular cognizing nodes. Correspondingly, the generic flux itself infects those provisionally specific nodes.

This single theme, economically summarized in (a)–(d) and brought to bear on the puzzle of (e), the constituted or constructed self, threads a disarmingly transparent path through much of the conceptual country of the most vigorously debated philosophies. But it is as instantly subversive as it is transparent. For it indicates how characteristically standard pretensions of universal fixities or even traditionally reliable regularities have presupposed the fixity of the self. What would remain, for instance, of the assured, reflexive, cognitive "beginnings" in the self, whether psychologically managed in the manner of Brentano or Chisholm or (more desperately) of Moritz Schlick[21] or egologically in the manner of Husserl, once the self, the locus of cognition, were admitted to be subject to the contingent vagaries of cultural construction? It is the presumption of the fixed nature of the self – the transformation (to put the matter provocatively) of the self into the immortal soul – that ensures the steady achievement of all familiar forms of foundationalism and the quest for the apodictic. That is the point of the original triumph of the Cartesian, well before the schism between naturalistic and phenomenological strategies was invented. Challenge the assured unity of the self over any temporal span of self-consciousness, challenge the fixed, self-referential disclosures of *what* the self-cognizing powers of the self are: the epistemic certainty of any particular "self-presenting states" would fall into fundamental question.[22] Without that assurance, analytic epistemologies become completely vacuous, entirely formal. They lack legitimating concerns addressed to the praxical sources from which they emerge.[23] The intended assurance is incompatible with every theory that views the self as constructed or societally constituted or subject to historicized variability. The logical need for a referentially individuated center of cognition is simply not equivalent to any substantive doctrine regarding the actual epistemic or ontological unity or cognizing power of any such center: the *unicity* of the self is hardly equivalent to its supposed *unity* and hardly entails an original apodictic power.[24]

Once this is clear, one sees remarkably easily that any constructive conception of the world – roughly, within the purview of doctrines (b) and (c) – similarly undermines all hope of achieving a uniquely correct, or essentialist, or universalistic, or even verisimilitudinous science. We may suggest another powerful benefit of this line of argument (to which we shall have to return by way of a fresh start). *If* there is anything to the constructive theory of the self, then to that extent all theories of the structure of human history – of the narrative form of actual human existence and of the texts of authentic histories and fictionalized surrogates – cannot presume any essentialist or traditionalist structure, cannot for example (as with Paul Ricoeur) presume that Aristotle's *Poetics* and St Augustine's *Confessions*, Book XI, *have* captured the abiding ontological structure of man's historical existence.[25] That, too, would transform the self into a simple and timelessly invariant soul. But these remarks are meant only as reminders of the strategic and ubiquitous effect of theorizing about the self.

The critical finding on which these remarks converge is simply that it remains entirely open to us to search for the universal structures of the cognized world or of the cognizing mind, without presuming thereby to confirm the validity of any universalism – or, by parity of reasoning, any foundationalism, cognitivism, essentialism, inductivism, extensionalism, and the like. Indicative first-order universals are entirely compatible with the rejection of self-confirming second-order universals that would fix our ultimate cognitive powers. The very forms of human tradition and human culture are too various (and have always been too various) to ensure any single, species-wide, convergent picture of the cognized world and the cognizing self; but that variety has not actually disabled the achievement of the sciences. Similarly, the constitution of the cognizing self through the variety of cultures in which it emerges cannot but subvert any reflexive pretension at marking the essential, innate, species-wide structure of the mind's way of functioning; but that concession cannot meaningfully preclude the role of cognition itself. The symbiosis of self and world is as neutral a posit as man seems capable of grasping, once we concede our salient sciences. Hence, even the pretense of *not* requiring an account of the methodological and epistemic puzzles of man's cognitive aptitudes – famously, in Hans-Georg Gadamer's retreat from the false models of "truth" and "method" he would dismiss – fails to escape a version of those same false models, fails to dislodge the need for a theory of world and self. Gadamer's retreat is prophetic of much of our philosophical age: the practice of the classical tradition of Greece, either by itself or by analogy, is somehow made (by Gadamer) to confirm the cognizing norms of the race and is made to do that without the need for any theoretical model of a methodological or epistemic sort. The truth is, it abandons any such inquiry because it ensures by "tradition," preemptively, what such an inquiry would otherwise have had to establish.[26]

II

The effect of the thesis of the technological self is perhaps most compellingly displayed in the views of those who apparently accept the flux of human history, who accept the unsystematizable, evolving, preformative conditions governing the emergence of the various kinds of selves the proliferating cultures of the world engender – and who, at the very moment of admitting that, somehow manage, albeit contradictorily, to secure their own favored fixities once again. These are the assured logocentric posits: transhistorical, ahistorical, totalized, timeless, context-free, originary posits and projections going well beyond Kuhn's more modest sort of *internal*, empirically idealized invariances.

Two brief examples should serve our needs well enough here. They are in fact closely related and dialectically opposed to one another, In one, Gadamer, counterattacking Jürgen Habermas's critique of his own *Truth and Method*, insists on what we are calling here the flux of the self – within the terms of his own hermeneutic orientation:

> Reflection on a given preunderstanding brings before me something that otherwise happens *behind my back* . . . only in this manner do I learn to gain a new understanding of what I have seen through eyes conditioned by prejudice. . . . It is the untiring power of *experience*, that in the process of being instructed, man is ceaselessly forming a new preunderstanding.[27]

Man's experience and relation to the world is, Gadamer insists, "essentially . . . universally . . . linguistical" – by which he means "a truth that goes questioningly behind all knowledge and anticipatingly before it." As a result, "hermeneutics is not to be viewed as a mere subordinate discipline within the arena of the *Geisteswissenschaften*."[28] Gadamer projects as a universal, "external," *constitutive* condition of human knowledge and understanding a condition idealized on the strength of "internal," empirically reflective experience alone. It is as close as he comes to a transcendental argument – and it *is*, effectively, such an argument. But it never presumes (though it should, logically) a cognitive privilege of its own in claiming such universality.[29] Hence, it also undercuts (by a sort of serendipity) Habermas's own pretensions; for, on

Habermas's view (as Gadamer argues), the "use of hermeneutics stands on the premise that it shall serve the methodology of the social sciences." The human "understander [that is, Habermas's critiquer, armed with a grasp of historicity, preformational prejudice, hermeneutic penetration] is [now] seen – even in the so-called sciences of understanding like history – not in relationship to the hermeneutical situation and the constant operativeness of history in his own consciousness, but in such a way as to imply that his own understanding does not enter into the event."[30]

For Habermas, the hermeneutic element is an "additional" instrument *for* the operation of an *independent* critique of society, an instrument serving "the emancipatory power of reflection," facilitating an escape from the "deceptions of language," leading to genuinely necessary, actually explicit universal conditions of rational understanding.[31] Correctly perceived by Gadamer, Habermas means to free *method* – therefore, also, rational political *control* – from the entanglements of historical tradition and hermeneutic prejudice: the "social engineer, this scientist who undertakes to look after the functioning of the machine of society, appears himself to be methodically alienated and split off from the society to which, at the same time, he belongs"; "unconsciously the ultimate guiding image of emancipatory reflection in the social sciences must be an anarchistic utopia."[32]

Nevertheless, the ironies of this well-known contest are more tangled, for Habermas and Gadamer each unmask the other and are each in turn unmasked. It is certainly clear that, in his opposition to Husserl's transcendental solutions and his (adjusted) adherence to Heidegger's account of *Dasein*, Gadamer opposes any notion of the fixity of the cognizing self within "the subject-object bifurcation."[33] He sees Habermas, therefore, as somehow restoring that older "objectivism" or "naturalism" in spite of Habermas's insistence of the praxical nature of human life – the point of the familiar jibe that Habermas is the last of the Enlightenment crowd. It is also the focus of Gadamer's emphasis on "linguisticality":

> Language is by no means simply an instrument, a tool. . . . The appearance of the concept "language" presupposes consciousness of language. But that is only the result of the reflective movement in which the one thinking has reflected out the unconscious operation of speaking and stands at a distance from himself. The real enigma of language, however, is that we can never really do this completely.[34]

We are ourselves endlessly constituted and reconstituted by the dialogue of social existence – we are very much like texts whose incompletable structure depends on the open and interpenetrating contribution of future–present prejudice within the fusion of horizons (*Horizontverschmelzung*).[35] Selves – the I and thou of dialogue – are never fixed and finished entities within any exchange; they are always reconstituted within a social dialogue, like problematic texts (which in a way they are) within the course of problematic interpretation. Habermas himself cites approvingly Gadamer's characteristic charge "The meaning of a text goes beyond its author, not only occasionally, but always. Understanding is therefore not merely reproductive but productive."[36]

The marvelous irony remaining at the bottom of the pool is simply that, for his part, Gadamer snatches, via the classical tradition, a Habermasian-like emancipation from the very flux of history; and that, for his part, Habermas subverts (as Gadamer correctly reports) his own acceptance of Gadamer's insistence on the inalienability of the historical tradition in which we live and move. Here, our opponents change places – each inconsistently. Gadamer resists conclusions tantamount to holding (by hermeneutic means) "that cultural tradition should be absolutized and fixed"; he offers instead the following alternative:

> whether . . . the function of reflection [is to bring] something to awareness in order to confront what is in fact accepted with other possibilities – so that one can either throw it out or reject the other possibilities and accept what the tradition de facto is presenting – or whether bringing something to awareness *always dissolves what one has previously accepted.*[37]

This *is* Gadamer's most consistent formulation of the "universality" of hermeneutic reflection within an ongoing tradition – a kind of hermeneutic *via negativa*. But it cannot sustain more than an interlocking sequence of something analogous to Wittgensteinian "strands of similarity"; certainly, it cannot ensure any hidden fixities within the flux of history. And yet, Gadamer asserts, in a famous passage of *Truth and Method*,

> The classical is fundamentally something quite different from a descriptive concept used by an objectivizing historical consciousness. It is a historical reality to which historical consciousness belongs and is subordinate. What we call "classical" is something retrieved from the vicissitudes of changing time and its changing taste . . . it is a consciousness of something enduring, of significance that cannot be lost and is independent of all the circumstances of time, in which we call something "classical" – a kind of timeless present that is contemporaneous with every other age.[38]

To speak thus is either to voice a mere empirical hope, which history cannot possibly ensure (and which is less than Gadamer requires), or else it is to cheat Gadamer's own deep adherence to the flux of human time. *The historical cultures of mankind are simply too diverse to sustain, as traditions, convergent normative notions of self and world.*

It may not be too intrusive, therefore, to remark here that (as already noted) Kuhn's insistence on the empirical invariances of man's neural constitution (what we have termed "indicative universals") is, pertinently and ineluctably, intended to convey in addition a legitimate sense of a deeper cognizing aptitude (unanalyzed but certainly adequate to the discovery of mere indicative universals) *by means of which* the shifting conceptual incommensurabilities of a historical science never preclude their diachronic resolution within the competence of a progressive science seeking and finding the nomic invariances of the actual world. So Kuhn, like Gadamer (and Popper, pursuing verisimilitude), is a closet essentialist: for, like Gadamer (and Popper and others), he means to rescue – however incoherently, however arbitrarily – the tacit, *second-order* invariances of cogniscence from the indicative regularities of the flux of the world, by means of which that flux is known to instantiate a timeless order of law or meaning.[39]

Gadamer favors the ontology of understanding – not its method, Habermas favors its would-be method – and hang the ontology. The one topples late Frankfurt School presumptions by way of hermeneutic preconditions; the other exposes the formality and shallowness of a hermeneutic sense of history that ignores the structured processes of effective social change. Gadamer recovers an invariance by an obscure "method" he cannot be entitled to; and Habermas constructs a "method" that cannot possibly deliver what his own insistence on human *praxis* will not allow. The one commands no more than the smallest piece of the complexity of the technologized self; the other, via Marxist and Frankfurt School themes, plainly holds a larger piece, but invariably misrepresents it as validly ensuring a set of determinate and normative fixities for human reason as such.[40] This is what is meant by characterizing both Gadamer and Habermas as "traditionalists," recovering (somehow) by way of the historical flux of cultural practices what essentialists or cognitivists would, ahistorically, have already delivered from the flux.[41]

This also marks the essential implication of that best-known paper of Habermas's, which begins, "The task of universal pragmatics is to identify and reconstruct universal conditions of possible understanding [*Verständigung*]."[42] Not all the indecisive fiddling with the difference between transcendental arguments and universal pragmatics can erase the full intent of that modal term – "possible." "I shall," Habermas avows

> develop the thesis that anyone acting communicatively *must*, in performing any speech action, raise universal validity claims and suppose that they can be vindicated [or redeemed: *einlösen*]. . . . The speaker must choose a comprehensible [*verständlich*] expression so that speaker and hearer can understand one another. The speaker *must* have the intention of communicating a true [*wahr*] proposition (or a propositional content, the existential presuppositions of which are satisfied) so that the hearer can share the knowledge of the speaker. The speaker *must* want to express his intentions truthfully [*wahrhaftig*] so that the hearer can believe the utterance of the speaker (can trust him). Finally, the speaker *must* choose an utterance that is right [*richtig*] so that the hearer can accept the utterance and speaker and hearer can agree with one another in

the utterance with respect to a recognized normative background. Moreover, communicative action *can* continue undisturbed only as long as participants suppose that the validity claims they reciprocally raise are justified.[43]

Now, these conditions must either be rationally binding upon, but not *constitutive* of, actual communication, or else be both regulative *and* constitutive. The second option is plainly false. Habermas hardly denies that speakers may successfully communicate without subscribing to the conditions given; also, he could hardly demonstrate that a breach of these conditions would necessarily disable communication. On the other hand, the first alternative would signify that the conditions were inessential for actual communication; their regulative validity would then be problematic. Even if they were empirically regular invariances, they would hardly yield as such the valid elements of any universal norm of inquiry.[44] To emphasize the cognitive competence of isolated individuals in order to *ensure* the satisfaction of the four conditions Habermas posits is to retreat to an objectivism Habermas's own critical approach must disallow; and to concede the socialized and historicized context of effective communication is to set as a conceptual problem the difference between merely recognizing successful piecemeal communication and demonstrating that successful communication in some way implicates determinate normative universals of discourse. The plain fact is that Habermas's conception of the historicized symbiosis of self and society makes it impossible for him to *show* (as opposed to his being able to dream or hope) that communication ever instantiates particular pragmatic universals of rational discourse – or, indeed, that such universals are ever really needed or possible.[45] To admit moderate incommensurabilities and the constructive nature of the self clearly challenges both Habermas's effort to remove the conditions of rationality from the historical flux and to recover the transhistorical conditions of communicative understanding from the flux itself. These are the marks of Habermas's Enlightenment mentality.

III

What we have sketched thus far are the lines of an argument by which, admitting the constructive nature of the world along the moderate (if somewhat muddled) lines of Kuhn's historicizing, we find ourselves obliged to admit the constructive nature of cognizing selves. Mark that (the constructive thesis) as *theme 1* of what we have termed the doctrine of the technological or technologized self. It exercises an immense economy in disqualifying at a stroke all forms of logocentrism – all essentialisms, all universalisms, all natural necessities of cognition, all totalizing, all closed systems, all apodicticity. But it is itself fragile and incomplete as an account of what the technologized self entails. It does not sufficiently identify what, minimally, the achievement of human communication requires. We have just taken note of the extraordinary ease with which Gadamer and Habermas ensure a comfortable fixity of humane or rational values within the traditions of human understanding – in virtue of which each (by different routes) insouciantly extends the destructuring power of historical process without the least loss of essential transhistorical invariances. What (we may well ask) if either would have had to defend his claim against the Nietzschean strategies of Foucault's genealogies? Regardless of Foucault's own conceptual predicaments, the tableaux would have exposed the unjustified traditionalism of each – the assurance that, within their own flux, changing histories could harbor sufficiently robust invariances to justify speaking of *the* classical tradition or *the* requirements of reason *tout court*. And yet, there can be little doubt that human communication *is* successful, works, functions – in a way that clearly facilitates the survival and reproduction of the species.

If we allow the proliferation of something like very thin Wittgensteinian forms of life to function unchecked, "conventionally," anarchically, abstractly, without detailed constraints of any sort except for whatever is said to be internal to the constituting "rules" of this or that life form, we should make an utter mystery of effective human traditions, of the viable plurality of cultures, of the relative smoothness of intersocietal (as well as intrasocietal) communication. We have already taken notice of Kuhn's rather naive effort to save – within the discontinuities of paradigm shifts – a certain fallback to an invariant physical order somehow not affected by that shift itself. *There* lies the incoherence threatening every historicized picture of science. It has already been energetically promoted in an anarchistic, even a deconstructive, spirit by Paul Feyerabend.[46] More recently, its aporetic nature has been even more diligently enhanced by Nelson Goodman.

Now, Kuhn actually cites Goodman approvingly for what he takes to be the latter's sympathy for his own thesis of "paradigm-determined" perception. In the context in question, Kuhn explicitly opposes "the attempt, traditional since Descartes but not before, to analyze perception as an interpretive process, as an unconscious version of what we do *after* we have perceived."[47] Kuhn may be taken to agree (implicitly) here with Gadamer in opposing the notion that we ever fix – antecedently, free of our historicizing paradigms – particular "texts" that, then and only then, we move to interpret: the "texts" of physical processes, say, as far as the sciences are concerned; but in doing that Kuhn also undercuts his own matched efforts to ensure certain trans-paradigmatic invariances. He cites approvingly Goodman's remark from *The Structure of Appearance*, "It is fortunate that nothing more [than phenomena known to exist] is in question [Goodman recommends restricting appraisals of 'extensional identity' to 'all cases that actually *are*,' omitting any and 'all cases that "might have been,"']; for the notion of 'possible' cases, of cases that do not exist but might have existed, is far from clear."[48] Kuhn favors the remark because he links the impossibility of a perceptually neutral vocabulary to the play of competing paradigms: "No language," he says, glossing Goodman, "thus restricted to reporting a world fully known in advance can produce mere neutral and objective reports on 'the given.' Philosophical investigation has not yet provided even a hint of what a language able to do that would be like."[49] Here Kuhn stresses only the puzzle of neutrality: he neglects Goodman's opposition between the actual and the possible. In doing that, he fails to show how the operative procedures for determining the boundaries of the "actual" may be reliably drawn from the play of paradigms. Given his view of paradigms, Kuhn cannot really accept – cannot even rightly understand – Goodman's assured distinction between "actual" and "possible" cases. And Goodman himself, certainly after having developed his own recent theories of world-making, can no longer draw reliably (if he ever could have) on the same distinction.[50]

We have come back then to the difference between a swinging stone and a pendulum – now with attention to our understanding one another, not merely with regard to the conundrum of a coherent science. Kuhn cannot but be unwilling to endorse Goodman's "constructionalist orientation" – the claim that we make "multiple actual worlds" through the bare activity of the "sciences, the arts, perception, and everyday practice . . . without even the consolation of intertranslatability."[51] Goodman, of course, is quite open about the implied divergence (between himself and Kuhn, which he never directly discusses): "there is" he says, "no version-independent feature, no true version [of the world] compatible with all true versions [of the world]."[52] Still, he seems merely reckless here. He does not bring his "worlds" together in any cognitively pertinent way – as Kuhn at least attempts to do. He does not discuss the consequences, on admitting his own constructionalism, of the symbiosis between world and cognizing self. He does not address in a cognitively pertinent way the distinction between the "actual" and the "possible." In Goodman's view,

> reality in a world, like realism in a picture, is largely a matter of habit. Ironically, then, our passion for one world is satisfied, at different times and for different purposes, in many different ways. . . . That right versions and actual worlds are many does not obliterate the distinction between right and wrong versions, does not recognize merely possible worlds answering to wrong versions, and does not imply that all right alternatives are equally good for every or indeed for any purpose.[53]

He loses the cognizing focus from which "right" and "wrong" versions could possibly be sorted – distributively. He abandons every effort to detail a theory of "entrenched" predicates – belonging to an earlier period[54] – that might have saved the minimal realism that still remains embedded in his recent "irrealism." In short, his theory is all but incoherent.[55] The reason is critical. It is precisely what separates Goodman from Quine. Quine's holism, of course, forbids his *mentioning* any determinate invariances; but he insists nevertheless that we cannot abandon admitting invariances – which counts as his attempt to reconcile pragmatism with his Duhemian-like stance. "At this point," Quine says in his most astutely guarded manner, "some heuristic value can be got from evolutionary considerations. There must be . . . an innate standard of perceptual similarity. It underlies our primitive inductions, and is accountable to natural selection by virtue of its survival value."[56] Quine *never* goes beyond this concession, but he also never fails to remind us of it. It is the breaking point between himself and Kuhn (which he would be unwilling to explore). For our present purpose, it is enough to remark that Quine's concession counts as the thinnest version of biological nativism that could possibly be formulated. It is obviously not enough – for the simple reason that any science worth its salt requires a large array of distributed truths aspiring to a measure of invariant order. Goodman's "entrenchments" are no more than a mere nostalgia for the theme; Quine's innate dispositions are at least a minimal provision on which, eventually, science may come to rest.

Paradoxically, both fail to place the cognizing self in a larger conceptual space in which the achievements of empirical science (taken holistically) could plausibly be grounded and in which those same achievements (taken distributively) could possibly be confirmed. The matching mistake of Gadamer and Habermas is of quite a different sort: by means of a conceptually hopeless maneuver, *they* struggle to ensure for science and inquiry a universalism their more promising picture of the historicized niches of actual human existence effectively disallows. Quine and Goodman merely husband their arbitrary pretensions regarding extensionalism, nominalism, physicalism; but in their more explicit moments they do really give up every form of universalism. (They remain logocentric while denying cognitive privilege or transparency.) Gadamer and Habermas inconsistently believe they can actually salvage a suitable universalism from the very flux of historicity. (*They* believe they can reconcile universalism and historicism.[57]) The first pair fail to link the cognizing feat of science with a deeper condition that does not itself betray a cognitive privilege – but they do abandon privilege. The second pair fail to abandon privilege even as they manage to limit an essential part of that deeper historicized condition – but their method is self-contradictory. The maneuver required must go deeper than Gadamer and Habermas do, must be more forthright than Quine and Goodman are prepared to be.

The better clue lies elsewhere – in the biologized philosophical anthropologies of the European tradition. Marjorie Grene, for instance, captures what we shall mark here as *theme 2* of the technologized self:

To be a person is to be a history. In what respects? In two respects, opposed but related. On the one hand, being a person is an achievement of a living individual belonging to a natural kind whose genetic endowment and possible behaviors provide the necessary conditions for the achievement. On the other hand, a human being becomes the person he is within, and as one expression of, a complex network of artifacts – language, ritual, social institutions, styles of art and architecture, cosmologies and myths – that constitute a culture. A culture, of course, is itself a sedimentation of the actions of past persons; but it is, nevertheless, preexistent with respect to the development of any particular person.[58]

Speaking with Helmuth Plessner, Grene stresses "the natural artificiality of man" – that "it is our nature to need the artificial"; and, with Adolf Portmann, she speaks of the first year of life as "the year of the social uterus."[59] The biology of man uniquely requires completion through cultural artifactuality, through historicity (*Geschichtlichkeit*), through the development of the technologically apt self. Technology, then, is the biological aptitude of the human species for constituting, by alternative forms of equilibration, a world suited to a society of emergent selves or a society of such surviving selves adjusted, diachronically, to such a world. We understand one another for the same reason we survive as a species. Technology is the flowering of our biological endowment and is *incarnate* in it.[60] But it flowers divergently, in historically diverse ways; and it flowers within the indicative invariances of the genetics of our species. Hence, both the divergences and invariances are posited within a deeper flux that affects *both* cognized world and cognizing self – that cannot be resisted at any legitimative, second-order level of reflection. Here, in fact, is the essential (transcendental) theme of the notion of the technological self.

This means that all communication, all understanding, all forms of knowledge, science, interpretation, action, cooperation, art, institutionalized life are biologically grounded, emergent with respect to – incarnations of – biological predispositions. Selves are constituted through the enculturing forms that our genetic endowment can support; and the diachronic reconstitution of selves accommodating successive such incarnations, generation by generation, must be (i) open-ended toward future cultural forms; (ii) minimally constrained by the empirically projectible limits of innate capacities (short of evolutionary change); and (iii) similarly constrained by the empirically projectible limits of what the real structures of the world may be taken to be. These are all *holist* constraints – *not* privileged in any cognitive way, projected from *within* the "internalist" resources of a reflective science and philosophy.[61] They are, also, always addressed to reconciling the strong *distributed* claims of our science with the deeper *holist* sources of its realism. This is the only formula consistent with (our) themes of the constructive nature of the technological self (*theme 1*) and of the need to account biologically for communicative successes of every sort (*theme 2*). It need not urge the cogniscent invariances favored by Gadamer or Habermas or Karl-Otto Apel; it need not flaunt the know-nothing anarchies of Feyerabend and Goodman; it need not resign itself to the vaguer and weaker empirical invariances of Kuhn and Quine. Its economy provides for the defeat of all forms of ontic dualism and functionalism; and it respects the intentional complexities of cultural emergence.

It favors, therefore, two characteristic themes: first, the very strong doubt that the causalities of cultural process can be reduced to the terms of a closed physicalism of any sort or of a merely biologized system of closed generative rules – hence, it opposes the views of Donald Davidson and Noam Chomsky and Claude Levi-Strauss; second, the very strong conviction that the underlying regularities, uniformities, similarities that make communication effective – as in the use of general linguistic terms – are themselves incarnate, technologized or praxical, resting on a tacit consensus about the tolerance of consensus, uncommitted to explicit (second-order) universals, viable through the interpretive accommodations of an actual society.[62] A Wittgensteinian resolution of the demarcation between the "actual" and the merely "possible" is more helpful than the resolution afforded by Goodman and Kuhn;[63] it also suggests how we may reconcile Gadamer and Habermas and Wittgenstein.

We must therefore, eschew the irrelevances of an extreme nominalism as well as of an extreme realism rearding universals: one fails to accommodate the incarnation of cultures in the biology of the species; the other fails to admit the distinction of the cultural altogether. Marjorie Grene apparently believes, for instance, that her own interesting approval of Plessner's formula can be reconciled with J. J. Gibson's theory of "affordances."[64] Unfortunately, that is quite impossible. Gibson's view disallow *any* real, emergent, constituted world that would subvert ecologically real invariances at the level of sub-cultural biology or that would require the open-ended interpretive powers of well-formed cognizing selves. To ground the sciences and cognizing activity biologically *and* to construe positing such a grounding in strongly historicized terms, in terms that concede the inextricable symbiosis of the realist and idealist aspects of human inquiry or in terms that concede the culturally con-structive nature of self and world, *is*, effectively, to disallow any universalism of the sort Gibson favors – either in the sense of a direct realism or in the sense of real universals somehow structuring the ambient world. Grene cannot possibly be consistent here. The technological theme is neither biologically reductive nor culturally functionalist. It is thoroughly committed to an emergence incarnate within the biological, and it must remain open-ended in the historicist sense.

IV

We come, then, to our third and final theme. On the argument sketched, even the perception of a pendulum is a technological feat. There is no disjunction, at the cultural level, between thinking, perceiving, desiring, on the one hand, and acting, intervening, producing, inventing, on the other. The human self is a technologized organism, groomed in a natural way – that is, merely by living among the apt adults of a viable society – *to* see and think and act in accord with the Intentionally significant modes the various historical cultures have formed over time.[65] Hence, extending the tally of the preceding section, (*theme 3*) theorizing is inherently praxical – in a double sense: first, because the very formation of the new selves of each cohort of infants depends on processes of internalizing the culturally emergent forms of viable life a given society generates and because the diachronic, gradual reordering of the constitutive forms of each such society must be similarly congruent with the innate aptitudes that underlie every cultural evolution; and, second, because the praxical achievement of man must be continuous with the sub-cultural aptitudes of other species, both instinctive and learned, that ensure their own viability under changing environmental conditions (notably, under conditions that man more and more extensively imposes). These themes lead to the *contextedness* of human life and to the *realism* due the cultural world. This is in part to say that, although the world is in a measure "constructed," it cannot be merely constructed (on pain of incoherence) and that its constructed phases must form a congenial and conservative set of biologically incarnate variations (on pain of excessive incommensurability).

Goodman offers a penetrating remark that *could* serve us here more flexibly than Quine's quite marginal innatism. To the extent that it is sufficiently explicit, it shows how easy it is to repudiate the heavy invariances favored by such historically oriented theorists as Gadamer and Habermas, *and* it suggests (without intending to) a reconciliation with the wilder post-structuralist currents of contemporary French thinking – of Foucault and Derrida, of Barthes and Bataille, of Lyotard, of Deleuze. Goodman offers a new way of defeating the correspondence theory of truth:

> truth cannot be defined or tested by agreement with "the world"; for not only do truths differ for different worlds but the nature of agreement between a version and a world apart from it is notoriously nebulous. Rather – speaking loosely and without trying to recover either Pilate's question or Tarski's – a version is taken to be true when it offends no unyielding *beliefs* and none of its own precepts.[66]

Let us consider Goodman's observation lightly.

First of all, Goodman's is a formula that is easily sustained without the extravagance of plural actual worlds. Secondly, it is a pragmatist and holist formula reconcilable with Quine's own holist intent (granting always that Quine's own view may be made sufficiently coherent). Thirdly, it is an analogue of Gadamer's hermeneutic recovery of the classical tradition, though without anything like Gadamer's strained insistence on a strong invariance: that is, it is also a version of the *via negativa*. But, fourthly, and against Goodman's own style of thinking, it is profoundly entangled in interpretive puzzles, caught up in the hermeneutic circle, dependent on the intentional regularities of particular cultures within which and with which particular sets of beliefs and desires and the like must be dialectically equilibrated. The last feature occasions no difficulty for our present line of theorizing. But Goodman, we must remember, had earlier insisted (and means to do so here as well) on disjoining the "actual" and the "might have been" and on restricting (to the actual alone) questions of truth and "rightness of rendering"; [67] whereas the hermeneutic and the praxical (as both Gadamer and Habermas attest) are futural, oriented to possible intentional extensions tested under conditions of consensus and viability.

It would not be difficult to interpret Goodman conformably – for he speaks of the true as of what "offends no unyielding *beliefs* and none of its own *precepts.*" It is hard to see how these concessions can fail to favor a very robust sense of the open and shifting context of social practices. Nevertheless, it is quite impossible to reconcile this way of reading Goodman with Goodman's own notorious nominalism: the very idea of spontaneously extending the use of general terms to new cases beyond any finite set of learned exemplars *cannot in principle* be reconciled with nominalism.[68] The defeat of nominalism and the rejection of a realism of innate or cognitively transparent universals[69] would oblige us to adopt a very strong contextualism (and, perhaps, a theory of universals that either is or is very much like a conceptualist theory). Only a marriage of views that combines the functional theme of Wittgenstein's "forms of life," Gadamer's historicized "fusion of horizons," and Habermas's (or of course Marx's) emphasis on the formative powers of the productive and reproductive processes of a society (its *praxis*) may be said to begin to provide a suitable setting for an adequate theory of effective communication and work within open-ended cultural contexts.[70] The denial of real contexts and real possibilities, the affirmation of nominalism, the retreat from distributed truth-claims to no more than a holist grip on realism, the avoidance of interpretive consensus, indifference to historicity, inattention to the conditions of social existence, all go hand in hand. They are, in effect, the symptoms of a weak grip on the praxical nature of theory – not necessarily entailing its denial but failing nevertheless to provide for the viability of science itself – especially its constructive features. There is that much difference at least between Kuhn and Goodman.

The fact is that something analogous to the human situation must be admitted even among thoroughly instinctual animals. Something like the *Ur*-form of the intentional unity of theory and *praxis* appears for instance in Niko Tinbergen's well-known studies of the stickleback. For, on the basis of Tinbergen's ingenious tests of the responsiveness of these agressive fish to color-spots and body shape and movement, it is quite clear that (in an instinctual way) they discriminate *abstract,* biologically pertinent universals; that is, they exhibit, *in their niches,* a behavioral responsiveness of an appropriate kind to runs of noticeably new physical stimuli *falling within approximate limits of some sort.*[71] Their behavior certainly invites intentional characterization (though Tinbergen would oppose the practice); and what they do within their niches would of course, in the human case (or among the higher animals), invite a fuller sense of intentionalized context.[72] The linguistic contexts of human intelligence preclude at one stroke both an extreme behaviorism and an extreme nominalism – since neither of those doctrines promises to analyze language itself in a completely satisfactory way.

The simple point remains that, among instinctual animals, there is no way to avoid postulating an internal information-processing mechanism of some sort that coordinates behavior and discrimination *within a range of invariance that clearly accommodates perceptual variances*. That is all one means in speaking of "universals" among such creatures; ironically, it is just such creatures rather than man who show the sense in which, *à la* Goodman, similarity can be confined to the "actual" as opposed to the "might have been." By enlarging the range of application from the one to the other, by rejecting any principled demarcation between the two, by raising ("indicative") universals to the status of a cultural achievement, by embedding learning in a natural form of life, by linking the shifting limits of conceptual tolerance and extension to intrasocietal consensus and interpretation, by binding the entire process to the embedding conditions of species survival, by refusing to disjoin the conditions of effective thought and perception and desire from those of effective action, by acknowledging the informality of consensual implicatures of relevance and context, we raise the primitive invariances of instinctual behavior to the conceptual invariances of the technologized life of humans. There, they are simply benignly workable indicative invariances of any first-order empirical inquiry, not the cognitively privileged invariances of any second-order universalism or essentialism or the like. *The technological self is the agent of that sort of aptitude.* This is precisely why, when he speaks of offending "no unyielding *beliefs* and none of its [that is, a 'world-version's'] own *precepts*," Goodman betrays his own indifference to the linkage between theory and practice and between culture and biology – and betrays his indifference to the ubiquity of the technological.[73]

Furthermore, if we remind ourselves of Kuhn's constructive view of reality (and concede thereupon the constructive nature of the self), we see at once that we cannot, in a consistent way, construe selves realistically without so construing the "made" world as well. In particular, since the emergence of the apt cognizing creatures we treat as persons depends on the formative and sustaining powers of their particular cultures, there is no plausible way in which to discredit the reality of cultural phenomena. "To be a person is to be a history," Marjorie Grene correctly affirms. To be a person is to be culturally constituted as such. To be real as a person or as a self entails the reality of those powers and attributes by which selves or persons are rendered real. Nevertheless, in our own time as in others, there remains a very strong tendency to confine the real to the merely physical – to movements rather than actions, to living bodies rather than persons, to pigments and blocks of stone rather than artworks, to strings of sound and strings of marks rather than speech or language. We have already taken notice of a certain similar tendency in Kuhn's worry about the relation between swinging stones and pendulums. It reappears in Davidson's and in Arthur Danto's much less troubled conceptions of action:[74] in the elimination of persons or selves altogether in cognitive psychology;[75] and in the tendency to treat the history, interpretation, and theory of art (a metonym for the whole of human culture) as no more than heuristic forms of rhetoric, favored *façons de parler* for viewing what, ultimately, are no more than "mere real things" – reductively, physical objects.[76]

One cannot refuse the bare option of the reduction or elimination of the cultural dimension of the real. But its intended prize has yet to be earned. The doctrine of the technological self is incompatible with the victory of that project; and, in fact, the separate vindication of its own characteristic claims – the constructed nature of reality and self, the incarnation of cognition, the praxical nature of theory – counts against a bifurcation of the real and the rhetorical, in virtue of which one might be otherwise tempted to endorse their ultimate rejection. Failing that, we are invited to make a fresh analysis of what is clearly salient in human history – of what, in the opposing view, tends to be neglected anyway.

Nevertheless, in achieving just this small advantage, we have not yet explained what the sense is in which the technologized self or its world *is* constructed and yet is not *merely* constructed. We have offered no more than a rationale for a fundamental reorientation in our thinking. One final specimen view may focus its radical possibilities in a useful and particularly memorable way.

We have noted, in passing, the thread of traditionalism (the recovery of second-order invariances of cogniscence solely on the basis of an arbitrary logocentric optimism about the import of the first-order invariances of "our" tradition) that may be drawn in different ways from the theories offered by Kuhn, Gadamer, Habermas, Apel – also, Peirce, Popper, Paul Ricoeur, Charles Taylor, Imre Lakatos, Hilary Putnam, Richard Boyd, Wesley Salmon, Adolf Grünbaum, Isaac Levi, Alasdair MacIntyre, Richard Bernstein, and many others. But there is reason to believe that all of these theorists are persuaded that, even admitting the complication of the historicized nature of knowledge and science, *there is an independent order of reality that inquiry somehow penetrates and does not alter or affect merely by attempting to fathom.* Traditionalists resist the frontal claim of a cognitive competence *to* penetrate that "mind-independent" order; they "merely" recover the fruit of what would have been such a claim, by way of second-order assurances internally gleaned from our first-order practices, without the pretense of the other.

The important point remains that the thesis in question is fundamentally equivocal: on one reading, it is essential to the claims of scientific realism; on another, it is essential to the claims of traditionalism. To grasp the full force of what we have been calling the notion of the technological self is to identify that equivocation and, in doing so, to free scientific realism from any necessary connection with traditionalism.

What may well be the most explicit and most telling use of the equivocation indicated can be found in the recent views of Roy Bhaskar, who quite clearly attempts to formulate a viable form of scientific realism in accord with a general Marxian conception of technology and *praxis*. In doing that, Bhaskar unwittingly identifies the essential arbitrariness of construing the independent order of reality as cognitively penetrable *as such* even *within* the opacities already mentioned. This is traditionalism pure and simple – if it is not (fairly construed as) a contradictory retreat to cognitive privilege itself.

The equivocation should be clear enough. The scientific realist (who is not a traditionalist) must, on the rejection of all forms of cognitive privilege, treat the *objective*, "mind-independent" *order of nature* (and whatever, problematically, may be regarded as the cultural analogue of an independent physical nature) *as a reasoned posit afforded within the space of first-order inquiries, consistent with the terms of our original tally (a)–(d)*. The traditionalist (normally a scientific realist of some sort) maintains that *that posit permits the recovery of determinate essences, invariances, natural necessities that are not merely "indicatively" idealized in first-order terms but actually legitimated by way of second-order invariances of cogniscence.* The traditionalist holds that such invariances are assured by what is internal to the ongoing tradition of inquiry and practice: he offers no apodictic or independent cognitive source – on pain of incoherence; but he affirms or insinuates his second-order claim nevertheless. The theorist of cognitive privilege straightforwardly goes one step better than the traditionalist.

In the sense of these distinctions, Bhaskar is an unusually instructive traditionalist. For, first of all, he offers an impeccable sketch of what scientific realism entails (which, contrary to familiar objections including his own, "idealists" such as Kuhn and "instrumentalists" such as Bas van Fraassen[77] actually support):

it becomes mandatory to make the distinction between the (relatively) unchanging real objects which exist outside and perdure independently of the scientific process and the changing (and theoretically imbued) cognitive objects which are produced within science as a function and result of its practice; that is, between the intransitive and transitive objects of scientific knowledge, and accordingly between the intransitive and transitive dimensions in the philosophy of science.[78]

Bhaskar's adoption of what we have called the notion of the technological self, within his own scientific realism, rests with his insistence on our inextricable dependence on the transitive dimension (TD) of science:

if the (intransitive) objects of scientific knowledge exist and act independently of the knowledge of which they are the objects, then such knowledge as we actually possess cannot be identical, equivalent or reducible to these objects, or any function of them. Rather such knowledge must consist in an element materially irreducible to these objects – that is to say, in more or less historically specific, symbolically mediated and expressed, praxis-dependent, ineradicably social forms.

Thus without a TD or philosophical sociology to complement the ID [the intransitive dimension] or ontology legitimated, any attempt to sustain the irreducibility of knowable being – the only kind of being of concern to science – to thought, and hence the discursivity (and hence the rationality) of science must ultimately come to grief.[79]

This is still quite straightforward. It actually makes a very plausible case for the "constructed" nature of the "cognitive objects" of our science, including ourselves, in accord with our own thesis. When, however, Bhaskar affirms, "constant conjunctions are praxis-dependent, but causal laws are not," "constant conjunctions are empirical, but causal laws are not" – in the context of asserting that "known laws cannot be *both empirical and universal*" – we begin to approach the incoherent solution of the traditionalist.[80] For Bhaskar means to preserve our *knowledge of both*, which (as we saw) are not the same at all (one being "transitive," the other "intrasitive").

It is true that a scientific realism must acknowledge an order of reality independent of inquiry, which inquiry somehow comes to know – what may be dubbed ontic externalism.[81] But that doctrine legitimates no distributive claims about such an order; alternatively put, whatever is distributively claimed about that order is claimed only on grounds *internal* to actual cognitive inquiries – to what may be dubbed ontic internalism, or to what Bhaskar dubs the "transitive objects" of science. This is quite enough to resist (with Bhaskar) "the reduction of events to experience" or "the reduction of being to knowledge" – what he calls "the epistemic fallacy."[82] *But it does not license any knowledge of "intransitive objects" except by way of "transitive objects"; and this entails that the invariances assigned "intransitive objects" are themselves artifacts of the regularities empirically discovered regarding "transitive objects."* To admit that is *not* to commit the epistemic fallacy; but it is also not to countenance invariances beyond the cognizable invariances of "transitive objects" except as reasoned projections of some sort *from* our knowledge of the latter objects *subject to whatever are the contingencies of our full tally (a)–(e).*

Those contingencies are never completely penetrable to Bhaskar's scientist (on his own theory) or to our own technological self. But, if so, then it is quite impossible to draw Bhaskar's conclusion – which amounts to a tradionalist's betrayal of a technologized or praxical account of science:

A world without human beings would contain no (human) experiences and far fewer constant conjunctions of events. For experiences always and essentially, and epistemically significant invariances normally, if contingently, depend upon human activity. But the generative mechanisms, structures, processes, relations, forces and fields of nature do not. Thus in a world without (wo)men *the causal laws that sciences have hitherto managed to discover would prevail*, despite the paucity of conjunctions and the absence of experiences to mark them.[83]

The point is that the *distributed* determinate laws science discovers cannot be known to obtain independent of science *except as an artifact of science itself.* The postulate of ontic externalism – or of Bhaskar's "intransitive objects" (now, an equivocal notion) – *is invariably holist*: no distributed formulations are possible that are not subject to the vagaries of a historicized science. There you have the fundamental confusion of the traditionalist, prettily betrayed (unfortunately) by a particularly staunch defender of a praxical conception of science. No distributed claim can ensure universality; and no claimed universality can fail to be an artifact of contingently discerned regularities. In that sense, the transfer of high technology to third-world countries dramatizes, precisely in the social dislocations it invariably generates, the most profound conceptual unity possible affecting the global prospects of theoretical science and the global prospects of sharing and assessing the practical fruits of a scientific technology. Wherever we speak of intelligent, purposive, deliberate, rational activity, we speak under the veil of the enabling praxical and technological aptitudes we internalize in coming to be formed as the historical creatures we are.

Notes

1 I have benefited here from the papers of the conference "Technology Transfer and the Third World: Issues in the History and Philosophy of Technology," held at Virginia Polytechnic Institute and State University, Blacksburg, Virginia, 15–18 July, 1987; I must single out particularly Edmund F. Byrne, "Globalization and Community: A Search for Justice," and Romualdas Sviedrys, "A Conceptual Framework for Understanding Technology Transfer to the Third World." I have seen these papers only in manuscript.

2 These issues are taken up in Joseph Margolis, *Science without Unity: Reconciling the Natural and Human Sciences* (Oxford: Basil Blackwell, 1987), chs 3–4.

3 See Joseph Margolis, *Pragmatism without Foundations: Reconciling Realism and Relativism* (Oxford: Basil Blackwell, 1986).

4 Thomas S. Kuhn, *The Structure of Scientific Revolutions*, 2nd, enlarged edn (Chicago: University of Chicago Press, 1970), p. 118.

5 Ibid., p. 121.

6 Ibid., p. 120.

7 Ibid., pp. 126–7.

8 Ibid., p. 195 (italics added).

9 Ibid., p. 193.

10 Ibid., p. 195.

11 Ibid., p. 200.

12 The point is essentially missed by Donald Davidson, "The Very Idea of a Conceptual Scheme," *Inquiries into Truth and Interpretation* (Oxford: Clarendon Press, 1984). The mistake is of the greatest importance.

13 The detailed argument is given in *Science without Unity*.

14   See Clyde Kluckhohn et al., "Values and Value-Orientation in the Theory of Action," in Talcott Parsons and Edward A. Shils (eds), *Toward a General Theory of Action* (Cambridge, Mass.: Harvard University Press, 1951); also Florence Kluckhohn and Fred L. Strodbeck, *Variations in Value Orientations* (Evanston, Ill.: Row, Peterson, 1981).

15   This may be taken to be part of the force of W. V. Quine's "Two Dogmas of Empiricism," *From a Logical Point of View* (Cambridge, Mass.: Harvard University Press, 1953). Quine's explicit remarks on this issue may be found in *Word and Object* (Cambridge, Mass.: MIT Press, 1960), pp. 11–12, 59–61.

16   See Isaac Levi, *The Enterprise of Knowledge* (Cambridge, Mass.: MIT Press, 1980), p. 375. Levi's own theory of knowledge and inquiry attempts to preserve a measure of methodological invariance while admitting our dependence, contextually, on a changing corpus of knowledge. It also entails a very curious view of "epistemological infallibility." See chs 1–3, for instance at pp. 67–8; also p. 13. See also the exchange on Isaac Levi's "Truth , Fallibility and the Growth of Knowledge," involving Israel Scheffler and Avishai Margalit, in Robert S. Cohen and Marx Wartofsky (eds), *Language, Logic and Method* (Dordrecht: D. Reidel, 1983).

17   For a specimen version of inductivism, see Hans Reichenbach, *Experience and Reduction* (Berkeley, Calif.: University of California Press, 1938); see also Karl R. Popper, *Realism and the Aim of Science* (from *Postscript to the Logic of Scientific Discovery*), ed. W. W. Bartley, III (Totowa, NJ: Rowman and Littlefield, 1983), pt I, ch. 1. For a specimen of extensionalism, see Donald Davidson, *Inquiries into Truth and Interpretation* (Oxford: Clarendon Press, 1984); see also Ian Hacking, *Why Does Language Matter to Philosophy?* (Cambridge: Cambridge University Press, 1975), ch. 12. Some specimens of the programs in question are examined in some depth in *Pragmatism without Foundations* and *Science without Unity*.

18   See Jacques Derrida, *Of Grammatology*, tr. Gayatri Chakravorty Spivak (Baltimore: John Hopkins University Press, 1976).

19   See W. V. Quine, *The Roots of Reference* (LaSalle, Ill.: Open Court, 1974), pp. 20–4.

20   See for example Edmund Husserl, *The Crisis of European Sciences and Transcendental Phenomenology*, tr. David Carr (Evanston, Ill.: Northwestern University Press, 1970), section 54; and Roderick M. Chisholm, *The First Person* (Minneapolis: University of Minnesota Press, 1981), ch. 7.

21   See Moritz Schlick, "The Foundation of Knowledge," tr. David Rynin, in A. J. Ayer (ed.), *Logical Positivism* (Glencoe, Ill.: Free Press, 1959). Schlick excludes the possibility of error associated with protocol sentences (under Otto Neurath's barrage) by insisting that we are capable of cognizing "the absolute fixed points" of empirical science – given by what Schlick came to call an "observation statement" (as opposed to a "genuine protocol statement"), "always of the form 'Here now so and so' . . . because in a certain sense [they] cannot be written down at all" (pp. 221, 223, 225).

22   The most subtle contemporary exploration of this question designed to salvage what can be salvaged from the Cartesian *cogito* may well be that of Roderick M. Chisholm – wherein Chisholm asks what is "discovered" in discovering that "I am me": "It is the discovery one makes," he says, "when one is first aware of the unity of consciousness; it is thus a discovery about those things one has been di-

rectly attributing to oneself. One suddenly becomes aware of the fact that they are all being attributed to the *same* thing. One realizes that there is a single thing that has all one's self-presenting properties and that *that* is the thing to which one makes all one's direct attributions. And *how* does one come to see this? It would be correct to say: 'One has only to consider it to see that it is true'. But it is, apparently, something that many people never happen to consider" – *The First Person* (Minneapolis: University of Minnesota Press, 1981), p. 90. See also Hector-Neri Castañeda, "He: A Study in the Logic of Self-Consciousness," *Ratio*, VIII (1966); Elizebeth Anscombe, "The First Person," in Samuel Guttenplan (ed.), *Mind and Language* (Oxford: Clarendon Press, 1975). One must notice, in Chisholm's statement, that he moves rather comfortably from one's becoming aware "of the fact that different attributions are all being attributed *de dicto* to the *same* thing" to "one's realiz[ing] that there is a single thing *de re* that has all one's self-presenting properties and that *that* is the thing to which one makes all one's direct attributions." There is an inescapable circularity here that Chisholm seems nowhere to have explored further.

23 The argument is given in *Pragmatism without Foundations*, ch. 10. Cf. also Alvin I. Goldman, *Epistemology and Cognition* (Cambridge, Mass.: Harvard University Press, 1986).

24 See Margolis, *Science without Unity*, ch. 3; also ch. 9, below.

25 See Paul Ricoeur, *Time and Narrative*, vols 1–2, tr. Kathleen McLaughlin and David Pellauer (Chicago: University of Chicago Press, 1984, 1985).

26 Apart from Gadamer, one may mention Taylor's and MacIntyre's views as specimens of traditionalism. See for instance Charles Taylor, "Philosophy and Its History," in Richard Rorty et al. (eds), *Philosophy in History* (Cambridge: Cambridge University Press, 1984); and Alasdair MacIntyre, *After Virtue*, 2nd edn (Notre Dame, Ind.: Notre Dame University Press, 1984).

27 Hans-Georg Gadamer, "On the Scope and Function of Hermeneutical Reflection," tr. G. B. Hess and R. E. Palmer, in Brice R. Wachterhauser (ed.), *Hermeneutics and Modern Philosophy* (Albany, NY: State University of New York Press, 1986), pp. 294–5.

28 Ibid., pp. 227–8.

29 For an account of transcendental arguments of this informal – non-apodictic – sort, see Margolis, *Pragmatism without Foundations*, ch. 12.

30 Gadamer, "On the Scope and Function of Hermeneutical Reflection," in Wachterhauser (ed.), *Hermeneutics and Modern Philosophy*, pp. 284–6.

31 Ibid., p. 297.

32 Ibid., pp. 296–8.

33 Hans-Georg Gadamer, "Text and Interpretation," tr. Dennis J. Schmidt, ibid., particularly p. 379.

34 Hans-Georg Gadamer, "Man and Language," *Philosophical Hermeneutics*, tr. David E. Linge (Berkeley, Calif.: University of California Press, 1976), p. 62; cf. also Hans-Georg Gadamer, *Truth and Method*, tr. Garrett Barden and Robert Cumming from 2nd German edn (New York: Seabury Press, 1975), pt II; and Kathleen Wright, "Gadamer: The Speculative Structure of Language," in Wachterhauser (ed.), *Hermeneutics and Modern Philosophy*.

35 Gadamer, "On the Scope and Function of Hermeneutical Reflection," in Wachterhauser (ed.), *Hermeneutics and Modern Philosophy*, p. 295.

36 Jürgen Habermas, "A Review of Gadamer's *Truth and Method*," tr. Fred R. Dallmayr and Thomas A. McCarthy, in Fred R. Dallmayr and Thomas A. McCarthy (eds), *Understanding and Social Inquiry* (Notre Dame, Ind.: University of Notre Dame Press, 1977). The passage is cited from *Truth and Method*, p. 280 (in the German edn). See also Joel C. Weinsheimer, Introduction to *Gadamer's Hermeneutics* (New Haven, Conn.: Yale University Press, 1985).

37 Gadamer, "On the Scope and Function of Hermeneutical Reflection," in Wachterhauser (ed.), *Hermeneutics and Modern Philosophy*, p. 228.

38 Gadamer, *Truth and Method*, p. 256.

39 There is, in Kuhn's work, a subterranean commitment, never explicitly reconciled with the notion of paradigm shifts (*within* the space of which the practices of science are first defined and flourish), to the fixity of natural laws and to their discernibility despite (or because of) the proliferation of such shifts. This may explain, for instance, Kuhn's extremely coy account of the relationship between science and the history of science, once (after the hubbub created by *The Structure of Scientific Revolutions* died down) he realized that a too-sanguine admission of the usefulness of *"external* history of science" (that is, a history that emphasized the social sources of evolving scientific practice) might obscure or even cast doubt upon the peculiar distinction of the sciences themselves – the discerning of the invariant laws of nature. So he complains mildly, somewhat against the effect of his own research, that, "If it becomes the exclusive approach, history of science could be reduced to a higher-level version of the tradition which, by leaving the science out, ignored the *internalities* which shape the development of any discipline." See Thomas Kuhn, "The Relations between History and History of Science," *Daedalus*, C (1971), repr. in Paul Rabinow and William M. Sullivan (eds), *Interpretive Social Science: A Reader* (Berkeley, Calif.: University of California Press, 1979), p. 300 (italics added). Kuhn has never managed to reconcile the theoretical status of invariant physical law with the historical contingency of paradigm shifts, *under the condition of repudiating any and all forms of cognitive transparency*. There is, therefore, a strong impression, in reading the essay mentioned, that the demarcation between "internal" and "external" is fixed by the fixity of laws and is obscured by the contingency of paradigm shifts. What, obviously, is called for is a more radical account of the nature of science, physical law, and scientific explanation.

40 The essential paradox of Habermas's theory is sketched in *Pragmatism without Foundations*, ch. 2. We may, therefore, identify it quite briefly here.

41 See ibid., chs. 2–3.

42 Jürgen Habermas, "What Is Universal Pragmatics?" *Communication and the Evolution of Society*, tr. Thomas McCarthy (Boston, Mass.: Beacon Press, 1979), p. 1.

43 Ibid., pp. 2–3; I have italicized the modal terms, See also Richard J. Bernstein, "What is the Difference that Makes a Difference? Gadamer, Habermas, and Rorty," in *PSA 1982*, vol. 2: *Proceedings of the 1982 Biennial Meeting of the Philosophy of Science Association*, ed. P. D. Asquith and T. Nickles (East Lansing, Mich.: Philosophy of Science Association, 1983). Bernstein takes note of this feature of Habermas's argument, although his own discussion homogenizes in much too sanguine a spirit the quite fundamental differences between Gadamer and Habermas – and Rorty (despite his assurance to the contrary).

44 See Margolis, *Pragmatism without Foundations*, ch. 2.
45 This single, essential weakness undermines, for example, the whole point of Habermas's otherwise extremely engaging attempt to recover modernism (and more than modernism) from the subversive arguments of the post-structuralist (and postmodernist) critique – roughly, of the Nietzschean tribe: Heidegger, Derrida, Foucault, Bataille. See Jürgen Habermas, *The Philosophical Discourse of Modernity: Twelve Lectures*, tr. Frederick Lawrence (Cambridge, Mass.: MIT Press, 1987), particulary Lecture XI. Habermas presupposes, there, the very argument we are challenging (pp. 297–301). There is in all the extended discussion of that very large book not a single advance on the conceptual difficulty here remarked. Habermas simply takes it for granted that he has met all the essential objections.
46 See Paul K. Feyerabend, *Against Method* (London: New Left Books, 1975).
47 Kuhn, *The Structure of Scientific Revolutions*, p. 185 (italics added).
48 Nelson Goodman, *The Structure of Appearance*, 2nd ed. (Indianapolis: Bobbs-Merrill, 1966), pp. 4–5; the phrase "than phenomena known to exist" is inserted by Kuhn.
49 Kuhn, *The Structure of Scientific Revolutions*, p. 127.
50 See Nelson Goodman, *Ways of Worldmaking* (Indianapolis: Hackett, 1978), particularly ch. 6, and *Of Mind and Other Matters* (Cambridge, Mass.: Harvard University Press, 1984).
51 Goodman, *Ways of Worldmaking*, pp. 1–3, and *Of Mind and Other Matters*, p. 21.
52 Goodman, *Of Mind and Other Matters*, p. 33.
53 Goodman, *Ways of Worldmaking*, pp. 20–1.
54 See Nelson Goodman, *Fact, Fiction, and Forecast*, 2nd edn (Indianapolis: Bobbs-Merrill, 1965).
55 See Hilary Putnam, "Reflections on Goodman's *Ways of Worldmaking*," *Philosophical Papers*, vol. 3 (Cambridge: Cambridge University Press, 1983).
56 Quine, *The Roots of Reference*, p. 22.
57 See Margolis, *Pragmatism without Foundations*, ch. 2.
58 Marjorie Grene, "The Paradoxes of Historicity," in Wachterhauser (ed.), *Hermeneutics and Modern Philosophy*, pp. 168–9.
59 Ibid., p. 169. Cf. Marjorie Grene, *The Understanding of Nature* (Dordrecht: D. Reidel, 1974).
60 For an account of the "incarnate," see Margolis, *Science without Unity*, ch. 9, and *Culture and Cultural Entities* (Dordrecht: D. Reidel, 1984), ch. 1; also ch. 6, below.
61 See Margolis, *Pragmatism without Foundations*, ch. 11.
62 See further, Margolis, *Science without Unity*, pt II.
63 See E. Rosch and B. Lloyd (eds), *Cognition and Categorization* (Hillsdale, NJ: Lawrence Erlbaum Associates, 1978); and Saul A Kripke, *Wittgenstein on Rules and Private Language* (Cambridge, Mass.: Harvard University Press, 1982).
64 Personal communication. See James J. Gibson, *The Ecological Approach to Visual Perception* (Boston, Mass.: Houghton Mifflin, 1979); and Marjorie Grene, *Descartes* (Minneapolis: University of Minnesota Press, 1985).
65 For a fuller sense of the use of the term "Intentional" (= $_{df}$ "cultural"), see Margolis, *Science without Unity*, chs 7, 9.
66 Goodman, *Ways of Worldmaking*, p. 17 (italics added).

67   Cf. ibid., ch. 7.
68   See Nelson Goodman, "Seven Strictures on Similarity," in Lawrence Foster and
     J. W. Swanson (eds), *Experience and Theory* (Amherst: University of Massachu-
     setts Press, 1970).
69   See Jerrold J. Katz, *Language and Other Abstract Objects* (Totowa, NJ: Rowman
     and Littlefield, 1981).
70   See for instance Jürgen Habermas, *Legitimation Crisis*, tr. Thomas McCarthy
     (Boston, Mass.: Beacon Press, 1975); also chs 4, 9, below.
71   See N. Tinbergen, *A Study of Instinct*, with a new introduction (New York:
     Oxford University Press, 1969); and Margolis, *Culture and Cultural Entities*, ch.
     3.
72   See David Premack, *Gavagai!* (Cambridge, Mass.: MIT Press, 1986).
73   It is worth remarking, in passing, that Goodman's unalterable opposition to
     admitting real possibilities is never brought to bear on the problems of quantum
     physics – where, that is, the classical distinction of the "actual" and the
     "possible" and the cognate distinction (basically Aristotelian) between the
     "potential" and the "actualized" need (certainly threaten to need) to be replaced
     by an altogether novel category, "potentialities," that cannot be captured by
     either the "actual" or the "possible" alone (or by their dialectical linkage). I am
     indebted here to a paper by Abner Shimony, "Physical and Philosophical Issues
     in the Bohr-Einstein Debate," which is to appear in print shortly. The point is
     that Goodman's resistance to the "possible" is not motivated by any empirically
     resilient attention to the puzzles of the actual sciences: quantum physics obviously
     requires a new conception linking the "possible" and the (actually) "potential."
     See, also, Erwin Schrödinger, "The Present Situation in Quantum Mechanics," in
     John A. Wheeler and Woycieck H. Zurek (eds), *Quantum Theory and
     Measurement* (Princeton, NJ: Princeton University Press, 1983).
74   Donald Davidson, "Agency," *Essays on Actions and Events* (Oxford: Clarendon
     Press, 1980); Arthur C. Danto, *Analytical Philosophy of Action* (Cambridge:
     Cambridge University Press, 1973).
75   See for instance Stephen P. Stich, *From Folk Psychology to Cognitive Science*
     (Cambridge, Mass.: MIT Press, 1983); also Margolis, *Science without Unity*,
     ch. 5.
76   The latter theme is pursued most systematically by Danto. See his *Transfiguration
     of the Commonplace* (Cambridge, Mass.: Harvard University Press, 1981), and
     The Philosophical Disenfranchisement of Art (New York: Columbia University
     Press, 1986). I have examined Danto's account in "Ontology down and out in
     Art and Science," *Journal of Aesthetics and Art Criticism*, forthcoming. Cf. also
     Joseph Margolis, *Art and Philosophy* (Atlantic Highlands, NJ: Humanities Press,
     1980); and ch. 8, below.
77   See Bas C. van Fraassen, *The Scientific Image* (Oxford: Clarendon Press, 1980).
78   Roy Bhaskar, *Scientific Realism and Human Emancipation* (London: Verso Books,
     1986), p. 51.
79   Ibid., pp. 51–52.
80   Ibid., p. 28; cf. also p. 31, where Bhaskar specifically mentions "knowledge of
     causal laws."
81   See further Margolis, *Pragmatism without Foundations*, ch. 11.
82   Bhaskar, *Scientific Realism and Human Emancipation*, pp. 23, 45.
83   Ibid., pp. 46–7 (italics added); cf. also pp. 252, 286.

3

Entailments from
"Naturalism = Phenomenology"

We intend, now, to support a heterodox thesis and, by extension from it, a whole series of further heterodoxies. The thesis affirms that "naturalism = phenomenology." What follows from it is most remarkable, so its defense invites a measure of care.

The relationship between naturalism and phenomenology has, of course, been memorably mapped by Edmund Husserl in a way completely opposed to the equation given, mapped with the implicit certainty that its defense could be little more than conceptual disaster. Nevertheless, the equation *is* defensible – and strategically important; and, it may be claimed, the entire movement of contemporary Western philosophy is effectively (and reasonably) committed to its support. If it were read in a suitably comprehensive way as addressing the entire range of first-order knowledge – roughly, as knowledge of physical nature and human minds and human culture, or of what is true, where what is "true" may not (on a theory) accord with what is merely actual or even merely "real," may, instead, address another "world" entirely (the "worlds" of logic or geometry or arithmetic or the "irreal" world Husserl dabbled in[1]) – then a very large number of powerful theorems may be shown to follow directly from our equation.

At the risk of excessive compression, we may effect an important economy. The argument to be considered goes more or less as follows. If naturalism = phenomenology, then

1   ontological and epistemological questions cannot be disjoined,
2   first- and second-order cognitive aptitudes cannot be disjoined, and
3   all forms of cognitive privilege – foundationalism or logocentrism – must be abandoned;[2]

and, if condition 1, 2, and 3 hold, then

4   knowledge of reality and truth cannot be disjoined from some form of *anti-realism* or intuitionism or a decidability program (not necessarily Michael Dummett's or L. E. J. Brouwer's[3]), and

5   no first- or second-order knowledge of any particular sector of inquiry
     can fail to entail some form of *critique* or critical legitimation regarding
     the preformative conditions of cognition (not necessarily Marxist or
     Frankfurt School or phenomenological or Nietzschean);

and, if conditions 3 and 5 hold, then

6   no knowledge can fail to support or instantiate some form of *historicism*
     or contextualism (not necessarily Hegelian or post-Hegelian or
     Heideggerian or Foucauldian or Wittgensteinian),
7   no claims of distributed knowledge can fail to fall within the holist
     constraints of some form of *pragmatism* (not necessarily Peirce's or
     Dewey's or James's or Quine's),
8   no adequate theory of knowledge can preclude or fail to instantiate
     some form of *psychologism* (not necessarily Descartes's or Locke's or
     Hume's or J. S. Mill's or Brentano's), and
9   no adequate theory of knowledge can disqualify or fail to instantiate
     some form of *relativism* (not necessarily the Protagorean's or the
     incommensurabilist's);[4]

and if conditions 4 or 5 or 6 or 7 or 8 holds, then

10   no claims of knowledge can preclude or fail to instantiate *praxism* –
     that is, the thesis that knowledge is grounded and emergent in *praxis*
     (not necessarily construed in Marx's or Nietzsche's or Heidegger's or
     Gadamer's or Habermas's particular sense).[5]

Furthermore, if the generic import of anti-realism, critique, historicism,
pragmatism, psychologism, relativism, and praxism may be abstracted from
the contingencies of the various, possibly disparate, forms of each, then,
effectively, assuming naturalism = phenomenology,

11   all of these doctrines are either equivalent to one another or are merely
     technically specialized distinctions within the scope of the original
     equation. (They could, or course, be developed in independent ways.)

Clearly, to make the case would require a generous reading of what *is* generic
with regard to each. But, with due allowance for terminological quarrels, the
thesis (*if* sustained) would prove a remarkably decisive and compendious
directive affecting future analyses of first-order inquiry and science and second-
order legitimation. The argument, therefore, is well worth pursuing; although,
for the sake of economy, we shall confine our attention primarily to the
equation itself and to its bearing on the programs of critique and psychologism.

I

If we admit that the real world is cognizable as it is independent of human inquiry, or if we admit that human agents are capable of knowing what is true of

that world or of a world altogether independent of their minds or independent of the actual or natural world itself,[6] or if we admit that human agents are capable of knowing the real structures and properties of a world they themselves constitute that is nevertheless not merely an artifact of some particular inquiry or flight of imagination, then there are only a limited number of conceptual strategies by which to ensure *that* human agents can achieve such knowledge. That is, there are only a limited number of strategies if the ones required are supposed to be sufficient in *first-order* terms. Call any such strategy *privileged*, in the sense that a second-order assurance of such first-order knowledge is taken (somehow) to be entailed in or abstractable from a given first-order competence. When the source of assurance lies in a reflexively detectable feature of first-order experience or cogniscent reports or the like, the legitimating argument may be said to be *foundationalist*; and, when it does not depend on such a feature but can be counted on nevertheless, the legitimating argument may be said to be *logocentric*.[7]

Foundationalist and logocentric arguments may be as arbitrary as you please, but in principle they suppose that our first-order inquiries somehow provide a basis for our second-order assurance; they suppose that, *distributively*, determinate first-order claims either ensure knowledge directly or provide the best, or at least a viable and privileged, source of or constraint on the body of knowledge. W. V. Quine, for example, in the very process of repudiating the pertinence of intentional complications with regard to the prospects of any empirical science,[8] clearly proceeds in a logocentric (but not in a foundationalist) way – in a way, in fact, that has dominated most Anglo-American theorizing about knowledge and science for nearly forty years. It would certainly not suit Quine to acknowledge only that his own regimented brand of extensionalism was *entitled* to an epistemological inning. Quine clearly intends to discharge intentionality as utterly irrelevant epistemologically: "If we are limning the true and ultimate structure of reality," he says – and he means what he says – "the canonical scheme for us is the austere scheme that knows no quotation but direct quotation and no propositional attitudes but only the physical constitution and behavior of organisms."[9]

It is possible that Quine is registering here an altogether undefended prejudice. But it is difficult to believe that reading in the face of his substained interest in the puzzles of knowledge and science, his persistent efforts over an entire career to entrench his extensionalism, and the seriousness with which his many followers have adhered to his apparent instruction. For the moment, our interest does not concern such maneuvers. It rests rather with the plain fact that the requisite first-order competence is taken to be a natural capacity of the members of human communities: to form, codify, discipline, enlarge, confirm, even improve those relatively systematic collections of distributed claims that they are pleased to treat as the core of the various sciences. Our concern, we may say, is almost nosological. The would-be legitimation of first-order knowledge is, trivially, a second-order matter. When the required assurance is taken to instantiate a specifically cognitive aptitude of its own, legitimation is (as remarked) either foundationalist or logocentric. When it is not – when the legitimation of first-order competence is denied any special competence or "privilege" – it functions (we may say) in the *pragmatist* manner.

It is conceivable (but indefensible) to favor first-order cognitive competence *and* to deny the pertinence or eligibility of second-order legitimation. For such a maneuver either tacitly installs, logocentrically again, some first-order aptitude (and so violates the pretended repudiation of second-order arguments) or it abandons every rational concern regarding the compared relevance and power of competing would-be resources. Where, however, moderate incommensurabilities obtain, or where we are confronted with discontinuities in research programs, contests between options regarding paradigm-like shifts, the radical underdetermination of explanatory theories relative to observational data, paraphrastic uncertainties and the like, there can be no defensible abandoning of second-order reflection and no segregating of first- and second-order inquiries. The supposed second policy (segregating first- and second-order inquiries) is now also called pragmatism – largely through the efforts of Richard Rorty. Pragmatism in the second sense calls for an end to traditional philosophy on the grounds that *any* legitimating inquiry cannot fail to be logocentric. Pragmatism in the first sense – in denying privilege but pursuing matters of legitimation – cannot but tend in the direction of holism, internalism, historicism, relativism, and an emphasis on the role of *praxis*. (We need not return to the details of the story.[10]) What concerns us rather is that both logocentric and pragmatist forms of legitimation are construed *naturalistically* – that is, as involving no cognitive powers other than those entailed or embedded or exercised in, or assignable to, the native capacities of human investigators. (They involve no cognitive titans or gods, no revelations.)

Needless to say, the first-order powers admitted *as* cognitively apt on pragmatist grounds are apt only in the sense of *salience*, not of privilege – that is, only in the sense of what, provisionally, perspectivally, reflexively, in a way internal to the very achievement to be accounted for, appear to be the most promising candidates (for the time being) for the *explananda* required. They are subject to revision or replacement for all sorts of reasons having to do with how salience itself may change. The importance of admitting salience is just that it precludes privilege and acknowledges the profound transience and contingent stability of what, in terms of the implicit consensus of actual societies pursuing inquiries of high discipline, *appears* to them to be their science and cognitive power (constitutes *Erscheinungen*). In short, the validity of second-order legitimations *is* an artifact of the relative stability of our informal saliences, which are themselves, quite frankly, affected by our own ongoing efforts at science and legitimation. So doubts regarding the force of legitimation cannot escape applying with equal relevance to the first-order standing of our scientific accomplishments. By the same token, endorsing the latter as at least sufficiently reliable and promising so that we may press on with our first-order work is tantamount to endorsing the legitimacy of legitimation.

Legitimation *need not* (and does not here) presuppose privilege or risk its constitutive and regulative function in abandoning privilege. In a word, the theme of salience serves to integrate

(a)   a preference for pragmatist or holist legitimation;
(b)   the symbiosis of first- and second-order discourse;
(c)   the consensual acknowledgement of a body of apparent sciences and their and other assorted truth-claims; and
(d)   the assignment of realist import to any and all distributed truth-claims, whether first- or second-order, entirely within the space of (a).

Put another way, the theme of salience is the theme of the *empirical* grounding of all science and philosophy shorn of any and all first-order or second-order privilege.[11] For example, it permits the acknowledgement of *invariances, universal laws, necessities, essences* within its scope; but, in permitting that, it obliges us to construe their discrimination *as* encumbered, as ineluctably grounded in whatever is given as salient – as whatever we cannot thus escape. Hence, by a simple maneuver, invariances, essences and the like are *posits* made under and within the tacit, endogenous, incompletely penetrable constraints of salience itself. Anything less would imperil realism (in the pragmatist sense); anything more would restore privilege. To anticipate, therefore: William James, whom Husserl credits with an important clue regarding the escape from psychologism, cannot convincingly be credited with actually having established (whether as a "precursor" of phenomenology or as an actual practitioner) a cognitive source or capacity embedded in "experience" but having apodictic powers (or powers approximating the apodictic) superior to whatever is the putative subjective correlate of the merely salient.[12] James's famous thought-experiment, for instance, distinguishing black and white, *may* therefore, even when it leads to the affirmation of "necessary and eternal relations" that "form a determinate system, independent of the order of frequency in which experience may have associated their originals in time and space,"[13] still be consistently (and convincingly) construed as *not* violating the limitations of the salient or empirical. To see this possibility is to anticipate the defeat of all arguments against psychologism, all phenomenologies that would exceed the limits of the salient.

Once we see matters in this light, once cognitive privilege is denied, it proves surprisingly easy to demonstrate that there is and can be no principled division or disjunction of an epistemically pertinent sort between what may be legitimated as naturalism and what may be legitimated as phenomenology. This goes entirely contrary, of course, to the main theme of Husserl's master-project, which, in a very real sense, could be said to be focused on ensuring the most profound disjunction possible between naturalism and phenomenology.

To press the "correction" against Husserl is to side with a good many who have been perceptibly influenced by Husserl's own attempt to correct naturalism's pretensions of privilege. It is to side, to a considerable extent, with the programmatic intentions of Heidegger, Merleau-Ponty, Sartre, Derrida, and (stretching things somewhat) Gadamer – insofar as those theorists mean to pursue phenomenological corrections *of* a naive naturalism; but it is also to insist on the obvious convergence (not necessarily intended) between their (quite varied) programs and such others (also eschewing logocentric advantage) as have evolved from, for example, American pragmatist sources (from Peirce and Dewey and James and Quine), European Hegelian and Marxist and Frankfurt School sources, and, of course, Nietzsche and his most recent adherents (Derrida and Foucault, in particular). For, the essential criticism made of Husserl – by this time almost banal though it is assuredly still effective – is simply that, in correcting the pretensions of privilege among the naturalists, Husserl failed to admit (indeed, resisted to a preposterous extent) the plain fact that the validity of *that* correction could not but extend to the pretensions of phenomenology as well. Husserl apparently "did not understand" what *he* was doing in demonstrating that the naturalists did not understand the limitations of their own undertaking.[14] On our reading of "salience," what this means is that the phenomenological correction of naturalism must take a pragmatist turn, in the sense of (a); that the distributed *and* holist correction of naturalistic claims cannot be denied (on pain of irrelevance) and cannot exceed the preformational opacities that do affect naturalism (on pain of cognitive privilege).

This is surely the neatly focused message of Merleau-Ponty's "adjustment" of Husserl's theme. (We may allow it to stand proxy for the convergent intent of the rather different figures just mentioned.) He comments,

> The perceiving mind is an incarnated mind. I have tried, first of all, to re-establish the roots of the mind in its body and in its world, going against doctrines which treat perception as a simple result of the action of external things on our body as well as against those which insist on the autonomy of consciousness (that is, against empiricism and rationalism as forms of naturalism or objectivism). These philosophies commonly forget – in favor of a pure exteriority or of a pure interiority – the insertion of the mind in corporality, the ambiguous relation which we entertain with our body and, correlatively, with perceived things.[15]

It is a message reinforced in the opening lines of *Phenomenology of Perception*:

> What is phenomenology? . . . Phenomenology is the study of essences; and according to it, all problems amount to finding definitions of essences: the essence of perception, or the essence of consciousness, for example. But phenomenology is also a philosophy which puts essences back into existence, and does not expect to arrive at an understanding of man and the world from any starting point other than that of their "facticity." It is a transcendental philosophy which places in abeyance the assertions arising out of the natural attitude, the better to understand them; but it is also a philosophy for which the world is always "already

there" before reflection begins – as an inalienable presence; and all its efforts are concentrated upon *re-achieving a direct and primitive contact with the world, and endowing that contact with a philosophical status.*[16]

Merleau-Ponty's intended corrective exhibits the necessary tact and subtlety of functioning *as* a corrective within the pale of Husserl's own deeply admired endeavor. It may be instructive, therefore (for a reason which will gradually become clear) to juxtapose without elaborate preparation a rather famous if somewhat primitive (but characteristic) remark of John Dewey's – already refined, in 1938, from earlier speculations going back before the turn of the century – that clearly converges (innocently) with the deeper intent of Merleau-Ponty's pronouncement but without having to work through the unfortunate disjunction Husserl imposed on his followers. It shows at a stroke the obvious, the marvelously simple, sense (within the American pragmatist movement) in which naturalism could be said to be "phenomenologically" constrained (natively) without ever having to pass through an official correction. In context, the passage in question was intended by Dewey to concede the preformational and incarnate biological and social world within which human inquiry cannot but proceed, the horizonal and contingent nature of its every effort, the place it affords withal for a viable logic and science, and (perhaps most important) the respect in which otherwise logocentric oppositions between cognizing subject and cognized world are already treated by Dewey as no more that abstractly posited *within* what (mythically) precedes such oppositions. The link with Heidegger's myth of *Sein* and *Dasein* is plain enough; it supplies the reason for linking Dewey and Merleau-Ponty as well.[17] The remark itself is drawn from Dewey's *Logic*:

> Inquiry is the controlled or directed transformation of an indeterminate situation into one that is so determinate in its constituent distinctions and relations as to convert the elements of the original situation into a unified whole.[18]

Dewey's essential point – one must bear in mind how early relative to phenomenology it was made – is that "the unsettled or indeterminate situation might have been called a *problematic* situation [and that, existentially, it is] precognitive."[19] The full import of these remarks remains still to be drawn out: they may actually be a little surprising. But for the moment it is perhaps enough to exhibit the unintended convergence between a "phenomenologized" naturalism and a "naturalized" phenomenology. For, by the device of the "problematic situation," Dewey genuinely intends to risk the fixity of *every* would-be structure of an "independent" world (including whatever, of would-be inquiring agents, is similarly "independent" of or prior to their explicit inquiry); and, in doing that, Dewey has surely avoided and completely bypassed the unnecessary traffic of the whole of official phenomenology.

Clearly, Merleau-Ponty means to offset the idealist and solipsistic possibilities that, though never intended by Husserl, invariably beckon from some point deep within Husserl's theory. Nevertheless, it is Merleau-Ponty himself, who, "adjusting" Husserl, still insists – ambiguously (in a sense very much like that in which James is ambiguous) – that "the world is always 'already there' before reflection begins – as an inalienable presence": so that all the efforts or philosophy "are concentrated upon re-achieving a direct and primitive contact with the world, and endowing *that contact* with a philosophical [that is, with an epistemically pertinent] status." Merleau-Ponty may have meant this *in* the "pragmatist" sense (or in a sense very much like it – holistically *and* mythically). That certainly would not be an unfair reading of a related late manuscript entry: "We will not admit a preconstituted world, a logic, except for having seen them arise from our experience of brute being, which is as it were the umbilical cord of our knowledge and the source of meaning for us."[20] So construed, the passage represents Merleau-Ponty's thoroughly *un*privileged (mythic) speculation about the conceptual connection between the "presence" of an unnamed and unnamable brute world – "there" prior to our objectifying inquiries – and the valid work of those same inquiries, also (ambiguously now, *as* the activity of "mobile bodies") precognitively "located" in that same brute world.

But the question still nags, whether and to what extent the "lived body," the "embodied subject," the original percipient source of science, is, as the very center of consciousness (*not* in the idealist's manner), also and for that reason the "source" of the cognizable world that surrounds it. "The whole universe of science," Merleau-Ponty remarks, "is built upon the world as directly experienced, and if we want to subject science itself to rigorous scrutiny and arrive at a precise assessment of its meaning and scope, we must begin *by reawakening the basic experience* of the world of which science is the *second*-order expression." He adds,

> I am *the absolute source*, my existence *does not* stem from my antecedents, from my physical and social environment . . . [it is through that original] consciousness, through which from the outset a world forms itself round me and begins to exist for me. To return to things themselves is to return to that world which precedes knowledge, of which knowledge always *speaks*, and in relation to which every scientific schematization is an abstract and derivative language. . . .[21]

Here, it is difficult to avoid the conclusion that, in an impossibly gymnastic way, the "second-order" pronouncements of science are *somehow* to be reconciled (in a cognitively pertinent way) with the *precognitive but* (seemingly) *distributed* encounters of "primary" perception. Otherwise, why say that science "speaks" of the things of the "world which precedes knowledge," and why mention the semiotized "relation" holding between the two? It is true that Merleau-Ponty insists that "our relation to the [originally perceived] world is not that of a thinker to an object of thought," and yet he explicitly says (and means) that the analysis of primary perception is essential to psychology (possibly to all the sciences, though, here, he hedges – inconsistently – under questioning).[22]

There is reason to believe that Merleau-Ponty did not resolve this difficulty – could not (and, in a way, did not want to). For, in insisting on the continuity of science and philosophy *and* on the continuity of science and primary perception, he characterizes science as *a second-order coding and systematization of whatever is given (albeit precognitively) in primary perception*; and that makes no sense unless what is thus given (in a "first-order" respect) bears in a cognitively pertinent (recoverable) way *on* our science. It is partly for this reason that he assigns intentionality to the "lived body" functioning below the level of explicit consciousness. He opposes innatism; but already in the primary biology of the human organism Merleau-Ponty finds a need for a somewhat equivocal vocabulary that is not *yet* fully "mental" (or behavioral in the mentally informed sense) but that still requires a mode of perception and experience that may serve to fix the "first-order" intentional life that discursive consciousness and science "refer" to in their "second-order" way. So he says, at the very close of *The Structure of Behavior*,

> The natural "thing," the organism, the behavior of others and my own behavior exist only by their meaning; but this meaning which springs forth in them is not yet a Kantian object; the intentional life which constitutes them is not yet a representation; and the "comprehension" which gives access to them is not yet an intellection.[23]

The best Merleau-Ponty makes of this oscillation between the recovery of the "first-order" experience of the lived body and the "second-order" representations of science is collected in his notion of the "tacit *cogito*":

> Behind the spoken *cogito*, the one which is converted into discourse and into essential truth, there lies a tacit cogito, myself experienced by myself. . . . The tacit *cogito*, the presence of oneself to oneself, being no less than existence, is *anterior* to any philosophy, and knows itself only in those extreme situations in which it is under threat: for example, in the dread of death or in another's gaze upon me. . . . The consciousness which conditions language is merely a comprehensive and *inarticulate* grasp upon the world, [it] *waits to be won back, fixed and made explicit by perceptual exploration and by speech*. Silent consciousness grasps itself only as a generalized "I think" in the face of a confused world "to be thought about." Any particular seizure, even the recovery of this generalized project by philosophy, demands that the subject bring into action powers which are a closed book to him and, in particular, that he should become a speaking subject. The tacit *cogito* is a *cogito* only when it has found expression for itself.[24]

This means, of course, that Merleau-Ponty does not intend to cheat in a foundationalist or logocentric way regarding our primary, precognitive, linguistically inarticulate, (but still) intentional "experience"; that he conforms, within his own idiom, to the constraints of the salient; that his view of the phenomenological recovery of invariant essences (linked to the recovery of primary experience) is inherently constrained by the contingencies of whatever is linguistically articulated; *and*, most important, that he therefore rejects entirely Husserl's sanguine commitment to an interior and separable phenomenological reflection that, pursuing intentions somehow prior to language (however linguistically expressed), leads in the direction of pure apodictic discoveries.[25]

To admit this much, however, *is* to naturalize phenomenology: Merleau-esque "in-variants" are never more than salient contingencies posited within the context of experience and directed to the most plausible recovery of the would-be invariances of (an inaccessible) "primary" experience; so they are doubly infected by the loss of privilege within the pragmatized space of linguistic reflection. Nevertheless, Merleau-Ponty does not always remember that what is thus recovered of "precognitive" primary experience is recovered only as a late artifact of "second-order" reflection.

Husserl's phenomenology is starker, more uncompromising, endowed with superior powers – but it is also less convincing: In Investigation I he says,

So far we have considered expressions as used in communication, which last depends essentially on the fact that they operate indicatively. But expressions also play a great part in uncommunicated, interior mental life. . . . It seems clear, therefore, that an expression's meaning, and whatever else pertains to it essentially, cannot coincide with its feats of intimation. Or shall we say that, even in solitary mental life, one uses expressions to intimate something, though not to a second person? Shall one say that in soliloquy one speaks to oneself, and employs words as signs, i.e. as indications, of one's own inner experiences? I cannot think such a view acceptable. Words function as signs here as they do everywhere else: everywhere they can be said to point to something. But if we reflect on the relation of expression to meaning, and to this end break up our complex, intimately unified experience of the sense-filled expression, into the two factors of word and sense, the word comes before us as intrinsically indifferent, whereas the sense seems the thing aimed at by the verbal sign and meant by its means: the expression seems to direct interest away from itself towards its sense, and to point to the latter.[26]

It is just this disjoining of the intentional and the linguistic matched with the notion that the phenomenological examination of (intended) meanings is so utterly disjointed from the naturalistic[27] that identifies Husserl's extraordinary advocacy of the apodictic. For example, it marks the fundamental difference between Husserl's and Frege's opposition to psychologism, since Frege lacked Husserl's conception of the intentional.[28]

These observations help to clarify the essential equivocation (*not* inadvertence) of one of Merleau-Ponty's characteristic pronouncements: "Our own body is in the world as the heart is in the organism: it keeps the visible spectacle constantly alive, it breathes life into it and sustains it *inwardly*, and *with it forms a system.*"[29] Nevertheless, that existentialized phenomenology *is* meant to support an opposition to every form of cognitive privilege – what we have unceremoniously associated with Dewey's seemingly thinner theme. The irony is that it is Dewey's pronouncement that is the clearer of the two and that helps to extricate Merleau-Ponty (conceivably, also, the phenomenological James) from his own dilemma: here, naturalism hurries to the rescue of phenomenology. The intentionality of the lived body need not be compromised; it must, however, either be raised to a mythic pronouncement (like Heidegger's or Foucault's) or else it must descend to the pronoucements of a tempered naturalism "critically" informed by that myth (as in Dewey's solution). But, in favoring the better alternative, we must not devalue or defuse Merleau-Ponty's actual equivocation. On the one hand, he asserts that "my existence does not stem from my antecedents, from my physical and social environment" and, on the other, that "Our own body is in the world as the heart is in the organism"; on the one hand, he affirms our presence in a "world which precedes knowledge" and, on the other, speaking of his notorious glass cube, that it is "by conceiving my body itself as a mobile object [*in that world*] that I am able to interpret perceptual appearance and construct the cube as it truly is."[30]

Viewed in the manner favored, phenomenology *is* a naturalism shorn of its own logocentric pretensions and attentive (especially) to the preformative conditions under which all inquiry proceeds; and, similarly viewed, naturalism *is* simply phenomenologized. The intended reconciliation is meant to be comprehensive: there is nothing left that, in principle (though not, of course, in determinate detail), needs to be added in order to ensure the viability of the first- and second-order epistemic concerns with which we began. Deconstruction, therefore, is merely the ultimately attenuated instruction of any such reconciliation: that is, the instruction that every particular such reconciliation is subject to the further *supplément* of a now-unfathomable future such adjustment; that the conceptual relation between the one and the other is and must remain opaque yet effective; that there is no sense at all to pretending to be able to project rational surmises of continuity, progress, verisimilitude, or totalizing based on cognitive sources external to the contingent work of just such surmises; and that every such surmise is, if internal to such work, fatally "infected" by an absence of privilege. In effect, these considerations mark the almost unnoticed common error of such varied projects as those of Peirce, Quine, Chisholm, Popper, Gadamer, Habermas, Apel – and Husserl.[31]

II

Now, then, what are the benefits of all this? Husserl had resisted the simple conclusion that naturalism = phenomenology, for the double reason that he (rightly) saw that naturalism could claim no cognitive privilege and that he (wrongly) supposed that phenomenology could. There are really three essential strategies on which Husserl and Merleau-Ponty diverge in this regard (taking Merleau-Ponty as proxy for all those who support the reconciling maneuvers intended). These are centered on

1   cognitive "voices" or sources;
2   intentional or propositional content; and
3   dependency or contingency on preformational processes.

A glance at the passages cited from Merleau-Ponty confirms that, for Merleau-Ponty, it is the same incarnated and "enworlded" mind that pursues naturalized perceptual truths and processes them phenomenologically; and that that dual enterprise is "factically" encumbered by the same *Lebenswelt* within which humans live and exercise these abilities. Merleau-Ponty, therefore, opposes any principled or privileged disjunction of cognitive voices between the naturalist and phenomenologist (1), although, as we have seen, he introduces a further, uneasy complication. He also opposes any pretense that phenomenological inquiry can escape the constructive role of the existential preconditions of "primary" or "lived perception" (3).[32] Furthermore, once his stand on matters 1 and 3 is declared, it bcomes clear that any further distinction regarding the special content of this or that inquiry can neither override the constraints just admitted regarding 1 and 3 nor escape whatever strictures are there imposed. Hence, for Merleau-Ponty, *any* distinction regarding 2 – even the phenomenological pursuit of essences – will be entirely neutral as regards the disjunction between naturalism and phenomenology. (To be sure, naturalism in Dewey's sense cannot be characterized as even interested in Merleau-Ponty's revision of the Husserlian pursuit of essences, the skillful work of eidetic variations. But the point of linking Dewey and Merleau-Ponty is not to erase such differences but to provide a fair sense in which the special work of the one could be quite easily fitted to the conceptual orientation of the other. In any case, the point of distinction 2 is just that it raises no epistemological issue of its own that would affect our findings regarding 1 and 3.)

Husserl implicitly opposes all three of Merleau-Ponty's stands and for the same reason. This may be seen, without actually explicating Husserl's entire theory, by juxtaposing two brief remarks of his on the role of the *Lebenswelt*. First, Husserl says,

Things, objects (always understood purely in the sense of the life-world), are "given" as being valid for us in each case (in some mode or other of ontic certainty) but in principle only in such a way that we are conscious of them as things or objects *within* the world-horizon. Each one is something, "something of" the world of which we are constantly conscious as a horizon.[33]

But then, secondly, he says,

Now, how can the pregivenness of the life-world become a universal subject of investigation in its own right? Clearly, only through a total change of the natural attitude, such that we no longer live, as heretofore, as human beings within natural existence, constantly effecting the validity of the pregiven world; rather, we must constantly deny ourselves this. Only in this way can we arrive at the transformed and novel subject of investigation, "pregivenness of the world as such": the world purely and exclusively *as* – and in respect to *how* – it has meaning and ontic validity, and continually attains these in new forms, in our conscious life. Only thus can we study what the world is as the ground-validity for natural life, with all its projects and undertakings, and, correlatively, what natural life and its subjectivity *ultimately* are, i.e., purely as the subjectivity which functions here in affecting validity. The life which effects world-validity in natural world-life does not permit of being studied from the attitude of natural world-life. What is required, then, is a *total transformation* of [cognitive] attitude, *a completely unique, universal epoché.*[34]

Segregating the cognitive voices of naturalism and phenomenology (1) and declaring the one but not the other subject to the preformative influence of the *Lebenswelt* (3), Husserl moves effortlessly to affirm that the pertinent cognitive pronouncements of particular (naturalistic and phenomenological) sciences are of profoundly different epistemic sorts (2). Husserl's position, then, depends entirely on his insistence on the cognitive privilege of transcendental phenomenology. He agrees (in effect) with Merleau-Ponty that the epistemic fortunes of 2 depend entirely on the resolution of the matters sorted under 1 and 3; but, for that very reason, Husserl and Merleau-Ponty part company. This bears directly, or course, on Husserl's fundamental criticism of Galileo's geometry and on his own attempt to ground geometry in some transcendentally apodictic, "primary" or "original meaning-giving achievement which, as idealization practiced on the original ground of all theoretical and practical life – the immediately intuited world (and here especially the empirically intuited world of bodies) – resulted in the geometrical ideal constructions."[35]

It may be, as Merleau-Ponty enthusiastically affirms, that Husserl was seeking "a way between psychology and philosophy – a mode of thinking – . . . which would be neither eternal and without root in the present nor a mere event destined to be replaced by another event tomorrow, and consequently deprived of any intrinsic value." But the characterization is more apt autobiographically. Hence, the following manifesto, possibly one of the most explicit Merleau-Ponty ever offered, points to the essential division between the two:

One may say indeed that psychological knowledge is reflection [Merleau-Ponty had just announced that "Reflection is historicity"] but that it is at the same time an experience. Acccording to the phenomenologist (Husserl), it is a "material *a priori*." Psychological reflection is a "constatation" (a finding). Its task is to discover the meaning of behavior through an effective contact with my own behavior and that of others. Phenomenological psychology is therefore a search for the essence, or meaning, but not apart from the facts. Finally this essence is accessible (only in and through the individual situation in which it appears. When pushed to the limit, eidetic psychology becomes analytic-existential.[36]

So seen, the "primacy" of perception is meant to account (*holistically*) for the (*mythic*) origination of a phenomenologized naturalism within the space of an existential, precognitive presence in the world, *and* to permit and enable an (*internalist* or *critical*) recovery of whatever, reflectively, can appear as the (*existentially*) thus-encumbered essences or meanings within the flux of experience. Ultimately, therefore, Merleau-Ponty refuses Husserl's "total change of the natural attitude."

What, however, is an unexpected bonus resulting from this otherwise curious review of the convergence and opposition of naturalism and phenomenology is the illumination (and resolution) of Husserl's famous diatribe against psychologism. Given 1–3 and the divergence between Husserl and Merleau-Ponty (and the mild promise of Dewey's seemingly thinner naturalism), the puzzle of psychologism cannot but prove shallower (in one sense) than Husserl supposed and incapable (in another) of a resolution favorable to his own exteme philosophical program (or to Frege's). Furthermore, even that profound issue proves, quite transparently, to be only one among a large family of expanding questions that the reconciliation of naturalism and phenomenology entails. These matters should prove instructive.

Before turning to them, we need to remind ourselves that, in Husserl, one finds all the principal forms of cognitive privilege, both foundationalist and logocentric. These include Husserl's reliance on

(a)   the *apodictic* (self-disclosure yielding unconditional cognitive certainty);

(b)   the *originary* (assurance regarding the ultimate source on which correspondence, essences, the epistemic link between the possible and the actual and between the necessary and the contingent depend); and

(c)   the *totalized* (achievement of the conceptual closure within which every considered possibility is related to the inclusive system of all such possibilities).

Ultimately, for Husserl, these three are only different aspects of one and the same transcendental source of epistemic assurance.[37]

It makes no difference that Husserl concedes (in a sense) the provisional, step-by-step, "infinite" exercise of what is required by his own notion of transcendental phenomenology. No such concession ever blunted, for Husserl, the full accessibility and necessity of the transcendental leap itself:

Instead of this universal abstention in individual steps [in effect, the naturalized approximation of the *epoché* Husserl requires], a completely different sort of universal *epochē* is possible [he insists], namely, one which puts out of action, with one blow, the total performance running through the whole of natural world-life and through the whole network (whether concealed or open) of validities – precisely that total performance which, as the coherent "natural attitude," makes up "simple" "straightforward" ongoing life. . . . An attitude is arrived at which is *above* the pregivenness of the validity of the world, *above* the infinite complex whereby, in concealment, the world's validities are always founded on other validities, *above* the whole manifold but synthetically unified flow in which the world has and forever attains its content of meaning and its ontic validity.[38]

Through the "liberation" thus effected, one can and does (that is, "the philosopher [now] situated *above* his own natural being and *above* the natural world"[39] can and does) discover "the universal, absolutely self-enclosed and absolutely self-sufficient correlation between the world itself and world-consciousness."[40] It is only this extraordinary great gasp of Husserl's that makes one uncertain of just how much (later) phenomenologists are willing to admit regarding the convergence between naturalism and phenomenology. Also, *to* retreat from Husserl's extreme position (to suggest even that Husserl himself relented) is to make utter nonsense of his own anti-psychologism. If we assume the force of our original equation, such a strategy would completely subvert the entire purpose of the transcendental function of Husserl's phenomenology. That is why, to risk a sly conjecture, the good-humored simplicity of Dewey's pragmatism (itself a deprivileged, delogocentric precipitate of Hegelianized "phenomenology") is enjoying such an inning at the present moment. (The recovery of Willam James was rightly bound to follow.[41])

We are not here concerned with the vagaries of why Husserl – or, in his own way, Merleau-Ponty – obscures the convergence indicated. The important thing is to draw out its lesson. This surely includes at least the following:

(i)   that naturalism unphenomenologized cannot fail to be logocentric;

(ii)   that phenomenology unnaturalized has no epistemic relevance whatsoever, and where it supposes it does it cannot fail to be foundationalist; and

(iii)   that, given (i) and (ii) – in effect, the symbiosis of first- and second-order knowledge – all science, the fruits of all acknowledged inquiry, cannot fail to be psychologized (psychologistic).

Admittedly, these are rather cryptic findings, but they have a surprising force. For one thing, (i) signifies that *any* first-order inquiry that posits an *epistemically* pertinent relationship between cognizing subject and cognized object or world, that is itself *not* construed holistically in the pragmatist manner as a precognitive artifact of the structuring power of the *Lebenswelt* within which we come to occupy such a cognising role, posits to that extent an initial or privileged transparency or correspondence or similarly favorable preharmony in virtue of which such first-order work succeeds as it does. This is, in fact, just the critical theme that Merleau-Ponty and Dewey explicitly enunciate (and unwittingly share): in Merleau-Ponty, the "relation" between "primary" and "reflective" experience; in Dewey, that between affirming the "problematic situation" and rejecting the "spectator" theory of perception and knowledge.[42] It shows not only

(i[a])   that any adequate epistemology must take the form of a realist–idealist symbiosis,

but also

(i[b])   that *that* symbiosis must be phenomenologically encumbered.

Kant ultimately fails to escape the logocentric predicament, though he does take the first step; he fails to question the conceptual preconditions for the transcendental arguments he sought to refine over an entire lifetime. It is an irony that Husserl takes the second step but converts it at once into a new Cartesianism; Husserl simply places the Transcendental Ego beyond the life-worldly encumbrances of the natural, the empirical ego.

What (ii) signifies, then, is that phenomenology has no other function but to experiment, *within* the life-worldly constraints of naturalistic science, *with* the conceptual variability of whatever saliently appear as the encumbering limitations, distortions, prejudices, interests, habits, and the like that (precognitively) affect the cognized horizons, invariances, regularities, universalities, necessities, essences, laws, rules, theories, principles, categories, concepts, and systems of concepts with which we organize the body of our particular disciplines. (The point may be usefully intruded, here, that Bertrand Russell's demonstration of the fatal paradox of Frege's original logicist account of arithmetic – the rightful mate and source of Husserl's anti-psychologism – decisively demonstrates that, even in the world of numbers [Frege's "third realm"], one cannot count on the required measure of self-evidence that Frege and Husserl needed for their respective versions of anti-psychologism.[43]

It needs but a step, therefore, to see that, once the reciprocity of (i) and (ii) is acknowledged, there *is* no principled *second-order* difference to be made out in legitimating the "critical" *first-order* functioning of Hegelian, Marxist, Husserlian, Frankfurt School, Nietzschean, Wittgensteinian, and pragmatist accounts of the preformative constitution of the subject-object relation: there remain only those first-order differences and their (now) deprivileged second-order mates. (Those differences, are, of course, well worth considering.) The reciprocity of (i) and (ii) also signifies that there *is* no science or serious inquiry except as it is the work of a community of actual inquiring agents (selves) who address *their* cognizing powers to this or that sector of the world. To paraphrase Kant, naturalism without phenomenology is blind, and phenomenology without naturalism is empty. The reflexive analysis of the preformative conditions constituting any inquiry need be no more blind or empty than the inquiry it purports to examine: indeed, it *is* that inquiry, seen through the reciprocity of (i) and (ii).

What needs to be remembered is

(ii^a)   that cognizing subjects (selves) are preformed by their environing world but in ways we can only guess at – reflexively, distributively, always "prejudicially" (in Gadamer's sense[44] – within the holist space of what we take our world to be;

(ii^b)   that what we *take* our world to be is, reciprocally, an artifact of what we take ourselves to be as the cognitively apt creatures that we are; *and*

(ii^c)   that both of these sorts of conjecture are assignable only to cognizing subjects, who regard themselves as addressing an objective world accessible to their native powers.

Since, however, our first- and second-order reflections are symbiotically linked – are intentional in that sense – and since, given (i) and (ii), self and world are similarly symbiotized, we may reasonably draw out another element of the dawning lesson:

(iv)   that science and the legitimation of science cannot be conceptually disjoined.

What we regard as the fruitful prospects and determinate promise of our *first-order* science are, ineluctably, the causal consequence and more of our *second-order* reflections on the nature of self and world.[45]

There you have the precise point of worrying the deep equivocation of Merleau-Ponty's insistence on the "primacy" of perception and the "relation" between science and the "brute" world. There you have, also, the clue to the essential pathos of Imre Lakatos's doomed effort to form, in first-order terms, a linear measure of the inherent promise of scientific research programs scrupulously compared across and within any interval of historical work.[46] Kuhn's and Feyerabend's discontinuities and incommensurabilities – the one meant mildly enough, the other more radically – completely subvert Lakatos's dream, merely by invoking (in their respectively thin ways) the phenomenological (or critical) theme.

It may then prove a further economy to add, as a consequence of these last remarks, another strand of the intended lesson drawn from the convergence of naturalism and phenomenology:

(v)   that (cognizing) self and (cognized) world are never more than historicized referents – possibly discontinuously, even incommensurably, certainly relativistically, posited referents – that cannot but be symbiotically linked.

That is, what the *nature* of self and world is and what the *cognitive relationship* between them is are artifacts of salient truth-claims that, on a theory powered by the very ability to make such claims, supposes every such conjecture to be preformatively constituted under diachronically shifting conditions about which we must also conjecture only from the vantage of the other. In a plain sense, therefore, *critique* is no more than the first-order inquiry (or its second-order legitimation) into the historically preformative conditions of distributed truth-claims engaging cognizing subjects and cognized world – *itself similarly affected*. Accordingly, *psychologism* is the second-order theory (or its narrow first-order application to logic, arithmetic, geometry, transcendental phenomenology) that holds that the legitimation of all such claims must forgo any and all forms of foundationalism and logocentrism; alternatively, it is the theory that the invariances or necessities of such judgments are posited only under the endorgenous contingencies of reflecting on the saliences of our experienced world. They are, therefore, never invariances *sans phrase*; but they *are*, *there*, reasonably posited as invariances. (This is also the point of steering a path between the disjunctive extremes of Platonism and constructivism regarding mathematical objects.[47]) It is easy to see that, however unlikely it may seem, critique and psychologism effectively require the same commitment: simply that naturalism = phenomenology (in the sense supplied).

Reviewed in terms of these distinctions, deconstruction is nothing but a negative idiom – almost a *via negativa* – by which (i)–(v) are affirmed or at least favorably featured. It is perhaps the most attenuated version possible of a purely (necessarily) mythologized instruction regarding the preformational contingencies affecting cognizing subject and cognized world. In what may well be one of Jacques Derrida's most felicitous formulations, the "critical," interventionist function of deconstruction is unmistakably acknowledged: "The *incision* of deconstruction," he says, "which is not a voluntary decision or an absolute beginning, does not take place just anywhere, or in an absolute elsewhere. An incision, precisely, it can be made only according to lines of force and forces of rupture that are localizable *in the discourse to be deconstructed*."[48] It effectively explains Derrida's resistance to any straightforward Marxist historicism (in his *Positions*), since historicism (in the French context) is taken by Derrida to conceal some logocentric privilege. But, in explaining that, it also demonstrates that deconstruction is the mythologized unity of all forms of discourse tempered in accord with (i)–(ii). In this sense, deconstruction catches up the historicizing theme common to Hegel, Marx, Nietzsche, Husserl, Heidegger, Merleau-Ponty, Lukács, Gadamer, Habermas, Derrida, Foucault (and Dewey). Nietzsche's "will to power" is, undoubtedly, the purest version of an exclusively deconstructive theme. Derrida's *"différance"* is merely an extraordinarily abstract adjustment of Nietzsche's theme fitted to (and intended to combat) recent preoccupations with structuralism, (Husserlian) phenomenology, Marxism, and historicism – all of which are clearly prone to logocentric excess. Foucault's "power/knowledge" is also a formula derived from Nietzsche but deliberately employed (with consummate skill) naturalistically, phenomenologically (that is, critically), *and* deconstructively at one and the same time.[49] (It is, in fact, just this complexity that has baffled Foucault's commentators and encouraged the simpler but altogether inadequate picture of the straightforward social critic and activist.[50])

Furthermore, it cannot (and certainly should not) be denied that Marx's notion of *praxis* plays a similar double role (critical and deconstructive) that, within the often opposed phenomenological tradition, is best exemplified by Heidegger's tale of *Sein* and *Dasein* (and Derrida's *différance*) – though, of course, with an entirely different message on its critical side. The double role involves the mythological genesis of symbiotized subjects and objects – cogniscent, sub-cognitively mobile (in Merleau-Ponty's sense), technologically active (in Heidegger's), praxically effective (in Marx's) – *and* the distributed critique of first-order life and work and inquiry informed by the second-order legitimating themes Marx happens to favor.

Clearly, it would not be easy to demonstrate that Marx does work deconstructively, but it is certainly not an unreasonable suggestion. In fact, in a particularly important passage in *The German Ideology*, in which he specifically criticizes Ludwig Feuerbach's conception of *praxis*, Marx observes,

> He does not see how the sensuous world around him is not a thing given direct from all eternity, remaining ever the same, but the product of industry and of the state of society; and, indeed, in the sense that it is an historical product, the result of the activity of a whole succession of generations, each standing on the shoulders of the preceding one, developing its industry and its intercourse, modifying its social system according to the changed needs. Even the objects of the simplest "sensuous certainty" are only given him through social development, industry, and commercial intercourse.[51]

This is certainly a passage that reminds one of the treatment of related themes in the thin naturalism of Thomas Kuhn, the anti-naturalistic phenomenology of Husserl, and the Nietzschean genealogies of Foucault. It may well be that, without acknowledging the "deconstructive" side of Marx's account of *praxis*, we risk failing to offset the familiar charge of incoherence so often leveled against him. That charge, tantamount to that of the incoherence of the sociology of knowledge, cannot stand, once the subject–object relationship is treated in the historicized and praxicalized way Marx treats it.[52] Once one concedes incommensurabilities at the conceptual or cognitive level, and once one construes these as historically and praxically generated, then the usual dilemma invoked – either incoherence (assuming the privilege of a cognitively fixed stance) or vicious regress (the self-referential stigma of construing knowledge as ideology) – cannot fail to dissolve. The sociological thesis need not, of course, be restricted to the Marxist idiom: it could be deconstructive in spite of being Marxist: and, as with Foucault, it could be Nietzschean as well.

III

In drawing out the lesson of the convergence of naturalism and phenomenology, we mentioned but did not actually pursue a constituent item of our earlier
tally – namely, (iii) that science cannot but be psychologized (psychologistic).
The meaning of the key term is a source of considerable quarrel. It could, for
example, merely mean what it usually means in the naturalistic tradition, as in
Quine's Millian conception of logic. On that view, logic, the study of the "laws
of thought," is a sub-study of the psychology of thinking. On Husserl's and
Brentano's view, a grasp of the laws or of the necessary, self-evident constraints
of logic may well require reflexive attention to the processes of thought in
which they are embedded; but the laws are not merely the contingent
regularities, or idealizations drawn from the regularities, of those processes.
They are not psychologistic in that sense, though they need not, for that reason
alone, entail the irrelevance of psychological process: what is reflexively
presented (to consciousness, say) may well be (initially) psychological, but what
is self-evident or apodictic *in* what is thus presented may (on an argument) depend on other grounds (psychologically embedded) that may be brought to
bear.[53]

This is, in fact, Roderick Chisholm's view, partially based on a reading of
Brentano's view;[54] it could also have accommodated Husserl's view (contrary to
Chisholm's intent) if we were (as we are not) prepared favorably to segregate
what we had sorted in an earlier tally as items 1 and 3, the difference between
distinct cognitive sources or "voices" (in Husserl's account, the empirical ego
and the Transcendental Ego) and the affirmation that the one but not
the other is preformatively encumbered by the *Lebenswelt*. On Chisholm's
reading of Brentano – and in his own name – a "person's self-presenting properties . . . are such that he can be absolutely certain that they are all had by one
and the same thing – namely, himself."[55] On Chisholm's (and Brentano's)
view, phenomena or appearances – the "elements of consciousness" – are
intentional: "a phenomenon or appearance is an appearance *to* something or *to*
someone"; hence, "there is something else to which [a phenomenon, even the
phenomenon of being that to which a phenomenon appears,] appears only as a
phenomenon, and . . . this something else exists in itself and is apprehended as
such."[56] The apodictic, therefore, on Brentano's and Husserl's (mature) views,
is drawn (on both accounts) from psychological phenomena, is not equivalently
or identically construed by them, and is viewed on neither account as
psychologistic. (James's view may stand closer to Brentano's; Merleau-Ponty's
to Husserl's. But we lack the decisive evidence for either finding: James did not
actually discuss his relationship to Husserl, and Merleau-Ponty never published
his *L'Origine de la verité*.[57]) As Chisholm summarizes the matter elsewhere, the
psychologistic "conception of the truths of logic, if it were tenable [which he
holds it is not], would reduce 'reason' as a source of knowledge, to our 'inner
consciousness' – i.e., reduce [what he earlier identified as] (4) to (3)," namely,

(3)   "Inner consciousness," or the apprehension of our own states of mind – for example, our awareness of our own sensations, of our beliefs and desires, of how we feel, or what we are undertaking to do;

(4)   Reason, as the source of our a priori knowledge of necessity – our knowledge, for example, of some of the truths of logic or mathematics.[58]

Chisholm's (and of course Brentano's) view *would* be construed psychologistically by *Husserl*. It is not so construed by Chisholm himself, apparently because his distinction between (3) and (4) entails a distinction between *any* phenomenal content presented to a cognizing self and *that self, and* because the certitude assigned to the awareness of what is thus presented depends on the self's reflexive awareness and *not* on (the mere awareness of) the psychological content of what is presented. On an interesting reading of Frege's anti-psychologism, Mark Notturno holds that all forms of psychologism that Frege opposed (Notturno actually manages to formulate four distinct forms) are committed to the thesis that "truth is . . . dependent upon the judging subject."[59] On Fregean grounds, then, truth *is* mind-independent:

A third realm [a realm of things other than spatio-temporal physical entities and other than mental ideas] must be recognized. . . . The thought, for example, which we expressed in the Pythagorean theorem is timelessly true, true independently of whether anyone takes it to be true. It needs no bearer. It is not true for the first time when it is discovered, but is like a planet which, already before anyone has seen it, has been in interaction with other planets.[60]

Husserl would not be satisfied with Frege's formulation – though of course Frege's criticism of Husserl's *Philosophy of Arithmetic* decisively influenced his own version of anti-psychologism – simply because Frege did not pursue (whereas Husserl required, for *his* transcendental phenomenology) a disjunctive distinction (as we have already seen) between the empirical ego and the Transcendental Ego. So Husserl's criticism of Chisholm (and Brentano) would have depended on Chisholm's conflating the two *while preserving apodicticity*. The attack on psychologism is, then, neither an attack on the (supposed) ineliminability of psychological sources of the materials on which *a priori* apodictic truths are alleged to depend nor a mere affirmation of the *a priori* or apodictic as such. This is often not appreciated.

Furthermore, as Chisholm goes on to say, to be able to grasp the absolute certainty of his self-presenting properties "is the closest [a person] comes – and can come – to apprehending himself directly. But this awareness that there is something having the properties in question is what constitutes our basis, at any time, for all the other things that we may be said to know at that time."[61] Unfortunately, *if* the phenomenological or critical theme of preformation is admitted, and *if* the very nature of the cognizing self is subject, in praxical and historicist terms, to diachronically changing preformational forces, then Chisholm's (and Brentano's) line of argument – in effect, Descartes's – cannot fail to be inadequate for any body of science sustained beyond the specious present; and in the specious present it would be pointless to affirm or deny the claim. The conceptual necessity of assigning the mere "possession" of conscious states to a cogniscent self (Strawson's rejection of "no ownership"[62]) is altogether independent of the apodictic standing of *anything* therein distributively presented. So there is a fair sense in which Chisholm's recovery of the apodictic is itself subject to the contingencies of the *Lebenswelt* and, for that reason, *is* ultimately psychologistic. The quick conclusion suggests itself at once: Frege's "third realm" is an entirely arbitrary posit, insufficiently motivated philosophically, question-begging; and Husserl's transcendental source of apodicticity is itself simply subject, contrary to his own argument, to the preformative forces of the *Lebenswelt*. The one inclines toward Platonism, which he does not address; the other inclines toward the purity of an apodictic cognitive source, which he does not vindicate. *If so, then there is no escape from psychologism.* More than that, one cannot fail to see that the vindication of psychologism is essentially the same as the vindication of the sociology-of-knowledge thesis. Both depend on a clear grasp of the force of historicist and praxicalist concessions within the terms of our original equation.

The naturalistic, therefore psychologistic, view is explicitly favored by Gilbert Harman, confessedly under Quine's direct influence. Psychologism, on Harman's view, maintains that "the valid principles of inference are those principles in accordance with which the mind works" – that is, the principles involved in "the working of the mind when nothing goes wrong: how it works ideally."[63] Harman's notion is that induction is the psychological process of "inference to the best explanatory statement" yielding, in real-life terms, what may be called "knowledge of the world." On that view, there is no "inductive logic": "Deductive logic is the only logic there is." Induction is inference – mental processing – directed (according to Harman's solution of the problem of induction) "to the best *total* explanatory account." "Deductive arguments," he adds, "are not inferences but are explanatory conclusions that can increase the coherence of one's view": "There are neither inductive arguments nor deductive inferences. There are only deductive arguments and inductive inferences."[64] For Harman, therefore, "reasoning is a mental process," "mental states and processes are functionally defined," reasoning itself is modeled by programs of inference the function of which lies "in giving us knowledge," and deductive arguments assign "an abstract structure consisting of certain propositions as premises, others as conclusions, perhaps others as intermediate steps" by which the successful functioning of actual processes of reasoning can be explained. In effect, the mapping of the reasoning process can be fitted to what appear to be the ideal formal conditions of success.[65] Both because deduction is *explanatory* of induction and because there are no independent sources of apodicticity that Harman would or could acknowledge, the theory is thoroughly psychologistic.

It is worth noting how extremely casual and straightforward is Harman's reference to "knowledge of the world," to how the mind works "ideally" to achieve knowledge, to how deductive logic serves as a theory of the structure of inferential processes yielding in real-life circumstances "the best total explanatory account" of the supposed events of the world. From Husserl's view, psychologism confuses and conflates the processes of the thinking of empirical egos or natural minds and the "processing" of certain *a priori* "pure ideal truths" (such as $2 + 2 = 4$ or the law of non-contradiction) "in whose meaning not the least is said about the spatio-temporal, factual world" – whose truth holds "irrespective of whether there is a world or not."[66] Quine, of course, had rendered the notions of logical necessity and apodicticity inherently problematic for naturalists: by rejecting, in the "Two Dogmas" paper, any principled analytic/synthetic distinction and by naturalizing epistemology. Harman effectively follows him in this, for he abandons the explicit use of the expression "logical necessity" and insists, without further explanation, on treating "truth-conditional structures" in a way that is relativized to given natural languages – but also so as not to preclude different such languages from exhibiting *the same such structures*. Harman nowhere discusses the conditions under which such structures are suitably "idealized." He merely claims universal scope for a suitable theory: "If all obvious implications could not be accounted for by means of a finite list of axioms, something would be wrong with the theory of logical form."[67]

Michael Dummett hints at an additional way of characterizing psychologism, but he does not carry the analysis out sufficiently. The Frege of "Der Gedanke," he says, "launches a renewed assault on psychologism, i.e. the intrusion of appeal to mental processes in the analysis of sense." He adds, "in doing so, [Frege] produces his most uncharacteristic piece of writing: for, in the process, he for once essays a criticism of the idealist thesis that we are aware only of our own ideas, and hence have no ground for believing in the existence of a world external to us."[68] The point at stake seems to be just that the domain of sense [*Sinn*] is not (whatever it is) the same as the domain of sensory experience, of psychological processes, or even of the "outer" world of normal experience and empirical science. But, as we have already seen, that distinction (our consideration 2) would affect absolutely nothing regarding the apodictic assurances with which *Sinn* could be examined. Dummett has nothing really to say about that; and, in fact, his own (self-styled) anti-realist insistence on decidability undermines, if it can be construed as relevant at all, any Fregean or Husserlian sources of assurance.[69]

Unless we actually link this theme – the specification of the intentional content or "objects" of logic or arithmetic, what logic or arithmetic is "about" – with some further, ramified theory of *the cognizable nature of the world or reality within which such "objects" may be found, the very question of psychologism simply does not arise at all*. In an odd sense, then, on Dummett's line of argument, in spite of what Harman openly declares, Harman does *not* actually opt for a psychologistic account of logic – in the narrow sense in which *he* confines logic to certain formal structures that *thinking* may instantiate in the mental processes of inference. It is only *when* he subsumes (as, of course, he does) *this* paired distinction under his more general naturalism that he rightly claims to be advocating psychologism. By a curious reversal, then, Frege remains a psychologist *manqué* (for all one knows), in the sense that (like Dummett after him) Frege neglects to explain what the nature of the privileged cognitive competence of man is by which the truths of the "third realm" may be assuredly grasped.[70] The short conclusion stares us in the face: that either psychologism is quite trivially avoided (by making too much of our consideration 2); or it is altogether unavoidable, once the equivalence of naturalism and phenomenology is conceded – the reciprocity of (i) and (ii) of the tally of the previous section.

Item (v) of that same tally now leads us to a further consolidation. For the point of (v) is just that *what* is posited as the symbiotized subject and object of cognitive inquiry is an artifact of the historically preformative conditions that *we* posit *in* some present interval of just such inquiry. But that, as we saw, is exactly what Marx intended in explicating (against Feuerbach) his own notion of *praxis*. Exactly the same lesson could be drawn from what, on its "critical" side, Heidegger and Foucault intend by the use of their respective myths of *Sein* and *Dasein* and "power/knowledge." Surprising as it may seem, therefore, *the issues of critique and psychologism are essentially the same.* By "critique" or "critical" philosophy – adhering to (i) and (ii) – one merely means the legitimation of first-order accounts of the preformational conditions under which any well-defined first-order science or inquiry (physics, mathematics, sociology, medicine, law) is said to be so constituted. Phenomenology, then, is simply a particular kind of generalized second-order theory of such preformational forces – as are, also, Hegelian, Marxist, pragmatist, Nietzschean, Frankfurt School and similar undertakings. Here, then, for sheer convenience, also as a memento of the needlessness of an entire philosophical history, also for the sake of a nice irony, we are deliberately collapsing the distinction between "phenomenology" and "critique" – that is, as far as their generic second-order function is concerned, though not, of course, in terms of their actual first-order claims or in terms of their particular (unprivileged) second-order policies or in terms of the agonistic roles particular champions may have pursued *vis-à-vis* one another.

One might well say that Karl Mannheim's thesis of the sociology of knowledge, extended, generalized, and (thereby considerably) altered from Marx's original critique of ideology, is the affirmative analogue, applied in the human sciences, to what (usually without explicit attention to historicist and praxical considerations) is criticized in the anti-psychologist's attack on psychologism. Mannheim speaks of "the characteristics and composition of the *total* structure of the mind of *this* epoch or of *this* group."[71] There is no way to make such specifications coherent without either retreating to a privileged access to a fixed and independent reality (the anti-psychologist's view) or to a frank admission of a serially historicized, preformative *passage* of cognitive orientations within the horizon of which the pluralized, relativized, potentially incommensurable structures "of the mind of this epoch or of this group" could possibly be said to be detected (the praxicalist's and the critiquer's view). That the latter maneuver places in jeopardy the entire question of what we should mean by objectivity goes without saying: it is in a sense just what Mannheim inherits from Max Weber's unresolved obsession with fixing the objectivity of sociology under the joint conditions of the "interested" status of presently active human agents and the historical conditions forming those same interests.[72] On the argument here advanced, the retreat to privilege has been cut off and the advance toward a recovered objectivity remains problematic. Be that as it may, we surely see the sense in which no other options lie at hand, and we surely see both the irresistibility and the force of affirming that naturalism = phenomenology.

There is perhaps one final benefit that we may extract from this review of the import of "naturalism = phenomenology," a benefit bearing primarily on the conception of persons or selves. We have seen how the abandonment of cognitive privilege contributes to phenomenologizing naturalism and naturalizing phenomenology. By the same token, that convergence leads to enlarging the scope of intentional ascriptions beyond the psychological or egological restrictions favored by Brentano and Husserl. The fact is that there is a distinct solipsistic thread that runs through the theories of both Brentano and Husserl. Chisholm may well have exploited this thread in Brentano as sanguinely as anyone could imagine. So he says, for instance, "the fact that a certain intentional property is exemplified . . . implies that there is an *individual thing* [a person – in an older idiom, a 'soul'] that has that property"; for he adds at once that it is a "feature of intentionality and of conscious properties generally [that] they could be had – they could be exemplified – even if there were only *one* individual thing."[73] But, of course, the properties of language, tradition, culture, institutions, and the like *cannot* be specified for one individual thing (even if specified for Robinson Crusoe) and, therefore, the linguistically and culturally freighted psychological and conscious properties of persons cannot be specified solipsistically or monadically (even if *some* intentional properties attributable to the animal powers of man could be solipsistically construed). (We have, already, of course, noticed a similar solipsistic tendency in Husserl.) But that means that, in naturalizing phenomenology and phenomenologizing naturalism, we are bound to enlarge the notion of intentionality beyond the (alternative) accounts of "aboutness" favored by Brentano and Husserl (assignable only to conscious or psychologically apt persons) to include the meaningfulness or significance or purposiveness or deliberately constrained regularity or the like of social practices; and in doing that – precisely because of the symbiosis of self and society, because of the irreducibility of self to the mere instantiation of social process and of the irreducibility of social process to the aggregation of distributed mental or behavioral processes – we are bound to disallow the maneuver that the social, cultural, or collective dimension of human existence is intentional only in a "derived" sense, a sense in which "aboutness" construed as in Brentano's or Husserl's view remains fundamental or primary.[74] The fact that only individual agents think, speak, and act does not show that the intentionality of social process is logically derivative; for *that* they think, speak, and act itself bespeaks their having internalized (and their having emerged as selves by internalizing) the collective intentionalities of their preformative and enveloping culture.

To see this is to see at a stroke the progression of alternative theoretical positions that moves from the solipsistic option to an intermediate position (like P. F. Strawson's, in *Individuals*) to the full recognition of the collective (symbiotized) dimension of human life – as, in various rather disparate ways, is manifest in Hegel, Marx, Nietzsche, Heidegger, Dewey, Gadamer, Wittgenstein, Habermas, and Foucault. For Strawson, who serves as a convenient marker here for a certain minimal but essential insight, refuses to countenance psychological predicates that do not accommodate matched univocal first- and third-person uses; nevertheless, Strawson nowhere discusses the societally implicated conditions (as in acquiring the linguistic aptitude for self-regarding and other-regarding ascriptions) by which his own account of psychological predicates becomes plausible and is rendered reasonably complete.[75] The ineliminability of psychologism, therefore, is tantamount to some form of theorizing about the ineliminability of social *praxis* in the very formation of distinctive human thought. The deeper significance of this concession contests the (methodologized or ontological) disjunction (in Husserl) between empirical and transcendental egos, affirms (with Foucault) the constructive, historicized nature of persons or selves and (therefore) the contingency of second-order necessities, universalities, essences, and the like. Psychologism ultimately precludes solipsism *and* cognitive privilege as it reinterprets the legitimacy of legitimation. We are forced to see the conceptual linkage between restricting *intentionality* to "aboutness" (*à la* Brentano and Husserl) and the tendency toward solipsism. It is prehaps no accident that many of the leading figures of the analytic currents, both Anglo-American and Continental European, are or tend to be (methodological) solipsists – Frege, Russell, Quine, Chomsky, Davidson, and nearly all the American theorists of psychology who favor reductive, eliminative, or cognitivist views of mental states.[76]

Notes

1   See Edmund Husserl, "The Task and the Significance of the *Logical Investigations*," tr. J. N. Mohanty, in J. N. Mohanty (ed.), *Readings on Edmund Husserl's "Logical Investigations"* (The Hague: Martinus Nijhoff, 1977), pp. 198–9; and Gottlob Frege, "The Thought: A Logical Inquiry," tr. A. M. and M. Quinton, repr. in E. D. Klemke (ed.), *Essays on Frege* (Urbana: University of Illinois Press, 1968).

2   A number of detailed analyses and arguments on which our equation depends –
    at some distance – are provided in Joseph Margolis, *Pragmatism without
    Foundations: Reconciling Realism and Relativism* (Oxford: Basil Blackwell, 1986).

3   See L. E. J. Brouwer, "Consciousness, Philosophy, and Mathemactics" (ex-
    cerpted), repr. in Paul Benacerraf and Hilary Putnam (eds), *Philosophy of
    Mathematics*, 2nd edn (Cambridge: Cambridge University Press, 1983).

4   Again, one should consult *Pragmatism without Foundations* for the discussion of
    these themes, with the exception of critique and psychologism. Critique is very
    briefly introduced there and is developed in a more focused way in *Science without
    Unity: Reconciling the Human and Natural Sciences* (Oxford: Basil Blackwell,
    1987). Psychologism will be pursued here as a fresh theme, and what we will
    need regarding critique will be supplied as well.

5   See ch. 4 below.

6   In effect, this is David Lewis's speculation about real but unactual worlds. Lewis,
    however, does not provide a full motivation for postulating such worlds, except
    by way of an apparent sympathy for Frege's "third realm" (which he does
    not directly examine and regarding which he does not diretly address the
    psychologistic question) and by way of (skillfully) debunking the largely
    primitive objections to his own account, which mean to resist the reality of
    alternative worlds. See David Lewis, *On the Plurality of Worlds* (Oxford: Basil
    Blackwell, 1986).

7   The term "logocentrism" was coined by Derrida, partly at least in criticism of
    Husserl. We are using it here more generally. The term appears in Jacques
    Derrida, *Of Grammatology*, tr. Gayatri Chakravorty Spivak (Baltimore: Johns
    Hopkins University Press, 1976) – see particularly "Translator's Preface." See
    also Jacques Derrida, "The Supplement of Origin," *Speech and Phenomena and
    Other Essays on Husserl's Theory of Signs*, tr. David B. Allison (Evanston, IU.:
    Northwestern University Press, 1973).

8   W. V. Quine, *Word and Object* (Cambridge, Mass.: MIT Press, 1960), p. 219.

9   Ibid., p. 221.

10 See further Richard Rorty, *Philosophy and the Mirror of Nature* (Princeton, NJ:
    Princeton University Press, 1979), and *Consequences of Pragmatism* (Minneapolis:
    University of Minnesota Press, 1982). The discussion is aired in *Pragmatism
    without Foundations* and constitutes an important point of contrast affecting the
    present program.

11 This is the sense of "empirical," equally apt for Quine's conception of logical
    truths, William James's empiricism, and Husserl's and Merleau-Ponty's
    phenomenology, that I intended in characterizing transcendental arguments as
    empirical. See Margolis, *Pragmatism without Foundations*, ch. 11.

12 See Edmund Husserl, *Logical Investigations*, tr. J. N. Findlay from 2nd
    German edn, 2 vols (New York: Humanities Press, 1970), vol. 1, p. 420 n. 1
    (Investigation II).

13 See William James, *The Principles of Psychology*, 2 vols (New York: Dover,
    1950), vol. 2, ch. 28, particularly pp. 641–2, 661. (There is a fresh edition, in
    three volumes, from Harvard University Press, 1981, under the general
    editorship of Frederick H. Burkhardt, Fredson Bowers, and Ignas K. Skrupske-
    lis.) The most favorable reading in phenomenological terms is summarized in
    James M. Edie, *William James and Phenomenology* (Bloomington: Indiana
    University Press, 1987), ch. 1.

14 Husserl's own intention and his usage of "naturalism" and "phenomenology" are conveniently given in Edmund Husserl, *Phenomenology and the Crisis of Philosophy*, tr. Quentin Lauer (New York: Harper and Row, 1965).

15 Maurice Merleau-Ponty, "An Unpublished Text by Maurice Merleau-Ponty: A Perspective of His Work," tr. Arleen B. Dallery, in *The Primacy of Perception*, ed. James M. Edie (Evanston, Ill.: Northwestern University Press, 1964), pp. 3–4.

16 Maurice Merleau-Ponty, Preface to *Phenomenology of Perception*, tr. Colin Smith (London: Routledge and Kegan Paul, 1962), p. vii (italics added).

17 This, indeed, is very close to the point of Rorty's deconstructive reading of Dewey (and Heidegger). See "Overcoming the Tradition: Dewey and Heidegger," *Consequences of Pragmatism*.

18 John Dewey, *Logic: The Theory of Inquiry* (New York: Henry Holt, 1938), pp. 104–5. The term "situation" is somewhat clarified on pp. 66–7. In a class on Dewey's logic that I attended at Columbia University, Ernest Nagel made a great deal of (that is, found utterly baffling, utterly untenable) the notion that it was the "objective situation" that was "indeterminate." Nagel preferred assigning the intended indeterminacy, bafflement, uncertainty, and the like to the inquiring subject. But, of course, Dewey was profoundly opposed (*avant la lettre*) to the "logocentric" implications of the simple, relatively constant relationship between subject and object. For an early anticipation of the doctrine of the *Logic*, actually directed against Peirce, see John Dewey, "The Supersition of Necessity," in *John Dewey: The Early Works, 1882–1898*, ed. Jo Ann Boydston et al. (Carbondale, Ill.: Southern Illinois University Press, 1972), vol 4, and "The Reflex Arc Concept in Psychology," ibid., vol. 5. See also R. W. Sleeper, *The Necessity of Pragmatism* (New Haven, Conn.: Yale University Press, 1986); Sandra B. Rosenthal, *Speculative Pragmatism* (Amherst: University of Massachusetts Press, 1986); and Joseph Margolis, "The Relevance of Dewey's Epistemology," in Steven M. Cahn (ed.), *New Studies in the Philosophy of John Dewey* (Hanover, NH: University Press of New England, 1977).

19 Dewey, *Logic*, p. 107 (in the context of pp. 105–7).

20 Maurice Merleau-Ponty, "Preobjective Being: The Solipsist World," *The Visible and the Invisible*, trs. Alphonso Lingis (Evanston, IU.: Northwestern University Press, 1968), p. 157.

21 Merleau-Ponty, *Phenomenology of Perception*, pp. viii–ix (only the expression "speaks" was italicized in the original). Cf. also pp. 203–6.

22 Merleau-Ponty, "The Primacy of Perception and Its Philosophical Consequences," tr. James M. Edie, in *The Primacy of Perception*, p. 12. Cf. p. 38, where Merleau-Ponty answers a question posed by a certain M. Césari.

23 Maurice Merleau-Ponty, *The Structure of Behavior*, tr. Alden L. Fisher (Boston, Mass,.: Beacon Press, 1963), p. 224. Cf. also pp. 170–6, 184.

24 Merleau-Ponty, *Phenomenology of Perception*, pp. 403–4, read in the context of the whole of part III, ch. 1 (italics, excluding the repeated use of "*cogito*", added). See also Maurice Merleau-Ponty, *Consciousness and the Acquisition of Language*, tr. Hugh J. Silverman (Evanston, Ill.: Northwestern University Press, 1973), and *Signs*, tr. Richard C. McCleary (Evanston, Ill.: Northwestern University Press, 1964), especially "Indirect Language and the Voices of Silence" and "On the Phenomenology of Language."

25 See Husserl, *Logical Investigations*, particularly vol. 2, pp. 828–34. See also

Jitendranath N. Mohanty, "Husserl's Theory of Meaning," and Ernst Tugendhat, "Phenomenology and Linguistic Analysis," in Frederick Elliston and Peter McCormack (eds), *Husserl: Expositions and Appraisals* (Notre Dame, Ind.: Notre Dame University Press, 1977); and Derrida, *Speeech and Phenomena*, particularly "Signs and the Blink of an Eye."

26   Husserl, *Logical Investigations*, vol. 1, pp. 278–9. See also ibid., ch. 8: "Prolegomena to Pure Logic."

27   See Edmund Husserl, *The Crisis of European Sciences and Transcendental Phenomenology*, tr. David Carr (Evanston, Ill.: Northwestern University Press, 1970), pp. 139, 141, 184–5.

28   See Mohanty, "Husserl's Theory of Meaning," in Elliston and McCormack (eds), *Husserl*, p. 21. See also Jacques Derrida, *Edmund Husserl's Origin of Geometry: An Introduction*, tr. John P. Leavey, ed. David B. Allison (Stony Brook, NY.: Nicolas Hays, 1978).

29   Merleau-Ponty, *Phenomenology of Perception*, p. 203 (italics added). In emphasizing a conceptual difficulty in Merleau-Ponty's presentation, we have not done full justice to Merleau-Ponty's distinctive invention – the sense in which each of us, distributively, must begin with and is forever bound to the temporal life of the body. The most sympathetic account of this theme is given in Marjorie Grene, "Merleau-Ponty and the Renewal of Ontology," *Review of Metaphysics*, XXIX (1976). But Grene does not press the difficulty noted.

30   Ibid., p. 203.

31   The details are provided in *Pragmatism without Foundations*. The issue regarding Husserl is developed further in *Science without Unity*, ch. 1 – and here.

32   Merleau-Ponty's distinction between first-order and second- order considerations is captured (in reverse order) by the neat (but difficult) formula "The knowledge of a truth is substituted for the experience of an immediate reality" (*The Structure of Behavior*, p. 176).

33   Edmund Husserl, *The Crisis of European Sciences and Transcendental Phenomenology*, tr. David Carr (Evanston, Ill.: Northwestern University Press, 1970), p. 143.

34   Ibid., p. 148.

35   Ibid., p. 49; see also Appendix VI: "The Origin of Geometry," and pp. 68–9.

36   Maurice Merleau-Ponty, "Phenomenology and the Sciences of Man," tr. John Wild, in *The Primacy of Perception*, pp. 92, 95.

37   A conveniently brief, sympathetic account of (what amounts to) these elements in Husserl is given in Timothy J. Stapleton, *Husserl and Heidegger: The Question of a Phenomenological Beginning* (Albany, NY: State University of New York Press, 1983).

38   Husserl, *The Crisis of European Sciences and Transcendental Phenomenology*, p. 150.

39   Ibid,. p. 152.

40   Ibid., p. 151.

41   The point is very briefly noted in Gerald E. Myers, *William James: His Life and Thought* (New Haven, Conn.: Yale University Press, 1986), p. 490 n. 35. Myers does give a number of leads, however, about the relationship between James's pragmatism and phenomenology proper: see particularly pp. 490 n. 35, and 504 n.30. There is, also, an intriguing, somewhat impressionistic chapter in John J.

McDermott, *Streams of Experience: Reflections of the History and Philosophy of American Culture* (Amherst: University of Massachusetts Press, 1986), that specifically associates Dewey and James and Merleau-Ponty. The sub-title of that chapter, ch. 9, is actually "A Phenomenology of Relations in an American Philosophical Vein." See also Edie, *William James and Phenomenology*; and Bruce Wilshire, *William James and Phenomenology: A Study of "The Principles of Psychology"* (Bloomington: Indiana University Press, 1968).

42   The clearest linkage between these two themes, in Dewey, is the following: "The new realism [Dewey's] finds . . . that thinking (including all the operations of discovery and testing as they might be set forth in an inductive logic) is a mere psychological preliminary, utterly irrelevant to any conclusions regarding the nature of objects known. The thesis of the following essays is that thinking is instrumental to a control of the environment, a control effected through acts which would not be undertaken *without the prior resolution of a complex situation into assured elements and an accompanying projection of possibilities* – without, that is to say, thinking" – John Dewey, *Essays in Experimental Logic* (New York: Dover, n.d.), p. 30 (italics added). The formula is clearly as phenomenological as it is naturalistic. In a similar vein, Dewey opposes the assumption "that knowledge has a uniquely privileged position as a mode of access to reality in comparison with other modes of experience" – *The Quest for Certainty* (New York: Minton, Balch, 1929), p. 106. I have consulted, here, Arthur E. Murphy, "Dewey's Epistemology and Metaphysics," in Paul Arthur Schilpp (ed.), *The Philosophy of John Dewey*, 2nd edn (New York: Tudor, 1951).

43   The point is effectively pressed in Mark Amadeus Notturno, *Objectivity, Rationality and the Third Realm: Justification and the Grounds of Psychologism; A Study of Frege and Popper* (Dordrecht: Martinus Nijhoff, 1985), ch. 6.

44   See Hans-Georg Gadamer, *Truth and Method*, tr. Garrett Barden and John Cumming from 2nd German edn (New York: Seabury Press, 1975).

45   This is the central issue explored in *Science without Unity*, pt I. The argument here sketched amounts to a *reductio* of Rorty's thesis in *Philosophy and the Mirror or Nature*.

46   See Imre Lakatos, "Falsification and the Methodology of Scientific Research Programs," *Philosophical Papers*, vol. 1, ed. John Worrall and Gregory Currie (Cambridge: Cambridge University Press, 1978).

47   See Charles Parsons, *Mathematics in Philosophy: Selected Essays* (Ithaca, NY: Cornell University Press, 1983), Introduction.

48   Jacques Derrida, *Positions*, tr. Alan Bass (Chicago: University of Chicago Press, 1981), p. 82 (I have italicized the final phrase).

49   See Michel Foucault, "Truth and Power," in *Power/Knowledge: Selected Interviews and Other Writings 1972–1977*, tr. Colin Gordon et al., ed. Colin Gordon (New York: Pantheon, 1980), and "Nietzsche, Genealogy, History," in *Language, Counter-Memory, Practice: Selected Essays and Interviews*, tr. Donald F. Bouchard and Sherry Simon, ed. Donald F. Bouchard (Ithaca, NY: Cornell University Press, 1977). The single most impressive example of Foucault's *application* of his (deconstructive) theme at the level of first-order naturalistic and phenomenological (critical) history may be found in Michel Foucault, *Discipline and Punish: The Birth of the Prison*, tr. Alan Sheridan (New York: Vintage Books, 1977); but see also Michel Foucault, *The History of Sexuality*, vol. 1, tr. Robert Hurley (New York: Random House, 1978).

50   See for example Mark Poster, *Foucault, Marxism and History: Mode of Production versus Mode of Information* (Cambridge: Polity Press, 1984).

51   Karl Marx (and Friedrich Engels), *The German Ideology*, excerpted in David McLellan (ed.), *Karl Marx: Selected Writings* (Oxford: Oxford University Press, 1977), p. 174. Nicholas Lobkowicz notes the passage but makes very little of it; see his *Theory and Practice: History of a Concept from Aristotle to Marx* (Notre Dame, Ind.: University of Notre Dame Press, 1967), ch. 25. Michel Henry is much clearer about the import of the passage. As Henry remarks, "As long as Marx remained Feuerbachian and understood reality as sensuous reality, sensuous representations had the meaning of reaching this reality in itself; images, dreams, religion were its 'mere representations.' But when reality is defined by praxis, *the ontological meaning of original representation, of the representation which presents being as an object and which in this presentation gives it as it is in itself, is lost. . . . The representation which reveals itself to be unequal to its ontological claims, which, as it gives us external being, cannot give us being but is only a mere representation of it, this representation is 'consciousness.'* " This Henry takes to be "the key concept to the whole Marxian interpretation of ideology." See Michel Henry, *Marx: A Philosophy of Human Reality*, tr. Kathleen McLaughlin (Bloomington: Indiana University Press, 1983), p. 161; also, further, the whole of chs 4–5 For an explicit comparison of Marx's efforts and deconstruction, see Michael Ryan, *Marxism and Deconstruction* (Baltimore: Johns Hopkins University Press, 1982), chs 2–3. It is interesting to compare here, on Heidegger, Reiner Schürmann, *Heidegger on Being and Acting: From Principles to Anarchy*, tr. Christine-Marie Gros and the author (Bloomington: Indiana University Press, 1987). The "soft" convergence between Marx's view here and the views, already examined, of Merleau-Ponty and Dewey is clear enough. See also Marx W. Wartowsky, *Feuerbach* (New York: Cambridge University Press, 1977).

52   For a recent, somewhat bland, sketch of the issue, see Anthony Giddens, *Central Problems in Social Theory: Action, Structure and Contradiction in Social Analysis* (Berkeley, Calif.: University of California press, 1979), ch. 5. See also Karl Mannheim, *Ideology and Utopia* (New York: Harcout, Brace and World, 1936), and *Essays on the Sociology of Knowledge* (London: Routledge and Kegan Paul, 1952).

53   See Husserl, *Logical Investigations*, vol. 2, ch. 2 (Investigation V), especially pp. 557–8, where Husserl identifies "two misunderstandings" on Brentano's part, regarding the "mental" (or the intentional): "first, that we are dealing with a real (*realen*) event or a real (*reales*) relationship, taking place between 'consciousness' or 'the ego', on the one hand, and the thing of which there is consciousness, on the other; secondly, that we are dealing with a relation between two things, both present in equally real fashion (*reell*) in consciousness, an act and an intentional object, or with a sort of box-within-box structure of mental contents" (p. 557). But see also Edmund Husserl, *Formal and Transcendental Logic*, tr. Dorian Cairns (The Hague: Martinus Nijhoff, 1969), p. 152, regarding an important restriction in Husserl's opposition to psychologism.

54   Roderick M. Chisholm, "Brentano's Descriptive Psychology," in Linda L. McAlister (ed.), *The Philosophy of Brentano* (Atlantic Highlands, NJ: Humanities Press, 1976).

55   Roderick M. Chisholm, *The First Person: An Essay on Reference and Intentionality* (Minneapolis: University of Minnesota Press, 1981), p. 89. This needs to be read

in the context of Chisholm's discussion of the whole of ch. 7. See also Franz Brentano, "On the Unity of Consciousness," *Psychology from an Empirical Standpoint*,
ed. Oskar Kraus (German edn) and Linda L. McAlister, (English edn), tr. Antos
C. Rancurello et al. (New York: Humanities Press, 1973), especially p. 160
(cited by Chisholm). This, incidentally, accounts for Chisholm's strong interest in
Thomas Reid's views. (Reid, of course, was Hume's principal opponent in
matters regarding the analysis of the self and self-consciousness.) See Keith Lehrer
and Ronald E. Beanblossom (eds), *Thomas Reid's Inquiry and Essays* (Indianapolis: Bobbs-Merrill, 1975); and Keith Lehrer, "Reid's Influence on Contemporary
American and British Philosophy," in Stephen F. Barker and Tom L. Beauchamp
(eds), *Thomas Reid: Critical Interpretations* (Philadelphia: Philosophical Mono-
graphs, 1976). See also Chisholm, *The Foundations of Knowing*, chs 5, 7.

56   Chisholm, "Brentano's Descriptive Psychology," in McAlister (ed.), *The
     Philosophy of Brentano*, p. 98.
57   See "An Unpublished Text by Maurice Merleau-Ponty: A Prospectus of His
     Work," in Merleau-Ponty, *The Primacy of Perception*.
58   Roderick M. Chisholm, *The Foundations of Knowing* (Minneapolis: University of
     Minnesota Press, 1982), pp. 114, 119; cf. also p. 155.
59   Notturno, *Objectivity, Rationality and the Third Realm*, p. 56; and cf. the rest of
     ch. 3.
60   Frege, "The Thought: A logical Inquiry," in Klemke (ed.), *Essays on Frege*,
     pp. 523–4.
61   Chisholm, *The First Person*, p. 89. (Add)
62   See P. F. Strawson, *Individuals* (London: Methuen, 1959). Cf. Margolis, *Science
     without Unity*, ch. 3.
63   Gilbert Harman, *Thought* (Princeton, NJ: Princeton University Press, 1973),
     pp. 18–19; cf. Preface, p. viii.
64   Ibid., pp. 20–1, 162, 168, 172 (italics added). The theme is quite Millian in
     spirit. See John Stuart Mill, *Logic*, ed. J. M. Robson (Toronto: University of
     Toronto Press, 1973).
65   Harman, *Thought*, pp. 43–4, 46–7, 48, 164; cf. ch. 5, section 2.
66   Husserl, "The Task and Significance of the *Logical Investigations*," in Mohanty
     (ed.), *Readings on Edmund Husserl's "Logical Investigations"*, pp. 198–9.
67   Harman, *Thought*, p. 76, in the context of ch. 5.
68   Michael Dummett, *Frege: Philosophy of Language* (New York: Harper and Row,
     1973), p. 659.
69   See Michael Dummett, *Truth and Other Enigmas* (Cambridge, Mass.: Harvard
     University Press, 1978).
70   See Dummett, *Frege: Philosophy of Language*, pp. 155–9; Hans Sluga, *Gottlob
     Frege* (London: Routledge and Kegan Paul, 1980); Notturno, *Objectivity,
     Rationality and the Third Realm*; J. N. Mohanty, *Husserl and Frege* (Blooming-
     ton: Indiana University Press, 1982), p. 43 and ch. 2; and the charge made in
     Isaac Levi, *The Enterprise of Knowledge: An Essay on Knowledge, Credal
     Probability, and Chance* (Cambridge, Mass.: MIT Press, 1980), ch. 18: "The
     Curse of Frege." Levi, it may be noted, treats Frege's curse as the imposition of a
     disjunctive choice between psychologism and anti-psychologism and claims to
     have begun to offer a third "alternative to suffering from its tyranny" (p. 428).
     But it is not clear that there can be a genuine alternative, and it certainly is not

clear how Levi wishes us to understand his own option as such an alternative. On the contrary, at least in terms of the distinctions here advanced, it seems to be a form of psychologism itself – that is, an option that could not demonstrate more than a naturalistic form of objectivity. Notturno presses the objection in a reasonable way, quite apart from his quarrel with Levi regarding Popper's objection to psychologism; see Notturno, *Objectivity, Rationality and the Third Realm*, pp. 216–17. A recent collection of new essays on Frege confirms, at least implicitly, Frege's neglect of the epistemological issue. See Crispin Wright (ed.), *Frege; Tradition and Influence* (Oxford: Basil Blackwell, 1984), particularly the papers by Peter Carruthers, Harold Noonan, Bob Hale, Gregory Currie, and John Skorupski.

71   Mannheim, *Ideology and Utopia*, p. 56 (italics added). See also Marx (and Engels), *The German Ideology, passim.*

72   See further Peter Hamilton, *Knowledge and Social Structure; An Introduction to the Classical Argument in the Sociology of Knowledge* (London: Routledge and Kegan Paul, 1974); Gunter W. Remmling, *The Sociology of Karl Mannheim* (New York: Humanities Press, 1975); Barry Barnes, *Interests and the Growth of Knowledge* (London: Routledge and Kegan Paul, 1977); and Ted Benton, *Philosophical Foundations of the Three Sociologies* (London: Routledge and Kegan Paul, 1977). Unfortunately, the issue of the sociology of knowledge has not advanced very far beyond the repetition of the original puzzle.

    The principal conceptual difficulty with the sociology of knowledge is simple enough. On the thesis, *knowledge* proves to be a "natural" ingredient in man's historical existence, in effect an ingredient produced in the process of larger efforts of human societies interested in survival and relatively successful in pursuing survival. The sociology of knowledge traces the changing conditions under which knowledge is thus structured or yielded – and variably structured and yielded; but it never quite comes to terms with the fact that *it* affords an objective account of same. This was certainly Mannheim's *pons*. Admittedly, the best clue to its resolution lies with a reasonably delicate grasp of the main themes of Marx's theory of *praxis* – not necessarily with Marx's or Engels's handling of their own theme, certainly not with, say, Lukács's (or Mannheim's) handling of that theme. See Karl Marx and Friedrich Engels, *The German Ideology* (London: Lawrence and Wishart, 1965); and Georg Lukács, *History and Class Consciousness: Studies in Marxist Dialectics*, trs. Rodney Livingstone (London: Merlin, 1971). The dispute about the import, in this general regard, of Max Weber's work is generally muddled. The evidence is that a Marxist framework *can* accomodate Weber's causal claims but only by rejecting a disjunction between "material" and "ideal" elements and a hierarchy of "substratum" and "superstructure" (reasonable in any case). On that issue, see H. R. Trevor-Roper, *Religion, the Reformation and Social Change.* (London: Macmillan, 1967). On the naturalistic emphasis of the sociology of knowledge, note particularly Barnes, *Interests and the Growth of Knowledge*, pp. 1, 86. See ch. 5, below.

73   Roderick M, Chisholm, "Intentionality: How We Refer to Things" (unpublished). This is a version of a number of views Chisholm has fornulated elsewhere. The paper was presented at a conference, "Philosophical Interface: New Beginnings," at Temple University, Philadelphia, Fall 1987.

74   In the conference at which Chisholm's paper was presented (see note 73), the

Husserlian version of solipsism was, in effect, implicitly championed by Robert Sokolowski, in a paper titled "Grammar and Thinking." The prevalence of solipsism in contemporary thought is rather underrated. See ch. 9, below.

75 Strawson, *Individuals*, ch. 3. See also ch. 9, below.

76 Husserl's attempt to overcome solipsism – or, perhaps more accurately, to incorporate the intersubjective within the solipsistic – is a notably strenuous and much disputed matter. I have benefited particularly from an unpublished manuscript by Ronald Bruzina, "Solitude and Community in the Work of Philosophy: Husserl and Fink, 1928–1938," presented at the annual meeting of the Society for Phenomenology and Existential Philosophy, University of Notre Dame, Fall 1987. Bruzina has examined Eugen Fink's notes and papers bearing on the issue. The solipsistic dilemma falls between (a) the intersubjective experience of living subjects that are not the absolute subject originating phenomena and (b) the identity of the reflecting subject with the solipsistic absolute subject. There seems to be no plausible way in which to account for the reality of social phenomena: in (a) the transcendental ego is too weak; in (b) it is too strong. Cf. also ch. 6, below.

4

Thinking, According to Praxism

However we characterize the process of *thinking* fitted to the high achievement of a rationally disciplined science, fitted to rigorous argument, to justified true belief, to confirmed knowledge, we face an inescapable choice between two opposed options: in one, thinking is governed by formal or quasi-formal constraints that match, *a priori*, whatever would ensure truth regarding some given sector of reality (geometry or arithmetic, say); in the other, any would-be such constraints are extrapolated, *a posteriori*, from an order of structured objects apparently cognized by (or salient to) an aggregate of apt subjects, themselves similarly identified by reflexive efforts inseparable from those concerning the other. Broadly speaking, the first stance is anti-psychologistic and the second psychologistic – more or less in Frege's sense.[1] The first requires a source of cognitive privilege. The second rejects the implied relationship affirmed by the first – *a fortiori*, the basis of its presumed privilege. In fact, the second may deny that, within the confines of human inquiry, thinking could possibly satisfy any conditions or criteria approximating truth in accord with the first stance; it would also then deny that there was any sense in which human science (genuine enough) could be characterized as satisfying conditions of knowledge or belief or argument however weakly keyed (logically) to such approximation. If, in accord with the second stance, one still adhered to the regulative (but now substantively impossible) ideal of objective knowledge according to the first stance, one would have subscribed to something very much like Karl Popper's theory of versimilitude – of an exclusively negative testing of scientific claims by scrupulous challenge (as by falsifiability) without the least pretense of ever satisfying epistemically sufficient conditions of confirmation or corroboration.[2] (Whether such a divided strategy is coherent is open to serious dispute. For, it is not clear that it makes sense to suppose – as Popper obviously does – that, regarding a realist science, one could in principle disjoin relevant conditions and criteria of criticism or falsification from the relevant conditions of confirmation and corroboration. This is not to say that we do possess an understanding of how to confirm factual claims, only that the

Popperian disjunction is question-begging.) Or, if, in accord with the second stance, one rejected the need for such a regulative policy but opted instead for epistemic constraints (whatever they might be) that were admitted to be no more than artifacts internally specified within some (blind) preformed symbiosis of cognizing subjects and cognized objects postulated under similarly postulated conditions, one would have subscribed at least to what is captured by affirming "naturalism = phenomenology"[3] – that is, a phenomenologized naturalism and a naturalized phenomenology within the space of which science (and all other forms of inquiry and commitment) and its critical placement within a historicized *Lebenswelt* are located at the same cognitive level. Alternatively, if one rejected both stances, one would have rejected every serious sense in which we speak of an epistemically disciplined science; one would have opted instead for skepticism. Psychologism (on Frege's reading) and skepticism are, therefore, very closely allied: Popper's characterization of his own theory of scientific knowledge as anti-psychologistic and anti-skeptical would then be no more than a terminological sport.

We may collect these distinctions in a more useful way. Eschewing all forms of privilege, we may say

1   that there is no cognitively pertinent sense in which truth or truth-like values can be distributively applied to scientific claims on grounds drawn from the prior structure, or in accord with prior norms governing the detection of the structure, of a mind-independent world;

2   that, admitting (1), there is no rational discipline for subsequently ensuring the "verisimilitude" of science *vis-à-vis* such a world; and

3   that, admitting (1) and (2), the epistemology of every science must be psychologistic and therefore subject to skeptical as well as critical challenge.

Furthermore, to subscribe to 1–3 entails – since doing so is tantamount to accepting "naturalism = phenomenology" –

(a)   denying any principled disjunction between practical and theoretical thinking;

(b)   denying any principled disjunction between individually and societally defined conceptual horizons or cognitive practices; and

(c)   affirming the preformational (precognitive) source of the uncognizable (holist) fit between alternative schemata of descriptive and explanatory categories of world and cognizing self and the conditions of species survival and reproduction.

(a)–(c) constitute, therefore, what may be termed *praxism* – what may now be fairly regarded as an alternative formulation of pragmatism.[4]

We may well ask ourselves what the novelty and special force of a praxical conception of thinking involves. The project divides itself in a natural way: it obliges us to be clear, first, about what it refuses and why; secondly, about what a minimally pertinent reorientation would require; and, thirdly, about what instructive new conceptual flexibilities regarding science and inquiry it makes possible. We risk, in so proceeding, losing a quick sense of the power of a praxical orientation, but we stand to gain a better impression of its scope and linkage to certain strategic questions in the theory of knowledge that are otherwise treated in a prejudically timeless and contextless way. It may be a benefit, therefore, to collect a slowly dawning sense of the relevance of canonical matters that their usual analytic treatment tends to ignore. In this way, we mean to approach the praxist thesis from a considerable distance. We shall proceed by rather deliberate stages, examining alien doctrines that, by their own palpable inadequacy, lead us inexorably and progressively to the praxist corrective. In doing that, however, we need to flag two important *caveats*: first of all, although we shall certainly be guided by Marx's conception of *praxis*, the argument here offered makes no claim to any adequate or narrow accuracy regarding Marx's own particular view or intentions; and, secondly, our account will be seriously truncated (and therefore defective) in addressing hardly at all the question of human or praxical freedom and politically pertinent action. These are serious admissions, to be sure. But the justification for adhering to the limitations mentioned lies (it is supposed) in the recovery of an essential strand of theorizing about *praxis* that is itself usually completely neglected in pursuing these other glossier themes. The intended implication is that it is the neglected strand that clarifies the issue of historically engaged action and that makes the quarrels about the viability of a Marxist science or Marx's consistency (or Marx's very distinction, for that matter) worth quarreling about at all. Freedom, for instance, is itself the praxical formation and transformation of — man. But the meaning of that formula would require much more than we could possibly justify introducing in the context of the present discussion. Hence, in probing the nature of *praxis*, we lay the essential groundwork for an adequate theory of human freedom, but we cannot claim to have plumbed the notion.

Consider, then, the first issue.

I

In explicating Leibniz's analysis of the nature of necessity, Alvin Plantinga introduces the notions of "a possible state of affairs" and of "a possible world" — since, as he remarks, "we can do no better" (than Leibniz, here).[5] Roughly, by "a possible state of affairs," he says, we mean "a *way things could have been*," a logically compossible condition, something normally captured by or corresponding to a proposition — in the way in which (as Plantinga offers) the possible state of affairs *Socrates's being snubnosed* is captured by or corresponds to the proposition *Socrates is snubnosed*. Perhaps there are two distinct entities here, states of affairs and propositions; or perhaps, as Roderick Chisholm holds, there is only one kind of entity (states of affairs).[6] "But not every possible state of affairs," Plantinga goes on to explain, "is a possible world. To claim that honor, a state of affairs must be *maximal* or complete" (which *Socrates's being snubnosed* is not); and "a state of affairs *S* is *complete* or *maximal* if for every state of affairs *S'*, *S* includes *S'* or *S* precludes *S'* . . . a possible world is simply a possible state of affairs that is maximal."[7] Plantinga then leaps to the finding, "Of course *the actual world* is one of the possible worlds; it is the maximal possible state of affairs that is actual, that has the distinction of actually obtaining."[8]

But the least reflection shows that we do not know – and we do not know how to show – that whatever actual *states of affairs* obtain actually could function to define (or characterize), *not* merely to designate, that possible world that *is* the actual *world*. By hypothesis, we already know that given states of affairs are actual states of affairs: they must, therefore, belong to the actual world; but we have no idea *how* to identify *that* actual state of affairs that *is the actual world* – as opposed, say, to identifying a possible (because actual) state of affairs that (trivially, as such) belongs to, or is only a part of, or obtains in, the actual world. There is good reason to think that, in a cognitively serious sense, we *never* know what the actual world (the "maximal possible state of affairs") is – we never know what the proposition is that, if true, would capture or correspond to the actual state of affairs that is the actual world; hence, we know only, in knowing what is actual, no more than that that is (for logically trivial reasons) part of, or obtains in, the actual world. In referring to the actual world, then, we refer to what is (to what we suppose to be) maximal or complete, but we never actually formulate (and have no idea how to formulate) the proposition corresponding to the determinate states of affairs in virtue of which that world *is* demonstrably maximal or complete. As Plantinga explains matters,

> for any possible world *W*, the book on *W* is the set *S* of propositions such that *p* is a member of *S* if *W* entails *p*. Like worlds, books too have a maximality property; if *B* is a book, then for any proposition *p*, either *p* is a member of *B* or else not-*p* is. And clearly for each possible world *W* there will be exactly one book. There is at least one, since for any world *W* and proposition *p*, *W* entails either *p* or its denial; so the set of propositions entailed by *W* will be maximal. There is also at most one; for suppose a world *W* had two (or more) distinct books *B* and *B'*. If *B* differs from *B'*, there must be some proposition *p* such that *B* contains *p* but *B'* contains the denial of *p*. But then *W* would entail both *p* and its denial, in which case *W* would not be a possible state of affairs after all. So each world has its book. Similarly, each maximal possible set of propositions is the book on some world; and the book on the actual world is the set of true propositions.[9]

Several objections fairly leap to the mind. First of all, with respect to the *actual* world, it is by no means clear that, for *every* proposition *p*, either *p* or the denial of p will, or will necessarily, be a member of B_A (the book on the actual world). *Whether any* given proposition is a member of B_A clearly depends (but only in part) on the truth of whatever propositions actually hold of W_A (the actual world), whether it makes sense to say that any and all propositions (or their denials) imputed to B_A hold of W_A independent of any cognitive or decidability procedure for determining whether there *are* conditions on which the truth of p or its denial can be decided, whether (therefore) one can convincingly claim as a necessary truth that the law of excluded middle holds of truth assignments on W_A.[10] In fact, if the law of excluded middle were abandoned, then the maximality of worlds and books would depend on relevance constraints; and, since those could not fail to be open to dispute and subject to epistemically favored considerations, the idea that there was a unique maximality property and a unique book for every world would be utterly unconvincing.

The salient difference between discourse about the actual world and discourse about possible worlds is simply that, relative to the first, we suppose that much is included in that world that is *logically* independent of whatever else is included; and that, relative to the second, we have *no* clues as to what comparable constraints or tolerances should be imposed on what is included, apart from constraints of logical consistency. This is why it is idle to speak about what is true in a possible world W "had W been actual." We may then sadly conclude that, apart from compossibility, with respect to the actual world we have no idea how to proceed to show that what we *take* to be the actual world *is* maximal or complete; and with respect to possible worlds we have no idea how logically to encumber the concepts of being maximal or complete, in order *to* distinguish between possible worlds and possible states of affairs within possible worlds. Of course, as we may suspect – and as Plantinga's own illustrations confirm – our notion of possible worlds is parasitic on our notion of the actual world, even though among those who use the possible-worlds idiom (Plantinga, in particular) the actual world is supposed to be individuated within the set of all possible worlds.

That we cannot actually individuate the actual world (maximally or completely) affects and complicates the import of Plantinga's account. For Plantinga goes on to say,

> Obviously *at least* one possible world obtains [that is, is actual]. Equally obviously, at most one obtains; for suppose two worlds W and W^* both obtained. Since W and W^* are distinct worlds, there will be some state of affairs S such that W includes S and W^* precludes S. But then if both W and W^* are actual, S both obtains and does not obtain; and this, as they say, is repugnant to the intellect.[11]

But Plantinga's conclusion presupposes that we are able to fix the actual world in some cognitively pertinent way: for, if we do, we will (so he claims) be rationally obliged to concede that there is at least and at most one actual world.

Not at all unreasonably, Plantinga introduces the thought that he does "not see that modality *de re* [in particular, necessity *de re*] is in principle more obscure than modality *de dicto.*" He offers as illustrations of the plausibility of this finding: "the necessity of a given proposition – $7 + 5 = 12, \ldots$ or *modus ponens*, or *Socrates is not a number.*"[12] But he nowhere considers the import of the preformational constraints entailed in "naturalism = phenomenology," in virtue of which (1) the *de re/de dicto* distinction would itself be an artifact within the space of that constraint; and (2) necessity, whether *de re* or *de dicto* and however reasonably ascribed, would be psychologistically constrained within that same space. Plantinga's maneuver with respect to B_A and W_A clearly presupposes logical constraints on reality or actuality that take precedence over (1) and (2) – for instance, as in maintaining that the law of excluded middle holds of any proposition p with respect to the book on W_A and in holding that, with respect to W_A, it is a necessary truth that there is some exclusively true book that is maximal for W_A. Furthermore, if "a proposition is true in the actual world if it is true," and if, for some possible world W, a proposition is "true-in-W" "if it *would have been* true had W been actual," then, on Plantinga's own view, compossibility in W cannot impose constraints stricter than those that obtain in W_A – now, notably intended to include constraints of formal consistency. Plantinga himself says, "it is the notion of existence *simpliciter* that is basic; existence-in-W is to be explained in terms of it."[13] Hence, if we have doubts about the necessity or decidability of the maximal book on W_A (even granting that the question is arguable), we cannot fail to have similar doubts about the book on any W.

Plantinga admits, further, that existence may be an "atypical" property,[14] but he does not develop the thesis further. It is reasonably clear that it cannot be applied distributively except in second-order terms that entail an appeal to cognitive specifications.[15] But *that* signifies an encumbrance affecting the entire question of the book on W_A – not merely of whether its maximal content can be specified in principle or in real-time terms but also of whether it even makes sense to claim that, for W_A (*a fortiori*, for any W), there *is* a book on it. (That is, to claim that some X_A exists entails claiming that X_A is actually perceivable or suitably detectable or that there is a determinable procedure for correctly deciding the question of X_A's existence and that that procedure would be – or is – satisfied. Clearly, this is *not* to define existence as such.)

What this shows is that compossibility for any W is a function of whatever constitutes possibility relative to W and that any *specification* of possibility-relative-to-W_A is itself an artifact internal to how W_A is specified within the constraints of "naturalism = phenomenology." (To deny this is to appeal to logocentric grounds Plantinga never supplies or defends.) Hence, it is entirely possible that *what* is taken to be possible or necessary relative to W_A may vary – synchronically as well as diachronically – within whatever are the terms in which we specify W_A or its parts. If we admit *that*, then we cannot subscribe to Plantinga's rule on the "maximality" or either Ws or Bs. But that, in fact, is just what Quine's "Two Dogmas" commits us to (that is, the rejection of Plantinga's rule) – read in terms of our guiding equation and not in terms of Quine's own favored forms of behaviorism or extensionalism.

For example, applying (in effect) Quine's thesis, Hilary Putnam remarks, "Could some of the 'necessary truths' of logic ever turn out to be false for empirical reasons? I shall argue that the answer to this question is in the affirmative, and that logic is, in a certain sense, a natural science."[16] Perhaps one familiar example will serve us here – Putnam's summary of the rejection of Euclid's parallel-lines axiom, which, in effect, is the denial of the impossibility of the following tableau or the denial of the necessity of the Euclidean axiom itself (*de re* – one supposes – on Plantinga's view):

> Consider the following assertion: two straight lines *AB* and *CD* are alleged to come in from "left infinity" in such a way that, to the left of *EF* [a line normal to both the others], their distance apart is constant (or, at any rate, "constant on the average"), while after crossing *EF* they begin to converge – i.e. their distance apart diminishes – without its being the case that they bend at *E* or *F* (i.e. they are really straight, not just "piecewise straight").

"Is it not 'intuitively clear'," Putnam teases, "that this is a contradiction? If one did not know anything about non-Euclidean geometry, relativity, etc., would the intuitive evidence that this is a contradiction, an impossibility, a complete absurdity, etc., be any less than the intuitive evidence that no surface can be scarlet (all over) and bright green at the same time? Or that no bachelor is married?" It turns out, Putnam concludes, that "what was yesterday's 'evident' impossibility is today's possibility (and even *actuality* – things as 'bad' as this really happen, according to the GTR [the General Theory of Relativity] – indeed, if the average curvature of space is not zero, then 'worse' things happen!)."[17] By analogy, even the behavior of the "classical" logical connectives may be affected by *operational* application to the quantum-mechanical world.[18]

In addition, there are actually at least two well-known, quite disparate ways in which Plantinga's claim has (implicitly) been challenged in recent years – both opposed to the Leibnizian option and both fairly characterized as pragmatist in motivation. W. V. Quine holds (and has always held) that "There is really only one world";[19] and, yet, Quine's holism with respect to science entails an "indeterminacy of translation" such that "manuals for translating one language into another [featuring, of course, what science would favor as forming the most reliable core of its findings about the real world] can be set up in divergent ways, all compatible with the totality of speech dispositions, yet incompatible with one another."[20] So, for Quine, the actual world is one, but what may count as true propositions and actual states of affairs is mediated by "analytical hypotheses"[21] in such a way that incompatibilities among sets of propositions governed by *them may* yet be tolerated as picturing or designating parts of the actual world (one as well as another) in spite of such distributed collisions. The reason is that, on Quine's argument, we have no other option. What this shows is that, for a world the properties of whose members cannot be assigned except on an "analytical hypothesis" (or, morely deeply, cannot be assigned except in accord with a pre-formational bias among indefinitely many possible alternative such biases), we can make no sense of the claim that *there is any book or a unique book* for the world in question; and that that difficulty is aggravated by the denial of any principled disjunction between logical and factual claims. On that view, Plantinga's claim proves to be a straightforward *non sequitur*: Quine simply gives up the sanguine conviction that, apart from whatever is holistically confirmed regarding the actual world, we can fix distributive truths uniquely within the holistic body of science.[22] To subscribe to our world is not (necessarily) to subscribe to one book on the world.

The other alternative is the one favored by Nelson Goodman. Goodman begins with a consideration very much like Quine's – that is, with the rejection of cognitive transparency or correspondence.[23] But, where Quine holds fast to one actual world, Goodman declares outright that "We are not speaking in terms of multiple possible alternatives to a single actual world but of multiple actual worlds."[24] Many, of course, have been puzzled by this claim; but, conceding for the sake of the argument that it is coherent, Plantinga will be found to have characterized a possibility as "repugnant to the intellect" that, on the evidence, need not be so at all. In any case, there surely *is* no way, from the vantage of Plantinga's stance, to decide in advance that Goodman's maneuver is an incoherent one – even if Goodman's specific version of the claim proves to be incoherent; also, as with Quine's option, it is quite possible that Goodman's could be freed from whatever difficulties prove local to his own formulation. So we may risk going the extra mile with Goodman.

Goodman identifies himself as an "irrealist," by which he means that he is both "an anti-realist and an anti-idealist"; coordinately, he is a "radical rela-tivist" with regard to these multiple actual worlds, in at least the double sense that he opposes "linguistic universals" (binding on whatever language is alleged to constrain true descriptions of the world) and that he subscribes to "ontological relativism" (which "does not imply that all world-versions [as he terms his central notion] are right but only that at least some irreconcilable ver-sions are right").[25] Also, since, for Goodman, "there is nothing non-actual," possible worlds are disallowed; but, "Since there are conflicting truths, there are many worlds if any, but no such thing as *the* world." So Goodman rejects correspondence, true representation, and any

> faithful reporting on "the real world." For there is . . . no such thing as the real world, no unique, ready-made absolute reality apart from and in-dependent of all versions and visions. Rather, there are many right world-versions, some of them irreconcilable with others; and thus there are many worlds if any. A version is not so much made right by a world as a world is made by a right version.[26]

Apparently, a "world" is (what we may term) the internal accusative of a "version": hence, Goodman, not altogether unlike Plantinga, must – if he is to individuate worlds – individuate versions; but he nowhere attempts to do so. Hence, quite frankly, Goodman has shown neither how to preclude Quinean-like "incompatibles" relative to a *given* "world-version" nor (as yet at least) what cognitively pertinent grounds we have (or could have) by reference to which particular (apparently) "conflicting truths" could be shown not to be (or to be different from) falsehoods relative to *various* "actual worlds" (or relative to the one actual world). But, if Goodman's maneuver were admitted, then, once again, Plantinga would have victimized himself by way of a *non sequitur*. For he would not have satisfactorily demonstrated that if there is an actual world there is at most one actual world; hence, he would not have demonstrated that there is a uniquely maximal book for the actual world (or, we might add, a maximal book for each of Goodman's actual worlds). Certainly, we would not know what to make of the claim that there was a maximal book for the actual world. Furthermore, since, on Goodman's view, there is no operative sense in which "worlds" and "world-versions" may be disjoined, Plantinga's speculation – that the actual world, even "possible worlds" (now no longer clearly intelligible), does or must, apart from our cognitive interest in formulating a coherent world, exhibit a unique maximality condition and submit to the law or excluded middle – seems threateningly arbitrary.

Up to this point Goodman's option looks coherent – though not entirely explicit – since the conceptual relation between "versions" and "worlds" and the very meaning of "world-versions" are unclear. On this (provisional) reading, Goodman sketches an option according to which Plantinga is multiply mistaken: for, (1) if there is at least one actual world, there are many actual worlds; (2) there is no sense in which actual worlds are members of the set of possible worlds (including non-actual worlds); and, (3) inasmuch as multiple actual worlds include "irreconcilable" worlds, there are or may be "conflicting truths" with regard to what is actual. The point again is that the option arises with respect to what we may say about human conceptualization and knowledge, *not* merely about formal constraints on consistency. Furthermore, if formal consistency cannot be freed from the contingencies of psychologism, then the specification of consistency itself must be internal to the specification of what we take to be the actual world (or worlds). Notice, also, that "world-versions" are made by "words" (according to Goodman) – which, in a way, corresponds to the contingent "analytical hypotheses" by which the representation of the one world (according to Quine) may yet yield incompatibilities (on the "classical" view of logic).[27] At any rate, quite apart from the weakness of Goodman's speculation, Plantinga could claim no privileged ground on which either the number of actual worlds or the maximality of any book on the world could be decided.

What is troublesome in a sympathetic way about Goodman's account is that he fails to address what is critical to his own philosophical program. For, for one thing, he does not tell us fully how to distinguish between competing ("irreconcilable") theories with regard to, or falling within, one and the same "world" or "world-version" and competing ("irreconcilable") "world-versions": this, as already remarked, returns us to a difficulty regarding what is "maximal" and "complete" in Plantinga's account. And, for another, he does not tell us fully what the relationship is between "version" and "world": and this, of course, affects what we should count as true among propositions, and "right" among would-be "world-versions." On Goodman's view, consistently with his irrealism, there cannot be any privileged vantage from which to determine which world-versions are "right" or which detailed propositions – about whatever falls within given world-versions – are "true." As he says, "there is no version-independent feature, no true version compatible with all true versions." Consequently, "everything including individuals is an artefact." Nevertheless, "right versions are different from wrong versions." How can this be? The answer Goodman gives is this: "If we make worlds, the meaning of truth lies not in these worlds but in ourselves – or better, in our versions and what we do with them,"[28] But, if *we* ourselves are not artifactually made within particular world-versions but *make* them instead, then it is difficult to see how Goodman can escape (some part of) the cognitive privilege he denies; and, if we *are* artifactually made within them, then it is difficult to grasp what it would mean to claim a distinction between right and wrong world-versions. There is no evidence that Goodman ever addresses the dilemma, or puts it to rest, or outflanks its apparent threat.

The closest Goodman comes to providing an answer returns us to his theory of projectability (at least as an illustration of the answer he apparently has not yet completely formulated). To the question, "what makes a category right?" he answers, "Very briefly, and oversimply, its adoption in inductive practice, its entrenchment, resulting from inertia modified by invention." So inductive validity is at least "an example of rightness other than truth"; and, although "we cannot equate truth with acceptability" (since "we take truth to be constant while acceptability is transient"), nevertheless "*ultimate* acceptability – acceptability that is not subsequently lost – is of course as steadfast as truth." In this sense, "although we may seldom if ever know when or whether it has been or will be achieved, [ultimate acceptability] serves as a sufficient condition for truth."[29]

But this won't do at all, since the rather Peircean long run ("entrenchment") that Goodman appears to count on would *require one* actual world with respect to which our versions are fallibilistically and progressively linked, would *require* a world that is not *merely* an artifact (of our conceptual world-versions), would *require* a universal community of inquiring minds functioning self-correctively *with respect to* the one world to which they belong. If he does not count on that much, we should be even more baffled about the "right" constraints to be imposed on the plural actual worlds we make. In other words, *if* Goodman's thesis is coherent, it must account for the *non-artifactual* aspects of what is actual – consistently with irrealism, relativism, and (a restricted) constructivism. It would still be different from Quine's view, but it would address the *cognitive* concern that it apparently espouses. Curiously, then, there is almost nothing in either Quine's or Goodman's accounts that directly addresses the conditions of actual human inquiry or cognition, any more than there is in Plantinga's – which confirms the vacuity or near-vacuity of talking about "the" one world or about many "worlds," actual or possible. But *that* difficulty does not offset the essential difficulty of Plantinga's account: it points to a further difficulty that dogs all three positions.

The difficulties peculiar to each of these theorists' views – Quine's, Goodman's and Plantinga's – do not enhance the plausibility of either of the others'. Furthermore, one may reasonably suggest (one can hardly pretend to have discovered) that to speak of "one" real or actual world is to do no more than to match the *unicity* (not the internal *unity*) of whatever are the intended referents of the cognitive work of similarly specified, reflexively engaged, merely unitary selves or subjects or cognizing agents.[30] We speak of one world not because we *can* individuate worlds and certainly not because we have any privileged grasp of the internal structure of what we may find in "it" (or in ourselves) but because what we claim to find as actual answers to the unicity of the inquiry *we* claim to pursue. From this point of view, it is entirely possible that, *within* the symbiotized space of cognized world and cognizing self, there *may* also be a point to individuating "one" world or "many" – perhaps non-exclusively; and, then, each of the projects favored by Quine, Goodman, and Plantinga may be appreciated and appraised but, now, utterly without their accustomed privilege. That would mean that the very reason for which each favors his own project would no longer assure an advantage from which the undertakings of the others (or of others even less disposed to agree with any of them) could be convincingly undermined.

What is instructive about our survey is that we see that constraints on our discourse about what is actual – whether in accord with alternative Leibnizian[31] or anti-Leibnizian idioms – *cannot* be pertinently motivated in purely formal terms, *either* in modal terms or in terms meant to be antecedently addressed to the operations of a human science. Quine's and Goodman's efforts signify the open-ended nature of theorizing about the conditions of empirical truth and intelligibility applied to what is actual, which the Leibnizian cannot preclude or relevantly guess at. But, for their own part, once we fully reject the cognitive transparency of the world and all logocentric advantage, Quine and Goodman are much too insouciant about the uncertain force of the global options each happens to favor. For instance, neither has a theory of the actual behavior of scientific thinking considered historically or in praxical terms. There's the trouble, for instance, with Goodman's notion of "entrenchment" – particularly, with his notions of "earned" and "inherited" entrenchment and his notion of "differences in *degree* of projectibility" – since, under historicized and radically relativized circumstances, the governing notion of "*ultimate* acceptability" and its regularized bearing on these other distinctions are rendered completely meaningless or inoperable.[32] Similarly, when Quine summarizes "the genesis and development of reference" applied "to either the individual or the race," when he supplies what he himself terms the "psychogenesis" of reference, he means only to have provided an *"imaginary"* reconstruction of how, in natural language, we *could* have developed the practice of objectual quantification.[33] There is no account in either Plantinga or Quine or Goodman of our conceptual resources considered as part of the historical development of human inquiry. In this sense, Quine and Goodman may be termed *formal pragmatists*, since, in rejecting the cognitive transparency of the world (or worlds), they conform minimally to what (both historically and as a useful term of art) is required by a pragmatist view of science.[34] In this regard, they do gain a small march on Plantinga, since the strongest arguments drawn from the most varied sources of current philosophy reject transparency, any cognitive reading of the correspondence theory, and all forms of logocentrism. Yet, on the argument offered, it remains quite impossible to decide between right and wrong "world-versions" (with Goodman) or between competing hypotheses under the conditions of a thoroughgoing scientific holism (with Quine), unless we can legitimate our reliance on particular, historically emergent, and contingently favored schemes for characterizing and testing the presence of what we take to be actual phenomena. Otherwise, the doctrines of those two gentlemen must appear logocentric (as they surely do). There is, therefore, a remarkably large lacuna in these thin pragmatisms.[35]

The characteristic maneuver of the logocentric is to posit, *a priori*, strong constraints on the cognizable structure of – of what may be discovered with respect to – any part of reality, and to do so in a way that does not obviously betray its apriorism. Plantinga assumes the extensionality of the set of true propositions about the actual world and its closure as a maximal book. Quine and Goodman are similarly committed to extensionalism: Quine, implicitly, to the demonstrable indeterminacy of translation with respect to any would-be "book" in Plantinga's sense; Goodman, explicitly, to the irreconcilability of conflicting truths about what is actual, without attention to any artifactual contingencies that may be due to interpretive intrusion, hence to the impossibility of even forming a "book." The same sort of finding applies to many others: to Popper, for instance, whose demarcation of science presumes the realist relevance of falsification (for verisimilitudinous purposes) in spite of his own insistence on the indemonstrability of the cognitive relevance of all inductive confirmatory and corroborative procedures; to Davidson, who regiments all human inquiry and science, however pursued in contexts first informally identified in terms of natural language and social history, as inexorably yielding to an extensionalism extracted (against the grain and without argument) from a Tarskian-like formal semantics and a token physicalism that appear to acknowledge the intransigencies of natural language and social history;[36] to Frege, who saves apodictic truth by improvising a "third realm" of necessary relations to which such truth can and assuredly does correspond;[37] and, of course, to Husserl, who simply announces a privileged "transcendental" source of cognition as the only way of ensuring apodicticity.[38]

The holism of the pragmatists corresponds in a thin way to the holism of the phenomenologists' *Lebenswelt*. The irony remains that the admission of each is never permitted to disallow the essential apriorism of its strongest champions – witness Quine and Husserl. Nevertheless, it confirms at the very least the polar opposition between logocentric and praxical conceptions of thinking and human inquiry, the opposition between antecedent constraints of a formal or quasi-formal sort ensuring extensionalism or apodicticity or totalization and the internally encountered, preformed informalities distributed among plural societies of the human species, surviving in the shifting contexts of their existence. Furthermore, the failure of programs such as Plantinga's and the failure (or flaunted limitation) of programs such as Quine's and Goodman's amply confirm the unlikelihood that we have any operative sense at all in which we may claim to ascribe determinate closure to the actual world or to be able to give a determinate sense to the notion of individuating possible worlds. Our finding is obviously congenial to the fortunes of praxism, though a little longwinded.

II

Viewed against this backdrop, the distinction of Martin Heidegger's *Being and Time* lies primarily in Heidegger's having attempted a comprehensive phenomenology of coming to know the things of the world under the most radical reading of the denial of cognitive transparency. This Heidegger achieves partly by characterizing man as *Dasein*: for, by that designation, Heidegger means to signify that man is essentially a historical (or historicized) being; that being such is the tacitly predisposing precondition for whatever in his temporal experience he may be said to come to know; that the things of the world and their natures are grasped by man (*Dasein*) in his existential or continually present activity in the world; and (most important) that, in being *Dasein* (the entity), man is essentially defined by the power through which the structure of things is "disclosed" to him (serially, contingently, without privilege, under prejudice), through his own interested activity, always subject to the blind fore-structuring of his cognitive and active capacity. Heidegger achieves his picture of man's cognitive role by identifying the objects thus disclosed (the "phenomena") as objects whose disclosed structure is a structure that itself depends on what can only be mythically specified as the "relationship" between *Dasein* and *Sein*. Such objects and their structures are constituted in being disclosed to *Dasein*: the cognizing self (the "existentiell" self) is included among such "objects." This is what Heidegger means by viewing matters phenomenologically.[39] In that process, *Dasein* reflexively comes to understand itself.

The following may be offered as a fairly perspicuous statement of Heidegger's own summary view, if we are prepared to tolerate the alien quality of Heidegger's prose as seen from the vantage of analytic philosophy:

> Dasein always understands itself in terms of its existence – in terms of a possibility of itself; to be itself or not itself. Dasein has either chosen these possibilities itself, or got itself into them, or grown up in them already [, and] the understanding of oneself which leads along this way we call *"existentiell"*. . . . So far as existence is the determining character of Dasein, the ontological analytic of this identity always requires that existentiality be considered beforehand. By "existentiality" we understand the state of Being that is constitutive for those entities that exist. But in the idea of such a constitutive [or ontic] state of Being, the idea of Being is already included [ontologically, not merely ontically]. . . . Sciences are ways of Being in which Dasein comports itself towards entities which it need not be itself. But to Dasein, Being in a world is something that belongs essentially. Thus Dasein's understanding of Being pertains with equal primordiality both to an understanding of something like a "world," and to the understanding of the Being of those entities which become accessible within the world. So whenever an ontology takes for its theme entities whose character of Being is other than that of Dasein, it has its own foundation and motivation in Dasein's own ontical structure [that is, in whatever of its own structure is disclosed in the ongoing "existentiell" way].[40]

This is certainly not what Quine or Goodman would ever say. But it is, correctly read, a way of historicizing what is common to the most radical denial of the cognitive transparency of the world – in Quine's holism, Goodman's irrealism, and Heidegger's existentialized phenomenology. It is a way of preserving the sense of man's effective survival in the world (a sense much more robust than either Quine's or Goodman's, more like Peirce's or James's or Dewey's – if we may extend the convergence of the pragmatist and phenomenological movements). In effect, Heidegger identifies the minimal conditions and preconditions of human knowledge a *pragmatist* conception of science requires: his analysis fixes the sense in which whatever structures science imputes to the world depend entirely upon and are formulable only within the historical processes of *praxis* and technology. In effect, Heidegger *legitimates* science technologically *and* holistically; in doing that, he probes what is ontologically (or phenomenologically) *prior* in *man's being capable of* cognitive discovery within-the-world – the (necessarily mythologized) precondition on which disputes about *distributed* claims in science must depend. (Putting matters this way – that is, favorably as far as Heidegger is concerned – should not obscure the fact that the account of *Dasein* in *Being and Time* remains unresolvably equivocal and aporetic: as being a frank myth projected from some "existentiell" vantage [in effect, pragmatically] or as being a new essentialism regarding the "ontic" nature of man [precluded by the first option].)

Speaking in this way may still obscure the peculiar power (and limitation) of Heidegger's contribution. A dialectical comparison between the formal theories offered by Quine and Goodman and Plantinga's refinement of a Leibnizian formalism shows

1 that would-be constraints of consistency and coherence imposed on our theory of the actual world *cannot* be given logical priority over our detailed interpretation of the world and our cognitive powers – *formalism is simply pointless, forever generates question-begging "necessities"*;

2 that reference to a "complete" and "maximal" world or worlds, actual or possible, never plays a *cognitively* productive role in developing a science – *the individuation of worlds is conceptually idle*; and

3 that the denial of the world's cognitive transparency affords a direct conceptual basis for viably accommodating the *permanent* presence of incompatible sets of truth claims – *alethic questions no longer take precedence over epistemic questions.*

So there is an enormous gain to be made in moving beyond

(A)   a Leibnizian formalism

to

(B)   a pragmatized formalism

to

(C)   a mythic phenomenology drawn from the technologized preconditions of inquiry.

Nevertheless, that gain is also a dead end if it is not supplemented (internally) by a further account of an effective and detailed theory of science. Neither Plantinga nor Quine nor Goodman nor Heidegger addresses the issue.

The point of the complaint is obvious enough: a holism regarding science or human inquiry is vacant without distributed detail; and such detail is critically irresponsible without a *correspondingly* detailed assessment of the horizon of such a holism. Plantinga's formalism makes no concession in the direction of preformative constraints; Quine's and Goodman's versions do, but they abort the concession in the interest of a still-favored formalism; Heidegger's formalism is deliberately mythologized in order (correctly) to avoid any logocentric charge, but Heidegger himself never descends to the internal discipline of distributed claims within the existential horizon of a (holistic) *Lebenswelt*. (Furthermore, Heidegger is never entirely consistent on the avoidance of essentialism.[41]) In effect, Heidegger provides what may be paradoxically but best termed a *formal praxism* – that is, a theory that understands thinking to be praxically conditioned in the most radical sense but that never ventures an account, *internal* to the space thus postulated, *of* whatever is distributively claimed to be true about the actual world. In a word, Heidegger never ventures an explicit *critique* of the praxical sort he recommends. One can only find such a critique articulated – variously, incompatibly, not always consistently, often piecemeal, with varying degrees of systematic comprehensiveness and detail – among the Hegelians, the Marxists, the Frankfurt School theorists, the Nietzscheans, and the Freudians. It is notably weakly developed among the hermeneuts, the pragmatists, the existentialists, and the phenomenologists; although here and there individual authors – Max Weber for instance, John Dewey on occasion, Jean-Paul Sartre in his literary work, and Husserl certainly in *The Crisis* – have made memorable contributions to such a discipline.

Heidegger's thesis fills a gap, then, by specifying an existential precondition affecting man's (or *Dasein*'s) *cognitive* power in two distinct (but inseparable) ways: first, in that particular cognitive claims are, necessarily, instantiations of *Dasein*'s peculiar mode of being *vis-à-vis* whatever of reality may prove to be cognitively disclosable; and second, in that the conceptual structure of particular such claims is always preconditioned by *Dasein*'s *already having been preconditioned* by its own cognitive (or "existentiell") history and by its having recovered that history under the same condition.

Technology is Heidegger's master-clue: not in the sense that cognitive discovery is exclusively technological but in the sense that disclosure through human technology is always primary, salient, effectively linked to what may be disclosed even by "another" avenue of *Dasein*'s capacity (poetry or art, for instance[42]). Technology draws attention to the inchoate sources within human existence itself – on which human viability depends – in virtue of which the world is seen to be aptly structured *for* cognitively informed activities of any kind; it is also drawn to the power of discontinuous, contingent, serial, variably overriding or influential such disclosures that continually reorient cognition and science historically and reveal to man his own profoundly historical nature. In this sense, Heidegger may not unreasonably be said to provide a phenomenological basis for the more anthropological theses advanced, in, say, Thomas Kuhn's account of normal and revolutionary science and Michel Foucault's account of the unpredictable seriality of the conceptual orientations of different historical ages.[43] But they, unlike Heidegger, do actually address quite detailed first-order claims.

There is no point to the phenomenological thesis about technology unless it is joined to an account (at the level of psychology, ideology, history, sociology, hermeneutics, critique – or of a more generalized philosophical anthropology) *of how the "technic" conditions or constrains the actual horizon of determinate inquiry*; on the other hand, there is a kind of systematic scatter in a collection of such accounts if we fail to relate their shifting conceptual tableaux to the conditions of man's existence. *There* is the point of featuring the peculiarly abstract formulations of Quine's holism and Goodman's irrealism. It is apparent to any reader of *Word and Object* that Quine never addresses the technological – or pragmatist – aspects of the mere survival of a human society, in virtue of which, say, a field linguist seeks to penetrate an alien language: it is surely only for this reason that Quine theorizes that the "analytical hypotheses" by which we parse a would-be language form a (perhaps) inescapable but (nevertheless) arbitrary imposition of one human society's conceptual orientation on another's. It is similarly apparent to any reader of *Fact, Fiction, and Forecast* and *Ways of Worldmaking* that Goodman never addresses the detailed practices of actual inquiry in terms of which to assess the projectability of particular competing categories of induction. The unexpected insight (regarding Quine and Goodman) that Heidegger's approach to the question of science provides is simply that its resolution cannot be derived from timeless or essentialist principles (with which, of course, Quine and Goodman would "formally" agree) but is, withal, existential (in fact, "existentiell"), plausibly imputed (not uniquely and not self-evidently) by attention to the *particular* technologized conditions under which given historical phases of human inquiry are seen to be ordered.

The Heideggerian view – which we are here rather unabashedly integrating with American pragmatism – may be conveniently fixed by a few brief citations and allusions. First of all, from the phenomenological point of view, we are to understand that what we come to know and treat as distinct worldly things (objects or phenomena) we do treat thus – "we encounter as closest to us" (as Heidegger puts it) – because of our "dealings" (*Umgang*) "in the world and *with* entities within-the-world."[44] That encounter is, then, not yet cognitive but only the precondition (holistically mythologized) of our being cognitively concerned with whatever is thus disclosed. The most reasonable interpretation of the thesis is that, at the very least, man's mode of existing (including the subterranean or tacit capacity for survival) skews or forms or founds whatever appear as objects-discovered-by-cognizing-subjects. Here Heidegger borrows the Greek term for things – *pragmata* – "that which one has to do with in one's concernful dealings (*praxis*)." But the Greeks (he claims) failed to explicate what such things are: they thought of them "'proximally' as 'mere Things' [and hence, were deceived by their metaphysics]. We," Heidegger adds, "shall call those entities which we [thus] encounter in concern 'equipment' [*das Zeug*]."[45]

From Heidegger's point of view, the categorizing of things cognized is, in some sense, originally generated by reflecting on what we emergently find suited to our existential dealings – suited to survival, in particular. Heidegger hastens to add here, "Taken strictly, there '*is*' no such thing as *an* equipment. . . . Equipment is essentially 'something in-order-to . . . ' ['*etwas um-zu* . . . ']. A totality of equipment is constituted by various ways of the 'in-order-to', such as serviceability, conduciveness, usability, manipulability."[46] This captures the complex idea that our classificatory schemes are not informed by the cognitive transparency of the actual world (the correspondence thesis); that the classificatory schemes we favor reflexively emerge from our existential dealings with the world in which we find ourselves (the phenomenological aspect of technology); and that these classificatory schemes have a historically contingent life, gradually replacing or affecting one another, legitimately within but only within the interval in which they thus function (the very meaning of *Dasein* itself). This is the reason – the reason for linking Heidegger with the essential themes of American pragmatism, the reason, then – that Heidegger says that " 'Nature' is not to be understood as that which is just present-at-hand, nor as the *power of Nature*": "the ready-to-hand is not thereby *observed* and stared at as something present-at-hand; the presence-at-hand which makes itself known is still bound up in the readiness-to-hand of equipment."[47]

Shorn of its somewhat picturesque terminology, what Heidegger is getting at is that the apparent, cognizable structures of objective nature or reality are originally founded upon the existentially historicized condition of human life itself, which – viewed as the precondition of our science – generates our shifting picture of the known world as an abstraction from what (reflexively) we must suppose *to have been* disclosed in our technologized mode of surviving. We are gifted enough to survive in a world in which we "deal" with "things" *before* we know what they are – and in which, therefore, we identify things *as* what they are (objectively) *because of* that contingent and changing linkage. (The general similarity of Merleau-Ponty's quite different approach is clear enough.) It would be too weak to say (in Heidegger's sense) that things are (then) first relationally identified in terms of their use as gear or equipment: no, in existing, in surviving, *we* reflexively see that we must have first tacitly *used* things *as* equipment. Our various classificatory schemes derive from *that* condition – *but not cognitively at the point at which that condition (mythically) obtains.*

Here, therefore, Heidegger seeks to go beyond the philosophical anthropology implicit in Kant's First *Critique*, to the phenomenological source of all such anthropologies. That theme, the theme that our cognitive abilities *cannot be cognitively grounded*, is the *sine qua non* for effectively rejecting foundationalism, the philosophy of presence, the correpondence theory, and the like. Formulated in terms of a realist science, the theme is also the central theme of pragmatism. Thus, the seemingly baffling puzzles of Quine's and Goodman's invention depend upon (accordingly, are also resolved by) attending to the *supposed* need – now impossible to satisfy – of grounding questions of objective truth in some account of the world's assured transparency. Quine's and Goodman's paradoxes only arise on a theory that they themselves disallow. *They* oblige us to give up that theory all right, but they do not withdraw their own associated (*a priori*) expectations: *hence* the apparent bite of the indeterminacy of translation and of the conflict of incompatible but actual plural worlds. Heidegger's thesis about technology, then, offers a felicitous (but still purely formal) way of rejecting the transparency doctrine *and* of disolving any puzzles that still adhere because we *once* subscribed to it. In particular, Quine's and Goodman's worries prove to be entirely vestigial.

Finally, let us risk a brief comparison between Heidegger and Dewey. The following is tantalizingly close (however alien) to Heidegger's idiom:

By its nature [says Dewey] technology is concerned with things and acts in their instrumentalities, not in their immediacies. Objects and events figure in work not as fulfillments, realizations, but in behalf of other things of which they are means and predictive signs. A tool is a particular thing, but it is more than a particular thing, since it is a thing in which a connection, a sequential bond of nature is embodied. It possesses an objective relation as its own defining property. . . . Man's bias towards himself easily leads him to think of a tool solely in relation to himself, to his hand and eyes, but its primary relationship is toward other external things, as the hammer to the nail, and the plow to the soil. Only through this objective bond does it sustain relation to man himself and his activities. A tool denotes a perception and acknowledgement of sequential bonds in nature.[48]

Notice that Dewey's notion of the "primary relationship . . . toward other things" corresponds to Heidegger's "totality of equipment" – *not* to what Heidegger terms "presence-at-hand" (This may be doubted at first.) Notice, also, that man's reflexive understanding is mediated by technologized activity and perception. The entire discussion, in fact, is set in terms of Dewey's opposition to all the dualisms he believed he could draw from the classic philosophy of the West. There's no question that Dewey was not attracted to anything like Heidegger's high-blown phenomenology. In this sense, he was perhaps more inclined toward a philosophical anthropology in the sense already suggested. Nevertheless, one can also find in Dewey remarks such as the following:

But if we free ourselves from preconceptions, application of "science" means application *in*, not application *to*. Application *in* something signifies a more extensive interaction of natural events with one another, an elimination of distance and obstacles; provision of opportunities for interactions that reveal potentialities previously hidden and that bring into existence new histories with new initiations and endings.[49]

This is an extraordinarily close approximation, within the idiom of American pragmatism, of Heidegger's contrast between *Vorhandenheit* and *Zuhandenheit*, with a splash of the existential history of *Dasein*. The point, however, is not to claim an identity of positions, only a strong convergent line of theorizing that promises the most balanced and most comprehensive account of the full meaning of technology. Furthermore, on the argument here developed, although there is a difference between the inquiries of a philosophical anthropology (or a transcendental philosophy) and a phenomenology of man, there is no difference that would legitimate a claim about the relative privilege or foundational nature of the one inquiry over the other. We may for convenience distinguish first- and second-order inquiries. But to treat technology as a theory of man's historicized existence is to deny the cognitive ascendancy of first- or second-order inquiries in either direction. Also, it must be said, it is *not* a substitute for any distributive, first-order science or for any first-order critique (for instance, Marxist, Frankfurt School, Freudian, or Foucauldian) of the governing prejudice, interest, ideology, horizon or the like with which some science or committed activity is effectively pursued. In Heidegger's hands (less explicitly in Dewey's), reference to technology is more of a second-order (or mythologized account of the source of second-order) reflections on the existential context of science and practical activity. In that sense, it offers what may be termed

(D) a formal praxism.

III

In an obvious sense, the foregoing merely brings us to the threshold of a praxical account of thinking. What we want to understand is its essential novelty and power. We need to proceed in a way that is not indifferent to the strongly partisan (even dubious) uses to which a praxical model has historically been put – notably, in the work of such figures as Hegel, Marx, Lukács, Horkheimer, Weber, Habermas, and, by extension, Foucault – but also in a way that is not captured by any particular such use. We have already linked praxism with an (enlarged) pragmatism, by way of exploiting the entailments of the equation "naturalism = phenomenology" – that is, by way of naturalizing phenomenology and phenomenologizing naturalism, by way of admitting the inextricability of a relational account of cognizing agent and cognized world and an account of the preformative *Lebenswelt* within which that relationship is taken to obtain. We must be candid enough to admit that, by that device, we have deliberately skewed the analysis of *praxis*.

The fact remains that the notion is embedded – notably in the views of Hegel and Marx – in doctrinal commitments that either are, or on plausible and prominent interpretations would be, utterly incompatible with pragmatism and the force of that equation. In particular, its analysis can be made, and has been made, to yield – on the part of either Hegel or Marx or both – an extreme collectivism or teleologism or essentialism or universalism or apriorism or holism or historical determinism or absolutism that only a god could afford to defend. Let it be said as directly as possible that those grand doctrines, so easily extracted from the canonical texts, are utterly preposterous and utterly indefensible. If they were honest heuristic or mythologized devices for effecting a unified world view of a certain sort (illuminating, perhaps, because of their peculiar facility as well as because of their deliberately favored distortions), why, well and good. But, if they are, so to say, the authentic train schedule for the actual odyssey of *Geist* or of its global "materialist" replacements, then Hegel and Marx deserve all the contempt that has been so cordially heaped on them. We have no need to follow them in this.

This sort of criticism had already been leveled at Hegel, at the earliest possible moment, in the deliberately restricted remarks Kierkegaard assigns to Johannes Climacus:

> Hegel is utterly and absolutely right in asserting that, viewed eternally, *sub specie aeterni*, in the language of abstraction, its pure thought and pure being, there is no either–or [and yet] Hegel is equally wrong when, forgetting the abstraction of his thought, he plunges down into the realm of existence to annul the double *aut* with might and main. It is impossible to do this in existence, for in so doing the thinker abrogates existence as well.[50]

An existentialized (or pragmatized) sympathy for Hegel and Marx signifies, roughly, that their own (at times) quite mad and impossible conceptual schemes do, nevertheless, manage (perhaps in a way that is more instructive than any other at their particular moment in history could have been) to "set the 'problematic' for [a more adequate inquiry into the nature] of human action."[51] We may concede the option as worth an argument. But it has the plural disadvantage of improving Marx and Hegel along lines they themselves clearly recommend; of correcting their own unbridled use of their schemata just where they signal a misplaced cognitive confidence; and, most important, of obscuring thereby what, perhaps dimly at times but surely not always, they first fixed as a much-neglected but essential distinction of human thinking.

Perhaps Hegel was a supreme ironist. Perhaps, in Alexandre Kojève's phrasing (though contrary to Kojève's own intent), Hegel did mean, in chapter VIII of the *Phenomenology of Spirit*, to indicate "what [absolute] *Knowledge* [the object of true Science] *must be*, what the Man *must be* who is endowed with a Knowledge that permits him completely and adequately to reveal the *totality* of existing Being."[52] Perhaps, in that sense, Hegel could at least construct a human picture of absolute knowledge – assigning to it a holistic, entirely regulative function. On that reading (particularly sympathetic to Adorno's negative dialectics), "totality" becomes a surd that plays no more than a negative role, that can never actually collect the determinate elements of the totality of the real.[53] Or perhaps Kojève is right, and, on Hegel's own say-so,

> it *is* Hegel, the author of the *Phenomenology*, who *is* somehow Napoleon's Self-Consciousness. And since the perfect Man, the Man fully "satisfied" by what he *is*, can only be a Man who *knows* what he is [who achieves absolute Science], who is fully *self-conscious*, it is Napoleon's existence as *revealed* to all men in and by the *Phenomenology* that is the realized ideal of human existence.[54]

Our own concern, of course, is only to recover a workable conception of *praxis* that escapes (with or without Hegel's or Marx's blessing) all the conceptually indigestible isms enumerated just above.

Here an economy is required. There are many variant conceptions of *praxis* that are incompatible, or at least not convergent, with one another; and there is no readily generic version that straightforwardly collects all that we want to collect for our own purpose. There is no single account that can be relied on to be clearly authoritative as well as adequate for whatever we may here deem essential; and there is none that is reasonably ramified that is not also inextricably bound up with moral or political or philosophical preferences and prejudices that we cannot really expect to redeem or vindicate.

For example, without presuming to fix, by mere mention, the systematic importance of what is entailed in the notion of *praxis* (introduced here as a term of art), it is certainly useful to remark that

(E)   praxism (as we shall understand that doctrine)

(i)   repudiates fetishism.

The meaning of "fetishism" pretty well conforms with what, in *Capital* and elsewhere, Marx signifies as "commodity fetishism"; but to be guided by the gist of Marx's account is not (necessarily) to subscribe to his particular analyses or theories – or, indeed, to discount or oppose them.

Summarily, on Marx's view,

> the mutual relations of the producers [workers], within which the social character of their labor affirms itself, take the form of a social relation between the products. The mystery of the commodity form, therefore, consists in the fact that in it the social character of men's labor appears to them as an objective characteristic, a social natural quality of the labor product itself, and that consequently the relation of the producers to the sum total of their own labor is presented to them [also] as a social relation, existing not between themselves, but between the products of their labor. . . . It is simply a definite social relation between men, that assumes in their eyes, the fantastic form of a relation between things.[55]

Commodity fetishism is distinctive of capitalism; capital fetishism is itself distinct from commodity fetishism; and Marx recognizes an enormous array of alternative forms of fetishism that have appeared in different historical societies. G. A. Cohen conveniently schematizes the narrow sense of commodity fetishism:

1   The labor of persons takes the form of the exchange-value of things.
2   Things do have exchange-value.
3   They do not have it autonomously.
4   They appear to have it autonomously.
5   Exchange-value, and the illusion accompanying it, are not permanent, but peculiar to a determinate form of society.[56]

The significance of (i) in the present context is simply that *praxis* (not by any means uniquely) denies the reducibility of persons to things, and denies the reducibility of behavior (or the properties of personal behavior or relations holding between persons) to physical events (or to the properties of physical events or to relations holding between mere physical things). Thus construed, praxism presupposes the untenability of all forms of physicalism, whether eliminative or reductive.[57] (There simply is no known strategy of reductive materialism by which the normative concerns of a praxical philosophy – Marxism in particular – could be convincingly generated.) Often, it may be admitted, the affirmation of (i) is motivated (notably by Marx himself) by overriding moral or humane considerations concerned with the critique of capitalism and rather less by the metaphysical analysis of persons. Nevertheless, it is reasonably clear that the validity of the objection does presuppose that, as a matter of fact, the reduction of persons to things is *not* philosophically viable; for if it were, commodity fetishism could hardly be convincingly so characterized, and the normative critique of it *and* of capital fetishism would, if viable at all, have to proceed in a radically different way (which is nowhere indicated). This is, also, not to deny that the validity of Marx's intended critique *and* the validity of his own socialist corrective may well fall under suspicion and be challenged for all sorts of interpretive and doctrinal reasons[58] – for example, as possibly not quite escaping a collectivism as dubious as Hegel's. Perhaps, for instance, "Marx's critique of fetishism . . . rests on the myth of a self-transparent and self-identical collectivity."[59] Still, for our present purpose, it is sufficient to emphasize that opposition to reductionism takes on a distinctly praxical cast only when (as anti-fetishism) it is also linked to a further array of distinctly praxical themes that do effectively preclude collective agents (though not collective properties) and all the varieties of cognitive privilege.[60]

Many of the items of that array merely need to be recovered here: they have been analysed (piecemeal) more perspicuously elsewhere, though some will need to be reconsidered. For the moment, it will serve us well to collect them under the same doctrinal umbrella. So, the citation from *Capital*, given above, reminds us that praxism

(ii) affirms the symbiosis, in man, of the individual and the societal.

Marx takes notice, for instance, of "the social character of labor": "From the moment that men in any way work for one another [that is, ubiquitously,] their labor assumes a social form."[61] (ii) may be made to signify that human beings are not mere aggregations of individuals whose cultural, historical, linguistic, productive aptitudes are analyzable entirely and adequately in terms of capacities that are only atomically and intrapsychologically assigned to isolable individuals as such; nor are they mere parts of some "trans-subjective" agent that (somehow) generates or realizes its own *geistlich* or class-collective history.[62] (ii) may also be made to signify that human selves or persons are culturally emergent, socially constituted entities formed from the members of a certain biologically apt species.[63] It is true that, in the passage cited, Marx intends to draw attention to the import of the division of labor (which need not have obtained in the most primitive societies and which links the dynamics of class relations to the dynamics of different modes of production).[64] This is just what makes fetishism possible. But Marx also mentions approvingly Aristotle's characterization of man as *zoon politikon* just where he dismisses as "twaddle" talk of the "productivity" (unless purely accidental) of isolated individuals:

> The human being is in the most literal sense a *zoon politikon*, not merely a gregarious animal, but an animal who can individuate itself only in the midst of society. Production by an isolated individual outside society – a rare exception which may well occur when a civilized person in whom the social forces are already dynamically present is cast by accident into the wilderness – is as much of an absurdity as is the development of language without individuals living *together* and talking to each other. There is no point in dwelling on this any longer.[65]

Themes (i) and (ii) also suggest that praxism

(iii)   admits the historicity of human nature;
(iv)   denies, therefore, that man has an essential or fixed nature; and
(v)   acknowledges that man transforms himself by his own labor and activity.[66]

Theme (v) is prominently pursued by Marx; in a way, it is just the kind of emphasis, true also of (i), that marks the recovery of all these themes as distinctively praxical. The point at stake is that Marx does not merely announce themes (iii)–(v) in a formal, or abstract manner – in which, for instance, one *might* have claimed to be able to draw them out from Heidegger's existential myth of cognition. No, he draws them from their own replete manifestations in actual human history. When, in a letter to P. V. Annenkov, he says by way of summary explanation,

> Monsieur Proudhon has very well grasped the fact that men produce cloth, linen, silks, and it is a great merit on his part to have grapsed this small amount! What he has not grasped is that these men, according to their abilities, also produce the social relations amid which they prepare cloth and linen. Still less has he understood that men, who produce their social relations in accordance with their material productivity, also produce ideas, categories, that is to say the abstract ideal expression of these same social relations. Thus the categories are no more eternal than the relations they express. They are historical and transitory products. For M. Proudhon, on the contrary, abstraction, categories are the primordial cause. According to him they, and not men, make history. . . .[67]

Marx is surely reviewing his own elaborately detailed studies of the interrelationship between changing modes of production and changing social relations. We need not here pursue the promise or fate of those structuralist accounts of "substratum" and "superstructure" that have dogged the history of Marxism[68] (and have all too often been tagged as the views of the authentic

Marx – in order to dismiss any recoverable gains as well). Their defeat would not, after all, disallow the gains of the praxical themes isolated as (iii)–(v), though it would affect the direction of the human sciences and the very viability of Marxism.

Similarly, the underlying biological or species characteristics of man confirm the eligibility of admitting general and persistent human traits ranging over historical change, despite the potentially radical import of (iii)–(v). This accords, for instance, with that remarkably perceptive (possibly anti-Aristotelian, certainly anti-Cartesian) pronouncement by Merleau-Ponty that "one cannot speak of the body and of life in general, but only of the animal body and animal life, of the human body and of human life; and the body of the normal subject – if it is not detached from the spatio-temporal cycles of behavior of which it is the support – is not distinct from the psychological."[69] It also accommodates the ("empirically") radical possibilities envisaged in Foucault's use of the Nietzschean genealogical myth. But, more to the point – anticipating further distinctions – it confirms the reasonableness of Marx's speaking of generic, relatively stable *human* features despite the validity of (iii)–(v).[70] It merely means that all talk of the generic, the essential, the rational, the universal, the characteristically human is empirical, first-order talk, not any second-order commitment to essentialism or the like.[71] Essences without essentialism and universals without universalism are the only possibilities compatible with a thoroughgoing praxism.

It follows at once that we may assimilate to that doctrine a very large array of additional commitments that, once again, remind us of pragmatism but now begin to bear more directly and more distinctively on the praxical conception of thinking. Praxism, then,

(vi)   repudiates apriorism, logocentrism, all forms of cognitive privilege;
(vii) anticipates and accommodates discontinuities and incommensurabilities among large movements of conceptual change;
(viii) anticipates and accomodates the ineliminability of pluralism and relativism in the confrontation of alternative conceptual schemes.

There are, also, a good number of themes belonging to praxism that bridge the difference between theorizing about man's nature and theorizing about the prospects and properties of human science and rational activity. Thus, praxism

(ix) denies any bifurcation between practical and theoretical thinking;
(x)   affirms the interested, purposive, teleologized, normatively oriented nature of thinking;
(xi) concedes the historicized preformation of man's conceptual horizons;
(xii) understands thinking to be tacitly oriented to and constrained by the productive and reproductive conditions of life, by the conditions for the survival of the species and the survival of particular societies; and

(xiii)   construes human thinking and informed behavior as tacitly and
         intentionally objective – that is, addressed to the real, mind-
         independant world, occupied with changing the world in order to
         realize the preferred values and normative goals of societies of men.
Of all these, there can be little doubt that themes (i), (v), (xii) and (xiii) are the
most salient themes in Marx's own notion of *praxis* – perhaps in all familiar
notions. But all of (i)–(xiii) appear to be favorably congruent with Marx's
Theses on Feuerbach, which, without doubt, is the *locus classicus* of the
contemporary notion. We may well discount (for purposes of pertinent
generality but not – at least here – in what Marx calls "practical–critical"
terms) the revolutionary intent of the *Theses*. (Our tally, of course, is not compatible with all of Marx, nor with every derivative current of the Marxist conception of *praxis*.) Here, Nicholas Lobkowicz's reading is surely not
unreasonable: Lobkowicz also reminds us that "there is nowhere in [Marx's]
writing anything resembling a definition of '*Praxis*'; in fact [he adds],
considering how central the notion is to his thought, one time and again is as-
tonished to see how relatively seldom Marx uses it."[72]
   Nevertheless, if one merely reviews the *Theses*, it will not seem unreasonable
to claim to have captured in (i)-(xiii) a great part of what Marx intends by
praxis. Thus,

(II)   The question whether objective truth can be attributed to
        human thinking is not a question of theory but is a practical
        question.

(VI)   . . . the human essence is no abstraction inherent in each single
        individual. In its reality it is the ensemble of the social relations.

(VIII) All social life is essentially practical.

(XI)   The philosophers have only interpreted the world, in various
        ways; the point is to change it.[73]

We may, then, fairly claim to have collected, in (i)–(xiii), the principal – rather
conventional – themes of the usual uses of *praxis*.

IV

What, however, is most decisive about praxism is still missing. This may be
guessed merely by noting that Aristotle, who appears to have been the first to
use the term *praxis*, means by it largely what belongs only to the political
activity of the free man.[74] Assuming Marx's profound historicism and rejection
of real essences (which he could hardly have shared with Aristotle), it is fair to
suppose that the use of the term *praxis* is meant, at least prominently, to entail
a radical conception of thinking. Others, notably G. A. Cohen, have

emphasized chiefly the congruity intended, in the *Theses*, between thought and reality: liberate thought so that it accords with reality; change reality so that it accords with the aspirations of thought.[75] That theme is surely there, but it does not quite touch on the nature of praxical thinking as such.

Richard Bernstein's view, also oriented to the *Theses*, seems initially more promising. "*Praxis*," he claims, "is itself the result of a dialectical critique of Hegel's *Geist*."[76] But in Bernstein's hands the motivation for pressing the connection is to set the stage for the more existentialized or pragmatized treatment of human activity in Sartre and Dewey. Hence, what Bernstein wishes to recover as Marx's contribution to our understanding of *praxis* is his "radical anthropology," by which – in a way more reliably pursued in Dewey than in either Marx or Hegel, admitting for instance Marx's own tendencies toward dogma and absolutism and acknowledging an intensified such disposition in Marx's self-appointed successors – Marx himself (Bernstein says) "seeks to overcome the dichotomies that have plagued modern thought and life: the dichotomies between the 'ought' and the 'is,' the descriptive and the prescriptive, fact and value."[77] So seen, Bernstein's approach is a kind of improvement on Cohen's, but it is also a reading of a similar stripe.

No, what is wanted is a bolder proposal that brings a clearly embedded feature of Marx's view of *praxis* (and of what is distinctly similar in Hegel's account of thinking, even if he does not address *praxis* as such) into accord with certain suggestive strands of a larger theory, quite variously pursued, possibly even opposed to Marx's particular projects, certainly differently motivated, that could be drawn together from analytic philosophy, from Wittgenstein, from Heidegger, from Foucault, and from other sources, to yield a surprisingly strong, coherent account of what, minimally, may be made of regarding human selves and persons as culturally emergent entities. In this sense, it would focus on the way thought itself is effectively structured.

If we leave to one side the troubled structuralist question of the priority of substratum and superstructure, then the key notion, in Marx, that bears on the missing theme is pretty well captured (but hardly analyzed in the sense we require) by such comments as the following:

> These social relations into which the producers enter with one another, the conditions under which they exchange their activities and participate in the whole act of production, will naturally vary according to the character of the means of production. With the invention of a new instrument of warfare, firearms, the whole internal organization of the army necessarily changed; the relationships within which individuals can constitute an army were transformed and the relations of different armies to one another also changed.
>
> Thus the social relations within which individuals produce, the social relations of production, change, are transformed, with the change and development of the material means of production, the productive forces. The relations of production in their totality constitute what are called the

social relations, society, and, specifically, a society at a definite state of historical development, a society with a peculiar, distinctive character. Ancient society, feudal society, bourgeois society are such totalities of production relations; each of which at the same time denotes a special stage of development in the history of mankind[78]

and

the greatness of Hegel's *Phenomenology* and its final product, the dialectic of negativity as the moving and creating principle, is on the one hand that Hegel conceives of *the self-creation of man as a process*, objectification as loss of the object, as externalization and the transcendence of this externalization. This means, therefore, that he grasps the nature of labor and understands objective man, true, because real, man *as the result of his own labor*.[79]

Add to these the remark, already cited, from Marx's letter to Annenkov: the missing theme begins to dawn.

We may say, innocuously enough – following the language of the *Theses on Feuerbach* (II) – that praxism

(xiv)   attributes objectivity or objective truth to human thinking as a practical rather than a theoretical matter.

The sense is clearly linked with Marx's criticism of Proudhon (in the letter to Annenkov). But what does that mean? It surely entails

(a)   rejecting a strong or comprehensive nativism or innatism with respect to concepts or conceptual categories;
(b)   construing the actual range of concepts and categories employed as artifacts of man's historical existence in particular societies;
(c)   conceding the transience, however conservative, of the conceptual horizon of different societies;
(d)   affirming the tacitly and preformationally technic or productive origin of a society's conceptual horizon; and
(e)   affirming the symbiotic and reciprocal effect of changing concepts on production and relations, of changing production on relations and concepts, and of changing relations on production and concepts.

Productive forces just *are* forms of knowledge objectified. As Marx observes in *Grundrisse*,

Nature builds no machines, no locomotives, railways, electric telegraphs, self-acting mules, etc. These are products of human industry; natural material transformed into organs of the human will over nature, or of human participation in nature. They are *organs of the human brain, created by the human hand*; the power of knowledge, objectified. The development of fixed capital indicates to what degree general social knowledge has become a *direct force of production*, and to what degree, hence, the conditions of the process of social life itself have come under the control of the general intellect and have been transformed in accordance with it.[80]

Theme (xiv), therefore, is committed also to

(f)   acknowledging that, *qua* productive, thought and science are as essential a part of the productive process as are physical nature and any determinate technology.

In fact, nature is *not* "productive" (productive in a historically or humanly significant sense) unless technologized; and (productive) technology just *is* knowledge objectified. Hence, (xiv) also favors

(g)   affirming that man transforms himself by his own productive activity, which, now, may be distributively characterized in terms of concepts, social relations, productive forces, or any combination of these.

Distinctions (a)–(g) capture a good part of (xiv) – perhaps the entire notion, if we understand them generously enough. These are, in fact, the themes of Karel Kosík's reading of Marx:

praxis is the exposure of the mystery of man as an onto-formative being, as a being that *forms* the (socio-human) reality and therefore also grasps and interprets it (i.e. reality both human and extra-human, reality in its totality). Man's praxis is not practical activity as opposed to theorizing, it is the determination of human being as the process of forming reality.
    Praxis is active and self-producing in history, i.e. it is a constantly renewing, practically constituting unity of man and world, matter and spirit, subject and object, products and productivity. . . . Praxis permeates the *whole* of man and determines him in his totality. Praxis is not an *external* determination of man: neither a machine nor a dog have or know praxis.[81]

Here, at a stroke, Kosík manages to identify the convergent import of the realist/anti-realist, materialist/idealist, and naturalist/phenomenologist disputes and the point of *rapprochement* between Marxist, Hegelian, and pragmatist orientations.

Still, there are at least two further lines of thought that ought to be explicitly mentioned in order to round out the account of what we are here calling praxism. They are quite closely related notions, though it may be said to be Marx's distinctive contribution to have shown us how to link them in a natural way. First of all, objectivity, the question of truth (Thesis II), arises only within a preformational order of the sort we have drawn out as an entailment of "naturalism = phenomenology" – in particular, of the sort we have associated with the somewhat different but converging views of Heidegger, Dewey, and Foucault.[82] There is, of course, hardly a comparison, at the level of empirically detailed first-order studies, to be made between Marx and either Heidegger or Dewey. Foucault has a better claim: he actually provides more than a fair sketch of how to accommodate an ampler, less structured schema of socially "productive" forces than Marx would ever have been disposed to favor. This is the point of Foucault's "genealogical" (or Nietzschean) orientation – as in *Discipline and Punish*; also, of Foucault's explicit critique of Marxist *and* Husserlian theories of thinking:

> [the] historical contextualization [I have favored, Foucault affirms] needed to be something more than the simple relativization of the phenomenological subject. I don't believe the problem can be solved by historicizing the subject as posited by the phenomenologists, fabricating a subject that evolves through the course of history. One has to dispense with the constituent subject, to get rid of the subject itself, that's to say, to arrive at an analysis which can account for the constitution of the subject within a historical framework. And this is what I would call genealogy, that is, a form of history which can account for the constitution of knowledges, discourses, domains of objects etc., without having to make reference to a subject which is either transcendental in relation to the field of events or runs in its empty sameness throughout the course of history.[83]

Foucault has in a way Nietzscheanized Marx and phenomenology and existentialism and pragmatism. But the point remains that, on first-order empirical grounds, we are not obliged to take exclusive sides for or against Marx or Hegel or Weber or Lukács or Habermas or Foucault; and, on second-order (legitimative or transcendental) grounds, a good argument can be made for affirming a strong convergence among all of these theorists (to the extent they themselves escape the theoretical traps exposed by our themes (i)–(xiv)). What follows is that praxism:

(xv) concedes the artifactually relativized status of the very posit of objectivity or objective reality.

Marx is simply too sanguine and too authoritarian here, too much tempted by presumptions of privilege regarding *what* is real. We must agree with him, of course, in his subtle and devastating attack on Proudhon – against the very notion of regarding mere "abstract" categories as entering into the "objective" description of anything as "objectively productive" or "practical." *But*, within the entire range of possibilities of how, distributively, we may construe human activity *as* practical or productive, *there simply is no compelling ground on which, in principle, Marx could disallow the claims of his proper competitors regarding what we should mean by "real" or "objective."* This is surely the great lesson of Weber's *Protestant Ethic*, for instance – which, of course, the Marxists were bound to assimilate (to the extent that Weber's thesis can be defended) or to modify congenially (to the extent that the undisputed data invite or require adjustment).[84]

In any case, *that* the cognitively accessible real world is "plural," conceptually unbounded, artifactually dependent on the self-transformative activity or productive human societies, objectively "there" only in a sense inextricable from the reflexive perception of man's technologized transformation of brute nature, yields the only reading of *praxis* compatible with "naturalism = phenomenology" and the only reading that (possibly at a heavy price) would render Marx's own doctrine entirely consistent. It is also a reading that confirms the non-individuative sense in which we speak of one actual world and in which to speak of plural worlds (actual or possible) is only to adopt a heuristic convenience, a *façon de parler*, for accommodating horizonal incommensurabilities and relativistic versions of objectivity. There is no principled sense in which, say, the "worlds" described and explained by Weber and Foucault are less real than Marx's "world" – or, that they are real only because they can be redescribed and explained in terms of the "productive" concepts Marx supplies for his "world". (Foucault, of course, remains profoundly paradoxical, since the "objectivity" relativized to the normalization of discontinuously entrenched *epistemes* is not straightforwardly recoverable as meaningfully objective across *epistemes*; and yet Foucault is clearly unwilling to relinquish the sense of the relatively independent discipline of his own genealogies.[85])

The second line of speculation needed concerns the actual detail of the conceptual categories we *affirm* as objective. The issues are extraordinarily hazy, albeit perennial. How, we may ask, does a general concept actually function in the space of objective human activity – even, or especially, granting the contingent, historicized, intentionalized, pluralized, relativized, horizonal, preformative, incommensurable, transient, interested, normatively infected, practical, and open-ended nature of alternative sets of conceptual categories in actual use? Two extremes may be dismissed at once, which, however, provisionally fix the range of options within which a plausible account may be rendered – and within which Marx's own broad hints afford our own best instruction.

At the one extreme, Kant is usually reported to hold that "a concept is always, as regards its form, something universal which serves as a rule." Thus, for instance, he says that "the concept of body as the unity of the manifold which is thought through it, serves as a rule in our knowledge of outer appearances. But it can be a rule for intuitions only insofar as it represents in any given appearances the necessary reproduction of their manifold, and thereby the synthetic unity in our consciousness of them."[86] In this spirit, though without necessarily subscribing to Kant's entire schema, many would be attracted to the notion that concepts are rules by applying which this or that is judged to instantiate or exhibit this or that feature (designated by the concept). Nevertheless, in an extraordinarily explicit passage, Kant himself makes it quite clear that that view must fail. It is a passage worth citing in full:

If understanding in general is to be viewed as the faculty of rules, judgment will be the faculty of subsuming under rules; that is, of distinguishing whether something does or does not stand under a given rule (*casus datae legis*). General logic contains, and can contain, no rules for judgment. . . . If it sought to give general instructions how we are to subsume under these rules, that is, to distinguish whether something does or does not come under them, that could only be by means of another rule. This in turn, for the very reason that it is a rule, again demands guidance from judgment. And thus it appears that, though understanding is capable of being instructed, and of being equipped with rules, judgment is a peculiar talent which can be practised only, and cannot be taught. It is the specific quality of so-called mother-wit; and its lack no school can make good. For, although an abundance of rules borrowed from the insight of others may indeed be proffered to, and as it were grafted upon, a limited understanding, the power of rightly employing them must belong to the learner himself; and in the absence of such a natural gift no rule that may be prescribed to him for this purpose can ensure against misuse. . . . [One] may comprehend the universal *in abstracto*, and yet not be able to distinguish whether a case *in concreto* comes under it.[87]

It may be disputed whether Kant means that those who are not gifted at judgment *err* in applying concepts (for which there are in principle rules determining necessary content but not application to would-be instances) or whether he (really) means that there are no rules *for* applying concepts to would-be instances (*and* that the only sense in which, *in the context of making judgments*, one can be said to understand a concept is the sense in which one *can* apply it to instances – that there is no fall-back sense in which there can be an antecedent grasp of a concept, regarding which the additional question of how to apply *it* arises). In the second sense, a concept is a special ability, not a rule – in particular, an ability to judge instances in a certain way that cannot, in principle, be assessed by reference to, or characterized as instantiating, any antecedent rule.

Jonathan Bennett tends to favor this second reading (with *caveat*s) and is inclined to treat Kant pretty well as having quite definitely anticipated Wittgenstein.[88] Now, it would be a very pretty argument that could show that, in his criticism of Proudhon's appeal to "abstract" concepts, Marx was in a way also anticipating Wittgenstein – but, *in doing that*, was also interpreting the entire exercise in praxical or "objective" terms. Construing matters thus, it might be said, in a provocatively instructive way, that, despite *his* complete indifference (in *Investigations*) to the historically replete details of a Marxian view of *praxis*, Wittgenstein's notion of "forms of life" does provide a generic formula for the praxical notion of objectivity itself – in the sense in which we may speak of applying concepts.[89] Such an argument would, in a remarkably economical way, capture the sense in which "objective" reality is plural (pluralized) along the lines already sketched. Proudhon's kind of abstraction would still be rejected – along the lines Kant had already supplied; although, *if any set of concepts in use within the practices of a historical society is admitted to function there thus, then the empirical question of objectivity, ideology, false consciousness, error, and the like (and the second-order legitimation of particular solutions of that question) remains unanswered merely in our having clarified the notion of what it means to have an objective concept.* To put the point quite bluntly: no pragmatist or praxical theory of objectivity could assume that the *holist* version of realism to which it is committed yields an exclusively correct *distributive* rule or criterion of objectivity (Marxist, Weberian, Foucauldian, Habermasian or whatnot) without violating its own constraint against cognitive privilege. This part of the argument is reasonably compelling: to what extent we may also favorably bridge the differences, among, say, Kant, Marx, Wittgenstein, and Foucault – along the lines indicated – is a textual question of distinctly reduced interest.

At the opposite pole, regarding the role of concepts in thinking, stands an unrelenting nominalism. The least biologized account of human nature concedes a natural propensity on the part of the human species (as in all percipient species) to favor or collect discriminations as linked similarities and dissimilarities. Quine may be the most candid of the nominalistically disposed (as, say, in opposition to Goodman):

> A standard of similarity is in some sense innate. This point is not against empiricism; it is a commonplace of behavioral psychology. A response to a red circle, if it is rewarded. will be elicited again by a pink ellipse more readily than by a blue triangle. Without some such *prior spacing of qualities*, we could never acquire a habit; all stimuli would be equally alike and equally different. These spacings of qualities, on the part of men and other animals, can be explored and mapped in the laboratory by experiments in conditioning and extinction. Needed as they are for all learning ,these distinctive spacings cannot themselves all be learned; some must be innate.[90]

Certainly, Quine's concession – offered in a very strongly extensionalized, empiricist, behaviorist, de-intentionalized spirit – is hardly very different (for all that) from Merleau-Ponty's treatment of the natural world of brute experience.[91]

On the other hand, Goodman is bafflingly unrelenting. He insists on a number of purely formal theorems: for example, "Dyadic likeness between particulars will not serve to define those classes of particulars that have a common quality throughout"; "Similarity cannot be equated with, or measured in terms of, possession of common characteristics"; "Similarity between particulars does not suffice to define qualities"; "any two things have exactly as many properties in common as any other two." So he concludes that, "As it occurs in philosophy, similarity tends under analysis rather to vanish entirely or to require for its explanation just what it purports to explain . . . similarity becomes entirely superfluous . . . a blank to be filled."[92] There are, however, two fatal limitations in Goodman's account: for one, he makes an utter (and insoluble) mystery of *any* cognitive discrimination; and, for another, he ignores the need to explain the smooth functioning of linguistic concepts spontaneously applied to *new* instances – to instances *not* included in whatever may be supposed to have been the exemplars in connection with which they were first learned. One *cannot* make sense of that phenomenon without admitting (1) some operative regularities of "prelinguistic quality space" (along the lines "shared" by Quine and Merleau-Ponty), (2) some culturally regularized habits of mind and speech embedded in the first (along the lines memorably marked in Wittgenstein's "forms of life"), and (3) some praxical sense in which pertinent human activities may be judged to be "objective" (along the lines sketched, say, in Marx and Foucault). That Goodman fails to touch on any of these matters merely confirms the ease with which one may be led to suppose that concepts (or "predicates" as Goodman prefers to say[93]) *used* in cognitively pertinent contexts can be managed in strictly nominalistic terms. But that is an utter, unmitigated delusion – or else a lapse of philosophical responsibility.

Within these two limits – between construing concepts (*a fortiori*, "objective" concepts) simply as rules formulating what is necessary to the content of a concept and, alternatively, construing concepts as (nominalistically) completely disconnected from all biological, historical, and praxical regularities – lies the only plausible prospect of a viable, non-question-begging, reasonably realistic resolution of the question of the nature of objective thinking. But that is as much as we dare venture in the present setting. By praxism, then, we shall understand a theory of effective human thinking and cognitively guided activity conforming with doctrines (i)–(xv) and committed to focusing a general clue about how the holist themes of what we are here calling pragmatism or the rapprochement of naturalism and phenomenology (as well as of deconstruction, if the question needs asking) may be brought to bear – without reverting to any form of cognitive privilege – on the development of a distributive realism of science and practical commitment. The theory of thinking praxism affords, that is, the theory of how we use concepts in thinking, must be of a *conceptualist* cast. It must accommodate at one and the same time:

(a) biological or nativist dispostions toward discerning similarities (minimally, *à la* Quine);

(b) a *praxis*-centered historicized habituation to favor similarities within the horizon of the determinable interests and biases of one's own society (minimally, *à la* Marx); and

(c) the improvisational capacity of the apt members of a given society to extend spontaneously their particular generalizing practices in a consensually tolerable manner (minimally, *à la* Wittgenstein).

In that way, we preserve the realism of cultural life without retreating either to an inadequate nominalism or to an inflexible and essentialist realism (regarding universals).[94]

By bringing praxism within the terms of pragmatism, we have, then, sketched an entirely plausible conceptual strategy for accounting for the realist pretensions of actual truth-claims and actual commitments, without in the least foreclosing on the viability of divergent, even antagonistic and incompatible, visions of "what there is" and of "what serves man." Let is be said only that a realism that would (1) reject all forms of privilege, (2) admit the historicized nature of the preformational condition of human cogniscence, and (3) legitimate the realism of the distributed claims and commitments of different societies, cannot fail to take a praxist form. There appears to be no other sufficiently flexible and comprehensive option. But in that sense, contrary to the usual accounts (not, however, at all distant from Marx's own reflections), the notion of *praxis* is primarily addressed to a radically novel analysis of the very process of forming and using concepts in the actual work of science and engaged practical activity. Thus applied, it facilitates *a holist rationale for a realist reading of the distributed claims and commitments of theory and practice*: it bridges, therefore, the second-order (holist and pragmatist) rejection of cognitive privilege and the first-order (distributive, empirical) work of every viable and productive society. Clearly, it plays an indispensable role.[95]

Notes

1   See ch. 3, above.
2   See Karl R. Popper, *Realism and the Aim of Science* (from *Postcript to the Logic of Scientific Discovery*), ed. W. W. Bartley, III (Totowa, NJ: Rowman and Littlefield, 1983), pp. 57–8.
3   See ch. 3, above.
4   See Joseph Margolis, *Pragmatism without Foundations: Reconciling Realism and Relativism* (Oxford: Basil Blackwell, 1986).
5   Alvin Plantinga, *The Nature of Necessity* (Oxford: Clarendon Press, 1974), p. 44.
6   Roderick M. Chisholm, "Events and Propositions," *Nous*, IV (1970), and "State of Affairs," *Nous*, V (1971). These are cited by Plantinga.
7   Plantinga, *The Nature of Necessity*, pp. 44–5.
8   Ibid., p. 45.
9   Ibid., p. 46.
10   This of course bears directly on Michael Dummett's anti-realism. See Michael Dummett, *Truth and Other Enigmas* (Cambridge, Mass.: Harvard University Press, 1978); and Joseph Margolis, *Science without Unity: Reconciling the Human and Natural Sciences* (Oxford: Basil Blackwell, 1987), ch. 1.
11   Plantinga, *The Nature of Necessity*, p. 27; cf. also p. 42.
12   Ibid., p. 45.
13   Ibid., pp. 46–7.

14   Ibid., p. 137. See also Alvin Plantinga, *God and Other Minds* (Ithaca, NY: Cornell University Press, 1967), ch. 2.

15   See Joseph Margolis, *Knowledge and Existence* (New York: Oxford University Press, 1973), ch. 4.

16   Hilary Putnam, "The Logic of Quantum Mechanics," *Philosophical Papers*, vol. 1 (Cambridge: Cambridge University Press, 1975), p. 174. The paper was originally titled "Is Logic Empirical?" The entire paper deserves close attention and calls into clear doubt the *logical status* of Plantinga's intuitions about necessities *de re* and *de dicto*. It may be admitted that necessities expressed *de dicto* can be replaced *de re* (and *vice versa*) – which is Plantinga's claim, against Quine (*The Nature of Necessity*, pp. 23–26,42). But it is Putnam's claim that would-be necessities must be examined *empirically* and may be found wanting. On that reading, *de dicto* formulations may be said to draw attention to, without specifying (so one may claim), the epistemological preconditions on which a given claim is tendered; whereas *de re* formulations may be construed as insinuating a structure in reality that our epistemologies would have to accommodate (that, for instance, there are *de re* necessities in nature). This may have been close to Quine's preference for *de dicto* modality rather than *de re*. See for instance, W. V. Quine, *Ways of Paradox and Other Essays*, rev. and enlarged edn (Cambridge, Mass.: Harvard University Press, 1976), p. 176; cited by Plantinga. Notice that Quine does not favor contingent or accidental properties over necessary properties, but only asymmetrically (and even there grudgingly), *de dicto* formulations over *de re* formulations. The only possible reason must depend on his well-known skepticism about certain determinable matters of fact.

There is a useful exchange on the empirical aspects of logic (and mathematics) in a relatively recent discussion by Dalla Chiara and Stachel. See Maria Luisa Dalla Chiara, "Some Logical Problems Suggested by Empirical Theories," and John Stachel, "Comments on 'Some Logical Problems Suggested by Empirical Theories' by Professor Dalla Chiara," in Robert S. Cohen and Marx W. Wartofsky (eds), *Language, Logic, and Method* (Dordrecht: D. Reidel, 1983). Stachel instructively opposes the strong disjunction of the sciences into "empirical" and "formal" sciences and argues that it is best to treat each of the sciences "as a theoretical practice, working upon and transforming given conceptual materials to produce the particular object of knowledge characteristic of that science at a certain stage of development. The whole hierarchical organization of the sciences into logic, mathematics, the empirical sciences – each earlier term supposedly founded independently of, and serving as part of the foundation for, the later ones – must be rejected as the consequence of an incorrect starting point in the division of formal and empirical sciences" (p. 92).

17   Putnam, "The Logic of Quantum Mechanics," *Philosophical Papers*, vol. 1, pp. 174–6.

18   Ibid., pp. 190–7. There is a helpful discussion of Quine's collapse of the *de re/de dicto* distinction in Paul Gochet, *Ascent to Truth: A Critical Examination of Quine's Philosophy* (Munich: Philosophia Verlag, 1986), ch. 7. Note particularly Gochet's example suggesting a useful difference between *de re* and *de dicto* constructions (pp. 167–8).

19   W. V. Quine, *Methods of Logic* (New York: Henry Holt, 1950), p. 200. Cf. also W. V. Quine, "Goodman's *Ways of Worldmaking*," *Theories and Things* (Cambridge, Mass.: Harvard University Press, 1981).

20 W. V. Quine, *Word and Object* (Cambridge, Mass.: MIT Press, 1960), p. 27.
21 Ibid., section 15.
22 Ibid., section 56. (There is no question, it should be added, that the thesis needs some adjustment in terms of Quine's actual statements, because Quine's formulation may well be incoherent as it stands. But it does not seem to be critical to the possibility at stake.) See further Joseph Margolis, "The Locus of Coherence," *Linguistics and Philosophy*, VII (1984).
23 Nelson Goodman, *Of Mind and Other Matters* (Cambridge, Mass.: Harvard University Press. 1984), ch. 2.
24 Nelson Goodman, *Ways of Worldmaking* (Indianapolis: Hackett, 1978), p. 2.
25 Goodman, *Of Mind and Other Matters*, pp. vii, 13.
26 Ibid., pp. 125–7.
27 See Putnam, "It Ain't Necessarily So," *Philosophical Papers*, vol. 1; and Goodman, *Ways of Worldmaking*: "We can have words without a world but no world without words or other symbols" (p. 6).
28 Goodman, *Of Mind and Other Matters*, pp. 29, 33, 38. In his brief review of the book, Quine appears to have found this line of thinking either incoherent or hopelessly extravagant. Cf. also Hilary Putnam, "Reflections, on Goodman's *Ways of Worldmaking*," *Journal of Philosophy*, LXXVI (1979); Israel Scheffler, "The Wonderful Worlds of Goodman," *Synthese*, XLV (1980); C. G. Hempel, "Comment on Goodman's *Ways of Worldmaking*," *Synthese*, XLV (1980).
29 Goodman, *Of Minds and Other Matters*, p. 38.
30 See Margolis, *Science without Unity*, ch. 3.
31 For an alternative to Plantinga's view of possible worlds, see for instance David Lewis: "Counterpart Theory and Quantified Modal Logic," *Journal of Philosophy*, LXV (1968); "Anselm and Actuality," *Nous*, IV (1970); and *On the Plurality of Worlds* (Oxford: Basil Blackwell, 1986), ch. 3.
32 Nelson Goodman, *Fact, Fiction, and Forecast*, 2nd edn (Indianapolis: Bobbs-Merrill, 1965), pp. 105–6.
33 W. V. Quine, *The Roots of Reference* (La Salle, Ill.: Open Court, 1973), p. 123.
34 See Margolis, *Pragmatism without Foundations*, ch. 7.
35 The term "pragmatism" is not inapt applied to Goodman's position, in spite of the fact that Goodman had, earlier on, indicated his (at least partial) opposition to pragmatism. For Goodman had, in developing his theory of projectibility with regard to both undetermined cases and truth, maintained that, "Since a hypothesis is true only if true for all its cases, it is true only if true for all its future and all its undetermined cases; but equally, it is true only if true for all its past and all its determined cases" (*Fact, Fiction and Forecast*, p. 91 n. 3; this must be read in the context of pp. 89–9). But now, conceding "conflicting truths," it is no longer clear that the required entrenchment of genuine projectibles can be measured or measured with respect to "ultimate acceptability."
36 See Margolis, *Science without Unity*, chs 2, 5.
37 See ch. 3, above.
38 Husserl's remarkable candor can be readily seen in his warnings regarding how he means to use the expression "transcendental philosophy." Note particularly: "Of course this most general concept of the 'transcendental' [what concerns the ultimate, apodictic grounding of all cognition] *cannot be supported by documents*; it is not to be gained through the internal exposition and comparison of the individual systems. Rather, it is a concept acquired by pondering the coherent

history of the entire philosophical modern period: the concept of its task which is *demonstrable only in this way*, lying within it as the driving force of its development, striving forward from vague *dynamis* toward its *energeia"* – Edmund Husserl, *The Crisis of European Sciences and Transcendental Phenomenology*, tr. David Carr (Evanston, Ill.: Northwestern University Press, 1970), p. 98 (I have italicized the phrases "cannot be supported by documents" and "demonstrable only in this way"); cf. also section 27.

39   Martin Heidegger, *Being and Time*, trs John Macquarrie and Edward Robinson from 7th German ed (New York: Harper and Row, 1962), p. 50. What is offered here, thus far, is of course an extremely abbreviated summary of a sprawling theme. But it is, perhaps not unfairly, offered as the nerve of the Introduction.

40   Ibid., p. 33; cf. p. 34.

41   See Charles B Guignon, *Heidegger and the Problem of Knowledge* (Indianapolis: Hackett, 1983).

42   Martin Heidegger, "The Origin of the Work of Art," *Poetry, Language, Thought*, tr. Albert Hofstadter (New York: Harper and Row, 1971).

43   See Thomas S. Kuhn, *The Structure of Scientific Revolutions*, 2nd, enlarged edn (Chicago: University of Chicago Press, 1970): and Michel Foucault, *The Order of Things: An Archaeology of the Human Sciences* tr. from the French (New York: Random House, 1970).

44   Heidegger, *Being and Time*, p. 95.

45   Ibid., pp. 96–7.

46   Ibid., p. 97.

47   Ibid., pp. 100, 104.

48   John Dewey, *Experience and Nature*, 2nd edn (New York: Dover, 1958), pp. 122–3.

49   Ibid., p. 162. I have it on pure hearsay that someone once gave Dewey a copy of Heidegger's *Sein und Zeit*. He is reported to have said that Heidegger's book reads rather like the effort of a Swabian peasant attempting to make sense of his own pragmatism. It may be a poor joke, but it manages to capture an unmistakable convergence from quite different sensibilities and intellectual orientations.

50   Søren Kierkegaard, *Concluding Unscientific Postscript*, tr. David F. Swenson and Walter Lowrie (Princeton, NJ: Princeton University Press, 1944), pp. 270–1. It is, incidentally, not unreasonable to hold that Hegel addresses the problems of *praxis* even if he does not use the term.

51   This is fairly close to the recommendation in Richard J. Bernstein, *Praxis and Action; Contemporary Philosophies of Human Activity* (Philadelphia: University of Pennsylvania Press, 1971), p. 165, in the context of Bernstein's entire argument.

52   Alexandre Kojève, *Introduction to the Reading of Hegel: Lectures on the "Phenomenology of Spirit"*, assembled by Raymond Queneau, trs. James H. Nichols, Jr, ed. Allan Bloom (Ithaca, NY: Cornell University Press, 1980), p. 31 (I have italicized the iterated modal expression "must be"). See also G. W. F. Hegel, *Phenomenology of Spirit*, tr. A. V. Miller (Oxford: Oxford University Press, 1977), Preface and ch. 8.

53   See Theodor W. Adorno, Introduction to *Negative Dialectics*, tr. E. B. Ashton (New York: Seabury Press, 1973).

54 Kojève, *Introduction to the Reading of Hegel*, pp. 69–70 (I have italicized the first two occurences of the copula "is"). Cf. *Hegel, Phenomenology of Spirit*, ch. VI. One interesting reading of the *Phenomenology* suggests "that Hegel's logic, at least in the *Phenomenology*, is a *logic of inadequacy*, a logic whose whole point is to remind us always of our limited vision, our unexposed presuppositions, our unwillingness to see the other side until forced to" – Robert C. Solomon, *In the Spirit of Hegel: A Study of G. W. F. Hegel's "Phenomenology of Spirit"* (Oxford: Oxford University Press, 1983), p. 637. Unfortunately, Solomon does not pursue the full implications of this "(tentative) conclusion." For example, he has nothing to say about the doctrine of "internal relations." A brief history of that matter is given by Richard Rorty, "Relations, Internal and External," in Paul Edwards (ed.), *The Encyclopedia of Philosophy* (New York: Macmillan and Free Press, 1967), vol. 7. See also Tom Rockmore, *Hegel's Circular Epistemology* (Bloomington: Indiana University Press, 1986).

55 Karl Marx, *Capital: A Critical Analysis of Capitalist Production*, vol. 1, tr. S. Moore and E. Aveling (New York: International Publishers, 1973), p. 72. See also Karl Marx, *Theories of Surplus Value*, vol. III, tr. Jack Cohen and S. W. Ryazanskaya (Moscow: Progress Publishers, 1971), p. 130.

56 G. A. Cohen, *Karl Marx's Theory of History: A Defense* (Princeton, NJ: Princeton University Press, 1978), pp. 116–7. Cohen adds (n. 2) that "statements 2, 3 and 4 explicate 'takes the form of' as it is used in statement 1."

57 See Joseph Margolis, *Philosophy of Psychology* (Englewood Cliffs, NJ: Prentice-Hall, 1984), and *Science without Unity*. Cf. ch. 6, below.

58 See for instance the recent review of the issue in Selya Benhabib, *Critique, Norm, and Utopia: A Study of the Foundations of Critical Theory* (New York: Columbia University Press, 1986), ch. 4, especially pp. 114–33; but see also Cohen, *Karl Marx's Theory of History*, ch. 5.

59 Benhabib, *Critique, Norm, and Utopia*, p. 115. Benhabib is reporting here – is somewhat critical of, but also somewhat attracted to – the charge of "a longing for a mythical, self-transparent utopia" on Marx's part (p. 116), as in the view (she cites) of E. M. Lange, "Wertformanalyse, Geldkritik und die Konstruktion des Fetischismus bei Marx," *Neue Heft für Philosophie*, no. 13 (1978). See also Shlomo Avineri, *The Social and Political Thought of Karl Marx* (Cambridge: Cambridge University Press, 1968), and "The Hegelian Origins of Marx's Political Thought," *Review of Metaphysics*, XXI (1967).

60 See Margolis, *Science without Unity*, ch. 12.

61 Marx, *Capital*, vol. 1, p. 71.

62 Benhabib presses the criticism of the "transubjective" (as opposed to the "intersubjective") against both Marx and Hegel – in preparing the ground for her own advocacy of an adjusted Habermasian critique. See *Critique, Norm, and Utopia, passim*, especially chs 3–4. By "transubjective" Benhabib means the perspective of a God-like or objective "observer" who grasps the "true" collective import of the aggregated behavior of the members of a society (p. 31). Cf. particularly G. W. F. Hegel, *Natural Law*, tr. T. M. Knox (Philadelphia: University of Pennsylvania Press, 1975). It is theoretically possible, on Benhabib's thesis, that a "collective agent" (the proletarian class, say) may, because of ideological blindness, not be able to produce a "transubjective" observer of its own collective life.

63   See ch. 2, above.

64   See for instance Karl Marx, *Grundrisse: Foundations to the Critique of Political Economy*, tr. Martin Nicolaus (New York: Vintage Books, 1973), pp. 158–60.

65   Ibid., p. 84; cf. also p. 85. This, of course, is just the point of Marx's opening the *Grundrisse* with his famous reference to "eighteenth-century Robinsonades." See ch. 9. below.

66   (iii) and (iv) are lightly pursued in *Science without Unity*.

67   From a letter of 1846 to P. V. Annenkov, in Cohen, *Karl Marx's Theory of History*, p. 144. For convenience, I have used the translation in David McLellan (ed.), *Karl Marx: Selected Writings* (Oxford: Oxford Univeristy Press, 1977) pp. 193–4, which gives a fuller sense of Marx's notion. I have relied substantially on Cohen's careful analysis, *Karl Marx's Theory of History*, ch. 6. A fuller version of Annenkov's letter appears in *Karl Marx and Frederick Engels: Selected Works in Two Volumes*, vol. II (Moscow: Foreign Languages Publishing House, 1951), pp. 400–10.

68   See for example the vexed question of the "primacy" of productive forces – an issue we need not pursue here. Cohen usefully cites the well-known passage from *The Poverty of Philosophy*: "Social relations are closely bound up with productive forces. In [or by] acquiring new productive forces men change their mode of production; and in changing their mode of production, in changing their way of earning a living, they change all their social relations. The hand-mill gives you society with the feudal lord; the steam-mill society with the industrial capitalist" (*Karl Marx's Theory of History* pp. 143–4). But, apart from the usual quarrels, it is reasonably clear that the "primacy" issue (between "substratum" and "superstructure") tends to become quite amorphous by the time it has reached our own disputatious world. See for example Maurice Godelier, *Perspectives in Marxist Anthropology*, tr. Robert Brain (Cambridge: Cambridge University Press, 1977), ch. 1, which perhaps worries the "primacy" question as convincingly as any.

69   Maurice Merleau-Ponty, *The Structure of Behavior*, tr. Alden L. Fisher (Boston, Mass.: Beacon Press, 1963), p. 181. This marks Merleau-Ponty's lifelong opposition to "layering" the human upon the animal. Cf. Maurice Merleau-Ponty, *The Visible and the Invisible*, tr. Alphonso Lingis, ed. Claude Lefort (Evanston, Ill.: Northwestern University Press, 1968), "Pre-objective Being: The Solipsist World," especially pp. 158–9. The theme is, of course, the master-theme of Merleau-Ponty's *Phenomenology of Perception*, tr. Colin Smith (London: Routledge and Kegan Paul, 1962).

70   Cohen is particularly good on this matter. See *Karl Marx's Theory of History*, pp. 152–6.

71   See further Margolis, *Pragmatism without Foundations*, pt I.

72   Nicholas Lobkowicsz, *Theory and Practice: History of a Concept from Aristotle to Marx* (Notre Dame, Ind.: University Of Notre Dame Press, 1967), p. 419, in the context of pp. 416–26.

73   Marx, *Theses on Feuerbach*, in McLellan (ed.), *Karl Marx: Selected Writings*, pp. 156–8.

74   See Lobkowicz, *Theory and Practice*, chs 1–2.

75   Cohen, *Karl Marx's Theory of History*, pp. 338–42. Cohen ultimately advises us to "abandon" Marx's view of "science" but not of "social science." In particular,

Cohen concludes that "it is futile to hope for the total transparency contemplated in the Hegelio-Marxism tradition" (p. 343). Cf. the whole of Appendix I. But it is not entirely convincing – with regard either to Hegel or to Marx – that, rightly read, their best formulations are actually committed to apodictic or privileged knowledge. On Cohen's reading, "Marxian socialism is, in its epistemic aspect, the fruition of Absolute Knowledge, since to have that knowledge is to know immediately, without ratiocination, the nature of the total spiritual world" (p. 341). *That* notion is clearly incompatible with praxism as we have characterized it – which is to say, with Marx's notion of *praxis* clarified in the *Theses* (cf. Cohen, *Karl Marx's Theory of History*, p. 341 n.2).

76   Richard J. Bernstein, *Praxis and Action: Contemporary Philosophies of Human Activity* (Philadelphia: University of Pennsylvania Press, 1971), p. 14.

77   Ibid., Epilogue, p. 307; cf. p. 315.

78   Marx, "Wage-Labor and Capital," in McLellan (ed.), *Karl Marx: Selected Writings*, p. 256. For an excellent impression (more than an impression) of the enlargement of Marx's theme, see Alvin W. Gouldner, *The Dialectic of Ideology and Technology: The Origins, Grammar, and Future of Ideology* (New York: Oxford University Press, 1976), particularly chs 1–2.

79   Marx, "Critique of Hegel's Dialectic and General Philosophy," in McLellan (ed.), *Karl Marx: Selected Writings*, p. 101 (italics added).

80   Marx, *Grundrisse*, p. 706.

81   Karel Kosík, *Dialectic of the Concrete: A Study on Problems of Man and World*, tr. Karel Kovanda with James Schmidt (Dordrecht: D. Reidel, 1976), p. 137. This need not commit us to Kosík's sanguine view of Marxist science; cf. ch. 1. A related theme is developed by Leszak Kolakowski. It is, of course, the essential basis on which one is obliged to insist on a radical disjunction between Marx's and Lenin's conception of truth – also, on a disjunction between Marx's and Engels's conception of correspondence (Lenin being dependent on Engels's). In *Toward a Marxist Humanism: Essays on the Left Today*, tr. Jane Zielonko Peel (New York: Grove Press, 1968), Kolakowski observes, "the compatibility of judgment with reality is no longer a relationship of 'resemblance' between the judgment and the world 'in itself'; it applies to the world upon which man has already imposed 'substantial forms' " (p. 57). See also Leszak Kolakowski, *Main Currents of Marxism*, vol. 1, tr. P. S. Fuller (Oxford: Clarendon Press, 1978), pp. 58–63. Professor Tom Rockmore drew my attention to Kosík's and Kolakowski's views. I have also benefited from Rockmore's reading of the draft of this chapter.

82   See ch. 3, above.

83   Michael Foucault, "Truth and Power," *Power/Knowledge: Selected Interviews and Other Writings 1972–1977*, ed. Colin Gordon, tr. Colin Gordon et. al. (New York: Pantheon, 1980), p. 117. There are other intriguing combinations of "Marxian" and "Nietzschean" themes or Nietzscheanized (or Freudianized) subversions of canonical Marxist notions of reality to be found in Jean Baudrillard, *For a Critique of the Political Economy of the Sign*, tr. Charles Levin (St Louis: Telos Press, 1981), and *The Mirror of Production*, tr. Mark Poster (St Louis: Telos Press, 1975); and Gilles Deleuze and Felix Guattari, *Anti-Oedipus: Capitalism and Schizophrenia*, tr. Robert Hurley, Mark Seem, and Helen R. Lane (Minneapolis: University of Minnesota Press, 1983). These and similar analyses attempt to uncover hidden essentialisms in apparently anti-essentialist programs,

142 THE CONTEXT OF THE HUMAN

but they have noticeable difficulty in reconciling theory and practice – as does Foucault, of course.

84 See Max Weber, *The Protestant Ethic and the Spirit of Capitalism*, tr. Talcott Parsons (New York: Charles Scribner's Sons, 1958). See also Max Weber, "Science as a Vocation," in *From Max Weber: Essays in Sociology*, tr. and ed. H. H. Gerth and C. Wright Mills (New York: Oxford University Press, 1946); Guenther Roth and Wolfgang Schluchter, *Max Weber's Vision of History: Ethics and Methods* (Berkeley, Calif.: University of California Press, 1979); and Hans Albert, *Treatise on Critical Reason*, tr. Mary Varney Rorty (Princeton, NJ: Princeton University Press, 1985), ch. 3; also H. R. Trevor-Roper, *Religion, the Reformation, and Social Change* (London: Macmillan, 1967). For an unusually perceptive, somewhat offbeat, comparison of Weber and Marx, which favors Weber's flexibility along methodological lines, see Peter T. Manicas, *A History and Philosophy of the Social Sciences* (Oxford: Basil Blackwell, 1987), ch. 7; and Max Weber, *Roscher and Kneis: The Logical Problems of Historical Economics*, tr. Guy Oakes (New York: Free Press, 1975), discussed by Manicas.

85 See Michel Foucault, "The Discourse on Language," tr. Rupert Sawyer, in *The Archaeology of Knowledge*, tr. A. M. Sheridan Smith (New York: Harper and Row, 1976): "True discourse, liberated by the nature of its form from desire and power, is incapable of recognizing the will to truth which pervades it, and the will to truth, having imposed itself upon us for so long, is such that the truth it seeks to reveal cannot fail to mask it" (p. 219). There is an instructive analysis of Foucault offered in Jürgen Habermas, *The Philosophical Discourse of Modernity: Twelve Lectures*, tr. Frederick Lawrence (Cambridge, Mass.: MIT Press, 1987), Lectures 9–10, which may be detached from Habermas's own program.

86 *Immanuel Kant's "Critique of Pure Reason"*, corr. tr. Norman Kemp Smith (London:Macmillian, 1933), p. 135 (A105–6); cf. also pp. 105–6 (A68–9), pp. 147–9 (A126–8).

87 Ibid., pp. 117–78 (A133–B172).

88 See Jonathan Bennett, *Kant's Analytic* (Cambridge: Cambridge University Press, 1966), section 36. I have benefited considerably from Bennett's analysis of the Kantian account, though I am not certain what Kant means us to understand by "an abundance of rules borrowed from the insight of others" regarding the application *of which* someone lacking judgment may fail. See Stephan Körner, *Kant* (Harmondsworth: Penguin, 1955), p. 71; cited by Bennett. See also Ludwig Wittgenstein, *Philosophical Investigations*, tr. G. E. M. Anscombe (New York: Macmillan, 1953), sections 199, 202, 219, 292. (There are, of course, an endless number of pertinent references in *Investigations*, pt I).

89 See Joseph Margolis, "Wittgenstein's 'Forms of Life': A Cultural Template for Psychology," in Michael Chapman and Roger A. Dixon (eds), *Meaning and the Growth of Understanding: Wittgenstein's Significance for Developmental Psychology* (Berlin: Springer-Verlag, 1987); pertinent portions of this essay are incorporated in ch. 9 below.

90 W. V. Quine, "Natural Kinds," *Ontological Relativity and Other Essays* (New York: Columbia University Press, 1969), p. 123 (italics added). Cf. also *Word and Object*, pp. 83–4, where Quine mentions a need for admitting a "prelinguistic quality space."

91 See Maurice Merleau-Ponty, *Phenomenology of Perception*, tr. Colin Smith (London: Routledge and Kegan Paul, 1962), ch. 2; also Joseph Margolis, *Culture and Cultural Entities* (Dordrecht: D. Reidel, 1984), ch. 6; and Eleanor Rosch, "Principles of Categorization," in Eleanor Rosch and Barbara B. Lloyd (ed), *Cognition and Categorization* (Hillsdale, NJ: Lawrence Erlbaum Associates, 1978), and "Wittgenstein and Categorization Research in Cognitive Psychology," in Chapman and Dixon (eds), *Meaning and the Growth of Understanding*.

92 Nelson Goodman, "Seven Strictures on Similarity," in Lawrence Foster and J. W. Swanson (eds), *Experience and Theory* (Amherst: University of Massachusetts, 1970), *passim*.

93 In a footnote Goodman remarks, "Of course as a nominalist, I take all talk of properties as slang for more careful formulations in terms of predicates" (ibid., p. 25 n. 9).

94 See further Joseph Margolis, "Berkeley and Others on the Problem of Universals," in Colin Turbayne (ed.), *Berkeley: Critical and Interpretive Essays* (Minneapolis: University of Minnesota Press, 1982); also the suggestive account of the *habitus*, sympathetic to both Marx and Wittgenstein, in Pierre Bourdieu, *Distinction: A Social Critique of the Judgment of Taste*, tr. Richard Nice (Cambridge, Mass.: Harvard University Press, 1984), ch. 3.

95 I should perhaps add that the Yugoslav Marxists (the *Praxis* group), particularly Gajo Petrović and Mihailo Marković, have, among the Marxists themselves, addressed these issues regarding the definition of *praxis* – of what may well be called cognitive or conceptual *praxis* – in the most sustained way. I should be pleased to think that my own account (hardly Marxist) might strike them as congruent with their own speculation, however differently oriented it is. See Gajo Petrović, *Marx in the Mid-Twentieth Century: A Yugoslav Philosopher Reconsiders Karl Marx's Writings* (New York: Anchor Books, 1967), particularly "Praxis and Being" and "What Is Meaning?"; and Mihailo Marković, *Dialectical Theory of Meaning* (Belgrade, 1961), which I came to know first only from Petrović's summary in "What Is Meaning?" It has now appeared in an English edition (Dordrecht: D. Reidel, 1984); see particularly the "Preface to the English Edition."

5

Human Space: Systems, Holisms, Structuralisms

I

Once the reliability of the model of invariances is seriously challenged – the model of second-order nomic universals governing the perceived physical world[1] – it becomes entirely reasonable to deny to the "world" or "worlds" of human culture such or similar invariances. This is not, of course, to disallow the contingent regularities of first-order inquiry. But first-order invariances or "indicative" universals are really empirical generalities projected as dialectical contenders for universal standing. Even mortality, for instance, reasonably essential as a condition of human existence, hardly precludes perpetual bionic tinkering and replacement of parts that would disrupt the salient fixities of our familiar world, within which that very regularity and its contextual kin might lose their compelling patterned presence. Our own historicized perception might well change the conceptual weight of every such fixity. So it is entirely possible to admit universals without subscribing to universalism, to admit essences without essentialism. Also, if we put in doubt the plausibility of construing the domains of the human and natural sciences as sufficiently homogeneous to justify applying to the human world any *exclusive* vocabulary, however powerful or effective, developed primarily for the description and explanation of the physical world, we cannot fail to be attracted to disciplined forms of inquiry that are not tightly dependent on the best success of the physical sciences. It is surely the complexities of intentional and intensional phenomena, and in particular the conditions involved in the construction and plasticity of human selves and human cultures, that have come to be recognized as providing a reasonable basis for distinguishing between the two ways of proceeding.[2] The search for a language adequate to the description and explanation of the human, the cultural, the institutional, the historical, the Intentional forces on our attention the complex matter of the conceptual relationship between the vocabularies we regard as suited to the physical and the human and the ontological relationship between what, actually, *is* physically and humanly or culturally real.[3] For the time being, let us set aside that extraordinarily delicate question.

There is, on a familiar presumption, a very strong prejudice that would view *as a system* the whole of nature or suitably selected sub-sectors of nature (including, now, sectors of the human or cultural world – language, for instance). That prejudice has been formulated as a most attractive intuition by the Danish linguist Louis Hjelmslev, who, though he clearly has a modification of Ferdinand de Saussure's conception of *langue* in mind, also implies a favorable analogy between theories adequate to the cultural world and theories adequate to the physical world. As Hjelmslev remarks,

> *A priori* it would seem to be a generally valid thesis that for every *process* there is a corresponding *system*, by which the process can be analyzed and described by means of a limited number of premises. It must be assumed that any process can be analyzed into a limited number of statements recurring in various combinations. Then, on the basis of this analysis, it should be possible to order these elements into classes according to their possibilities of combination. And it should be further possible to set up a general and exhaustive calculus of the possible combinations. A history so established should rise above the level of mere primitive description to that of a systematic, exact, and generalizing science, in the theory of which all events (possible combinations of elements) are foreseen and the conditions for their realization established.[4]

The domains affected may be distinguished in the following way:

1   they are all treated extensionally (non-intensionally);
2   they are all treated as systems (closed with respect to a finite set of generational operations ranging over a finite set of elements, adequate for describing and explaining – and generating – all the features and processes of the domains in question;
3   they all exhibit either causal or formal (structural or syntactic) order or a mixture of the two deployed over time (synchronically or diachronically); and
4   the ontic status of the elements and generative regularities adduced are, characteristically, all treated in a realist manner, or, if realism is in principle inaccessible, they are treated as ensuring the sole avenue to a suitably disciplined, universalized science.

Item 4 collects and separates such programs as the unity of science, Chomsky's nativism, and the analytic structuralism of Saussure, Hjelmslev, and Lévi-Strauss: the first two are fiercely realist; the third denies realism outright, as in insisting on the arbitrary nature of world-to-sign regularities, or else toys (as does Lévi-Strauss, for instance) with the mooted possibility of a deeper but unfathomable invariance in the nature of man. In any case, the structuralists are quite certain that a science of man cannot but take the form of the distinctive system they advocate, a matter rendered all the more certain by the inherent unmanageability of the materials of natural cultures for any serious science. This is the point and meaning of Saussure's influential summary of how the science of linguistics *replaces* the elements of a natural domain with the *relata* of the minimal system a linguistics would require:

> Instead of pre-existing ideas then [the terms of a natural language, or the concepts for which they are supposed to stand], we find in all the foregoing examples [the would-be analysis of those linguistic terms] *values* emanating from the system. When they are said to correspond to concepts, it is understood that the concepts are purely differential and defined not by their positive content but negatively by their relations with the other terms of the system. Their most precise characteristic is in being what the others are not.[5]

In a curious way, it is just the arbitrariness of linguistic signs (*parole*) and the lack of (scientifically) penetrable order in the context of the natural use of signs (*langage*) that ensures the peculiar sort of science the structuralist advocates (the analysis of *langue*); for, "In separating language from speaking we are at the same time separating: (1) what is social from what is individual; and (2) what is essential from what is accessory and more or less accidental."[6] It is also just this insistence that Chomsky opposes, in distancing himself from any taint of structuralism: first, in denying the arbitrariness of speech; secondly, in insisting on the realist standing of speech and its underlying structure; thirdly, in treating the analysis of the linguistic in terms of a radically individualistic (effectively, solipsistic) psychology (or biology).[7]

Item 3 also invites enlargement. Causal order is classically construed as involving discrete, relatively fixed elements among which temporally prior changes or movements in certain ones are said to produce, generate, or effect changes in others and, in doing that, to yield canonical explanations of such effects; the power to effect such changes is said to inhere in the very nature or properties of the first sort, within a space that includes elements of the second. This, broadly speaking, identifies the extensional model of classical or mechanistic physics. It may be challenged in quite a number of ways – but in two in particular, still within the terms of reference of a "system." It may be that the "system" that includes the physical world cannot be captured by the simple "explicate order" (to employ David Bohm's provocative term) that the classical model of physics favors, and it may be that the "system" suited to parts of the real world (human culture in particular) must be characterized in terms that are fundamentally not causal at all.

Bohm's view is interesting in spite of its overwhelming vagueness, because it attempts to incorporate the whole of the real world within the terms of reference of a single model, but without reducing the human to the physics of the classical model: it tries instead to enhance the physical with features drawn from the saliencies of human culture – said to be found (on Bohm's view) at least in part *in* relativity and quantum physics. Bohm holds, then, that the ("preexistent") "explicate order" is no more than a restricted but useful abstraction – "secondary, derivative, and appropriate only in certain limited contexts" – drawn *from* some more inclusive and more basic "implicate order," drawn from the laws of the larger physical world the new physics addresses. These laws are said to be *not* causal in the classically extensional or explicate sense and are said to be "ultimately unknowable in their totality." At any level at which it is introduced, the explicate order is an abstract, fragmented, perspectivist, heuristic, and instrumental schema.[8]

Bohm's implicate order, it must be admitted, is difficult to unpack. (We are not wedded to it.) It appears to conflate at least two entirely different notions, which we may simply, in detailing, take advantage of for our own particular purpose:

(i)   a model for reforming physics itself – and, by extension, a model thought to be apt for biological and conscious phenomena, in effect a model thought to be apt for all sub-sectors of the cosmic order – drawn (at least in part, though it is uncertain *how*) from recent relativity and quantum physics; and

(ii) a myth of the total cosmos that favors (i) and, in effect, affirms a Heraclitean sense of the flux of reality – rhetorically akin to the preformational themes of phenomenology, the "nihilizing" strains of Nietzscheanism, as well as a sanguine persistence (withal) of a naturalistic science functioning quite effectively under such constraints.

Thus Bohm affirms, "Not only is everything changing, but all *is* flux. That is to say, *what is* is the process of becoming itself, while all objects, events, entities, conditions, structures, etc., are forms that can be abstracted from this process."[9] Certainly, this *should* mean that the displacement intended in (i), at least as far as quantum physics is concerned, is every bit as inadequate, relative to (ii), as is the old "explicate order"; and yet, of course, the defense of (i) requires a kind of approximative verisimilitude that (ii) would itself preclude. This identifies the threatening incoherence of Bohm's characteristic elaboration of (i):

The implicate order has its ground in the holomovement [the "undefinable and inescapable" movement of what is ultimately real, "total," "one"] which is vast, rich, and in a state of unending flux of enfoldment and unfoldment [the ultimate, noncausal, implicative, "rational" order], with laws most of which are only vaguely known, and which may even be ultimately unknowable in their totality. Thus it cannot be grasped as something solid, tangible and stable to the senses (or to our instruments). Nevertheless, . . . the overall law (holonomy) may be assumed to be such that in a certain sub-order, within the whole set of implicate order, there is a totality of forms that have an approximate kind of recurrence, stability and separability. Evidently, these forms are capable of appearing as the relatively solid, tangible, and stable elements that make up our "manifest world." The special distinguished sub-order indicated [the order of discrete, independent, preexistent, fixed elements], which is the basis of the possibility of this manifest world, is then, in effect, what is meant by the explicate order.[10]

Here, Bohm attempts (impossibly) to reconcile the unanalyzable totality of which every explicate or causal order is said to be an approximation and the compared standing of every such derivative order within the space of the other. In the process, he introduces two sorts of physics, which may themselves be graded with respect to the "holomovement."

The difference between the two kinds of *physics*, Bohm thinks, may be modeled by contrasting the heuristic conceptual strategies afforded by the photographic lens and by the hologram. Roughly, the *lens* suggests the explicate order, by encouraging the generalization that there is a point-for-point correspondence between actual object and perceived image, or between cogniscent instrumentation and the application of realist theory. The *hologram*, on the other hand, precludes any such one-to-one correspondence ("between parts of an 'illuminated object' and parts of an 'image of this object on the plate' ") and replaces it with another conception in which every discriminated region within the object or order thus given represents (on an interpretation) the "whole [interlocking, implicate,'undivided'] structure" of that order: "a *total order* is contained, in some *implicit* sense, in each region of space and time."[11] In a television broadcast, for instance, the implicate ("part" to " total"/"total to "part") relationship between visual image and temporally ordered radio wave is (linearly, discretely) "*explicated*" by the (television) receiver in order to present an intelligible visual image (to us) "to 'unfold' the [implicate visual image] in the form of a new [explicate] visual image."[12] So it does seem (thus far) as if *every* specification of the implicate order yields a partial or fragmentary explicate order. Even the hologram favors that interpretation: it simply replaces one extensionalized order for another (one "explicate" order for another, one might have said, had not Bohm preempted the term for the classical model). In any case, Bohm surely conflates the part–whole relation of the model of the hologram (i) and the "part"–"whole" relation of the totalized image of his own myth (ii). He never really explains how the mathematization of the new physics would differ from that of classical physics apart from replacing the particular "explicate" model in place; that is, he does not really tell us whether, with what large results, and in what way (why or why not) the new physics would employ an extensional model in shifting from the explicate to the putatively implicate order. It looks as if extensionalism would not be disturbed, though the classical explicate model would be. Bohm never brings his reflections on the implications of the flux and the peculiarly derivative standing of *any* cognitive articulation of structure to bear on the common features of those two competing models.[13] Nevertheless, it is clear that Bohm's holism, or holist system, is quite opposed to that of the structuralists, as it is also to the reductive system of the unity-of-science program. For, on the one hand, Bohm treats the "implicate order" that the new physics ushers in as fully realist, in a comparatively sanguine sense; and, on the other, the new physics itself exhibits properties favorable to the description and explanation of psychological and cultural phenomena that resist the reductionism of the old "explicate order." It is in this sense that Bohm's speculation, while it has yielded no firm results, remains intriguing. It may well be the most visible contemporary specimen of a nonreductive physicalism, informed by an advanced physics, that claims to discern structures *in* the physical world intimating the presence of real structures that cannot be reduced to the physical – a construction usually favored by theories that would (at the very least) bifurcate the natural and the human sciences.

There is a pertinent, much leaner speculation in S. W. Hawking's cosmology that may capture a part of Bohm's intent. Hawking offers the suggestion, associated with Mach and Dirac, that "local [physical] laws are determined by the large scale structure of the universe"[14] – which suggests what may be salvageable in Bohm's notion of the "holomovement" *and* what must be utterly unsalvageable in Bohm's notion of the "rheomode" – that is, the idiom we apparently must invent for capturing truth and falsity in an order of reality in which "*all* is an unbroken and undivided whole movement, and [in which] each 'thing' is abstracted only as a relatively invariant side or aspect of this movement."[15] (The rheomode, of course, would be the death of discursive language.)

For his part, Hawking adds, immediately following the remark mentioned, that:

> There is of course a large extrapolation in the assumption that the physical laws one determines in the laboratory should apply at other points of space–time where conditions may be very different. If they failed to hold we should take the view that there was some other physical field which entered into the local physical laws but whose existence had not yet been detected in our experiments, because it varies very little over a region such as the solar system.[16]

Hawking's governing intuition appears to be that present physical theory strongly indicates that "singularities" have obtained through the interval of the evolution of our universe; that "the actual point of creation" of our universe was such a singularity; that the collapse of stars (producing black holes) is, in a sense, the "time-reverse" phenomenon of the original expansion; that "It seems to be a good principle that the prediction of a singularity by a physical theory indicates that the theory has broken down, i.e. it no longer provides a correct description of observations"; and that, as with all singularities, "the actual point of creation, [that] singularity, is outside the scope of presently known laws of physics."[17] Hawking's point is that all physical theory is provisional and partial (abstracted from the "holomovement," if you like), that the failure of every theory signifies the presence of singularities which elude the law-like regularities thus far posited by our theories (the structure of "holomony" is inherently unknowable, if you like), *and* that all explanatory models, laws, law-like elements, and the posited origins of the universe itself are always particularized *artifacts* symbiotically formulated only with respect to whatever we take, distributively, to be the sub-structure of the world we claim to be examining ("all *is* flux," if you wish).

Thus seen, on Hawking's view, we must be prepared for indefinitely many quite different models of the universe, given the shifting, enlarging, reflective, preformed, biased, and fragmentary nature of human inquiry. Taken as a holistic myth, Bohm's implicate order may be thought to capture Hawking's insight about singularity and totality; but, taken as a specific alternative to a distributively applied explicate model, it is itself either insufficiently explicit or only very loosely applied (by analogy) to the different domains to which it is fitted, or else it is utterly unworkable.

(One important emendation should be mentioned here. Bohm *may* mean – in his more recent statements, surely does mean – to include an irreducible informational dimension embedded – "incarnate" – in the physical or biological domains. There is evidence that he does mean something of the sort, though it introduces a holism that is plainly different from that posited on the strength of the image of the hologram. Hawking's line of reasoning, on the other hand, has nothing to do with Bohm's attempt to find, *in* physics, law-like structures recognizably congenial to the salient phenomena of psychology and human culture. In this respect, Hawking is much more inclined, intuitively, to emphasize in a naturalistic manner the fragmentary and preformed nature of theorizing itself. The picture of Bohm's account rests largely, it should be said, on *Wholeness and the Implicate Order*. There is a naiveté in that book that Bohm has considerably eliminated in his later reflections. He now is inclined to regard quantum physics as only *part* of a larger order that includes conscious, psychological, cultural, and cosmic phenomena the structure of which, much as was true of the older "explicate" order, it has no decisive clue about. Bohm still has only an inkling of the enlarged conceptions his model would require. What is striking, however, is his persistent openness to the sort of enlargements needed, his continued resistance to the usual reductionism a comprehensive physics characteristically inspires.[18] It is clear, however, that he remains very much committed to the search for an inclusive system – which the pertinent evidence cannot be said to vindicate; his own acknowledgement of a duality of "somatic" and "significative" dimensions – in a somewhat Spinozistic manner – is still too primitive to be of more than heuristic use.)

Now, then, to turn back to our original line of argument: the model of classical physics (Galilean or Newtonian physics, say) may be challenged by invoking a model that (as Bohm claims) recent physics requires, that cannot rightly be captured by the specific model of the "explicate [classical] order." *That* challenge, however, has nothing directly to do with the ulterior challenge of the holistic, preformational, horizonal nature of physical theorizing itself – which affects, in precisely the same way as it affects the explicate model, *whatever* Bohm means by the "implicate order" narrowly restricted to the new physics. There is no reason to believe – Bohm surely offers none – that the improved physics would not behave in an extensional way every bit as much as the old physics (which might then also be said to be "explicate"); or to believe that the new physics could not be coherently reconciled with the old explicate order; *or*, indeed, to believe that the new physics would ever abandon the notion of systematic closure. The argument against closure and system has rather to do with the import of the original myth of the flux and with its rhetorical bearing on what (by an economy, I hope not too precipitate) concerns the interrelationship between naturalism, phenomenology, and deconstruction.[19] Hence, to be able to sort out the excessive economy or simplicity Bohm's theory seems to exhibit, however congenially, could be to vindicate – possibly eccentrically – our own "reasonable prejudice": *that the human world is no system of any sort.* The human world is also not an "open system," in the sense in which open systems are equilibria or dynamically changing sub-complexes identified within and only within the space of systems in the technical sense here sketched.[20]

Furthermore, in this sense, all would-be natural systems, whether applied to physical nature or to human culture, are no more than provisional artifacts generated from *within* the space of actual human existence and inquiry. In principle, therefore, the compared advantages of different would–be systems are utterly indifferent to and unaffected by that larger constraint. It is, indeed, in this sense, that the proposal of a system is constrained by holist, internalist, pragmatist limitations.[21] So, for example, the introduction of a top–down model in psychology, in which molar persons are admitted, *does* introduce a form of holism in which the would-be "elements" of psychological functioning *are distributively specified only as functionally interrelated and intensionally qualified.*[22] Such a schema may be said to be an "implicate order," but the explicate orders that, *factorially*, it may subtend are quite different from those that may be *approximatively introduced*, as in Bohm's account of the holographic model: first, because Bohm does not introduce or feature intensional complexities in his implicate order (though he hints at them); second, because his model is designed *for* extensional (however inexhaustive) approximation favoring (even if not restricted to) causal accounts.

This helps us to see that there may be many different conceptions of system in accord with which the human world may be thought to be suitably dissected. Bohm's intuition is merely one of these – which hardly progresses beyond the rather Cartesian pronouncement that *whatever* the features of consciousness and whatever rightly serves to contrast conscious minds and anything that exhibits "extension and [discretely divisible] separations" will, *ipso facto*, be assignable *to* the implicate order : "The implicate order has just this latter quality, so in a certain sense Descartes was perhaps anticipating that consciousness has to be understood in terms of an order that is closer to the implicate than it is to the explicate."[23] Clearly, this cannot be taken quite seriously. The implicate order is, now, little more than a grab-bag for *whatever* fails to be reducible to the classical explicate order.

In any case, we have been stalking Bohm because of his rather heroic effort to find a unitary theory within which explicate and implicate orders are graded with respect to one another, grounded in physical structures, and treated as never more than provisional abstractions within some larger, perhaps more complex, all-inclusive totality ("the totality of all that is"[24]). For, in thus searching, Bohm appears to have been convinced that there is an ultimately adequate system integrating transiently generated implicate orders as well as the explicate orders they subtend.[25]

What we have been doing, therefore, in stalking Bohm is collecting, informally, a compendious sense of the principal varieties of system-mongering that might be fitted to Hjelmslev's sketch of a system – in order, frankly, to get clearer about what sort of theories must be rejected in rejecting the thesis that the human world forms a system. We are bound to reject explicate systems of the sort Bohm criticizes: they would be reductionist or eliminationist. We are bound to reject (or to postpone assessing) Bohm's own would-be model: it really has little as yet to say about the nature of the human world or its relationship to the physical. We shall (shortly) discover that we are bound to reject structuralist models. And we are bound to reject (as we shall also see) developmental systems that mean to use or combine, within some diachronic process, elements from any of these other models.

II

We may now present our survey in a somewhat more orderly form, anticipating the finding we intend. The following tally introduces varieties of system that are or have been thought to be promising or reasonably adequate for description and explanation *within the space of human existence*:

1   theories of explicate order, based on the descriptive and explanatory practice of classical physics and allied disciplines – in effect, all forms of physicalisms, heuristic functionalism, eliminationism, unity of science, and the like;[26]

2   theories of Bohm's sort, of implicate order, at least insofar as they are drawn primarily from relativity and quantum physics;

3   analytic structuralist theories ("implicate," perhaps in a sense richer than Bohm's, because irreducibly relational and informational and addressed to the human world primarily);

4   developmental theories that yield merely diachronically phased forms of emergence with respect to synchronic systems of type 1 or type 2 – for

instance, as in unity-of-science accounts or accounts closely akin to them (such as those in accord with Oppenheim and Putnam's well-known early paper or Herbert Feigl's views), or somewhat more specifically, the account tendered by Mario Bunge,[27] or the theory (even more specifically and suggestively) applied to evolutionary biology by theorists such as François Jacob;[28]

5 developmental theories based either on type 3 or on type 4, of specifically cultural phenomena – for instance, as in Jerry Fodor's treatment of concepts or Chomsky's treatment of generative grammar (certainly closer to type 4 than to type 3)[29] or, alternatively, the use of the notion of morphological variation (closer to type 3 than to type 4), as in Vladimir Propp's well-known account of the folktale;[30] and

6 theories of psychological or related development that are systematic insofar as their diachronic sequences are minimally controlled at some initial stage and their developmental phases are both empirically regular and (formally or informally) taken to entail the occurrence of an immediately preceding stage – notably as in Piaget's well-known interactional model.[31]

It needs to be said that, in a narrow sense, "structuralism" is rightly applied only to theories subsumed under item 3; but, informally, theories of all these sorts are "structuralist," however incompatible they may be with one another. Also, there is a reasonable sense in which Hegel's conception of history and nineteenth-century post-Hegelian histories are structuralist, or in which Louis Althusser's version of Marxism invokes a structuralist-like conception of system. But these are notably much more informal speculative conjectures that claim to identify, piecemeal, what forms a "system"; they do not actually specify a system by reference to some fairly explicit operative rule or law or principle of the relatively fine-grained sort favored among items 1–6 just given, or intended in Hjelmslev's account.[32]

Let us, now, arrange in a tidier way a reasonably comprehensive tally of the senses in which "holism" has been advocated. The topic has obviously been intruding in our discussion here and elsewhere, and needs to be sorted in a manageable way. A number of these senses will surely clarify the issue of system, since systems may be said to manifest a form of holism; other senses will bear on larger, rather different, questions regarding man's cognitive endeavor; and still others may serve to yield a picture of the entire range of possible options that lie before us, that have been historically pursued or pursued in different cultures, and that identify a family of contexts within which the very speculation about system first gains a footing. The general drift of our tally will serve (we may anticipate) to fix the sense in which *whatever of holism proves distinctive of human space marks it convincingly as not forming a system at all*. Some varieties of holism, of course, are entirely neutral to the claims of system; and some relevantly preclude system altogether. A simple tally should be enough for our needs. The order favored is one of convenience only: after all, the items to be arrayed cannot be made to support any single or converging doctrine.

(Many of the distinctions intended even lack a familiar or established usage, and some have overlapping application.)

Here, then, is our tally. By "holism" one may mean

(a)   the *pragmatist* thesis, the thesis that the second-order legitimation of realist claims is, as cognitively unprivileged, restricted to a holist or nondistributive legitimation of the claims of science and disciplined inquiry;[33]

(b)   the *indeterminacy* thesis, either a corollary of (a) applied to first-order science and inquiry (as by Quine) or itself a first-order claim not necessarily taken as an application of the other, denying distributed evidentiary force to the particular members of any set of propositions by which to test the truth or falsity of the members of another (whole) set or (unified) theory, again taken distributively (a view more characteristically advanced by Duhem than by Quine[34]);

(c)   the *preformational* thesis, historically most closely associated with phenomenology and critical theory (notably, as in Heidegger, Merleau-Ponty, and Marx), in accord with which, eschewing cognitive privilege, the horizon of any inquiring subjects *vis-à-vis* the world they inquire into is restricted, deformed, or constrained by legitimative or second-order conditions of worldly existence (principally historical) that are themselves not able to be distributively specified except under the same holist constraint;[35]

(d)   variations of the indeterminacy thesis (b), or analogues of the same, formulated with regard to (c), usually in historical terms (as, in different ways, suggested at least by Heidegger, Gadamer, Foucault, and Kuhn[36]), in accord with which the preformational influences affecting distributed first-order claims are themselves subject, holistically, to ulterior diachronic forces – a view perhaps fairly termed the *historicist* thesis;

(e)   the *deconstructive* thesis, or the mythic "generalization" of the import of (a)–(d), to the effect that every distributed claim, however minor, depends on a conceptual categorization of the ultimate surd of Reality, with regard to which the intended fit is beyond all legitimation or confirmation, and which poses a barrier that no version of any discursive schema permitting truth-claims could itself claim to overtake, or with regard to which no schema could claim to achieve any meaningful representational completeness or verisimilitude – except by tacit commitment to another such conceptual scheme arbitrarily and antecedently thus privileged (preeminently expressed in the views of Nietzsche and Derrida[37]);

(f)   the corollary of the preformational or historicist thesis (c) or (d), or an analogue of the same, possibly drawn also from (e), to the effect that the *cogniscence relationship* – the relationship of cognizing subject and cognized world – is itself an artifact of preformational or historicist forces (as in the praxical naturalism of Marx, or Dewey's thinner pragmatist counterpart, or Heidegger's explicitly mythologized, existential phenomenology[38]);

(g) the *denial of distributed cognitive privilege* or transparency, in part the counterpart of (a), in the sense in which all inquiry, first- and second-order, stands before the epistemic tribunal of the undifferentiated totality of whatever appears to be the world, utterly without distributed differential epistemic weighting (as, notably, in Quine's well-known view and, in a sense, also in Heidegger's[39]);

(h) the *artifactuality* thesis, to the effect that all distributed claims are artifactually encumbered by the collective, contingent background of would-be knowledge, belief, conceptual distinction, and prejudice presupposed in pursuing the particular claims we favor testing and holding (perhaps best associated with (e) or (g));

(i) the *piety* thesis, to the effect that all human inquiry is forever fragmentary, transient, contingently favored, partial, biased, never determinately comparable with that possible whole or total or encompassing state of knowledge of which, in principle, any present or particular inquiry is an incalculable part, and by its defective relationship to which it is incalculably affected; also, inconsistently, the thesis to the effect that, in spite of that, the comparative verisimilitude of different programs of inquiry *can* be assessed (as, as already noted above, in Bohm's view, and, notoriously, in Peirce and Popper[40]);

(j) the thesis of *emergence*, to the effect that, at some first-order level, properties may be attributed to ensembles, aggregates, collectives, or systems of elements that cannot be attributed to those elements taken distributively (as notably described by Bunge[41]);

(k) the *factoring* thesis, to the effect that, in first-order inquiry, notably in the context of biology, psychology, the societal, historical, and information disciplines, the functional parts of particular entities (organisms, societies, institutions, machines and the like) cannot be appropriately described in terms of any "explicate order" (as Bohm and Jacob remark[42]) or must be at least initially described in terms of sub-functional factors of some molar functioning (or homunculi, as Daniel Dennett concedes only provisionally[43]);

(l) the *informational* thesis, to the effect that, in first-order inquiry, phenomena obtain (notably, in biology, psychology, the social, historical, and information sciences) in which informational coding is real and embedded (incarnate) in some physical or biological or societal order; and that, relative to whatever may be the structure of the embedding (or incarnating) order, information is causally efficacious as such and exhibits an irreducible, therefore holist or "implicate" or relational order with respect to the functioning of the embedding order (as in both Jacob and Bohm[44]);

(m)   the *hermeneutic* thesis, the thesis of the hermeneutic circle, to the
effect that, at the first-order level (normally supplemented by second-
order, legitimative conjectures), all distributed interpretive claims
regarding the "parts" of given "texts" or text-like phenomena are
symbiotically inseparable from the interpretation of the "whole" text,
and *vice versa* (notably, among contemporary exemplars, in the
opposed accounts of Gadamer and E. D. Hirsch, Jr[45]);

(n)   the *structuralist* thesis, to the effect that, at the first-order level, all
pertinent distributed claims are claims made about "*relata*," which,
in principle, exhibit the properties they do only as functions of their
function within a total system of *relata* (notably, as maintained by
Saussure, Lévi-Strauss, and Trubetzkoy[46]);

(o)   the *functionalist* thesis, whether realist or heuristic, to the effect that,
at the first-order level, all pertinent claims assign a function to some
distributed element *vis-à-vis* an indissoluble, whole, or contextually
undifferential complex, regardless of how, at other levels of analysis,
such complexes may be analyzed (as, for instance, maintained in the
so-called *modularism* of Zenon Pylyshyn and Jerry Fodor or in the
homuncularism of Dennett or even in the role-playing theory of
persons, as favored by Wilfrid Sellars[47]);

(p)   the *monadist*, or holographic, thesis, to the effect that, at the first-
order level, every discriminable region or part of a pertinent domain,
fixed or transient, contains complete information about the total
domain of which it is a sub-region or part (as proposed, for instance,
by Leibniz and Bohm[48]);

(q)   the *contextualist*, or Intentional, thesis – in effect, a generalization of
(m) or a generalized analogue of the same – to the effect that all
human thought, behavior, work, production, history, deeds, and
the like are intensionally significant; and that their significance is a
function of whatever may be ascribed as the similarly specified
significance of the whole undifferentiated or at least distributively
inexhaustible context of such thought and practice, usually societally
defined (as in Wittgenstein's "forms of life," or the cognate devices
of the hermeneuts, the Hegelians, the Marxists, the Frankfurt School
theorists, the Nietzscheans, and others[49]);

(r)   the thesis, similar to (q) but applied so as to yield a determinate and
closed system of a global *Geist* or *Geist*-like problematic, that,
distributively, infects everything within the domain it encompasses
(as in nineteenth-century post-Hegelian *romantic historicism* or in
Althusser's *structuralist Marxism* or, more loosely, despite his
demurrer, in Foucault's *archaeologies*[50]);

(s)   the *collectivist* thesis, to the effect that, at the first-order level,
whether in heuristic or realist terms, the agents of significant action
and history are or include collective or organic entities (nations,

peoples, socioeconomic classes, or the like) that cannot be reduced in terms of aggregates of individual persons and their actions (as, for instance, identified, however quarrelsomely, in Popper's well-known critique of Hegelian and Marxist thought[51]); and, finally,

(t) the *ineffability* thesis, to the effect that the Real is indefinably One, that all predicative distinctions whatsoever utterly fail to accord with its unbreachable wholeness or unity – possibly an unconditionally extreme, reversed analogue of (e) – which is still somehow meaningfully accessible or intelligible (as appears to be claimed in certain Hindu and Buddhist doctrines[52]).

It should now be reasonably clear that the "prejudice" here favored – to the effect that the space of human life does not form a system – is convergently supported by strengthening nearly any combination of items (a), (c), (f), (g), (h), and (q). But these particular items are notably strong doctrines in their own right, either nearly universally conceded at the present time or particularly difficult to defeat, assuming the inconclusiveness of the efforts of the system-mongers. In any case, it is surely a prejudice entitled to a very generous inning.

What, to round out our present account, we must now consider are several specimen disputes focused on the prospects of construing human or cultural space as forming a system. The two principal theories that have been developed and that still attract adherents are those of *analytic structuralism* and *nativism* – both adjusted to the pertinent phenomena of the human world. There are no other models of comparable power and attractiveness at the present time that (1) form systems; (2) are meant to fit the usual saliencies of human existence; (3) are not excessively reductive or eliminative with respect to these; (4) are congruent with the general thrust of the unity of science or are at least designed to apply extensionally; and (5) are actually applied under reasonably explicit, comprehensive operational rules.

We must, of course, remember that the general purpose for introducing the claims of system is to dismiss them ultimately as untenable, inadequate, arbitrary, defective, unconvincing, or at least not exclusively apt for the whole of human space.

III

The condition essential for treating the whole or any sector of physical nature as a system is its subsumption under nomic invariants or nomic universals. There is no narrowly observational (or Humean) resource for confirming such invariants, or relevantly confirming the failure to falsify such invariants – that is, effectively, for converting "constant conjunctions" into nomic universals. This is the point of the question-begging charge laid against inductivism and against the peculiar naiveté of falsificationism: that the "Humeans" can never make their case, and that the "Popperians" fail to grasp the fact that they can never subvert in an empirically pertinent and decisive way the presumption that some promising conjunction may still approximate the required invariance.[53] Indicative regularities are converted, idealized, deformed, replaced, or radically reinterpreted as nomic invariances only under the presumed transcendental import of the realist work of scientific explanation; but the relevant argument is neither ineluctable nor spare enough to be decisively favored competitively.[54] On the other hand, once the reductive strategies of physicalism, eliminative materialism, heuristic functionalism and the like are defeated or at least rendered philosophically harmless,[55] the thesis that the whole or any sector of the human world – however sorted: psychologically, linguistically, institutionally, historically – forms a system depends on a strategy of argument of a radically different sort from that favored in the theorizing about the physical sciences. It is a strategy that will have to appeal, at least initially, to utterly different considerations, even though, if it succeeded, it might arguably help to restore the usual presumption regarding the physical sciences. This, for example, is the obvious strategy of Donald Davidson's so-called anomalous monism: the presumed invariances collected by applying Tarski's formal semantics to natural languages (suitably adjusted to the analysis of behavior) is then reconciled with the presumed nomic causal invariances of the physical sciences (again adjusted to the analysis of behavior).[56] The result is a sly but utterly fatuous restoration of the longings of the unity-of-science program. This part of the story is reasonably clear – though we shall make use of our specimen in a novel way in a moment.

At the risk of some misunderstanding, or at least at the risk of deliberate provocation, we may say that all theories that construe the human world or any of its sectors as a *system, without first claiming or establishing the validity of some form of reductive materialism*, may rightly be regarded as a form of *structuralism*. Generically, then, as a term of art, we may characterize as "structuralist" any theory that posits structural invariances of a sector of the human world that are not themselves, either initially as such or ultimately, rightly characterized as nomic or causal invariances of the sort canonically favored in theorizing about the physical sciences. Davidson's theory, then, *is* a form of structuralism, in the plain sense that Davidson's advocacy of a Tarskian-like (perhaps not a strictly Tarskian) reading of the formal syntax of natural languages presumably depends on grounds that need not *first* invoke the exceptionless scope of the universal causal laws of the physical sciences. Davidson's theory is, furthermore, a remarkably instructive specimen of the structuralist mentality – however heterodox it may appear to be to insist on the point – simply because Davidson *does not* attempt to establish the validity of his formal semantics by way of empirically cumulative fieldwork: he is, one may say, committed *a priori* (logocentrically) to the indefeasibility of that venture as well as to its theoretical advantage within the terms of a realist science and philosophy of science. This is the reason he is tempted by the prospect of an eventual integration of his (Tarskian-like and Quinean) structuralism and the quite different grammatical structuralism favored by Noam Chomsky.[57]

We ought not to proceed further, however, without acknowledging quite straightforwardly that neither Davidson nor Chomsky would relish being called a structuralist. Davidson does not seem to have addressed the matter, at least in his best-known papers; and, of course, Chomsky explicitly rejects the term. So also does Michel Foucault – notoriously.[58] So does Jean Piaget.[59] So also would Louis Althusser, Lucien Goldmann,[60] and many others who have been dubbed structuralists (*manqués*) if, indeed, they have not, somewhere, actually repudiated the label. Their protests need not trouble us, however, so long as we recognize that, among themselves – for instance, as between Chomsky and Piaget – they may actively repudiate one another's views (hence, on our own terms, may repudiate one another's version of structuralism) and may explicitly oppose the classic form of (analytic) structuralism. The advantage of insisting on our term of art is just that it permits us to fix quite directly the various senses in which the human world is said to form a distinctive system and to sort the conceptually decisive varieties of that very claim.

Roughly speaking, Davidson's, Chomsky's, Piaget's, and Lévi-Strauss's "structuralisms" are of rather different sorts. For instance, of the four, Chomsky's is the only one that is explicitly *modular*; Piaget's is the only one that pretends to have discovered an *open system*; Lévi-Strauss's is the only one that is put forward as *totalized*. Chomsky's and Piaget's structuralisms, explicitly pitted against one another, are the only ones that are clearly treated as *empirically* confirmed or empirically favored (in some sense) in *first-order* terms. Piaget's is, as remarked, an open system; Chomsky's is committed to the model of a *closed system* (a genetic system, in fact), which, therefore, though its invariances are clearly not natural laws, are regularities that cannot fail to exhibit difficulties analogous to those that dog inductivism and falsificationism (even though Chomsky is not a partisan of either methodological strategy). Davidson's (Tarskian-like) system is also intended as a closed system, but it is not (as is Chomsky's) modular.

Lévi-Strauss's is explicitly advanced on the strength of the view that indicative, first-order claims favoring systems are empirically – also, in principle – incapable of supporting any closed system (as may be seen from Lévi-Strauss's diatribe against Jean-Paul Sartre[61]) *and* on the view that science requires the use of suitably formed such systems. So Lévi-Strauss's notion of a totalized (closed) system is distinctly linked to *second-order, legitimative* arguments. Davidson's is the only one that is undeniably *logocentric*, in the sense that it attempts no first-order inquiry of Chomsky's or Piaget's gauge though it means to apply its system empirically to natural languages, and in the sense that it implicitly legitimates its own preferment (its formal semantics) without actually providing the second-order argument that that would require. Conveniently, these four specimen views (Chomsky's, Davidson's, Lévi-Strauss's, and Piaget's) appear to capture the generically important features of all candidate theories. That may well be too sanguine a claim. But no harm need follow if we remain alert enough to variations that may from time to time oblige us to make finer or larger distinctions. For instance, Gérard Genette's narratology,[62] as well as the historicized proto-structuralisms of the Russian and other Slavic sources Genette has been influenced by, may indicate both the potential range of "open systems" in the cultural world and the conceptual significance of the historicized orientations of a Hegelian, Marxist, or Nietzschean bent that may yield distinctive versions of system.

In any case, casual though our schematism may be, our conception of structuralism may, even without further adjustment, be made to yield findings of considerable power. For example, once we appreciate that the pretensions of structuralism are initially interesting only on the assumption that no form of physical reductionism obtains, and if we understand the fully cultural world of man to be (1) *real*, (2) *emergent*, (3) *incarnate*, and (4) *causally efficacious* (which are, after all, the minimally worthwhile implications of rejecting reductionism in the context of the human sciences),[63] then it is reasonably clear that a *modular* structuralism – for example, one like Zenon Pylyshyn's or Jerry Fodor's[64] – must either (i) be restricted to a physiologically *factored* functional component of the molar functioning of human beings as human beings, or (ii) depend on the fortunes of the closed systems (modular or not) of the sort Chomsky and Davidson afford, which are expressly addressed to the salient features of the (as yet unreduced) human world – which are addressed, in particular, to the structures of natural languages. It is, therefore, hardly surprising that Fodor (rather more adventurously than Pylyshyn) subscribes to both a Davidsonian view of "concepts" and to a Chomskyan-like innatism;[65] and that Pylyshyn has retreated (more plausibly than Fodor) to the search for the empirical existence of physiologically mediating modules functioning, as such, sub-functionally *within* the molar functioning of what must be jointly described in biological, informational, and culturally relevant terms – for instance, human visual perception.[66] Pylyshyn, therefore, goes in search of *transducers*, which, in effect, are the empirical, first-order *conditiones sine qua non* of any modular structuralism that tolerates, at least initially, our constraints (1)–(4) following the repudiation of reductionism.[67] (Transducers could, in fact, also service a reductive structuralism.) On Pylyshyn's view, a transducer is a physical process that falls under some nomic invariance that can, at another, *independent* "level" of analysis – say, cognitive – be mapped in a computationally isomorphic way with the elements of that second level. It functions, therefore, as a transition device linking the physical or biological and the psychological or "symbolic."[68] So a modular structuralism (or modularism) requires a domain closed under invariant physical laws that can be mapped into another, a "symbolic" or computational or psychological, domain that is itself, on independent grounds, closed with respect to some set of invariant computational rules. What makes a system modular is that it possesses modules or sub-domains that are characterized as above, whether or not the functional behavior of the entire domain can be compositionally or hierarchically generated from the interlocking and interacting functioning of its modules. Pylyshyn does not insist on the more strenuous thesis (having, perhaps, visual perception in mind); Chomsky does insist on the more strenuous thesis (having language in mind).

The essential weakness of a modular structuralism is that the culturally or linguistically (or similarly relevant) system it proposes must be shown *to be a system* before or independent of showing that *that* system functions entirely as a co-functioning network of interacting modules (Chomsky's thesis: which, of course, Chomsky never attempts to demonstrate) or that that system includes (at least) *some* physiologically and informationally sub-functional modules within whatever may be the range of the molar functioning of human beings (Pylyshyn's thesis). The important thing is that the success of a project like Pylyshyn's does not show or even reasonably suggest that the phenomena of the human world will actually yield, in first-order terms, a full structuralist account (either modular or not) and cannot even advance its own claim *at the level of such phenomena* without first being reconciled with a structuralist account (modular or not) *of* such phenomena. (Language, or course, as many have argued, may be said not to be structured at all in the structuralist's sense – *a fortiori*, not to be modularly structured; *a fortiori*, not able to yield transducers. It is entirely conceivable, however, that, although, taken globally, it may not exhibit a structuralist order, language may exhibit sub-functional modules that *are* of a structuralist sort: for such, then, there could, in principle, be found a first-order transducer. Also, the fortunes of the analysis of language need hardly be the fortunes of an analysis of visual perception: there is that much to be said against the strange but suggestive "organ" analogies Chomsky has famously pressed.[69]

Be that as it may, we surely are entitled to raise *first-order* objections against the would-be closed systems Davidson and Chomsky mean to champion. The reasons are fairly straightforward and need not occupy us very strenuously. For one thing, as already remarked, nomic invariances – *a fortiori*, rule-like invariances – are subject to the empirical difficulty that indicative regularities cannot be said to confirm or support (in an evidentiarily pertinent sense) *any* such invariances, without prior appeal to some independent argument (which, on its face, cannot be compelling or decisive, cannot fail to be logocentric[70]). To admit the need for such an argument is to make the search for genuinely universal or necessary invariances (hence, structuralist systems) conceptually unavoidable. But *there is no known compelling argrument of that sort.* Certainly, neither Chomsky nor Davidson advances any.

We have, of course, slipped, unobserved, from first-order to second-order objections against closed systems. But that is simply how the matter stands: there is no first-order supporting evidence, and there cannot by any in second-order terms, because there cannot be any for the nomic invariances of the physical sciences themselves. Which is *not* to say that it would be unreasonable to pursue empirical matters within the terms of reference of a system closed in such a way. It only means that such an undertaking must be carefully monitored in first-order terms *and* that the model of a closed system (in the structuralist sense as well as in the sense of the unity-of-science program) *is no more than regulative or heuristic* – not supported, that is, by any sort of Kantian transcendental argument. That would be quite good enough, however, if it were the case (which it is not) that there is a decisive body of evidence empirically or "instrumentally" favoring such a model to the exclusion of others of an opposed sort. Here, the difference between Chomsky and Davidson is hard to ignore. Chomsky, after all, *has* amassed an impressive body of empirically respectable, interlocking, generative, indicative invariances (or near-invariances); Davidson (like his followers) has done almost no fieldwork at all and has never really addressed the salient objections to his own project.[71] (The same, it may be said, is true of Fodor's theory of predicative concepts modelled, by way of a borrowed nativism, on Davidson's presumption regarding his Tarskian-like program.)

In a nutshell, *both* the Davidsonian and the Chomskyan programs are, as first-order undertakings, probably worth pursuing. Neither is entitled, however, to the second-order presumption both insinuate (and at times explicitly insist on). Still, all the first-order empirical work Chomsky has collected may, without the least disadvantage, be continued independently of whether we or he subscribes to structuralism, to a nativist structuralism, or to a modular nativism. For all his insistence, there is not a single argument that Chomsky offers that shows that we must subscribe to his view, that it is the rationally exclusive option under the circumstances, that it is even a fully plausible option given certain larger considerations about human cognitive efforts or the nature of science. If we treat Chomskyan linguistics as the fruitful empirical work of a genial philosophical prejudice, well and good. There is no reason to carp at it. But if it is meant to be more, then we must politely insist

1 that Chomsky give us an account of the intermodular functioning of the grammatical *and* non-grammatical *competences* he posits, on the basis of which his own modular nativist "structuralism" regarding grammar alone obtains;

2 that he explain what the relationship is between the methodological resources of his own favored form of inquiry and the empirical and pre-formational limitations that affect all forms of human inquiry; and

3 that he offer us a sketch at least of the relationship between the historical societies within which humans are born and mature and the actual process by which individual persons access and use what they acquire through the forms of social communication – in terms relatively independent of the thesis Chomsky claims to support empirically.[72]

It is entirely fair to say that Chomsky has hardly addressed issues 1–3. It is perhaps a compliment to him to insist that he should do so. On the other hand, there is *nothing* in the way of first-order evidence that Davidson assembles for his nonmodular, non-nativist "structuralism"; and what there is in the way of second-order argument is entirely logocentric – simply because Davidson's program presupposes a reasoned assurance that the extensional mode of analysis of a Tarskian-like formal semantics *must* fit in an empirically perspicuous way the actual structure of natural languages, *and because Davidson never attempts to give us the argument for his extensionalism.* Once again, if it is to be viewed as the work of a genial prejudice, let it bloom among a thousand other flowers. But why should it be viewed as more? There is, it may be admitted, a fair sense in which nativists such as Chomsky and Fodor economize on the legitimative grounds favoring their sort of theory and conflate first- and second-order arguments. Fodor is particularly open in this regard, summarizing the import of a rather famous confrontation between Chomsky and Piaget:

> It seems to me that there is a sense in which there *isn't* any theory of learning, and this is quite compatible with Chomsky's point that maybe there is no general learning mechanism that applies equally to perception, language, and so on. I'll argue not only that there is no learning theory but that in certain senses there certainly *couldn't* be; the very *idea* of concept learning is, I think, confused. . . . I am saying that an inductive logic [that is, a theory of the fixation of beliefs; that is, a theory of learning in the only sense in which there *are* theories of learning] can't tell you how the concept *miv* is acquired because it presupposes the availability of that concept when it assumes that *miv* occurs in the confirmed inductive hypothesis. As far as I know, nobody except the nativists has addressed the question of how the concept *miv* [that is, *red and square*] is acquired, and what they have said is that it *isn't* acquired.[73]

There is an obvious charm in Fodor's candor. But there is more in what Fodor says. First of all, Fodor means to treat the theory of "concept acquisition" in a realist sense. Secondly, he offers a straightforward *reductio* as effectively disallowing any alternatives but nativist ones – which supplies the reason he believes he can conflate first-order and second-order objections, bypass more strenuous transcendental arguments, and confidently turn to explore how best to integrate (empirically) the distinct but quite compatible closed systems advocated by Chomsky and Davidson. Thirdly, he gives us notice that the nativist solution will be of a modular sort (differentially adjusted, say, to language and perception). And, fourthly, his adversaries – explicitly identified as Piaget and such allied theorists as Lev Vygotsky and Jerome Bruner – are characterized as partisans of open systems (as opposed to closed), of general learning mechanisms (as opposed to modular systems), and of (broadly) non-innatist processes of acquisition and learning (as opposed to exclusively nativist resources). So the battle lines are trimly drawn.

The nerve of the argument remains the *reductio*. Fodor applies it most tellingly to a reading of Piaget's alternative notion: on the Piagetian view, according to Fodor, if we tried to characterize

> the computational capacities of the [developing human] organism [over time] in terms of some very general constraints on the character of the concepts available to it . . . what [we] would get is a fundamentally different galaxy of constraints on the organism's concepts [developmentally deployed]. Morever, this difference would have the following important characteristic: the logic instantiated by the system of concepts at any i^{th} stage is *weaker than* the logic instantiated by the $i - 1^{th}$ stage. [I take this to be implied by such remarks as that children at certain stages "don't have" reversibility, and so on]. In short, if [we] look at the organism as a succession of logics, then it is a succession of increasingly powerful logics, and powerful in some fairly rigorous sense: as for example that the set of truths that could be expressed by using the concepts available at i is a subset of the set of truths that could be expressed by using the concepts available at $i + 1$.[74]

(It needs, perhaps, to be said that Fodor's characterization of Piaget's view is one that Piaget is entirely willing to apply to his own view.[75])

The argument is a most strategic one and disarmingly simple. It certainly is true that theories of thinking (in an empirically realist sense concerned with "the actual" process) are peculiarly vague and primitive. Nevertheless, there are some considerations that may be mentioned that distinctly temper the force of Fodor's argument even before we move to examine its specific charge: first, there is no standard sense in which we may examine in an empirically straightforward way the "logic" of thinking, as if such structures were palpably and publicly independent phenomena; secondly, we are at least as unclear (ontologically) about what, in a realist sense, concepts *are* as we are about facts and propositions; hence, thirdly, in admitting the reality of thinking, belief, the use of concepts, and the like, we are not bound to insist that our *modeling* of such processes is or need be intended in realist terms – we may well be restricted to representing only heuristically what we have reason to believe has a realist structure.[76] It is not unreasonable to hold that, if we are not transparent to ourselves, then there must be an ineliminable interference phenomenon involved in analyzing what exactly we are doing when we think. The constraints mentioned hardly seem prejudicial. Certainly Fodor offers no reason for disallowing them. And yet, once granted, they completely defuse the ingenious way in which Fodor has trapped us into subscribing to an updated version of Socrates's argument about Meno's slave's mastery of the Pythagorean theorem (which the slave boy has obviously not learned).

What we have managed to do, then, is to reject the *reductio*, both the ancient Platonic version and Fodor's – without having (as yet) rejected or subverted Fodor's substantive claim, now complexified as requiring a clearer use of first- and second-order arguments. One may readily appreciate that Chomsky, too, must have been led to a similar *reductio* affecting all those who opposed his own strong nativism,[77] although Chomsky is more circumspect than Fodor in this regard. But it clearly won't work, quite apart from whether the modular structuralisms Chomsky and Fodor favor do, or do in a competitively favorable first-order sense. Now, then, there is a handsome *reductio* that can be easily drawn from Fodor's substantive argument about concepts, that *shows* (once our preliminary *caveats* are in place) that there *are* conceivable alternatives to his own theory (and Chomsky's); that they actually accommodate Piaget's line of theorizing (without, in doing that, vindicating Piaget's own claims); *and that such alternatives are themselves entailed within the range of Fodor's own alternative, once his own reductio is set aside.* What such an argument would help us to see is

(i) that the peculiar force and exclusiveness of Fodor's and Chomsky's claims essentially depend on the compelling nature of a strong modularism;

(ii) that theories favoring such a modularism themselves depend on higher legitimative arguments, if a Fodorian-like *reductio* fails;

(iii) that, in the absence of such a *reductio*, there is no way in which to preclude, in either first- or second-order terms, non-nativist, open, or developmental systems of language, concept acquisition, learning or the like; and

(iv) that disputes about our heuristic models of concepts and thinking ought not to be confused with disputes about the real structure of concepts and thinking, and that inferences moving in either direction need to be constrained by what we take to be the inherent limitations of our theories.

There is a considerable instruction, then, in the argument we intend to mount, for there can be little doubt that many have been profoundly puzzled as to why the Chomskyan strategy is so difficult to subvert while at the same time it appears so implausible – actually, even inattentive to the general thrust of contemporary philosophies of science.

Now, Fodor's thesis (effectively, a variant or analogue of Chomsky's) is that "The organism is a closed system proposing hypotheses to the world, and the world then chooses among them in terms explicated by some system of inductive logic."[78] So, once again, the "fixation of belief" provides the normal or most distinctive form of learning among humans, and the learning of concepts (which is itself a form of fixing belief) presupposes a modular and innate conceptual resource. In an early account that appears still reasonably close to his current view (though he has changed his theory of the complexity of concepts in the innate pool), Fodor characterizes the learning process in the following way (clearly integrating Chomsky and Davidson):

Learning a language (including, of course, a first language) involves learning what the predicates of the language mean. Learning what the predicates of a language mean involves learning a determination of the extension of these predicates. Learning a determination of the extension of the predicates involves learning that they fall under certain rules (i.e., truth rules). But one cannot learn that *p* falls under *R* unless one has a language in which *p* and *R* can be represented. So one cannot learn a language unless one already has a system capable of representing the predicates in that language *and their extensions.* And, on pain of circularity, that system cannot be the language that is being learned. But first languages *are* learned. Hence, at least some cognitive operations are carried out in languages other than natural ones.[79]

The short way with this argument dictates that the theory of conceptual learning and the theory of an innate language are both heuristic stratagems; and *that*, therefore, the (Socratic) paradoxes regarding learning whatever we do not already "know" or regarding "knowing" what we first learn to know we "know" are themselves artifacts of those heuristic strategems. There is absolutely no need to be bound by them: the idea that the analysis of thinking must be cast in terms of the very categories by which the analysis of language would itself proceed – *because* human thinking is essentially linguistic – is a complete *non sequitur.* Fodor's model just cited is the product of just such a *non* sequitur, even if it is the case that there are heuristic advantages in employing it. The entire claim that "nobody except the nativists has addressed the question of how [a] concept . . . is acquired, and what they have said is that it *isn't* acquired" is a product of that same *non sequitur.* Once we give it up, we may admit theories aplenty: the Socratic paradoxes will no longer dissuade us. Here, then, is a very pretty and painless finding: the *Piagetian* thesis itself (which Fodor neatly summarizes) suddenly becomes entirely eligible and non-paradoxical *and*, as we have yet to show, may (once the *non sequitur* is disallowed) actually be drawn out of Fodor's own argument. Furthermore, it is surely preposterous to deny that Piaget *has* addressed (however convincingly or unconvincingly) the question of the acquisition or learning of concepts: *it is only the intrusive effect of adopting the Socratic* reductio *that could possibly lead to denying that non-nativists have ever addressed (or addressed as plausibly as the nativists) that most difficult question.*

We do need a little more patience, however, to get to the end of the argument. On Fodor's view,

Both [Empiricists and Nativists] assume that the space of concepts potentially available to any given organism is completely determined by the innate endowment of that organism. This follows from the assumptions that (a) the set of potentially available concepts is the closure of the primitive concepts under the combinatorial mechanisms. [that may be postulated]; (b) the set of potentially available primitive concepts is fixed; and (c) the combinatorial mechanisms available are themselves innately specified. [Regarding (c):] if concept learning is hypothesis confirmation, and if you need the combinatorial apparatus to specify the hypotheses that are available for the organism to confirm, then the one thing that *can't* be a consequence of concept learning is the availability of the combinatorial apparatus. This dilemma is conceptual, and loose talk about bootstrapping will buy you nothing.[80]

But the dilemma is an artifact of the heuristic use of Socrates' *reductio*. It could hardly mean that

1 there *is* an innate set of primitive concepts with which we learn whatever we do learn; or

2 that there *is* a fixed and finite set of innate "combinatorial mechanisms" by which we learn whatever we learn; or

3 that the only (or the most plausible) sense in which our learning capacity is "completely determined" by our "innate endowment" *favors* either 1 or 2 or any modularism; or

4 that, even admitting an original innate endowment, such an endowment *logically* precludes acquiring concepts that cannot be generated from a supposed original source of concepts, or *logically* precludes developing (perhaps *because* of acquiring new concepts) an enlargement of our "combinatorial mechanisms" (if we actually are, in the first place, prepared to employ such a model of mental processing).

There you have the *reductio* of Fodor's *reductio*; and there you have the sketch of a strategy by which Piaget's own thesis may be drawn out of a Fodorian-like argument – once Fodor's executive *reductio* is set aside, which, after all, is not itself part of the *first-order* postulation of innate mechanisms and resources.

It may be useful to add a very brief word about Fodor's categories – the Empiricist and the Nativist, which he pretty well takes to be exhaustive of the "classical theories . . . of mental representations" (versions of what he calls "the Representational Theory of Mind"). Roughly, the Empiricist holds that complex concepts are somehow "learned" or generated "from experience" (by certain combinatorial operations on primitive concepts), and that "primitive concepts are merely triggered by experience," by some "non-rational, hence non-learning, mechanism."[81] The Nativist, by contrast, holds

either that (a) all or most lexical concepts have *no* internal structure [are not complex in the Empiricist's sense], or (b), if they are internally structured, nevertheless the fact that they are plays no role in the explanation of their acquisition. To put the same point another way, according to the Nativist view the story that Empiricists tell about *sensory* concepts also holds for a wide [not necessarily exhaustive] range of *non-sensory* lexical concepts: viz. that they are triggered but unlearned.[82]

Both Empiricists and Nativists, then, subscribe to some form of innate endowment. But, of course, so does Piaget – who is neither an Empiricist nor a Nativist.

We need not follow Piaget's line of argument as closely as Fodor's. The important point is that it is internally coherent, not at all wrecked by Fodor's *reductio*, at least moderately congruent with the first-order empirical data of developmental psychology, *and* (of course) subject to the same constraints of heuristic modeling as we have imposed on Fodor. In what is very nearly his last formulation of his own thesis, Piaget offers the following remark (which we may construe in just the terms Fodor summarizes, which Piaget willingly accepts):

> Nor do any a priori or innate cognitive structures exist in man; the functioning of intelligence alone is hereditary and creates structures only through an organization of successive actions performed on objects. Consequently, an epistemology conforming to the data of psychogenesis could be neither empiricist nor preformationist [Nativist], but could consist of a constructivism, with a continual elaboration of *new concepts and structures*.[83]

Now, then, from this alone – which, in effect, is the denial of the exclusive viability of a nativism or modularism – *any* learning process of the sort Fodor is prepared to consider empirically (without first reducing the forms of internal processes to the Nativist's devices) cannot fail to make room (*logically*) for developmental processes of the Piagetian sort. Dialectically, only if we already construe nativism as the exclusive option before us could the learning of concepts preclude "constructivist" possibilities. In that sense, the very thrust of Fodor's argument must provide (both empirically and conceptually) for the Piagetian alternative. (*Punkt*: as Fodor is fond of saying.) But that, of course, neither defeats nor confirms either Fodor's or Piaget's *first-order* thesis. It is, however, fair to say that, just as Chomsky has the edge over Davidson in terms of fieldwork, so, too, has Piaget over Fodor.

(It needs to be borne in mind, in gathering the argument against nativism, that we are, quite indirectly, also mustering evidence in favor of a constructivist account of selves or persons. But that connection has yet to be made.[84])

The constraints Piaget admits are essentially biological and developmental in the biological sense; but such constraints, quite correctly judged, do not *logically* preclude either an increase in concepts beyond whatever, at any stage of development, may be supposed to be already in place (that is, from which "new" concepts may somehow be generated) or an increase in the "structures" of intelligence (which, similarly, are said to be in place at any stage of development). Simply by minimizing hereditary restrictions and by rejecting the Socratic *reductio*, closed structuralisms, nativisms, modularisms are denied privilege of place in a second-order sense. Once the point of the strategy is grasped, it is clear that only an "open structuralism" such as Piaget's (that is, a first-order theory of indicative invariance, reasonably capturing the equilibria and developmental phases of the growth of intelligence) is likely to be empirically supportable (as a structuralism). Such a "structuralism" is hardly quarrelsome in the large (second-order) sense that nativism is, whether or not Piaget is reasonably correct in his conjectures.[85]

IV

The picture regarding structuralisms, nativisms, modularisms is more complicated, or course.

Zenon Pylyshyn, for instance, correctly preceives the dependence of modularism on a functionally defined isomorphic linkage between physical and "symbolic" invariances. ("Symbolic" is a term Pylyshyn uses for any and every cognitively pertinent dimension of life congenial to the characteristic cultural and psychological manifestations of the human world – though without a varied and detailed study of its different forms or of their structural congruity relative to his own thesis.) Hence, he goes in search of transducers; and, probably in pursuing that line of inquiry, naturally allies himself with Fodor, who, as a modularist[86] and functionalist, is similarly symbiotically drawn to Pylyshyn. Chomsky is, in a very indirect sense, also drawn to something like the transducer issue; but he is quite content to treat (without independent genetic evidence) the invariances of deep grammar as genetically determined. Their articulation, in Chomsky's hands, does not require in the least any constant or regular or even intitial appeal back to the specific physical invariances of what, as a bridge between the biological and grammatical orders, may be determinately specified as a transducer. Ther complex structure of (whatever of) language yields to Chomsky's structuralism is not construed, by Chomsky himself, as standing in need of confirming that given linguistic regularities, analyzed in terms of syntactic invariances, are at every step empirically linked with the determinate, law-like invariances of the biological order. The same is true of Fodor, though Fodor takes pains to assure us (again, without empirical detail) that the appropriate transducing invariances do obtain. In this, he generalizes over sensory perception and language.

One may see in these theoretical variations an explicit concern to bring the most strategically placed human sciences (linguistics, the psychology of human sensory perception) into line with the master themes of the unity-of-science program,while at the same time they are meant to accommodate the peculiar complexity of an (as yet) unreduced human science. The same is true in a way of Davidson's program, except that Davidson does not require transducers; for, on his view, some form of "token identity" surely obtains;[87] and, independently of that truth, the invariances of a Tarskian-like analysis of natural languages can be counted on. (Of course, as already remarked, Davidson has never offered the slightest empirical or philosophical evidence that either view would be sufficiently productive.) The important clue here is that the advocacy of a *closed* structuralism, whether modular or not, is very strongly guided by an intended linkage to the unity program.[88] In the hands of a theorist such as Piaget, disregarding the empirical adequacy of Piaget's particular thesis, structuralism need never abandon its commitment to an "open system"; hence, Piaget is opposed to reductionism, invariances of a closed (structuralist) nature, and any second-order presumptions favoring a strong unity of science. Nevertheless, his *empirical* work (he believes) supports a robust but relatively informal extension of the sense of rigor associated with the unity program. The impression is probably strengthened in at least two ways: first, the phases of cognitive development (Piaget claims) are empirically quite regular for the species, and the "structures" that govern every particular level of development exhibit strong formational and transformational invariances that may be captured extensionally;[89] secondly, all the forms of intelligent or cognitively informed development among humans tend to be empirically uniform and tend to converge in terms of the same equilibrative and self-regulative structures.[90] The upshot is that, in terms of the philosophical (second-order) import of structuralism, Piaget's may well be the logically least troublesome version of the thesis applied to relatively strenuous materials: it is essentially a first-order claim (whatever Piaget's own ulterior vision) and it is explicitly an open structuralism (committed to an "open system").[91]

These distinctions prepare us, in effect, for a brief review of classic or analytic structuralism, which (as with Lévi-Strauss) may ultimately be linked with some form of reductionism (true also of Chomsky's program). The inspirational theme of all structuralisms of the "French" variety more or less associated with Saussure's view of language is captured by the following two famous claims:

> Taken as a whole, speech [*parole*] is many-sided and heterogeneous; straddling several areas simultaneously–physical, physiological, and psychological – it belongs both to the individual and to society; we cannot put it into any category of human facts, for we cannot discover its unity.
>
> Language [*langue*] on the contrary, is a self-contained whole and a principle of classification.[92]

> Instead of pre-existing ideas . . . we find in all the foregoing examples [of linguistic regularities] *values* emanating from the system. When they are said to correspond to concepts, it is understood that the concepts are purely differential and defined not by their positive content but negatively by their relations with other terms of the system. Their most precise characteristic is in being what the others are not.[93]

The first remark denies that actual human discourse is conceptually accessible to being treated as a science; the second introduces a peculiarly extreme conception of what the appropriate science of language would be like. Saussure's views are cranky in these respects, and he appears to have had severe misgivings about the standing of his own work.

In the hands of such a virtuoso as Lévi-Strauss, however, aided by the mediating views of N. Troubetzkoy, Saussure's somewhat lame doctrines have taken on a remarkably disciplined form. For, in the first place, Lévi-Strauss replaces Saussure's first thesis with an opposition between "history" and "anthropology" – that is, replaces it with an opposition between historically contingent and preformed pronouncements that could never form a genuine science and a fully formed system of conceptual interrelationships applied to social life in a way that accommodates all conceptual possibilities and so escapes the contingency of the other: "History organizes its data in relation to conscious expressions of social life, while anthropology proceeds by examining its unconscious foundations."[94] The contrast is not merely one of method, but is one of privileged access to reality. One of the distinguishing aims of anthropology is "totality"; for it "regards social life as a system of which all the aspects are organically connected" – a condition impossible for history (or any merely empirical discipline) to discern and a condition essential for the pretension of scientific status among the human studies.[95]

Secondly, Lévi-Strauss explicates his conception of a structuralist science (whether a structuralist linguistics or a structuralist anthropology) by adapting one of Troubetzkoy's statements. The structuralist method is "reduced to four basic operations":

First, structural linguistics shifts from the study of *conscious* linguistic phenomena to [the] study of their *unconscious* infrastructure; second, it does not treat terms as independent entities, taking instead as the basis of analysis the *relations* among terms; third, it introduces the concept of *system* . . . ; finally, structural linguistics aims at discovering *general laws* . . . .[96]

We may add the following amplification: that analytic structuralism regards *systems* as sets of formational and transformational laws that exhaust all possible forms of significative events belonging to a given domain of cultural life (kinship, for instance); that actual events of the relevant sort exist but, for explanatory purposes, must be conceptually replaced by *relata* synchronically generated within the system of which they are a part; that human societies, like individuals, do no more than "choose certain combinations from a repertory of ideas which it should be possible to reconstitute";[97] and that, as *relata* within a totalized domain, events have no significance except in terms of the relational differences holding among all surrogate instantiations of the *relata* of which they themselves are also idealized or deformed instantiations.

Lévi-Strauss certainly construes his account as Saussurean. By that characterization, he intends his own anthropological studies to accord with his conception of a structuralist science. Those studies are, then, in the descriptive and explanatory regard in which they achieve the status required,

(i)   *not* empirical, though they are addressed to subsuming, by way of an approximative replacement (by *relata*), the otherwise intractable materials of empirical observation and reflection;

(ii)   *not*, as a reconstruction of a fully rational system within which the phenomena to be considered are included, epistemically addressed first or primarily or even critically to the sensitive or reflexive reports or intuitions of participants or field linguists or anthropologists;

(iii) *not* addressed to collecting indicative, first-order empirical near-invariances, as of a causal sort, in the manner of standard inductive efforts; and

(iv)   *not* self-corrective in the fallibilist manner, by incrementally accommodating new empirical discoveries that tax the apparent invariances mentioned in (iii).

Lévi-Strauss specifically objects to construing the notion of totalizing (the essential key to a structuralist science) as nothing more than the inductive or empirical or approximative or conventional or progressive hypotheses of theorists consciously trying to formulate the laws of linguistic or societal behavior. So he says,

> Linguistics . . . presents us with a dialectical and totalizing entity but one outside (or beneath) consciousness and will. Language, an unreflecting totalization, is human reason which has its reasons and of which man knows nothing . . . [for human] discourse [spontaneous speech, *parole*] never was and never will be the result of a conscious totalization of linguistic *laws*.[98]

The very system that makes the adequacy of speech possible cannot be the result of deliberate reflection, historically or dialectically developed, upon the laws or conditions of *such* speech; they must be presupposed by it. That is why – so far, correctly – Lévi-Strauss says that "dialectical reason can account neither for itself nor for analytic reason"[99] – that is, neither for the discovery of the limitation of any would-be hypothesis about the deep totalizing power of language nor for the proposal of any such totalized hypothesis in the first place. This presumably is what Jean-Paul Sartre is unable (on Lévi-Strauss's view) to accommodate within the generalized (but misleadingly dubbed) historical method of his *Critique of Dialectical Reason*.[100] Also, of course, this is what accounts for Lévi-Strauss's conception of a human science that penetrates below the level of the conscious (like Freudian psychology) and even below the level of the personal (anticipating Foucault, for instance).

This way of putting matters favors Lévi-Strauss – at least initially. But it ought not obscure the important fact that "totalizing" is conceived in radically different ways by Lévi-Strauss and Sartre – in ways that bear decisively on the prospects of a human science. For Lévi-Strauss, *totalizing* is

1   an innate, determining capacity – probably "bio-chemical" or genetic in some suitably physicalist reduction of the mind and social existence[101] – that, at the level of species-specific manifestation, generates significative activity subject to finite, universal, and invariant laws; and

2   the empirical speculations of the anthropologist to construct totalized systems of laws that permit the deduction of all significative possibilities within the domain examined – that, by dialectical reform mediating the native tendencies of both investigators and examined societies (*dédoublement*), leads us to approximate to the invariant totalizing power of the human species itself (a power necessary, in fact, to account for the advent of such speculation).

Sartre, on the other hand, never means, by totalizing, the existence or discernibility of *any* system of finite, universal, and invariant laws of social life (*contra* 1); hence never means, by totalizing, any empirical approximation to such laws (*contra* 2). For Sartre, totalizing is always an incompletable process, generated out of social *praxis*, intended to give direction to but also to accommodate the improvisational freedom of the population involved (the proletariat, for instance), diachronically conditioned by antecedent praxical tendencies to totalize as well, out of which the associated individuals of a present historical interval manifest their own freedom by repledging themselves to what they provisionally totalize as the significance of their own praxical role.

Lévi-Strauss views all empirically proposed totalities as variant arrangements of an invariant system; and Sartre views all proposed totalities as the free work of a creative community, that can never validly take the form of a closed and universally adequate system. Thus, Sartre says (having Lévi-Strauss expressly in mind) that, "although always capable of being rearranged, the functional organization has to be in question by the whole group, either through a *reflexive* attitude of each of its members, or by some specially differentiated organ, in order to realize the coordinations, modifications, adaptations, etc., when they come to be necessitated by the totalizing *praxis*."[102] (Admittedly, it is difficult not to see in this a touch of Rousseau's disastrous collectivistic tendencies.) Still, Sartre adds that we may call "these structures, in so far as their inorganic materiality has been freely interiorized and reworked by the group, the necessity of freedom."[103] The issue is irrelevant within Lévi-Strauss's conception of a science.

A "totality," it seems, is, for Sartre, "*created*," functions only "as the correlative of an act of imagination." It is for that reason that, as we may guess (struggling with his extraordinarily dense but perceptive prose), Sartre declares that

totalization has the same statute [collective source] as the totality, for, through the multiplicities [the collective life of man], it continues that synthetic labor which makes each part an expression of the whole and which relates the whole to itself through the mediation of its parts. But it is a *developing* activity, which cannot cease without the multiplicity reverting to its original statute [that is, without becoming "*inert*"].[104]

In effect, then, for *both* Lévi-Strauss and Sartre, *Lévi-Strauss's* "totalizing" is the work of "analytical reason" – that is, the attempt to reduce the human sciences to the natural sciences, the attempt to reduce the human world to the "inert," "external," "inorganic" elements of physical nature. For Sartre, "totalizing" is instead the living work of "dialectical reason" – that is, the active, praxical "transformation" of brute nature into the significant order of human life, the resistance of the "practico-inert" tendency of man's created world to appear as (and therefore to function as) "neutral," "exterior," "there" as far as human intervention is concerned:

> Thus analytical reason, as the pure, universal schema of natural laws, is really only the result of a synthetic transformation or, so to speak, a particular practical moment of dialectical Reason: this latter, like animal-tools, uses its organic powers to make certain regions of itself into a *quasi-inorganic residue deciphering the inert by means of its own inertia*; scientific thought is synthetic in its internal movement (*creation* of experiments and hypotheses), and (in the case of the sciences of Nature in their present state) analytical in its noemic projection of itself.[105]

There is a curious inadequacy that each theorist perceives in the view of the other: and there is an equally curious undefended assumption essential to the work of each. These assumptions are in fact radically opposed variations of the same ulterior assumption. Lévi-Strauss correctly observes that Sartre has no way of ensuring that an understanding of history, itself historically contingent and clearly capable of bias and error, is able to count as an objectively valid account of actual history, if he (Sartre) can be said "to have valued history above the other human sciences": "historical facts are no more *given* than any other," says Lévi-Strauss. "It is the historian, or agent of history, who constitutes them by abstraction and as though under the threat of an infinite regress."[106] So Lévi-Strauss manages to demonstrate that Sartre entangles himself in an irresolvable paradox: he "invokes the criterion of historical consciousness" to discern the meaning of history; but that criterion cannot fail, in performing its intended work, to be completely "ahistorical." The process of history is "impossible to know" merely by means of historical consciousness; the "superstructures" by which man claims to understand his own meaning are, says Lévi-Strauss in a memorable remark, "*faulty acts* which have 'made it' socially" – that is, distinctions that are merely the spontaneously persuasive but utterly contingent categories of self-analysis.[107] Lévi-Strauss has surely put his finger on the *aporia* of Marxism as well as of Sartre's existentialized and phenomenologized version of Marxism. The irony remains, of course, that the structuralist (Lévi-Strauss) recommends his own view as the guardian of historical understanding.

For his part, Sartre implicitly raises the double question of how Lévi-Strauss can account for the cognitive privilege (under existential conditions) of claiming that his own totalizations actually and objectively fit the apparent motley of human behavior[108] and of how he can possibly claim to have

succeeded in discerning the invariant system of the sufficient laws of cultural
life – that no merely historically conditioned understanding could ever
discover. So Sartre says, with his usual luminous complexity, that

> what we are dealing with here is not a totality [a prior, truly "exterior"
> system obtaining independently of man's cognitive and praxical interven-
> tion] but a totalization, that is to say, a multiplicity which totalizes itself
> in order to totalize the practical field from a certain perspective, and that
> its common action through each organic *praxis*, is revealed to every
> common individual as a developing objectification.[109]

Underlying structures Sartre does not deny; but they are never more than historically provisional, general, open-ended, compelling but freely accepted
uniformities that implicate man's own *praxis* – he speaks, here, of their
practical necessity within a society as "only the external appearance of [a] freely
created inertia."[110] Sartre has surely put his finger on the *aporia* of
structuralism construed as a science: that is, the impossibility of discerning,
under historical conditions of inquiry and with regard to the historicized nature
of human existence itself, finite invariant structures of meaning that
nomologically order all possible forms of historical emergence.

On Lévi-Strauss's view, Sartre makes a myth of history; and, on Sartre's
account, Lévi-Strauss cannot but be committed to the myth of the timeless
unity of historical flux. And both, therefore, are committed (certainly without
conceptual justification) to an epistemically privileged foundation for their
respective systems of accounting for human events – which, to intrude an
instructive point, is precisely what Derrida, writing about Lévi-Strauss and
Rousseau particularly, had in mind in speaking (in his own cryptically
expansive way) of "the originary violence of a language [that is, any language]
which is already a writing" (Lévi-Strauss and Rousseau having made so much
of the absence of a written language among primitive peoples – say, the
Nambikwara[111] – and, *therefore*, of *their* [the Nambikwara's] being better
placed than we to reveal the essentially innocent and transparent grasp of reality
by natural man).[112] The two views are incompatible, though they both aspire
to cognitive privilege.[113]

The upshot of their confrontation is to drive any warily realist account of historical or cultural understanding (which, of course, infects the invariances of
natural science as well) *in the direction of praxical and hermeneutic processes.*
That is surely the upshot of rejecting the conceptual possibility of structuralist
totalization, the repudiation of cognitive privilege, the acknowledgment of the
preformational orientation of human interests and effective and cognitive
aptitudes, the tacitly artifactual nature of what we identify as the cognizable
world, the technological and praxical sources of the formation of effective
human agents, the inevitable division of social (and, in particular, communicative) labor, the admission of science and inquiry as undeniably productive, the
capture of critique under these same conditions, and the consequently shifting

horizonal nature of every conceptual focus. In a word, Lévi-Strauss's option is preposterous, and Sartre's is only mildly suggestive, much too primitive for the questions that need to be addressed.

Apart from the extraordinary pretension of adopting a God's-eye view (which is what Derrida chiefly rails against – if we understand by that that not only Lévi-Strauss [explicitly] but all theorists [at least implicitly] are drawn to totalizing), analytic structuralism combines two fatal errors, each of which would have been decisive alone. First of all, it is committed to a form of the doctrine of internal relations, since, on the structuralist view, no predication made of any putative referent is logically independent of *any* predication that is true of it.[114] Even if that doctrine were coherent in a formal sense, it would be impossible to apply under the real-time terms of human inquiry. Secondly, totalization in the structuralist sense, viewed merely in terms of the applicability of concepts without regard to truth, would entail that one could not even understand the meaning of a particular concept without understanding the totalized system within which *alone* it *was* meaningful and had the meaning it had. But there are no formulable grounds on which to ensure that any putatively totalized schemes consciously assigned to an actual domain are in fact totalized; and there is no clear sense in which concepts are ever characterized, explained, or applied in terms of any such totalized scheme. (No conceptual scheme can be completely cast in relational terms even if to understand a concept is to understand how it is related to other concepts.) If we concede that systematically linked alternative possibilities ("possible worlds") are generable only relative to a governing theory, the very idea of totalized possibilities ("all possible worlds") is bound to be vacuous. The objection may be put in a word: the slightest change in a would-be structuralist system logically entails altering that entire interrelated system. Hence, (1) there can be no meaningful *approximation* to the putatively totalized system fitting any domain; (2) no inquirer lacking a grasp of the totalized system can understand any putative part of it; and (3) no pair of inquirers lacking a common system can understand one another at all.

These are, of course, utterly mad consequences – however ineluctably they follow from Lévi-Strauss's conception. Obviously, *his* anthropologists are bound to cheat around the edges of their would-be systems; but, insofar as they do so, they must yield in Sartre's direction *at least* – without necessarily subscribing to Sartre's own particular proposals. This is just what is meant to be captured in remarking that no theory of human history and culture, either on its ontological or its epistemological side, can fail to be committed to a praxical and hermeneutic orientation. To say that much, however, is by no means to subscribe to any particular account of the relevant processes – Marxist, Habermasian, Gadamerian, Foucauldian or any other. It is merely to identify the dialectically indicated field within which alone a viable solution would (if any could) be possible.

Analytic structuralism is the most extreme and the most contrived attempt to link the recalcitrant materials of the human world to whatever, by canny attenuation and retreat, may still aim to preserve some sufficient vestige of the unity-of-science program. "Totalizing" cannot fail to be an artifact of a theorist's *Lebenswelt*; and, within the space of a *Lebenswelt*, effective "totalization" is quite impossible. We understand our world and ourselves only within the flux, if we may be said to understand our world and ourselves at all.

Hjelmslev's intuition is singularly flawed and unpromising.

Notes

1 See Joseph Margolis, *Science without Unity: Reconciling the Human and Natural Sciences* (Oxford: Basil Blackwell, 1987), ch. 8; also Nancy Cartwright, *How the Laws of Physics Lie* (Oxford: Clarendon Press, 1983).

2 See Margolis, *Science without Unity*, chs 7, 9; and ch. 9, below.

3 See ch. 6; below.

4 Louis Hejelmslev, *Prolegomena to a Theory of Language*, rev. edn, tr. Francis J. Whitfield (Madison: University of Wisconsin Press, 1961), p. 9.

5 Ferdinand de Saussure, *Course in General Linguistics*, tr. Wade Baskin, ed. Charles Bally et. al. (New York: McGraw-Hill, 1959), p. 117. See also Jonathan Culler, *Ferdinand de Saussure* (Harmondsworth: Penguin, 1976).

6 Saussure, *Course in General Linguistics*, p. 14.

7 See for instance Noam Chomsky: *Aspects of the Theory of Syntax* (Cambridge, Mass.: MIT Press, 1965), ch. 1, section 1; *Current Issues in Linguistic Theory* (The Hague: Mouton, 1970), ch. 1; *Reflections on Language* (New York: Pantheon, 1975) ch. 1. See also Fred D'Agostino, *Chomsky's System of Ideas* (Oxford: Clarendon Press, 1986), ch. 1.

8 Bohm also characterizes the classical model as "Euclidean," "Cartesian," "Newtonian," even "manifest." See David Bohm, *Wholeness and the Implicate Order*, corr. edn (London: Routledge and Kegan Paul, 1981), pp. 182–6, 114.

9 Ibid., p. 48.

10 Ibid., pp. 185–6.

11 Ibid., pp. 144–7, 149.

12 Ibid., p. 149.

13 This helps to clarify the peculiar disconnectedness of chs 2–3 of *Wholeness and the Implicate Order*. Bohm records, in passing, a debt to A. N. Whitehead, *Process and Reality* (New York: Macmillan, 1933).

14 S. W. Hawking and G. F. R. Ellis, *The Large Scale Structure of Space–Time* (Cambridge: Cambridge University Press, 1973), p. 1.

15 Bohm, *Wholeness and the Implicate Order*, p. 47, in the context of ch. 2.

16 Hawking and Ellis, *The Large Scale Structure of Space–Time*, p. 1.

17 Ibid., pp. 362–4.

18 I have had the opportunity of confirming this continued searching on Bohm's part, in an informal conversation with him during some talks he presented recently at a conference on the status of quantum physics and its bearing on

psychological and cultural phenomena, organized at Temple University, Philadelphia, Fall 1987, by Dr Gideon Carmi. Bohm has kindly let me see a recent unpublished paper of his, "Soma-Significance: A New Notion of the Relationship between the Physical and the Mental," which confirms his continuing sympathy for the views of J. Krishnamurti. I have not had a full opportunity to read Bohm's most recent book, *Science, Order, and Creativity* (co-authored by F. David Peat) (New York: Bantam Books, 1987), especially chs 4–5, which pursues some of these same themes.

19 See ch. 1, above.

20 See Karl R. Popper, *The Open Universe: An Argument for Indeterminism* (from *Postscript to the Logic of Scientific Discovery*), ed. W. W. Bartley, III (Totowa, NJ: Rowman and Littlefield, 1982), pp. 172–4; and Ilya Prigogine, *From Being to Becoming: Time and Complexity in the Physical Sciences* (San Francisco: W. H. Freeman, 1980). See also Margolis, *Science without Unity*, ch. 10.

21 See Hilary Putnam, *Meaning and the Moral Sciences* (London: Routledge and Kegan Paul, 1978), particularly Lecture II of the John Locke Lectures, 1976; and Judson C. Webb, "Gödel's Theorems and Church's Thesis: A Prologue to Mechanism," in Robert S. Cohen and Marx W. Wartofsky (eds), *Language, Logic, and Method* (Dordrecht: D. Reidel, 1983). See also ch. 1, above.

22 See Margolis, *Science without Unity*, ch. 5.

23 Bohm, *Wholeness and the Implicate Order*, p. 197. See further pp. 196–213 and, for a sense of how tenuous Bohm's speculation about the implicate nature of quantum physics and its extension to consciousness is, ch. 4.

24 Ibid., p. 213.

25 Cf. ibid., p. 201. In indicating here, his relationship to Leibniz and Whitehead, Bohm pretty well summarizes his entire thesis.

26 Extensive discussions of these alternatives are collected in Joseph Margolis, *Philosophy of Psychology* (Englewood Cliffs, NJ: Prentice-Hall, 1984), *Culture and Cultural Entities* (Dordrecht: D. Reidel, 1984), and *Science without Unity*, *passim*.

27 These views are discussed in *Science without Unity*, ch. 10.

28 See François Jacob, *The Logic of Life: A History of Heredity*, tr. Betty E. Spillman (New York: Pantheon, 1973), issued in Great Britain as *A Logic of Living Systems: A History of Heredity*. Cf. for example pp. 306–7. One can begin to see here the sense in which Bohm's speculation is simply an exemplar for a very large variety of theories. See also Theodosius Dobzhansky and Ernest Boesiger, *Human Culture: A Moment of Evolution*, ed. Bruce Wallace (New York: Columbia University Press, 1983).

29 Aspects of Chomsky's and Fodor's speculations are explored in *Science without Unity*, chs 6, 9; also ch. 9, below.

30 See V. Propp, *Morphology of the Folktale*, 2nd, rev. edn, tr. Lawrence Scott, ed. Louis A. Wagner (Austin: University of Texas Press, 1968). Goethe's notion of the *Urpflanze* is not an altogether inapt model to mention, though it was not applied to specifically cultural phenomena. The morphological model, diachronically deployed, appears also, more ambitiously, in Northrop Frye, *The Anatomy of Criticism: Four Essays* (Princeton, NJ: Princeton University Press, 1957); and in Hayden White, *Metahistory: The Historical Imagination in Nineteenth-Century Europe* (Baltimore: Johns Hopkins University Press, 1973).

31   See Jean Piaget, *Structuralism*, tr. Chinanah Maschler (New York: Basic Books, 1970); and Massimo Piattelli-Palmarini (ed.), *Language and Learning: The Debate between Jean Piaget and Noam Chomsky* (Cambridge: Harvard University Press, 1980). The application of the Piagetian model to moral development appears in Lawrence Kohlberg, *The Philosophy of Moral Development* (New York: Harper and Row, 1981); see also Jean Piaget, *The Moral Judgment of the Child*, tr. Marjorie Gabain (New York: Free Press, 1965). See also, for clues regarding the dubiousness of Kohlberg's project, Carol Gilligan, *In a Different Voice: Psychological Theory and Women's Development* (Cambridge, Mass.: Harvard University Press, 1982); and Joseph Margolis, "Does Kohlberg Have a Valid Theory of Moral Education?" in Matthew Lipman and Ann Sharp (eds), *Growing Up with Philosophers* (Philadelphia: Temple University Press, 1978). Freud, it may be fairly claimed, holds a developmental theory of a structural sort similar to Piaget's. See particularly Erik Erikson, *Childhood and Society* (New York: W. W. Norton, 1950); Philip Rieff, *Freud: The Mind of the Moralist* (New York: Viking, 1959).

32   See further ch. 8, below.

33   This is the sense introduced and defended in Joseph Margolis, *Pragmatism without Foundations: Reconciling Realism and Relativism* (Oxford: Basil Blackwell, 1986).

34   See Sandra G. Harding (ed.), *Can Theories Be Refuted? Essays on the Duhem–Quine Thesis* (Dordrecht: D. Reidel, 1976).

35   See chs 3–4, above.

36   Heidegger and Foucault may offer the best specimens, although Heidegger's account is essentially abstract. See for instance Martin Heidegger, *Being and Time*, tr. John Macquarrie and Edward Robinson (New York: Harper and Row, 1962), sections 5–6; and Michel Foucault, "Docile Bodies," *Discipline and Punish: The Birth of the Prison*, tr. Alan Sheridan (New York: Random House, 1977).

37   See for instance Friedrich Nietzsche, *The Will to Power*, tr. Walter Kaufmann and R. J. Hollingdale, ed. Walter Kaufmann (New York: Random House, 1967), sections 473–4, 544, 556, 585; and Jacques Derrida, "The End of the Book and the Beginning of Writing," *Of Grammatology*, tr. Gayatri Chakravorty Spivak (Baltimore: Johns Hopkins University Press, 1976).

38   See ch. 4. above.

39   See W. V. Quine, *Word and Object* (Cambridge, Mass.: MIT Press, 1960), sections 6–7, 12, 14–16, 56; and Margolis, *Pragmatism without Foundations*, ch. 8.

40   See Margolis, *Pragmatism without Foundations*, ch. 7.

41   See Margolis, *Science without Unity*, ch. 10.

42   Jacob affirms, "At the extremes [of modern biology] are two great tendencies, two attitudes in fundamental opposition. The first [which Jacob favors] may be called integrationist (or evolutionary). Not only does it claim that the organism cannot be separated into its components, but also that it is often useful to consider it as an element of a system or higher order – group, species, population or ecological family. Evolutionary biology is concerned with communities, behavior, the relationships which organisms set up with one another or with their environment" (*The Logic of Life*, p. 6).

43   See Margolis, *Science without Unity*, ch. 5.
44   See Jacob, Introduction to *The Logic of Life*, particularly with regard to what Jacob calls the "programme"; also Margolis, *Science without Unity*, ch. 6.
45   See Hans-Georg Gadamer, *Truth and Method*, tr. Garrett Barden and John Cumming, from 2nd German edn (New York: Seabury Press, 1975); and E. D. Hirsch, Jr, *Validity in Interpretation* (New Haven, Conn.: Yale University Press, 1967), ch. 5.
46   We shall consider the structuralists shortly.
47   These theories are fully analyzed in *Science without Unity*, ch. 9.
48   See Gottfried Wilhelm Leibniz, *Philosophical Papers and Letters*, 2nd edn, tr. and edn. Leroy E. Loemker (Dordrecht: D. Reidel, 1970), items 63vii, 66, 67.
49   See Margolis, *Science without Unity*, chs 7, 9, 11; also chs 8, 9, below.
50   See ch. 8, below; also Louis Althusser and Etienne Balibar, *Reading Capital*, tr. Ben Brewster (London: New Left Books, 1970), pt I; and Michel Foucault, *The Order of Things: An Archaeology of the Human Sciences*, tr. from the French (New York: Random House, 1970).
51   See for instance Karl R. Popper, *The Poverty of Historicism*, 3rd edn (New York: Harper and Row, 1961), and *The Open Society and Its Enemies* (Princeton, NJ: Princeton University Press, 1950); also Margolis, *Science without Unity*, ch. 12.
52   See for example Keiji Nishitani, *Religion and Nothingness*, tr. Jan Van Bragt (Berkeley, Calif.: University of California Press, 1982), chs 3–4; and Kitaro Nishida, "The Intelligible World," *Intelligibility and the Philosophy of Nothingness*, tr. Robert Schinzinger (Honolulu: East–West Centre Press, 1958). Nishitani, Nishida's student, and Nishida himself represent the'influential views of the so-called Kyoto School (of Buddhism). There is, however, a quite noticeable inclination on their part to read the Buddhist doctrine of *śunyātā* ("emptiness") in a way that clearly derives from Heidegger's myth of *Dasein* (as well as, notably in Nishida, from Hegelian themes).
53   This appears to be the master-theme of Roy Bhaskar's strenuous, rather too sanguine distinction between the "intransitive" and "transitive" dimensions of the sciences – that is, Bhaskar's realist commitment to invariances and his admission of the inadequacy of epistemic sources to reveal them as such. See Roy Bhaskar, *Scientific Realism and Human Emancipation* (London: Verso Books, 1986). See also Imre Lakatos, *Proofs and Refutations: The Logic of Mathematical Discovery*, edn. John Worrall and Elie Zahar (Cambridge: Cambridge University Press, 1976).
54   See Cartwright, *How the Laws of Physics Lie*; and Margolis, *Science without Unity*, ch. 8
55   See Margolis, *Philosophy of Psychology*, and *Science without Unity*, chs 5, 6, 9.
56   See Donald Davidson, *Essays on Actions and Events* (Oxford: Clarendon Press, 1980). The objections to Davidson's program are laid out in *Science without Unity*, chs 1, 5.
57   See Donald Davidson, "Semantics for Natural Languages," *Inquiries into Truth and Interpretation* (Oxford: Clarendon Press, 1984).
58   Cf. Foucault, Foreword to the English Edition of *The Order of Things*.
59   Piaget identifies himself as a structuralist in the sense in which he, as other structuralists of whatever stripe, is concerned "with self-regulating transformational totalities." He is, however, explicitly opposed to Lévi-Strauss's version, as noted

in the oblique remark "We must admit that we do not really understand why the mind is more truly honored when it is viewed as the as yet unfinished product of continual self-construction." See Piaget, *Structuralism*, pp. 97, 114, in the context of ch. 6.

60 Cf. Lucien Goldmann, *Cultural Creation*, tr. Bart Grahl (St Louis: Telos Press, 1976), especially Appendix 3.

61 See Claude Lévi-Strauss, *The Savage Mind*, tr. from the French (Chicago: University of Chicago Press, 1966), ch. 9.

62 See Gérard Genette, *Narrative Discourse: An Essay in Method*, tr. Jane E. Lewin (Ithaca, NY, Cornell University Press, 1979); for another, not altogether dissimilar specimen of openness regarding structuralism see Jurij Lotman, *The Structure of the Artistic Text*, tr. Gail Lenhoff and Ronald Vroon (Ann Arbor: University of Michigan, 1977).

63 The general grounds for the elaboration of the argument are given in *Science without Unity*, chs 9, 10, and in *Culture and Cultural Entities*, ch. 1. But we shall have to return to these issues again.

64 See Zenon W. Pylyshyn, *Computation and Cognition* (Cambridge, Mass.: MIT Press, 1985); Jerry A. Fodor, *The Modularity of Mind* (Cambridge, Mass.: MIT Press, 1983) and *Representations* (Cambridge, Mass.: MIT Press, 1981). Their views are canvassed in *Science without Unity*, ch. 6. Apparently, Pylyshyn and Fodor are currently at work on an extended defense of a modular account of aspects of human intelligence: Pylyshyn, more with regard to visual perception; Fodor, more with regard to language and purposive behavior. (Personal communication). It will be interesting to see to what extent we have anticipated the force of their argument.

65 See Jerry A. Fodor, *The Language of Thought* (New York: Thomas Y. Crowell, 1975), chs 1–2, and "On the Impossibility of Acquiring 'More Powerful' Structures," in Massimo Piattelli-Palmarini (ed.), *Language and Learning*.

66 I am guessing, here, at Pylyshyn's current line of inquiry from some informal remarks of his. Cf. David Marr, *Vision: A Computational Investigation into the Human Representation and Processing of Visual Information* (New York: W. H. Freeman, 1982).

67 The concept of a transducer – in particular, Pylyshyn's – is critically examined in *Science without Unity*, ch. 6.

68 Pylyshyn, *Computation and Cognition*, pp. 152–5.

69 See Noam Chomsky, *Rules and Representations* (New York: Columbia University Press, 1980), ch. 1, for instance at p. 39.

70 See Margolis, *Science without Unity*, ch. 8.

71 For a quick summary of what may well be the decisive difficulty of Davidson's entire venture in this respect, see Ian Hacking, *Why the Philosophy of Language Matters* (Cambridge: Cambridge University Press, 1975), ch. 12.

72 See Margolis, *Science without Unity*, ch. 12.

73 Fodor, "On the Impossibility of Acquiring 'More Powerful' Structures," in Piattelli-Palmarini (ed.), *Language and Learning*, pp. 144, 146. The bracketed material appears in the original text.

74 Ibid., p. 147. The sentence in brackets beginning "I take this . . ." appears thus in the original text.

75 In the Discussion following the presentation of Fodor's paper, ibid., p. 150.

76   The general argument for the heuristic modeling of real minds (for instance, the modeling of animal minds as well as the reflexive modeling of our own) is given in *Science without Unity*, ch. 9; cf. also, *Culture and Cultural Entities*, ch. 3.

77   See Margolis, *Science without Unity*, ch. 12.

78   Fodor, "On the Impossibility of Acquiring 'More Powerful' Structures," in Piattelli-Palmarini (ed.), *Language and Learning*, p. 152.

79   Fodor, *The Language of Thought*, pp. 63–4.

80   Fodor, *Representations*, p. 277.

81   Ibid., p. 275.

82   Ibid., p. 279.

83   Jean Piaget, "The Psychogenesis of Knowledge and Its Epistemological Significance," in Piattelli-Palmarini (ed.), *Language and Learning*, p. 23 (italics added). See also Piaget, *Structuralism*; and Joseph Margolis, "Thinking about Thinking," *Grazer Philosophische Studien*, XXVII (1986). Recent studies appear to confirm that the physical structures and modes of functioning of the brain and neurophysiological pathways are actually and progressively altered, developed, and made more complex as a result of the graded learning of the developing human organism. If so, Fodor must be wrong on empirical grounds; if not, or not yet, he is wrong about the conceptual possibilities. See for instance Gerald M. Edelman, *Neural Darwinism* (New York: Basic Books, 1988); and William T. Greenough and Janice M. Juraska (eds), *Developmental Neuro-psychobiology* (Orlando, Fla: Academic Press, 1986).

84   See chs 8, 9, below.

85   See for example Richard F. Kitchener, *Piaget's Theory of Knowledge: Genetic Epistemology and Scientific Reason* (New Haven, Conn.: Yale University Press, 1986); Margaret A. Boden, *Jean Piaget* (New York: Yale University Press, 1986); Philip N. Johnson-Laird, *Mental Models* (Cambridge, Mass.: Harvard University Press, 1983): and Ulrich Neisser, *Cognition and Reality: Principles and Implications of Cognitive Psychology* (San Francisco: W. H. Freeman, 1976).

86   See Fodor, *The Modularity of Mind*.

87   See Donald Davidson, "Mental Events," *Essays on Actions and Events*.

88   See Margolis, *Science without Unity*, ch. 10.

89   See Piaget, *Structuralism*, *passim*; also Jean Piaget, *Genetic Epistemology*, tr. Eleanor Duckworth (New York: W. W. Norton, 1971), ch. 1.

90   See Jean Piaget, "Autobiography," in E. G. Boring et al. (eds), *A History of Psychology in Autobiography*, vol. 4 (New York: Russell and Russell, 1952). See also C. H. Waddington, *The Nature of Mind* (Edinburgh: Edinburgh University Press, 1972) and *The Development of Mind* (Edinburgh: Edinburgh University Press, 1973).

91   See Massimo Piattelli-Palmarini, "How Hard Is the 'Hard Core' of a Scientific Program?", in Piattelli-Palmarini (ed.), *Language and Learning*, pp. 5–9.

92   Saussure, *Course in General Linguistics*, p. 9.

93   Ibid., p. 117.

94   Claude Lévi-Strauss, *Structural Anthropology*, tr. Claire Jacobson and Brooke Grundfest Schoepf (Garden City, NY: Anchor Books, 1967), p. 19.

95   Ibid., pp. 362, 33. See also Lévi-Strauss, *The Savage Mind*, ch. 9.

96   Ibid., p. 31.

97   Claude Lévi-Strauss, *A World on the Wane*, tr. John Russell (London: Hutchinson, 1961), p. 160. This is a translation of part of *Tristes tropiques*, tr. John and Doreen Weightman (New York: Atheneum, 1981).
98   Lévi-Strauss, *The Savage Mind*, p. 252.
99   Ibid., p. 253.
100 See Jean-Paul Sartre, *Critique of Dialectical Reason*, tr. Alan Sheridan-Smith, ed. Jonathan Rée (London: New Left Books, 1976).
101 Claude Lévi-Strauss, "Introduction à l'oeuvre de Marcel Mauss," in Marcel Mauss, *Sociologie et anthropologie* (Paris: Presses Universitaires de France, 1968); cf. Thomas Shalvey, *Claude Lévi-Strauss: Social Psychotherapy and the Collective Unconscious* (Amherst: University of Massachusetts Press, 1979), ch. 7.
102 Sartre, *Critique of Dialectical Reason*, p. 488.
103 Ibid., p. 489.
104 Ibid., pp. 45–6. An informal but useful impression of this doctrine may be found in Gila J. Hayim, *The Existential Sociology of Jean-Paul Sartre* (Amherst: University of Massachusetts Press, 1980), ch. 4.
105 Ibid., p. 53.
106 Lévi-Strauss, *The Savage Mind*, pp. 256, 257.
107 Ibid., p. 254.
108 See for example the subtle subversion of Lévi-Strauss's methodological orientation in Pierre Bourdieu, *Outline of a Theory of Practice*, tr. Richard Nice (Cambridge: Cambridge University Press, 1977).
109 Sartre, *Critique of Dialectical Reason*, p. 492.
110 Ibid., p. 491.
111 See Lévi-Strauss, *Tristes tropiques*, ch. 28.
112 See Derrida, *Of Grammatology*, p. 106.
113 It may be said, by the way, that Sartre has constructed a peculiarly closed system for preserving the inherently asystematic nature of human existence.
114 The doctrine of internal relations was strenuously debated in England and America particularly with regard to the viability of F. H. Bradley's philosophy and of the philosophy of one of his principal supporters, Brand Blandshard. See Brand Blanshard, *The Nature of Thought*, 2 vols (London: Allen and Unwin, 1940); A. J. Ayer, *Language, Truth and Logic* (London: Victor Gollancz, 1936), ch. 8; "Monism and Pluralism"; G. E. Moore, "External and Internal Relations," *Philosophical Studies* (London: Allen and Unwin, 1922); and Timothy Sprigge, "Internal and External Properties," *Mind*, LXXI (1962). There is also a summary account of the issue, "Relations, Internal and External," by Richard Rorty, in Paul Edwards (ed.), *The Encyclopedia of Philosophy*, (New York: Macmillan and Free Press, 1967), vol. 7.

Part Two

The Reality of the Human

6

Constraints on the Metaphysics of Culture

Realism is essentially a theory about the epistemic fit or relationship between human inquirers (their cognitive aptitudes and particular claims) and reality (the actual world). What the nature of that fit is is, hardly innocuously, a function of the nature of human inquiry *and* of the nature of the world. Since it is clear that a supposed realist science must, to be assigned such status, have already raised as a viable question the question of why we should suppose there is a fit of the right kind and that our science satisfies it, and since it is clear that in addressing that question we must intend to answer it (if we mean to answer at all) under the constraint of whatever may be the unspecified as well as specified cognitive powers humans would exercise in answering, we cannot suppose, taking realism seriously, that theorizing about *reality* – as it enters into the "relationship" realism posits – is an illicit undertaking merely because human efforts will have infected the question and its answer. It merely signifies that theorizing about reality as it is apart from the relationship assigned in a realist science cannot fail to be pursued under the same constraints as bind such a realist science. On the rejection of all forms of cognitive transparency, such speculation is at least of an "internalist" sort, not merely in the trivial sense (acceptable to the partisans of privilege) that it must depend on and instantiate whatever are or may be the cognizing capacities of humans, but also in the hardly trivial sense that we cannot (speaking informally) claim to demarcate the world or reality-as-it-is-independent-of-human-inquiry except as a posit internal to what we take to be the world-as-it-is-cognitively-encountered-by-us. The naive terms contrasted signify principally the awkwardness of the question posed, but they do not in any obvious sense disallow it. On the contrary, the first term (the "independent" world or "mind-independent" world, as it is usually dubbed nowadays) as well as the second (the "mind-dependent" world, as we may say) are both used in a distributive and a holist sense but never quite univocally in either of these two ways.[1] In fact, it is the reading of the *holist* sense of the first term that is peculiarly open to quarrel.

There are many who would agree with the following as a fair formulation of a *minimal* (uncompromising) realism:

To say the world determines truth . . . is to say roughly that given the way(s) the world is, there is one and only one way truth-values can be distributed over our whole sentences (whether or not we could ever know what this distribution is). But only interpreted sentences can have a truth-value. So we should say

> WDT1. The world determines truth iff, given the way(s) the world is, for each interpretation of our language there is one and only one way the truth-values can be distributed over our whole sentences as thus interpreted.[2]

This formulation (by John Post) need not be unacceptable to so-called anti-realists (in Michael Dummett's sense of anti-realism). (Dummett himself, of course, is an anti-realist in the sense of opposing "verification-transcendent truth"; but he is also a realist in the sense in which anti-realism would be entirely content to adopt something like Post's formulation.[3]) Anti-realists appear to be obliged neither to revise classical logic (as Dummett believes) nor to subscribe to all of it (for instance, to the law of excluded middle) – *qua* anti-realists.[4] We should also notice, reviewing Post's formulation, that

1 theorizing, as it does, about how "the world" (or reality) affects the realist relationship, Post's formulation is entirely (and rightly) unconcerned about epistemic (*a fortiori*, anti-realist) complications;
2 it is, therefore, entirely unaffected by disputes about vagueness, interpretation, cognitive privilege, or even the range of truth-values or truth-like values that may be assigned statements and other entities that take truth-values;
3 it presupposes but does not supply a theory about what the nature of reality must be in order for WDT1 to obtain; and
4 it does at least, as far as the issue raised by item 3 is concerned, draw out a distributive consequence regarding truth-values from what must be a holist (or global or undistributed) constraint imposed on any suitable answer to 3.

To the question of what, in his account, we should understand by "determination," Post answers straightforwardly enough that "When we say one thing determines another, we mean merely that given the way the first is [causally or noncausally (say, logically), or in any other admissible way], there is one and only one way the second can be."[5] And to the question of what we should understand by "a world," Post answers that "We may construe a [possible] world W as a structured domain, namely a triple $\langle D, P, R \rangle$ where D is the set of W's entities, P is the set of their genuine properties, and R is the set of their relations."[6]

We must bear in mind that Post is here attempting to capture the minimal, relatively uncontroversial, distinctly intuitive, essentially ubiquitous sense of what *realism* entails and of how *reality affects the realist relationship*.

Nevertheless, there are at least two telltale qualifications that Post here insinuates – that he does not pursue in context – that suggest that his notion (as applied to the actual world) may be much more partisan and more complex than he himself supposes. For one thing, in explicating the expression "a world," Post insouciantly characterizes the introduced triple as collecting the "*genuine*" properties and relations of the entities of that world (and, one supposes, therefore, the "genuine" entities of that world – *a fortiori*, of the actual world). For another, in a note clarifying his intended usage, he adds that "The properties and relations are to be construed extensionally."[7] Now, it looks as if Post must mean that the real or actual world must be such that all its entities, properties, and relations are "there," crisp enough in a mind-independent sense, that there are no "structured" indeterminacies among such items such that the determination thesis would be false or would not hold (though there may be indeterminacies of other sorts – vaguenesses, for instance) for at least part of whatever is *in* the actual world; secondly, that at least properties and relations are so crisp, in this regard, that they may, with assurance, be said to behave extensionally. Both claims, however, *may be quite false*. It is even intuitively clear why they may be false.

Suppose, for example, that a sculpture, Michelangelo's *Pietà*, is a real entity in our world, has real properties and enters into real relationships; and suppose that among its properties is the property of representing the mourning of Christ's death. It is not clear that that property behaves extensionally though it be a "genuine" property; and it is not clear that, if it is a genuine property, there cannot be certain "structural indeterminacies" in the very nature of the sculpture that possesses it (*not* regarding any cognitive difficulties *we* may have in discerning what it is, as with vagueness) *in virtue of which WDT1 is false*. The *Pietà* may, for instance, be such that the full meaning of its real representational property (its *real* content) *can only be imputed to it – is real but not crisply "there" for discovery* (determinately, or even in the way baldness may be said to be) – *for ontological, not epistemological, reasons.* There is no compelling *a priori* reason for precluding such a possibility. There is no way to settle the matter without a detailed account of the actual nature of our world. There are very good reasons for supposing that the world of human culture at least – chiefly, persons, artifacts, artworks, words and sentences, actions, institutions, and the like – *are* ontologically affected, as the real phenomena they are, in the manner just sketched. Post is unaccountably silent on the matter. Furthermore, if this much be conceded, then, on the argument that the physical or natural world is itself (in one sense, though not in another) an artifact internally posited only within the symbiotized cognitive space of a realist science (rejecting all forms of transparency and privilege), the determination thesis may (arguably) also be adversely affected by an extension of the same concession.

To say this much is *not* to retreat from ontological to (merely) epistemological issues: it is, rather, to complicate considerably the very question of what we could possibly mean in speaking of "a structured domain" (in Post's sense) in any sense in which *distributed structures* – however realist in the "mind-independent" way – could be ontologically assigned, except as structures artifactually *dependent* on (*not* "determined" by) the symbiosis (the *Lebenswelt*) of cognized world and cognizing agent.

On a theory according to which the distributed structures of the mind-independent world are posits (however reasonably made) drawn from the world-as-cognized, from a world in which realist and idealist elements cannot be disjoined in principle,[8] Post's assumption cannot but appear tendentious and completely unguarded. Also, the theory is peculiarly hospitable to a *realist* ontology of cultural entities and phenomena that holds that such entities do have structures incompatible with Posts's formulation, structures of such a sort that one can only (and because of that, is thereby invited to) impute – say, within the practice of familiar interpretive traditions – the *real* intentional import of this or that property (representing the mourning of Christ's death, let us say) in ways that cannot be squared with the principle of excluded middle (and *that*, not merely for epistemological reasons). The thesis is at least eligible – is in fact coherent and quite reasonable.[9]

We are, of course, hardly entitled to draw the findings indicated without an argument; but we *are* entitled to challenge Post's intuition about minimal realism. The truth is that a genuinely minimal realism says no more than

(a)   that there are real physical or natural phenomena that exist or obtain mind-independently;

(b)   that there are, or at least may be, real cultural phenomena that, though they cannot exist entirely "mind-independently," do exist in a way that depends on the reality and real efficacy of persons and in a way that is relatively mind-independent of any particular persons taken distributively;

(c)   that human inquirers are related to the real world in such a way that they are capable of discerning a significant range of its entities and their properties and relations.

Items (a)–(c), however, are completely *holist* assumptions, without the least distributed import of the sort Post insists on. It must surely be obvious, therefore, that, in (a)–(c), we have a leaner conception of minimal realism than Post's WDT1 or the thesis of determination. It is but a step to grasp that what we choose to favor in our theory of the range of truth-values applied to what we may claim regarding the world (in the realist sense – in a sense reasonably thought to be shared by Post and Dummett, say) cannot but be strategically affected by our theory of *reality* itself – which, after all, enters into the realist "relationship." That is just the point of the *Pietà* example. It is also the knockdown reason why Michael Dummett, for instance, may be charged, *on* anti-realist grounds, with having failed to vindicate his own thesis of *tertium non datur* while giving by bivalence.[10] The point of crucial importance here is simply that questions regarding the logic of inquiry, the presumptions of realism, and the structure of reality are ineluctably interrelated and cannot be separately managed. Post's otherwise elegant proposal is simply a victim of not having sufficiently attended to the complexity of this important triad – just as the *a priori* repudiation of all forms of relativism may mislead us (certainly cannot be expected to settle essential questions) about the actual structure and nature of the real world.

We have, in effect, just laid the ground for a sympathetic review of the onto-logical peculiarities of the world of human culture. There are no good arguments for denying the reality of human persons; and there are no convincing arguments for denying the reality of the entire cultural world if we admit the reality of persons – particularly if, as is reasonable, persons are them-selves seen to emerge and exist only within a cultural space.[11] But, of course, *if* cultural phenomena – especially persons – are part of *reality* in as robust a sense as are physical or natural phenomena, then there cannot be, even in prin-ciple, a disjunction between a fully "mind-independent" sector of reality reserved for cultural phenomena (as there may be for physical phenomena) and the symbiotized *Lebenswelt* within which both sectors are defined. Both the reality of culture and the realism of a science of culture require an entirely dif-ferent characterization. Once we admit that much, there remains no prior reason for thinking that our ontological and epistemological models addressed to the *physical* phenomena of the principal natural sciences must, or are even likely to, be adequate or suitable for *cultural* phenomena. After all, on the sketch provided, *cultural phenomena may exhibit properties that cannot be described, explained, or even located in a purely physical space; as a result, such properties may not be able to be characterized in just the way in which our intu-ition about the reality of the physical world seems to be characterizable.* It would be preposterous to insist on the privilege of our physicalist models (Post's, for instance) if we conceded what our mere musing on the *Pietà* has already ob-liged us to consider. At a stroke, therefore, we can grasp the essential weakness of Post's very attractive attempt to convey the plausibility of our sense of re-ality – and of its "determination" of truth – by way of the following (his) intu-ition regarding the "can" of WDT1:

> WDT2. The world determines truth iff, given the world and given any other world that is relevantly similar, under each interpretation the same sentences have the same truth-values in both.[12]

The fact is that, on the argument already provided, it may well be the case that, in interpreting the *real* representational property of the *Pietà* – that is, in trying to fix the real (interpreted) content of the *Pietà* – it proves impossible to do so, for *ontological* reasons, in a way that, in principle, would never countenance violating WDT2 in *realist* terms. There you have the essential challenge of acknowledging the world of human culture and the reason, of course, for the zealous multiplication of all those familiar efforts to exorcise the "folk" world of physics as well as of art and politics. The reduction or elimination (or at least the "regimentation") of the cultural world in terms congenial to our developing picture of the physical world (the point of WDT2) would, if it could have worked, have made things extremely tidy. We need, however, to examine much more closely why such exorcisms are unconvincing and what, if anything, would actually be the conceptual price of acknowledging the full reality of the cultural world.

I

Culture may be metaphorically identified as the space proper to persons, artworks, language, history, institutions, civilizations, states, ideologies, myths, and deeds. In saying that, one signifies that the phenomena of these remarkably varied sorts have much in common that distinguishes them from merely physical or natural phenomena. They have in common whatever demarcates the cultural, and they obtain only in contexts formed by related phenomena. Artworks, for example, are produced by persons; persons are whatever they are, not without some aggregative sharing of language; and the histories of political states are projections of some kind that depend on the deeds of ideologically linked individuals. These are the commonplaces of what is common to the phenomena of culture. They are not as such systematically instructive; for, although they collect what is relevant, their explicitness does not touch as yet on the principle of cultural space itself. Nevertheless, the indirection is an economy. It permits us to sort, in a naive way, certain salient clues about the testing of any would-be analysis of the cultural, that might otherwise easily be lost in its own complexities.

Two such clues are particularly instructive. They are connected with one another by the same strategy. In one, we must consider what results (by way of example) from impoverishing our conception of artworks and artifacts relative to a rich account of agents competent to produce them – that is, persons; and in the other, we must consider what results from impoverishing our conception of persons, the primary bearers and agents of culture. If we pursue these strategies, what we discover are relatively, or provisionally, compelling constraints by which to guide our speculations about the ontology of artworks and artifacts and persons or of cultural entities and phenomena in general. We may anticipate that it is bound to be quarrelsome to hold that we have discovered the necessary, or necessary and sufficient, or essential, or universal, marks of the cultural. There may be alternative, nonconverging, even incompatible findings that these thought-experiments will yield. Nevertheless, we gain thereby a sense of at least provisional restrictions hovering between strongly general, salient, characteristic, but perhaps not binding, regularities and more sanguine projections aspiring to the essential and the universal. Dialectically, to achieve even this much would be an enormous simplification of our task – one in fact that could well afford to leave unresolved the deeper question of the possible powers of historicized inquiries, begun somehow in the middle of things, to discern and to know that regularities have been discerned that are confirmably universal in scope. (Any retreat, in fact, from resolving the "deeper" question cannot fail to affect adversely arguments meant to support anything like Post's WDT1 and WDT2 – though it will do so via epistemological doubts.)

Turning to tableaux directed to the first clue, we may take it that any impoverishment of the concept of an artwork (perhaps the most complex order of artifacts) will be served by treating all or as many as we wish of the usual attributions made of artworks as mere imputations made of objects otherwise conceptually indistinguishable from non-artworks. For example, a stone that, *qua* stone, may be supposed to be suitably and completely described in terms of a certain range of physical properties, may, in the spirit of the impoverishing strategy, be said to be imputed, but not to possess, as a property intrinsic or proper to itself, a certain sacred power. It "has" the power only in the deriva-tive sense that, on the basis of certain *relations* holding between the physical stone and suitably endowed persons – and featuring the intentional states of those persons (for instance, a certain imaginative interest) coloring that relation – the stone is thereupon treated as if the power imputed was an intrin-sic attribute not thus dependent. The difference, then, between a skeptical view of the stone's power and the belief of a convinced believer is, in an important sense, ontological: there is a conceptual difference between them regarding the real structure of the attribute the shared predicate is thought to designate. Cor-respondingly, we may construe (or at least attempt to construe) the attributes of artworks, for example the property that Michelangelo's *Pietà* has of representing the mourning of Christ's death, as no more than an attribute intentionally projected onto a certain chunk of marble and thereupon treated logically *as if* it were an intrinsic or proper attribute of *that piece of marble*, which (on the hypothesis) it is not.[13] (One should begin, here, with a variety of objects – for example, with stones that remain absolutely untouched by human hands but are "functionally" assigned or imputed sacred power, and then move, say, to something like the monumental stone slabs of Chaco Canyon, in New Mexico, somewhat tooled and adjusted, functioning as the equipment of an Anasazi observatory, and move then to something like Michelangelo's *Pietà*.[14])

Even these homely examples are most complicated. Let us proceed naively. We are supposing that persons are so endowed that *they* are capable of working the marble in the manner of making a sculpture like the *Pietà* and of treating the marble thus worked as if, on the basis of their own rich intentional life, *it* posssessed as intrinsic or proper attributes of itself (*qua* chunk of marble), properties merely imputed to it because of the imaginative or intentional re-lationship holding between particular persons and that particular piece of marble. The marble could not be said to possess the property of representing the mourning of Christ's death in virtue only, or without reference to more than any, or all, of its merely physical properties. Its possessing the representational property must depend in some way on the intrinsic powers of human persons and (merely amplifying what we should mean by such powers) on the history of its creation and social reception: whether it is said to have that property intrinsically (for instance, *qua Pietà* – that is, because it *is* a sculpture, an artwork, and not merely a physical block of marble) or whether it is said to possess the property only by way of the complex parasitic imputation we are entertaining here in accord with the impoverishing strategy. Even Alberti's technique of seeing images in the materials of nature requires the concession.

Richard Wollheim, worrying the same – or a closely related – question is strongly attracted to what he calls the "physical-object hypothesis," for paintings and sculptures but not for literature and music. He has some misgivings, for instance about representational and expressive properties, but these are somewhat wrongly directed (by Wollheim) to the supposed "incompatibility of property between works of art and physical objects" or to the supposed need to save so-called "aesthetic" properties of artworks,[15] whereas the critical problem concerns a certain puzzle of what may be called *adequation* – that is, the conceptual congruity or fit between *being a thing of a certain kind or nature* with respect to which it is individuated as the thing it is and, as such, *being capable of possessing as intrinsic or proper attributes of itself such and such properties.* Anything that may be mentioned may, by way of an interest persons take in it, be imputed properties treated as intrinsic to it that are thus ascribed parasitically because and only because of that interest or intentional relation. Thus, a mere stone may be ascribed sacred powers because *we* believe it to have those powers. On the argument, imputing the imputable property presupposes that persons themselves do possess intrinsic properties suitably congruent with (adequate for) *that* imputation, whether or not the object to which it is imputed also possesses suitably congruent intrinsic properties. In short, the first impoverishing strategy appears to work, at first glance, because and only because, although there is a failure of adequation between the intrinsic properties of the merely physical object and those imputed to it as an artwork, *the property of the property's being thus imputed* as well as the property thus imputed *are* (one supposes) adequated to the intrinsic properties or powers of the persons who presumably either make artworks or treat particular objects as if they were artworks possessing properties such as that of representing the dead Christ or of expressing a certain attitude toward Christ's death. (The notion of adequation, here, is not of course that of the familiar account of truth but rather that of what may be called ontic coherence or sufficiency – rescued, so to say, from the doctrine of the gradation of being. It will need to be explicated.)

The minimal sense of what, for natural and culturally specified particulars, could be an intrinsic or proper attribute of such particulars is simply this:

(i)   that particulars are individuated as being of this or that kind or nature;

(ii)   that properties ascribed to particular things in virtue only of being of that kind or having that nature are said to be *intrinsic* or *proper* attributes of such particulars;

(iii)   that such ascriptions are, as such, specified only formally – that is, in a way as yet indifferent to whatever specifically and actually *there is* in the world (indifferent to what may belong "within reality");

(iv)   that whatever properties are contingently ascribed to particulars thus individuated must, if also taken as intrinsic or proper to those particulars – hence, not merely in virtue of their being particulars of given kinds – be suitably and conceptually congruent (adequated) with whatever is intrinsic or proper to such kinds;

(v)   that no relational properties involving distinct particulars are as such intrinsic or proper attributes of those particulars; and

(vi)   that, insofar as the explanation of any of the effects, states, processes, relations, and the like involving given particulars depends on the behavior or condition of those particulars, such explanation must be made in terms of the intrinsic properties of those same particulars.

(It may be unnecessary but still useful to intrude the thought that these six distinctions may be viewed either naturalistically or phenomenologically, either ontically or eidetically, provided only we accept the thesis "naturalism = phenomenology" and its supporting arguments.[16] That is, the invariances will hold only as reasonable *saliences* within a phenomenologized naturalism or a naturalized phenomenology – and are certainly subject to pluralistic and relativistic readings.)

On the impoverishing strategy, representational and expressive properties cannot be proper or intrinsic properties of artworks *if* discourse about artworks is always and only (as we are hypothesizing) discourse about physical objects the intrinsic properties of which are all and only physical properties. There is one *caveat* of course: if, by some argument, the *predicates* for representational and expressive (and similar) properties could always be fairly translated, paraphrased, replaced, or eliminated – preserving something of the point of the original discourse – then the impoverishing strategy would not actually be impoverishing; *or*, more subtly, if the would-be intrinsic *properties* of artworks, initially introduced by *predicates* that are not physical predicates could be replaced in principle if not in actual practice here and now by physical predicates (without a reductive or eliminative reading), then the impoverishing strategy would not actually be impoverishing. The point of the strategy is to attempt to account for ascriptions made of particular objects that, though treated as if they were intrinsic to those objects, are actually not (for instance, saying of a mere block of marble that it represents the mourning of Christ's death). The strategy is impoverishing because no adequation (in the sense given) obtains; but it is viable nevertheless, both because of a compensationg adequation involving persons who make the required imputations (hence, because relations between the two do not exceed, in terms of conceivability, what the separate instances of adequation would jointly support) and because, one supposes, the discourse developed is otherwise internally coherent.

The issue is quite complex. Once again, Post is instructive (though, again, contrary to his own purpose). He introduces the slogan "No difference without a physical difference" in the context of reviewing Quine's so called "Full Coverage Principle."[17] He quite reasonably rejects what he calls the "Reductive Discernibility Principle" – which, in effect, corresponds to the first version of the *caveat* mentioned just above:

> RD. If there is a distinction between x and y expressible by terms from some domain, then there are terms solely from physics which express that same distinction.[18]

But he does introduce – and subscribe to – what he calls the "Modal Nonreductive Discernibility Principle":

> MND. For any P-world W [that is, for any physically possible world W], if x and y are N-discernible in W [that is, are discernible by the use of "non-physical" predicates, not yet otherwise specified], then they are [in the modal sense] P-discernible in W.[19]

This gives, Post feels, a defensible *and adequate* nonreductive account of "No difference without a physical difference" that accords with his own notion of a "minimal" nonreductive physicalism and that accommodates the emergent phenomena of the cultural world. It is, we may say, also, the painful pivot of a puzzle Goodman had introduced and memorably addressed and had never quite satisfactorily resolved: namely, the puzzle of forgeries in art (and elsewhere). Of an original, apparently indiscernible forgery, Goodman observes,

> Although I see no difference now between the two pictures in question, I may learn to see a difference between them. I cannot determine now by merely looking at them, or in any other way, that I *shall* be able to learn. But the information that they are very different, that the one is the original and the other the forgery, argues against any inference to the conclusion that I *shall not* be able to learn. And the fact that I may later be able to make a perceptual distinction between the pictures that I cannot make now constitutes an aesthetic difference between them that is important to me now.[20]

The matter is quite complicated, in ways that are irrelevant for our present purpose. But it is certainly clear (and reasonable) that one may never be able to make a *perceptual* (that is, narrowly, a sensory or sensorily perceptual) distinction between the original and the forgery that relevantly bears on their being "original" and "forgery"; and similarly, one may never be able to make a *physical* distinction that would be relevant to the distinction in question; *and*, Goodman pretty well admits this but is uncomfortable with the fact.[21]

Furthermore, in a way that is more interesting and more challenging than is Goodman's view, Arthur Danto has pretty nearly deluged his readership with all sorts of ingenious examples involving artworks and natural objects that are not artworks, or artworks and other artifacts that are not artworks, the differences between which are perceptually and physically indiscernible in *demarcating artworks and natural objects and artifacts that are not artworks*.[22] Goodman had fiddled uncompellingly but suggestively with the contrast between individuative strategies for artworks based on historical considerations (history of production, for instance: "autographic" marks, in Goodman's terminology) and strategies based on notational compliance of given artworks (as in different pianists performing one and the same musical composition: "allographic" marks.).[23] Danto, on the other hand, frankly embraces the formula "To see something as art requires something the eye cannot *decry* – an atmosphere of artistic theory, a knowledge of the history of art: an artworld."[24] Danto's considerable body of work on the peculiarities of contemporary art shows, conclusively, both the plausibility and coherence of introducing what, in effect, are *intentionally complex considerations* relevant to the individuation and discernibility of art *and* the incapacity of Post's MND to accommodate such distinctions. There are many other such puzzles that could be mentioned that the history of art would readily support; but these are enough to show the difficulty of any *physicalist* account of reality, of however attenuated, guarded, non-reductive, and skillful a sort we may imagine.[25] (Certainly, Post is most skillful in meeting any number of objections to a supple physicalism, generated by phenomena that are not culturally complex.)

Troublesomely, the conclusion begins to loom that there may only be *intentionally complex* grounds – involving theories, paradigms, frames of reference, histories, and ontologies diverging from those of the physical world (if even that much need be conceded) – in accord with which cultural phenomena may be discerned. *Nothing* Post says shows the slightest reason to discount that possibility. Furthermore, on the concession indicated, it may well be that the properties ascribed to *one and the same artwork*, say, may not (and need not at all) be discernible in a way that Post's WDT1 and WDT2 would require or accommodate. This would be the case, for instance, if a relativism with regard to the interpretation of artworks were ontologically grounded.[26] Of course, we have been treating artworks, here, as a convenient metonym for the whole of human culture; and we have hardly conceded that our physical science is not a part of that culture or (therefore) not infected with the same conceptual poison that infects the world of art and action.

There is an obvious implausibility in supposing that there just *are* no artworks, no objects possessing as intrinsic properties representational, expressive, symbolic, stylistic, genre, intentional, significative, historical, or otherwise semiotic properties. This may seem a blackmail argument; and in a way it is. But its objection is not a pointless one, in the sense that discourse about and interest in art – in making paintings, collecting them, putting them on view, writing and speaking about them, buying them, instituting laws governing their status as property, as well as our entire emotional and intellectual involvement with them – is difficult to reconcile with the thesis, *intended in a realist sense*, that those properties putatively intrinsic to artworks are all and only parasitically so imputed, only projections from the real states and condition of interested persons and from their relations with pertinently impoverished objects. On the impoverishing strategy, we are restricted, as it were, to predicates merely masquerading as designating the real or intrinsic properties of artworks – by way perhaps of imagination, fiction, *façon de parler*, heuristic convenience, assignment of ulterior function or role, or something of the sort. The blackmail argument is hardly conclusive. But it must remind us of Locke's thesis that the concept of a person is the concept of something more fundamental (a self, a center of consciousness) that thereupon functions "forensically" as a person only by being treated *in addition* in terms of responsibility and law; or it may remind us of the extreme worry of Wilfrid Sellars's remarkably influential thesis: to speak of something as a person "is not to *describe* him as one might describe a scientific specimen . . . one does something more . . . . It is not to *classify* or *explain*, but to *rehearse* an *intention* . . . . The conceptual framework of persons is not something that needs to be *reconciled with* the scientific image, but rather something to be *joined* to it" as a functional but not for that reason a realist addition.[27]

II

Here we begin to see the close connection between the two forms of impoverishing strategy. For what, relative to real persons, may be attempted with regard to artworks, may also be attempted with regard to persons.

The first version of the strategy seemed promising only because we admitted suitably richly endowed persons; but the second may prove to be a remarkably radical strategy, since, being deprived of the usual forms of adequation accorded to persons, it may have to favor some further reductive strategy – by way of translation, equivalence of truth-value, theoretically legitimated successor theories, or ultimate elimination of an allegedly outmoded "folk" idiom of persons.[28] The crucial consideration here (to which we shall return shortly) is that the first version of the strategy in question is not strongly reductive or eliminative, in the sense that it ignores the question with respect to persons. But the second version would be reductive or eliminative, unless it could be shown (as Post, for instance, believes it can be) that whatever is culturally emergent may be reconciled with a minimal physicalism.

We can afford to be a bit informal here, since, on the argument sketched, we are taking it as likely that no physicalism will do. Post neatly specifies what the "minimal physicalist principles" are. Roughly, they include principles MND (which we have already examined); TT, which runs

TT.   Given any two P-worlds [physically possible worlds], if the same P-sentences are true in both, then the same N-sentences [sentences employing non-physical predicates, as yet otherwise unspecified] are true in both[;][29]

and what Post identifies as INV (or some variant of same) – that is (cobbling Post's account a little), that everything is a spatiotemporal entity or part of a spatiotemporal entity included in a set that "satisf[ies] a positive predicate on the list [drawn] from [current] physics [or from what would correct and complete our physics], or else [it is an entity included in a set that is 'built on a ground level of concrete physical entities' of the sort mentioned in the first clause]."[30] In effect, our objections to MND apply to TT with equal force, particularly since TT is identified by Post as "the principle of the determination of all truth by P-truth" and since Post is disposed to treat his determination thesis in such a way that "the world determines not only physical truth but also whether it is true that physical truth determines all truth [TT]."[31] INV is meant only as an "Inventory Principle," identifying as carefully as one can the range of entities that a (minimal) physicalist (who is not a reductionist or eliminationist) would be willing to countenance. For our purposes, then, no refinement of INV is likely to make the slightest difference to the failure of the physicalist program, simply because it never addresses the peculiar nature and properties of the culturally emergent entities *that it does not intend to ignore or mischaracterize.* (It is perhaps worth remarking that the rejection of *physicalism*, even in the attenuated form Post intends, is not tantamount to the rejection of *materialism.* On the contrary, it is just the conceptual treatment of emergent cultural phenomena that spells the difference between Post's physicalism and the nonreductive materialism here intended.[32] That is, by *physicalism* we may understand any theory that subscribes to Post's [nonreductive] formula MND, or to any more strenuous formula of a similar sort – type- or token-identity, eliminationism, or "successor" theories [in Sellar's sense]. By *materialism*, by contrast, we may understand any theory [including physicalism] that holds that whatever entities are actual, whatever really exist in the world, are composed of, or essentially depend on what are composed of, matter only. Hence, the materialist, but not the physicalist, can admit that the structures and properties of what is actual, as distinct from the compositional material or "stuff" of actual things, may not be able to be captured by physical predicates – whether by paraphrase or near-paraphrase or extensional equivalence or near-equivalence. The analysis of ultimate matter may be left empirically open.)

There are two elementary objections to the first impoverishing strategy: first, insofar as we speak at all of real particulars, we are disposed (at least saliently) to treat as real whatever we perceive or make or move or deliberately change

– or, in doing that, talk about, analyze, invest our energies and interests and feelings in; second, if, by the first objection, we do admit artworks as real or as real particulars (though, to be candid, there are deep puzzles about the individuation of artworks[33]), then whatever we should admit as the intrinsic properties of such entities could not be specified by drawing only on whatever properties are intrinsic to mere physical objects – unless of course the *caveats* mentioned earlier on obtained. So, at least provisionally, short of some reductive materialism or similar doctrine, the impoverishing strategy cannot be expected to make a good case for the parasitic idiom we have been trying to test. If persons are real, then the salient phenomena of their world are real.

Artworks are normally individuated as being of a kind that would permit intentional, purposive, semiotic, representational, expressive and similar *intrinsic* properties; and these appear to require an idiom of a culturally developed sort that simply does not lend itself perspicuously to their being reduced to mere physical properties. Notice, for instance, that it is characteristically claimed by the partisans of physicalist reduction – for example, Donald Davidson[34] – that the physical world is homonomic: that is, that physical phenomena are describable and explicable adequately and solely in terms of purely physical properties and physical laws. David Lewis has put the point in an admirably candid form: "We who accept the materialistic working hypothesis," he says, hold "that physical phenomena have none but purely physical explanations."[35] This suggests an important part of the motivation for both forms of the impoverishing strategy. For, *if* artworks and persons are not suitably reducible, then, if they enter into causally efficacious relations, the homonomic character of the physical world will have been decisively breached. Culture, in short, may well affect nature – without that fact itself being explicable solely in physical terms. The gathering argument is reasonably clear:

1   if cultural phenomena are emergent (emergent$_M$, in an idiom developed elsewhere[36]), emergent in a sense not expressible in physical terms suited to the description and explanation of physical phenomena, then cultural phenomena cannot be conceptually captured within the nomological net of the physical world;

2   if such phenomena are causally efficacious (as they plainly appear to be) in virtue of their cultural attributes, then even the physical world cannot be causally homonomic, and causality cannot be taken to entail nomologicality;[37]

3   if cultural phenomena are real, under conditions 1 and 2, then physicalism (both reductive and nonreductive) is false *sans phrase*, and both cultural entities and cultural attributes require a distinctive ontological account; and,

4   if conditions 1–3 obtain, then the human sciences cannot fail to be top-down disciplines.[38]

The conceptual landscape may be taken in at a glance, but its vista is breathtaking.

There are, correspondingly, two elementary objections to the second impoverishing strategy: first, the reduction of persons in terms favorable to the supposed closure of the physical sciences normally ignores the fact that the activity of reduction must itself be explained, that persons are at once objects to be reduced as well as skilled agents pursuing that reduction, that science itself is a culturally significant enterprise; second, the admission of the reality of human language, art, political history, and the like entails the admission of entities apt for being the primary agents making, using, and affecting whatever belongs within those very large categories of cultural phenomena. Yet, when Sellars, for example, promotes the "scientific image" against the "manifest image," he say, "To complete the scientific image *we* need to enrich it *not* with more ways of saying what is the case [that is, not with ways of treating discourse about persons as discourse saying what is the case], but with the language of community and individual intentions [that is, with a merely *nonrealist* way of heuristically assigning or imputing further functions to whatever is real]."[39] In a similar spirit, another popular analytic theorist, Daniel Dennett, declares, "The personal story . . . has a relatively vulnerable and impermanent place in our conceptual scheme, and could in principle be rendered 'obsolete' if some day *we* ceased to *treat* anything (any mobile body or system or device) as an Intentional system – by reasoning with it, communicating with it, etc."[40] On the other hand, there is at the present time no known way and no prospect of describing and explaining even the phenomenon of natural language in purely physicalistic terms or in any terms that could genuinely be called sub- or prelinguistic. It would be philosophically irresponsible in the highest degree to suppose that language and the linguistic behavior of humans were not part of whatever may be construed, however economically, as actual or real – whatever felicitous analysis we may recommend.

There is, in fact, an indefeasible symbiosis between the concept of a person and the concept of the phenomena of culture. Persons are the primary agents who use and make and affect changes in language, art, history, and the like – they are the primary bearers of culture; in fact, they function *as* such agents *because* they have, possess, understand, and learn how to use language, traditions, practices, institutions that, as the agents they are, they do not actually make or institute *from a condition originally deprived of such resources.* They are and function as cultural agents because they are the bearers of cultural powers: they possess the requisite properties.[41] The formula is, plainly, a version of the adequation thesis. If this were not so, then, indeed, the impoverishing strategy would be the correct one; for it would then be possible and necessary to account for the emergence of cultural phenomena in terms of a vocabulary restricted to the sub-cultural. (We still owe an argument if we are to meet the challenge of a nonreductive physicalism of Post's sort.)

This is an instructive but most mysterious finding. Because it is reasonable to suppose that the complexities of cultural life do emerge in some natural way from a precultural world. Nevertheless, given the irreducibility of language, its reality, and its apparent function as the *sine qua non* and very paradigm of the cultural, the explanation of its own emergence cannot but be a reflexive artifact that already and always presupposes its own (*sui generis*) attributes; hence, its explanation is peculiarly speculative in the same sense in which Jean Piaget's studies of the genetic epistemology of *pre*linguistic infants is speculative, though not therefore without interest. In short, attempts at explaining the emegence of the culturally complex *reflexively* concede the cultural, and then speculate on what *could have led* to *its* emergence from simpler, sub-cultural or *pre*cultural phenomena; but no attempt can be made that will not prove reductive that shows that the cultural is actually *not* conceptually more complex than the domain from which it emerges. Thus, the explanation of the cultural in terms suitable to the explanatory models favored in the physical sciences must ultimately invoke the impoverishing strategy, because otherwise there is no way to ensure the closure of physical nature and the homonomic nature of physical laws. If one sees the matter rightly, then one sees that the thesis is really nothing more than an indirectly focused formulation of the so-called hermeneutic circle and of the contrast between the natural and the human sciences. That is, *any* attempt to explain how cultural phenomena emerge from the physical world, in the sense in which the intended account must confine itself to whatever (however generously) may be *first* identified as the actual range of entities of the physical world – for instance, in a way that accords with something like Post's INV – cannot fail to be reductive: it cannot, for the very simple reason that, even if we suppose cultural emergence to depend, in a critically enabling sense, on the processes of physical or biological emergence, particular instances of the first cannot be adequately explained on the basis only of the causal powers of the second. On the hypothesis,

(a)   discernible differences of a cultural sort need not be matched by discernible differences of a physical sort;

(b)   where there are no discernible cultural differences among numerically distinct cultural phenomena, we cannot preclude discernible physical differences critical to the actual occurrence of the other; and

(c)   in general, we cannot discern culturally relevant phenomena solely on the basis of mere physical criteria.

To offer the barest illustration of these charges (partly collecting what has already been said): (a) may be exemplified by the difference between an original and a forged oil painting; (b) may be exemplified by making precisely the same chess move in moving a pawn with one's left hand or right hand; and (c) may be exemplified by the fact that we cannot tell conversationally (think of the Chinese Room puzzle) whether someone's uttering a string of sounds that normally would be uttered in using Chinese sentences signifies that the utterer does or does not understand Chinese.[42] (These are not crude cases, though they are not presented here in a particularly careful way.)

It may be helpful to mention that Herbert Feigl, hoping to formulate a reductive physicalism that would prove empirically reasonable, was, throughout his career, candidly worried about what he called the "many-many" problem.[43] By this he meant a doctrine very close to what we have collected as (a)–(c). For, on Feigl's view, it might well be (though *he* did not believe it true) that, for any physical predicable, there could be indefinitely many psychological predicables "associated" or (even) "correlated" (as Feigl would say, somewhat loosely) with it that, because there was no principled (or nomological) connection between the one and the other, could not be systematically determined or collected by reference to that physical predicable; and that, for any psychological predicable, there could be indefinitely many physical predicables similarly associated that could not be systematically determined or collected by reference to that psychological predicable. The "many-many" problem is, plainly, the decisive empirical difficulty confronting all versions of physicalism, both reductive and nonreductive.

Also, of course, *if* the many-many problem cannot be resolved in a way favorable to physicalism, *if* the intentional complexities of culture cannot be managed extensionally, and *if* (in addition) the complexities of culture (the complexities of representation, expression, meaning, signification, purpose, intention) are such that, although robustly real, they cannot in principle be (or always be) uniquely determined,[44] then the ontology of culture itself provides an ineluctable rationale for supporting a relativistic account of valid truth-claims.[45]

There is only one possible line of solution to the irreducibility issue. The phenomena to be explained (for instance, in explaining the emergence of language – by linguistic means) impose a conceptual barrier below which we cannot see how to go, if we mean to identify and explain (within our present resources, possibly within any improved resources) the very phenomena in question.

No doubt there are many things we suppose exhibit such a pattern but are simply mistaken about: it is possible, for instance, that the manic-depressive syndrome, elaborated in florid psychodynamic terms, may (in a certain sense) prove to be pertinently characterizable (etiologically) in terms of a certain biochemical imbalance; and we may suppose that *many* quite complex phenomena will, in time, yield to that sort of reformulation. *But language, culture, history, artworks, persons, institutions, actions are simply not mere details of such a sort.* *Their* emergence, explained in a manner congenial to the program of the "minimal physicalist," *would* be profoundly reductive (even though Post – whom we have been stalking somewhat mercilessly albeit with respect – has no intention of being reductive), in the perfectly straightforward sense that it *would deny that the properties intrinsic to cultural phenomena are not discernible in physical terms* (even if they are not, when applied in Post's sense, applied in any canonically reductive ways: by translation, say, or by extensional equivalence or by succession or the like). Let us say that failure to meet the conditions of emergence in the physicalist sense (what, in effect, violates the rule of emergence favored by the unity-of-science program or its near-analogues[46]) constitutes *conceptual discontinuity*.

On the theory here favored, then, cultural emergence need not be "ontologically" discontinuous with respect to the physical or natural order of real things, but it is "conceptually" discontinuous: in the sense (1) that there is no reason to believe that there are any causal discontinuities between the emergence of biological phenomena and the emergence of cultural phenomena, and (2) that the explanation of the emergence or causal generation of cultural phenomena can, at least, because of the conceptual interference involved, only be managed *top-down* – that is, by first admitting the phenomena in question or the conceptual resources adequate for identifying those phenomena – which, by hypothesis, we take it cannot be described, "determined" (in Post's sense), "discerned" (again, in Post's physicalist sense), or causally explained in merely physical terms. The explanation of their causal generation and emergence will, in principle, already make reference *to an order of real cultural phenomena*. The thesis is entirely coherent, eligible, and even plausible. It is, in fact, in agreement (thus far) with one of Jerry Fodor's very perceptive observations:

> Any psychology must attribute some endogenous structure to the mind (really unstructured objects – bricks, say – don't have beliefs and desires and they don't learn things). And it's hard to see how, in the course of making such attributions of endogenous structure, the theory could fail to imply some constraints on the class of beliefs that the mind can entertain.[47]

Generalize Fodor's charge so that it applies to the very activity of theorizing about what an adequate psychology might include, and, in making the thesis reflexive, construe that thesis as entailing an *ontological* limitation implicated in whatever is really involved in exercising our theorizing power – you will have admitted the plausibility of top-down accounts of (cultural) emergence and causality.[48] Doubtless, if such a condition obtained, it would affect in the most profound and fundamental way our notion of the norms of reasonable explanatory practice in the sciences. But why should we deny its likelihood?

It is important, however, to realize that, although individual persons are primary agents and bearers of cultural process – in the plain sense that they alone possess the required intrinsic properties: intention, purpose, intelligence, cognitive power, desire, interest and the like – the description and explanation of cultural phenomena need not, and cannot actually, be formulated solely in terms of the intentional activities or real powers and properties of such persons. This is, of course, the famous puzzle of so-called methodological individualism. It is worth noting that Karl Popper, who is perhaps the most energetic advocate of such individualism – a doctrine opposed to what Popper calls "holism," which, for its own part, posits the effective agency of social groups, "group-spirits" and the like (Hegelian and Marxist views particularly, on Popper's view) – does manage to concede that "the social sciences are comparatively independent of psychological assumptions, and that psychology can be treated, not as the basis of all social sciences, but as one social science among others." In the same spirit, in fact invoking Tolstoy's *War and Peace*, Popper stresses the need for an analysis of "the *logic of situations*"; also, of "studies, based on methodological individualism, of the social institutions through which ideas may spread and captivate individuals, of the way in which new traditions may be created, and of the way in which traditions work and break down."[49] Here, Popper acknowledges, but does not quite manage to reconcile with the thesis of individualism the causal efficacy of cultural practices and institutions that cannot themselves be analyzed or accounted for solely in terms restricted to the specific powers and properties of aggregates of individual persons – hardly, therefore, solely in terms restricted to sub-personal physical properties.[50]

Similarly but more surprisingly, in his recent account of the narrative nature of human history, Paul Ricoeur has substantially confused the import of the symbiosis of individual persons and their cultural practices and traditions. Ricoeur says, for example, that "history . . . remains historical to the extent that all of its objects refer back to first-order entities – peoples, nations, civilizations – that bear the indelible mark of concrete agents' participatory belonging to the sphere of praxis and narrative."[51] But "peoples, nations, and civilizations" cannot be "first-order entities" in any realist sense in accord with the actual intentional life of effective agents – as, for instance, would be understood by methodological individualism or as we have every reason to believe Ricoeur himself intends in his detailed analysis of Augustine's *Confessions*, book XI, and Aristotle's *Poetics*, on which his own account of the so-called "three fold *mimesis*" of history and of "historical intentionality" depends. In short, Ricoeur believes that the concept of historical time integrates the structure of the lived time of *individual persons* (the "prenarrative structure of [personal] experience"[52] so movingly developed in Augustine's *distentio animi*), plotted as "a configuration [extracted] from a succession . . . following . . . the 'arrow of time' "[53] (more or less guided by Aristotle's paradigm suited to individual agents), and read back or interpreted as "a life story [that] proceeds from untold and repressed stories in the direction of actual stories the subject [or others] can take up and hold as constitutive of his personal identity" (so-called "mimesis").[54]

It is certainly true that this largely biological or biographical notion of historical time – which, by the way, corresponds most closely to R. G. Collingwood's conception of historical agency, though not necessarily to Collingwood's conception of history itself[55] – cannot be eliminated from the purview of historical narrative; but that model is quite insufficient to provide the essential schema of all historical narratives, as Ricoeur apparently supposes. The inclusion of collective entities as "first-order entities" obscures the option of more varied forms of historical narrative (since such entities do not, *pace* Spengler, conform to the "arrow of [biographical] time"). Also, Ricoeur has considerable difficulty in reconciling the large structural histories favored by the Annalistes (particularly, Braudel, whose study of the Mediterranean world he explicitly discusses), which significantly depart from the theme of methodological individualism as well as from the paradigms of narratized biography.[56] Processes within the cultural world may well be efficacious *through* the agency of aggregated individuals without being reducible to such agency; and both the structure of historical time and that of historical narrative may accommodate such forces, without being restricted to the forms of biographical narrative and without being incompatible with them. Once again, to pursue this very slight detour, the point of these deficiencies must count as an indirect approximation to the general charge against romantic hermeneutics (Schleiermacher, for instance) as well as against the premature reductive themes of methodological individualism and the simple bifurcation of the natural and cultural sciences (Dilthey, for instance).[57] The deeper point, of course, of permitting ourselves the luxury of what would otherwise seem a mere aside is that the complex structure of cultural space – particularly, the historically, institutionally, intentionally complex features of a "culture" – cannot, by any known means, be adequately characterized in terms first addressed to atomically individuated human beings, whose own aptitudes and attributes would *then* (one might philosophically hope to prove) be analyzable either in reductive physical terms or along the lines of a nonreductive physicalism of Post's sort (one committed, say, to TT). The prospect of either sort of physicalism hardly seems worth admitting, wthout some prior effort to do justice ("nonreductively") to the nature of historical institutions. Failing such an effort, it looks very much as if an ontological constraint such as MND must prove to be an entirely arbitrary posit at best.

These and similar findings come to rest in two pivotal observations: for one, persons mediate in some way between the physical and cultural domains and belong to both; and, for another, they do so in a way adequated to the effective processes and powers of both. If one grasps these themes correctly, then it is at once obvious that, although persons, artworks, words and sentences, institutions, practices, traditions, states, and the like are not to be confused with one another, the metaphysics of persons and artworks, for instance, as well as that of the others, must be *generically* the same. For artworks (and words and sentences) must belong jointly to the physical and cultural domains, must be adequated to both and to one another; persons and the traditions and practices of art and language are symbiotically linked in that sense in which a reductive individualism – a psychologism of the sort Popper opposes – or worse, a subpersonal or sub-cultural reduction of persons (in Sellars's sense) or a moderate physicalism (of Post's sort) cannot account for the phenomena of actual personal and cultural life. (In all candor, of course, these are promissory notes.)

The constraining clues bearing on any would-be solution of this puzzle – of how to construe persons, artworks, cultural phenomena in general – are reasonably clear. We have only to keep in mind that such clues are not meant to be timelessly invariant, assuredly essential, indefeasibly universal. They are in-variants only in that dialectical sense in which a historically sensitized, metaphysics (or phenomenological thought-experiment) tests, within whatever horizon it can command, all salient challenges to the adequacy of such candi-date notions. It depends on a strategy at once conceptual and *vécu*, perhaps quite close to the sense Merleau-Ponty was struggling to the end of his life to explain:

> Fact and essence can no longer be distinguished, not because, mixed up in our experience, they in their purity would be inaccessible and would subsist as limit-ideas beyond experience, but because – Being no longer being *before me*, but surrounding me and in a sense traversing me, and my vision of Being not forming itself from elsewhere, but from the midst of Being – the alleged facts, the spatio-temporal individuals, are from the first mounted on the axes, the pivots, the dimensions, the generality of my body, and the ideas are therefore already encrusted in its points.[58]

An essence, on that view, is "an in-variant," what conceptually and otherwise appears best or most successfully (but only provisionally thus) to resist change, absence, alteration, denial, destruction, or the like *within the range of change* – in order to remain the same thing, always within the horizon of an embodied life that cannot and need not claim the fixed and timeless invariances of Cartesian spectators.[59] It is, in this respect, hardly proof against the pressures of relativism and the shifting consensus of a society of mutually interpreted and mutually interpreting lives. This large consideration, then, colors our efforts to fix the meaning of the intrinsic properties of persons, artworks, and related cultural phenomena.

III

The beauty of our strategy is that its frankly conceded prejudice (in the sense Gadamer has made so appealing[60]) does not depend on any ramified theory of persons, artworks, language, or culture in general. On the contrary, it seeks to lay a dialectical trap for itself as well as for its antagonists, a sense of a reasona-bly shared space of pertinent questions and answers without yet introducing any fully explicit contending theories. We have been confining ourselves to initial clues regarding what may be minimally required of a theory of culture as well as to what seems to be inadequate in theories that resist such minima. Drawing on what has already been inferred, we may risk positing a small num-ber of promising "in-variant" constraints that the better contenders had better either satisfy or show why they need not. Consider at least the following:

1 persons, artworks, and other cultural phenomena must in some integral way inhabit both the world of physical nature and the world of human culture;

2   such entities are so linked with their environing worlds (particularly the
     cultural) that their intrinsic properties must be adequated there to
     whatever changes they effect and to whatever distinctive powers of those
     worlds they are the primary bearers or possessors of;
3   within the world of culture, persons are the primary agents of effective
     intentional change and production and, therefore, their intrinsic
     properties must be adequated to those of artworks, linguistic episodes,
     historical events and the like that they effectuate;
4   the world of culture that environs persons, artworks, linguistic episodes,
     historical events, and the like has properties that cannot be reductively
     described or accounted for only in terms of the prior specific powers of
     individual persons or of any sub-cultural order of physical nature – for
     instance, the properties of institutions, traditions, period trends, rules,
     practices and the like (just the "non-eventworthy history" the
     Annalistes favor[61]) – but that also do not exceed the powers of whatever
     may be adequated to the intrinsic properties of persons, the primary
     bearers and agents of culture;
5   granting (what we have termed) conceptual discontinuity, causal
     regularities of cultural phenomena need not be subsumable under the
     putative nomic universals of mere physical phenomena; and
6   the causal efficacy distinctive of the cultural world obtains in virtue spe-
     cifically of culturally intrinsic properties and powers – primarily, of the
     intelligent and purposive agency of humans and of the artifacts they ef-
     fectuate in their environing world.[62]

We may bring all of this to bear in a particularly telling way by recalling the
example (Post's) of the Anasazi Chaco Canyon observatory. Post's intention is
to call into question certain claims about "the asymmetry of [causal]
explanation" linked to the presumption, in much of science, of hierarchically
ordered asymmetries of explanation leading to "ultimate explanations."[63] The
question is posed whether "the positions and dimensions of the [stone]
slabs – their total configuration – explain, in conjunction with the angle of the
sun, the patterns of light and shade" or whether "the patterns [of light and
shade] explain the configuration." Post's plausible account finds that

> the patterns [do] explain the configuration of the slabs [contrary to the
> expected asymmetrical claim], since the slabs were made that way in
> order to cast precisely those shadows, just as the moving shadow of a sun-
> dial explains the shape and orientation of its gnomon. From this point of
> view, the shadows are not at all an accidental feature of the slabs, any
> more than a sundial's shadow is inessential to its gnomon.[64]

Post is dead right, of course. But he has reined in his very pretty puzzle much
too quickly. The pressure point is this: Post merely seeks to explain the physical
configuration of the stones; he does not consider with the same seriousness the
Anasazi's having placed the slabs in the configuration they have (if, indeed, they

were the creators of the observatory). The latter phenomenon is not – and, on the argument here intended, could not be – explained in physical terms, or in terms confined to the regularities or invariances of physical laws of the sort adduced for Post's case. Post does go on (later in his account) to suggest this difficulty; but he does not pursue it systematically. He offers several observations (to which we shall return) that fix the essential weakness (as well as promise) of the moderate physicalist's position. For the moment, let us merely make a note of his remarks:

> It is only because these physical states [the configuration of the slabs] *are realized* by the slabs in the wider cultural context that they are [really constitute] a solar marker.[65]

> Presumably, the property of being a solar marker is *emergent* with respect to physics and indeed natural science. For a solar marker is such only in virtue of certain intentions, and intentions are widely supposed to be irreducible to natural properties or relations. Assuming that the property of being a solar marker is emergent, Chaco Canyon yields a clear case in which the physical truths about *x* in isolation (the system of the slabs) hardly suffice to determine that *x* does (or does not) *instantiate* a certain emergent property. A much wider set of truths *at the level of physics* must be brought in. Such truths will determine *whatever it is about the Anasazis* and the slabs that determines that the slabs are a solar marker.[66]

This is indeed what a physicalist must say. On our own argument, it is fatally flawed.

All of the puzzles that the constraints we have tallied collect are neatly focused in that most equivocal expression, "human nature." For to speak of human nature is to speak at once, in however bifurcated or integrated a way, of both whatever is understood physically, biologically, psychologically, and socially regarding what falls entirely under the category of *Homo sapiens* and of whatever falls under the ampler categories of "self" or "person" (where, at least, the powers of cultural life – language in particular – are conceded to be such that they may not be completely subsumable under the physical or biological: *Homo sapiens*). Recall here that Noam Chomsky has advanced a peculiarly radical notion of man, in construing "universal grammar . . . as a study of the biologically necessary properties of human language," which therefore forms "a part of natural science."[67] If Chomsky were right in this conjecture, then there would be good reason to suppose that there need be no "bifurcation" of the sciences (that is, at least no radical irreducibility of the cultural to the physical);[68] although, on Chomsky's view, the physical itself would have to be suitably enhanced beyond the usual terms of physics and its allied disciplines. So our criticism of the impoverishing strategy is contingent on the defeat of this interesting and powerful line of argument and of others like it – that are not, let it be said, committed to the merely eliminative maneuvers already noted in Sellars's program.

Beyond this relatively secure point of reflection, speculation about what further we may say regarding persons of selves, artworks, practices, traditions, histories, languages, and the like becomes noticeably more quarrelsome – not confused or uncertain, only infinitely more complex, plural, open-ended, partisan, tentative, and strongly persuasive in intent. There is, for one thing, the question of why such categories as persons and artworks should be singled out in attempting to determine the intrinsic properties of cultural phenomena; or of why the cultural itself should be thought to be worth contrasting with the natural. The answer is roughly a double one: these categories strike us irresistibly as the salient ones pertinent to our own historical horizon and practice; and, drawing on our intuitions thus grounded, in a sense sufficiently convergent for the most disparate of thinkers, we are bound to invest in the study of invariances collected by the notions of such things as promise the most comprehensive, least distorting, most coherent, most economical, and most perspicuous conceptual pictures of our world. There is no guarantee that all such inquiries will converge in a unique way; but there is no reason why they should.

Marcel Mauss, in a strange and rather wonderful lecture, once proposed to demonstrate that, and how, "the idea of the 'person', the idea of the 'self' (*moi*)," was not at all "natural," "innate," "precise" or "completely serviceable" in all of us but rather "was slowly born and grew through many centuries and many vicissitudes, to the extent that even today it is still hesitant, delicate, precious and requires further elaboration."[69] Mauss seems to have intended to give an account of certain modern views of persons, particularly bearing on the moral role of persons; but he somehow presented his account as if it were a study of the origination of the very concept. He cannot quite have meant this, however, for he goes on to concede, almost casually, "In no sense do I maintain that there has ever been a tribe or a language in which the word '*je-moi*' . . . did not exist and did not express something clearly represented . . . there has never been a human being without the sense not only of his body, but also of his simultaneously mental and physical individuality."[70] Mauss's thesis is contestable of course, but it is, nevertheless, the perception of a sub-critical "in-variant" (in Merleau-Ponty's sense: in the sense of a characteristic, tacit, perceptual "faith common to the natural man and the philosopher"[71]), not actually and determinately invariant, not incontestable, but still noticeably difficult to drop or eliminate or alter without conceptual penalty – also, intuitively felt to provide the ground for a good beginning to our speculation. (Of course, Mauss's view, here, goes contrary to the thesis Julian Jaynes espouses, while at the same time it tries to preserve a sense of the historicized nature of consciousness.[72])

Yet, in saying what he does, Mauss very nearly, in effect, defeats his intended project; for, on his own view, there *is* an invariance (or in-variance) that belies the thesis of the slow historical emergence of the concept of persons. Whatever the modern version of that concept, Mauss apparently believes that persons always and everywhere are capable of self-reference of a sort that distinctly involves bodily boundaries and bodily individuation and the possessing of psychological attributes in a comparably individuated way. The thesis has been contested many times, perhaps most strenuously in recent years by Derek Parfit, in a series of somewhat phenomenological experiments with the conceptual variants of the central notion of identity.[73] There is no need, here, to argue the sufficiency of its defense or defeat. (In any case, in supporting the in-variance of positing a self or person, we need not contest the culturally formative and variable nature of what emerge as persons within historically different societies: we can insist on the *unicity* and ineliminability of persons in cultural contexts and deny the transcultural invariance of specific forms of internal *unity* or internally structured natures. That sort of accommodation would be quite sufficient to permit a sympathetic airing, here, of such different accounts of persons as are offered by Mauss, Vygotsky, G. H. Mead, Bruner, Marx, Hegel, Foucault, Jaynes, and Harré.) Our present concern is only to take note of certain salient (but by no means automatically decisive or totalized) tactics for exploring the concept of persons *vis-à-vis* providing a systematic account of the relationship between nature and culture. One notices, for instance, that the notions of self-reference and self-individuation already signify a straddling by persons of both worlds; for it is one thing to make claims about criteria adequate for the numerical identity of persons, and it is quite another to make claims about certain developed linguistic skills (innate skills being denied by Mauss) the exercise of which, and of which alone, entails a suitable (reflexive) grasp of one's own numerical identity.

This confirms in a very light way the sense in which the notion of "human nature" is equivocal. When we ask for a tabulation of the most generic traits of humans, characteristically the conceptual puzzle of the "relationship" between culturally specialized persons and members of *Homo sapiens* is very nearly never raised – understandably so. Thus, for instance, we get such lists as Clyde Kluckhohn's universal categories of human culture[74] or Mauss's own related schemata. But the pressure of philosophical concerns pretty well requires that, if human nature is to be analyzed, then it must be analyzed relative to such major themes as those of reference and individuation and self-reference, ultimately provided in terms that directly address such problematic issues as (1) favoring a strongly reductive (or impoverishing) tactic; (2) avoiding a Cartesian-like dualism; or (3) providing a third tactic that, while acknowledging the nonreducibility of cultural phenomena, affords a clear sense of the unity and integrity of such entities as persons, artworks, words and sentences differentiated somehow among themselves within the generic commonalities of cultural phenomena. Contemporary dispute is clearly polarized between versions of the first and third tactics: the first is certainly not yet convincing in the least; the third is largely unexplored; and the second is very nearly universally conceded.

Another well-worked salience regarding persons – perhaps incompatible with the thrust of Mauss's would-be history but strongly represented in the literature that has puzzled about persons (notably, in Locke's and Joseph Butler's speculations) – is collected very trimly in some probing remarks offered by Charles Taylor, in an effort to understand the distinction of purposiveness beyond mere teleology and the distinction between responsible action and the mere capacity to have intentions and to act in accord with them. Taylor clearly thinks animals as well as men are capable of acting purposively and with intention; but the import of what he develops seems to signify (quite reasonably) that only men (human persons) exhibit responsible behavior: "the distinction between action and non-action," he says, "hangs not just on the presence or absence of the corresponding intention or purpose, but on this intention or purpose having or not having a role in bringing about the behavior."[75] The ulterior import of Taylor's observation bears on the nonreducibility of the descriptive and explanatory features of the human sciences (and even of the behavioral psychology of animals) to the allegedly canonical features of the physical sciences. The purpose of his study is essentially critical of certain reductive tendencies – it serves, then, as a sort of clearing of the air. But, although it is reasonable to suppose that Taylor's conception of responsibility, rationality, specifically human existence, bridges the natural world and the world of culture,[76] these interconnections are not actually systematically developed.

Nevertheless, Taylor's remarks do go some distance toward collecting the line of argument that would be favored by any theorist who treated cultural phenomena as

(a)   real;
(b)   emergent in the strong sense of "conceptual discontinuity";
(c)   causally efficacious within the physical or natural world;
(d)   not analyzable or explicable in terms of a dualism of substances (so-called Cartesianism); and
(e)   including among its own phenomena the very existence and intrinsic aptitudes of persons or selves.

Item (b) is clearly the decisive consideration separating physicalists of every stripe and those (even including materialists who are not physicalists – that is, those who subscribe to (d) at least) who pursue a theory of *reality* and a *realism* (of science) fitted to the peculiarities of the cultural world. Taylor's remarks feature the ineliminable causal efficacy of intentional attributes of a sufficient complexity to permit ascriptions of responsibility and rational agency. What Taylor does not quite insist on, what separates Post's views, for instance, from his own, is the failure or success of such doctrines as MND, TT, and INV. The "bifurcation" of the sciences ultimately depends (if the case can be made at all) on the *ontological* inadequacy of those three (or any similar) doctrines.

Ironically, pressing once again Mauss's confusion of the self-referential powers of persons and the modern history of the concept of a person, a further important salience suggests itself: the essential historicality (*Geschichtlichkeit*) of human existence, a theme that owes so much of the thrust of its current exploration to Heidegger, and that has inevitably infected our conception of the other phenomena of man's cultural world – artworks and texts, for instance. Like self-referentiality and responsibility, historicality cannot be suitably explicated without attending to the intimate connection between the worlds of nature and culture.[77] Again, of course, the conceptual distinction of the historical, both in the sense of human time and human narrative, has been substantially contested, particularly with regard to intentional and intensional complexities – as by Popper and Carl Hempel and Adolph Grünbaum.[78] Nevertheless, we have, meanderingly, managed to collect here what are surely the leading saliences of human nature pertinent to our present concern:

(i)   self-reference and self-individuation;
(ii) effective and responsible or rational agency;
(iii) the social sharing of language and practice; and
(iv) historicality.

We have even begun to take note of a certain interdependence among these notions and of the likelihood of a viable adequation between the intrinsic properties of persons and of whatever else belongs within the cultural world of which humans are the paradigm members. These minima (these in-variants) are entirely compatible with robust speculations, for example along Foucault's lines,[79] regarding the profound historical contingency and diversity of the specific nature and internal unity of the *kind* of persons or selves appearing in different societies. (It is true, nevertheless – a point Parfit fails to grasp – that the ineliminability of selves is conceptually tied both to the formal unicity entailed in self-reference and to a unity or internal coherence sufficient at least for such reflexive reference.)

What dawns, then, is the necessity of sorting these and related saliences regarding human nature in such a way that

1   some set of intrinsic properties is ascribed to persons;
2   this set of properties is adequated to the entire range of cultural phenomena that persons make, effectuate, use, possess, and are the (symbiotic) bearers of (such as language, traditions, and practices);
3   all such saliences in accord with 1 and 2 are further integrated with efforts to resolve larger questions regarding alternative forms of reductionism, dualism, and nonreductive or emergentist accounts of the cultural.

Of course, the kinds of entities and phenomena at stake – persons, artworks, semiotica, responsible actions – serve both as the principal objects of direct description and explanation and as part of the background world influencing and influenced by such objects. These generate a notably parallel set of puzzles engaging issues 1–3: schematically, persons/human organisms, artworks/physical objects, words/sounds or marks, actions/movements. In the art-world, paintings and sculptures, precisely because they seem to encourage the notion that artworks are after all nothing but physical objects, help to fix the relative uniformity with which the entire world of culture poses the questions we have been trying to put in order. Richard Wollheim unintentionally makes this parallel quite compelling – by way of his own tentatively yielding affirmation of the "physical-object hypothesis." Thus, worrying that hypothesis in order to support it, Wollheim appeals in effect to Leonardo's recommendation to painters to "find" landscapes and figures in damp walls and promisingly colored stones – to offset, that is, the idea that "representational seeing," the perception of representational images, is incompatible with, or not "co-extensive" with, or significantly different from, "our seeing of any physical object whose surface exhibits any substantial degree of differentiation." "Once we allow this fact," says Wollheim, "it then surely seems absurd to insist that representational seeing, and the judgments to which it characteristically gives rise, implicitly presuppose a denial of the physicality both of the representation itself and that on which it lies.[80]

But the conclusion is a *petitio* and a complete *non sequitur*: the perception of mere physical objects does not show the absurdity of supposing that persons are not mere physical objects or mere biological organisms; and the fact that *in* perceiving a representation one must perceive physical objects does not show the absurdity of supposing that representations are not themselves mere physical phenomena – or that they cannot be discerned or explained *as such* solely in terms restricted to a physicalist vocabulary (as on Post's view). Wollheim himself offsets a primitive resemblance theory of representation by aptly noting that "what counts as a representation of what or how we represent things, is a culturally determined matter."[81] In any case, the question cannot be answered without a theory of adequation involving intrinsic properties. Wollheim goes on to consider, by a sort of rhetorical concession, that,

> though there is nothing other than a physical object that has representational properties, there is something other than a physical, or at any rate a purely physical object that has expressive properties: namely, a human body and its parts, in particular the face and certain limbs. So now we wonder, . . . How can anything purely physical be expressive?[82]

But he satisfies himself even here by observing that some sort of "physiognomic percepion" of emotional or expressive properties in physical objects can hardly be "independent of what is for us the supreme example of the relationship between inner and outer: that is, the human body as the expression of the psyche." Once the connection is conceded, however, then, "to the question, Can a work of art be a physical object if it is also expressive?, it now looks as though we can . . . give an affirmative answer."[83] Once again the conclusion is a *petitio*. For some curious reason, Wollheim does not invoke, with regard to expression, the same cultural considerations as he invokes with regard to representation; although he does note, in passing, that

> the qualities of gravity, sweetness, fear, that we invoke in describing works of art seem essential to our understanding of them; and if they are,

they cannot be extrinsic to the works themselves. They cannot be, that is, mere attributes of the experiences or activities of Masaccio, of Raphael, of Grünewald – they inhere rather in the Brancacci frescoes, in the Granduca Madonna, in the Isenheim Altarpiece.[84]

These, of course, are clear indications of the essential puzzles of adequation and intrinsic properties, with which we began. It is, in fact, precisely the same unresolved issue that Arthur Danto raises so promisingly in introducing his well-known epithet "the *is of artistic identification*" – which, he says, is not meant in the sense of identity, predication, existence, identification, "or some special *is* made up to serve a philosophic end."[85] It is rather the sense, common even with children, in which, pointing to a spot in a painting, I say to a friend, "That white dab is Icarus."[86] True. But *what* is that sense? Danto never says; in fact, he had not resolved a similar puzzle in an earlier account of the nature of human action (which is generically the same).[87] And almost no one has attempted the issue in a systematically nonreductive way.[88] It is no less and no more than the world-knot linking nature and culture – conceptually affecting all of its conjoint creatures.

We are bound to diverge somewhat, one from another, in answering the large questions we are posing here. The saliences regarding persons, artworks, linguistic utterances, actions and the like cannot fail to strike different minds in different ways. The presumption that, if there is a fair answer to these questions, there must be a unique, ideally adequate one is both unconvincing and unnecessary. They remain, however, a relatively neglected range of issues: probably because physicalist reduction, extensionalism, and allied doctrines have been so overwhelmingly fashionable in our age that one senses a certain unspoken embarrassment and uncertainty in finding it necessary to depart from their characteristic constraints; because dualism is itself a conceptual scandal; and because the alternative of nonreductive or emergentist metaphysics appears so inchoate at the same time it seems so daunting and bewildering. There is, however, no longer any excuse for avoiding these questions, and there is no reason why we should.

IV

We cannot leave our topic without addressing a little more formally the issue of adequation. Of course, as already conceded, we have not actually ventured a particular ontology of cultural entities, though we may have dropped clues ecough for the required account. We have confined ourselves to certain minimal constraints on what an adequate ontology is likely to be like. Adequation is clearly our central constraint; but, since it is a constraint that, once admitted, applies uniformly to nature and culture, it cannot have any bite without some inkling of what distinguishes the cultural from the natural. Still, it can be applied conditionally and critically (as in effect we have) in testing would-be proposals that admit culturally pertinent attributes and then assign them to entities characterized in such a way that a little analysis confirms a failure to meet the adequation condition.

In the most elementary sense, one supposes that it is literally false that stones speak or smile. Some may say that such remarks are not false but meaningless, incoherent, nonstarters, category mistakes, or the like, in the sense in which our conception of what it is to be a stone either precludes or does not make conceptual provision for the attribution in question. Whether to treat would-be statements involving such alleged conceptual mistakes as uniformly false or as generating truth-value gaps – in a sense paralleling a familiar quarrel about the use of referring expressions that lack reference[89] – is a question that need not tax us here. In fact, the entire issue of the adequation condition is much simpler than whatever the requirements of a general theory of categories or of real essences or of meaning and nonsense or of truth-conditions and truth-value gaps in natural languages would demand. It may be formulated as a modest regulative constraint imposed on would-be ontological analyses: *true (positive) ascriptions made of admitted entities may and ought to be adequated to the admitted natures of those entities*. In this sense, smiling and talking stones are (literally) "category mistakes," if the normal "nature" of stones be admitted – though, of course, only and always in a sense consistent with the demurrers just given.

An excellent (unintended) example may be drawn from John Searle's discussion of the mind/body problem. It is reasonably clear from the following that Searle is effectively concerned with the adequation question:

> the mind and the body interact, but they are not two different things, since mental phenomena just are features of the brain. One way to characterize this position is to see it as an assertion of both physicalism and mentalism. Suppose we define "naive physicalism" to be the view that all that exists in the world are physical particles with their properties and relations. The power of the physical model of reality is so great that it is hard to see how we can seriously challenge naive physicalism. And let us define "naive mentalism" to be the view that mental phenomena really exist. There really are mental states; some of them are conscious; many have intentionality; they all have subjectivity; and many of them function causally in determining physical events in the world . . . . Naive mentalism and naive physicalism are perfectly consistent with one another. Indeed, as far as we know anything about how the world works, they are not only consistent, they are both true.[90]

It is, to say the least, baffling that Searle offers not the slightest evidence that his implicit adequation claim is true or even viable. Mental "phenomena," mental "features," mental "states" just are (are rightly), he says, attributed to the physical brain: "all that exists in the world are physical properties and relations." Searle is clearly opposed to reductionism, identity theories, eliminationism, heuristic functionalism and similar doctrines. But, if we were to say "Yes, of course. But how do you explain the *conceptual fit* between the physical brain and its mental states?" Searle would not answer. If we recall, for instance, David Lewis's manifesto, "We who accept the materialistic working hypothesis [hold] that physical phenomena have none but purely physical explanations," or if we recall Post's MND or TT, we cannot suppose that Searle's announcement would be compatible, at the critical juncture, with either of these. To say that is not to insist that it should be, but only to give point to the request that Searle explain himself. He never actually does. It is certainly clear that there is no body of first-order empirical "science" (of any description) that could be said to support Searle's claim straightforwardly. The adequation issue constantly looms. If the mental includes, as he says, the conscious, the intentional, the subjective, and the causally efficacious (within the physical world), then we need to know how to understand – and how to be able to defend – Searle's claim. To insist on physical emergence is not enough; nor is it enough to add something such as the following:

> To put it crudely, and counting all of the central nervous system as part of the brain for our present discussion, everything that matters for our mental life, all of our thoughts and feelings, are caused by processes inside the brain. As far as causing mental states is concerned, the crucial step is the one that goes on inside the head, not the external or peripheral stimulus. And the argument for this is simple. If the events outside the central nervous system occurred, but nothing happened in the brain, there would be no mental events. But if the right things happened in the brain, the mental events would occur even if there was no outside stimulus.[91]

Apart from the very strong temptation to say that this is flatly false, the essential question remains entirely unanswered. To press into service, here, one of Searle's own lovely illustrations (invented for an entirely different purpose) – that of an American soldier who in the Second World War was captured by Italians and asked them, in the only German he knew from his high-school days, "Kennst du das Land, wo die Zitronen blühen?": *how*, conceptually, are we to understand that his real intention – to deceive his captors into thinking him a German officer – was "caused by processes inside the brain?"[92]

At the risk of being boringly explicit, we require at least a theory of language acquisition. Searle, in fact, means to improve on Chomsky's nativism, by advancing the "much simpler hypothesis . . . that the physiological structure of the brain *constrains* possible grammars without the intervention of an intermediate level of rules or theories."[93] Nevertheless, this "simpler hypothesis" does not noticeably strain our tolerance for conceptual adequation because it merely mentions physical constraints on the acquisition of a language. What, however, is troublesomely introduced in the same context – and what our initial citation draws attention to – is Searle's stronger thesis: "What [on his summary] is psychologically relevant about the brain is that it *contains* psychological processes and that it has a neurophysiology that causes and *realizes* these processes."[94] Now, the use of "contains" and "realizes" must count as specifically adequational claims, whereas "constrains" raises (it is true) an adequational issue but only indirectly in making a claim of quite another sort. Also, the adequational claim entailed in the use of "constrains" is globally or holistically satisfied merely by the rejection of ("Cartesian") dualism whereas the use of "contains" and "realizes" is meant in a distributively adequational sense. On the latter count Searle has all but nothing to say. (In fact, the adequation question recalls, not too implausibly but altogether informally, the well-known dispute about impredicative definition. To the extent that it invites the analogy, it is also rather less controversial; although the muting of objections against the other also depends on the sense of first fixing the independence of the sets or phenomena in virtue of which particular members or instances may be noncircularly said to exhibit the properties in question.[95])

Not surprisingly, we must turn back to Post for a more candid appreciation of the adequation issue. Post acknowledges quite a variety of physicalisms and, as we have already seen, argues that "the weakest [version of the relevant theses] one could accept and [still] remain a physicalist" would include (read in terms of his own carefully crafted MND, TT, and INV): "(i) 'Everything is physical'; (ii) 'No difference without a physical difference'; (iii) 'All truth is determined by physical truth'. . . ."[96] This is an instinctively strong way of addressing the adequation issue. Now, in airing unconvincing, stronger versions of physicalism, Post quite straightforwardly considers the intended relationship between two sets of "*terms* – one nonphysical [the terms invoked in what, elsewhere, he identifies as '*N*-discernibility' (as we have already seen)], the other from physics."[97] He mentions in this connection "talk about persons, intentions, consciousness, and the functional states of organisms"[98] – which pretty well accords with Searle's list of concerns about the "mental." The truth is that Post nowhere offers an analysis of "nonphysical" terms any more than Searle does of the "mental."

In fact, the simple contrast between "physical" and "nonphysical" ("*P-*" and "*N-*" terms) strongly suggests that the specification of the "non-physical" should involve no explicit attention to (and no ontological involvement of) "physical" features of any kind. *If*, of course, Post intends such a disjunction – which he clearly does not, but regarding the clarification of which he has nothing further to say (beyond his physicalist "constraints") – then, since on his own account (as well as on Searle's) the "mental" or "nonphysical" is both real and causally efficacious in nature, the admission of the "nonphysical" would be tantamount to subscribing to (some form of "Cartesian") dualism. For, surely, if the nonphysical is real and efficacious, then it must be a property of real entities; and, on the adequation thesis, there must be something in the intrinsic nature of those entities (designated by their putative intrinsic properties) *in virtue of which* their nonphysical properties *are* causally efficacious. It is for a similar reason that, reviewing the Chaco Canyon "secret," Post remarks (as we have already seen) that "A much wider set of truths *at the level of physics* [wider than whatever, regarding the slabs, would not yet 'suffice to determine that *x* does (or does not) instantiate a certain emergent property' – being a solar marker] must be brought in [to] determine whatever it is about the Anasazis and the slabs that determines that the slabs are a solar marker."

This convoluted account of Post's does not explicitly concede (but it also does not preclude the possibility) that the "determining" relationship involves causal as well as conceptual or logical distinctions. If it precluded the causal, it would thereby restrict the "nonphysical" to epiphenomenal status; and, if it conceded the causal, it would clearly implicate a conceptual gap between a ("Cartesian") dualism and all the reductive physicalisms Post is at pains to avoid. There is no evidence that Post here meets his own adequational requirement satisfactorily. There is also no need, here, to recapitulate an argument that has been provided elsewhere. But it can be shown – perhaps it is already reasonably clear – that the properties wanted, ranging from culturally informed psychological attributes such as that of thinking linguistically to the culturally explicit attributes of the (nonpsychological) artifacts of human culture, such as the representational property of the *Pietà*, must be *incarnate properties*.[99]
That, to make a long story short – granting only that properties such as consciousness, intentionality, functionality (involving the linguistic, the purposive, the historical, the institutional, the semiotic, and the like) are

   (a)   real,
   (b)   causally efficacious (within physical nature),
   (c)   not reducible in physicalist terms,
   (d)   incompatible with any ("Cartesian") dualism –

is, then, also to admit that they are

   (e)   emergent (in the sense of being "conceptually discontinuous," and
   (f)   indissolubly complex, monadic (with respect to the level at which they are emergent).

But to meet conditions (a)–(f) is just to be *incarnate.* On the argument, then, to be an incarnate property also entails being

   (g)   disruptive of any and all physically homonomic accounts of reality, and
   (h)   subversive of any and all versions (however attenuated – even along Post's lines) of a scientific realism conformable with the unity-of-science program or with its essential themes.

In particular, on the most reasonable review of the entire span of cultural or culturally informed psychological properties, the salient incarnate properties of the human world are just those that are intentionally complex; are just those that are, specifically, intensionally complex intentional properties – what, by a term of art, we have elsewhere termed *Intentional* properties[100] (which, clearly, the significative or semiotic features of the representational function of the *Pietà* may be said to instantiate). In fact, *the Intentional is the mark of the cultural*. Even if one believed (for example, along the lines Davidson for one has supposed) that intentionality could be neutralized with respect to intensional puzzles and that intensionality itself may be regimented extensionally (along Tarskian-like lines), an honest research program would oblige its adherents to demonstrate the empirical plausibility or correctness of those very conjectures. No one has been able to do so as yet. The upshot is that to admit (a)–(h) is, effectively, to accept that the incarnate is

(i)   disposed to endorse the realist standing of an ineliminable number of top–down sciences.

The irony is that the reductive physicalist *does* have an account of just the properties we have designated as incarnate and Intentional: they are, if they are real, all physical properties pure and simple. It is the nonreductive physicalists – Post and Searle, for instance – who have no account of the properties in question; hence, they have no purchase on the adequation question. On the reductive physicalist's view, the pertinent properties (*N*-properties, say) are all properties of the same physical entity that physical properties (*P*-properties) are properties of, *because persons, artworks and the rest are nothing but physical objects or physical phenomena*. If N-properties are not reducible to *P*-properties (drawn, remember, from some suitably amplified and corrected physics), then either one must be able to account adequationally for their ascription to physical entities or, preserving adequation, *there must be some more complex entities involved*. When, therefore, Post remarks that "embodiment versions of physicalism . . . are not really versions of physicalism [because] they posit an extra sort of entity,"[101] he is absolutely right. In fact, as we shall see in a moment, what he initially calls "embodiment" physicalism is *misnamed* a form of physicalism: it is really intended to be a form of *materialism*, in the straightforward sense that it rejects reductive, eliminative, *and* nonreductive physicalisms (nonreductive, in Post's interesting sense) and embraces items (a)–(i) of our tally regarding incarnate properties.

Post has Margolis's account of embodiment in mind.[102] He quite correctly remarks that his own

> minimal version [of physicalism] avoids [or at least intends to avoid] the embodiment relation, relying instead on relations of *instantiation* or *realization* to characterize the relations between bodies and properties or states of persons in such a way that persons do not exceed the physicalist's inventory of what there is [INV], and yet are not nothing but physical things.[103]

Now, the *embodiment* relationship is a complicated one. First of all, it is a relationship taken to hold between particulars only – that is, between particular entities. Second, it is a relationship taken to hold among all and only cultural phenomena. And, third, it is a relationship taken in such a way that an (ontic) adequation may be shown to hold between entities and their attributes in the cultural world. *If* what has been said about the need to admit incarnate properties – in particular, Intentional properties – is allowed, and *if* the adequation question is conceded to be a proper one, *then all physicalisms fail and an "extra entity" cannot be avoided.* Embodiment theories are merely one sort of answer to the adequation question under that condition.

Take persons and members of *Homo sapiens*, and the *Pietà* and a certain block of marble, as exemplars of the putative embodiment relation. Then, on the original tally Post rejects, the necessary and sufficient conditions of one particular's being embodied in another are the following:

(i) two particulars thus related are not identical; (ii) the existence of the embodied particular presupposes the existence of the embodying particular; (iii) the embodied particular possesses some (at least) of the properties of the embodying particular; (iv) the embodied particular possesses properties that the embodying particular cannot possess; (v) the embodied particular possesses properties of a kind that the embodying particular cannot possess; (vi) the individuation of the embodied particular presupposes the existence of some embodying particular; (vii) the embodying particular is not a proper part of the embodied particular.[104]

If we understand condition (v) to involve incarnate properties – in particular, Intentional properties – then it is reasonably clear that embodiment cannot be reduced to identity or composition, and, if we understand embodiment itself to be a relationship between particulars, then it is reasonably clear that it cannot pertinently be replaced in a systematic way by instantiation or realization (Post's preferences), unless identity or composition (or some similar relationship) obtains – since instantiation and realization are meant to hold only between entities and their attributes.[105]

There are, to be sure, all sorts of queries that may be made of the comparative force of the embodiment proposal. For example, reading (vii) in terms of the indissoluble complexity of incarnate properties enables us to avoid the fatal weakness of P. F. Strawson's theory (otherwise rather sympathetic to the embodiment proposal) in which both persons and physical bodies are, on his account, treated as "basic particulars." For, if they are "basic," then, contrary to his thesis, two distinct entities that are not proper parts of one another may (and even must) occupy the same spatiotemporal place in the world; and, if either is a proper part of the other, then, once again contrary to his thesis, that entity cannot be a basic particular. The dilemma is insoluble on Strawson's terms – which may be said to regard persons as emergent entities indissoluble, compositionally, in terms of any other basic particulars.[106]

We cannot pursue all the lines of inquiry that the embodiment proposal invites us to consider. But it may help to say that it is a proposal that makes sense *primarily* when matters of scientific description and explanation are viewed at least in terms of (h) and (i) of our tally regarding incarnate properties – that is, bearing on the realist standing of top–down sciences, So seen, Post's remark that the admission of persons and artworks and similar culturally emergent entities and phenomena posits "an extra sort of entity" is merely tendentious. For, for one thing, *his* own parsimony seems not (yet) to conform with Ockham's razor – whereas postulating embodiment does so conform; and, for another, the postulation of physical bodies is itself, on our reading of a preformative *Lebenswelt* affecting the very undertaking of an objective science,[107] in some respect an artifact of the cogniscent capacities of human inquirers. It is not prejudicial, therefore, that, within the framework of a top–down science, we may speculate, *bottom–up*, that persons and artworks emerge with respect to the physical world. Nothing could be more natural. We may also, of course, view the embodiment proposal as a heuristic device intended to service a realist conception of cultural entities. This is a particularly plausible suggestion in dealing with the complexities of artworks.[108] But we are not obliged to settle this question one way or the other; and, if we incline in the direction of the robust relativism earlier favored (particularly with regard to ontological indeterminacies affecting the real, interpretable properties of artworks and whatever may function similarly), then there is really no point in insisting on a exclusive resolution of the matter.[109]

It should suffice, then, to say that cultural entities *are* adequated to their incarnate and Intentional properties by defining or characterizing them as possessing, intrinsically, such incarnate and Intentional properties. The solution is logically trivial; but it is hardly trivial as far as the theory of scientific explanation is concerned. If the behavior and causal functioning of anything is to be explained – if it is said to be explained in any but the most elliptical sense – then it must be explained in terms of the putative *nature* of whatever is being considered. In that sense, the very notion of explanation in science is constrained by the adequation question. And in that case, on the argument, only a theory more or less in accord with the postulated embodiment relation and the admission of incarnate (and Intentional) properties could possibly suffice when cultural phenomena are involved.

We must, however, not lose sight of the fact that the adequation question has been brought to bear on what we suppose are the minimal ontic concessions regarding a realist conception of cultural phenomena. The meaning of realism and adequation remains unchanged in our shifting between physical nature and human culture, but the phenomena encountered in these two spaces are of significantly different sorts – primarily because of the Intentional structures present in cultural and absent in natural phenomena. It is true that, abandoning cognitive privilege, admitting the contingent and historically variable preformation of our cognitive aptitudes, and conceding that what we take to be independently real is a posit made under the condition of such intransparency, we cannot completely escape the intrusion of intentional complexities in speculating about the entities of the physical world. Nevertheless, we seek in the physical sciences certain physicalist economies. Many have tried to provide something similar in the sphere of culture – but they have failed and may forever fail. In accommodating what, on that failure, we seem obliged to concede, we see that, among cultural phenomena, we cannot (as we can, among physical phenomena) segregate what we take to be real independent of our inquiries and what we judge our inquiries yield in the way of cognitional clues about the other.

It is in fact the peculiar intimacy of human culture that confirms

1   that, however incarnated or embodied they may be, the properties and entities of the cultural world are discerned primarily in terms of their intentional features rather than of their physical features (which wrongly encourages the charge of ontic dualism);

2   that, whatever the fixity of their physical features or boundaries, culturally emergent properties and entities have no assured fixity of determinate boundaries, properties, or nature as far as their intentional features are concerned (which wrongly encourages the prejudice that they are unreal or merely heuristic);

3   that, whatever our reflexive doubts or suspicions about our understanding of our own cultural world, there is no conceivably cognitive source pertinent to discerning its intentional features that is not constitutively as well as regulatively dependent on some form of societal consensus (which wrongly encourages the suspicion that the human sciences are incapable of objectivity);

4   that, whatever may reasonably be imputed as the intentional features of given cultural phenomena cannot, for purely formal reasons, preclude, synchronically or diachronically, the reasonable imputation of intentional features that, on a bipolar model of truth-values, would be incompatible or contradictory (which wrongly encourages the worry that one is courting intellectual anarchy or nihilism);[110] and

5   that, whatever we may now impute as the intentional features of given cultural phenomena, other intentional features may be imputed to those same phenomena as a result of changing and different histories and changing and different funds of experience (which wrongly encourages the charge that admitting intentional features entails admitting that real phenomena change solely as a result of redescription and that, in this regard, "anything goes").

We may, in the name of the human sciences, collect what is affirmed in 1–5 regarding the ontic reality of cultural phenomena simply by observing that cultural realism is essentially hermeneutic: that the real properties and entities of the human world are, in their intentional aspect, inseparable from the interpretive consensus of those within whose Lebenswelt or Lebensform or praxis or episteme they obtain or exist. To admit this much is not to say anything as yet about what may count as objective criteria regarding the testing of particular truth-claims. It is, however, to concede that the culturally real is not *determinate* in its intentional features in the way in which physical objects are physically determinate; although it *is* intentionally *determinable* in ways suited to claiming that the human sciences enjoy a measure of *objectivity* and are entitled to claim a measure of *realism*. Only a prejudice carried over from the exemplars of the physical sciences could, in the absence of a successful physicalism, refuse those epithets.

V

Having said all this, it must be admitted that we have taken it for granted that discourse about persons and about ordinary physical objects are of a piece, that the predicative and referential features of constatations are uniform and entirely apt for discourse about both. This has been contested, chiefly by a putatively profound analysis or extension of Heidegger's (or Husserl's or Martin Buber's) notion of subjectivity. It needs to be briefly considered, but it is an entirely untenable (and unnecessary) conceptual extravagance. It is undoubtedly linked with Heidegger's concern for the technologizing of human "subjectivity" – of the unique human capacity for self-reference.[111] *That* issue *is* certainly decisive for any theory of persons; but it is a mistake to think that it adversely affects the ubiquitous application of the assertive, constative, predicative structures of discourse (of the "apophantical as," as Heidegger characterizes the logical structure in question – said to be radically contrasted with the "existential-hermeneutical as" of "primordial" interpretation from which it derives[112]). Admitting subjectivity, however, does not entail denying the relevance of constatation.

Heidegger is perhaps correct in worrying about the threatening erasure of the difference between the *natures* of persons and mere things, due to the conceptual totalitarianism of modern technology (of the cybernetic revolution, in fact[113]). So he warns, with hope and against hope, that "the matter of philosophy is subjectivity" – that is, that there is a decisive and ineluctable dependency of the "apophantical" on *alētheia*.[114] But, if we deny, as we have, the originary role of "subjectivity," if we deny the hierarchical ordering of (metaphysical) naturalism and (existentialized) phenomenology – Heidegger's "ontic"/"ontological" distinction – while preserving the difference between the natures of persons ("subjects") and of things, we must deny the *logical* inadequacy or inappropriateness of *applying constative discourse to persons* (or "subjectivity").[115]

The most uncompromising version of this insistence on the logical inaccessibility of "subjectivity" to constative discourse may well have been championed by Emmanuel Levinas. In a conversation on his most distinctive work, *Totality and Infinity*, Levinas provides a succinct (though characteristically florid) clue to his account of subjectivity ("the Other"). Speaking of the significance of the face, Levinas remarks,

> I think . . . that access to the face is straightway ethical. You turn yourself toward the Other as toward an object when you see a nose, eyes, a forehead, a chin, and you can describe them. The best way of encountering the Other is not even to notice the color of his eyes! When one observes the color of the eyes one is not in social relationship with the Other. The relation with the face can surely be dominated by perception, but what is specifically the face is what cannot be reduced to that . . . . The face is signification, and signification without context. I mean that the Other, in the rectitude of his face, is not a character within a context [a professor at the Sorbonne, say]. Here, to the contrary, the face is meaning all by itself. You are you. In this sense one can say that the face is not "seen." It is what cannot become a content, which your thought would embrace; it is uncontainable, it leads you beyond. It is in this that the signification of the face makes it escape from being, as a correlate of a knowing. Vision, to the contrary, is a search for adequation; it is what par excellence absorbs being . . . to speak truly, the appearance in being of these "ethical peculiarities" – the humanity of man – is a rupture of being. It is significant, even if being resumes and recovers itself.[116]

The fatal difficulty is a dual one: first of all, the individuative reference to the "Other" presupposes a conceptual relationship between predicative discourse and *any* supposed ethical responsibility; secondly, the very *nature* of the Other, accessed through the "face" and essentially determinative of the propriety of one's ethical stance (on Levinas's view), is open to fundamental dispute both in itself and with regard to phenomenal clues – and cannot possibly be resolved without appeal to constative distinctions. One has only to consider whether, as some feminists might well claim, gender differences entail essential differences in one's responsibility *vis-à-vis* the Other – similarly, racial differences, ethnic and cultural differences, historical differences, psychiatric differences, even biological differences between species.[117] Levinas holds both that the "Other" is "beyond" (conceptually inaccessible to) what Heidegger identifies as the "metaphysics" of being – recall, here, Heidegger's critique that "Philosophy is metaphysics"[118] – and that nevertheless one confronts the Other by (somehow) attending to the "face." Clearly, Levinas cannot have it both ways.

The issue may be put more directly. *If* we were thoroughgoing essentialists, we might hold that the nature of everything, persons as well as ordinary objects, could in principle be exhaustively described by the use of general predicates. Quine holds the unusual view that this is true of all individual things, in spite of the untenability of essentialism. That is the point of his having introduced the general predicates "socratizing" and "pegasizing."[119]

Apart from this small dispute about essentialism, what we may say is this:

no natural language can do without the constative function of discourse or, serving that function, no natural language can do without predicative and referential devices (the apophantical, as Heidegger puts it) *applied to everything it is used to discourse about.* A natural language need not, in principle, distinguish in an essentialist way between particulars and individuals – that is, between merely numerically individuated instances of the predicables in question (otherwise undifferentiated *"particulars,"* let us say, canonically indexed quantificationally by the use of "some" or "there is" or the existential quantifier or the like) and unique, numerically individuated entities that are taken to instantiate the predicables in question (*"individuals,"* let us say, canonically indexed by proper names, definite descriptions, indexical pronouns, the iota operator, or the like). An essentialist's use of singular terms or singular referring devices need only be construed as a grammatical convenience under real-time conditions. But, if, although (on something like Quine's apparent use of a Leibnizian strategy without essentialism) everything that could be individuated could in principle be taken to be uniquely specified by some set of predicates, we could never exhaustively determine such a set for all that we need or wish to individuate, then singular referring terms would be indispensable in our language and would bear a good part of the weight of actually individating things.

Singular and general (existential) statements are so interrelated that truly predicating something of an individual (in a singular statement) is normally taken to entail the truth of a logically weaker (relevantly linked) existential statement about some *particular.* But *there is no sense* in introducing individuals *of any kind* if (1) those individuals cannot be individuated; and (2) of them nothing can be meaningfully predicated. Now. Levinas's formulation regarding the Other risks incoherence inasmuch as, in the context of his account, the "rupture of being" that is intended risks violating (1) and (2) – may, in fact, actually violate those constraints – while, at the same time, Levinas means *to* individuate the Other, in order to be able to say *of* the Other *that apophantical discourse does not apply to it.*

On our argument, the Other may be as "other" as you please: it must be accessible apophantically (or, more neutrally, referentially and predicatively), because even assigning it its elusive distinction as Other logically depends on that condition. The "face," in Levinas's idiom, must function individuatively, on this side of the divide, if we are ever to say (or discern) regarding the Other, on its side of the divide, that it is the Other. (The language is terribly purple, but the distinction is quite simply black and white.) It makes no difference how exotic or alien the Other is supposed to be: if *we,* speaking mundanely (taking "mundane" in the literal sense), speak of *it* (in the referential sense, not meaning to deny the supposed alien quality of the Other), then there must be a constative form of discourse by which we can individuate it and make quite mundane predications of it.

A final word is in order. One may, canvassing the extravagances on this side of the divide, sympathize with the seemingly welcome simplicity of the physicalist's conceptual program. But we must be ready to admit its inadequacy at the same time as we disallow those self-defeating excesses (purporting to address "subjectivity") that make it impossible to discourse at all about persons or selves.

Notes

1 These issues are formally addressed in some detail in Joseph Margolis, *Pragmatism without Foundations: Reconciling Realism and Relativism* (Oxford: Basil Blackwell, 1986) chs 5, 11.

2 John F. Post, *The Faces of Existence: An Essay in Nonreductive Metaphysics* (Ithaca, NY: Cornell University Press, 1987), pp. 26–7.

3 See Michael Dummett, "Truth," *Truth and Other Enigmas* (Cambridge, Mass.: Harvard University Press, 1978), p. 14.

4 See for example Crispin Wright, "Realism, Bivalence, and Classical Logic," *Realism, Meaning and Truth* (Oxford: Basil Blackwell, 1987), which offers a very persuasive argument against Stig A. Rasmussen and Jens Ravnkilde, "Realism and Logic," *Synthese*, LII (1982) as to the logical commitments required of realists and anti-realists; see also Wright's "Anti-Realism and Revisionism" in *Realism, Meaning and Truth*.

5 Post, *The Faces of Existence*, p. 26.

6 Ibid., pp. 27f; cf. also p. 170. The sense of how this is to be used is given in section 4.1. Cf. also, G. H. Merrill, "The Model-Theoretic Argument against Realism," *Philosophy of Science*, XLVII (1980), which Post indicates he favors here, though "inessentially." The "possible worlds" idiom is at least "a heuristic device to help analyze various modal assertions," Post suggests (*The Faces of Existence*, p. 170); but it may well be that it cannot be merely heuristic – the matter is not entirely resolved (cf. pp. 170–3). See also William G. Lycan, "The Trouble with Possible Worlds," in Michael Loux (ed.), *The Possible and the Actual* (Ithaca, NY: Cornell University Press, 1979); Geoffrey Hellman and F. W. Thompson, "Physicalist Materialism," *Nous*, XI (1977); and Fabrizio Mondadori and Adam Morton, "Modal Realism: The Poison Pawn," *Philosophical Review*, LXXXV (1976). (These papers are discussed, in passing, by Post.)

7 Post, *The Faces of Existence*, p. 28 n. 5.

8 See Joseph Margolis, *Science without Unity: Reconciling the Human and Natural Sciences* (Oxford: Basil Blackwell, 1987), ch. 4.

9 I have for many years been advocating such a thesis – paradigmatically but not exclusively with respect to artworks. See Joseph Margolis, *Art and Philosophy* (Atlantic Highlands, NJ: Humanities Press, 1978), ch 6, 7; also "Puzzles of Pictorial Representation," in Joseph Margolis (ed.), *Philosophy Looks at the Arts*, 3rd edn (Philadelphia: Temple University Press, 1987). Cf. also ch. 8, below, for a brief discussion of Roman Ingarden's rather different view of the indeterminacy of the literary work of art.

10 The relevant argument is given in *Science without Unity*, ch. 1.

11 See Joseph Margolis, *Culture and Cultural Entities* (Dordrecht: D. Reidel, 1984).

12   Post, *The Faces of Existence*, p. 27.

13   See ch. 8, below, for an analysis of a related example developed by Arthur Danto.

14   I am happy to borrow the Chaco example from Post, *The Faces of Existence*, section 2.6 and pp. 200–3.

15   See for example Richard Wollheim, "Art and Its Objects," *Art and Its Objects*, 2nd edn (Cambridge: Cambridge University Press, 1980), pp. 4, 5, 11–12, in the context of supplementary essay III.

16   See ch. 3, above.

17   The discussion in Post, *The Faces of Existence*, appears primarily in section 4.2. See also W. V. Quine, "Goodman's *Ways of Worldmaking*," *Theories and Things* (Cambridge, Mass.: Harvard University Press, 1981), and "Facts of the Matter," *Southwestern Journal of Philosophy*, IX (1978).

18   Post, *The Faces of Existence*, p. 174.

19   Ibid., p. 176. See also Hilary Putnam, "Reflections on Goodman's *Ways of Worldmaking*," *Philosophical Papers*, vol. 3 (Cambridge: Cambridge University Press, 1983).

20   Nelson Goodman, *Languages of Art* (Indianapolis: Bobbs-Merrill, 1968), pp. 103–4.

21   It is interesting to note that Post has Goodman's view in mind, but does not address the issue. Notice, also, that a physical mark distinguishing the original and the forgery presupposes an independent difference between them.

22   See for instance Arthur C. Danto, *The Transfiguration of the Commonplace* (Cambridge, Mass.: Harvard University Press, 1981).

23   See Goodman, *Languages of Art*, ch. 3; also Joseph Margolis, "Art, Forgery, and Authenticity," in Denis Dutton (ed.), *The Forger's Art: Forgery and the Philosophy of Art* (Berkeley, Calif.: University of California Press, 1983).

24   Arthur C. Danto, "The Artworld," *Journal of Philosophy*, X (1968), 162 (italics added).

25   For an overview of a number of these further puzzles, see Margolis, *Art and Philosophy*, pts I and II. For an assessment of Danto's compendious view of art, with reference to other parts of his philosophical theory, see Joseph Margolis, "Otology Down and Out in Art and Science," *Journal of Aesthetics and Art Criticism*, forthcoming. In that paper, I try also to take account of the analogous puzzle T. S, Kuhn raises regarding paradigm shifts: in which, say, "pendulums" and "swinging stones" are not (on Kuhn's view) the same things but which look very much as if they could not be distinguished in any straightforward way that would support Post's doctrine. On the contrary, on an intuitionistic reading of double negation, the kind of failure Kuhn has in mind could not serve as ammunition favoring Post's MND. See Thomas S. Kuhn, *The Structure of Scientific Revolutions*, 2nd, enlarged edn (Chicago: University of Chicago Press, 1970), pp. 118–35. See also ch. 8, below.

26   This is the thesis of *Art and Philosophy*; cf. particularly ch. 7. See also *Pragmatism without Foundations*, pt I.

27   Wilfrid Sellars, "Philosophy and the Scientific Image of Man," *Science, Perception and Reality* (London: Routledge and Kegan Paul, 1963), pp. 39–40.

28   See for example the account, inspired by Sellars, offered in Stephen P. Stitch's *From Folk Psychology to Cognitive Science: The Case against Belief* (Cambridge, Mass.: MIT Press, 1983); also Paul M. Churchland, *Scientific Realism and the*

Plasticity of Mind (Cambridge: Cambridge University Press, 1979). These views and others are thoroughly canvassed in *Science without Unity*, chs 5, 6.

29 Post, *The Faces of Existence*, pp. 184, 189.

30 Ibid., p. 169, with simplifications drawn from p. 168 and section 3.1. On Post's own view, his account is close to that offered in Hellman and Thompson, "Physicalist Materialism," *Nous*, XI.

31 Post, *The Faces of Existence*, pp. 192, 185.

32 The general lines of the difference in question are, in effect, developed in Joseph Margolis, *Persons and Minds: The Prospects of Nonreductive Materialism* (Dordrecht: D. Reidel, 1978). I have, I believe, improved the account given there in *Culture and Cultural Entities*, ch. 1, particularly with regard to the matter of functional and (what I term) incarnate properties, of which more in a moment. Cf. also *Science without Unity*, ch. 9.

33 Cf. Margolis, *Art and Philosophy*, ch. 4.

34 See Donald Davidson, "Mental Events," *Essays on Actions and Events* (Oxford: Clarendon Press, 1980).

35 David K. Lewis, "An Argument for the Identity Theory," *Journal of Philosophy*, 63 (1966). See also David Lewis, *Philosophical Papers*, vol. 1 (Oxford: Clarendon Press, 1983).

36 See Margolis, *Science without Unity*, ch. 10.

37 See ibid., ch. 8.

38 See ibid., ch. 5.

39 Sellars, "Philosophy and the Scientific Image of Man," *Science, Perception and Reality*, p. 40 (I have italicized "we" in the citation).

40 Daniel C. Dennett, *Content and Consciousness* (London: Routledge and Kegan Paul, 1969), p. 190 (again, I have italicized "we" in the citation).

41 This is the strongest theme in the "social construction" of persons, institutions, the social world itself. See for example Rom Harré, "The Conditions for a Social Psychology of Childhood," in M. P. M. Richards (ed.), *The Integration of a Child into a Social World* (Cambridge: Cambridge University Press, 1974); and Harré's *Social Being: A Theory for Social Psychology* (Oxford: Basil Blackwell, 1979). See also Peter Berger and Thomas Luckman, *The Social Construction of Reality* (Harmondsworth: Penguin, 1967). John Shotter, who also subscribes to the general theory, draws attention, in his *Social Accountability and Selfhood* (Oxford: Basil Blackwell, 1984), to a passage in Vico that gives what is surely one of the first formulations of the doctrine. See *The New Science of Giambattista Vico*, tr. Thomas Goddard Bergin and Max Harold Fisch (Ithaca, NY: Cornell University Press, 1948), section 331; also ch. 9, below.

42 See John Searle, *Minds, Brains and Science* (Cambridge, Mass.: Harvard University Press, 1984), ch. 2. (This is not to endorse Searle's resolution of the puzzle.)

43 The term does not appear to be used in Herbert Feigl, *The "Mental" and the "Physical": The Essay and a Postscript* (Minneapolis: University of Minnesota Press, 1967). I have, however, heard Feigl use the term several times and believe it to be his own usage. In fact, it may well be one of his principal contributions – the thesis as well as epithet.

44 See for example Morris Weitz, *"Hamlet" and the Philosophy of Literary Criticism* (Chicago: University of Chicago Press, 1964).

45 See Margolis, *Pragmatism without Foundations*, pt I.

46 See Margolis, *Science without Unity*, ch. 10.
47 Jerry A. Fodor, *The Modularity of Mind* (Cambridge, Mass.: MIT Press, 1983), p. 125.
48 See Margolis, *Science without Unity*, ch. 5.
49 Karl R. Popper, *The Poverty of Historicism*, 3rd edn (New York: Harper and Row, 1961), section 7, pp. 142–9. Cf. also Popper's later discussion of the reality and "partial autonomy" of what he calls World 3, in *The Open Universe* (*Postscript to the Logic of Scientific Discovery*, vol. II,) ed. W. W. Bartley, III (Totowa, NJ: Rowman and Littlefield, 1982), particularly Addendum 1, "Indeterminism Is Not Enough: An Afterword."
50 It is quite extraordinary how widely these puzzles of the reduction of collective properties to individual properties, of persons to sub-personal entities, and of persons to mere nodes within collectivities, have been pursued in the social and psychological sciences – within sub-disciplines relatively ignorant of one another's work. I have caught a reflexive sample of this in the sociological literature, from a reading of Douglas V. Porpora, *The Concept of Social Structure* (New York: Greenwood Press, 1987), particularly regarding what is called Structural Sociology, which holds as reductively as possible to the Durkheimian conception of "social structure as a body of relationships [solely] among social facts" (p. 1). See, for specimens, Peter M. Blau, "Objectives of Sociology," in Robert Bierstedt (ed.), *A Design for Sociology: Scope, Objectives and Method* (Philadelphia: American Academy of Political and Social Science, 1969), and *Inequality and Heterogeneity: A Primitive Theory of Social Structure* (New York: Free Press, 1977); also Bruce Mayhew, "Structuralism versus Individualism," pts I–II, *Social Forces*, LIX (1980, 1981). See also ch. 9, below.
51 Paul Ricoeur, *Time and Narrative*, tr. Kathleen McLaughlin and David Pellauer (Chicago: University of Chicago Press, 1984), vol. 1, p. 181. See also Margolis, *Science without Unity*, ch. 12.
52 Ricoeur, *Time and Narrative*, vol. 1, p. 60.
53 Ibid., pp. 66–7.
54 Ibid., p. 74.
55 See R. G. Collingwood, *The Idea of History* (Oxford: Clarendon Press, 1946).
56 Cf. ibid., ch. 6; also Paul Veyne, *Writing History*, tr. Mina Moore-Rinvolucri (Middletown, Conn.: Wesleyan University Press, 1984).
57 See ch. 8, below.
58 Maurice Merleau-Ponty, *The Visible and the Invisible*, tr. Alphonso Lingis (Evanston, Ill.: Northwestern University Press, 1968), p. 114.
59 Cf. ibid.,p. 111; also Margolis, *Pragmatism without Foundations*, ch. 11.
60 See for instance Hans-Georg Gadamer, *Truth and Method*, tr. Garrett Barden and John Cumming from 2nd German edn (New York: Seabury Press, 1975).
61 See Veyne, *Writing History*, ch. 2.
62 On the issues of distinguishing causality and nomologicality and of characterizing agency, see *Science without Unity*, ch. 8. It is clear, of course, that on constraints 5 and 6, in context, the "structuralist" insistence on nomological regularity linking the physical and the cultural orders – in Pylyshyn and Fodor (and, in a different sense, in Lévi-Strauss) – are neither required nor likely to be empirically supported or supportable. See ch. 5, above.

63 Post, *The Faces of Existence*, section 2.6. The example is an ingenious counterexample to a well-known instance posed by Sylvain Bromberger; cf. Bas C. van Fraassen, "The Pragmatics of Explanation," *American Philosophical Quarterly*, XIV (1977), mentioned by Post.

64 Post, *The Faces of Existence*, p. 108.

65 Ibid., p. 200 (italics added).

66 Ibid., p. 200 (italics added).

67 Noam Chomsky, *Rules and Representations* (New York: Columbia University Press, 1980), p. 29.

68 Cf. ibid., ch. 1.

69 Marcel Mauss, "A Category of the Human Mind: The Notion of Person, the Notion of 'Self'," in *Sociology and Psychology*, tr. Ben Brewster (London Routledge and Kegan Paul, 1979), p. 59.

70 Ibid., p. 61.

71 Merleau-Ponty, *The Visible and the Invisible*, p. 3.

72 See ch. 1, also ch. 9, below, on Rom Harré's view.

73 See Derek Parfit, *Reasons and Persons* (Oxford: Clarendon Press, 1984), pt III; also Margolis, *Science without Unity*, ch. 3.

74 See Clyde Kluckhohn, "Universal Categories of Culture," A. L. Kroeber (chairman), *Anthropology Today* (Chicago: University of Chicago Press, 1953).

75 Charles Taylor, *The Explanation of Behavior* (London: Routledge and Kegan Paul, 1964), p. 33.

76 See for instance Charles Taylor, "Interpretation and the Sciences of Man," in Paul Rabinow and William M. Sullivan (eds), *Interpretive Social Science: A Reader* (Berkeley, Calif.: University of California Press, 1979), and "Rationality," in Martin Hollis and Steven Lukes (eds), *Rationality and Relativism* (Cambridge, Mass.: MIT Press, 1982).

77 See Marjorie Grene, "The Paradoxes of Historicity," *Review of Metaphysics*, 33 (1978).

78 See Carl G. Hempel, "The Function of General Laws in History," *Aspects of Scientific Explanation* (New York: Free Press, 1965); and Margolis, *Science without Unity*, ch. 8.

79 For instance, Foucault observes, "'What is called Christian interiority is a particular mode of relationship with oneself, comprising precise forms of attention, concern, decipherment, verbalization, confession, self-accusation, struggle against temptation, renunciation, spiritual combat, and so on. And what is designated as the 'exteriority' of ancient morality also implies the principle of an elaboration of self, albeit in a very different form. The evolution that occurred – quite slowly at that – between paganism and Christianity did not consist in a gradual interiorizaton of rules, acts, and transgressions; rather, it carried out a restructuration of the forms of self-relationship and a transformation of the practices and techniques on which this relationship was based" – Michel Foucault, *The Use of Pleasure* (*The History of Sexuality*, vol. 2), tr. Robert Hurley (New York: Pantheon, 1985), p. 63. The entire chapter ("Enkrateia") in which the remark appears, repays attention.

80 Wollheim, "Art and Its Objects," *Art and Its Objects*, p. 16.

81 Ibid., p. 21.

82 Ibid., p. 22.

83   Ibid., pp. 32–3.

84   Ibid., p. 24.

85   Danto. "The Artworld", *Journal of Philosophy*, X; cf. also Danto's *The Transformation of the Commonplace*.

86   Danto, "The Artworld," *Journal of Philosophy*, X.

87   See Arthur C. Danto, *Analytical Philosophy of Action* (Cambridge: Cambridge University Press, 1973).

88   Regarding the theory of action, one obtains a very clear sense of how unsatisfactorily the matter has been managed by reviewing the account in Alvin I. Goldman, *A Theory of Human Action* (Englewood Cliffs, NJ: Prentice-Hall, 1970). For a clearer sense of the ontological issues, but not a solution, see Myles Brand, *Intending and Acting: Toward a Naturalized Action Theory* (Cambridge, Mass.: MIT Press, 1984). See also chs 8, 9, below.

89   The best-known discussion of truth-value gaps regarding reference is surely to be had in P. F. Strawson, "On Referring," *Mind*, LIX (1950). But, of course, Strawson does not hold that would-be statements generating truth-value gaps are nonsense or absurd or senseless. An approach to that position is probably best known from the discussion of so-called "category mistakes" in Gilbert Ryle, *The Concept of Mind* (London: Hutchinson, 1949). Strawson suggests that Ryle "came later to abandon, if he ever held, the view that there could be such a thing as a theory of categories – a clear and general explanation of the notion of sameness and difference of category and hence of the notions of category-confusion and category-mistake" – P. F. Strawson, "Categories," *Freedom and Resentment and Other Essays* (London: Methuen, 1974), p. 109.

90   Searle, *Minds, Brains and Science*, pp. 26–7.

91   Ibid., p. 18.

92   The example is given is John Searle, "What Is a Speech Act?" in Max Black (ed.), *Philosophy in America* (London: Allen and Unwin, 1965), repr. in Jay F. Rosenberg and Charles Travis (eds), *Readings in the Philosophy of Language* (Englewood Cliffs, NJ: Prentice-Hall, 1971), p. 615.

93   Searle, *Minds, Brains and Science*, p. 51 (italics added).

94   Ibid., p. 50 (italics added).

95   See Kurt Gödel, "Russell's Mathematical Logic," in Paul Arthur Schilpp (ed.), *The Philosophy of Bertrand Russell* (New York: Tudor, 1951); Charles Parsons, Introduction to *Mathematics in Philosophy: Selected Essays* (Ithaca, NY: Cornell University Press, 1983).

96   Post, *The Faces of Existence*, p. 161.

97   Ibid., p. 160 (italics added).

98   Ibid.

99   See Margolis, *Science without Unity*, ch. 9.

100 See Margolis, *Science without Unity*, ch. 9 (p. 316).

101 Post, *The Faces of Existence*, p. 164.

102 As originally presented in *Persons and Minds*.

103 Post, *The Faces of Existence*, p. 164 (italics added).

104 Margolis, *Persons and Minds*, p. 235.

105 Cf. Post, *The Faces of Existence*, p. 164.

106 See P. F. Strawson, *Individuals: An Essay in Descriptive Metaphysics* (London: Methuen, 1959), pt I.

107 See chs 1, 3, above.

108 See Margolis, *Art and Philosophy*, ch. 4.

109 See further, chs 8, 9, below.

110 See Margolis, *Pragmatism without Foundations*, pt I.

111 The theme appears, perhaps most characteristically, in "The Question Concerning Technology," tr. William Lovitt, and "The End of Philosophy and the Task of Thinking," tr. Joan Stambaugh, repr. in Martin Heidegger, *Basic Writings from "Being and Time" (1927) to "The Task of Thinking" (1964)*, ed. David Farrell Krell (New York: Harper and Row, 1977).

112 Heidegger remarks, linking the ontic and the ontological, the "objective" and its generation by *Dasein*, that "assertion cannot disown its ontological origin from an interpretation which understands. The primordial 'as' of an interpretation (*hermeneía*) which understands circumspectively we call the 'existential-hermeneutical "as" ' in distinction from the '*apophantical* "as" ' of the assertion" – Martin Heidegger, *Being and Time*, tr. John Macquarrie and Edward Robinson from 7th German edn (New York: Harper and Row, 1962), p. 201 (p. 158 in the German edn). The distinction is clearly linked with Heidegger's account of technology. See J. N. Mohanty, "Heidegger on Logic," *Journal of the History of Philosophy*, XXVI (1987). (I have had the opportunity of seeing this paper in galley sheets, after completing this section of the chapter.) See also Errol E. Harris, *Formal, Transcendental, and Dialectical Thinking: Logic and Reality* (Albany, NY: State University of New York Press, 1987), ch. 4. Husserl, of course, segregates quite deliberately the "apophantic analytic" laws of thought, which depend entirely "on pure categories of meaning [as] distinct from ontological-analytic laws, which rest on formal-ontological categories (such as object, property, plurality etc)" – Edmund Husserl, *Logical Investigations*, 2 vols, tr. J. N. Findlay (New York: Humanities Press, 1970), vol 2, pp. 523–4. But Heidegger reintroduces ontology at the heart of phenomenology (*Being and Time*, pp. 56, 265–6; pp. 33, 223 in the German edn) because of the receptive role he assigns *Dasein* – hence (it seems) he cannot admit, in Husserl's sanguine way, the distinction of apophantical logic (which bears on the issue of psychologism). See ch. 3, above. There is an extremely clear summary of Husserl's view of the distinction between apophantic and objective judgment and its relations to apophantic logic in Robert Sokolowski, *Husserlian Meditations* (Evanston, Ill: Northwestern University Press, 1974), Appendix: "Logic and Mathematics in *Formal and Transcendental Logic*."

113 Cf. Heidegger, "The End of Philosophy and the Task of Thinking," *Basic Writings*, p. 376.

114 Ibid., p.383 (in the context of the entire essay).

115 See ch. 1, above.

116 Emmanuel Levinas, *Ethics and Infinity: Conversations with Philippe Nemo*, tr. Richard A. Cohen (Pittsburgh: Duquesne University Press, 1985), pp. 86–7. See also Emmanuel Levinas, *Totality and Infinity*, tr. Alphonso Lingis (Pittsburgh: Duquesne University Press, 1979). Thus, although Levinas remarks that our "relation" to the Other (*Autrui*) "is language" (*Totality and Infinity*, p. 39), that relation "implies relations with what is not given, of which there is no idea . . . [which signifies or entails] non-adequation [constatively construed]" (p. 34). Levinas has carried Heidegger's prioritizing and disjoining

of (something very much like) the existential-hermeneutic over the apophanti-cal beyond the conditions of coherence. This may be easily seen by considering the following typical passage: "The Other is not other with a relative alterity as are, in a comparison, even ultimate species, which mutually exclude one another but still have their place within the community of a genus – excluding one another by their definition, but calling for one another by this exclusion, across the community of their genus. The alterity of the Other does not depend on any quality that would distinguish him from me, for a distinction of this nature would precisely imply between us that community of genus which already nullifies alterity . . . . The Other remains infinitely transcendent, infinitely foreign; his face in which his epiphany is produced and which appeals to me breaks with the world that can be common to us, whose virtualities are inscribed in our *nature* and developed by our existence. Speech proceeds from absolute difference" (p. 194). The fact is that the Other is in some sense individuated or identified, and yet, of course, individuation and identification are essentially constative or apophantical (cf. pp. 36, 39, 42, 45, 47–8, 51).

117 I have benefited greatly, in developing this point, from a conversation with David Wood and Adriaan Peperzak, on the occasion of Peperzak's interpreta-tion of Levinas ("From Intentionality to Responsibility") presented at the annual meeting of the Society for Phenomenology and Existential Philosophy, at Notre Dame, Indiana, Fall 1987. See Hélène Cixous, "Sortie," and Luce Irigaray, "This Sex Which Is Not One," in Elaine Marks and Isabelle de Courtivron (eds), *New French Feminisms; An Anthology* (Amherst: University of Massachusetts Press, 1980); also Levinas, *Totality and Infinity*, section 3.

118 Heidegger, "The End of Philosophy and the Task of Thinking," *Basic Writings*, p. 374.

119 See W. V. Quine, *Word and Object* (Cambridge, Mass.: MIT Press, 1960), sec-tions 38–9.

7

The Grammar and Ontology of Reference

It needs to be said as firmly and as directly as possible that the formal, grammatical, syntactic, structural, formal-semantical, formal-pragmatic features of language have no direct ontological or epistemological consequences of the sort that have, in the extended history of the philosophy of language, been so often made to appear to favor physicalism and/or extensionalism and realism. Such gains are all either faked or the result of invoking substantive assumptions in the process of analyzing particular linguistic practices. W.V. Quine is entirely straightforward, therefore, when, in the opening pages of *Word and Object*, he remarks,

> So the proposition that external things are ultimately to be known through their actions on our bodies should be taken as one among various coordinate truths, in physics and elsewhere, about initially unquestioned physical things. It qualifies the empirical meaning of our talk of physical things, while not questioning the reference.[1]

Quine is still entirely noncommittal when, on the same page, he says,

> We shall find, as we get on with organizing and adjusting various of the turns of phrase that participate in what pass for affirmations of existence, that certain of these take on key significance in the increasingly systematic structure; and then, reacting in a manner typical of scientific behavior, we shall come to favor these idioms as the existence affirmations "strictly so-called."[2]

Interestingly, however, Quine indexes the second remark under "Ontology, commitment to," even though neither the expression nor any of its cognates actually appears on the page. He is preparing us, in effect, for a *policy* that he himself usually supports with great care, but which many have somehow misread (which, to be candid, Quine himself has been known to misread from time to time), which goes as follows:

> In our canonical notation of quantification . . . the objects we are to be understood to admit are precisely the objects which we reckon to the universe of values over which the bound variables of quantification are to be considered to range. . . . To paraphrase a sentence into the canonical notation of quantification is, first and foremost, to make its ontic content explicit, quantification being a device for talking in general of objects.[3]

Hence, when Quine considers the paraphrase of such sentences as "Tom believes that Cicero denounced Catiline" and remarks that "you cannot quantify into an opaque construction,"[4] he is certainly not denying that "Cicero" and "Catiline" denote, respectively, those Roman gentlemen, only that their referential or denotative function is opaque within the terms of his policy (regardless of his own ulterior convictions of how else we might proceed). It is also no accident, of course, that, on Quine's view, opacity is bound up with our failure to eliminate intensional (nonextensional) constructions in natural language. But, even there, there is no clear sense given that it is really the formal structures that bear the ontological import. It is, if we so choose, our policy.[5]

It is an illusion of the history of the question, particularly in the English-language analytic tradition (whatever may have been its Continental European lineage in the interval from Frege to Carnap before it jumped the Channel to be taken up by Russell), that announcing this particular policy or similar policies is, somehow, merely announcing as a policy what would already accord with an independent finding about the true ontic and epistemic import of the formal properties of natural language. Quine himself, in a famous paper published well before *Word and Object*, clearly contributed to that confusion (unintentionally and not at all by way of an actual mistake, it may be said) when, addressing the same matter of realist reference and denotation, he declared, "But this is, essentially, the *only* way we can involve ourselves in ontological commitments: by our use of bound variables."[6] That sentence is an expression of philosophical ardor, not of an ontological discovery of the natural match between the world (or between our commitment to the world) and the devices of first-order logic. But, when, for instance, shifting our focus not quite as abruptly as it may appear, Donald Davidson affirms – advancing his well-known attempt to generalize Tarskian formal semantics for natural languages – that "what is invariant as between different acceptable theories of truth is meaning [and] translation [of meaning] is a purely syntactic notion. Questions of reference do not arise in syntax, much less get settled,"[7] there is a sea-change to be reckoned with – more insinuated than declared, but certainly all but declared.[8] Grammar has become the metagrammar of ontology; although, by denying the ineliminable conceptual linkage between reference and truth, it may (it will) have rendered itself incoherent in the process.

We need to attend to these *caveats* because we have, only a moment ago,[9] favored an account of cultural entities and phenomena that, on the evidence, cannot be reconciled with Quine's policy or with Davidson's "finding." We must assure ourselves that such peculiarities (our own proposals) need not (and cannot convincingly be made out to) violate any *a priori* formal canons governing the use of reference, predication, or truth-ascription. The argument required demands something of a detour and, in fairness, a suitable inning for the principal contending views. We may center on reference chiefly, partly as a convenience, partly because of its pointed relevance in the setting of our own concerns, partly because extensionalism cannot be so readily confined (by trickery, of course) to purely formal considerations.[10] We may begin with an aside on our detour.

I

In the history of the philosophy of science, theoretical entities have been confidently assigned, by different hands, a remarkable variety of incompatible ontological functions. Wilfrid Sellars's view, for instance, voices the radical sentiment of all those who still adhere to the main convictions of the unity-of-science program (now, historically, more of the right than of the left), who have focused their energies on eliminating all aspects of the cognitive salience as well as privilege of the "folk" orientation of perceptually endowed and perceptually centered human investigators. Speaking of the "relationship" between the macroscopic objects of practical life and the unobservable micro-theoretical entities of high-level physics, Sellars unflinchingly affirms,

> microtheories explain why inductive generalizations pertaining to a given domain and *any refinement of them within the conceptual framework of the observation language* are at best approximations to the truth . . . theories explain [inductive, phenomenological] laws by explaining why the [observational] objects of the domain in question obey the laws that they do to the extent that they do.[11]

Sellars goes on to draw the inevitable conclusion: "According to the view I am proposing, correspondence rules would appear in the material mode of statements to the effect that the objects of the observational framework *do not really exist – there really are no such things.* They envisage the *abandonment* of a sense and its denotation."[12] Of course, the micro-theories posited are all, on Sellars's view, tethered (however attenuatedly) to observational clues; also, by hypothesis, the properties of the real entities of the micro-theories in question cannot, in principle, be explicated in observational terms. Nevertheless, Sellars apparently is able to preserve "a sense and its denotation" with respect to such entities. On the evidence, it is the universal invariance of micro-theoretical laws that fixes the reality of the entities of the associated theories – in virtue of which observational regularities may be said to "obey . . . to the extent that they do" those particular invariances – and confirms (if anything can) the true referents of our world. On the other hand, such invariances are themselves hostage in a double sense: first, because they must be the adjusted idealizations *of* given empirical regularities, for which there is no independent evidence of their "approximative" realism; and, second, because continuous corrections of such idealizations must rely on a confident inductivism that is itself a creature of the vagaries of the shifting history of the sciences.[13]

Bas van Fraassen, who borrows from Sellars the title of his own discussion of the same matter, reverses Sellars's claim and conviction as completely as one can. The scientific realist (Sellars, for instance) holds that "a physical theory is completely adequate only if it is true. My own view," van Fraassen goes on to say, "is that physical theories do indeed describe much more than what is observable, but that what matters is empirical adequacy, and not the truth or falsity of how they go beyond the observable phenomena":

> To present a theory is to specify a family of structures, its *models*; and secondly, to specify certain parts of those models (the *empirical substructures*) as candidates for the direct representation of observable phenomena. The structures which can be described in experimental and measurement reports we can call *appearances*: the theory is empirically adequate if it has some model such that all appearances are isomorphic to empirical substructures of that model.[14]

Van Fraassen substitutes a "conceptual model" of a theory for Sellars's realist micro-theory – the result being that, on a suitable isomorphism between theory and empirical data, a scientist "*accepts* the theory but . . . does not *believe* it; [that is,] *accepts the theory as empirically adequate*, but does not *believe it to be true*."[15] He does not believe the theory to be true unless "one of its models correctly represents the world . . . the real one."[16] On van Fraassen's (anti-realist) account (what he calls "constructive empiricism"), "*Science aims to give us theories which are empirically adequate; and acceptance of a theory involves as belief only that it is empirically adequate.*" It will be empirically adequate "exactly if what it says about the observable things and events in this world, is true – exactly if it 'saves the phenomena'."[17]

Nevertheless, van Fraassen admits that the disjunction between "observable" and (theoretical) "unobservable" is subject to the constraint that "all our language is thoroughly theory-infected," that "the point at issue for the realist is . . . the reality of the entities postulated in science, [and that] the term 'observable' classifies putative entities, and has logically nothing to do with existence." He adds, "even if observability has nothing to do with existence," even if "what counts as an observable phenomenon is [only] a function of what the epistemic community is (that *observable* is *observable-to-us*)," "it is, on the face of it, not irrational to commit oneself [and science] only to a search for theories that are empirically adequate."[18] What the relationship is between empirically fixing the distributed truths thereby collected ("truths-to-us") and the pragmatic (Duhemian-like) holism within the space of which we "save the phenomena" – given the changing history of science and given the tacit dependence of what we count as observable (within that span of change) on our changing theories and conceptual schemes – is never entirely clear enough to confer on the use of the epithet "empirical adequacy" authority beyond the punctual moment that (one supposes) van Fraassen means to assign it.[19]

Finally, by an ingenious third route that opposes Sellars's form of realism but also opposes van Fraassen's form of (empiricist) anti-realism, Nancy Cartwright declares,

> Realists are inclined to believe that if theoretical laws are false and inaccurate, then phenomenological laws are more so. I urge just the reverse. When it comes to the test, fundamental laws are far worse off than the phenomenological laws they are supposed to explain . . . the falsehood of fundamental laws is a consequence of their great explanatory power.[20]

Cartwright agrees in a limited formal sense with van Fraassen – against the scientific realist – that "the appearance of truth [of the realist's theoretical laws] comes from a bad model of explanation, a model that ties laws directly to reality"; whereas the correct "route from theory to reality is from theory to model, and then from model to phenomenological law. The phenomenological laws are indeed true of the objects in reality – or might be; but the fundamental laws are true only of objects in the model."[21] The crux of her argument – now, as much against van Fraassen as against Sellars – is that "explanation [as such] is [not] a guide to truth [but nevertheless] causal reasoning [as in experimental situations] provides good grounds for our beliefs in theoretical entities."[22] Her view, then, is that "we can reject theoretical laws without rejecting theoretical entities."[23]

It is surely clear that the vagaries of the philosophy of science itself are such that not only the empirically descriptive incompleteness of would-be theoretical entities but also the disputatiousness of their very existence indicates that a firm disjunction between the real referents of our world and merely fictional, heuristic, instrumental, or model-theoretic entities, and between the real referents and what, for whatever reasons, we happen to commit ourselves to ontologically, is by no means a secure one. To admit that much is not yet to counsel skepticism. But, to avoid the threat of a vigorous skepticism, it seems reasonable to construe the referential devices of our language as supple enough not to be completely done in, misled, drawn into hopeless falsities, rendered in-effectual, merely by the smooth shifts of normal discourse moving between the observational and the theoretical, between the actual and the imaginary, and between what at any moment we suppose to be real and what actually is real.

There appear to be only two lines of strategy open to the non-skeptic: on one, he can determine once and for all what in a distributively determinate sense *are* the real entities and phenomena of the world, and then hold his referential and (associated) predicative devices to those precise constraints. Presumably, this is fairly close to what Frege and Russell intended by the reform of the use of proper names.[24] Or, he can permit those devices to play as they will, without fear that they are in any formal sense disabled merely by our ontological uncertainties and occasional failures. Since, on the evidence, the first is an impossible prospect, we can hardly resist subscribing to the second. Nevertheless, it is a fact that the general history of the theory of reference is overwhelmingly committed to alternative accounts of the sort the first strategy requires and alone favors – not, of course, in the narrow sense that grammar determines "what there is" but in the sense of ontological commitment in which an appropriately "deep" or "scientific" grammar determines what we should or must mean to take as real or true about what is real, in uttering sentences having the structure they have.

It is extremely important to concede that the referential and predicative acts we utter in natural discourse (leaving aside for the time being contentious theories of what we actually do do in making reference and in predicating whatever we do predicate of our would-be referents) *are*, for the most part, as effective as we suppose language in general to be – are, therefore, however surprisingly, hardly subverted by all our swirling theoretical disagreements about ontological resources and ontic commitments, hardly affected by our obviously diverse, even uncertain, referential intentions.[25] The important point is that, in natural language at least, reference and predication are generally inseparable and that the resources of both (partly because of that fact) cannot preclude – for either ontological or epistemological reasons – indeterminacies of a range even wider than whatever we may be obliged to admit by theorizing about cultural entities and cultural phenomena.

On a Duhemian view (to which, in rather different ways, van Fraassen and Quine adhere[26]), on a view favoring Quine's "Two Dogmas" argument,[27] on a view favoring Thomas Kuhn's notion of paradigm shifts (for example, regarding Galileo's and Aristotle's sighting of pendulums),[28] on a view favoring Sellars's general discounting of the realist import of observationality, it is clearly uncertain what may rightly be claimed to be the crisply determinate form and nature of the distributed, empirically discernible objects of our familiar world. On the positivist frustration at the inaccessibility of empirical paraphrases of the characterization of putative theoretical entities,[29] on the anti-realist theme favored by van Fraassen, on the realist tolerance of views favored by Cartwright (hardly bothered at all by the dearth of observational characterizations of our would-be theoretical entities), on the general admission of error and the need for altering (not always clearly correcting) our accounts of both observational and theoretical entities, under the influence of historical and praxical change and preformational bias, we cannot be quite sure of the lineaments of the phenomena of the physical and biological world even "before" we venture to characterize the cultural. In being thus uncertain about substantive ontological matters – both first-order and second-order – it is more than difficult to see how we could ever suppose that grammar holds the clue to all minimally admissible ontologies.

This is a roundabout way of saying that admissions of all the sorts mentioned count as profoundly intentionalized (or, Intentionalized) commitments on the part of the most stubbornly extensionalist speculations we are ever likely to assemble – even where the phenomena in question are central to the physical sciences; and that, therefore, the thesis that, on an argument already given,[30] cultural entities are *embodied* entities possessing *incarnate* proprerties – the admission that they can only be designated in Intentionally complex ways, that they manifest Intentional properties, that they may be ontologically indeterminaate in certain respects that the law of excluded middle could not accommodate – cannot by itself, or by reflecting on the formal requirements of reference and predication and ascriptions of truth, justify discounting its plausibility. In short, the puzzles of ontic indeterminacies with respect to both reference and predication inhere in the use of both, simply because, on the most promising view, neither the formal features of reference nor those of predication (nor, *a fortiori*, those of ascribing truth-values to "whole sentences") is likely to vary – or to vary nearly as widely or as wildly – as do our extreme theories of them. We may confirm the point (and gain the advantage) by reviewing the principal accounts of reference and by attempting to construct an ontologically neutral theory of reference itself.

Turn, then, to the theory of reference, and consider that the mere notion that reference is relational already harbors a certain realist metagrammar that is bound to play havoc with ontologies that are frankly Intentionally complex.

II

There are many strategies by which to try to ensure or, opposing the thrust of much of current analytic philosophy, to redeem the intuitive thesis that we may refer to fictional, intensional, or modal "entities" – granted not to exist – despite the fact that thay do not exist. Many recent theorists reject such attempts, arguing that for instance the fictional *is* actual or does exist as part of the real world.[31] Others argue that we cannot recover reference to the fictional since we cannot refer to what does not exist and since the fictional does not exist.[32] It is, however, not implausible to hold that the fictional is not real or actual: with care, that reading may be extended (or refused extension) to what is often meant in speaking of the intensional or modal – for instance, regarding the number of possible fat men in an actual doorway.[33] What is peculiarly problematic is the issue of whether, *if* would-be referents are fictional or nonexistent, "they" can be successfully referred to – and, in what sense and with what consequences. The argument that it is unreasonable to construe the fictional as part of the real world is quite another matter from that of whether, though nonexistent, the fictional can be referred to. Also, whether if reference to the fictional is possible it need be denied that extraneous complications regarding would-be reference can arise with respect to particular instances of the fictional or intensional (as with the real world itself) is quite another matter from that of whether any such reference can be viably admitted at all. Here, we shall be largely concerned with the latter question.

Still, at this moment in the lengthy history of the attempted resolution of the matter, it will pay us to approach the issue a little gingerly – in a way that may encourage initial sympathy as least for an effort that will be taken at once to defy the established canon. There is a sense in which the perceived force of a solution depends on one's affording (in the process of attempting to provide it) an impression of having grasped its bearing on constraints assumed to have accumulated through the entire philosophical tradition – and, in doing that, of having to some extent offset those constraints wherever they would have disallowed *ab initio* the very alternative to be advanced. Thus perceived, there is good reason to suppose that there is a common thread of objection (to the project at hand) that may be drawn from the views of such disparate thinkers as Parmenides, Bertrand Russell, and W. V. Quine. Parmenides's formalism is, of course, not at all easy to place, let alone assess; and although Russell and Quine are both strongly committed to versions of extensionalism, Russell is an empiricist who holds very robust views about distributed knowledge of the actual world – by distributed acquaintance; and Quine is an extreme holist regarding science, also an extreme empiricist opponent of any and every form of cognitive privilege. It is not at once clear that the selection of these three figures can be brought together in a convenient and perspicuous way, in any effort to break out of certain well-established prejudices regarding referential acts; but there can be little doubt that the most focused accounts rarely stray very far from the rather different light each has chosen to cast in reflecting on the shadowy topic of referential discourse.

We shall have to risk conceptual scatter, then, by first setting in place a loose or loosened sense of the limited effectiveness – against our undertaking – of arguments that might be drawn from these and like-minded theorists. It may be hoped that a margin of play may be fairly claimed (and conceded) within which to reconsider would-be strategies regarding fictional reference in particular. Otherwise, the attempt to treat such reference *as* reference may be dismissed out of hand as simply irresponsible. The argument is not primarily intended to clinch an account of fictional reference opposed to the familiar analytic treatment of the matter. It is intended rather – and first – to introduce such a line of reasoning. Should it prove positively compelling, so much the better. But it is too much to expect that it will do so straight off.

About Parmenides: one may plausibly argue that he was profoundly mistaken, and in at least two distinct ways. For one thing, of what Is[34] (whatever that may be), one may suppose or believe that it Is Not or that there Is nothing that there (truly) Is: or that what Is has (merely) come into being (which, on Parmenides's view, apparently means that it Is Not). And, of what Is Not, one may similarly conjecture that it Is or that there (truly) Is what (truly) Is Not. This is not to deny that "What Is, Is" and "What Is Not, Is Not" are true – necessarily. It is only to say that that is quite irrelevant to the possibility being broached (the possibilities of what we may *think*) and hardly affects its coherence. There is surely no antecedent reason for supposing that when we think (when we think, as we say, of "objects," of this and that) we always think and can only think of what – quite independently of our thinking – *Is*. It would be most extraordinary if such a constraint obtained. It would be extraordinary, also, if when we thought of "anything," we invariably or necessarily thought that "*it*" *Is*. We might, for instance, think of what Is Not (or of what we *think* Is Not) that it Is Not.[35] Rejecting or entertaining such possibilities need not adversely affect Parmenides's dictum, although it does suggest its own remarkably limited importance and the profound ambiguity that surrounds its interpretation. Secondly, although one may know that "What Is, Is" and "What Is Not, Is Not" are necessary truths, such knowledge is vacuous in a distributive sense, in that knowing *that* entails nothing regarding human knowledge of the real world (whatever that may be or include). To know that what Is, Is and what Is Not, Is Not is not to know *what* Is or *what* Is Not. To say that what is impossible to think cannot possibly be is vacuously true, insofar as that hardly informs us of *what* is thinkable or not thinkable or of what the limits of *human* thinking (for instance) may be. (This last possibility, of course, is akin to the *caveat* of the so-called anti-realist.[36]) *If* he actually meant to hold that *what* Is is known, not merely *that*, of whatever Is, it is necessarily true that it Is, Parmenides nevertheless never shows that what Is *is* suitably transparent to our cognition – so that we can both know *what Is and* know, of *that* (other than formally or vacuously), that *it* Is. A convenient way of expressing the distinction at stake is simply to acknowledge that "What Is, Is" and "What Is Not, Is Not" are entirely uninterpreted formulae and tell us absolutely nothing about actual referential intentions or the proper way of speaking of the world we take it we inhabit. We must, in all cases, distinguish between assessing the truth of any thesis about what is the most perspicuous way of viewing our discourse about the actual world (which, we take it, we are in touch with, in some sense cognitively, in a distributed way) and assessing the truth of and any thesis about what is the inclusive range of intelligible human discourse (insofar as it may or may not be confined to the actual world).

One commentator, favoring a well-marked trail, affirms, "The intellect is the criterion, and what it can think, exists; what it cannot think, does not exist."[37] But that is both textually extravagant and intellectually wedded to some version of the cognitive transparency of reality – which our own contemporary tradition is largely persuaded cannot be defended.[38] Still, there is an important insight lurking in this commentator's oversimple reading: one may perhaps argue that "Being is the only possible object of thought"[39] – not that mere thinking somehow entails the existence of what Is and what is thought. Even that thesis is either necessarily false or taken as necessarily true because of an equivocation. For Parmenides himself affirms that (of what Is Not) "you could neither recognize that which IS NOT, nor express it."[40]

"Objects" of thought (whatever they are) must be specifiable in some sense in order to enable Parmenides to affirm what we have just noted he affirms. What this will involve must be of some diverse sort, since even to "think" of square circles is not (yet) relevantly explained by merely analyzing the declared denial of the possibility of there being a square circle – as, say, "Necessarily, it is not the case that there is a this or a that that is both circular and square"; and, since, even if it were so explained, it would not help in understanding what is involved in "thinking" about something as existing that, contingently, happens not to exist, not to exist any longer, never to have existed, or to have been merely and deliberately imagined to exist with the full knowledge that what is thus imagined could never exist – just because it is "only" being imagined to exist. Put very simply, there is no obvious way in which to derive an account of what may be actually *thought* from an analysis or recommendation regarding any set of *sentences* that we introduce – or, for that matter, from an analysis or recommendation regarding the use of "What Is" and "What Is Not" in the entirely formal and otherwise uninterpreted sense assigned Parmenides. The upshot is that Parmenides's dicta do not really help in the analysis of natural languages – with regard to reference, denotation, intention, or the kinds of "objects" of thought we normally acknowledge within the range of familiar discourse. If Parmenides had meant to deny these things, then, as argued, he was profoundly mistaken; but, of course, it is entirely possible that he did not mean to construe his own dicta in any way contrary to what we are here insisting on.

Moving rather abruptly forward in time: the theory of reference, as it has been generally pursued in the interval between the appearance of Russell's "On Denoting"[41] and Quine's "On What There Is," may not unreasonably be taken to have set the principal, relatively unified project for nearly all Anglo-American analytic accounts of reference down to our own day. Nevertheless, there is a salient naiveté and narrowness about that project, partly betrayed by its own internal features and partly exposed by reference to a larger context of speculation: these weaknesses jointly suggest a conception of reference entirely at variance with the master-theme that Russell and Quine more or less share – and that Parmenides is sometimes made to share. Russell of course pretty well conflates the issues of denotation and reference, essentially because of his overly sanguine view about a strong form of knowledge by acquaintance and because, as Strawson has so convincingly shown, of his failure to distinguish between propositions and speech acts.[42] But there is also a fundamental difference between Russell's and Quine's speculations about reference, since Quine, pretty much in accord with his thesis about the indeterminacy of translation – his rejection of any strong form of knowledge by acquaintance and his relegation of reference to a distinctly subordinate and parasitic role within the theory and practice of language – could hardly wish to ground an account of reference in anything like Russell's way. Nevertheless, in the same spirit in which he presses an empiricist program at the very moment he opposes the "dogmas of empiricism" (for instance, against Carnap),[43] Quine pursues something very much like Russell's empiricist program of reference (with regard to proper names as well as predicates) just when he introduces his own form of ontological relativism, his pragmatic and somewhat skeptical views of knowledge, and his firm emphasis on incompletely analyzable background conditions affecting the articulation of reference and denotation. There is no other way to understand Quine's proposals about "pegasizing" and the "inscrutability [or opacity] of reference."[44]

The strict upshot of Quine's account is that Quine largely abandons reference in favor of "ontic commitment" – which means *both* that he cannot and will not fix reference in realist terms that are epistemically reliable in just that regard, and that reference (such as it is in thought and speech, in the *use* of sentences) becomes a distinctly intentional notion. This of course goes entirely contrary to the usual reading of Quine's main purpose, said to agree with Russell's and Carnap's at least in attempting to provide an entirely extensional analysis of the whole of what is important in language. But, in speaking of (ontic) "commitment" rather than of what we may safely claim to know there is in the world, Quine clearly makes the articulation of what we *take* it there is, *internal – opaquely internal – to our own thought and speech.*[45] And yet, at the same time, the very point of proposing to read "Pegasus" as a uniquely satisfiable general predicate – not even a definite description – makes no sense if we lack in principle (or even in real-time terms) any distributed epistemic access to the world, in terms of which fair approximations to a *complete* account of the truth-conditions of familiar predicates can be given. (It may be observed here, in passing, that Quine approaches rather dangerously and surprisingly close to Leibniz's view about confining individual things to one world – the one actual world, in Quine's case – and about the unchangeability of even the accidental properties of every such individual.[46]) The fact is that, in natural-language contexts *and* on Quine's theory applied to natural-language contexts, reference is more nearly invariably "story-relative" than "pegasized" (extensionally manageable) and is, as such, quite adequate for our purposes. But this is an entirely heterodox way of reading Quine – one that makes him the unintended champion of the intentionalists (or intensionalists).[47]

There is no obvious way to guage the power and usefulness of Quine's recommendaton – in the light of his own philosophical claims – except as a somewhat nostalgic sketch of what might have been possible with regard to reference and denotation *if* Russell or Carnap had been more or less right (which, on Quine's view, is not possible at all). And, yet, Quine himself urges us to pursue "empiricism without the dogmas." So he says, quite characteristically,

in point of epistemological footing the physical objects and the gods differ only in degree and not in kind. Both sorts of entities enter our conception only as cultural posits. The myth of physical objects is epistemologically superior to most in that it has proved more efficacous than other myths as a device for working a manageable structure into the flux of experience.[48]

This cannot be true in any sense that could actually support the treatment of "pegasizing" as the predicate Quine wants; for that would require that, whatever our epistemic myths, we could actually, distributively, sort *the entire system* within which we introduce reference and denotation. And that's not possible.

This is the fatal weakness of Quine's otherwise intriguing encouragement: "*Total* science, mathematical and natural and human, is [like the algebra of numbers] similarly but more extremely underdetermined by experience. The edge of the *system* must be kept squared with experience . . . ."[49] In Quine's world, there *can* be no epistemic grasp of the *total* range of science or of its entire *system* or, for that matter, of the *distributed* features of any empirically encountered order of things whether systematically closed or not. But our not being able to gain such a grasp essentially affects the pursuit of universal laws and the exclusively extensional treatment of predicates, definite descriptions, and proper names.

Now, then, the irony of this part of the history of theories of reference and denotation is just that the two themes that are most characteristic of Quine's general philosophy are also most characteristic of the leading currents of contemporary Continental European philosophy – *and*, in the context of Continental philosophy, they lead to a radically different theory of how we may parse natural language terms and structures with regard to normal referential and denotative functions.[50] In fact, they lead to a theory that is frontally opposed to Quine's – and, *a fortiori*, to Russell's and, by reasonable extension, to what is usually made of Parmenides's pronouncements. The two themes are these:

1   that there is no cognitively privileged access to reality, that reality is not cognitively transparent, that foundationalism is untenable; and
2   that cognitive inquiry is inextricably preformed by the background conceptions embedded in the natural language we acquire, that questions of meaning and questions of truth cannot be disjoined at any point, that there are indefinitely many alternative conceptual schemata that, in terms of effectiveness, cannot be cognitively discounted if the one we happen to favor is itself found to be moderately effective, that the "ultimate" testing of the adequacy of any part of our theories depends on being able to test the adequacy of any would-be total and exhaustive system of such theories, (but) that that condition cannot be satisfied and cannot be known to be satisfied.

If, conceding 1 and 2, reference may be said to obtain *only if* a suitable relationship obtains between our actually using a referential device and some particular entity or phenomenon *external* to the restrictive range of 1 and 2 that, within that range, we intend to make reference to, *then there are no referents* (whatever the "independent" world may independently harbor).

The problematic nature of Quine's would-be solution is deepened considerably when we realize that whatever *is* sanguine in Quine's epistemological outlook depends on the thesis that the extensional adequacy of *sentences* for (the whole of) science *can* be fixed independently of fixing *any* of the *terms* of such sentences – by which the activities of reference and denotation are effectuated. This is the point, of course, of that famous remark of Quine's, "Occasion sentences and stimulus meaning are general coin, terms and reference are local to our conceptual scheme"[51] – to which Quine adverts even in his recent autobiography.[52] But the thesis is an utter nonstarter, since there is no way to segregate sentence and term conceptually or to test, however provisionally, the truth of sentences without *some* commitment both to the referential import of what such sentences are about and to what those who are to test them are prepared to admit and recognize they are about. Once the connection is grasped, the naiveté of the extensionalist program (earlier charged) becomes quite clear – at least as far as the issue can be expected to bear on whatever else may be thought to be of promise in the program. It is *terms* that threaten the extensionalism of Quine's program; and so, to preserve that program, Quine demotes metaphysics, the parsing of sentences into terms, reference itself – to the "inscrutable" – so that, in effect, we are obliged to "intentionalize" ontic commitment (to speak of what we "take it" there is, without ever fixing or being able to fix what there actually is). Skepticism and holism rule out a signal role for reference; but preservation of truth, *contra* Quine, forces us to concede the symbiosis of word and sentence. There is, therefore, no conceptually feasible way to prise truth and reference apart, once we support the possibility of an empirical science.

This, of course, is the fatal mistake that Davidson and Putnam and others have inherited from Quine – that ensures the incoherence of any formal grammar or formal semantics of natural language meant to be applied to the same empirically accessible world in which natural language is at home.[53] Empirically, the gauge of truth is the same as the gauge of reference – even in a Duhemian world. Quine's (confessedly) ersatz program of fixing the "stimulus-meaning" of *sentences* cannot escape fixing the "stimulus-reference" of *terms* since they are presupposed and entailed *in* fixing the other.

The point may be pressed a step further, if we recall – in the Quinean spirit, in the spirit of an empiricism exorcised of its own dogmas, in the spirit of an extensionalized treatment of dependently introduced (empirical) terms and predicates within an antecedently extensionalized (formal) treatment of sentences, in the spirit of construing meanings in terms of truth-conditions and of denying reference a primary role in the theory of language – that Donald Davidson has actually sought to apply Tarski's formal semantics to the theory of sentences fitted to the work of the empirical sciences.[54] Davidson, however, makes no attempt to explain, in an epistemically detailed way, how to resolve problems of coextensive but semantically different predicates within real-time constraints; or how to treat the predicates of natural languages in exhaustively extensional ways; or how to fit the predicates of natural languages to an antecedent syntax that is strictly extensionalized along Tarskian lines; or how to replace such predicates with others that empirically preserve what is scientifically wanted and at the same time meet the formal requirements Davidson wishes to impose. Lacking answers to these questions, we would not be unfair if we characterized Davidson's treatment of reference and denotation as a particularly careful attempt to protect the Quinean program against its own unheeded concessions: it is, therefore – like Quine's program – a formulation of what it *might* have been possible to defend if only we had cognitive access to the world (in the way affirmed in Russell's or Carnap's view, or at least in accord with a more sanguine form of access than Quine concedes) that (on the theory and on independent grounds) we clearly lack.

The irony stares us in the face that, *if* we could recover such a cognitive assurance, we neither could, nor would need to, downgrade the executive function of reference itself (along Quine's – and Davidson's – lines); correspondingly, *if* we mean to recover the full empirical role of science, we cannot segregate the would-be syntax of empirical sentences from our cognitively informed (semantic) constraints – that is, from an understanding of just how far we may support an extensionalized treatment *of empirical predicates.* Furthermore, *whether* we support a sanguine picture of science or retreat to Quine's holism, there is no longer any conceptual objection to be posed against admitting reference to fiction and the nonexistent – or to the ontically uneasy theoretically entities we entertain. So seen, the continuum of theories of reference from Russell to Davidson suffers from attempting to preserve a strongly extensional life (for rather different reasons) in the face of the recalcitrant consequences of the two themes, 1 and 2, that actually link Anglo-American and Continental European philosophy at the present time, though without intergrating their respective projects along common lines.

III

The Quinean strategy – therefore, the strategy of Davidson and Hilary Putnam[55] – must assign reference an entirely subordinate function in the characterization of scientific inquiry. It must do so because (a) it espouses a strong holism, (b) it rejects all forms of cognitive privilege, and (c) it construes the parsing of sentences employed in empirical inquiry as subject to the preformational influence of the background theories we tacitly absorb in learning our native language and native culture. The Russellian strategy can (within limits) afford to conflate reference and denotation because (a) it espouses a strong form of distributed epistemic acquaintance on which the whole of science depends, and (b) it discounts the permanent effect of distortions due to one's personal or cultural history as far as the prospects of a realist science are concerned. Hence, reference (as Russell treats it) is always central to his theory of language. This perhaps explains why he has no need to distinguish between would-be referents (or *denotata*) that contingently never existed and fictional referents that (also but necessarily) never existed – why there seems to be no difference, for Russell, between "the present King of France" and, say, Sherlock Holmes.[56] The Parmenidean strategy seems to deny that one can discourse at all about what Is Not. But Parmenides never quite explains (a) how this claim constraints discourse about the actual world or human cognition in general, or (b) how it bears on his own discourse about the (apparently) actual world, which, on his own hypotheses, must be characterized (in some way) in terms of what Is Not. Perhaps John Searle's would-be Axiom of Existence is the most familiar modern, watered-down version of Parmenides's dictum.[57] But it remains completely undefended, offers no linkage to Parmenides's actual notion, and in effect cheats with regard to reference to fiction.[58]

The surprising upshot is that, relative to Parmenides, Russell, and Quine – and that very large army of theorists who converge in various ways toward their very different views – we really have no comprehensive theory of reference and no theory that satisfactorily disallows reference to fictional, intensional, or modal "objects . . . as such." Of course, it may be that certain uses of modal objects – Quine's fat man in the doorway, for instance – may not be wanted or allowed in a reasonably workable theory of the functions of natural languages; but such restrictions may be *added* for reasons that have nothing to do with any universally binding objection against referring to nonexistent "objects." Here, we should take passing notice of the fact that "*denotata*" are often treated as requiring that we take "them" to be actual or real, whereas "referents" – intuitively construed intentionally – are often permitted to "include" the nonexistent. This bears, of course, on relational and nonrelational theories of reference, to which we shall soon turn. Before we consider the nonrelational option directly, however, we must enlarge our account a little, to include Gottlob Frege's influential thesis, in order to round out our sense of the disadvantages of the relational option.

Frege clearly believed that natural languages could be replaced – in order at least to exhibit perspicuously and unambiguously certain essential logical forms that all communicative discourse requires. So, for example, in a footnote to "Naming and Necessity" ("Über Sinn und Bedeutung," 1892) Frege observes, "In the case of an actual proper name such as 'Aristotle' opinions as to the sense may differ. . . . So long as the reference remains the same, such variations of sense may be tolerated, although they are to be avoided in the theoretical structure of a demonstrative science and ought not to occur in a perfect language."[59] Russell took *Principia Mathematica* to have laid the reliable groundwork for such an extensionally "perfect language," in virtue of which he candidly says, in the paper on denoting, that "All the difficulties with which I am acquainted [regarding denoting phrases] are met, so far as I can discover, by the theory which I am about to explain."[60]

Russell took "denoting phrases" to range over definite and indefinite descriptions. Rather curiously, he took "a man," as an example of expressions that "denote ambiguously," to denote "not many men, but an ambiguous man"; also, his examples of definite descriptions – notoriously, "the present King of France" and "the present King of England" – simply divide the field between denoting expressions that do and those that do not denote any definite particular (actual) object. Hence, Russell treated fictional objects as "non-entities" and included their putative descriptions, along with "the present King of France" – and " 'the round square,' 'the even prime other than 2,' 'Apollo,' 'Hamlet,' etc., . . . satisfactorily . . . [as] denoting phrases which do not denote anything."[61]

Frege, of course, as is well known, spoke of the sense and reference of sentences (admitting the usual translation) in addition to speaking of the sense and reference of names. It was in fact in the context of analyzing the sentence "Odysseus was set ashore at Ithaca while sound asleep" that he concluded that, although that sentence clearly had a sense it lacked a reference (that is, a truth-value). As he remarks, "Whoever does not admit the name has reference can neither apply nor withhold the predicate" – the famous truth-value gap problem that Russell appeared to avoid and Strawson appeared to embrace.[62] One implication of this view, seldom emphasized, is that Frege clearly thought of the order of reality as including the True and the False as referents; hence, since he also thought we could be straightforwardly successful in fixing such reference, Frege held a sanguine view regarding the powers of human cognition and thought and the conformable transparency of reality; although, of course, he approached the question as if it would yield to a prior formal analysis of the logical structure of the sentences of a "perfect language" rather than to a close study of the actual cognitive powers of man. This is the profound point of the full distinction between *Sinn* and *Bedeutung*, linked to sentences and not merely names, *and* operative in contexts generating truth-value gaps both with respect to fiction (as in the Odysseus sentence) and with respect to the contingently nonexistent (as in the present-King-of-France sentence [or assertion] – as in Strawson's application of Frege's distinction to Russell's specimen cases).[63]

Most of this is familiar history. But there is a great difference between working confidently within the tradition to cover all contingencies that yeoman investigators are liable to turn up, and questioning, from outside the tradition, its very capacity to gather in an increasingly adequate and convincing way a thoroughly extensional account of reference. For example, to press Russell and Frege very lightly at this point, both seem more concerned with what is now called denotation than with reference – a distinction indelibly focused by Strawson's careful review of Russell's original paper; but neither explains *what* sort of process or act or whatnot *denoting* is or *why* successful denoting should be restricted to real or existing objects or real particulars of any sort. In fact, almost no one seems to have answered these questions except *within* the extensionalist tradition itself – which is in a sense already too late, as the accumulating record confirms.[64] Certainly, it is not convincing to lump the name "Hamlet" with "the round square" and "the present King of France" as simply failing to denote *sans phrase* – when what is meant is that it is logically impossible that anything should satisfy the literal description "the round square"; that there is (now, at the moment of speaking) nothing satisfying the description "the present King of France"; and that, at least in speaking naturally, though hardly fully in a philosophically responsible way, "Hamlet" appears to denote Hamlet (that is, without prejudice to what a fictional entity might be supposed to be *and* without prejudice to what denoting anything might be supposed to be).

It is reasonably clear that, through the entire analytic tradition, nearly everyone who has put his hand to the question (surely, at least, nearly everyone who has attracted sustained professional attention) has assumed that denotation or reference is a *relationship* of some sort. In fact, when, in "On Referring," Strawson declares his intention to show that "Russell's Theory of Descriptions . . . embodies some fundamental mistakes" in conflating denoting and referring,[65] he, too, is very clearly committed to treating both denotation and reference as, or as entailing, relationships of some essential sort. So, in introducing what he calls "the 'uniquely referring use'" of expressions, Strawson signifies that these are used "to mention or refer to some individual person or single object or particular event or place or process, in the course of doing what we should normally describe as making a statement about that person, object, place, event, or process."[66] The emphatic restriction to the actual is unmistakable. Despite his impressive enlargement of the topic of denotation and reference, therefore, and despite his disagreements with both Frege and Russell, Strawson shows his profound allegiance to the underlying commitments Frege and Russell share. For the truth-value gap problem obtains only within a relational interpretation of denotation (Frege) or of reference (Strawson), within an extensionalist model of natural language; and it is (or could be) eliminated, on that interpretation, only by providing a solution like Russell's or Carnap's (or whatever might serve as its analogue in referential contexts). If one denied that denotation and reference were relational in some sense fixed independently of mere intention, one would challenge at a stroke the entire project and purpose of the extensionalist tradition; and, if, on independent grounds, extensionalism were found systematically defective (for example, in eliminating opaque contexts of reference, or in applying Tarski's so-called Convention T to natural languages without remainder, or in fixing belief states and other psychological states extensionally so as to facilitate mind/body identity claims, or in eliminating intensionally specified actions and actual causes), then perhaps the alternative to an extentionalist account of reference (denotation) would be welcome or at least hospitably received – and the single-minded direction of the analyses of reference and denotation would be called to account.

One useful way of posing the contrast is to concede at once that a relational treatment of reference need not (on every interpretation) be opposed to a nonrelational treatment: it may be, merely, a heuristic convenience provided *within* a basically nonrelational account, or such a convenience additionally and independently supported by and brought into accord with whatever we take to be our distributed cognitive powers (facilitating any effective science). A strong relational treatment that positively precludes the nonrelational must be either (1) committed, rather as with Russell, to some robust notion of cognitive privilege with regard to reality, or (2) committed, apart from that, to a strenuous conception of what it is possible to think, along the lines already examined in connection with Parmenides's dictum, or (3) both. The import of the arguments already sketched clearly indicates that the required cognitive privilege is both alien to current Anglo-American *and* Continental European views and utterly rejected by Quine for example and by similar-minded extensionalists; and that no independent reasons of sufficient fortce have ever been advanced for showing that one simply *cannot* intend to refer (or, consequently, succeed in referring) to what one merely imagines or imagines to exist (which, therefore, is meant to remain nonexistent), or that, even if one supported a more sanguine cognitive privilege of Russell's sort, such a commitment would adversely affect the possiblity of being able to refer to what does not exist. There is, in short, a palpable lacuna in the usual extensionalist argument; and there are clear prospects surfacing here that a nonrelational, nonextensionalist account of reference may be quite coherent, sufficently resilient, and even distinctly to be favored. In any case, the strong relatonalist view must restrict itself to the thesis that there *are* objects (of what sort does not here matter), to which we may be *related* by way of reference; whereas the nonrelationalist can accommodate instances of reference that could not be relational (since the would-be referents in question may be said to be – may even necessarily be – nonexistent: fictional entities, for example), without precluding relational reference (by way of a further, epistemically supplemented adjustment). (The details may be postponed for a bit, though it is important, here, to take note of the enlarged opportunities.)

Certainly, it is clear that to deny a relational account is to opt for a radically intentional one; in effect, an account that would concede ineliminable nonextensional (that is, intensional) constraints on every relevant effort to formulate the effective extensional marks of denotative or referential structures. As Russell originally said, "a phrase is denoting solely in virtue of its form" – which is the extensionalist's confidence, unguardedly affirmed.[68] But *Russell's* reason for taking the formalist line was his own ulterior confidence regarding knowledge by acquaintance – regarding empiricist privilege. Deny the latter (as with Quine, despite Quine's adherence to empiricist policies on other grounds): the entire rationale for confidence in (a) a relational (an ontologically relational) conception of reference *and* in (b) a formalist account of ontic commitment utterly collapses. This is what relationalists regarding reference fail to see and what extensionalists who eschew cognitive privilege appreciate (in denying, as they do, a conceptual parity between reference and truth). But the first policy can be no more than arbitrary; and the second, no more than incoherent.

The intentionalist with respect to reference or denotaton or both will deny the sufficiency of logical form to mark the phenomena in question: the intensionalist will, instead, insist on the intensional structures of thinking. Matching Russell's account, but (understandably) moving away from mere logical form to linguistic convention, Strawson explicitly says,

> The requirement for the correct application of an expression in its referring use to a certain thing is something over and above any requirement derived from such ascriptive meaning as the expression may have; it is, namely, the requirement that the thing should be in a certain *relation* to the speaker and to the context of utterance. Let me call this the contextual requirement.[69]

Furthermore, when, very briefly, he considers the use of referring expressions in the context of *Pickwick Papers*, Strawson makes it clear that, though (as G. E. Moore remarked) "some of the statements in *Pickwick Papers* are *about* Mr Pickwick," "it would not *in general* be correct to say that a statement was about Mr X or the so-and-so, unless there were such a person or thing."[70] In general, on a strong relationalist view, there must, on independent grounds, be an actual "object" to which, by way of reference, we can be related. This is why Fregean truth-value gaps imply a sufficiently strong view of human cognitive powers, such that, on the condition of actual assertion, validly designated gaps entail the pertinent nonexistence of what names (or their surrogates) – functionally identified in terms of formal structures alone – rightly serve to denote. A purely formal theory of the structure of reference, however, cannot possibly show why (short of charging incoherence) a nonrelational view of reference must be rejected; and the use of such a theory in cognitive contexts cannot possibly fail to favor some sort of cognitive privilege, though not necessarily of just the sort Russell or Carnap or Strawson might favor.

In his original paper, Strawson had characterized the fictional use of sentences and referring expressions as a "spurious" use – which is to say, as really generating truth-value gaps where they appear not to, as presuming an actual relationship of the required sort where none can be found. But in a footnote Strawson relents and speaks rather of " 'secondary' uses" of such sentences and such expressions – which seems to concede that, in the "secondary" context at least, there need not be any truth-value gaps after all.

John Searle has developed this "secondary" use in a surprisingly robust sense (that, doubtless, Strawson would not endorse). In a complex passage favoring Russell's solution of Meinong's Golden Mountain paradox – in which he indicates his indebtedness to Frege and Strawson and subscribes to what he calls "the axiom of existence"[71] – Searle simply announces that "References to fictional (and also legendary, mythological, etc.) entities are not counter-examples [to the axiom]. One can refer to them as *fictional characters* precisely because they do *exist in fiction*."[72] Searle is quite explicit about his view of reference: "by reference," he says, "I mean not predication, or truth, or extension but *reference*, the *relation* between such expressions as definite descriptions and proper names on the one hand, and the things they are used to refer to on the other."[73] Hence, consistently with this thesis, Searle holds that when, say, Iris Murdoch

> pretends [without intending deception] to refer to a [certain] person [Lieutenant Andrew Chase-White, for instance, in *The Red and the Green*] she creates a fictional person. Now once that fictional character has been created, we who are standing outside the fictional story can really refer to a fictional person. Notice that in the passage about Sherlock Holmes [cited just] above, I really referred to a fictional character . . . I did not *pretend* to refer to a real Sherlock Holmes; I really referred to the fictional Sherlock Holmes.[74]

Searle neglects to tell us *what* a "fictional person" or "character" actually is, but his strategy is obviously to bring fictional discourse into line with the relational conception of reference and thereby to preclude truth-value gaps that, on Strawson's sterner view, might well have been generated. He does say that the usual things said about actual persons ("taken as a piece of serious discourse") would "certainly not be true" of fictional persons;[75] but, apparently, discourse about fictional persons taken as such *is* also a piece of serious discourse. Surely, if "fictional persons" are abstract "entities" somehow created by an author *out of words and images*, it would be very difficult to understand ascriptions made of such entities that appear to parallel (as Searle wishes them to) what we might ordinarily ascribe to actual persons (for instance that "there did exist a Mrs Watson because Watson did get married").[76] Searle apparently wishes to treat the fictional world (created) as a special sub-world in which whatever could "seriously" be said of the creatures of the actual world (our world, so to say) could not similarly be said of those of the other, but in which things of "the same kind" could be "nonseriously" true. But he fails to explain how this could possibly be. Furthermore, it would be difficult to provide a sense in which such entities would not be "ontologically incomplete" (in a sense usually associated with Meinong's theory); so that truth-value gaps might well continue to haunt the account with a peculiar vengeance.[77] At the very least, Searle does not explicate what he himself counts as an "ontology" of fictional characters[78] or whether he agrees, say, with Terence Parsons's attempt to resurrect Meinongian objects (with which at least a part of his formulation appears to converge).[79] But how difficult this maneuver is likely to be may be guessed from Parsons's quite courageous remarks: "We know, e.g., that

Pegasus *is* a winged horse (in the real world), not just that he is a winged horse in *some* world"[80] – which preserves at enormous cost the relational thesis again. Also, at the risk of further complication, it may be remarked that to concede the reality of an author's invention of a *"fictional" character* is not necessarily to concede (or even to address the question of) the existence or (nonexistent) reality of a *fictional entity*. All we need observe is the usual equivocation of "fictional" on what (a) an author invents (perhaps theoretical entities abstractable from and somehow embedded in actual stories) as opposed to what (b) we merely imagine to exist (but cannot possibly exist) even if the activity of so imagining be guided and responsibly encumbered by literary and related constraints drawn from actually invented characters.

One extremely simple and direct way to undermine all ontological accounts of fiction (hence, to dissolve their attendant puzzles) is to affirm, without qualification, that fictional entities Are Not – do not exist, are not actual, in any sense at all. For, once we do this, *the theory of fictional reference can only be a theory of certain of the structures of human thinking*; all attempts to state what are the minimal constraints on actual "objects" that are or happen to be fictional lose their point at once: for example, insistence (as with Nicholas Wolterstorff) on the requirement of conforming, exhaustively with regard to all possible predicates, to the principle of excluded middle,[81] or on Searle's play with the distinctive "nature" of fictional as opposed to living persons, or on Parsons's concern with "incomplete" nonexistent objects as well as with "native" and "immigrant" objects of fictional discourse.[82] (Parsons, of course, has a robust sense of what "exists," and does not take it that "exists in fiction" means at all that *what* "exists in fiction" exists; although he recognizes that existent "objects" – London, for instance – may, as "immigrants," also exist-in-fiction.) Perhaps it is unnecessary to add here – but let us risk the luxury – that the usual attempt to treat reference to fiction relationally is meant to ensure the universal adequacy not only of the relational account but also of a strongly extensional reading of the relational account.

As soon as one distinguishes between "there exists" and "there is," however, *acts of reference* are readily restricted to "there is" constructions, *without precluding* the parallel use of "there exists" constructions; but, if that is so, then reference ceases to be exclusively relational, cannot fail to be intentional in opting between the two constructions, and (most important) is antecedently constrained by what we take it we can *think about* rather than by *any putative ontology* of what "exists" or "is" (nonexistently). This helps to expose the extravagance of solutions such as Wolterstorff's, the irrelevancy of solutions such as Searle's, the too-easy conflating of "exists" and "is" of solutions such as Peter van Inwagen's (favoring ontological readings), the unnecessary complication of Parsons's (otherwise useful) distinction between "exists" and "is" (still favoring an ontological reading).

Parsons is right to refuse to countenance "exists in fiction" as marking a distinction of the same ontological sort as "exists" – although (on his view), within fiction, reference may be made to what exists *and* to what does not exist. But, when he introduces the further distinction between "there exists" and "there is," so that (against van Inwagen, for instance) "there is" may range over what does not exist, he still encumbers that expression (and its cognates) in an ontologically freighted way (as does van Inwagen, who simply equates the force of the two expressions).

Here, one can only repeat that we have a free choice; and that, *if* (as seems likely) the "ontological" reading leads to systematic difficulties, we can always fall back to construing "there is" and its cognate expressions as signifying no more than reference to the internal "objects" of one's thought (or speech) – without prejudice to any analysis of such "objects," except that they must be specified *nonrelationally, non-ontologically, in a way restricted to what is internal to our thinking.* Thinking need not be restricted to "objects" internal to itself: one may think of actual things. But to think of what is actual may be characterized – heuristically, by way of a grammatical convenience – as affirming that the internal "object" of our thinking is identical with some particular actual object. Both the relational import of our referential intention and the ontological standing of the "object" thus intended are independently assignable, on cognitive grounds that inform some putatively minimal referential act.

There is only one strategy that meets these and similar conditions: referential "objects" are, as such, objects only in a grammatical sense or, relative to thinking, no more than intentional in that sense in which they can only be grammatically fixed. Put another way, referents are identified, by the heuristic use of grammar, as "objects" to which we are *related*, by way of thinking, speech, behavior, and the like; but *that* relational device is itself introduced solely as a dependent conceptual convenience by which to manage the analysis of such monadic, indissoluble, but complex phenomena as mental states and mental acts. Nothing that links us to an actual robust world (of whatever description we may favor) is lost or jeopardized by that maneuver; for ontological *and* cognitive questions regarding what exists can always be added to and reconciled with a nonrelational account of reference. All one needs is a policy (intentionally characterized) for identifying what we (intend to) refer to and what, in the real world, is *that*. Also, such provisions are themselves primarily heuristic, even piecemeal. For, if we admit that fictional reference cannot actually be relational (there being no actual *relatum* to relate to), in spite of the fact that reference is most conveniently treated relationally, then it is impossible that our explicative devices will fail to have a touch of the piecemeal about them. That, once again, confirms the difference between the provision of grammatical and logical structures by which to explicate what is involved in thinking and the analysis of ontological claims or commitments conveyed in our thinking. We thereby gain a flexibility denied to the strict relationalist reading of reference. Notice, also, that Parsons's willingness to countenance "impossible objects" (round squares, for instance) as (ontologically) among "what is" (though not among "what exists") is summarily – and happily – avoided.[83]

IV

There are, it should be noted, deeper, easily detailed, ironies generated within the relationalist program. They can all be described as variations on the difficulty – ranging from empirical uncertainty to conceptual indeterminacy – *of fixing the actual referents of any piece of discourse.* For, if that difficulty is genuine, then, *if denotation and reference are or entail relations between words and worldly things,* either we forever risk failing to achieve reference or we forever risk failing to know whether we ever achieve it. But both those possibilities are intellectual scandals. Under such circumstances, imposed by prevailing views of the cognitive intransparency of reality, of the historically contingent and largely tacit background conceptions against which referential claims are made, as well as of inherent uncertainties and alternative possibilities of ontological parsings of discourse, it makes good sense – if the maneuver is viable at all – to retreat to a broadly grammatical account of reference and to eschew all strongly relational accounts that require more ontological reliability than can be guaranteed.

Quine is probably the most explicit and systematic recent skeptic about fixing the actual objects of reference, despite the fact that, in a very broad sense, he is clearly a realist with regard to science and reference. "It is only," he says,

> by [the] outright projection of prior linguistic habits that the [field] linguist can find general terms in the native language at all, or, having found them, match them with his own; stimulus meanings never suffice to determine what words are terms, if any, much less what terms are co-extensive. . . . The point is not that we cannot be sure whether the analytical hypothesis [by which the matching of linguist's and native's terms is accomplished] is right, but that there is not even . . . an objective matter to be right or wrong about.[84]

How, then, in accord with the subtleties of recent realist, idealist, irrealist, realist–idealist theories of the world, could we possibly ensure the referential (or denotational) *relationship,* in virtue of which reference and denotation could succeed – or be known to succeed? There is and can be no answer. But, we may insist, *if* we reject as linguistically incoherent Quine's disjuncton between the assignment of truth-value to "whole" sentences and the subsequent fixity of reference due to the parsing of those sentences *and* of the referential and denotative expressions of other sentences employed to test *their* truth, then (contrary to Quine's and Davidson's and Putnam's views and those of an army of others) it is similarly incoherent to speak of empirical truth without implicating reference *at that very instant.*

The irony, of course, is that it is the extensionalist's own sense of rigor that assigns a deeper and deeper constitutive role to the transient or at least diachronic conceptual networks in terms of which reference and denotation, relationally construed, must make their difficult way. Notice that it is a foregone conclusion that, *if* "fictional entities" can be denoted or referred to, despite the fact that they do not exist, "are" not, are not real or actual, then the so-called causal theory of reference, said to be advocated by Saul Kripke and Keith Donnellan, would be utterly untenable. The reason is that the causal theory and its variations presuppose some version of the relational conception of denotation and reference (thought, because of the allegedly extensional nature of causal contexts, to strengthen th extensionalist program). Nevertheless, Kripke himself has rather neatly observed – speaking of both reality and fiction – that

real reference can shift to another real reference, fictional reference can shift to real, and real to fictional. In all these cases, a present intention to refer to a given entity (or to refer fictionally) overrides the original intention to preserve reference in the historical chain of transmission. The matter deserves extended discussion. But the phenomenon is perhaps roughly explicable in terms of the predominantly social character of the use of proper names emphasized in the text [this remark is a final footnote]; we use names to communicate with other speakers in a common language. This character dictates ordinarily that a speaker intends to use a name the same way as it was transmitted to him; but in [some cases], the "Madagascar" case [discussed, in which either "Madagascar" designates a mythical locality or was erroneously applied by Marco Polo to an island, though it was originally the name for a part of mainland Africa], this social character dictates that the present intention to refer to an island overrides the distant link to native usage.[85]

Here Kripke obviously marks the limitations of the causal theory and introduces, without full development, the possibility of overriding intentional considerations that could be made to challenge a thoroughgoing extensionalism.[86]

Certainly the indeterminacy of fixing what there is in the world – an even more fundamental question than whatever the vagaries of fictional discourse or such puzzle cases as the "Madagascar" case might generate – quite precludes the possibility of construing a completely relational account of denotation and reference. Here, again, Quine provides the extreme option. For, contrary to the usual extensionalist reading of Quine, Quine *never* commits himself to anything like the axiom of existence or to anything like an extensionally relational reading of denotation. This may seem surprising. But a careful reading of the essay "On What There Is" and the many adjustments of Quine's account of reference and denotation should convince one that Quine never strays beyond the question of ontological *commitment* – as opposed to addressing the question of what, ontologically, *there is*. To have gone beyond mere commitment – mere intention, that is (desire or hope or confidence, if you like) – would have been to contradict the very strong statement from *Word and Object* that we considered somewhat earlier. But, should there be any doubts, the following remarks are surely enough to dispel them:

> We can very easily involve ourselves in ontological commitments by saying, for example, that *there is something* (bound variable) which red houses and sunsets have in common [that is, considering the reality of universals and the like]. . . . But this is, essentially, the *only* way we can involve ourselves in ontological commitments: by our use of bound variables . . . To be assumed as an entity is, purely and simply, to be reckoned as the value of a variable . . . a theory is committed to those and only those entities to which the bound variables of the theory must be capable of referring in order that the affirmations made in the theory be true.[87]

Still, if Quine is right about ontological indeterminacy, what could he possibly mean by claiming that he has specified the *only* way to make an ontological commitment – or, for that matter, that his is even one way of making such a commitment? Why not treat commitment – and therefore denotation and reference – intentionally and then spell out what, on independent grounds, we take it is actual? The pretense that an exclusively extensional and relational idiom will work at all seems, on the argument, utterly arbitrary. In effect, Quine is an out-and-out intentionalist who, as with his commitment to analytical hypotheses, denies his own Word thrice.

The question now presents itself most forcefully: what would a nonrelational theory of reference or denotation look like? How would it accommodate the natural sense in which we are related to the things of the actual world, which we do denote and make reference to? And what economies would it possess, or what paradoxes would it avoid, in competition with other theories? The extraordinary thing is that the answer is absolutely elementary. Nothing more is needed than to treat reference and denotation as *grammatical* or *linguistic* distinctions, to free the relevant acts or processes of *all* epistemological and ontological entanglements, and then to recover whichever such entanglements we wish to preserve by suitably *interpreting* sentences employing denotational and referential devices as having just such import. Naturally, a theory of language acquisition and language use is bound to feature the realist import of ordinary language; but that need not be jeopardized at all. The only thing at stake is to construe reference and denotation as grammatical or linguistic *abstractions* from the fullblooded use of natural languages. They, then, are provided, initially, with intentional "objects"; and reference and denotation are initially construed monadically rather than relationally. But, precisely because they are such abstractions (from, say, the full activity of a viable human society), we can, by a suitable, simple, story-relative device, introduce a grammatical (intentional) relationship between denoting term and intended *denotatum*; and, where suitable, we can interpret *that* relationship in whatever existentially rich sense we wish. All we need is a strategy for grammatically detaching the internal "objects" of intentional discourse as (intentionally) dyadically specified objects of denotation (or reference). The parallel that suggests itself comes quite naturally from pictures and portraits. A painting of a centaur, we may say (pretty much in Nelson Goodman's sense), is a centaur-picture, a monadically construed representational piece; but a portrait of Wellington is not only a Wellington-picture but also, *on an interpretation*, a (dyadic) portrait *of* Wellington.[88]

Now, it is decisive to appreciate that, in natural language, quite apart from the complexities of any idealized canon, we already possess effective devices for the required linguistic detachment and interpretation. For example, when we speak of dreams, we do not normally suppose that what are detailed *in* dreams are independent objects that, contingently, others can "have" or relate to instead of the dreamer (who dreams the given dream) – that is, as in having another's toy. And yet, equally normally, we are prepared to talk about what can be discriminated *in* a dream as if "they" were indeed objects to which we can refer and to which the dreamer is somehow related. To twist a famous phrase: we can denote and refer to "sakes" if we wish, even though there are none (none exist). We can replace, *grammatically*, an indissoluble (intentional) monadic predicate by polyadic relational ones *within* the terms of a grammatically altered construction. Similarly, *if* one wishes to treat events as particulars – for instance, to articulate natural entailments that seem too difficult or perhaps impossible to manage directly from natural-language sentences (for example, the obviously intended relationship among the sentences "Sebastian strolled," "Sebastian strolled in Bologna," "Sebastian strolled in Bologna at 2 a.m.," and the like) – it does appear that we would need a merely *grammatical* device for constructing a suitable nominalizaton in virtue of which seemingly monadic predicates would permit us to introduce polyadic predicates of whatever complexity we required. *Whether* we wished to construe any particular such maneuver as having ontological import would depend on whether, for instance, we would be prepared to subscribe to Quine's test or not.[89] So its economy and convenience are obvious.

In effect, we have by a most elementary stroke enriched the suppleness of the extensionalist program itself – precisely by detaching the treatment of ontological and epistemological questions from all questions of a narrowly linguistic or grammatical sort, without, however, damaging in any way the natural presumption that the viability of any language confirms a strongly realist function. Nothing, then, has been lost of whatever disputes about the nature of reality or about the relationship between languages and reality we might care to pursue. One of the direct benefits of this way of viewing matters – perhaps little more than a symptom of a much larger benefit – is that we are thereby able to talk about fictional entities in any natural way we require, without *any* pressure to deny that "Mr Pickwick" denotes Mr Pickwick or that, in using "Mr Pickwick" in the usual way, we are referring to Mr Pickwick. We need not, in so speaking, commit ourselves to the existence or reality of Mr Pickwick (and so need not seek to explain just what kind of queer entity Mr Pickwick is). Give up the relational conception of denotation and reference, construe both primarily as grammatical or linguistic processes, assign their "objects" initially an entirely intentional status, provide a further grammatical device for intentionally detaching their "objects" as dyadically linked for purposes of discourse only, and interpret such relations (where one would) in some ontologically more robust sense on independent grounds: *nothing else affecting the extensionalist program need be altered*, although particular candidate theories about what the formal canon ought to be would doubtless be much affected. For example, all formulas paraphrasable as involving the denotative or referential use of "to be" ("There is . . . ," "Some *x* is . . . ") will, on the theory, lack all existential import *except* on an interpretation or in accord with a given presupposition. Sentences or utterances would no longer be automatically construed, logically, as invariably favoring discourse about the real world unless a special operator were employed. But adjustments of this sort would hardly affect the smooth expectations of the seasoned speakers of a natural language.

This seems like a remarkably small price to exact. In a sense it is; but in a sense, of course, it isn't. For example, a device will have to be provided for construing "existence" as a second-order predicate or for introducing more complex quantifiers that take up the ontologically neutral ones for use in a suitably interpreted domain of discourse.[90] But from another point of view, the preserved power of extensionalism depends entirely on the sufferance of some prior, intentionalized context linking man and his world, at least neutral to, if not actually inimical to, the standard foundational or essentialist or logocentric convictions that have traditionally informed Western philosophy.[91]

Still, to concede that much is not, it must be emphasized, to rush to that other quite mad extreme – defended by the so-called Yale deconstructivists, particularly Hillis Miller and to some extent Paul de Man, theorizing under the rather dangerous influence of Nietzsche – that reality itself is only a supreme fiction, that we live entirely in language, that reference is simply a lie or an utterly inescapable illusion.[92] To avoid the danger that Russell feared (Meinong's paradox), we need hardly subscribe to Russell's own solution. And to reject that solution and all other straightforwardly extensionalist accounts hardly drives us to the extravagance of the Nietzscheans. We can in fact agree with Russell: "With our theory of denoting, we are able to hold that there are no unreal individuals; so that the null-class is the class containing no members, not the class containing as members all unreal individuals;"[93] but to say only that entails absolutely nothing of importance regarding constraints on the functions of reference and denotation. Broadly speaking, we must avoid two extravagances: (1) the (Nietzschean) extravagance of rejecting the contrast between fiction and reality, so that all discourse is in a sense fictional; (2) the (extensionalist) extravagance of insisting that all reference is relational and succeeds only when either its *relata* are existents or nonexistent reals.

In fact, the charm of our proposal is ultimately this: that, so speaking, we can denote and refer to anything we please, without ontological extravagance; *and*, at the same time, we can commit ourselves *globally* to whatever realist conception of the relationship between language and the world we wish to sustain, without *any distributed* commitment to the reality of *denotata* or referents that a rigorous inquiry could not support. There are no other advantages to consider. The extensionalist's account simply embarrasses us by its premature strictures and undefended pretensions (that is, that an extensionalist program of meaning and truth, involving reference, or even demoting it to second-class standing, is the only pertinent one to pursue and the only one that can be progressively satisfied in a strongly realist sense).[94] *Whatever* advantages it can actually yield, *piecemeal*, remain entirely available under suitable interpretation. But its naively realist (or objectivist) pretensions – normally under conditions of ontological skepticism or indeterminacy (witness Quine) – seem oddly incongruous.[95]

As for the narrower issue of reference itself, the point of the argument may be put rather slyly: the generous atheist, we could say, could easily say to the theistic extensionalist (Alvin Plantinga, for instance), I grant that you are referring to God in your argument – whether God exists or not.[96] The same answer could be given to the eliminative materialist, who, like Wilfrid Sellars, believes that the existence of the micro-theoretical entities of the physical sciences entails denying the existence of the macroscopic objects of the familiar human landscape.[97] The theory of reference can be detached from ontological and epistemological considerations, but reference and denotation within a living language cannot be. In a word: there *are* no referents, but human thinking individuates them, and that is sufficient. An impish Quine might well have warned: to be or not to be is is to be the value of a bound variable.

V

One final issue suggests itself. It is sometimes supposed that the difference between the natural sciences and the human sciences lies in the fact that the natural sciences, pursuing explanation (*Erklären*), must achieve reference to the things of the physical world *external* to the entanglements of culturally contingent schemata, conceptions of reality, man's absorption with himself and his projects, the tentacular space of social history; and that the human sciences, incapable of such explanation, abandon such reference in contenting themselves with understanding man's intentional world (*Verstehen*). This oppsition, in truth only distantly in accord with Dilthey's division between *Naturwissenschaften* and *Geisteswissenschaften*, is quite explicitly advanced by Charles

Taylor, for instance, in a well-known and influential paper, "Interpretation and the Sciences of Man," and elsewhere.[98] In the "Interpretation" paper, speaking of human situations – for instance, "the 'meaning' of a given predicament" – Taylor distinguishes a type of meaning that he calls "experiential meaning" (to contrast it with what he calls "linguistic meaning"). "Meaning in this sense," he says, "is for a [human] subject, of something [thought about or similarly intentionally accessed], in a [humanly or socially or culturally contextual] field. Linguistic meaning is for subjects and in a field [characteristically, the natural or physical world], but it is the meaning of signifiers and it is about a world of [independent referents]."[99] Elsewhere, in the same spirit, he contrasts "truth-functional theories of meaning" with what he calls "the triple-H theory" (signifying the theory he proposes, based on the views of Humboldt, Herder, and Heidegger), which (he says) may also be termed "the 'Romantic' [or romantic hermeneutic] theory" or the "expressive" theory.[100]

His intention is to undercut the global adequacy of strongly extensional, truth-functional, or strongly "designative" theories of meaning (where the number of the latter has declined in any case, as we have seen and as Taylor remarks, with the subordination of reference to truth and of word to sentence). Taylor believes that the latter sort of theory *is* apt for the natural sciences but fails to accommodate the inherent peculiarities of the expressive use of language – primarily because, in the human world, language "constitutes" the phenomena that we might refer to and make truth-claims about:

> The t-c theorist [the theorist of truth-conditional theories of meaning] maps the words uttered on to their putative truth-conditions in such a way as to preserve plausibility of propositional attitude ascriptions. . . . But this requires that we identify the putative truth-conditions independently of the target language. That is, we must have a way of formulating our own adequate grasp of the truth-conditions independent of the formulations of the target language. For our coming to understand these formulations, on this view, just consists in our being able to match them systematically with the descriptions of truth conditions. Hence it is acknowledged that the language in which we formulate the right-hand side of our T-formulae [that is, truth formulae, perhaps in accord with something like Davidson's use of Tarski's semantic conception of truth] must be one we already understand.[101]

Taylor's objection to the global adequacy of the "t-c" theory is that the required condition of independence from "the target language" used to express, make public, manifest "our emotions, aspirations, goals, our social relations and practices" cannot obtain: "The reason is that these [emotions and the rest] are already partly constituted by language, and you have to understand this language to understand them."[102] "I believe with Gadamer," Taylor holds, "that something analogous [to what goes on in the expressive use of language within our own society] goes on in cases where there can be no living exchange with the target people, when we study past societies, for instance. . . . Now this is incompatible with adopting what I called the detached observer's standpoint, the kind we naturally adopt towards the natural world."[103]

In a sense, Taylor is right; but he is right for the wrong reasons, and his being wrong falsifies the standing of both the natural and the human sciences and their relatonship to one another. It is characteristic, ironically, of the tradition from Dilthey to Gadamer and Habermas that, for some reason, the *human* status of the natural sciences is not rightly acknowledged or grasped by the partisans of their common doctrine. If it were, then what Taylor contrasts as "experiential meaning" and "linguistic meaning" *could not* be sorted as he claims they are. Linguistic meaning, he says, "has a four- and not a three-dimensional structure," as (apparently) experiential meaning does.[104] (So Taylor means to favor a relational theory of reference for the physical sciences alone.) But this is doubly and desperately mistaken. For, first of all, *if* the natural sciences are formed and pursued in the same human space in which "experiential meaning" holds sway, then the *four*-dimensionality of those sciences ineluctably depends on the *three*-dimensionality of the other – which makes a mystery of their achievement; and, *if* the human sciences (or, the structure of experiential meaning on which they rest) are to achieve a valid grasp of the intentional world of human space, then they, too, must provide for the use of "signifiers" and "a world of referents" (even if not by way of independence of the target language or culture) – hence, they must provide a "four-dimensional" structure as well. This confusion, by the way, is precisely what gives aid and comfort to the rather preposterous longings (already noted) in Paul de Man's account of the relationship between fiction and reality. The human sciences must be referentially competent and capable of supporting a cultural realism.

Taylor is right to oppose "mainstream social science" – reductive behaviorisms and the like – because, as he remarks, "If we have a science which has no brute data, which relies on readings, then it cannot but move in a hermeneutical circle. . . . We can only [in trying to improve our understanding] continue to offer interpretations; we are in an interpretive circle." *That*, however, is not sufficient to justify his going on to say, "but the ideal of a science of verification is to find an appeal beyond differences of interpretation. . . . This ideal can be said to have been met by our natural sciences. But a hermeneutic science cannot but rely on insight."[105] No. *If* the natural sciences can do that, the human sciences must be able to do that as well, since, *ex hypothesi* (or, on pain of Taylor's reverting to the brute data" thesis), they do so by virtue of our mastering our "triple-H" language. The simple trick is that the "fourth" dimension (assigned to the natural sciences) is an artifact projected from *within* the space of the other, dependent on the regularities of the hermeneutic world, and justified in terms of its apparent grasp of the structures and regularities of the physical world. It is a mistake to think that, because what we *posit* as physical phenomena lack intentionality, their being thus *posited* is free of the intentionality of man's cognitive and praxical concerns. There is good reason to believe that the human sciences cannot equal the quantificational precision and the indifference to historical novelty that the natural sciences feature, but that alone does not preclude predictive or quantificational work in the human sciences, conceptual parity regarding "four-dimensionality" (if we can free the notion from "independence of the target language"), even the muting or restraint of intentional variation for particular purposes within the human sciences, *or* the hermeneutic complexities of the *natural* sciences.[106] There simply is no principled disjunction between the two sorts of science; and Taylor surely courts inconsistency in claiming that there is. The non-Intentional (non-intensionalized) phenomena of the natural sciences are restrictively sorted within the space of the other; something quite similar may, within limits, be contrived in the human sciences *if we wish*. The trouble is only that what would then be restricted is often just what we are interested in in pursuing the human sciences.[107]

Notes

1   W. V. Quine, *Word and Object* (Cambridge, Mass.: MIT Press, 1960), p. 4.
2   Ibid.
3   Ibid., p. 242.
4   Ibid., p. 166
5   See William P. Alston, "Ontological Commitment," *Philosophical Studies*, IX (1958).
6   W. V. Quine, "On What There Is," *From a Logical Point of View* (Cambridge, Mass.: Harvard University Press, 1953), p. 12.
7   Donald Davidson, "Reality without Reference," *Inquiries into Truth and Interpretation* (Oxford: Clarendon Press, 1984), pp. 225, 221. See also Joseph Margolis, *Science without Unity: Reconciling the Human and Natural Sciences* (Oxford: Basil Blackwell, 1987),ch. 1.
8   See for instance Donald Davidson and Gilbert Harman (eds), *Introduction to The Logic of Grammar*, 2nd edn (Encino, Calif.: Dickenson, 1975).
9   See ch. 6, above.
10 See also Margolis, *Science without Unity*, ch. 1.
11 Wilfrid Sellars, "The Language of Theories," *Science, Perception and Reality* (London: Routledge and Kegan Paul, 1963), p. 123.
12 Ibid., p. 126; cf. also "Philosophy and the Scientific Image of Man," in the same volume.
13 See Margolis, *Science without Unity*, ch. 8.
14 Bas C. van Fraassen, *The Scientific Image* (Oxford: Clarendon Press, 1980), p. 64. Cf. Patrick Suppes: "What Is a Scientific Theory?" in Sidney Morgenbesser (ed.), *Philosophy of Science Today* (New York: Basic Books, 1967); and *Probabilistic Metaphysics* (Oxford: Basil Blackwell, 1984).
15 Van Fraassen, *The Scientific Image*, pp. 191, 46.
16 Ibid., p. 47.
17 Ibid., p. 12.

18 Ibid., pp. 14, 18, 19.

19 Cf. ibid., ch. 5, for instance p. 130.

20 Nancy Cartwright, *How the Laws of Physics Lie* (Oxford: Clarendon Press, 1983), pp. 3–4.

21 Ibid., p. 4.

22 Ibid., p. 6. See also Ian Hacking, *Representing and Intervening: Introductory Topics in the Philosophy of Natural Science* (Cambridge: Cambridge University Press, 1983); and Joseph Margolis, *Pragmatism without Foundations: Reconciling Realism and Relativism* (Oxford: Basil Blackwell, 1986), ch. 5.

23 Cartwright, How the Laws of Physics Lie, p. 6.

24 See Gottlob Frege, "On Sense and Reference," tr. Max Black, in *Translations from the Philosophical Writings of Gottlob Frege*, 2nd edn, by Peter Geach and Max Black (Oxford: Basil Blackwell, 1960); and Bertrand Russell, "Philosophy of Logical Atomism," *The Monist*, XXVIII (1918), and "On the Nature of Acquaintance," *The Monist*, V (1914). Both papers are reprinted in Bertrand Russell, *Logic and Knowledge: Essays 1901–1950*, ed. R. C. Marsh (London: Allen and Unwin, 1956.)

25 For a recent overview of these issues, with regard primarily to sorting out, from among the contending theories, an adequate account of the uses of language in literature, see Thomas G. Pavel, *Fictional Worlds* (Cambridge, Mass.: Harvard University Press, 1986), chs 3–4. Pavel affords a natural and convincing introduction to the vagaries of knowing "which" world we are making reference to or within, across the space of natural discourse. The upshot (as I would put it) is to entrench "story-relative" reference as generally adequate and ineliminable. On story-relative reference, see P. F. Strawson, *Individuals: An Essay in Descriptive Metaphysics* (London: Methuen, 1959), ch. 1, particularly p. 18.

26 See Quine, *Word and Object*, ch. 1.

27 See W. C. Quine, "Two Dogmas of Empiricism," *From a Logical Point of View*.

28 See Thomas S. Kuhn, "Revolutions as Changes of World View," *The Structure of Scientific Revolutions*, 2nd, enlarged edn (Chicago: University of Chicago Press, 1970).

29 See for instance Carl G. Hempel, "Empiricist Criteria of Cognitive Significance: Problems and Changes" and "Postscript (1964) on *Cognitive Significance*," *Aspects of Scientific Explanation and Other Essays in the Philosophy of Science* (New York: Free Press, 1965).

30 See ch. 6, above.

31 See Peter van Inwagen, "Creatures of Fiction," *American Philosophical Quarterly*, XIV (1977).

32 See John R. Searle, *Speech Acts* (Cambridge: Cambridge University Press, 1969); cf. pp. 77 and 78.

33 See Quine, "On What There Is," *From a Logical Point of View*.

34 I have used the idiom favored in Kathleen Freeman, *Ancilla to the Pre-Socratic Philosophers* (Oxford: Basil Blackwell, 1952).

35 The point – at least part of the point – is nicely noted in Jay F. Rosenberg, *Linguistic Representation* (Dordrecht: D. Reidel, 1974), p. 7 ("representing falsehoods"), but it is deliberately left undeveloped.

36 See Michael Dummett, *Truth and Other Enigmas* (Cambridge, Mass.: Harvard University Press, 1978).

37   Kathleen Freeman, *Companion to the Pre-Socratic Philosophers*, 3rd edn (Oxford: Basil Blackwell, 1953), p. 147. A more disciplined, convenient summary of the interpretive problem is offered in Alexander P. D. Mourelatos, "Some Alternatives in Interpreting Parmenides," *The Monist*, LXII (1979). The account suggests, in effect, the irrelevance of Parmenides for the question of reference – since reference is rightly confined to (or enlarged to include) the "Doxa."

38   It is convenient to take note, here, of the fashionableness of Richard Rorty's thesis, in *Philosophy and the Mirror of Nature* (Princeton NJ: Princeton University Press, 1979), which many would defend by use of strategies rather different from Rorty's – and with quite different consequences.

39   Freeman, *Companion to the Pre-Socratic Philosophers*, p. 147.

40   Freeman, *Ancilla to the Pre-Socratic Philosophers*, p. 41.

41   Bertrand Russell, "On Denoting," *Mind*, XIV (1905); repr. in Herbert Feigl and Wilfrid Sellars (eds), *Readings in Philosophical Analysis* (New York: Appleton-Century-Crofts, 1949).

42   P.F. Strawson, "On Referring," *Mind*, LIX (1950); repr. in P.F. Strawson, *Logico-Linguistic Papers* (London: Methuen, 1971).

43   Cf. W. C. Quine, "Two Dogmas of Empiricism," *From a Logical Point of View*.

44   Quine, *Word and Object*, chs 4–5.

45   See Joseph Margolis, "The Axiom of Existence: *Reductio ad Absurdum*," *Southern Journal of Philosophy*, XV (1977).

46   Cf. for instance Benson Mates, *The Philosophy of Leibniz: Metaphysics and Language* (New York: Oxford University Press, 1986), chs 7–8.

47   See Paul Gochet, *Ascent to Truth: A Critical Examination of Quine's Philosophy* (Munich: Philosophia Verlag, 1986), ch. 3; and Jules Vuillemin, "On Duhem's and Quine's Theses," *Grazer Philosophische Studien*, IX (1979).

48   Quine, "Two Dogmas of Empiricism," *From a Logical Point of View*, p. 44.

49   Ibid., p. 45 (italics added).

50   See further Margolis, *Pragmatism without Foundations*, ch. 8.

51   Quine, *Word and Object*, p. 53. Cf. Joseph Margolis, "Behaviorism and Alien Languages," *Philosophia*, III (1973).

52   W. V. Quine, *The Time of My Life* (Cambridge, Mass.: MIT Press, 1985).

53   See for instance Davidson, "Reality without Reference" and "The Inscrutability of Reference," both repr. in *Inquiries into Truth and Interpretation*.

54   See Davidson, *Inquiries into Truth and Interpretation*.

55   See Davidson, "The Inscrutability of Reference," *Inquiries into Truth and Interpretation*; and Hilary Putnam, "Reference and Truth," *Philosophical Papers*, vol. 3 (Cambridge: Cambridge University Press, 1983).

56   See Russell, "On Denoting," *Mind*, XIV.

57   Searle, *Speech Acts*, p. 79.

58   Ibid., p. 78. See also Strawson, "On Referring," *Logico-Linguistic Papers*, pp. 13–14.

59   Frege, "Of Sense and Reference," *Translations from Philosophical Writings*, p. 58.

60   Russell, "On Denoting," in Feigl and Sellars (eds), *Readings in Philosophical Analysis*, p. 103.

61   Ibid., p. 113.

62   "On Referring," *Logico-Linguistic Papers*, pp. 12–13.

63   See Michael Dummett, *Frege: Philosophy of Language* (New York: Harper and Row, 1973), ch. 11.

64   See Richard Cartwright, "Negative Existentials," *Philosophical Essays* (Cambridge, Mass.: MIT Press, 1987).

65   Strawson, "On Referring," *Logico-Linguistic Papers*, p. 2.

66   Ibid., p. 1.

67   It may, at some risk, be worth remarking that Husserl's quarrel with Brentano's analysis of intentionality is clearly linked to Husserl's disjunction between a naturalistic (metaphysical – therefore relational) program and a phenomenological (eidetic – therefore nonrelational) program of analysis. This bears particularly on Husserl's restriction of the "apophantical." See Edmund Husserl, *Logical Investigations*, 2 vols, tr. J. N. Findlay (New York: Humanities Press, 1970), vol. 2, ch. 2 (Investigation V). This is, of course, not to endorse Husserl's vision of apodictic phenomenology.

68   Russell, "On Denoting," in Feigl and Sellars (eds), *Readings in Philosophical Analysis*, p. 103.

69   Strawson, "On Referring," *Logico-Linguistic Papers*, p. 19 (italics added).

70   Ibid., p. 13.

71   See Margolis, "The Axiom of Existence: *Reductio ad Absurdum*," *Southern Journal of Philosophy*, XV.

72   Searle, *Speech Acts*, p. 78.

73   John R. Searle, *Expression and Meaning* (Cambridge : Cambridge University Press, 1979), p. xi (I have italicized "relation").

74   Ibid., pp. 71–2.

75   Ibid., pp. 70.

76   Ibid.

77   See for example Nicholas Wolterstorff, *Works and Worlds of Art* (Oxford: Clarendon Press, 1980), pp. 137–141 (regarding the Principle of Exemplification and The Principle of Completeness). Wolterstorff himself, it should be said, treats fictional characters as (actual) *kinds* in order both to satisfy the Principles mentioned and also to subscribe (in effect) to the axiom of existence. But Searle cannot, on his own account, avail himself of this solution (which in any case yields unsatisfactory results). See Joseph Margolis, *Art and Philosophy* (Atlantic Highlands, NJ: Humanities Press, 1980), ch. 12.

78   Cf. Searle, *Expression and Meaning*, p. 70.

79   See Terence Parsons, "A Meinongian Analysis of Fictional Objects," *Grazer Philosophische Studien*, I (1975).

80   Ibid., p. 86. Cf. also David W. Smith, "Meinongian Objects," *Grazer Philosophische Studien*, I (1975).

81   Wolterstorff, *Works and Worlds of Art*, pt 3.

82   See Terence Parsons, *Nonexistent Objects* (New Haven, Conn.: Yale University Press, 1982); contrast van Inwagen, "Creatures of Fiction," *American Philosophical Quarterly*, XIV.

83   Parsons, *Nonexistent Objects*, pp. 21–2.

84   Quine, *Word and Object*, pp. 70, 73. The whole of bks 1–2 are instructive in this respect.

85   Saul A. Kripke, "Addenda to Saul A. Kripke's Paper 'Naming and Necessity,'" in Donald Davidson and Gilbert Harman (eds), *Semantics of Natural Language*,

2nd edn (Dordrecht: D. Reidel, 1972), pp.768–9. Pavel mentions an unpublished paper of Kripke's (which I do not know), "Existence: Vacuous Names and Mythical Kinds" (1979), that may well pursue this theme further. See Pavel, *Fictional Worlds*, p. 154 n. 16; cf. further ch. 3, *passim*.

86 Notice, incidentally, that the admission of intentional considerations does not preclude altogether the relevance of causal factors even in determining reference to fictional entities. It does show, however, that a causal account that is *not* dependent on prior overriding intentional considerations will not work. The point is missed in, for instance, Gareth Evans's account of the use of proper names: *The Varieties of Reference*, ed. John McDowell (Oxford: Clarendon Press, 1982), ch. 11. It is also clear that Evans never considers, in advancing his own quite sanguine relational account of reference, any of the deep puzzles of the loss of transparency, the preformational contingencies and complexities of knowledge and belief, the historical contingency of our conceptual schemes, or even, for that matter, the implications of the illicit assurance that, if we have holist reasons for sustaining realism (pragmatism), we must also have good realist grounds for ensuring reference distributively. The fact remains that reference is often "story-relative." It is entirely possible to believe that causal factors determine the reference of proper names despite the fact that their effective use in actual use may not depend on a correct knowledge of such factors – on anyone's part.

87 Quine, "On What There Is," *From a Logical Point of View*, pp. 12, 13–14. This is not to say that Quine holds to precisely this formulation throughout his writings; but he never compromises with the notion of commitment to entities as opposed to the notion of our being able reliably to determine what entities there are. Cf. also Margolis, "The Axiom of Existence: *Reductio ad Absurdum*," *Southern Journal of Philosophy*, XV.

88 See Nelson Goodman, *Languages of Art* (Indianapolis: Bobbs-Merrill, 1968), pp. 27–31. We need not subscribe here to Goodman's fuller account.

89 This, of course, is a commitment Donald Davidson is quite prepared to make but the rest of us are not yet obliged to make. See for instance his discussion of Roderick Chisholm's view of events: "Events as Particulars," repr. in Donald Davidson, *Essays on Actions and Events* (Oxford: Clarendon Press, 1980). See also Richard Montague, "On the Nature of Certain Philosophical Entities," in Richard H. Thomason (ed.), *Formal Philosophy: Selected Papers of Richard Montague* (New Haven, Conn.: Yale University Press, 1974).

90 See Joseph Margolis, "Fiction and Existence," *Grazer Philosophische Studien*, XIX (1983).

91 Probably the most popular American criticism of Western philosophy along these lines – hardly the most powerful or most original – is provided in Rorty, *Philosophy and the Mirror of Nature*.

92 See for instance Paul de Man, *Blindness and Insight* (New York: Oxford University Press, 1971); and *Allegories of Reading* (New Haven, Conn.: Yale University Press, 1979); J. Hillis Miller, "Georges Poulet's 'Criticism of Identification'," in O. B. Hardison (ed.), *The Quest for Imagination* (Cleveland: Case Western Reserve University Press, 1971).

93 Russell, "On Denoting," in Feigl and Sellars (eds), *Readings in Philosophical Analysis*, p. 114.

94 Donald Davidson's attempt to extend a Tarski-like program to natural language

is a leading specimen; see for instance "In Defense of Convention T" and "Reality without Reference," both repr. in *Inquiries into Truth and Interpretation*. In the latter paper Davidson actually maintains "We don't need the concept of reference; neither do we need reference itself, whatever that may be" (p. 224). Nevertheless, he intends his theory, the extension of a Tarski-like theory of meaning to natural languages, to be empirically productive and testable. It seems impossible to avoid a referential function, even in a Quinean sort of context (which he favors), for he himself holds that "We may take reference to be a relation between proper names and what they name, complex singular terms and what they denote, predicates and the entities of which they are true" (p. 216) – which catches up both the extensionalist orientation *and* the empirical realism he means to favor. He does not, however, address objections to his extreme thesis. But see further Michael Dummett, "What Is a Theory of Meaning? (II)," in Gareth Evans and John McDowell (eds), *Truth and Meaning: Essays in Semantics* (Oxford: Clarendon Press, 1976), which strongly indicates the ineliminability of a referential component in the empirical analysis of any language, and worries the realist import of such a theory as Davidson's – that is, a theory of meaning that takes truth as its central notion.

95   See for example Michael Dummett, "Realism," repr. in *Truth and Other Enigmas*.

96   See Alvin Plantinga, *God and Other Minds* (Ithaca, NY: Cornell University Press, 1967) and *Does God Have a Nature?* (Milwaukee: Marquette University Press, 1980).

97   See Sellars, "The Language of Theories," *Science, Perception and Reality*, pp. 123–6.

98   See Charles Taylor, "Interpretation and the Sciences of Man," repr. as the lead paper in his *Philosophical Papers*, vol. 2 (Cambridge: Cambridge University Press, 1985); also "Language and Human Nature" and "Theories of Meaning," *Philosophical Papers*, vol. 1 (Cambridge: Cambridge University Press, 1985).

99   Taylor, "Interpretation and the Sciences of Man," *Philosophical Papers*, vol. 2, pp. 22, 23.

100 Taylor, "Theories of Meaning," *Philosophical Papers*, vol. 1, p. 256.

101 Ibid., pp. 274–5. Taylor has specifically in mind Davidson, "Radical Interpretation," *Inquiries into Truth and Interpretation*; John McDowell, "Truth-Conditions, Bivalence and Verificationism," in Evans and McDowell (eds), *Truth and Meaning*; and Mark Platts, Introduction to Mark Platts (ed.), *Reference, Truth and Reality: Essays on the Philosophy of Language* (London: Routledge and Kegan Paul, 1980).

102 Taylor, "Theories of Meaning," *Philosophical Papers*, vol. 1, p. 275.

103 Ibid., p. 281.

104 Taylor, "Interpretation and the Sciences of Man," *Philosophical Papers*, vol. 2, p. 23.

105 Ibid., pp. 52–3.

106 *This*, ultimately, is the upshot of Kuhn's recent flirtation with hermeneutic concerns – which he rightly perceives are implicit in his entire effort. See Thomas S. Kuhn, Preface to *The Essential Tension: Selected Studies in Scientific Tradition and Change* (Chicago: University of Chicago Press, 1977).

107   I believe this is precisely what Ricoeur has been struggling to save, in much of his discussion of the human sciences. See for instance Paul Ricoeur, "The Model of the Text: Meaningful Action Considered as a Text," repr. in Paul Rabinow and William M. Sullivan (eds), *Interpretive Social Science: A Reader* (Berkeley, Calif.: University of California Press, 1979); also *Hermeneutics and the Human Sciences*, tr. and ed. John B. Thompson (Cambridge: Cambridge University Press, 1981). (The Rabinow and Sullivan volume, as it happens, includes the Taylor and Ricoeur pieces side by side.) Ricoeur's discussions are, it must be said, difficult to endorse, because of their tendency to homogenize the views of utterly disparate thinkers – on which Ricoeur himself builds in too sanguine a way. Ricoeur's best insight here – a very good one, too – is simply that *Verstehen* and *Erklären* (somewhat against Dilthey's bifurcation, which Ricoeur typically begins with) mutually entail one another in the context of the human sciences. This is very close to the point of the criticism of Taylor's view, above. Ricoeur's point is to object to all theories in which "Explanation has been expelled from the field of the human sciences" – "What Is a Text? Explanation and Understanding," *Hermeneutics and the Human Sciences*, p. 151.

8

Texts and Histories

In admitting the symbiosis of cognized world and cognizing agents within the preformative spaces of the *Lebenswelt*, we need not disallow the distinction between natural and cultural phenomena. It is true that that concession entails that any moderate extensionalism is an artifact of a more inclusive Intentionalized activity. That is the point of the convergence of naturalism, phenomenology, praxism, deconstruction, and similar doctrines. But within the terms of that precondition there is no reason why a relatively clean disjunction cannot be made between physical bodies (and organisms) and persons (and artworks).

It is true that, when Quine associates what he terms "analytical hypotheses" with his well-known doctrine of the indeterminacy of translation, he means us to understand his notion as installing a moderate sort of skepticism, a barrier beyond which we cannot pass, a range within which inquiry makes sense but regarding the details of which "there is no fact of the matter":

> The point is not that we cannot be sure whether the analytical hypothesis [introduced by us to translate, say, a native speaker's nonobservational sentences] is right, but that there is not even, as in the case of "Gavagai" [because, presumably, "Gavagai" may be regarded as open to being "stimulus . . . synonymous"] an objective matter to be right or wrong about . . . Just as we may meaningfully speak of the truth of a sentence only within the terms of some theory or conceptual scheme, so on the whole we may meaningfully speak of interlinguistic synonymy only within the terms of some particular system of analytical hypotheses.[1]

One could also argue, along Quinean lines, that there is no fact of the matter *anywhere*, since there is no way to determine, inter- or intralinguistically, *which* "system of analytical hypotheses" anyone actually subscribes to. It is, apparently, only on the strength of Quine's pragmatism – on the strength of tacit, prior, holist analytical hypotheses preforming our deliberately proposed field hypotheses – that "observation sentences" and "truth-functions" can be translated at all; beyond that, "stimulus-analytic sentences" and even the "stimulus synonymy" of "nonobservational . . . occasion sentences" can only be "recognized" – not translated.[2] So indeterminacy sets in very quickly for Quine. Nevertheless, that hardly dissuades him from championing physicalism and extensionalism: "If we are limning the true and ultimate structure of reality, the canonical scheme for us is the austere scheme that knows no quotation but direct quotation and no propositional attitudes but only the physical constitution and behavior of organisms".[3]

It may, with some justice, be said that Quine does not fully appreciate the extent to which his own conception of analytical hypotheses is a not-too-distant cousin of the ampler notion of the *Lebenswelt*. To admit the family resemblance would be to concede (against Quine) that, if observation sentences and truth-functions can be translated, then it is quite unconvincing to insist that translation cannot be extended to nonobservational sentences as well – on the strength of Quine's own rejection of the "dogmas" of empiricism, on praxical grounds, and on the grounds that there is no reason, within the context conceded, for restricting the testing of translation to the mere behavioral signs Quine prefers. The skepticism he "saves" is an arbitrary trick that his own admission neither requires nor actually condones. It is simply introduced to make room for the rejection of every Brentanoesque appeal to intentionality (which, hardly secretly, is viewed by Quine as making room for an irreducible intensionalism).[4] But our point is not to revive that piece of gossip, only to draw attention to the fact, via Quine's appealing intolerance, that an extensionalist treatment of physical phenomena is hardly precluded under the most severe intentional constraints. (Read "there is no fact of the matter" to signify that, if there *were*, it would have to be resolved Intentionally.) On the argument, extensionalism cannot possibly be more (if it is to remain empirically defensible) than a first-order program fitted to the work of the sciences as well as it can. But the very enterprise of undertaking that *fit* implicitly reserves a range of phenomena that may not, in the same first-order sense, be made to fit as well or at all.

In theorizing that all and only cultural entities and phenomena are embodied phenomena, intrinsically characterized as possessing incarnate attributes – possessing Intentional attributes in particular – we have already provided for a range of the world's real entities being identifiable as such only in Intentional terms:[5] *not* merely because all discursive distinctions obtain within the space of some symbiotized *Lebenswelt* – or within the terms of something like Heidegger's or Dewey's myth for conveying that condition[6] – but also because the intrinsic properties imputed to such entities cannot, within that very space, be treated in a way that favorably compares with the way physical objects are extensionally identified *within the same space*. The pivot of this contrast is just that the master-extensionalist, Quine, ignores the full implication of his own extremely subtle extensionalism: in following his strategy, the entire tribe of contemporary physicalists, reductionists, eliminationists, heuristic functionalists can claim no excuse for refusing to address what their own more original, understandably absorbed leader may simply have missed or may have been unwilling to discuss. The hegemony of their peculiar stubbornness within professional circles accounts for the equally odd absence among them of any sustained analyses of the cultural world. It is an economy too dearly bought – quite intolerant and quite intolerable.

Effectively, then, we shall have to collect, somewhat meanderingly at first, a sense of the range and local complexities of cultural phenomena before we are able to focus directly on the special complexities of certain of their generic features – in particular, their being interpretable and having histories. Please allow, therefore, an initial impression of drift to exert its own small charm. Its decentered purpose is meant to be redeemed.

I

If we treat the analysis of artworks metonymically as the analysis of the generic features of cultural entities, then it is very much to Arthur Danto's credit to have fixed as memorably as he has the essential clue to the ontological peculiarity of art: "To see something as art requires something the eye cannot decry – an atmosphere of artistic theory, a knowledge of the history of art: an artworld."[7] There is a sense, certainly related to what Danto says but also certainly also quite different from the sense of Danto's remark, in which, as Thomas Kuhn intriguingly claims, "Lavoisier . . . saw oxygen where Priestley had seen dephlogisticaled air and where others had seen nothing at all"; or, "Jean Buridan and Nicole Oresme, the fourteenth-century scholastics who brought the impetus theory to its most perfect formulations, are the first men known to have seen in oscillatory motions any part of what Galileo saw there . . . the Aristotelians [saw only a] swinging body . . . falling with difficulty [from a higher position to a state of natural rest at a lower one]."[8] The complexities of the theory-laden nature of perception cannot be gainsaid in either the world of science or the artworld. But there is an essential, double difference between them nevertheless: first, in the physical sciences but not in the arts, *what* we fix perceptually, however disputatiously and variably within the range of discontinuous conceptual changes Kuhn associates with paradigm shifts (as oxygen or as a pendulum), is referentially first marked for what it is in a way its sponsors treat and can treat entirely extensionally; and, second, in science but not in art, *what* we describe, however problematically, as the intrinsic nature of what is thus fixed, once given that determinate reference, is treated and can, in principle, be treated as open to adequate description and explanation in a way that is similarly entirely extensional.

What Danto is saying (what it is reasonable to take as his intent) is that, first, artworks are referentially identified as such only in terms that behave logically in nonextensional ways; and, second, that their description (*a fortiori*, explanation of their possessing whatever they can be descriptively – and/or interpretively – assigned) is essentially addressed to attributes that behave predominantly in nonextensional ways. There may be a certain seepage in both directions that would distress any effort at an absolutely complete disjunction between the usual entities of the sciences and the arts: the very treatment of predicates as extensional depends on larger Intentional considerations; the sciences are arts; the preformative conditions of cognition affect every inquiry and activity in the same global way; and cultural entities do possess physical properties. But there is a fair disjunction to be made out, nevertheless; and, if one denied it, it would not, on the argument being mounted, be at all to the advantage of the extensionalist.

The immense force of this single concession is terribly easily missed. For example, it may not be seen that, once admitted, every *realist* effort at physical reduction (not, therefore, content with either an eliminative or a functionally heuristic reading of the psychological, the cultural, the linguistic, the historical, the semiotic or significative, the purposive, the intentional, the deliberate, the rational, the appreciative) must – for principled reasons – fail to vindicate any and every mind/body or cultural/natural identity claim (type- or token-) or any plausible successor function in terms of which an identity or equivalence claim could thereupon be supported.[9] It is, in fact, just this remorselessly explicit distinction that ensures the bifurcation of the sciences and the significance of the intellectual war to save or liquidate the entire "folk" orientation.[10] Here, we shall take it as settled that the mentioned disjunction actually holds. How does it affect the fortunes of inquiry?

At least two considerations are decisive. For one, we must collect the sense in which certain puzzles of individuation obtain in cultural space, are satisfactorily resolved there, but are not resolved by invoking extensionally managed distinctions keyed to physical entities or to their intrinsic properties. This concerns the peculiarities of the embodiment "relation" (the relation between "embodied" and "embodying" entities) and the cognate "relation" of incarnation (between 'incarnated'' and "incarnating" attributes). For another, we must specify what it distinctively means for entities of the embodied sort to persist through time – by way of comparison with the persistence of physical objects. This concerns the nature of human history.

It is part of our argument that all and only cultural entities

1   are embodied, and   *no*
2   have histories.

But it is also part of that argument that cultural entities are additionally sui generis in that they

3   are tokens-of-types.

In fact, the seemingly anomalous individuative puzzles about cultural entities are all linked to the fact that particulars instantiating condition 1 also instantiate condition 3. We are attempting, in other words, to fix the essential ontological properties of cultural entities – "essential," in the sense, of course, of being saliently "in-variant" or of defining the necessary and sufficient features of our deliberately selected exemplars or "core specimens" or provisional "stereotypes." In that sense (broadly speaking, Hilary Putnam's sense of definition in science[11]), it would not be a conceptual embarrassment or a conceptual disaster at all to admit, without change of meaning, actual specimen cultural entities that failed in some way to meet the defining conditions. Fish with a four-chambered heart, lacking scales, possessing rudimentary pedal appendages, lunged, or the like are hardly contradictions in terms any more than is *l'art trouvé* (said, say, quite literally of a piece of driftwood either mounted but otherwise untouched or merely professionally noted in moving along the beach).[12] But their categorial standing would need to be explained.[13]

There is, for our present purpose, a convenient and well-known set of cases bearing on personal identity that Bernard Williams has canvassed over the years, and that very neatly serves to fix two important puzzles affecting, separately, our condition 1 and the bearing of 3 on 1 – puzzles that Williams himself does not satisfactorily resolve. In reviewing them here, we intend only to demonstrate, by example, how conditions 1 and 3 – and their neglect – affect the fortunes of would-be extensionalist accounts. (We shall not pursue them in very great detail, therefore.)

In reviewing the case of a certain Charles who claims to be a reincarnation of Guy Fawkes on the strength of apparent memories, Williams maintains, "It is a necessary condition of making the supposed identification on non-bodily grounds that at some stage identifications should be made on bodily grounds. Hence any claim that bodily considerations can be absolutely omitted from the criteria of personal identity must fail . . . "[14] But, since Williams is concerned to investigate the possibility, coherence, and defensibility of changes in personal identity involving both "bodily continuity" (Charles's body being not pertinently different in the interval in which he comes to believe he is a reincarnation of Guy Fawkes) and radical physical discontinuities or differences (Charles's believing he is Guy Fawkes in spite of his having a different body from that of the originally manifested Fawkes), the conclusion mentioned would require that there was some sort of conceptual blunder or incoherence necessarily involved in Charles's conviction.

There is, it may be said, a distinct congruity between Williams's theory of selves or persons and John Post's version of physicalism, and between Williams's conclusion (drawn here) and Post's so-called Modal Nonreductive Discernibility Principle (MND), mentioned earlier.[15] At any rate, there is a similar ambiguity in Williams's use of "non-bodily" and Post's use of "non-physical": if either term could designate what is not, or is not merely reducible to, a physical property (an incarnate property, say), apart from whether it could also designate a property that had no physical aspects at all, then Williams's (cited) conclusion may well harbor a decisive equivocation. For it may be that it is true that "any claim that bodily considerations can be absolutely omitted from the criteria of personal identity [Locke's claim[16]] must fail"; but that objection is certainly easily accommodated (by introducing incarnate properties) without admitting, or without entailing the admission, that if "the supposed identification [is made] on non-bodily grounds," then, "at some stage identifications . . . on bodily grounds [*alone* should also be successfully made]." The latter conclusion would require either a strong reductive argument (which Williams opposes) or something like Post's nonreductive physicalism (which seems close to William's own preference but which he does not actually develop).

The upshot is that Williams is quite unable to draw the conclusion he desires: for, if it is construed in a nonreductive physicalist manner, it would require that the intrinsic Intentional features that mark persons as persons in the first place be shown to be extensionally replaceable in something like Post's way (which Williams nowhere addresses and which has already been shown to be a defeated strategy); and, if persons are admitted to be embodied and to possess incarnate properties, then all the forms of physicalism fail and William's argument proves irrelevant.[17] Certainly, to hold that "bodily identity is always a necessary condition of personal identity"[18] (Williams's thesis) is open to a deep equivocation, which Williams himself never sorts: on one reading, personal identity always depends on incarnate properties, which signifies that *some* embodying body is a necessary condition of personal identity (opposing, say, disembodied existence); on another reading, personal identity (the continued numerical identity of *this* person) always depends on the continued numerical identity of *this* body (favoring "one person, one body"). The two readings are clearly not the same or equivalent: the first seems undeniable; the second will be taken to be true or false (or at least not proved false) depending on how we should interpret "non-bodily" or personal attributes ascribed to persons. Williams does not address the matter in a sustained way. But, *if* "non-bodily" attributes were construed as incarnate, *if* (along functionalist lines) different instantiations of incarnate properties were treated as Intentionally the same though not the same *qua* incarnated, and *if* personal identity (say, in terms of reincarnation, multiple incarnations, transposed-body cases, and the like) were decided on the strength of satisfying a sufficient number of the Intentional features of the incarnate properties decisive for the identity of this or that person, then it would be entirely possible to admit all the cases Williams denies – without the least incoherence.

Williams offers an additional difficulty: *if* Charles may make the claim, then Charles's brother may make the same claim; and then, since Charles and Robert (the brother) are clearly not one and the same, we should be unable to avoid "the reduplication problem."[19] There are many ways of resolving this difficulty, but one that services other puzzles regarding the individuation and numerical identity of cultural entities (artworks in particular) – one that Williams unaccountably ignores – involves our condition 3. *If* it is not the case that the precept "one person, one body" (which Williams shares with P. F. Strawson[20]) is a conceptually necessary truth, if it is no more than an empirically normal regularity (if multiple personality phenomena may be so complexly developed that we may occasionally postulate plural persons "inhabiting" one body[21]), if reincarnation is not conceptually incoherent (however false or unlikely relevant claims may be), then the alleged difficulty is simply too weak to be taken seriously. In any case, if persons, as cultural entities, may be *tokens-of-types*, then it is entirely possible that, assuming reincarnation, Charles and Robert may *both* by Guy Fawkes (may both be token incarnations of Guy Fawkes, different from one another and from the earlier, "original," singular incarnation usually taken to *be* Guy Fawkes) – just as different performances of a particular Bach cantata may all be (token) instances of the same (type) cantata or just as different (token) prints of Dürer's *Melancholia I* may all be said to be the same (type) etching, *Melancholia I*.[22] It is entirely irrelevant, in allowing this conceptual device to be employed, that the different tokens are qualitatively or physically or in other ways different from one another: this is, in fact, the essential reason for invoking it in the context of the arts – and for invoking it now (similarly) in speaking of persons. Normally, it is true, "one person, one body"; but also, normally, it is true, "one sculpture (the *Pietà*, say), one block of marble." There is, however, no logical reason why marble sculptures could not, for technically novel reasons, be treated in the same way as Rodin's many castings of *Le Penseur*, which are all *Le Penseur*. (Notice, by the way, that Rodin and Dürer need not have made all the tokens of their singular creations any more than Bach had to play all the true performances of his cantata in order that any and all of the tokens in question *be* the work in question.) Furthermore, *if* an abstract, functional, or informational feature may be incarnated in different physical or biological attributes (conceptually "detachable" but indissolubly incarnate in any instantiation), and if different entities, physically quite different, may be ascribed the same incarnate attribute on the strength of a functional analysis (*plus some* suitable incarnation), then plural incarnations (both diachronic and synchronic, involving both persons and artworks) are quite easy to imagine – would, in fact, capture what is entirely plausible in the functionalist's theory (without risking dualism). (This is, in fact, the same conclusion we drew a moment ago.)

Naturally, we need to be clearer about the use of the notion "token-of-a-type." We may construe it as a device for individuating real entities by way of introducing a heuristically assigned relationship, logically different from both the member–set relationship and the instance–kind relationship. It is

(a) restricted to the individuation and numerical identity of cultural entities;

(b) heuristically read as a relationship between different *particulars* rather than between particulars and universals;

(c) conceived as a *sui generis* relationship different from identity, class membership, or composition, a kind of instantiation (of one particular by another); and

(d) assigned in virtue of a given particular's possessing certain Intentional properties, in accord with certain Intentional criteria.

It is, therefore, a device that does not lend itself to the assured extensional treatment suited to the individuation of physical entities. Furthermore, it does not

require that "token" or "type" be construed as having any disjunctive or separate realist use. It is a term of art that applies to cultural entities that are, *qua*
real, particulars: notably, persons, artworks, words and sentences, actions. Its
intended use is readily grasped in considering that, in counting the words of the
English language, one would not wish to count every utterance of every
"Word"; but, in admitting the utterance-of-a-word, we need hardly
countenance a heaven of Platonic Words. "Token-of-a-type" is an indissoluble
device for enabling us to count plural incarnations-of-Guy-Fawkes without
supposing there is a (type) Guy Fawkes of which the incarnations are mere instances; or for enabling us to avoid denying that two violinists may give quite
different performances of the same piece of music, identified by reference to the
composer's score (or, invoking the same distinction once again, by reference to
its own token scores, which, in a musically embodied sense, is not the "music"
at all but does justify our collecting, numerically, that composer's particular
compositions). Our device is a pretty one, in the sense (clear from the music
case) that, say, Bach's cantata (a particular cantata) cannot be equated with or
exhausted by a finite set of performances, that every admissible performance is
a performance of the same cantata, and that every performance-of- the-cantata
is one and the same cantata (by being a token-of-a-type) without being the
same performance. There *are* no types, and there are no instances (of cultural
entities) except instances-of-a-type – which is quite a different matter from
being an instance-of-a-kind.

Persons and artworks, then, serve very neatly as the paradigms of cultural entities. They are what they are in virtue of their distinctive, intrinsic properties:
artworks possess Intentionally incarnate properties because they are created to
be such by suitably apt (adequated) persons; and persons possess Intentionally
incarnate properties because, *in* incorporating (and *as* they incorporate) their
native culture and language, *they* emerge as entities (adequatively) apt for
behaving, uttering, producing, effectuating entities and phenomena that do
possess Intentionally incarnate properties. By a convenient term of art, we may
now say that cultural entities and phenomena – entities and phenomena that
satisfy conditions 1–3 or are the parts or properties or relations holding only
among such entities and phenomena – are *texts*, or the parts and properties and
relations of texts. Saying that, we thereby signify that all and only things that
meet conditions 1–3 meet a further condition: they

4   intrinsically invite, sustain and justify *interpretation.*

Whatever is interpretable, or anything insofar as it is treated as interpretable, is
a text; and whatever is a text, or anything insofar as it is treated as a text, is
interpretable. Cultural phenomena are, paradigmatically, texts and are real *qua*
texts; and physical phenomena, particularly as caught up in theories (which are
obviously texts), are themselves derivatively treated as texts – for example, as
in interpreting the Olduvai Gorge or in interpreting a skin rash. (Needless to
say, to construe physical phenomena as texts in the derivative sense of being

treated as interpretable does not entail also invoking the ontic distinctions tallied as 1–3.)

We may risk mentioning here an even more profound distinction – moving perhaps a bit too quickly – by adding the important condition we have had occasion to broach elsewhere (in regard to ontic adequation[23]): namely, that cultural entities

5   possess a nature that is not determinately fixed or closed with respect to their interpretable properties.

It is, precisely, condition 5 that confirms the deep sense in which the human sciences – the study of the whole of human or cultural life – are ineliminably hermeneutic, in a way in which the physical sciences are certainly not. Still, because every science centers on theories and descriptions and categories for classifying things, there is, as Kuhn somewhat belatedly came to see, a hermeneutic dimension in the physical sciences as well.[24]

This leads us to several additional (largely housekeeping) distinctions segregating nature and culture. Insofar as persons *are* texts, human societies (also texts – or the intertexts of texts)

6   comprise aggregates of mutually interpreting texts, agents whose effectiveness and whose very nature are functions of consensually constrained interpretation, and whose interpretations are a function of their socially and naturally effective agency;

and the intelligible world (also, then, "a" text) – the real world *as* humanly grasped, the ensemble of cultural phenomena –

7   constitutes the inclusive symbiotized artifacts of man's interpretive and agental aptitudes.

Conditions 6 and 7 collect, respectively, the preformational indissolubilities of person and society and of cognizing selves and cognized world, as well as the historicized capacity for change or the vulnerability of any and all of the elements of these pairs to change or to being affected in intrinsic ways under the accumulating influence of actually exerted human agency. Condition 6 catches up the theme of methodological individualism; and 7, the theme of praxism.

This is a large basketful, no doubt. But there is a convenience to having brought together in one small place all of these distinctions. Also, of course, it is really only conditions 1 and 3 that may fairly claim to be significantly new in the context of what we have already discussed.

II

Conditions 1–7 are striking. Taken together, they constitute a radical ontology of culture.[25] It is an ontology more ignored or (quite literally) thoughtlessly precluded than actually denied. Its principal novelty lies in the elaboration of the consequences, for the human sciences and for every form of deliberate inquiry and activity, of featuring the detection of Intentional properties. Because, *if* the Intentional is ubiquitous in cultural space and if it is not discernible, translatable, explicable, or even workable in the extensional terms suited to the physical sciences – if, indeed, the extensional regularities of the physical sciences are themselves artifacts formed within the competence of agents apt for managing Intentional distinctions – then

(i)   it is a foregone conclusion that the unity-of-science program together with all its trailing vestiges is hopelessly misguided, entirely off the mark;

(ii) there must be, in the life of human societies, a natural process by which, as successive infant cohorts of *Homo sapiens* emerge as distributed persons (apt speakers of some native language, apt agents of some native culture), they actually develop by mastering the practice of discerning and manipulating the Intentional attributes of things – of themselves, of one another, of the artifacts of their world, and (derivatively) of the things of the physical world; and

(iii) there is and can be, in the praxical sense, no principled distinction between theory and practice, between the discovery of the structure of the real world and the intelligent direction of human life itself.

To favor brevity: (i) is simply the bifurcation thesis (or, multifurcation, if the term be allowed[26]); (ii) leads directly to that most remarkable of contemporary conceptions, Wittgenstein's "forms of life";[27] and (iii) is a reminder of the encompassing new pragmatism[28] that, dawningly, continues to assemble all the groping disclosures of this interminable study. To insist on (i)–(iii) is, among other things, to disallow any systematic disjunction between ascriptions of causality and ascriptions of import or meaning – hence, to disallow the crudities of a Marxism that essentializes the distinction between (causal) substratum and (interpretive) superstructure or of similarly impoverished doctrines. The preformational theme precludes them as it precludes the disjunction of history and structure, of science and philosophy, of ontology and epistemology.[29] In opposing these and similar disjunctions, it symbiotizes the subject–object relationship and it subordinates all extensional programs within the Intentionalized world of every inquiry. In doing that, it confronts us with a perennial conceptual puzzle – the puzzle of how our practices can legitimately claim a measure of coherence, of rationality, of effectiveness under conditions weaker than our own visions of rigorous system can imagine.

One clue fits all. Consider only that

(a) there is no definable limit on the (embodying) physical movements by which a particular chess move or speech act may be made;

(b) there is no bridge rule correlating physical and functional distinctions in accord with which an (embodied) chess move or speech act is and may be shown to be entailed by a particular physical movement; and

(c)   the smooth efficiency of no apt chess-player or native speaker is the least bit discomfited by the extensionally troublesome features of (a) and (b).[30]

This is precisely what Herbert Feigl was fond of dubbing (and prone to worry as) – in the context of the mind/body issue – the "many-many problem."[31]

It means, very simply, that humans have – could not survive without – a capacity for fixing referentially (at least as effectively as they require) what is and can be discerned only Intentionally, as well as a capacity for discerning (again, as rigorously as they require) the Intentional attributes of such entities so identified. Furthermore, they are able to do this under the constraints

(A)   of the constructivist or culturally formed nature of their own selves;

(B)   of the synchronically varied and diachronically shifting nature of different cultures, different sub-cultures, generationally different strata of the same culture;

(C)   of an absence of antecedently fixed rules, either innate or acquired, for interpreting or applying such Intentional distinctions;

(D)   of a need to improvise new Intentional distinctions in accord with historically and contingently changing sensibilities, and to be able to discern smoothly and spontaneously such improvisations generated by others; and

(E)   of a cultural world the ontology of which accords with the items of our previous tally 1–7 – particularly 5.

It is entirely reasonable to anticipate, as we have already in effect remarked,[32] that no satisfactory account could possibly be made of this entire complex that did not integrate at least the main themes of Husserl's "*Lebenswelt*," Wittgenstein's "forms of life," Marx's "*praxis*," Gadamer's "*Horizontversch-melzung*," and Foucault's "normalization." Admittedly, this is an unguarded assertion. But to say this much is both to give notice of the direction in which our best theories must surely converge and to indicate quite openly what, in the opinion of the present account, are the most rewarding contributions of our time – and, of course, to yield nothing, in doing that, in the way of scruple or rigor.

The underlying difficulty confronting the ontology sketched – the difficulty, particularly, of presenting a convincing account of its consequences for any reasonably plausible theory of the descriptive and explicatory powers of the human sciences – is, quite frankly, philosophical inertia. It is an open secret that within the last generation or so, when, precisely, American philosophers have come increasingly to influence the direction and conceptual ideology of professional inquiry, the English-language tradition has hardly been hospitable to any sustained analysis that emphasizes the recalcitrance of the cultural world to physicalist and extensionalist models. It is impossible to ignore the gathering influence of that narrowing tradition over the more recent years, not merely for sociological reasons or for reasons contributing to partisan advantage and disadvantage, but also *for* distinctly philosophical reasons: because the proper effectiveness of philosophical argument cannot be detached from the ambience of persuasion that soaks through its collecting history.

To dispute the adequacy of extensionalism, for instance, is, to a very great degree, to attempt to displace one set of exemplars with another and (in a sense) to "colonize" in their name as much of the charted (and uncharted) territory of the field as dialectical contest may support. That is certainly one fair way of construing the quarrels we have been assembling. It is, also, it may be said, a direct consequence of rejecting transparency and of committing ourselves to reconciling naturalism with its erstwhile opponents – phenomenology and deconstruction. At any rate, in trying to understand the power of, and resistance to, a set of given philosophical arguments, one must try to penetrate the process of thought by which favored contentions are gradually brought into line with the "correct" paradigms of debate or the totem specimens of satisfactory analysis that, for a time at least, clearly govern and "confirm" our philosophical intuitions. There is no way to formalize *that* process in extensionalist terms. Argument, therefore, is, in a deeper and more subversively skewed sense than Aristotle's *Rhetoric* would have us believe, a thoroughly rhetorical undertaking, an undertaking the rigor of which (including the use of relatively stable logical forms) is inseparable from the actual, interpreted practice of a living society.[33] The very theory of what may be accomplished philosophically is drawn from the same conceptual cloth as the theory of what may be accomplished by the first-order disciplines philosophy sets itself to monitor. We are likely to see this best when the "normal" practices of philosophy appear inadequate to their developing task. That match is *not* a normal question but the driving force of the very rhetoric of "rational" inquiry.

One brief example may help to fix the need for fresher models. Around 1970 Alvin Goldman formulated a rather interesting alternative to what (understandably enough) he termed "the identity thesis" – that is, the thesis, applied to acts (of either the type or token sort), that "if X and Y [individuatable acts identified under the designations 'X' and 'Y'] are identical, then X must have all and only the properties that Y has."[34] Of course, Goldman did not object to the formulation of the identity rule. He objected to its application to discourse regarding acts identified under different descriptions, maintaining that "we shall find . . . that some of the pairs of acts which are alleged to be identical do not share all the same properties."[35] As things transpired, however, Goldman adduced not a single clear case in which the violation of the identity rule could be shown to obtain – where, that is, the kinds of cases usually offered in accord with the thesis were directly confronted (pairing acts, that is, not acts and events that are not acts).[36]

The identity thesis is somewhat complicated by the fact that some of its adherents (Elizabeth Anscombe and Eric D'Arcy,[37] for instance) were clearly opposed to a physicalist or reductive reading of the thesis, while others (notably, Donald Davidson[38]) subscribed to a distinct physicalist reading (token–physicalist, in Davidson's case). Goldman's principal objection rested on causal considerations. The details are not especially important for our present purpose, particularly since the counterinstances Goldman offered all fail: it is, rather, the meaning of that failure that is important; and that may be readily retrieved without a full revival of the cases themselves.

Goldman clearly favored causal determinism, though he emphasized that "I offer no proof of the thesis that acts are determined." (Quite reasonably, he wished to disjoin the questins of determinism and of causal prediction.) Nevertheless, regarding events and acts Goldman maintained, "If a proposition describing event e is deducible from propositions expressing laws of nature and prior events $c_1, c_2, \ldots, c_k$, the events $c_1, c_2, \ldots, c_k$ will be said to *causally necessitate* event e. What I am assuming, then, is that if acts are determined, wants and beliefs are among the factors which causally necessitate them."[39] It appears, both because of the "causal necessitation" formula and because of Goldman's specimen list of so-called "basic act-tokens" – extending one's arm, moving one's finger, opening one's eyes, turning one's head[40] – that acts *are* events of some sort. (There is, however, a certain coyness in this regard, in Goldman's account.[41]) If we allow that that class inclusion obtains, then we may fix the force and intent of Goldman's theory straightforwardly enough. He holds (1) that, "if the identity thesis is correct, then the distinction between basic actions and non-basic actions must be abandoned;"[42] and (2) that "nothing can be a basic act-token unless it is intentional – i.e., caused in the indicated way by wants (and beliefs) of the agent."[43] Since he opposes the identity thesis, he opposes the reduction of intentional causes to neural states – at least in the strong type-identity sense.[44] In effect, he favors the irreducibility of nomic functional regularities involving wants (and beliefs) and acts to nomic neural regularities involving those same acts.

His reason for all of this apparatus – and much more, involving non-basic acts (generated either causally or noncausally from basic acts) – is to facilitate rejecting the identity thesis, to preserve what (mistakenly) he believes are logical errors regarding the identity of acts under alternative descriptions, *and* (most important) to preserve the strong extensional treatment of acts and actions (once identified) in accord with the model extensional treatment of physical phenomena. Essentially for much the same reasons as Davidson favors,[45] Goldman wishes to preserve the extensional behavior of causality (while admitting the intensionality of causal explanation). Believing (mistakenly) that the intentional features fixed in different act-descriptions preclude the acts in question from actually being one and the same – because intentions may be or are causes – Goldman produces would-be paradoxes to show that the identity thesis applied to *acts* or *events* under such different descriptions ("John's playing the piano = John's putting Smith to sleep = John's awakening Brown" is his example in a specimen tableau) cannot be the same. But the counterinstances fail. For example, Goldman (quite unacountably, given his vignette) maintains that "while John's playing the piano caused (e_1), Smith's falling asleep, John's awakening Brown did *not* cause (e_1)."[46] But, of course, *if* the identity mentioned holds, than what has just been specified under different descriptions just *does* possess the same causal property; and, *if* the identity does not hold, then, to be sure, these different events need not possess the same causal property. But whether they are or are not the same does not depend upon, and cannot be determined by merely considering, the completely contingent *descriptions* under which they happen to be identified. Goldman quite literally confuses the (alleged extensional) conditions of causality and the (admitted intensional) conditions of causal explanation. If that were the only potentially viable objection (which does seem to be the case), then Goldman's resistance to the application (1) of the identity thesis to apparently paired acts would simply collapse (as it does). It would then not yet be relevantly applicable (2) to the *identity of act and mere physical event or physical movement* (Davidson's thesis). The marvel is that Goldman never considers this fallback problem, never really addresses the second use of the identity thesis, because *he* believes he *has* established his own argument against the first use: *if* he had done *that*, then, since one and the same physical event would (on the thesis) be merely "associated" (speaking noncommittally) with plural acts that were clearly numerically different from one another, the identity thesis would utterly fail *against the second use*. What Goldman's effort demonstrates, therefore, is the ease (the obsessive ease) with which the general relationship between physical nature and human culture – here, instantiated in terms of the relationship between physical movements and the purposive behavior of a human agent – can be completely ignored in the interest of inventing ingenious backroom maneuvers to save as much of the unity of science program as possible.[47]

If, however, we think only of Dante's writing the *Commedia* or Hitler's negotiating his infamous pact with Stalin or Nixon's trying to cover up the Watergate conspiracy – if we think of these as complex but not untypical human acts – then it is embarrassingly clear that,

(i) beyond assuming (if we allow the idiom, or another of comparable power) that acts are normally embodied in physical movements, we are often entirely indifferent to the local *physical* properties of the "embodying" movements in which they obtain, largely because such features are usually (not always and not entirely) accidental to any pertinent explanatory effort;

(ii) the individuation and identity of culturally complex acts are normally (though not always and not entirely) of little interest in relevant descriptions and explanations and serve well enough even when quite approximate; or story-relative;

(iii) we normally regard the act in question as one and the same (though not always and not entirely) even when a wide range of physical details regarding the embodying movement prove quite other than whatever we might have guessed them to be;

(iv) in identifying a complex act referentially, we normally do not suppose that we have thereby fixed the individuation and identity of that act (though not always and not entirely), nor do we normally

suppose we have thereby fixed its nature, its (Intentional) properties, or its spatiotemporal limits (again, not always and not entirely); and
(v) in accommodating all the indeterminacies of (i)–(iv), we never doubt or disallow for one moment the reality and causal efficacy of the vast range of complex phenomena we would not hesitate to call human acts and actions.

In legal contexts, it is true, negligence and omission are often merely imputed, not embodied at all; and, in the law again, precision is sometimes required that goes well beyond the needs of ordinary usage.[48] But, by and large, acts are excellent specimens of what we have called *texts*: paradigmatically, together with persons, artworks, words and sentences, they instantiate condition 5 of our previous tally. Certainly, if the human sciences are preeminently occupied (as they are) with the description, interpretation, and explanation of human acts, and if extensionalist strategies ranging, say, from Davidson's to Goldman's maneuvers all fail (as they do), then there is nothing for it but to turn to an entirely different conception of the human sciences (and their cognate ontology).

Let us be quite clear, however. The reality or *actuality* of acts is ensured by their physical incarnation: their *nature* is largely determined by what is (Intentionally) incarnated. Whatever uncertainty or indeterminacy affects the latter cannot be obviated by any insistence on the former. One notorious example should serve us here. That Heidegger maintained his membership as a National Socialist throughout his career until 1945, that this alone contradicts the *Spiegel* interview with Heidegger published after his death, that he intervened as Rector of Freiburg University to oppose the admission of a colleague (Baumgarten) to the SA and to a chair in philosophy, that he favored Röhm against the faction supported by Rosenberg and Krieck, that he urged Hilter (by telegram) to stiffen the right ideological resolve and commitment of the German universities, that he published his essay on Plato's theory of truth through the direct intervention of Mussolini over the objection of Rosenberg, all of these and similar unhappy acts and actions are reasonably well established both as to their actuality and as to an essential part of their Intentional import. But what the full nature of those events is is neither fixed nor closed by such findings nor (if validly documented) infinitely malleable, alterable, or able to be denied.[49] The realism of the cultural is not an excuse for erasing the demarcation between the actual and the imaginary.[50] But it also does not disallow a fundamental difference regarding what is determinate and indeterminate as between physical and cultural phenomena.

III

We have been thrashing around among a variety of strategies dominating so-called analytic accounts of human or cultural phenomena – most lately,

Quine's (regarding linguistic meaning), William's (regarding persons), Goldman's (regarding actions). They all exhibit the same contempt for the complexities of cultural history – that is, for the ontological and epistemological bearing *of* such complexities *on* the conceptual analysis of language, persons, actions, and related phenomena. It is hardly enough to savage each one in turn, tracking them to their own fatal errors and inadequacies. That would only be to play the analyst's game again – in an even meaner spirit. Is there, we may ask, a better intuition?

There is at least one, extraordinarily compelling and straightforward. Think only of this: that the specimen acts mentioned a moment ago – Dante's composition of the *Commedia*, Hitler's concluding a pact with Stalin, Nixon's covering up the Watergate – *were* causally efficacious, did produce real, relatively traceable consequences in the human world. That's all. Think of that, and you will see at once that such acts characteristically yield *changes in human history that are new and are seen and judged to be new by the very agents of those changes and by those whose lives are affected*. It is important to introduce the theme naively, in a way that is conceptually uncluttered. Because we are recommending a shift of attention, not or not merely a particular doctrine. The ulterior finding to be drawn, of course, is that such phenomena require the replacement of the physicalist, extensionalist, transparent, ahistorical, contextless, totalized models of analysis that, in our own time, have nearly triumphed. But the trick is to preserve a clear sense of what they *omit* – of how what they do omit would or might affect what they do *admit* – and, only then, of what an alternative conceptual strategy would be like.

Two themes prove salient. First, the causal efficacy of cultural events and processes produces *intentionally emergent novelty*, novelty that cannot be captured under the nomologically universal nets of any physical science (if no form of physicalism holds – ranging, say, from Carnap and Smart and Davidson to Post and Pylyshyn and Searle and Williams and Goldman[51]) and that cannot be captured under the nomologically universal or universal rule-like acts of any "structuralist" human science (*if* no totalized system of a functional, syntactic, or informational or even historical sort holds of any sector of human culture – ranging, say, from Saussure and Lévi-Strauss and Hjelmslev and Trubetzkoy to Chomsky and Fodor and Piaget and Davidson and Hegel and Althusser[52]). And, secondly, *that* novelty is *culturally quite real, consensually constrained though not entirely determinate, causally potent in a futural sense*, and, therefore, *ontologically open-ended and resistant to determinable closure or fixity*. For example, part of the causal effect of the Watergate matter undoubtedly ramifies through the so-called Iran–Contra affair, ten years later. Part of the effect of Dante's having produced the *Commedia* undoubtedly ramifies (in some small way) through the rise of the Muslim world to a new prominence in our time, the culture of which is known to have provided an Islamic paradigm for the structure of Dante's poem – which, therefore, is not likely to fail to bear on attempts at a *rapprochement* of Christianity and Islam. Part of the effect of the Molotov–Ribbentrop pact is the perpetuation of the mutual mistrust between the United States and the Soviet Union in their ongoing negotiations regarding nuclear weaponry. But also, *if* these futural powers of the past are, somehow, potential "in the past" in spite of the now-paradoxical fact that the historical future includes the emergence of the culturally novel, *then* it must also be true that the process of present history "affects and alters the past" thus potentiated. The intrinsic properties of Dante's composition of the *Commedia* – an act conveniently fixed in clock or calendar time at least for certain of its elements – cannot themselves fail to be affected, to be alterable, within the continuous historical process in which, emergently, they influence (as a function of their assignable past) our present grasp of the profound linkage between Christianity and Islam. To reject such conceptual puzzles out of hand is to impoverish every theory of history and culture; and to assume that they are mere illusions or artifacts of a certain heuristic idiom of intentional discourse – one that can in principle be discharged or at least regimented with the installation of an adequate physicalism – is no more than a pipedream. Human culture and human history are real, if human persons are real; and, if they are real, they cannot fail to appear paradoxical to an imagination that invariably yields pride of place to the physical: to the supposed origin of all that is real, the source of all adequate categories, the very guardian of truth. Nevertheless, in saying all this, we are *not* subscribing to backward causation or challenging the directionality of causality itself within the range of physical nature (*a fortiori*, within the range of changes affecting incarnate properties). (Nor, it should be said in all candor – though adding the admission may muddy the waters – are we committed to the *a priori* incoherence of such possibilities.[53])

Our two themes are inextricably linked, then. They are the principal clues to an alternative model of cultural phenomena construed as *texts*: the interconnection between *history* and *interpretation*. Histories are the Intentional careers, *or* the Intentionally interpreted careers, of texts; interpretation is the consensually and historically generated characterization, or such characterization ontically implicated in actual agental generation, of the Intentional attributes of texts; and, in cultural space, there is and can be no principled disjunction (in contrast with what we normally suppose obtains in physical nature) between the real and what is cognized and cognizable as real. There can be nothing, in cultural space, for instance, to support the familiar dispute between realism and anti-realism in Michael Dummett's familiar sense.[54] The ontology of culture is against it. Histories are what they are because they are understood to be what they are, by those who make them what they are and, in doing and understanding that, become what *they* are. In drawing this conclusion, we have reached an extraordinarily important finding that contrasts the physical and cultural worlds and the physical and cultural sciences: namely, that the quarrel between so-called realist and anti-realist theories of our knowledge of the natural world[55] simply dissolves in the context of the world of human culture. There *are* no cultural phenomena that, *on any reasonable theory*, exist independently of human agency and psychological states.[56] But that is not to say that the cultural is not real or actual. It is only to say that admitting its reality entails cognitive strategies significantly at variance with canonical unity views of what we may posit *as* the real physical world as it is independent of inquiry.

There you have the unifying thread that runs through Hegel and Marx and Nietzsche and Dilthey and Meinecke and Droysen and Troelsch and Heidegger and Gadamer and Ricoeur and Habermas and Foucault.[57] Both "history" and "interpretation" are equivocal notions, because, in cultural space, what is real is what humans make and do, and what they make and do is what they understand themselves to make and do – diachronically as well as punctually. Once admit that persons are texts, have or are histories themselves: it becomes quite impossible to fix the ontological or Intentional closure of their careers and natures – *even after their physical death*. What, after all, *are* the intrinsic properties of Socrates, Jesus, Gautama, Mohammed, and how can those properties be historically or physically confined to their mortal span? Leibniz's formula is clearly wrong or wrongly focused: it is essential to the nature of each human being that that nature be logically incapable of definition or closure in terms of any set of its physical attributes or (indeed) in terms of any set of its Intentional attributes specified at any moment of physical (or historical) time; but *no* particular Intentional attribute can, in principle, be fixed at any given time, such that no subsequent change of history or interpretation could ever alter it *ontologically*.[58] Also, on the argument being developed, no merely physical property (Socrates' being snubnosed, for instance) could, in principle, be an essential trait of a *person* unless suitably mediated by some incarnate Intentional trait, which (also on the argument) can always be "altered" by the course of history.[59] (It is clear, of course, from these few observations, that the causal theory of names is normally made to presuppose, first, "one person, one body" and, second, that there is no serious conceptual problem linking identifying bodies and identifying persons "possessing" those bodies.[60] Both presuppositions have their difficulties.)

It should also be said, regarding proper names, that

(a) proper names need not be logically proper names (in Russell's sense);

(b) the effective use of proper names may well be "story-relative" (in Strawson's sense) and function quite well as such in normal contexts;

(c) proper names need not have "originate[d] in a baptism" or in a determinate practice that amounts to "a demonstrative reference to *x* [some particular individual]" or the like (as in Gareth Evans's view);

(d) proper names need not be introduced through the identification of distributed causal linkages of any kind between some individual name and some actual individual, but may depend on quite general background information and context (again, against Evans);

(e) proper names may, therefore, be assigned, nondeviantly, within a practice in accord with (a)–(d), to fictional, imaginary, mythical, legendary, ontologically uncertain, and Intentionally specified individuals; and

(f) the practice of introducing particular actual individuals by name (or similarly) does not impose necessary conditions on the distributed referring use of proper names as such.

It seems false or tautological to say, therefore, as Evans does (to single out one prominent discussion), that

> the expression [the proper name] does not become a name for x unless it has a certain currency among those who know x – only then can we say that x is *known as NN*. Any producer [that is, an apt member of the "core group," who were, in effect, demonstratively first introduced to the proper use of the name] can introduce another person into the name-using practice as a producer by an introduction ("This is NN"), and x may introduce himself.[61]

(Evans does not, of course, require this practice to be a "formal introduction.") The point at stake is that *to* function adequately as a name requires, *distributively*, a certain intentional stance; failure of reference (say, regarding actual individuals) does not subvert the referential use of names, and their successful use is still "epistemological" and not merely "semantic." Referential failure cannot, in the nature of the smooth functioning of natural language, be massive, but story-relative reference (invoking a division of labor) is often quite enough; and "reference" itself is an equivocal notion – oscillating between (at least)

(i) the intentional structure, of a certain (dependent) speech act,

(ii) the successful picking-out of that referent that one intended to refer to (also story-relatively), and

(iii) the initial naming of *that* individual.

It is clear from what has been cited from Evans that Evans sets (iii) above both (i) and (ii) in conceptual importance. But it is not obvious that Evans's "producer/consumer" analogy is any more perspicuous than Putnam's "division of linguistic labor" analogy.[62]

Our *natures* are saliencies only, histories, reflexive and consensual interpretations incarnate in the biological powers of the members of a gifted animal stock. And, yet, to say that is certainly not to say that, given provisionally in-variant Intentional properties of particular persons, particular physical properties (that the other are incarnate in) cannot be usefully (*then*) proposed as "essential" properties – by which one never means (absolutely) inviolate or unalterable properties but perhaps, more often, *sine qua non* properties stronger than merely necessary, unless overridden, superseded, defeasible, or the like under circumstances that cannot be antecedently formulated.[63]

How radical the thesis is is plain enough. The marvel is not that it is opposed by physicalists and extensionalists but that it is almost never formulated clearly and explicitly enough to be defeated or attacked at all. One obvious, obviously strenuous, paradox must be mentioned here that is bound to add fuel and fire to the contest. On the thesis given, history, the production of Intentional phenomena, must have a retroactive power: the future clearly affects the historical past.

This is the marvellously strenuous point so unfortunately mismanaged by Thomas Kuhn when, in his best intuitive moment, he says "examining the record of past research from the vantage of contemporary historiography, the historian of science may be tempted to exclaim that when paradigms change, the world itself changes with them."[64] "Lavoisier," as already noted, "saw oxygen where Priestley had seen [only] dephlogisticated air and where others had seen nothing at all": "Lavoisier saw nature differently . . . [he] worked in a different world."[65] Here, by our own cognizing efforts, the world – inseparable from the intelligibilizing symbiosis of the realist and idealist elements we theorize (after the fact) ensures the intelligibility of the physical "world" we subtract from the other within the space of the other – indissolubly incarnates the intentional features of our historical understanding as its own tacit structure. By the serial efforts of science, then, we subtract what we are able to subtract as the physicalist minima our sciences require. (This supplies at least a mythologized picture of the intentional features of the physical world.) So, on Kuhn's intuition, the physical world "changes" historically as a result of a paradigm shift in our theories. Aristotle, for instance, saw "only swinging stones" where Galileo saw true pendulums: "Pendulums were brought into existence by something very like a paradigm-induced gestalt switch."[66] That means both (1) that the physical world changes as a result of the intentionally altered vision of the scientists who investigate it (not merely as a result of their piecemeal causal tinkering with – their physically moving – particular stones or particular laboratory equipment); (2) that the intentional features of those who lived in the past are really altered as a result of the ongoing processes of present and future history (Aristotle, after all, "now," saw only swinging stones "then").

How? However history does that, it need not violate any of the constraints of physical time, since, on the argument, there is no adequate physicalist account of Intentionality anyway; and, in affecting the Intentional structure of the past, it does not and need not violate any of the constraints on the fixity of physical reality, since, also on the argument, cultural entities are, ontologically, not determinately fixed or closed with regard to their real Intentional attributes. (This, was, precisely, the point of item 5 of our earlier tally on the ontology of culture.) Furthermore, in affecting the past thus, history and interpretation do not simply erase what "had been" real in the historical past: somehow, in the process of their own historical present, they incorporate into what they there and then reconstruct of any entity's history whatever of "that" past they thus alter and thus incorporate. There is, therefore, no limit to such pasts or such histories of such entities; and, for that reason, there is also no limit to their assignable natures or futures. The principal puzzle is not one of conceptual coherence (although that is strenuous enough[67]), but one of cognitive control and variability in moving among them. (But of course, in saying that, we must not suppose that we have satisfactorily resolved the paradox. We shall return to the matter shortly.)

We must, at this point, move forward with a little more deliberation and care. Turn back, therefore, to the Intentional. Flatly stated, *the Intentional = the cultural*. The term is meant to range over incarnate attributes in virtue of which inten*s*ional properties that are inten*s*ionally informed are indissolubly emergent with respect to (what may be abstractly identified as, but cannot in any instantiation be separated from) physical or biological properties. Whatever the range of intentional and intensional distinctions,[68] the "Intentional" is, as a term of art, meant to collect those real attributes of things in which the intentional is inherently ascribable to entities (persons) in virtue of and only in virtue of their mastery or exercise of some native language and culture, or to entities (artworks, for instance) in virtue of and only in virtue of their having been produced, done, created, effectuated by persons exercising their linguistic and cultural aptitudes (or because of their having exercised such aptitudes, causing, as through the mediating effects of collective institutions, further cultural effects). If the inten*s*ional is confined to the linguistic or language-like or cultural insofar as it depends upon, incorporates, manifests linguistic or language-like features, then inten*s*ionality may be ascribed to sub-cultural animals as incarnate properties but as precluding *I*ntentionality. We may extend the intentional and the intensional as generously as we please; and we may admit a heuristic, functionalist sense in which the intentional and the intensional may be ascribed to things regarding which we do not bother to determine whether their natures can or cannot be adequated to such ascriptions. In the latter case, the intentional (the informational, the significative, the semiotic, the formal) is either applied metaphorically or is construed as applying to purely abstract attributes. But the intentional and the intensionalized intentional (that is, the Intentional) can only be construed as real attributes if – avoiding reductive physicalism and dualism *and* heuristic functionalism – they are taken as incarnate.[69]

A moderately useful tally suggests itself. We may say of the Intentional that it is

(a) incarnate,
(b) real,
(c) causally efficacious,
(d) not reducible in physicalist terms,
(e) the essential mark of the cultural, and
(f) not, except for finite segments of some domain or as intentionally restricted for a special purpose, open to simulation or generation by some extensional device.

Item (f) is clearly the most controversial. We shall take (f) as a first-order empirical generalization – certainly not as an *a priori* constraint. It is easy to show that, for any known empirically extensionalized program – structuralist, Chomskyan, Tarskian-like, machine-programmed – there are always many non-marginal, nondeviant phenomena belonging to any open-ended cultural domain under analysis that cannot be generated or simulated by the algorithms of *that* program, cannot, that is, in the modestly empirical sense that its known resources are *still* inadequate for *them and* that its current achievement cannot be shown, in principle, to be a suitably strong approximation to the complete system it supposes the segment in question to be a proper part of. Frankly, the ultimate quarrel between extensionalists and anti-extensionalists is not, as far as anyone has been able to show, a matter on which either side can claim to have won outright. The reason is elementary: to win, the extensionalist side would have to be able to demonstrate that, in more than mere principle, a given sector or the whole of actual human culture formed or might form an extensional system[70] – in effect, for real-time concerns, did form a network sufficiently system-like for it to be the case that, distributively, in its central and regularly extended application, the presumed such system would, for all practical purposes, function as a system.[71] The anti-extensionalist would, for his part, have to show (which he cannot) that the other is incoherent or impossible.

Our argument is, therefore, a conditional one. Assuming (f), or being unable to defeat (f) either empirically or *a priori*, there are good conceptual reasons for believing that the domain of human culture exhibits all the properties collected in our earlier tally 1–7. This is, in effect, the short form of the entire argument here broached. Furthermore, if one grants it, then all the puzzles of Intentionality, history, interpretation instantly bear in on us and must be directly resolved. Hence, even the physicalist or the extensionalist who *thus far* has failed to provide a sufficiently promising empirical program must concede that the phenomena in question invite, in the interim at least, alternative strategies of analysis the plausibility of which *cannot* be made to depend on adhering exclusively to physicalism, extensionalism, or any combination of the two. To put the point in an old-fashioned way: any strong claim to the contrary could not be a gentleman's claim.

IV

We come, now, to a peculiarly treacherous issue. What is the historical past? Is it alterable, and, if it is, how and in what sense can it be changed? Broadly speaking, the nearly universal answer, with only minor adjustments, has been: if it is real, then the past is fixed and unchangeable; although

(a)   it can acquire new *relationships* with an evolving present, and

(b)   we can always abandon, for cause, a previous *characterization* wrongly taken as historically true, on the basis of new, even hitherto nonexistent, evidence.

Admittedly, this thesis, properly clarified, that is (a)–(b), is philosophically quite comfortable. In fact, it is an essential part of that theory of history (if, indeed, there is to be a theory of history) that is required by

(i) any nonreductive physicalism;[72]
(ii) any theory that holds that causality, whether physical or historical, is and must be nomologically constrained;[73]
(iii) any theory that holds that truth is, in principle, effectively decidable;[74]
(iv) the correspondence theory of truth (however adjusted and freed from its familiar excesses);[75] and
(v) traditionalism, which repudiates relativistic truth-values, even as it admits the flux of history and refuses the blandishments of transparency claims.[76]

The secret of the nature of history – the secret nature of history – rests, as the deconstructionists might say, with its alterity, its absence. Certainly, the risk of a genuinely radical conception of history is plainly suppressed by all those accounts that, one way or another, signal their allegiance to one or another of the attenuated themes of the unity-of-science program. To secure the point is to expose in an unexpectedly compelling way the genuinely subversive implication of refusing to ignore the ontological *différences* of culture.

There is no more convenient and no more telling specimen theory to mention in this regard than Arthur Danto's, since Danto, memorably drawn in opposite directions – toward a nonreductive and toward a reductive physicalism at the same time – acts to save as much as possible of what is distinctive of history (that is, of what Danto can admit of history) that would be compatible with not actually choosing sides between the two versions of physicalism. But it is just there that the suppressed absence unmistakably betrays itself. *What is* suppressed is simply this: the conceptual option that, *perhaps, the historical past is both real and not fixed in its intrinsic properties.* There is no developed theory that takes this turn, unless (in all fairness) it is the theory of the Nietzscheans. Nietzsche himself had no patience with the kind of detail we here require; and, in any case, he was drawn much too quickly, by that very option, to his own larger concern with the Eternal Return. And Foucault never managed to address and resolve the *aporia* of actually being able to write a disciplined and accurate history under the Nietzschean banner.[77]

Danto's own theory introduces, and requires, the dialectic of "history-as-reality" and "history-as-science." He is entirely right in pressing this distinction and, with it, he furnishes an instrument of considerable subtlety and power. The following somewhat extended remarks capture his important notion conveniently and fairly:

> To hold an historical belief is to hold that there is (was) some bit of history-as-reality it describes, external to the belief in question. And this is so even though the beliefs themselves . . . compose a portion of

historical reality. Historical beliefs are thus internal and external to historical reality, and it was the curious muddle of relativism to have denied the latter by having discovered the former.[78]

> . . . it is not what [for instance] the [Paris] Commune was, but what it has come to mean to radical and conservative alike which determines the political complexion of the present. . . . But to point out, as good scholars repelled by falsehood, how off the mark [they and their age may] have been relative to the *en soi* of [the] times [in question], is in a way to forfeit a proper understanding of their age *from within*. . . . And indeed, we treat them as historians-as-scientists when we raise the question of the truth or falsity of their representations. . . . Representations, historical or any other kind, are within and without reality at once.[79]

Representation, historical representation in particular, has a dual nature: we are what we are, changeably, in believing what we believe about the world; and what we believe about the world, historically or otherwise, is true or false if the part of the world thus designated is or is not such as declared. "Reference," says Danto, "makes realists of us all. *Historical* reference then is simply reference in a certain temporal direction relative to the referring expression itself."[80] Notice that Danto's account of what a history is intends a seamless conceptual connection between physical science and human history. There is no need, apparently, to sort out ontologically appropriate objects. History is concerned entirely with the description of *anything* viewed with respect to a certain temporalized reference (in, say, the physicist's sense). In any case, the theory of historical reference is a purely formal matter, indifferent as such to *what* it is a history about.

Now, this *would* be true – or it could at least be straightforwardly claimed to be true – *if* one believed (as Danto apparently does) that the historical world behaves with respect to truth in the same way as does the physical world, if (say) something like a nonreductive physicalism (or even a reductive physicalism) obtained. It is not merely (or not yet at least) that Danto's is a false claim about history. It is rather that Danto never lays a proper ground for his own particular claim. (We shall need some patience here. The issues are unusually shy, difficult to draw out though they are forever near.)

The key question to press upon Danto asks *what* is it in the real world that historical truths are supposed to be true about. In answer, Danto offers a story in which certain stones used in market scales in Roman times find their way into the structure of Christian churches built on the market sites. Regarding the details of that story Danto says,

> the self-identical stones have come under different and non-overlapping descriptions for differing sets of peoples who, though they shared these stones, lived in *different worlds*. . . . To enter another world, as I am now using this expression, would be to see the same objects under different descriptions and against the background of different sets of historical and causal beliefs.[81]

It is here, Danto supposes, that the method of *Verstehen* has its inning, because "some reference to the *beliefs* of agents [in either the Roman or the Christian world] is required in the explanation, hence the understanding of their [respective] actions [with regard to the stones]."[82] Naturally, one is inclined to speak of the history of the *actions and beliefs* (and the like) of the Roman merchants and Christian believers involved. But what of the history of the *stones*? Also, is it so clear that the stones of "the one world" *are* the same as those of the other? And, what is the meaning of "same" in this rather complicated context? Danto never supplies an explicit answer to any of these questions.

There is much more here than meets the eye. Consider, first of all, that, in his extremely well-known account of the distinction between artworks and "mere real things," Danto quite seriously maintains – through the device of an appealing spoof – that a "mere rectangle of red paint" that, by hypothesis, is not a painting, an artwork, but might for all the world be sensorily indistinguishable from a "clever" Moscovite painting, "Red Square," or a penetrating Danish study, "Kierkegaard's Mood," or, indeed, Kierkegaard's own "witty" painting of the Israelites crossing the Red Sea, would, "by dint of an *ontological* classification [be] unentitled to titles." That, says Danto, would be "because it is a thing, and things, as a class, lack aboutness just because they are things. 'Untitled,' by contrast [offered as a title by a sullen young artist who has indeed produced a canvas sensorily indistinguishable from the others], is an artwork, and artworks are, as the description of my [imagined] exhibition shows, typically about something."[83]

Presumably, it is in just that sense, in just the sense in which he distinguishes between artworks and "mere real things," that it is true that all "mere" real things – the stones of the earlier vignette, for instance – utterly lack "aboutness" and, therefore, utterly *lack histories*. Human actions and beliefs do have histories, in spite of the fact that they are not (or at least need not be) artworks: because, apparently, they *do* possess "aboutness", intentionality – though not in any simple or unitary sense. They may even yield representations, for instance – "mere" diagrams perhaps, possibly even diagrams of a fictional invention: they could therefore have content or meaning or make accessible to us an entire imaginary world. *They* would still be "categorically" different from a "set of shapes" that are not "inscriptions" at all. Of the latter, mere "shapes," Danto says, "It is not just false to ascribe these properties [the intentional properties collected by 'aboutness'] to mere marks; it is categorically false."[84] On that reading, the *stones*, lacking "aboutness" *qua* stones, lack histories. Diagrams, on the other hand, though not artworks, do have histories because they possess "aboutness." The stones could also, perhaps, *be said* to have a history – but only *accidentally*, only by way of being *relationally* encumbered by our beliefs and actions involving them.

However, the same pressure (strangely enough) may actually be brought to bear on Danto's conception of actions, because Danto himself favors the identity of "basic actions" and certain physical or physiological events. On that

thesis, the difference between an action and a physical movement would essentially be one of *description* only, *not of intrinsic or real properties.*[85] Hence, history would (apparently) *never address real culturally emergent phenomena* (there
would be none), but only (apparently) physical events and the like "under certain descriptions." That would mean, for instance, that the *Pietà* – a "stone,"
after all – *had no history*; similarly, Dante's composing the *Commedia* would
have no history. It is hard to believe Danto means this, though it is not easy to
see how he can escape it. In any case, it is a completely untenable thesis, *if* we
mean to acknowledge the (emergent) reality as such of cultural entities and
phenomena. Put another way, Danto could escape the extreme of reductive
physicalism by way of nonreductive physicalism, *if* he could solve the
adequation problem for cultural entities. But this he *never* addresses: he
invariably falls back to descriptions – or to beliefs about particular phenomena
ontologically identical with physical phenomena.

This is really why he objects to Peirce's well-known remark to Lady Welby:
"Our idea of the past is precisely the idea of that which is absolutely determinate, fixed, *fait accompli*, and dead, as against the future which is living,
plastic, and determinable."[86] It is *not* that Danto believes the past is not fixed,
but rather that he believes it is open *only* by way of *relational* innnovations
regarding our beliefs and how we act with respect to the (intrinsically) fixed
past.[87] History concerns *that* connection preeminently. The point is very close
to the one Bernard Williams both usefully and misleadingly applies against
reductive physicalism – against the objection, that is, that, "If persons are
material bodies, then all properties of persons are material properties." That,
Williams says, "is false," for the simple reason that (borrowing the point, as he
says, from Sidney Morgenbesser) the thesis would exclude such (relational)
properties as "observed by physicists."[88] The trouble is that that objection is
not actually strong enough to resist reductionism; similarly, Danto's emphasis
on *relational* accretions involving the future (which, *contra* Peirce, do "affect"
the past) really do no such thing, since they do not "affect" the inherent or
intrinsic properties of "things." So the strategy utterly fails.

We must be careful, here. What we are laboring to preserve is the sense in
which

(a) the "historical past" can be "affected" in a realist sense by present historical novelty;

(b) the effects of that are fully compatible with human time (which is
more complex than anisotropy) and the isotropy of physical time (if
the latter be conceded);

(c) the resolution of the apparent paradox of (b) depends on correctly sorting causality with respect to the physical properties of real phenomena
and "influence" or "effectivity" with respect to the Intentional
features of incarnate properties;

(d) real phenomena characterized in accord with (c) are also, as incarnate, causally efficacious *in* the physical or natural world; and, therefore,

(e) the admission of cultural phenomena as real confirms that causality does not entail nomologicality.[89]

These tallied items, (a)–(e), collect the principal ontological oddities of history, interpretation, Intentional phenomena in general, in virtue of which the "spare" theorizing policy Quine, for one, has so effectively recommended is, in turning to cultural matters, judged to afford an early escape from conceptual grief. But that policy will not do *if*, as appears to be the case, cultural phenomena are real, satisfy conditions 1–7 of our earlier tally, and may be said, now, to play a causal and effective role in accord as well with conditions (a)–(e), just mentioned. Since Danto is (really) committed to physicalism, he cannot but treat history as extrinsic to what is real. (But, of course, he would resist that characterization.)

The deeper trouble is that Danto's theory is ultimately incoherent – and that *that* incoherence infects the theory of history and art he proposes, and that *that* forces us to an entirely different answer regarding what historical truths are supposed to be true *about* and regarding what historical and art-critical interpretations are supposed to *be*. Consider only that, on Danto's view, there will be two quite different histories affecting the use of the stones he mentions, because, "though [the Romans and the Christians] shared these stones," the "self-identical stones have come under different and non-overlapping descriptions for differing sets of people who [therefore] lived in *different worlds*,"[90] and because the histories directly concern, are generated by, the *use* of the stones (that otherwise would lack a history) and not the stones themselves. (One must, with inevitable irony, recall, here, Kuhn's deeper but more difficult puzzle about the "swinging stones" Aristotle and Galileo are said to have "seen." Those certainly are *not* the same stones, Kuhn says, because "they" (the "mere" swinging stones and the pendulums) belong "in different worlds."[91] Belonging in different worlds, they are not one and the same: they actually "have" different, even incompatible, properties; and, more important, they could not even be said to be "seen" in the same way – *since visual perception itself belongs "in different worlds."* Danto *never* concedes the point and never addresses it – which, of course, would completely disable his otherwise pretty story of the numerically different but otherwise "perceptually" indistinguishable "red" paintings and "mere red canvasses."[92]

On the other hand, if the stones *are* real and if the "different and non-overlapping descriptions" concern the real properties *of* (the real properties *intrinsic* to) the "stones," then the Roman stones cannot be the same stones as the Christian stones, just as a vase and a bowl made of the same clay are neither the same vase nor the same bowl (the Roman stones being *weights* and the Christian stones *relics*, as Danto tells it). Otherwise, the intentional properties assigned (the ones exhibiting "aboutness," in virtue of which the Roman and Christian stones – like the *Pietà* and Galileo's pendulum, at least on Kuhn's story – *would have histories*) would not (and could not) be the real properties of the "mere" stones. They could only be *relationally* associated with those "mere" stones, by way of *use*, in accord with particular *beliefs and actions*. The *stones*, then, could have histories only in a relational, external sense (by association with our beliefs). Histories, then, would only and always be relational and external. But they could not be such for persons and their cultural world, for persons possess beliefs and perform actions: unless, that is, persons, actions, and beliefs can be physicalistically identified and characterized, so that the relational histories required are relativized *to those reduced referents that, by hypothesis, are not intrinsically affected by history*. In short, the failure of physicalism may be shown to entail the paradoxes of history. That is certainly an unexpected economy.

Either, then, Danto is a reductive physicalist, and history (both as part of reality and as representation of reality) is peculiarly restricted to beliefs and actions (whatever the difficulty with them); or else he is a non-reductive physicalist, and the objects he supposes to be "one and the same" simply are not or cannot be shown to be – or, worse, are such that we have no idea how to show that "they" are one and the same. The dilemma is a hopeless noose. Either Danto has no theory of history, according to which the stones do have a proper history – are adequated, as we have earlier argued, to their possessing (intrinsically to their very nature) Intentionally complex properties; or else he suppresses the required theory because it would expose

(i) the inconsistency of having claimed that the referents of the two histories are or could be one and the same;
(ii) the impossibility of merely collapsing the ontologies of physical and cultural entities in order to preserve the conceptual distinction of human history itself;
(iii) the impossibility of merely adding extrinsic *relations* involving belief, action, use and the like to "mere real things" in order to preserve the intended distinction of history;
(iv) the inescapable pertinence of Kuhn's puzzle regarding *the cultural and historical nature of perception itself*, in resolving Danto's question adequately; and, therefore,
(v) the complete failure (on Danto's part) to identify properly *what*, ontologically, are the referents of history.

The answer to all these buried questions is the same. *History is the Intentionally complex career of real cultural entities, or it is the Intentionally complex characterization of such careers.*[93] Of course, it is a further direct consequence of our argument that, granting the reality of cultural phenomena and granting that their real properties would, on a bipolar model of truth-values, yield incompatible attributes or ascriptions of attributes, the ontology here favored obliges us to adopt a relativistic model of truth-like values.[94] In any case, the two go hand in hand.

V

It is a crucial part of Danto's resolution of the puzzle of history, by way of what he calls "narrative sentences" that the latter "refer to at least two time-separated events though they only *describe* (are only *about*) the earliest event to which they refer":[95] for example, the sentence "The Thirty Years War began in 1618," which Habermas reports with considerable favor, and which – that is, the theory underlying (which that is, Danto's theory of history) – Habermas criticizes only for its tendency to favor "an inexpungeable subjective factor," itself a dialectical alternative to a false "ideal of complete description as a meaningful historiographical ideal."[96] But Habermas does not actually address Danto's ontology of history, which he quite mistakenly associates with Gadamer's notion of *Wirkungsgeschichte* (roughly, the casual effectiveness of ongoing historical processes); and, of course, as we have seen, Danto himself really neglects the topic. In any case, Danto's theory of narrative sentences is entirely compatible with – in fact, it was in a sense introduced to *be* compatible with – the notion of the fixity or closure of the past. Habermas would have needed some such notion anyway, since, as Gadamer slyly and correctly observes, Habermas (we may as well say, also, Danto) must (as a late Enlighter-ment figure) fix the referents of historical discourse *ahistorically* – in such a way as not to subvert the objectivity of history; in a way that(seemingly) respects the process of history but still does not make it difficult to reconcile the objectivity of historical narrative with those conditions of objectivity that bind the physical sciences themselves.[97]

This is the meaning of Danto's insistence that *"any* piece of history must (*a*) report events which actually happened; and (*b*) report them in the order of their occurrence, or rather, enable us to tell in what order the events did occur." Danto never pauses to consider that historically significant events themselves may not always be able to be fixed as referents by straightforwardly attending to the movement of clock or calendar time, that fixing their time thus involves an ontological relationship between cultural and physical phenomena, and that fixing their order in clock time may not even be essential to a *bona fide* and reasonably defensible history. It is not obvious, for instance, in dealing with such complex events as Dante's composition of the *Commedia* (as opposed to the question of when the battle of Waterloo took place or when Naram-Sin built the Sun Temple at Sippar – Danto's specimens) that we can always, or are even clear about how to proceed to, sort the temporal (that is, clock- or calen-dar-time) order of the participant events, or would even need to. *Some* measure of reference to the *physical* order of events is surely required to set minimal con-straints of relevance and coherence. But it is not as important as Danto makes out (particularly in complex histories); and *how*, conceptually, it is actually to be done Danto nowhere discusses. In fact, it is a question that cannot fail to worry his account because (as we have seen) Danto himself insists that the difference, say, between a "mere" red square and the (hypothesized) painting

"Red Square" *cannot* be discerned on physical grounds or on criteria suited to "mere real things."

In short, cultural phenomena *are conceptually invisible to any and every form of physicalism*; hence, their spatiotemporal reference is impossible without an account of how actually to fix the identity of such entities. *There* is the essential lacuna in all of Danto's many analyses of the cultural world. It is, in fact, the same one as we have been tracing in Post's generic nonreductive physicalism, Quine's discussion of meaning, Searle's discussion of mind, William's discussion of persons, Goldman's discussion of actions, Wollheim's and Danto's discussion of artworks, and, now, Danto's discussion of history. But, in removing that lacuna, one may not be able to eliminate certain ontic indeterminacies that bear on the nature of the Intentionally complex phenomena that constitute the cultural world.

Danto *seems* to sense the difficullty but he never really does. With caution, he openly favors Ranke's maxim, for instance; to report what actually happened in history (*wie es eigentlich gewesen*). "Indeed, I might regard it," he says, "as a variant statement of what I have called the minimal historical aim." Where he does take serious issue with Ranke concerns the openness of the *past* that results from the openness of the future – "since a narrative itself [historical as well as fictional] is a way of organizing things, and so 'goes beyond' what is given, involved in something one might call 'giving an interpretation'."[99] We must bear in mind that Ranke, influenced by Schleiermacher's hermeneutic orientation, was also prepared to entertain interpretation; but, since he also held that "every epoch is immediate in God" and "must be seen as something valid in itself," Ranke could only have rejected what Danto quite dubiously (on his own account) regards as the open "contingency" of the past – actually, for reasons linked to his own opposition to the pretensions of the Göttingen historians who preceded him (whom Danto somewhat resembles).[100]

The "contingency" of the past is, on *either* a physicalist reading (Danto's) *or* on a version of the romantic hermeneut's conception of the legibly holist *Geist* of a historical era (Ranke's), *never concerned with the real, intrinsic properties of a given age or the events of that age*. For, on Danto's thesis, the contingency is entirely extrinsic, relational, real only insofar as, intentionally, it involves the actual beliefs, actions, uses, narrative interpretations of *present* agents; and, on Ranke's thesis, the contingency is merely epistemic, the manifestation of error, distortion, the failed interpretation by *present* agents of the authorially explicable documents of the age in question. Danto's mistake has to do only indirectly with history: it lies with his imposition of a physicalist model on history (on art,on action) – whatever history might be. Ranke's failure, on the other hand, has to do with the general failure of the Romantic tradition to grasp the full historicity of human life itself – *a fortiori*, to grasp the historicity of the interpretation of history. As a historical phenomenon, hermeneutics was simply overwhelmed by Heidegger's influence; with it, principally through the work of Gadamer, relevant theories came to be confronted with the *doubly* historicized nature of human existence: with the interminably Intentional nature of interpreting the Intentional nature of man and his works, inasmuch as man's nature *is* what it is historically interpreted to be. (To say that, of course, is not to license epistemic anarchy.[101])

The ontic indeterminacies of history are simply the ontic indeterminacies of culturally emergent entities and phenomena – indeterminacies due to their intrinsically possessing intentional properties. These concern

(a) initially fixing the cultural referents in question;
(b) determining the inten*s*ional import of properties ascribed to them;
(c) determining whether given properties are actually possessed by, or merely imputed to, them;
(d) reidentifying one and the same referent through a continuing history, particularly with respect to predications involving historically novel but apparently intrinsic properties; and
(e) determining the nature or integral boundaries of given referents, particularly with respect to the ascription of "incongruent" properties.

By *incongruent* properties, we mean properties that

(i) may be ascribed as real;
(ii) would, on a bipolar model of truth and falsity, yield (when admitted to be real) a contradiction with another such ascription; but
(iii) would not now, in context, yield such a contradiction.

Hence, incongruent properties – or, incongruent judgements about such would-be properties – presuppose setting aside the law of excluded middle, adopting truth-values or truth-like values logically weaker than those of the bipolar model, embracing relativism, and favoring relevance constraints (themselves subject to historical change) regarding matters of reference, predication, description, interpretation.[102] (a)–(e) are merely schematized concerns: they need hardly be formalized or sharply isolated from one another, but they do approximately define what we may term the *porous* nature of cultural entities or texts.

Our thesis straightforwardly affirms, then, that any would-be rigorous inquiry or science regarding the Intentionality of cultural phenomena must come to terms with their ontological features, that its methodology cannot be fixed *a priori*, that the appropriateness of a two-valued or many-valued logic is, in a fair sense, an empirical issue. It is, therefore, not in the least incoherent to suppose that cultural phenomena are such that their historical pasts are real; that they collect their intrinsic properties; that they are subject nevertheless to effective "influences" through their later history in ways that affect and alter such properties ascribed earlier; *and* that such judgements cannot be construed merely as registering limitations, disagreements, shifts of evidence, changes of mind or the like regarding such entities. *Cultural entities and their real histories are actually subject to the ontological peculiarities indicated – are porous texts.*

Is is clear enough that, if the case were made, the radical difference between the natural and human sciences could not be denied. It is equally clear that, rather ingeniously, Danto and Ranke (taken as exemplars) have hit on the only two strategies by which to deny this finding. Danto impoverishes history so that the study of culture is methodologically indistinguishable from that of natural phenomena (though it must, of course, address local complications involving intentionality); and Ranke ahistorically freezes the full intentional complexity of human history so that the method of studying history (*Verstehen*) at once distinguishes the human cultural sciences from the natural sciences but in a way that does not deny such studies a fully comparable form of objectivity.[103] The one retires to the minimal assurances of the unity-of-science model; the other to those of the Kantian-inspired clean bifurcation of the sciences. The one effectively restricts history to extrinsic relations involving "things," within the changing range of human belief, human action, the human use of "mere things"; the other sets no such restriction but treats the historical process itself as ontologically fixed, once and forever, for a correct re-covery (in principle) at any later time and place.[104]

We need, before proceeding further, to pause briefly to remind ourselves that our notion of causality springs from two different intuitions: the agental model, the model of persons effectuating in the world what they mean to do or produce or bring about; and the regularity or nomological model, the model of events and processes designated as causes only if they fall under appropriate law-like regularities that accord with certain norms of explanation.[105] The agental model is fully able to accommodate the other, as an artifact of human efforts at science; but the regularity model is not clearly able to accommodate the agental: for either it must reduce or eliminate the other or else it must risk obvious empirical counterevidence. It cannot fail to risk such evidence *if* we admit (as we have) culturally emergent, Intentionally complex phenomena: such phenomena cannot be shown *a priori* to be subject to nomological regular-ities ranging over all their real properties, and cannot, on empirical grounds, be shown actually to conform to particular such regularities. The agental model functions primarily by analogy from admittedly effective acts, at least case-by-case and, more adventurously, by exploiting whatever advantage presents itself in terms of empiric "folk" regularities. There is no reason, therefore, why agen-tal causes need violate whatever reasonable constraints obtain on mere physical causality. But the latter cannot be sufficient to account for all agental causality, simply because (1) causality does not as such entail nomologicality; and (2) causal processes involving incarnated factors bear directly on the very for-mulation of reasonable causal regularities – *in* psychological, actional, and cultural contexts, *a fortiori*, ranging over the whole of the real world.

Now, the important point to bear in mind is that the agental model accom-modates both *causality* – as that is intuitively admitted in distributed instances in the physical world (complicated, of course, by the admission of the causal efficacy of incarnate properties and processes – and the *"effectivity"* of historical processes with regard (restrictedly) to the Intentional features of incarnated properties. The regularity model, it is true, is often applied to cultural phenomena (to actions and history, for instance, as by Goldman and Danto); but that is usually done (as indeed it is by Goldman and Danto) without regard at all to the peculiar ontological traits of cultural phenomena. (The characteristic strategy is to turn from real properties to mere descriptions.) It may, therefore, merely be a terminological issue whether we should regard "historical influence" or "effectivity" as a form of causality proper. *If* we did, then, of course, causality would inevitably entail backward causation of at least a restricted sort. On the other hand, it remains true that, even assuming the general directionality of human time congruent with agency (leaving aside, entirely, the question of the irreversibility of mere physical processes), the same beliefs, actions, intentions, and the like that enter into "historically effective" relations also enter into "causal" relations. Terminologically (but without prejudice to realist concerns), it seems best to keep the two relations distinct, so as not to mislead. (Nevertheless, thus construed, effectivity must be incarnate in causality.) Accordingly, this entire discussion should be taken as neither endorsing nor precluding familiar heterodox views regarding physical time and causality involving physical phenomena. There are heterodoxies enough in what remains.

VI

In a curious way, the pattern of the maneuvers we have been examining exposes as well the essential nerve of the well-known dispute between Habermas and Gadamer – just where *both* fail to grasp the distinction of history. Each hits on the fatal weakness of the other. Each acknowledges a deeper historicity in human existence than either Danto or Ranke will admit (due, we may say, to the direct influence of Heidegger, Marx, Nietzsche, the early Frankfurt Critical movement at least). And each flinches at the last moment, against the apparent encroachments of relativism, for much the same reasons as sway Danto and Ranke. Consider, for instance, the following summary assessment of Gadamer, by which Habermas both compliments Gadamer and (justifiably) subverts the would-be autonomy of hermeneutics:

> An interpretive (*verstehende*) sociology that hypostatizes language to the subject of forms of life and of tradition ties itself to the idealist presupposition that linguistically articulated consciousness determines the material practice of life. But the objective framework of social action is not exhausted by the dimension of intersubjectively intended and symbolically transmitted meaning. The linguistic infrastructure of a society is part of a complex that, however symbolically mediated, is also constituted by the constraint of reality – by the constraint of outer nature that enters into procedures for technical mastery and by the constraint of inner nature reflected in the repressive character of social power

relations. . . . *Social actions can be comprehended only in an objective framework that is constituted conjointly by language, labor and domination.* The happening of tradition appears as an absolute power only to a self-sufficient hermeneutics: in fact it is relative to systems of labor and domination.[106]

Habermas is entirely correct, of course. But in his turn, as Gadamer effectively demonstrates, *he* neglects to mention that the "objective" *praxis* he refers to is itself hopelessly infected in the same historicist sense. For example: "Habermas," Gadamer says, "sees the critique of ideology as the means of unmasking the 'deceptions of language.' But this critique, of course, is in itself a linguistic act of reflection." Hence, the universalized "emancipatory power of reflection" Habermas favors risks failing to acknowledge just that reflexive complication:

> I maintain [says Gadamer] that the hermeneutical problem is universal and basic for all interhuman experience, both of history and of the present moment, precisely because meaning can be experienced even where it is not actually intended. The universality of the hermeneutical dimension is narrowed down, I think, when one area of understood meaning (for instance, the "cultural tradition") is held in separation from other recognizable determinants of social reality that are taken as the "real" factors.[107]

Habermas escapes the threatening indeterminacies of historical *praxis* by securing a genuinely objective, universalized critique of communication; and Gadamer makes his escape by reclaiming the essential tradition of humanity as preserved by classical Greece.[108] The one returns (in effect) to the Diltheyan theme; the other, more mysteriously, to an arbitrary confidence within the Heideggerian flux. And both pretend – both merely pretend – to draw their findings from the very process of history.[109]

These maneuvers pretty well exhaust the options – force us back to the ontic indeterminacies of history. There is one essential clue that brings all of our puzzles together. The *time* of history is

(a)   always the present of human cognition and interest (or the past posited from that present);

(b)   Intentional (not merely physical);

(c)   "about" Intentional phenomena (not physical phenomena, unless heuristically, functionally, or metaphorically construed, or relationally or extrinsically bound within a larger Intentional context);

(d)   real, in the sense in which the cultural world is real; and, most important,

(e)   governed by the ontic constraints of the hermeneutic circle.

Historical time is therefore, like all cultural attributes, incarnate in physical attributes. Hence, by the particular assignment of such incarnation, disciplined references and reidentifications regarding cultural phenomena are *aided*, not *determined*. Also, by "internalist" appeals to cultural materials that lend themselves to such devices as the "*Geisten*" of the romantic hermeneuts, or the phases of the "*Weltgeist*" of Hegel, or the history of class conflict in Marx, or the plural "*problématiques*" of Althusser, or the various manifestations of the "*Lebenswelt*" in Husserl or Wittgenstein's "*Lebensformen*," or the forms of "*normalisation*" in Foucault, the threatening anarchism of the hermeneutic puzzle is *constrained*, not in principle *eliminated*.[110] Conditions (a)–(e) ensure that there need be no formal incompatibility between the retroactive influence of historical time and the generally acknowledged (but puzzling) asymmetric "flow" of natural time.[111]

The required rule is quite straightforward: there can be no distributed retrocative causal influence of the future on the past, insofar as the order of *physical* nature is concerned (*a fortiori*, insofar as whatever of the physical is indissolubly entailed in incarnate properties is concerned) – unless a general and pertinent defense of backward causation can be provided.[112] There can, therefore, be no retroactive causation in which, say, acting at t', I am able to prevent an accident that had occured at t (earlier than t'). But that is *not* a reason for denying that the Intentional structure (or Intentionally abstractable features) of entities or phenomena possessing incarnate properties could not be retroactively affected or historically influenced by Intentionally significant behavior and interpretation. The matter would not be a serious one, except for the fact that cultural phenomena *are* real, *have* Intentional properties, and *are* causally efficacious in the physical world in virtue of their (incarnated) Intentional properties. Furthermore, since we ourselves are *causally affected* by the Intentional features of the things of our *Lebenswelt* (quite apart from the paradoxes of backward causation or historical influence), it is impossible to treat all forms of causality – even causality among physical phenomena – as necessarily bound by nomic universals, unless, of course, contrary to the argument here favored, reductive materialism or a nonreductive physicalism of Post's sort obtained.[113]

The reason for emphasizing these puzzles is not to encourage extravagance but, on the contrary, to offer conceptual economies sufficient for the *realism* rightly accorded persons, the artifacts of human culture, and human history. Our concern has been to demonstrate that no incoherences need result from acknowledging either the ontic indeterminacies of cultural phenomena or the prospect, because of those indeterminacies and the peculiar nature of Intentionality, of the retroactive effectiveness of historical phenomena on the intrinsic properties of real things. The key, as already remarked, lies with the hermeneutic circle, *because the circle designates an ontic attribute of human existence*, not merely an epistemic limitation or a methodological maxim governing inquiries into the cultural world – into *texts*, as that term has been introduced here.

The literary theorist E.D. Hirsch offers a reasonably straightforward characterization of the circle – which he explicates procedurally (and which, it may be added, he himself reads in the Romantic way, vexed though he is by the inevitable essentialism that that approach commits him to). First, Hirsch introduces "the paradox that objectivity in textual interpretation requires explicit reference to the speaker's subjectivity [roughly, the author's intentions in uttering his text, or, inevitably, the reconstruction of such intentions from the supposed 'genres' of relevant such utterings that belong to a particular culture at a particular time]." He goes on to explain,

> The paradox reflects the peculiar nature of coherence [in textual interpretation] which is not an absolute but a dependent quality. The laws of coherence are variable: they depend upon the nature of the total meaning under consideration. . . . The fact that coherence is a dependent quality leads to an unavoidable circularity in the process of interpretation. The interpreter posits meanings for the words and word sequences he confronts, and, at the same time, he has to posit a whole meaning or context in reference to which the submeanings cohere with one another. The procedure is thoroughly circular; the context is derived from the submeanings and the submeanings are specified and rendered coherent with reference to the context.[114]

Heidegger (whom Hirsch effectively rejects) clearly construes the hermeneutic circle as implicated in the *existentialia* of *Dasein*, hence as affecting at one and the same time "ontic/ontological" questions and questions of interpretive understanding.[115] Heidegger's principal clues, which we need only mention here, are "An interpretation is never a presuppositionless apprehending of something presented to us";[116] and "An entity [*Dasein*] for which, as Being-in-the-world, its Being is itself an issue, has, ontologically, a circular structure."[117] Gadamer discusses Heidegger's account at some length, of course; but his principal purpose is to emphasize that, both ontologically and interpretively, "prejudice" – historical preformation linked to our present interest in the past – is ineliminable in principle; that, therefore, the "meaning" of a historically uttered text cannot be assigned free of such prejudice; and that the process of human understanding marked by the hermeneutic circle is an open-ended and unending one.[118] Perhaps the following short passage is as representative as any is of Gadamer's conception of the circle – and, in particular, of his own influential thesis of the "fusion of horizons" (*Horizontverschmelzung*), which is itself the correlate of what he calls "effective history" (*Wirkungsgeschichte*):

> The circle, then, is not formal in nature, it is neither subjective nor objective, but describes understanding as the interplay of the movement of tradition and the movement of the interpreter. The anticipation of meaning that governs our understanding of a text is not an act of subjectivity, but proceeds from the communality that binds us to tradition, in the constant process of education. Tradition is not simply a precondition into which

we come, but we produce it ourselves, inasmuch as we understand, participate in the evolution of tradition, and hence further determine it ourselves. Thus the circle of understanding is not a "methodological" circle but describes an ontological structural element in understanding.[119]

For Gadamer, therefore, what we are here calling a text – "the true historical object" –

> is not an object at all [either in the sense favored in physical nature or in romantic hermeneutics], but the unity of the one and the other [the inseparability of the utterance of the past and the interpretation of the present], a relationship in which exist both the reality of history and the reality of historical understanding. A proper hermeneutics would have to demonstrate the effectivity of history within understanding itself. . . . Understanding is, essentially, an effective-historical relation.[120]

This shows very clearly that Gadamer is notably perceptive about the ontological indeterminacies of cultural and historical phenomena, the inescapable "backward" influence of historically generated interpretation, and the conceptual relation between these two themes and the theme of the hermeneutic circle. We cannot "understand" the past except as *we* understand the past: in doing that, we cannot fail to affect (without erasing) the real intrinsic properties of textual phenomena. For every imputation of the real meaning or intentional content of historically recovered texts (using that term in our broad sense – which, let it be said, Gadamer would refuse, though Schleiermacher would not[121]) is made from a particular historical present. The disciplined consensus that posits a distinction between real and merely apparent such meanings, therefore, itself becomes an artifact of the continuum of just such efforts. Hence, the theory (quite apart from Gadamer's use of it) does suggest how to reconcile (1) the realism of cultural phenomena; (2) their ontic indeterminacies; (3) methodological rigor regarding pertinent truth claims; and (4) what Gadamer is at pains to oppose – the vindication, both ontologically and methodologically, of a moderate form of relativism.

The point of having run through these alternative conceptions is to show how central Gadamer's version of the problem is for contemporary philosophy. For, if we abandon cognitive transparency, essentialism, the ahistorical conception of history (Danto), and the frozen historicality of history (the Romantics or romantic hermeneuts), and if we admit the symbiosis of the ontic and interpretive aspects of history and texts, then

(i) it is impossible to avoid the retroactive effectiveness of the hermeneutic process;

(ii) it is impossible to formulate the ontological conditions under which [i] obtains except in terms of the real Intentional indeterminacies of cultural phenomena; and

(iii) it is impossible to concede (ii) without committing ourselves to a moderate form of relativism (within the scope of a cultural realism).

Gadamer clearly sees the inexorability of (i)–(iii) but he will not allow it. Hence, just in the context in which he develops his account of the relational fusion of a "past" that is still able to "speak" to us in our own "present" – however prejudiced, tacitly preformed our aptitude for understanding the past may be (that is, if anything at all obtains that *could* be called understanding history or a historical text) – Gadamer converts the implicated cultural sharing into some peculiarly transhistorical (*not* an ahistorical) unity. Gadamer is clearly motivated to escape the sinister possibilities of a relativism that may border on complete anarchy; but his conceptual maneuver is entirely unnecessary and remains an intellectual scandal. With one voice, he (coherently) affirms that "The historical movement of human life consists in the fact that it is never utterly bound to any one standpoint, and hence can never have a truly closed horizon. The horizon is, rather, something into which we move and that moves with us. Horizons change for a person who is moving." And, with another voice, he (quite arbitrarily) adds,

> When our historical consciousness places itself within historical horizons, this does not entail passing into alien worlds unconnected in any way with our own, but together they constitute the one great horizon that moves from within and, beyond the frontiers of the present, embraces the historical depths of our self-consciousness. It is, in fact, a single horizon that embraces everything contained in historical consciousness.[122]

The obvious difficulty is that the "one horizon" – in effect, the humane values of the classical world – has "both a normative and an historical side."[123] No ground, however, has been laid for any such unitary and comprehensive norm; *and* the culturally constructed, historicized nature of man himself (human persons, *Dasein*) positively precludes it or at least anything like its empirical likelihood. In an odd way, then, Gadamer and Habermas converge from quite different paths.[124] Both need to recover universal norms within the flux of history. But there are none that can be secured *if*, as Gadamer says, "history does not belong to us, . . . we belong to it."[125] For, if persons are culturally constructed as the culturally apt beings they are, then the viability of plural societies, of intersocietal communication, of transhistorical understanding is quite intelligible within the scope of disparate, "prejudiced," somewhat local traditions. Without a suitable structuralism or essentialism, there is no prospect of confirming Gadamer's vision.

We must give up the pretense of substantive universal rationality somehow preserved in the flux of history (Habermas) or of a universal tradition somehow conservatively recovered within that same flux (Gadamer). The openness of history is against such findings – "Hegelian" findings, in that sense Heidegger so effectively exposed – findings of an ahistorically assured invariance within the flux of history or of grounds for believing that the merely salient, first-order regularities (or "in-variants") within the world of the flux, seen only from our contingent vantage within it, somehow ensure their continuance come what may.[126] (This, of course, may well be a view of history Hegel formulates only for a deeper ironic and instructional purpose.) Such claims (Habermas's and Gadamer's) may require only the thinnest of teleologies, practically invisible ones, but the trace of their halo remains unmistakable.

We may, nevertheless, recover a minimal conception of history that centers unblinkingly on the historicity of human nature: *to understand things historically is to understand how one understands oneself and how one understands one's understanding of other things – including nature, other persons, the phenomena of one's culture – under the constraint of one's self-understanding.* The historicity of human existence marks the radical defeat of second-order, cogniscent, transcendental, logocentric invariances. It is itself, of course, a *second-order* projection of the *via negativa* by which the first-order uniformities of any empirical understanding are refused the presumption of the sort of "Hegelian" assurance Gadamer and Habermas would rescue from the flux.[127] It does posit a universal that eschews universalism, a rhetorical conjecture synthetic and *a priori* in intent, functioning provisionally only within the admitted contingencies of its own internalist reflection; its posit is certainly not to be construed as *synthetic a priori*, and it expends itself in monitoring and disallowing all affirmative invariances, however decentered, of a second-order cogniscent sort (such as those of rationality and tradition). For, not only is the self culturally constructed; it is also aware of the deep contingency and change, even development, of its beliefs, intentions, desires, projects, actions, and remembered changes throughout its apparent career. Hence, it is aware of the ineluctably historicized contingency with which it understands how it understands – how whatever it posits in any reflexive interval is conditioned by that tacit historicity. (In a fair sense, this *is* Heidegger's conception of *Dasein*.)

The point at stake is the very irony of the penetrating exposé Gadamer directs against Dilthey's reclamation of the "scientific knowledge of the historically-conditioned as *objective science* [the point of Dilthey's Kantian-like critique]" under the conceptual schema of presupposing "that the historian can disengage himself from his own historical situation."[128] For it is the same insight that links Gadamer (and Habermas) to the fate of Dilthey, Ranke, Droysen, Schleiermacher – and Hegel. But that hardly erases Gadamer's genuine clarification of the import of saying that "man . . . is a being who only becomes what he is and acquires his 'bearing' by what he does, by the 'how' of his actions [that is, by his 'cultural know-how' – not by a knowledge of immutable rules or principles or objectivist structures; by acting in the world through having internalized the open practices of his culture and tradition; by acquiring, in Wittgenstein's terms, a form of life]."[129] Nor does it erase the prospect of a measure of objectivity with respect to the human sciences, *within* the constraints Gadamer (equivocally) believes can yield no objectivity. "Historical knowledge," Gadamer proclaims, "cannot be described according to the model of an objectivist knowledge because it is itself a process which has all the characteristics of an historical event. . . . Objectivism is an illusion."[130]

He is right, of course. But he neglects to add that, for that very reason, objectiv-*ism* is untenable in the *natural* sciences, though obectiv*ity* is not; and that, for analogous reasons, some form of objectivity regarding history, the interpretation of texts, and the like is entirely open to defense. His objection to Dilthey's Kantianism may be allowed. But that hardly leads to the (implied) blunderbuss objection "In history, nothing is incomprehensible. Everything is understood since everything resembles a text."[131] Ricoeur is also wrong in this regard, being too sanguine about the recovery of objectivity within a somewhat Diltheyan view of social space.[132] But the right calibration of the defense of objectivity already concedes its eligibility. Gadamer is too fearful about the long arm of positivism and the Enlightenment conception of science; and Ricoeur is too sanguine about the ease with which Dilthey's solution can be adjusted within a "distantiated" world; and both rely illicitly (in a transcendental sense) on the universal invariance of humanity. Thus Ricoeur affirms,

> only man *has a world* and not just a situation. In the same manner that the text frees its meaning from the tutelage of the mental intention, it frees its reference from the limits of ostensive reference. For us, the world is the ensemble of referents opened up by the texts. Thus we speak about the "world" of Greece, not to designate any more what were the situations for those who lived them, but to designate the non-situational referents which outlive the effacement of the first and which henceforth are offered as possible modes of being, as symbolic dimensions of our being-in-the-world. For me, this is the referent of all literature; no longer the *Umwelt* of the ostensive references of dialogue, but the *Welt* projected by the non-ostensive references of every text that we have read, understood, and loved. To understand a text is at the same time to light up our own situation, or, if you will, to interpolate among the predicates of our situation all the significations which make a *Welt* of our *Umwelt*.[133]

There can be no doubt that this *is* Gadamer's thesis presented in the guise of a recovery of an objectivity due to the reciprocal contribution of *Verstehen* and *Erklären* (which Gadamer himself would reject). Even the appeal to the Greek world is the same.

To say that much, of course, is to salute Heidegger once again – but in the leanest way. It is, in fact, just to collect the gathering theme of the materials we were collecting only a short while ago – among which Marx's forms of *praxis*, Foucault's more contingent, arbitrarily cohering cultural ensembles, and Wittgenstein's historically flat but structurally acute template of alternative "forms of life" remain, by far, the best large clues we have regarding the process of the symbiosis of emergent persons and emergent societies. For the moment, however, they merely bring us to the edge of the puzzle. We have still to answer how that symbiosis yields the distinctive objectivity of the human world.

VII

It remains to add a closing word about the ontology of cultural entities and phenomena – *texts*, in the sense we have fixed by a term of art – under the condition of history here elaborated. For, the theory of history we have been developing leads, both in itself and in application to texts, to a very bold, distinctly heterodox account. The pieces of what we want are scattered in what has already been said. We may collect them in a tally.

The single most important finding is this:

(a)   every text (that is, artworks, actions, linguistic or lingual utterances, institutions, practices, personal lives, the behavior of entire societies) has, as a history or insofar as it is intrinsically historicized, plural historical pasts generated by its changing historical present(s).

The (or a) historical past is a past intrinsic to the individuated career of a particular text, relationally linked to its current present or linked to that present via some past present that is linked to it. A text has indeterminately many pasts relationally linked to its evolving historical present(s). The past of clock or calendar time, fixed anisotropically, cannot be counted on to disallow the generation of such (historical) pasts.

The same considerations that confirm (a) confirm

(b)   the historical present(s) of any text is (are) its *Intentional presence*: that is, its present import or significance as interpreted by *those* particularly apt "texts" – human persons – that are exclusively capable of interpreting themselves and other texts and that similarly exhibit evolving histories.

From (a) and (b) it follows that

(c)   every historical (Intentional) present is a historically interpreted posit, every historical past is relationally implicated in some such posited present, every historical present attributed to an individuated text is generationally constrained by the sequence of past presents or future pasts (and *their* pasts) that still form the "effective" past of that text.

If, as we have already argued,[134] reference and individuation are intentionally, contextually, even "story-relatively" managed, then we need not fear that these confessedly strenuous admissions will inevitably violate any of the usual constraints of reference and reidentification. (In effect, for porous texts, we attenuate unity without sacrificing unicity.)

Having said this much, we may add

(d)   what is *intrinsic* to particular texts is not determined by appeal to anything like natural kinds (or by appeal to anything that merely falls under presumed physical laws – although, because cultural entities and cultural attributes are, respectively, "embodied" and "incarnate," as we have argued,[135] we may well be guided by the physical saliencies of embodying and incarnating entities and attributes; what is intrinsic is, rather, a historically changing posit open to constant reinterpretation keyed to the "Intentional presence" of the entire field of distributed texts accessible or salient to the self-interpreting "texts" (persons) among them.

For example, George Santayana's excellent reading of Goethe's *Faust* assigns the essential import of that text on the basis of a review of the peculiarly compelling congruities of the span of Western history from Goethe's *to* Santayana's own time as assembled by Santayana.[136] What is intrinsic to texts is itself historicized – hence, Intentional and interpretive. The causal and law-like models of the intrinsic or essential or natural as drawn up in the physical sciences are largely irrelevant here and, if insistently pressed, utterly misleading. There is no reason why texts should have a single historical past or future, or why what is designated as intrinsic to a text on one assigned history should, if evidentially supported, be comfortable with what is assigned on another assigned history.

Some further ontological peculiarities may serve to round out this account: notably, at least that

(e)   texts or cultural phenomena are causally efficacious in the embodied world in which they appear – hence, are causally effective in the physical and biological world in which texts are embodied.

This is the very point of admitting human agency.[137] It is also the point of admitting the reverse process – namely, the causal influence of one's constant and continuing enculturation. Perhaps the conversion of Saul on the road to Damascus may be allowed to stand as proxy for the numberless instances in which conversation, reading, the perception of events, participation in cultural activities, and the like actually affect us in ways that cannot be denied genuine causal force.[138] We may also add,

(f)   admitting the Intentional, interpretive, historicized, plural nature of what is intrinsic to texts, texts are *ontically indeterminate* (porous) in their Intentional features, even if they are not in their embodying and incarnating features.[139]

Texts are ascribed determinate Intentional attributes; but such assignments, even if vindicated, do not preclude ascriptions that would be incompatible with other such ascriptions on a bipolar model of truth-values.[140] The indeterminacy is at least triple-headed: first, because "incongruent" ascriptions (that is, ascriptions that on a bipolar model would be incompatible but on a relativistic model would not) cannot be precluded; second, because the validation of any ascription depends on the interpretive practice of a consensually supporting society that is itself historicized in the way all texts are, because we cannot determinately fix the limits and internal structures of individuated texts apart from or independently of the consensual practice of interpreting them; and, third, because texts are historicized and the intrinsic properties assigned them are themselves artifacts of that historically developing practice. The reasonableness of a particular interpretation is a function of the historical practice of interpreting texts and of interpreting *that* text *and* of the open-ended possibility of altering the general and the particular practice.

There is only a consensual constraint that ultimately affects what we judge to be a reasonable interpretation of given texts. But such a constraint can only be holistically applied, is itself open to interpretation and change, and cannot be counted on to disqualify pluralized and relativistic practices within its own space. It is clear that, to make our theory of texts workable, provisional strategies would be needed to permit us to mark off, within specific disputes, errors, corrections, inconsistencies, relevance constraints, and the like. There is no reason in the world why policies on all such matters could not be worked out. More to the point, there is no reason to believe that such policies are not actually in place – in all the relatively settled inquiries that our society supports but cannot forever fix, by means of whatever current methodological strategy it happens now to favor or what we may come to favor in the future in accord with unforeseeable "paradigm-like" shifts.

It would not be unreasonable, therefore, to add explicitly the finding already entailed in (f):

(g)   texts may have indefinitely many *plural interpretive presents*; for that is tantamount to saying that texts are ontically indeterminate but interpretively determinable.

In that sense, texts have open historical futures. Perhaps, then, in the spirit of the same explicitness, we may take note of the deeper import of (b), particularly in the light of (f) and (g): namely,

(h)   the reality of texts is ontically inseparable from the *collective* cultural world generated by the aggregated Intentional interests and Intentionally qualified causal interventions (actions) of some actual persons.

We may, then, as a convenience of art and with an eye to contrasting our (internalist) *presuppositions* about the nature of what is real within the domains of the physical and human sciences, say that *texts*, the principal entities of cultural space, are *"real!"* in satisfying (a)–(h); that physical entities are (merely) *"reall"* in being ontically independent of what governs the real!; though they are themselves ineluctably posited as such only within the space of the real!; and thet (redundantly) the real! is invariably embodied in the reall. To play a useful trick with typography, it is sufficient to hold that the real! is *real*, though not reall, because (1) the reall is ontically independent of (however it may be causally encumbered by) the interests and interventions of particular or aggregated human agents; and (2) the real! is ontically embodied in what is real!. The demonstration of the failure of physicalist elimination and reduction, therefore, is simply the obverse side of the elaboration of the nature of texts. Hence, the adequacy and scope of the physical sciences themselves are a function of the theory of texts.[141]

There are further distinct benefits only minimally touched on here. First, the theme of (h) may easily be detached from (a)–(g), in order, if wanted, to suggest a reduced sense in which mathematical entities could be said to be real! as opposed to the Platonist sense in accord with which such entities could be said to be real! (again, in a way reduced from the sense appropriate to physical entities) – for example, in accord with Henri Poincaré's constructivist account of mathematical entities.[142] Secondly, the recent spate of puzzles about the fixity of literary texts that are clearly open to interpretation is manageably resolved by any of a number of working commitments congruent with acknowledging that literary works are real! and that their individuation (despite Intentional indeterminacies and contextedness) is facilitated by the individuation of inscriptions functioning indexically and in ways significatively constrained by what we take them to embody minimally. This helps to resolve, for example, the apparent paradoxes of such accounts as those of Wolfgang Iser and Stanley Fish or of even more strenuous theorists.[143]

The cultural world, then, is, though embodied in the physical world, decidedly different from it.

Notes

1   W. V. Quine, *Word and Object* (Cambridge, Mass: MIT Press 1960), p.75; cf. the full context, pp. 68–79.

2   Ibid., p. 68.

3   Ibid., p. 221.

4   Cf. ibid., pp. 219–21.

5   See ch. 6, above.

6   See ch. 4, above.

7   Arthur C. Danto, "The Artworld," *Journal of Philosophy*, X(1968), p. 162.

8   Thomas S. Kuhn, *The Structure of Scientific Revolutions*, 2nd, enlarged edn (Chicago: University of Chicago Press, 1970), pp. 118–29. See also Norwood Russell Hanson, *Patterns of Discovery: An Inquiry into the Conceptual Foundations of Science* (Cambridge: Cambridge University Press, 1965).

9   This, ultimately, is the fatal weakness (papered over) of Donald Davidson's anomalous monism. See for instance his "Mental Events," *Essays on Actions and Events* (Oxford: Clarendon Press, 1980); also Joseph Margolis, *Science without Unity: Reconciling the Human and Natural Sciences* (Oxford: Basil Blackwell, 1987), ch. 5. See also ch. 6, above.

10 See further Margolis, *Science without Unity*, chs 7, 9.

11   See Hilary Putnam, "The Meaning of 'meaning'," "The Analytic and the Synthetic," and "Is Semantics Possible?" *Philosophical Papers*, vol. II (Cambridge: Cambridge University Press, 1975). This is not to endorse Putnam's account without reservation. He himself, now that he has demoted the role of reference in his own theory, would require a significant reformulation of the view he here presents. See, further "Language and Reality" in the same volume, and "Reference and Truth," *Philosophical Papers*, vol. III (Cambridge: Cambridge University Press, 1983). Cf. Joseph Margolis, *Pragmatism without Foundations: Reconciling Realism and Relativism* (Oxford: Basil Blackwell, 1986), ch. 9.

12   See Joseph Margolis, *Art and Philosophy* (Atlantic Highlands, N. J: Humanities Press, 1980), ch. 2.

13   See for instance the polite discussion of titless whales in Keith Donnellan, "Necessity and Criteria," *Journal of Philosophy*, LIX (1962).

14   Bernard Williams, "Personal Identity and Individuation," *Problems of the Self* (Cambridge: Cambridge University Press, 1973), p. 11.

15   See John F. Post, *The Faces of Existence: An Essay in Nonreductive Metaphysics* (Ithaca, NY: Cornell University Press, 1987), p. 146; also ch. 6, above.

16   See John Locke, *An Essay Concerning Human Understanding*, 2 vols, ed. Alexander Campbell Fraser (Oxford: Oxford University Press, 1894), bk ii, ch. 27; also Anthony Quinton, "The Soul," *Journal of Philosophy* XLIX (1962); and Geoffrey Madell, *The Identity of the Self* (Edinburgh: Edinburgh University Press, 1981), particularly pp. 50–74.

17   See further Joseph Margolis, *Persons and Minds: The Prospects of Nonreductive Materialism* (Dordrecht: D. Reidel, 1978), ch. 6.

18   Williams, "Personal Identity and Individuation," *Problems of the Self*, p. 1.

19   Bernard Williams, "Are Persons Bodies?" ibid., p. 77.

20   See P. F. Strawson, *Individuals: An Essay in Descriptive Metaphysics* (London: Methuen, 1959), p. 92.

21   The literature on multiple personality is suprisingly meager and often disappointing. For a sample of what there is, see Bennett G. Braun (ed.), *The Psychiatric Clinics of North America*, vol. 7, no. 1 (March 1984): "Symposium on Multiple Personality" (Philadelphia: W. B. Saunders, 1984); and Richard P. Kluft (ed.), *Childhood Antecedents of Multiple Personality* (Washington, D C: American Psychiatric Press, 1985).

22   The details of this device used with respect to the arts are given in Margolis, *Art and Philosophy*, ch. 4; cf. also Joseph Margolis, *Culture and Cultural Entities* (Dordrecht: D. Reidel, 1984), ch. 1.

23   See ch. 6, above.

24   Cf. Thomas S. Kuhn, Preface to *The Essential Tension: Selected Studies in Scientific Tradition and Change* (Chicago: University of Chicago Press, 1977), p. xv. Cf. Paul Ricoeur, *Hermeneutics and Human Sciences: Essays on Language, Action and Interpretation*, tr. and ed. John B. Thompspon (Cambridge: Cambridge University Press, 1981), particularly "The Task of Hermeneutics," "The Hermeneutical Function of Distanciation," "What Is a Text? Explanation and Understanding," and "The Model of the Text: Meaningful Action Considered as a Text."

25   It is perhaps worth reporting that there is no entry in the *Library of Congress Subject Headings*, 10th edn, 2 vols (Washington, DC: Library of Congress, 1986),

covering the metaphysics or ontology of culture or any of its cognate topics. Evidently, there is no large collection of books discussing the topic in a focused way.

26 I believe I owe this term to Abraham Edel. I hope I am right in this.

27 See ch. 9, below.

28 See ch. 1, above; also Ernst Tugendhat, *Self-Consciousness and Self-Determination*, tr. Paul Stern (Cambridge, MIT, 1986), particularly Lectures 11 and 12.

29 See for instance the classic reference in Karl Marx, *Capital: A Critique of Political Economy*, vol. 1. tr. Ben Fowkes (New York: Random House, 1976), pp. 477–9, that counters the simplistic reading of Marx in terms of a strong disjunction between "substratum" and "superstructure." An excellent account centered on the threatening inadequacies of Marxism and structuralism in the context of cultural anthropology (but also itself somewhat threatened by the tendentiousness of structuralism) is provided in Marshall Sahlins, *Culture and Practical Reason* (Chicago: University of Chicago Press, 1976).

30 See for instance the research of K. M. Colby on "artificial neurosis," in "Computer Simulation of a Neurotic Process," in S. S. Tomkins and Samuel Messick (eds), *Computer Simulation of Personality: Frontiers of Psychological Research* (New York: Wiley, 1963); and *Artificial Paranoia* (New York: Pergamon, 1975). For a balanced discussion of the matter, see Margaret A. Boden, *Artificial Intelligence and Natural Man* (New York: Basic Books, 1977), ch. 2.

31 See Herbert Feigl, *The "Mental" and the "Physical": The Essay and a Postcript* (Minneapolis: University of Minnesota Press, 1967).

32 See chs 1, 4, above.

33 This, of course is not the place to attempt an analysis of philosophical argument itself; although it would be a mistake not to draw attention to its bearing on the substantive issues in question. I have offered an account of transcendental arguments, however, along these lines, in *Pragmatism without Foundations*, ch. 11.

34 Alvin I. Goldman, *A Theory of Human Action* (Englewood Cliffs, NJ: Prentice-Hall, 1970), p. 2.

35 Ibid.

36 Cf. Joseph Margolis, review of Alvin I. Goldman, *A Theory of Action*, in *Metaphilosophy*, V (1974).

37 See G. E. M. Anscombe, *Intention* (Oxford: Basil Blackwell, 1957); Eric D'Arcy, *Human Acts* (Oxford: Clarendon Press, 1963). Both are cited by Goldman.

38 Donald Davidson, "Actions, Reasons, and Causes," *Essays on Actions and Events* (also cited by Goldman).

39 Goldman, *A Theory of Human Action*, pp. 172, 173.

40 Ibid., p. 18.

41 See ibid., p. 3 (which gives Goldman's would-be counterinstances to the identity thesis), for the use of "event" and "act," which pretty well ensures that, for Goldman, acts must be included in the class of events. For example, even though moving one's finger *may* be a "basic act-token," the "basic act-type" of which it is a member need not be restricted (it seems) to events that are act-tokens: one's finger may, for instance, move as a result of a nervous spasm. Unfortunately, in his most recent book, admittedly on another topic, Goldman finds no occasion to return to clarify the central notions of "causality," "act,"

and "event." See Alvin I. Goldman, *Epistemology and Cognition* (Cambridge, Mass.: Harvard University Press, 1986) – for instance at ch. 2. A careful critique of Goldman's view is offered in Raimo Tuomela, *Human Action and Its Explanation: A Study on the Philosophical Foundations of Psychology* (Dordrecht: D. Reidel, 1977), ch. 2. Tuomela is quite candid about the "scientific realist" orientation of his own account (p. 2), which, on the general argument being developed here, fails to demonstrate satisfactorily (as does Wilfrid Sellar's realism, which Tuomela pretty well follows) the unity with which physical and cultural phenomena may be examined methodologically – in particular, with regard to the fact that the human or cultural does *not*, as "non-sentient" physical phenomena do, obtain independently of the experience, observation, reflection of individual human agents. Cf. ibid, ch. 1.

42 Ibid., p. 6.
43 Ibid., p. 63.
44 Cf. ibid., ch. 5, for instance section 5.
45 See Davidson, "Actions, Reasons, and Causes," *Essays on Actions and Events*.
46 Goldman, *A Theory of Human Action*, p. 3.
47 Cf. Arthur C. Danto, "What We Can Do." *Journal of Philosophy*, LX (1963) and "Basic Actions," *American Philosophical Quarterly*, II (1965) – which Goldman mentions as being responsible for the term "basic action." A difficulty very much like the one indicated dogs Danto's account as well, which is all the more curious because of Danto's developed interest in the arts and in culture in general. See Arthur C. Danto, *Analytical Philosophy of Action* (Cambridge: Cambridge University Press, 1973); and Margolis, *Art and Philosophy*, ch. 1.
48 See for instance H. L. A. Hart and A. M. Honoré, *Causation in the Law* (Oxford: Clarendon Press, 1959).
49 These matters, of course, have all been raised afresh by the recent appearance of the sensational book by Victor Farias, *Heidegger et le nazisme*, tr. Myriam Bennaroch and Jean-Baptiste Grasset (Paris: Verdier, 1987). Of the remarkable European coverage accorded the book, the most significant includes a piece by Nicolas Tertulian, "Trois témoignages: Löwith, Jaspers, Marcuse," in *La Quaintaine littéraire*, on 1–15 November 1987; an interview with Derrida in *Le Nouvel observateur*, 27 November–3 December 1987, and Farias's reply to Derrida in the same issue of *Le Nouvel observateur*. There appears to be no challenge to Farias's facts, though how they should be construed and what their import is are, needless to say, much contested.
50 There is much debate just at the moment regarding whether, for instance, a hermeneutic approach to the cultural – in particular, an approach favoring Heidegger's philosophical stance, or indeed the stance of such a person as Paul de Man (himself recently exposed as an active contributor to anti-semitic, pro-Nazi newspapers in Belgium during World War II), is peculiarly closely linked to facilitating a principled denial that the past or the meaning of texts can be objectively established. There is reason to think that there are excessive and arbitrary claims on both sides of the question; and there is good reason to think that the issue will remain a lively one for some time to come.
51 See for instance Rudolf Carnap, "Psychology and Physical Language," tr. George Schick, in A. J. Ayer (ed.), *Logical Positivism* (Glencoe, Ill.: Free Press, 1959); J. J. C Smart, *Philosophy and Scientific Realism* (London: Routledge and Kegan Paul, 1963); and Margolis, *Science without Unity*, ch. 10.

52 See ch. 5, above; also Louis Althusser and Étienne Balibar, *Reading Capital*, tr. Ben Brewster (London: New Left Books, 1970); and Fredric Jameson, *The Political Unconscious: Narrative as a Socially Symbolic Act* (Ithaca, NY: Cornell University Press, 1981).

53 I have benefited considerably, here, from the elegant discussions of these and related topics in Paul Horwich, *Asymmetrics in Time: Problems in the Philosophy of Science* (Cambridge, Mass.: MIT Press, 1987), particularly chs 3, 6, 8. Horwich provides an ample bibliography (and discussion) of the leading accounts.

54 See Michael Dummett, *Truth and Other Enigmas* (Cambridge, Mass: Harvard University Press, 1978); also Margolis, *Pragmatism without Foundations*, ch. 5.

55 See Margolis, *Pragmatism without Foundations*, pt II.

56 There is a somewhat theologically motivated attempt to fix the reality of the cultural (say, of "fictional worlds") independently of human agency by assigning its Intentional *content* to God (or to a realm of Platonic Forms). See Nicholas Wolterstorff, *Works and Worlds of Art* (Oxford: Clarendon Press, 1980). So Wolterstorff maintains that the artist (a novelist for instance: Gogol as the author of *Dead Souls*) does not "bring into existence" the (intentional) "world" that the artist "projects" by the sentences of his story: "Neither is it something that the artist makes occur. The world of *Dead Souls* [for instance] existed apart from Gogol's activity as writer; and neither he nor anyone else has made it occur. The artist's activity consists in projecting an already existent but normally non-occurrent state of affairs by way of indicating certain states of affairs. Of course that state of affairs which the artist projected was not the world associated with his artefact until he composed that artefact and thereby projected the world. Yet all the while that conjunctive state of affairs which is in fact the world associated with the text of *Dead Souls* existed [apparently timelessly], waiting to become the world of his book. The text is made and associated with the world rather than the world made and associated with the text. World projection is a mode of selection, not a mode of creation" (pp. 129–130). But this has the unhappy consequence – requiring either God's providence or an unusually rich Platonic world – that the describable "world" of Gogol's *Dead Souls does not in any way depend on the actual history of nineteenth-century Russia* on which its imaginative "projection" seems to rest. Wolterstorff's technical reason for championing this unusual theory is in part at least that "states of affairs" – in particular, the state of affairs delineated by *Dead Souls* – have *kinds* as "components," and that "kinds" exist (ibid., pp. 143, 46-58). See further Nicholas Wolterstorff, *On Universals: An Essay in Ontology* (Chicago: University of Chicago Press, 1970), ch. 11. All such Platonisms can be obviated by treating artworks as (indissolutely) tokens-of-types – that is, as *particulars that are made or created* – and by treating predicates as not entailing the *existence* of properties or kinds. See Margolis, *Art and Philosophy*, ch. 4.

57 I have benefited considerably, here, from a close reading of an unpublished book manuscript of a younger associate, Gabriel R. Ricci, *"The Logic of History: Philosophy and History in Ernst Troelsch and Martin Heidegger."* I had not appreciated, until reading Ricci's account, the profound mediating role of Ernst Troelsch, in particular, in the development of Heidegger's and Gadamer's conceptions of human and hermeneutic history.

58 The strenuousness of Leibniz's formula (or, alternatively, the uncertainty of

what it means – restricting the existence of each object to one world and linking the indiscernibility of identicals to the necessity of what obtains in that world – may be sampled in Alvin Plantinga, "Transworld Identity or World-bound Individuals?" in Milton Munitz (ed.), *Logic and Ontology* (New York: New York University Press, 1973). Plantinga notes particularly the thesis of Leibniz's letter to Arnauld, 14 July 1686.

59 One cannot avoid recalling here, perhaps quite idly, J. B. Bury's well-known "Cleopatra's Nose," in *Selected Essays of J. B. Bury*, ed. Harold Temperly (Cambridge: Cambridge University Press, 1930), which speculates that an accidental physical trait (the length of Cleopatra's nose) may well have been an "essential" factor in shaping the history of ancient Rome.

60 See for instance Keith Donnellan, "Reference and Definite Descriptions," *Philosophical Review*, LXXV (1966); David Kaplan, "Quantifying In," *Synthese*, XIX (!968); Saul A. Kripke, "Naming and Necessity," in Donald Davidson and Gilbert Harman (eds), *Semantics of Natural Language* (Dordrecht: D. Reidel 1972).

61 Gareth Evans, *The Varieties of Reference*, ed. John McDowell (Oxford: Clarendon Press, 1982), p. 376f.

62 Cf. ibid., p. 377. In particular, it is doubtful that "the notion of using a term to refer [already equivocal between (i) and (ii)] is a less fundamental notion than the notion of understanding a term in such a use [(iii)]; [even conceding that] it is a perfectly intelligible possibility, occasionally realized, that someone can use an expression to refer without being himself in a position to understand the reference [(ii)]" (p. 398). This is not because story-relative identification is not "less fundamental" than understanding in a demonstrative sense that *this* name names *this* particular individual – when the latter is the relevant concern; but because the same general background conditions and realist assumptions are involved in the normal use and understanding of referring expressions as are involved in understanding, distributively, that this name names this particular individual. *Understanding* reference is here not the same as *knowing* referents (cf. pp. 400–402). One important reason for pressing these distinctions is to forestall insouciant and naive forms of realism, drawn inaptly from "practices" or Wittgensteinian "forms of life" (cf. pp. 398–404). Another is to offset the presumption that there is one practice that is epistemologically prior and more important than the others in the relevant sense. Otherwise, there is no real point in resisting Evans's maneuvers. Cf. ch. 9, below.

63 See particularly H. L. A. Hart, "The Ascription of Responsibility and Rights," in A. G. N. Flew (ed.), *Logic and Language*, 1st ser. (Oxford: Basil Blackwell, 1951); and Kripke, "Naming and Necessity," in Davidson and Harman (eds), *Semantics of Natural Language*. Both experiment, though in different ways, with the possibilities of overriding considerations.

64 Kuhn, *The Structure of Scientific Revolutions*, p. 111.

65 Ibid., p. 112

66 Ibid., p. 120 (italics added).

67 There is a particularly trim speculation about actual and possible and fictional and mythological and impossible and indeterminable and interminable worlds that I should like to mention here – with which the present remarks will be seen to be very much in sympathy. See Thomas G. Pavel, *Fictional Worlds* (Cambridge, Mass.: Harvard Univerity Press, 1986), chs 3, 4. The solutions

proposed, here and there, must, of course, go their own way – a warning born only of philosophical prudence and of a wish not to encumber Pavel. It is true, however, that certain large notions of fiction – Nietzschean notions, one may as well say – are due to reflections on the puzzles of the peculiar reality of historical cultures *and* the plausibility of construing whatever we assign as the "objective," "mind-independent" structures of the physical world as undeniable artifacts generated within the space of the other. That is, I believe, very close to Pavel's inspiration. In fact, if one asks for more robust evidence, it might well be noted that, at just this moment of writing, the American edition of Peter Wright's *Spycatcher: The Candid Autobiography of a Senior Intelligence Officer* (New York: Viking, 1987) has just been released. Reflecting on the interpenetrating "myths" of the world of espionage – and, prehaps, assimilating to it the motivation for the novels of John LeCarré, the floating and competing "near"-paradigms of local science (in Thomas Kuhn's sense), the extravagant (but hardly for that reason implausible) contexts of "heteroglossia" that Bakhtin takes to operate in everyday life, and much more – one can begin to see that *system*, even complete and completely testable *coherence*, is neither required nor to be expected in the affairs of men. See Mikhail Bakhtin, "Discourse in the Novel," in Michael Holquist (ed.), *The Dialogic Imagination: Four Essays by M. M. Bakhtin*, tr. Caryl Emerson and Michael Holquist (Austin: University of Texas Press, 1981).

68 There is an extended and compendious account of intentionality in *Science without Unity*, chs 7, 9. It would be impossible and pointless to attempt to provide a comparable summary here. We shall have to be content with a few brief clues.

69 This supplies, it may be mentioned, the critical failure of Hilary Putnam's well-known comparison of minds and machines – which he himself has now repudiated. See Putnam, "Minds and Machines," *Philosophical Papers*, vol. 2. Cf. also Fred I. Dretske, *Knowledge and the Flow of Information* (Chicago: University of Chicago Press, 1981).

70 On system, see ch. 5, above.

71 I have been influenced to some extent, here, by my reading of Judson C. Webb, "Gödel's Theorems and Church's Thesis: A Prologue to Mechanism," in Robert S. Cohen and Marx W. Wartofsky (eds), *Language, Logic, and Method* (Dordrecht: D. Reidel, 1983). I cannot claim sufficient mathematical expertise to have grasped the full force of Webb's account. But I have never supposed that the defeat of extensionalism in cultural contexts depended on a decisive contradiction, incoherence, or a transcendental argument of the Kantian sort. In any case, the issue rests with the difference between the domain of mathematics and the domain of human culture. For instance, Webb introduces two theses: (C) "Every 'precisely described' piece of human behavior can be simulated by a suitably programmed computer"; (CT) "Every 'effectively computable' function is general recursive [in Church's sense] (and vice-versa)," (pp. 310, 311). Of Daniel Dennett's argument, in effect linking the two, Webb says that "Dennett says that (C) 'is, or boils down to, some version of' (CT), but this may be claiming too much, for there are functions which are 'precisely described' in the literal (classical) sense [of mathematics] without being computable" (p. 311). (CT) is Alonzo Church's thesis, and (C) is the general formula of the extensionalist's committment regarding psychological, behavioral, and cultural

phenomena. Cf. Daniel C. Dennett, "Why the Law of Effect Will Not Go Away," *Brainstorms* (Montgomery, Vt: Bradford Books, 1978). Webb goes on to say, "Still, (CT) comes very close to implying (C), and is a major inspiration for it" (ibid.). The rest of Webb's paper supplies the sense in which this is so. I find no reason to dispute the point. My own objection concerns the interpretation of (C) or of any analogue of (C) *drawn from the study of human culture and generalized from the sample to the nature of the domain of which it is a sample.* Put another way, to make the argument, extensionalists would have to be able to *show* that this or that sector of culture *was* subject to (CT), not that a generalized successor to that natural sector, artifactically formulated from a given sample or the like, could be satisfactorily so characterized. The difficulty still stands; but it is, so to say, a matter for gentlemanly disagreement. Cf. also the pretty paradox Webb summarizes against the "anti-mechanist" ibid., pp. 339-40; but also pp. 342, 344).

72 See Post, *The Faces of Existence.* History does not play a distinct *ontological* role in Post's system, given his physicalism: it cannot, granting, for instance, his MND Principle (p. 176).

73 See Carl G. Hempel, "The Function of General Laws in History," *Aspects of Scientific Explanation and Other Essays in the Philosophy of Science* (New York: Free Press, 1965). Hempel's main – well-known – thesis is pretty well caught up in the following remarks: "By a general law, we shall understand a statement of universal conditional form which is capable of being confirmed or disconfirmed by suitable empirical findings" (p. 231); "The main function of general laws in the natural sciences is to connect events in patterns which are usually referred to as *explanation* and *prediction*" (p. 232); "the logical structure of a scientific prediction is the same as that of a scientific explanation, . . . the customary distinction between explanation and prediction rests mainly on a pragmatic difference" (p. 214) – which Hempel subsequently changed his views about; and "The preceding considerations apply to *explanation in history* as well as in any other branch of empirical science" (p. 215).

74 See Crispin Wright, "Anti-Realism and Revisionism" and "Realism, Bivalence and Classical Logic," *Realism, Meaning and Truth* (Oxford:Basil Blackwell, 1987). Again, history does not play a distinct *ontological* role in Wright's account of truth, since no reasons are adduced by him for characterizing different sectors of reality as affecting the question differentially. In effect, Wright treats the question of truth in epistemological terms, hence uniformly.

75 See Arthur C. Danto, "Narrative Sentences" and "Historical Language and Historical Reality," *Narration and Knowledge* (New York: Columbia University Press, 1985). The book incorporates the whole of the earlier *Analytical Philosophy of History* (Cambridge: Cambridge University Press, 1965). Since we shall be looking at Danto's theory more closely, there is no need to supply full details here. Nevertheless, see pp. 318, 306, 310 (of *Narration and Knowledge*).

76 Hans-Georg Gadamer, Paul Ricoeur, Charles Taylor, Richard Bernstein – and, among the theorists of the physical sciences, Karl Popper and Thomas Kuhn chiefly – are the most natural exemplars that spring to mind. So-called traditionalism is discussed in *Pragmatism without Foundations*, ch. 2.

77 See for example the interview titled "The History of Sexuality," in Michel Foucault, *Power/Knowledge: Selected Interviews and Other Writings 1972-1977*, tr. Colin Gordon et al., ed. Colin Gordon, (New York: Pantheon, 1980). This

pretty well shows the extent to which Foucault straightforwardly considered *Discipline and Punish* and *The History of Sexuality* histories, even if not straightforward histories. Also, Foucault's final remark betrays the sketchiness of his conceptual model: "one 'fictions' history on the basis of a political reality that makes it true, one 'fictions' a politics not yet in existence on the basis of a historical truth" (p. 193). The account has a loosely Marxist cast at best (cf. p. 188). A stronger statement of his theoretical orientation appears, of course, in "Nietzsche, Genealogy, History," in Michel Foucault, *Languange, Counter-Memory, Practice: Selected Essays and Interviews*, trans. Donald F. Bouchard and Sherry Simon, ed. Donald F. Bouchard (Ithaca, NY: Cornell University Press, 1977). But Foucault does not actually show how he reconciles his different conceptual attitudes to the *writing* of history.

78 Danto, "Historical Language and Historical Reality," *Narration and Knowledge*, p. 330.

79 Ibid., pp. 326–7.

80 Ibid., p. 67.

81 Ibid., pp. 336–7.

82 Ibid., p. 337.

83 Arthur C Danto, *Transfiguration of the Commonplace* (Cambridge, Mass.: Harvard University Press, 1981), pp. 1–3.

84 Ibid., p. 139.

85 Danto, *Analytical Philosophy of Actions*, pp. 63–4.

86 Cited by Danto in "Narrative Sentences," *Narration and Knowledge*, p. 143, from Irwin Lieb (ed.), *Charles S. Peirce's Letters to Lady Welby* (New Haven, Conn.: Whitlock's, 1953), p. 9.

87 Cf. Danto "Narrative Sentences," *Narration and Knowledge*, pp. 143–8; also "Future – and-Past – Contigencies," in the same volume.

88 Williams, "Are Persons Bodies?" *Problems of the Self*, p. 75.

89 See Margolis, *Science without Unity*, ch. 8.

90 Danto, "Historical Language and Historical Reality," *Narration and Knowledge*, p. 336.

91 Kuhn, *The Structure of Scientific Revolutions*, p. 120.

92 I offer a reasonably thorough review of Danto's theory of art in "Ontology Down and Out in Art and Science," *Journal of Aesthetics and Art Criticism*, forthcoming. The essential incoherence rests with both historicizing and not historicizing perception (in Kuhn's sense) and with both contrasting and conflating different senses of "perception" in the context of his account of the red canvases (and elsewhere).

93 Cf. Margolis *Science without Unity*, ch. 9.

94 See further Margolis, *Pragmatism without Foundations*, pt I, and Introduction to *Science without Unity*.

95 Danto, "Narrative Sentences," *Narration and Knowledge*, p. 143.

96 Jürgen Habermas, "A Review of Gadamer's *Truth and Method*," tr. Fred Dallmayr and Thomas McCarthy, repr in Brice R. Wachterhauser (ed.), *Hermeneutics and Modern Philosophy* (Albany, NY: State University of New York Press, 1986), pp. 256–60. The translation first appeared in Fred R. Dallmayr and Thomas A. McCarthy (eds), *Understanding and Social Inquiry* (Notre Dame, Ind.: University of Notre Dame Press, 1977). Actually, Danto's sentence, examined as if it might have been written in 1618, was "The Thirty

Years War begins now" ("Narrative Sentences," *Narration and Knowledge*, p. 152). The phrase "an inexpungeable subjective factor" occurs at p. 142 ("History and Chronicle").

97 See Hans-Georg Gadamer, "On the Scope and Function of Hermeneutical Reflection," tr. G. B. Hess and R. E. Palmer, in Wachterhaucer (ed.), *Hermeneutics and Modern Philosophy*. There is no question that Gadamer has gotten the better of the implicit argument between himself and Habermas (cf. Habermas's review, mentioned above). We shall return to the issue in a moment.

98 Danto, "History and Chronicle," *Narration and Knowledge*, p. 117.

99 Ibid., pp. 139–40; cf. "A Minimal Characterization of History," in the same volume. See Leopold von Ranke, *The Theory and Practice of History*, tr. Wilma A. Iggers and Konrad von Moltke, ed. Georg G. Iggers and Konrad von Moltke (Indianapolis: Bobbs-Merrill, 1973); also Georg G. Iggers, *New Directions in European Historiography*, rev. ed. (Middletown, Conn.: Wesleyan University Press, 1975), ch. 1.

100 Ranke, *The Theory and Practice of History*, p. 53; cited by Iggers. I have relied, here, on Igger's account.

101 The entire episode is reviewed, in place, in Hans-Georg Gadamer, *Truth and Method*, tr. Garrett Barden and John Cumming from 2nd German edn (New York: Seabury Press, 1975). Understandably, the account is favorably oriented – somewhat against Heidegger's own radicalism, certainly against the romantic hermeneuts – to accomodate Gadamer's important notion of *Horizontverschmelzung*. In our own time, the principal victim among the hermeneuts is undoubtedly Emilio Betti (whom Gadamer discusses, along with Ranke), who had, roughly at the time of the appearance of Gadamer's masterwork, just produced the most comprehensive *pre*-Heideggerian hermeneutic theory. For an impression of Betti's point of view, see Josef Bleicher, *Contemporary Hermeneutics: Hermeneutics as Method, Philosophy and Critique* (London: Routledge and Kegan Paul, 1980), ch. 2 and Reading I. Cf. also E. D. Hirsch, Jr, *Validity in Interpretation* (New Haven, Conn.: Yale University Press, 1967), particularly Appendix II, in which Hirsch, as a distinct romantic hermeneut, energetically opposes Gadamer's account.

102 This accords, of course, with the concept of relativism developed in *Pragmatism without Foundations*, pt I. We must not, however, fail to mention Roman Ingarden, because Ingarden, preeminently, addresses the question of the ontic indeterminacy of artworks: both in his *The Literary Work of Art: An Investigation on the Borderlines of Ontology, Logic, and Theory of Literature*, tr. George G. Grabowicz (Evanston, Ill.: Northwestern University Press, 1973); and in the later *The Cognition of the Literary Work of Art*, tr. Ruth Ann Crowley and Kenneth R. Olson (Evanston, Ill.: Northwestern University Press, 1973).

The main impression of Ingarden's strenuos efforts to specify the "mode of existence" of a literary work of art (and, by rather indirect analogy, other cultural phenomena) is that, ultimately, he is unable to answer his own question satisfactorily. It is true that in the second book he manages to eliminate the strong idealist, even Platonic, features of his earlier account; but he remains saddled with an ontologically unwelcome compromise. In *The Cognition*, apparently summarizing what is to be salvaged from *The Literary Work of Art*, he maintains that "the literary work as such is a purely intentional formation which has the *source* of its being in the creative acts of conciousness of its author and its physical *foundation* in the text set down in writing or through other physical means of possible reproduction (for instance, the tape recorder) . . . so that it becomes an intersubjective Intentional object, related to a community of readers. As such it is not a psychological phenomenon and is transcendent to all experiences of consciousness, those of the author as well as those of the reader" (p. 14; italics added).

More interestingly, in *The Literary Work of Art*, working with a disjunctive ontology of "real objects" and "ideal objects" (which he clearly finds inadequate), Ingarden cannot characterize the literary work as real: primarily because it is not "ontically autonomous." What Ingarden means (among other things) is that literary works depend for their existence on the intentional acts of authors. But this, of course, would mean that *no* cultural phenomena (excluding persons apparently or, perhaps, their acts) could be real – a thesis bound to generate unwanted difficulties, since persons, actions, histories, sentences and the like all invoke intentional analysis and interpretation. The literary work, Ingarden notes, is not "ontically independent of any cognitive act directed at it" (p. 10).

Several other distinctions offered are equally troublesome. (These are by no means all that Ingarden mentions.) But he says, "Whereas on formal-ontological grounds, . . . it is not possible for an objectively existing, ontically autonomous state of affairs to contain mutually exclusive material elements, a purely intentional state of affairs with mutually contradictory elements is quite possible. Likewise, if it is to exist at all, a really [*realiter*] existing state of affairs must be completely, *unequivocally, determined.* This does not pertain to the contents of purely intentional sentence correlates" (p. 142). Evidently, Ingarden does not consider the possibility of an intermediary category of complex, emergent cultural entities possessing incarnate properties. The irony is that he restricts "spots of indeterminacy of represented objectivities" *entirely* to the intentional (ideal) *content* of the "sentences" on which the work is said to depend (cf. section 38) and, correspondingly, takes a very strong line on the determinateness of "real" objects (pp. 246–7). From our point of view, the ontic indeterminacies of cultural entities are real but are not due to the fact that intentional content is *schematic* (determinable but not determinate: "colored, say, but not this or that particular red" – on one of Ingarden's explanations, pp. 247–8). Ingarden concludes that "every literary work is in principle *incomplete* and always in need of further *supplementation*; in terms of the text, however, this supplementation can never be completed" (p. 251; italics added) This is an unnecessary extravagance and produces a monstrous view *if*, as clearly Ingarden wished to maintain (but could not quite declare), the artwork is real. What we can say is that cultural entities are *ontically complete in that they are actual individual "things," but are, nevertheless, ontically indeterminate in that their intrinsic properties are (a) not "ontically independent of any cognitive act directed at [them]"* (in Ingarden's words); and (b) *subject, given (a), to "historical influence" in an open-ended and retroactive sense.* Ingarden was clearly struggling with related issues.

103 Cf. Wilhelm Dilthey, *Pattern and Meaning in History: Thoughts on History and*

Society, tr. and ed. H. P. Rickman (New York: Harper and Row, 1962) – first issued as *Meaning in History* (London: George Allen and Unwin, 1961); and Heinrich Rickert, *The Limits of Concept Formation in Natural Science: A Logical Introduction to the Historical Sciences* (abridged), tr. and ed. Guy Oakes (Cambridge: Cambridge University Press, 1986). See also Rudolf A. Makkreel, *Dilthey: Philosopher of the Human Studies* (Princeton, NJ: Princeton University Press, 1975), ch. 1; and Michael Ermarth, *Wilhelm Dilthey: The Critique of Historical Reason* (Chicago: University of Chicago Press, 1978), ch. 5.

104 This is rather close to what many have intuitively taken to be the affinity to romantic hermeneutics of Collingwood's notion of an essentially unchanging (therefore empathetically recoverable) human nature. See R. G. Collingwood, *The Idea of History* (Oxford: Clarendon Press, 1946).

105 See Margolis, *Science without Unity*, ch. 8.

106 Habermas, "A Review of Gadamer's *Truth and Method*," in Wachterhauser (ed.), *Hermeneutics and Modern Philosophy*, p. 273.

107 Gadamer, "On the Scope and Function of Hermeneutical Reflection," ibid., pp. 287-8

108 See Jürgen Habermas, "What Is Universal Pragmatics?" *Communication and the Evolution of Society*, tr. Thomas McCarthy (Boston, Mass.: Beacon Press, 1979); and Gadamer, *Truth and Method*, pp. 253-8. See also Margolis, *Pragmatism without Foundations*, chs 2-3.

109 There is an intriguing exchange between Gadamer and Jacques Derrida occasioned by a conference, in April 1981, convened by Philippe Forget at the Goethe-Institut in Paris. Derrida's brief "Three Questions to Hans-Georg Gadamer," tr. from the French by Richard Palmer, with attention to the German version, has circulated informally in typescript. I have not seen the French version, in *Révue internatinale de philosophie*, 1984 or the German, in *Text und Interpretation*, ed. Philippe Forget (München: Fink Verlag, 1984). But Derrida raises, in his usual oblique way, very much the same issue as is here raised agaist Gadamer. "Gadamer's Reply to Derrida's Remarks" continues the comedy of errors loosed by such remarks as "Whoever opens his mouth wants to be understood" offered in response to Derrida's questions, themselves apparently offered in an effort to understand Gadamer's position more fully than was possible by way of Gadamer's paper for the occasion. I am grateful to my colleague Richard Shusterman for letting me see these papers.

I must also mention, here, a very spirited paper by John D. Caputo, "Gadamer's Closet Essentialism: A Derridean Critique" (to appear in an anthology edited by Richard Palmer for the State University of New York Press), that presses Gadamer's arbitrary essentialism from an openly Derridean orientation. I have read the essay only in manuscript; but, from other nibbles of Caputo's papers, it is reasonable to anticipate a very much more developed and ramified analysis of the problem within the tradition of Heidegger and Nietzsche, in Caputo's *Radical Hermeneutics: Repetition, Deconstruction and the Hermeneutical Project* (Bloomington: Indiana University Press, 1987).

110 The meaning of "internalist" as used here is essentially Hilary Putnam's, though disengaged from his own "internal realism." See further Margolis, *Pragmatism without Foundations*, ch. 11.

111 See Horwich, *Asymmetries of Time*, particularly chs 1–3.
112 See, ibid., Horwich's discussion of time travel, for instance; also Kurt Gödel, "A Remark about the Relationship between Relativity Theory and Idealistic Philosophy," in Paul Arthur Schilpp (ed.), *Albert Einstein: Philosopher Scientist* (LaSalle, Ill.: Open Court, 1949), mentioned by Horwich, which gives a glimpse of the baffling possibilities of speaking of "the relativity of simultaneity" (p. 557). Einstein indicates in his "Reply" that the puzzle has occupied his attention (pp. 687–8).
113 See Margolis, *Science without Unity*, ch. 8, particularly section v.
114 Hirsch, *Validity in Interpretation*, p. 237.
115 See Martin Heidegger, *Being and Time*, tr. John Macquarrie and Edward Robinson from the 7th German edn (New York: Harper and Row, 1962), section 32. Cf. Hirsch, *Validity in Interpretation*, Appendix II.
116 Heidegger, *Being and Time*, p. 191f (p. 150 in German edn).
117 Ibid., p. 195 (p. 153 in German edn).
118 See Gadamer, *Truth and Method*, pp. 235–67.
119 Ibid., p. 261. See also David Couzens Hoy, "Hermeneutic Circularity, Indeterminacy and Incommensurability," *New Literary History*, X(1978); and John D. Caputo, "Hermeneutics and the Discovery of Man," *Man and World*, XV (1982).
120 Gadamer, *Truth and Method*, p. 267.
121 See Joseph Margolis, "Schleiermacher among the Theorists of Language and Interpretation," *Journal of Aesthetics and Art Criticism*, XLVI (1987).
122 Gadamer, *Truth and Method*, p. 271.
123 Ibid., p. 254, in the context of pp. 253–8.
124 Cf. ibid., p. 250, where Gadamer introduces in a favorable way the notion of "traditionalism." Cf. also, Margolis, *Pragmatism without Foundations*, ch. 2.
125 Gadamer, *Truth and Method*, p. 245.
126 See Heidegger, *Being and Time*, sections 5–6. See also ch. 3, above.
127 See Margolis, *Pragmatism without Foundations*, ch. 11.
128 Hans-Georg Gadamer, "The Problem of Historical Consciousness," tr. Jeff L. Close, in Paul Rabinow and William M. Sullivan (eds), *Interpretive Social Science: A Reader* (Berkeley, Calif.: University of California Press, 1979), p 120.
129 Ibid., p. 136.
130 Ibid., p. 145.
131 Ibid., p. 127f.
132 Paul Ricoeur, "The Model of the Text: Meaningful Action Considered as a Text," repr in the same volume.
133 Ibid., p. 79.
134 See ch. 7, above.
135 See ch. 6, above.
136 See George Santayana, *Three Philosophical Poets: Lucretius, Dante, and Goethe* (Cambridge, Mass.: Harvard University Press, 1910).
137 See Margolis, *Science without Unity*, ch. 8.
138 See Carol C. Gould, *Marx's Social Ontology* (Cambridge, Mass.: MIT Press, 1978); Margolis, *Culture and Cultural Entities*, ch. 4.
139 See ch. 6, above.

140 See Margolis, *Pragmatism without Foundations*, pt I.

141 Ricoeur, who, because of his attempt to distingusih between and yet reconcile the human and natural sciences and because of his central concern with hermeneutic complications, might well have been counted on to explore an option rather like that of our tally (a)–(h), rather disappointingly fails to address the essential puzzle of the ontology of historical time. See Paul Ricoeur, *Temps et récit*, vol. 3 (Paris: Editions du Seuil, 1985), pt I, ch. 3. Ricoeur thinks rather of a completed *past event* and, therefore, of the paradoxes of its "recovery" in the present. It seems reasonable to suggest that he is at pains to avoid the appearance of relativism. Hence he says, "A travers le document et au moyen de la preuve documentaire, l'historien est soumis *à ce qui, un jour, fut*. Il a une dette à l'égard du passé, une dette de reconnaissance à l'égard des morts, qui fait de lui un débiteur insolvable" (p. 204). That is, Ricoeur makes the hermeneutic "debt" of recovering the past that is now completed an infinite task because of our changing and increasing distance from that fixed past; whereas our account denies that the historical past *is* ontologically fixed at all just as the interpretable intentional structure of actually existent texts is not fixed.

142 See Henri Poincaré, *Science and Method*, tr. Francis Maitland (New York: Dover, 1952) and *Mathematics and Science. Last Essays*, tr. John W. Bolduc (New York: Dover, 1963). See also Morris Kline, *Mathematics: The Loss of Certainty* (New York: Oxford University Press, 1980), chs 9, 10, 14: and the papers of pt II of Paul Benacerraf and Hilary Putnam (eds), *Philosophy of Mathematics: Selected Readings*, 2nd edn (Cambridge: Cambridge University Press, 1983). I have benefited here from seeing a manuscript portion of Janet Folina's forthcoming book, *Poincaré and the Philosophy of Mathematics*.

143 See Wolfgang Iser, *The Act of Reading* (Baltimore: John Hopkins University Press, 1978); and Stanley Fish, *Is There a Text in This Class?* (Cambridge, Mass.: Harvard University Press, 1980). See also Joseph Margolis, "What Is a Literary Text?" in Herbert L. Sussman (ed.), *At the Boundaries: Proceedings of the Northeastern University Center for Literary Studies, Vol. 1, 1983* (Boston, Mass.: Northeastern University Press, 1984), and "How to Theorize about Texts at the Present Time: Deconstruction and Its Victims," in Peter J. McCormick (ed.), *The Reasons of Art* (Ottawa: University of Ottawa Press, 1985).

9

Enculturing Psychology

Having introduced the notion that cultural entities are "texts" and that persons or selves are those uniquely apt texts capable of and interested in interpreting all texts including themselves, we are bound to try to come to terms with the symbiosis of the psychological and the societal. The most strategic themes that that effort must intend to make plausible include at least

1 the nonreducibility of the societal to the psychological and of the psychological to the societal;
2 the nonreducibility of the societal (or cultural) to the biological; and
3 the ineliminability of employing collective societal traits in any adequate characterization of human persons.

There are immensely many counterstrategies that would subvert any or all of themes 1–3. But, ultimately, the vindication of the *sui generis* nature of the human sciences and allied disciplines depends on the fate of 1–3. So let us make a final effort in their favor.

I

Psychology is a reflexive discipline, however cleverly it may camouflage its practice in surveys and experiments. The observers and observed are one. All the human sciences are infected with that benign disease. Hence, on a reasonable theory, even the physical and formal sciences owe their objective standing to a steady orderliness perceived within the flux of the other. It is that reflexiveness, of course, that accounts for the otherwise extraordinary speculative leap that connects the fate of our theories of persons and selves to the fortunes of the largest philosophical puzzles. How else might we understand why the dialectical possibilities of phenomenology or deconstruction or praxism or the like should bear so intimately on what we take to be a fair theory of the formation of persons and selves? In a word, there can be no merely first-order psychology. The reflexive nature of discovering our nature implicates the ontologized prejudice of doing so. We can hardly abandon that study: it permeates the most unlikely inquiry; and we can hardly correct for its intrusion: every would-be correction is another instance of it, if any correction there be. Reflection, therefore – hardly reducible to the introspection and self-perception favored by canonical empiricists and rationalists – is at once a first-order and a second-order undertaking. Every empirical statement of what man is is perceptibly encumbered by assumptions, however inchoate, of what it would be coherent and tenable to suppose are the conditions under which distributed such pronouncements may be responsibly put forward. There is enough in that admission to refute, globally, any disjunction between science and the legitimative reflections of philosophy that might pretend to secure the self-corrective autonomy of any merely first-order empirical inquiry.[1]

There is a match, therefore, between the lack of fixity in our ontologies and epistemologies and the lack of fixity in our theories of persons and selves, between the uncertain fixity of any particular theory and the salient absence of assured fixity in the world and in ourselves. Whatever we posit as the structure of world and self is accompanied by an intuition of ontic – especially historical – flux. It was, in fact, with just that intuition that we began this entire reflection by reviewing Julian Jaynes's intriguing worry that the human mind must have had a history, and a radical one at that.[2] The same intuition has prompted many contemporary theorists of individual or personal or developmental psychology to favor what has come to be called a "social-constructionist" account of selves and to investigate, in adopting that view, the formational process the emergence of selves involves. Rom Harré, for instance, has advanced the thesis that "public conversation is prior to individual mind" and that "most of the features of properties of mind are derived from and sometimes actually reducible to features of public conversation" (*social constructionism*).[3] The thesis has a Durkheimian ring. It is not surprising, therefore, that Harré actually cites Jaynes's account rather hospitably:

> Even if Jaynes's claim (*The Origin of consciousness in the breakdown of the bicameral mind*) to have identified the moment when mankind invented self-consciousness . . . is fantasy, the fact that his claim is clearly intelligible (and might conceivably be defensible) demolishes the neccessary universality aspect of Kant's claim [in the Transcendental Dialectic]. To put it crudely, we learn to be conscious, and many amongst our fellow humans may learn to be conscious, to organize experience, in different ways.[4]

The trouble, of course, which Harré himself is well aware of, is simply that

1   the speculation about suggested varieties of psychological development, about the absence of selves, about alternative forms of selves, is ineluctably governed by reflections at and under the influence of our

own historical present and our own incompletely fathomed, historically preformed psychological powers;

2 generalizations such as those regarding "public conversation" and "individual mind" are equivocal, as between an application to the diachronic formation of distributed selves within a society (new infants) and an application to the synchronic, aggregated possibilities of psychological functioning within an entire viable society (apt adults); and

3 the various first-order possibilities that may be entertained (as by Jaynes and Harré) must be reconciled with our second-order speculations about the minima of functioning cognitive "sites" (persons, selves, or whatnot) in virtue of which the proliferating forms of the other are seen to justify psychological ascriptions in the first place.

Thus, for example, in one sense – in the process of an infant's acquiring a natural language – "public conversation *is* prior to individual mind"; but in another – *in* the process of public conversation itself – it *cannot* be prior; only "individual minds" (creatures suitably apt) engage and can engage in conversation, whatever we may suppose "engaging in conversation" to be.

These seemingly plausible reminders prove, however modest, surprisingly powerful. For one thing, they hint at the untenability of collective agency, and explicitly indicate how to avoid that troublesome concession. For another, they suggest that the structural varieties of persons and selves must nevertheless fall within the pale of certain constraints, below which the use of the categories in question would prove psychologically inappropriate. Both are conceptual issues of some importance. Harré is not always sufficiently explicit on these matters. For example, it is clear that "societies" and "families" – even "species" – may be "possible subjects of mental predications" but they cannot literally be subjects of predications of agency (that entail the other).[5] They lack intention, desire, belief, volition, and the like in any but a metaphorical sense, and the ascription of beliefs, moods, feelings, even actions, collectively (rather than aggregatively), clearly involves the subtle abstraction of a unified tendency drawn from the other. Harré rightly insists on "a conception of causality tied to real productive mechanisms," which, he plainly says, "involves a competence/ performance psychology of individuals who as members create social collectives, but who are created by those collectives in a thoroughly reciprocal fashion."[6]

But he does not explicitly distinguish between attributions of collective properties to individual or aggregated individual agents and the individuation of actual collective agents. In fact, he is inclined to introduce the term "collective" entitatively, in the logically bland but socially realist sense of "that" to which collective properties are directly ascribed. So he says, quite typically, "it should be noticed at the outset that the distinction between collectives and individuals is a relative distinction. An individual considered with respect to one kind of collective may be able to be treated as a collective with respect to another kind of individual."[7] Distinctions of this sort fail to explicate the full role of persons in "public conversations": in the very context in which Harré admits "collective actions" and in which he declares that "the fundamental human reality is a conversation, effectively without beginning or end, to which, from time to time, individuals may make contributions."[8]

There is a further double benefit in resisting Harré's easy *passage* between collective attributes and collective entities. First, collective states and processes (fashions as opposed to trends, institutional habits as opposed to average and median behavior, *Geisten* as opposed to theoretical types) are causally efficacious, even if not in the manner of *agency*; they function through the mediating causal processes *of* aggregated human agency, since they are collective attributes incarnate in such incarnate aggregated attributes. The infectious quality of the recent Iranian revolution offers a most plausible specimen. Second, the stipulation of the influence or causal efficacy of collective processes is characteristically subject to retrospective historical interpretation, in the same sense as but by a route different from that of the "effectivity" of individual or aggregative agency. Tolstoy's account of the Battle of Borodino may serve as a problematic specimen. In particular, the very notion of the causality of collective processes confirms the impossibility of freeing explanation in the human sciences from a certain hermeneutic complexity that cannot be reconciled with any straightforward empirical conception drawn from the natural sciences or favoring a unity model.[9]

Harré himself supports the following distinction between "persons" and "selves":

In the primary structure [persons in conversation] people appear as locations for speech acts. As such they are metaphysically simple without internal structure, just as the point locations of physical space are. Real human beings, however, are not mere locations: they are "internally" complex. This internal complexity I call the secondary structure. . . . [I support, therefore, "a new duality (in) the metaphysics of psychology,"] a duality between person and self. Persons as social individuals are locations in the primary structure, and so are identifiable by public criteria. The intentionality of their actions and speeches is interpreted within a social framework of interpersonal commitments rather than as the outward expression of some inner state. Selves are psychological individuals, manifested in the unified organization of perceptions, feelings and beliefs of each human being who is organized in that fashion in their own regard.[10]

This cannot possibly serve Harré's purpose, for the simple reason that there is no way in which to define *speech acts* without attention to the psychologically internal intentions, beliefs, desires, and the like of what Harré calls selves. He himself concedes that "necessarily all human beings who are members of moral orders are persons, social individuals, but the degree of their psychological individuality [their status as selves], I take to be contingent."[11] This hardly justifies the thesis that

- (a) there are genuine speech-act contexts that function without the functioning of "selves"; *and*
- (b) that, in whatever sense (a) may be conceded to obtain, it obtains as logically or temporally or metaphysically prior to the emergence of selves.

Harré explicitly indicates that, by "person," he means "very much the concept as elucidated by P. F. Strawson in his *Individuals*" – "the socially defined, publicly visible embodied being, endowed with all kinds of powers and capacities for public, meaningful actions."[12] But Strawson, of course, disallows the use of the term except where

- (i) "we ascribe to ourselves . . . things of a kind that we also ascribe to material bodies [for instance] to which we should not dream of ascribing others of the things we ascribe to ourselves [thoughts and feelings, for instance]";[13] and
- (ii) our psychological predicates "have both first- and third-person ascriptive uses, that they are both self-ascribable otherwise than on the basis of observation of the behavior of the subject of them, and other-ascribable on the basis of behavioral criteria."[14]

This certainly shows that, for Strawson, it is quite impossible to segregate in a realist way what Harré distinguishes as persons and selves.

It is true, as we have already noted, that Harré is somewhat sympathetic to the conceivability of Jaynes's story; but *that* would not justify his own theory of real persons in speech-act contexts. For, even in John Searle's theory of speech acts – which Searle characterizes congruently with his thesis that "speaking a language is engaging in a rule-governed form of behavior"[15] and which, surely would afford the best sort of theory for Harré's purpose – it is entirely clear that Searle builds into the defining conditions of particular speech acts factors that refer back to what Harré calls the "secondary structure" (the structure of selves). Thus, for example, in developing his well-known account of the exemplary case of promising, Searle offers the following "general hypothesis" in the context of acknowledging that his proposed "analysis into necessary and sufficient conditions [of particular speech acts], are likely to involve (in varying degrees) *idealization* of the concept analyzed":

Wherever there is a psychological state specified in the sincerity condition [making a promise or a statement sincerely], the performance of the act counts as an *expression* of that psychological state. This law holds whether the act is sincere or insincere, that is whether the speaker actually has the specified psychological state or not.[16]

The point is that, on Searle's theory (*a fortiori*, on J. L. Austin's[17]), the rule-like, behaviorist-like treatment of speech acts cannot but be an idealization or normative abstraction *from* the actual pattern of speech and conversation in the context of natural languages; and that *there* the usual features attributable to "selves" appear to be ineliminable. Jaynes's theory, as we have suggested, obscures or falsifies the degree to which, among the cultures Jaynes reviews, psychological complexities rather close to those of our own world cannot really be denied – even if they can be reasonably attenuated. Harré himself makes a very plausible case to the effect that "Eskimos, though sharing a concept of social identity of persons with ourselves, have a weaker sense of personal identity, that is, they do not use a concept of 'inner' unity of self comparable to ours, by which each individual organizes his or her own experience, memory and so on." Ironically, he makes a poorer case for the Maoris, who, he claims, "seem to have a stronger sense of personal distinctiveness, inviolability and power of self-activation than we do."[18] (In the case of the Maoris, it appears that that people do have a "stronger [or rather, a different] sense" of personal individuation, but it is not at all clear that that amounts to a more developed notion of self.) In any case, the theory of Harré's "primary structure" must, on the argument, be an abstraction for heuristic purposes from the "primary," real context of speech acts – even if or because, by attenuation, speech acts may be ascribed to Jaynes's bicameral people.

The truth is that Harré wishes to treat the "self" – "the central constructing concept of individual human psychology" – as

> a theoretical concept whose source analogue is the socially defined and sustained concept of "person" that is favored in the society under study and is embodied in the grammatical forms of public speech appropriate to talk about persons. Our personal being is created by our coming to believe a theory of self based on our society's working conception of a person.[19]

There are really two issues here, concerning

1   the separability of persons and selves and the alleged realist priority of persons over selves; and
2   the question of whether selves, formed in the way Harré indicates, are experienced as such or are only "theoretical" posits that (by analogy with what we posit in the physical sciences) may reasonably be regarded as real.

On the first, there can now be no doubt that Harré *does* believe persons to be prior to selves and to function as such in the context of "public conversation." He seems clearly mistaken in this, though it is a matter crucial to his entire constructinist account. Nevertheless, persons are (as we have already noted) "created" by social collectives – on Harré's view; it is simply that, as being not yet selves, the question of *their* reflexively experiencing themselves (in Hume's sense) does not yet arise. Harré's point is that selves cannot be experienced, are, and are reasonably (even necessarily), constructed as theoretical posits of that to which psychologically complex predications are made.[20] He is primarily concerned to oppose what he takes to be the Cartesian thesis.[21]

What we need to appreciate is that Harré's solution to question 2 does not entail his solution to question 1, and that the solution to 2 does not (as he himself admits) affect the realist standing of the self.[22] On the contrary, in a very strong – "top–down" – sense, Harré dramatizes (by his constructionism) the puzzling fact that "animate beings are persons if they are in possession of a theory – a theory about themselves." By way of acquiring that "theory," "a being orders, partitions and reflects on its own experience and becomes capable of self-intervention and control."[23] Our own thesis, therefore, may be construed as simplifying (in one sense) Harré's account: that is, by maintaining that persons (who, *qua* persons, always manifest *some* range of the functions of selves) are socially constructed if selves are constructed. Persons are not different entities from selves, and the division of functions (whatever that may be made to be) is a convenience with regard to one and the same entity. In another sense, however, *since* persons, though "created" socially, are *not* theoretically constructed even if they are not directly experienced, neither are selves. Even on Hume's view, contrary to the usual reports, the self is implicated in sensory awareness, even if it is not identifiable as a "simple idea."[24] Reference to the self cannot be coherently invoked as a theoretical entity posited (by persons?) to account for the unitary referents of given experiences: it is already entailed and presupposed *in* the apt behavior of (Harré's) persons and it invariably involves the range of experience regarding which persons are (however emergently) able to make predicative ascriptions. The real benefit of Harré's account is that it provides an approximate sketch of the kind of developmental process that, distributively, must be supposed to obtain between generations.[25]

George Herbert Mead's conception of the formation of the self (on which Harré relies to some extent) differs in a radical way from Harré's own, in that, although, for Mead as for Harré, the self is socially formed or constructed, it is not, as such, primarily a theoretical posit (somehow) reflexively achieved, or a heuristic fiction or anything of the sort, but an actual formation developing over time through the maturational process of childhood. It avoids, therefore, the insoluble paradox (a bit like that of Rousseau's social contract) of having to acknowledge functional powers (of self) apt for forming the very power of constructing the self. Furthermore, for Mead, the emergence of the conscious self is accounted for by the activation of a certain species-wide biological responsiveness to social stimuli:

> Two dogs playing with each other will attack and defend, in a process which if carried through would amount to an actual fight. There is a combination of responses which checks the depth of the bite. But we do not have in such a situation the dogs taking a definite role in the sense

that a child deliberately takes the role of another. . . . When a child does assume a role he has in himself the stimuli which call out that particular response or group of responses. . . . In the play period the child utilizes his own responses to these stimuli which he makes use of in building a self. The response which he has a tendency to make to these stimuli organizes them. He plays that he is, for instamce, offering himself something, and he buys it. . . . A certain organized structure arises in him and in his other which replies to it, and these carry on conversation of gestures between themselves.[26]

It is essential to Mead's view that the emergent, constituted social individual be the product of formative, *biological*, "primitive human impulses" proceeding, originally, in a way more or less analogous to what is both rehearsed and quickened in the specimen case of playing Indians. In this sense, for Mead – as for Lev Vygotsky and Jerome Bruner (and contrary to Chomsky), for instance – the formation of the self is biologically predisposed but socially determined.[27]

It would be unfair to suggest that Harré does not share this orientation. Indeed he does. But his own view appears to separate the formation of the person (apparently not a matter of theoretical posit) from the formation of the self, and to postpone the formation of the latter so that it can (somehow) be construed *as* a theoretical posit made by persons, of that to which their own powers belong (which, then, induces a natural disposition to acquire, and identify subjectively, particular experiences). The account shared in a general way by Mead, Vygotsky, and Bruner, on the other hand, is empirically more convincing and simpler, and not conceptually paradoxical in the way Harré's account is. Furthermore, it has the great merit of identifying a line of theorizing about human cognitive competences that views them as (1) open-ended; (2) socially acquired; (3) historicized; (4) linked to the culturally variable formation of the self; (5) not profoundly due to biologizing culture or language (in the manner of the nativists); (6) not, therefore, requiring the postulation of a closed system; and (7) symbiotized with regard to the reality of self and society. These seven considerations identify the dialectical advantages of a third conceptual strategy between a simplistic empiricism and a preposterously implausible structuralism (that, in effect, excludes the full functional relevance of cognitively active and inventive selves) or an equally unlikely nativism (that, in effect, assigns to our genes what clearly seems to be the work of cultural existence).[28] But to have brought these themes together in this way is to have obliged ourselves to provide an account of the enculturing processs itself.

The decisive finding we have been testing is the viability and adequacy of a concept of societal practices that are naturally acquired and naturally sustained: that acknowledges the full play of individual persons as the actual agents of linguistic and cognate cultural activity; that is thoroughly historicized; *and* that does not (in positing a viable society) require that that society form a closed system in any of the various senses favored by the unity of science, nativism, or structuralism. (The term "natural," or "naturally," signifies, here, that the practices of an actual society are acquired by the members of each generation merely by living as developing children among the apt adults of that society.)

From this point of view, it may be usefully noted that such doctrinal quarrels as that between "vulgar" Marxists and "vulgar" structuralists is an entirely local matter. Grant only that, whatever may be defended as an empirical account of social causation, there can be no principled ontological contrast between "base" and "superstructure" that would oblige us to construe the ideational dimension of human life as merely epiphenomenal. Grant only that, Marxist theories must then accommodate the structuralist's objection. On the other hand, grant only that, whatever may be the rule-like (or syntax-like) structures of a particular society in accord with which pertinent practical behavior may be shown to be distinctly constrained, those very structures must themselves have been causally generated, must have had a history, and can enjoy no ontological priority over the forces of practical life manifested in the aggregated behavior of individual agents that instantiates them. Grant only that, structuralist theories cannot fail to be grounded in the same praxical sources as the Marxist. The deeper quarrel, then, concerns the viability of a model of description and explanation in the human sciences that accommodates relevant cultural complexities – what we have earlier marked as "embodied" and "incarnate" – without presuming or assuming that societal existence forms a closed system.[29]

We have worried Harré's account in a pointed way because it is one of the few that admit (a) the real formation of selves, (b) the reality of causally efficacious societal processes and, apparently, (c) the temporal and logical priority of societal process with respect to formed selves. Broadly speaking, this is a way of mediating between Mead and Vygotsky, on the one hand, and Durkheim, on the other, that somewhat favors structuralist themes within historicized or open-ended systems. On the argument, it remains unsatisfactory because (as we have already seen, pursuing Jaynes's ingenious account) *the Intentional life of human cultures*, specified as language, tradition, history, institutions, artifacts, and the like, *cannot, for conceptual reasons, obtain independently of aggregated agental activity. Any* admission of speech, production, deeds, interpretation, purpose, cognitive states presupposes and entails the formation of persons or selves of some sort reasonably congruent with ourselves – who are, after all, the apt exemplars in these regards, formed within the same species. But the particular historicized *nature* of the agents of different historical societies may be as varied as you please, as discontinuous in their *epistemes* as the contingency of formative cultures may allow, as incommensurable in their categories of understanding as mutual understanding may support. Nothing need be lost of the first-order studies regarding the causal or formative role of societal processes or regarding second-order speculation about the societally preformative conditions under which all reflexive first-order work is pursued. Any retreat from this constraint is either clearly defective and question-begging (for instance, as in Lévi-Strauss, Peter Blau, the Annalistes, and Immanuel Wallerstein), and any sustained insistence on the elimination or late arrival of the self ultimately risks incoherence (for instance, as in Althusser, Foucault, and, more uncertainly, Harré).[30]

II

It is, of course, not altogether clear what conceptual boundaries should be imposed on the legitimate issues of what we may call enculturation or enculturing or developmental psychology. At one extreme, for instance, Marxist and Hegelian speculations about the historical conditions of human consciousness seem entirely eligible – quite convincingly so, if one considers only the promise and obvious power of the line of investigation favored by Vygotsky and Luria and its increasing attraction for Western psychologists and theorists otherwise hard put to formulate a resourceful account of the dynamics of social history within the context of which individual development may be effectively located.[31] At the other extreme, it is impossible, at the present stage at which psychology and the so-called cognitive and information sciences are conventionally taken to be interconnected, to disallow questions of the machine simulation of human intelligence to count as professionally pertinent regarding the study of individual development.[32] Also, within the implied span marked by these two extremes, the more biologically centered quarrels about the nature of developmental processes cannot be more instructively focused than they are in the well-known debate between Jean Piaget and Noam Chomsky[33] – which obliges us to weigh the competing claims of versions of nativism and of interactional models, both, of course, peculiarly slimly occupied with the structure and structuring functions of living societies. Nor, within those same limits, can the bare complexity of the diachronic processes of societal history (pertinent to our issue) be more clearly glimpsed than in texts largely ignored in standard discussions of such psychologies – for instance, in Pierre Bourdieu, in Gadamer, in Habermas, in Mikhail Bakhtin, and in Michel Foucault.[34]

It is in some such prepared setting that one is struck by the perspicuousness of Wittgenstein's conceptual *template* for analyzing enculturation. Obviously, despite the profound sense in which Wittgenstein was (perhaps best viewed as) a speculative mind centered on the puzzles of developmental psychology, even his most pertinent reflections cannot be easily incorporated within the usual canonical literature. Both Wittgenstein's style of comment and his well-known double messages regarding philosophical or conceptual theorizing tend to block any ready reference to his views, at the level of first-order empirical psychology.[35] Nevertheless, within a framework of the large sort just sketched, it seems entirely natural to test the power of his conception.

Indeed, once it is so posed, the general shape of the answer – at least a viable and pertinent answer – stares one in the face. Put somewhat indirectly, for the sake of tact and the advantage of strategy, what Wittgenstein contributes most is a sense of the proper *balance* and *gauge* of work most central to the field. These terms are, of course, terms of art designed to postpone confrontation until certain preparations are in place. The point to be pressed is simply that Wittgenstein himself failed to develop even very promisingly what is most promising in his own conception of the conditions of human development; that what *is* promising about it may be forcefully recommended; and that that cannot be effectively pursued without going well beyond the usual boundaries of developmental studies, to just the sort of text already mentioned: that is, to texts not usually consulted, texts that link such undertakings to the whole array of human science, social science, cultural criticism – texts that, on review, prove preeminently "Wittgensteinian" in the minimal sense here intended.[36] So placed, or preplaced, the required argument is entirely straightforward. However that may be, we must concede that its theme is, obviously, somewhat removed from first-order developmental studies, much more concerned with recommending a certain cast of mind, a perspective, a conceptual orientation within which to pursue any of a variety of such studies than with actually pursuing them.

There is no mystery in this, but there is an initial breakthrough that is both peculiarly powerful and elusive. The essential clue may be marked casually enough, but its extraordinary force is remarkably difficult to fathom at first – precisely because of its simplicity just at the point of its most radical conceptual adjustment. It may be put this way: we live and function well as the members of a human community – speaking a language, engaging in the ordinary practices of our society, acquiring a store of skills that we exercise spontaneously and inventively without ever having mastered or ever needing to have mastered or even ever having to refer to an official or formulizable set of rules or norms or criteria governing our entire behavior. That's all. Adopting Wittgenstein's orientation in this sense precludes a great many alternative orientations and radicalizes others that, on the historical record, have resisted or opposed just this simple theme – though they need not have. The line of investigation that Wittgenstein facilitates involves, then, challenging any and all presumed fixities of cognitive, calculational, volitional, experiential, actional, habituative, significative sorts – both substantive (involving particular truths) and "praxical" (that is, concerned with the way the mind processes any psychologically or culturally pertinent materials). "Don't always think that you read off what you say from the facts," Wittgenstein warns; "that you portray these in words according to rules. For even so you would have to apply the rule in the particular case without guidance."[37]

The challenge is not directed against conservative findings or against even psychological or cultural universals – *or* against the use of rules and criteria. It is directed against every manifestation of *apriorism* in our thinking about the development of persons or selves as culturally apt creatures adjusted to their particular social world, and against every tendency to enshrine any one viable way of acting or of characterizing how we act as an exclusive option at either of these levels or at any other level of understanding.

Wittgenstein himself collects his theme in the following way – in a notorious and much-contested passage:

> This was our paradox: no course of action could be determined by a rule, because every course of action can be made out to accord with the rule. The answer was: if everything can be made out to accord with the rule, then it can also be made out to conflict with it. . . . What this shews is that there is a way of grasping a rule which is *not* an *interpretation,* but which is exhibited in what we call "obeying the rule" and "going against it" in actual cases. And hence also "obeying a rule" is a practice. [*Darum ist "der Regel folgen" eine Praxis.*] And to *think* one is obeying a rule is not to obey a rule. Hence it is not possible to obey a rule "privately": otherwise thinking one was obeying a rule would be the same thing as obeying it.[38]

The mistake that is being patiently unearthed runs through the entire course of human learning and apt mastery: the mystification of every form of presumed understanding that takes it that every socially acquired or socially pertinent *practice* (and *thinking itself is a practice*) is acquired, must be acquired, functions, must function by *first* acquiring, by *matching* practice with, by confirming or interpreting or justifying practice by *reference to*, higher-order rules somehow antecedently fixed. " 'Before I judge that two images which I have are the same [goes the deep error], I must recognize them as the same.' "[39] To grasp how this elementary theme ramifies through the whole of man's thought and behavior – and through our theories about them – is to grasp the reason (and need) for pausing to examine a mere "template" for the enculturing process, in advance of any of the rich theories about learning, social apprenticeship, the mastery of skills, habituation, institutions we already possess.

The terms "balance" and "gauge" may be taken, respectively, as epithets signifying the horizontal and vertical dimensions of an ideally organized enculturing theory: whereas "balance" signifies the proper placement of our discipline within the range of overlapping issues shared by the biological and social sciences, "gauge" signifies the proper model of the dynamics of – the forces and conditions affecting – the relevant processes of development. The charm and power of Wittgenstein's contribution, then, lies with the intuitive simplicity with which he manages to articulate the most difficult issues regarding both dimensions – through his inimitable conceptual vignettes – so as to suggest how, favorably, to resolve theoretical questions affecting all forms of rational inquiry and what, dialectically, must be assigned the central role in any of the alternative explanatory accounts likely to be relevantly formed and debated. Nevertheless, in doing that, Wittgenstein proceeds in a noticeably formal and schematic way – that is, in a way that does not address either biologically or historically detailed constraints on enculturation.

It will come as no surprise to those familiar with Wittgenstein that the dual benefit may be traced to the notion of "a form of life" (*Lebensform*). One commentator, Henry Finch, usefully observes that the expression occurs only five times in the *Philosophical Investigations* (it does occur elsewhere), and that Wittgenstein makes no attempt to define it.[40] It is certainly one of the masterconcepts of Wittgenstein's entire "later" philosophy, possibly the most strategic – and it is the one most intimately connected with our theme. But, although he correctly objects to construing the expression as making merely "factual or quasi-factual" distinctions as opposed to "grammatical or semantic" ones (the easy linkage of "grammatical" and "semantic" is itself an unintended warning that something is wrong), Finch takes it that those interested in the social sciences will probably understand that

> *forms of life* are roughly what they call "social facts" or "institutional facts"; only for Wittgenstein they are not mere "facts," but units of meaningful action which are carried out together by members of a social group and which have a common meaning for the members of the group. . . . [that is, not really as] *facts*, but rather as *forms* which means possibilities of meaning, analogous to language-games, but in the area of human social actions. Forms of life [then] are established *patterns of action* shared in by members of a group.[41]

Insofar as this is nearly right, it hardly says more than Wittgenstein himself makes mention of; but, insofar as it is wrong, it is quite disappointingly misleading – precisely because it fails to feature what is so remarkable about Wittgenstein's much-admired theme. Roughly, what Finch does not altogether fail to note, what nearly everyone who reads Wittgenstein can hardly miss, is part of the essential clue about what we have dubbed the "balance" of the account: *the proper placement of enculturation or developmental psychology within the context of societal life.* This is surely part of the obvious thrust of Wittgenstein's notion.[42] But Finch gets the "gauge" wrong, *the point and nature of the descriptive and explanatory model of human behavior construed generically in developmental terms.* One senses this in, for instance, the choice of such terms as "units of meaningful actions," "common meaning," and "established patterns of action." These are the terms of "system" that may be said to be shared, possibly, by the *Tractatus*, the structuralists, the Chomskyans, the theorists of formal semantics, the positivists, and those favorably disposed to the progressive simulation of human behavior by finite machine programs construed as exhibiting artificial intelligence. By "system," we may understand any domain construed as

1 determinately structured;
2 deterministic;
3 homonomic with respect to a match between descriptive and explanatory vocabularies;
4 closed with respect to finitely many universal explanatory principles, laws, rules, or the like;

5   totalized with respect to all possible phenomena pertinent to that
     domain and to its explanatory concerns;
6   ideally capable of being thus characterized synchronically.[43]

The two principal (quite dissimilar) models of systems developed in our own
time are those of the unity-of-science program (which favors physicalist
reduction) and of (chiefly French) structuralism (which favors "unconscious,"
formal, generative syntaxes or related schemata and which, thereby, effectively
eliminates the agency of actual individual persons from affecting the structures
of a given society).[44] Wittgenstein was certainly utterly opposed to conceptions
of these sorts insofar as he invoked the notion of forms of life. To grasp the
linkage between the two issues (balance and gauge) is the essential key to the
Philosophical Investigations and to its promised contribution (together with the
rest of Wittgenstein's "later" philosophy) to the theory of encultured or
enculturing psychology.

     The correction of Finch's suggestions is not here intended in a merely
exegetical sense: it is meant rather to assist us to recover the peculiar power and
distinction of Wittgenstein's quite original notion, while at the same time it
prepares us for recognizing the need to flesh out that notion in ways
Wittgenstein never really pursued – and may well not actually have ever
considered.[45] First of all, forms of life are *not* analogues of language-games
merely fitted to the context of action; for, as Wittgenstein pointedly remarks,
"Disputes do not break out (among mathematicians, say) over the question
whether a rule has been obeyed or not. . . . That is part of the framework on
which the working of our language is based (for example, in giving
descriptions)."[46] It is not that "human agreement decides" what is true and
false: what humans say *may* be true or false. They agree "in the *language* they
use. That is not agreement in opinions but in form of life."[47] Language-games
are not really *based on* although they are *grounded in* our forms of life – but
never by way of antecedent rules or criteria: forms of life are that through which
a particular language "works [*wirkt*]."[48]

     It is easy to understand the confusion, but it is important to correct the error.
Wittgenstein says, quite remarkably, "You must bear in mind that the
language-game is so to say something unpredictable. I mean: it is not based on
grounds. . . . It is there – like our life."[49] Wittgenstein's uniquely powerful
point moving through these various passages is that, though we *may* formulate
what we take to be the "rules" of mathematical or linguistic practice – or their
counterparts in social behavior of other sorts – the would-be rules themselves
are, rather, based on our forms of life (to which in a sense we "agree"), where
agreement itself cannot be captured by further rules, cannot be independently
determined with certainty or on epistemic first grounds or the like, and
nevertheless does "work." Also, to say *that* is *not* to say that the rules are
uncertain, or to say that we do not proceed *by* following rules. This is just the
essential mistake of a very large number of fashionable interpretations of

boundary cond. do not have rules within system

Wittgenstein, of which Saul Kripke's is perhaps the most elaborate and impressive.[50] The point is that Wittgenstein's thesis identifies the conceptual space (a) within which, *holistically*, all our determinate, socially formed practices (including thinking) obtain; and (b) within which, in virtue of our having been introduced, in a natural way, to the particular forms of life it manifests in our society, we achieve a certain normal "praxical" aptitude. There cannot be rules or criteria by which to fix that particular space: fixing the rules in any sense presupposes our sharing it. A *fortiori*, there cannot be "truth-conditional" rules for determining such mastery (which Kripke attributes to the *Tractatus* and which he believes the *Investigations* repudiates); there cannot be "assertability-condition" rules (which Kripke believes *is* Wittgenstein's solution to the "rule-skepticism" issue); and there cannot be "community-agreement" rules (which Christopher Peacocke particularly favors). But to say *that* is not to say that there are no rules that are mastered *in* mastering the forms of life of one's own society. It is, in effect, to deny that that mastery can ever be formulated as a system, as a system of rules, say, more or less in accord with conditions 1–6 mentioned just above.

There is also some evidence that the "community-agreement" notion – that is, the notion of coming to share, as by implicit contract, the rules of a linguistic or cultural community, in developing linguistic aptitude – appears to go contrary to the facts, at least with regard to the formation of first-language sign language among deaf children whose parents do not use sign language, and the first-generation creolizing of pidgins among children whose parents cannot be said to exhibit a greater mastery of a particular pidgin than do those children.[51] The interesting thing is, first, that the formation of an idiosyncratic (as opposed to an idiolectic) language here appears quite plausible; second, that such empirical materials are entirely in accord with Wittgenstein's rather unexpected reading of the Robinson Crusoe story (against Kripke, Peacocke, and others); third, that such formations seem, empirically, to depend on other (apparently more primary) forms of enculturation, probably strongly biologized (say, along the lines Jerome Bruner favors[52]); and, fourth, that these materials do not actually confirm or preclude either a strong nativism or a strong enculturation thesis or any graded mixture of the two. However complex, the issue appears to be an empirical one. Empirical objections to a very strong nativism of the Chomskyan sort, for instance, rest on the absence of sufficiently developed analogues, or the indecisiveness of the analogues we have, for comparing semantic resources, the mastery of arithmetic and quantitative reasoning, and the functioning of visual perception[53] – *and* on both the probability that some mixture of nativist and enculturation elements cooperate in the development of all these aptitudes and the improbability that language could prove unique in the strong nativist sense.

It is a flat *non sequitur*, however, to argue (as Trevor Pateman appears to) that "there is no principled case against treating some dimensions of language as properties of the individual; language phenomena are not necessarily social."[54] The so-called "home-signing" deaf child need not (and does not, on the evidence) enter into a "community-agreement" arrangement (in G. P. Baker and P. M. S. Hacker's terms); but, as already remarked, Wittgenstein himself in effect accommodates this point – indeed, goes further. To admit that, however, is not tantamount to admitting that home signing is not socialized behavior in a sense more profound than mere social stimulation would require (perhaps minimally construed along Chomsky's lines). It is true that the nativist position cannot be shown to be incoherent on "Wittgenstein-ian" grounds. But the "Wittgensteinian" treatment, the treatment of language within the terms of "forms of life," is itself neither implausible nor incoherent nor irreconcilable with *some* nativist concessions (not necessarily Chomskyan), *and* (on independent grounds) not reducible to the "community-agreement" thesis rejected both by Baker and Hacker and by Pateman. If one admits (*contra* Chomsky) that the syntactic dimension of language is inseparable from the semantic and pragmatic or is affected by the contingencies that affect the semantic and pragmatic, *if* the unique nativist standing of language is implausible within an array of equally fundamental and ubiquitous functions among developed humans, and *if* a strong accommodation of something like Wittgensteinian forms of life appears to be empirically required to account satisfactorily for these other functions and may be flexibly fitted to language as well (without precluding *some* nativist concessions), then there *is* a "principled case against treating some dimensions of language as properties of the individual" (in the sense intended).

On Wittgenstein's view, the linkage between encultured behavior and form of life is such that our behavior remains "unpredictable" – in the profound sense that both *it and* the putative rules by which it functions are grounded in the same way and for the same reason: in the sense that the extension of such behavior is *also* the extension of the "rules," in the sense that there is no rule for continuing or changing the rules, that behavior is never really determined by the rules to which (in some regard) it does conform or may be said to conform. "Language-games" is an expression Wittgenstein characteristically uses when he refers to a restricted practice parasitic on richer natural-language practices or abstracted from such richer practices or recognizable as a thin imagined analogue of such practices; it is linked, therefore, with the equally abstracted notion of a formal rule. "Forms of life" designate the ultimately *unsystematiz-able* complex of actual societal life on which any *provisionally formulable regularities or rules* of behavior are *based* – habitually but not cognitively.

So, one essential theme in Wittgenstein's notion of a form of life is that *it is not a system of any sort.* This is what is missing in Finch's account, and what separates Wittgenstein's fundamental theme from those of thinkers like Chomsky or Saussure and Lévi-Strauss.[55] Wittgensteinian "forms of life" enable and oblige us to focus on the actual careers of aggregated human agents within their divergent social milieux – without presuming that their development is explicable solely in nativist terms (Chomsky) or in interactional terms (Piaget) that largely preclude any determining (*holist*) reference to their having internalized their own contingent cultures. The Wittgensteinian model eliminates neither biological (sub-cultural) constraints or determinants nor (contrary to the analytic structuralists) individual human agents as actual, effective entities – within the descriptive and explanatory scope of the human sciences. Wittgenstein's perspective permits us to address developmental questions (i) without invoking systems; (ii) without grounding human practices in foundationalist terms; and (iii) without ignoring the essential symbiosis between the individual and the societal at the level of human psychology. In particular, Wittgenstein would doubtless have opposed a strong disjunction (à la Chomsky) between any socially significant "competence" and "performance" (including but not restricted to language).[56]

It is true that Wittgenstein occasionally invokes the notion of a "system" as when, in *On Certainty*, he remarks that our beliefs and our knowledge form "a whole system of propositions," "an enormous system."[57] But, in speaking thus, he never construes a system in the sense given by conditions 1–6, tallied above. He means rather to emphasize the distinctive features of how we acquire the beliefs and practices of an actual, viable society, in a way that precludes the need for any privileged certainty about single propositions, or foundational rules for reliably fixing (proposition by proposition) what we may rightly claim to know, or determinate criteria by which to demonstrate our conformity with the governing or consensual practices of our own society. By "system" Wittgenstein means that what we learn in growing up is the presence of an *interconnected*, not altogether determinate, not universally fixed, variable and slowly changing network of beliefs or propositions – which preclude any reliance, *claim by claim*, on foundational propositions, and bypass the need for any such reliance within the stable practices of our society. It is not closure, therefore, that Wittgenstein intends but the idea of the habituated reliability or palpable presence of a complex world that, however open-ended in the extension of its practices, "dawns" on those it grooms from childhood – as a "system" that "holds fast" because of what we sense (and need only sense) "lies around" our every particular, explicit belief.[58] Wittgenstein's use of the term, then, actually supports the thesis that forms of life are cognitively and praxically effective despite the fact that they do not form or are not known to form any system in the sense defined above. Forms of life are contingently stable, diachronically slowly shifting, structurally open-ended, Intentionally habituated, naturally inculcated, horizonally skewed, stylistically congruent societal spaces within which the aptitudes of aggregated individuals issue in

(a) spontaneous acts ("performance") generally tolerated or socially allowed, instantiating

(b) skills and habits ("competence") specific to the forms of life of their society, regarding which

(c) rules, norms, structures, and the like are no more than posits internal to (a) by which individuals theorize about and influence congruities between (a) and (b), all the while

(d)   their improvisations, within the scope of (a) and (b), extend particular
practices in a way that invites or requires a gradual revision of (c).

In this respect, the Wittgensteinian model (*Lebensform*) differs fundamentally from the Husserlian (*Lebenswelt*) – or, at best, the latter only very
tentatively begins (toward the end of Husserl's work) to approach the import
of the former – in the quite specific sense that Husserl had great difficulty in
conceding and assigning a central role to the historically pluralized, contingent,
and shifting forms of social experience and practice and in resolving the puzzle
of the relationship between the societally generated nature of personal
experience and the originary role of the transcendental ego in his own system.[59]
By a contrast of an opposed sort, the Wittgensteinian template is also
fundamentally at odds with the new connectionism that is taking form in the
cognitive sciences. For, in spite of the fact that connectionism casts doubt on
the adequacy of Turing models to simulate the forms of natural intelligence –
hence, casts doubt on linear computational systems in the full-blooded sense –
connectionist views remain entirely indifferent to the molar societal role of
persons as agents who have internalized parts of the "life-world" or "form of
life" of their particular societies in ways that cannot be satisfactorily
characterized in either biological or computational terms.[60] In a sense,
therefore, connectionism may be even more radically "bottom–up" then
canonical cognitive science, since the latter favors a "top–down" strategy of
modeling knowledge or symbolic representation even if in the interest
ultimately of a bottom–up objective.[61] Simulation may seem to be within
closer reach, but the full nature of the interdependencies of actual processing
may actually have become more obscure.

Rules, on Wittgenstein's view, are, relative to actual societal life, neither
empirically nor conceptually prior to, nor separable from, nor metalinguistically
fixed with respect to, the practices of such life. They are invariably no more
than abstractions and projections (in generalized form) from merely finite
manifestations of our forms of life reflexively reviewed – but, as such, they may
well be apt or inapt, "correct" or "incorrect," as far as they go. This is surely
part of the meaning of that famous paragraph – possibly one of the most profound in Wittgenstein – "If language is to be a means of communication there
must be agreement not only in definitions but also (queer as this may sound) in
judgements. This seems to abolish logic, but does not do so . . . . what we call
"measuring" is partly determined by a certain constancy in results of
measurement."[62] On any reasonable reading, one sees that Wittgenstein *must*
have intended (could not possibly otherwise have explained) that the relevant
forms of agreememt are more tacit than explicit *and* involve both the different
forms of life of historically contingent societies and the generic societal
dispositions of the entire species, humankind. Differences between species
affect the possibilities of grasping or entering into the practices (or language-
games) of particular societies within this or that species: thus, "If a lion could

talk, we could not understand him"[65] (whether or not Wittgenstein is right in this regard).

Similarly, he remarks, in the same general passage, that "one human being can be a complete enigma to another," even whole *human* societies whose language we may even have mastered. In this sense, the relative constancy of "agreement" is not an outcome of inquiry, it is the *precondition* of any consensus regarding its outcome; also, it is not determinate (certain, fixed, incontrovertible) but only the generic precondition that we must assume obtains if any effective social action, social communication, science, or the like also obtains. It is, so to say, the precondition

(i) of determinate collective attributes peculiar to any one society as distinct from any other;

(ii) distributively applicable generically – that is, variably manifested from one individual to another within a given society; and

(iii) biologically incarnate in aptitudes preceding and contraining the variety of historically different cultures.

In fact, items (i)–(iii) may well be hospitable to such phenomena as creolizing – *pace* Derek Bickerton. It is certainly the case that admitting forms of life is *not* construing linguistic or similar rules merely dispositionally or consensually.[64]

In fixing the sense of Wittgenstein's notion of forms of life, we shall not yet have fixed the "gauge" of his model – but we shall be well on our way. What we may conclude, fairly broadly, are at least the following:

1 "forms of life" is to be construed as the most fundamental, most comprehensive category bearing on the description and explanation of human life – possibly of other species if capable of language or language-like behavior;

2 it makes no sense to talk of possible or imagined forms of life, unless parasitically, since the primary function of that notion concerns the description and explanation of actual life;

3 forms of life are essentially assigned actual human societies (or their surrogates if there be any), both in the sense of plural, historically contingent communities within the species and in the sense (presumably projected by comparing communities) of the common, species-wide "society" of man (that is, the capacity of the species to understand alien cultures);

4 forms of life designate the entire complex of the behavior and activity of viable human societies (and of whatever regarding thinking, desire, intention, and the like is involved in such behavior and activity);

5 "agreement" regarding forms of life signifies the tacit (essentially praxical) conditions obtaining within human societies, with regard to which individual members are "naturally" groomed from infancy to

adult competence (that is, merely in growing up in a society of apt practitioners);

6 forms of life are not systems in any sense – that is, closed domains of activity actually subject to formulable, finite sets of rules that govern, influence, generate, or in any fundamental sense explain the behavior or regularities of behavior of the aggregated members of a given society;

7 the sense in which rules, practices, and "agreement" regarding rules and practices are "grounded" in forms of life is not cognitively definable or confirmable, but signifies roughly the actual viability and survival of a human society insofar as such survival depends upon (is mediated by) such effective "agreement";

8 rules and practices of actual societies are, therefore, conceptually symbiotic, not hierarchically linked, and not universalizable in any transhistorical way;

9 individual behavior is intelligible only within the framework of particular forms of life, though the variations of socially interpreted (such) behavior may support the projection of alternative would-be rules, and may, as socially tolerated improvisations, lead, over time, to significantly distinct alternative would-be rules;

10 "changes" in social rules (actually, changes in our projections of what, relative to finite specimens of behavior, we formulate as the rules such behavior fits) are as much a part of our forms of life as patterns of behavior that seem not to require altering our sense of such prevailing rules;

11 forms of life, therefore, never enter in any distributed or determinate description or explanation of human behavior, but signify rather the distinctive nature of the description and explanation of human behavior itself;

12 our cognitive reflection on the properties and regularities of whatever falls within the scope of our form of life is itself part of that form of life and subject, therefore, to the same contingencies as the phenomena thus examined; and

13 there is no escape or exit from our form of life, just as there is no escape or exit from our natural languages: to be human is to share a form of life, in the sense of sharing a natural language and whatever that entails and makes possible.

Items 1–13 constitute the Wittgensteinian "template" but rest on empirical comparisons between the fit and promise of fit of competing templates.

Armed with this schematized account, we may now consider what the "gauge" of Wittgenstein's model is – and what its distinctive promise is for the issue of enculturation. Once again, the principal clue is quite simple and straightforward: Wittgenstein never, except accidentally, addresses (in speaking of forms of life) any particular empirical hypothesis about developmental processes; he offers instead the largest conceptual template (in his own view) for any and all empirically promising developmental theories and hypotheses. In effect, his model rules out – with cause – potentially competing ways of construing cultural learning, development, linguistic and other social aptitudes, the very formation of a socially apt self. Thus, even if it were true (as many have wrongly supposed) that Wittgenstein was a behaviorist, his "behaviorist" hypotheses (such as they are) may well be defeated without at all affecting his larger conception; also, such hypotheses would themselves have to be suitably reconciled (in terms of coherence) with that very conception. The doctrine of the forms of life is "empirical" in that large sense in which it is to be dialectically fitted to the widest range of pertinent data – against competitors – that we can claim to address; but it is not empirical in the narrower sense that it never takes the form of a determinate, middle-sized theory. It is, rather, the generic template for an indefinitely extendable set of middle-sized theories of one sort rather than of another. The question it addresses, we must remember, concerns what kind of model it is best to favor if we are to point developmental psychology and allied studies in the most fruitful direction we can imagine. The issue, therefore, concerns that vexed no-man's-land between "empirical" philosophy and empirical science. And, although Wittgenstein eschews philosophy, there can be little doubt that he practices it in the sense in which he draws attention to what he himself takes to be most compelling about his proposed template. It is, in short, a particularly perspicuous version of all top–down conceptions of the ontology of human nature and of a methodology of the human sciences attuned to such an ontology; and it has the peculiar advantage (of its own limitation) that it can accommodate empirically any of a variety of theories of a certain sort (congruent with our tally 1–13 provided just above – and even more) without the least distortion.

III

No one who considers the question of psychological maturation can fail to locate the phases of both biological and cultural development within the bounds of viable societies. This can be said just as well of Skinner and Hull and Freud and Chomsky and Piaget (and even, grudgingly, of Althusser and Lévi-Strauss) as it can of Vygotsky and Luria and Bruner and Bronfenbrenner and Bourdieu and Mead. But there remains an essential difference nevertheless. On the argument already sketched, the former theorize in ways that make an (as yet) unresolved or unresolvable puzzle of psychological development; and the latter are at least broadly "Wittgensteinian" in their orientation.

There is, therefore, a conceptual weakness involved in comparing, say, Quine's The Roots of Reference[65] with Bruner's Child's Talk; or Bruner's book with Piaget's The Language and Thought of the Child.[66] The weakness is this: the comparison of apparent developmental sequences is not sufficiently grounded by either Quine or Piaget, for instance, in their respective theories of the relationship between the human person and physical or biological order. The result is a peculiarly disengaged sense in which Bruner may be said to agree in this or that detail with Quine and Piaget; or in which Chomsky opposes details in Quine's or Putnam's views of linguistic acquisition.[67] We simply do not know enough of what should be made of the notion of a "person" or "human society" or "natural language" or "human thought and activity," among theorists of the first sort, to be sure that comparisons of detail between theorists of the two sorts will make coherent sense in terms of the relatively developed interpretation of these notions among thinkers of the second sort.

The latter do not agree among themselves, of course. But their differences are, largely, differences among competing empirical theories of developmental accounts formulated within what we are here calling Wittgenstein's conceptual space – the space of forms of life. When, therefore, Urie Bronfenbrenner introduces the notion of an "ecology" of human development, we must seize the central point: that it is a human, a societal, ecology that he has in mind – not merely a generic, environmental, or biological setting but one that is cultural, diachronically or historically shifting, distinctly institutional in nature. There is a world of difference between Bronfenbrenner's use of "ecology" and, say, J. J. Gibson's notion of "ecological optics" – which has, really, no cultural or historical or societal structure as such, even though "social" factors may affect perception within particular ecological niches.[68] (In fact, in Gibson, there are, once again reductively, no persons or perceptual agents to acknowledge, in discoursing about perception – that is, no agents who process perceptual input in terms of culturally structured experience and beliefs.) Again, when Bronfenbrenner favorably airs Luria's empirical studies of Asian Soviet communities offered in the spirit of a Marxist analysis of psychological development, we readily see that the convergence between their respective views lies as much in the congruity of their notions of the conceptual space within which their differences may be compared as it does in the narrow agreement of their actual views within that space.[69]

This is the reason why we are singling out Wittgenstein's conception of forms of life – and resisting more detailed questions about developmental sequences themselves. Let us say that Mead, Dewey, Vygotsky, Luria, Bourdieu, Bruner, Bronfenbrenner all converge more or less on the master themes of that notion of life we have already summarized. One could add to the list indefinitely many others – notably, among Continental European philosophers, Gadamer, Habermas, Ricoeur, Tugendhat,[70] and, among English-language philosophers, R. S. Peters, David Hamlyn, Rom Harré, Peter Winch, Charles Taylor: all focused to one degree or another on the problems of developmental psychology within a social context. But the master-theme remains

(i)   that persons are, relevantly, neither reducible in sub-personal terms nor adequately characterized as mere nodes of the primary intersecting

forces of the real structures of suprapersonal systems, nor are "persons" biologically fixed or developmentally evolved in any sense essentially disengaged from the processes of cultural formation; and
(ii) that, although only human agents are actual effective agents (which is not to deny non-agentive causal forces in social contexts), human agency is essentially socialized – in the sense in which language, human institutions, historical styles and the like are assignable as such only or primarily to entire societies, to social ensembles.

This is the double force of Wittgenstein's "gauge" of enculturation or psychological development. Natural language is irreducibly societal, but only individual human persons speak: we know of no convincing way to account for phenomena at that level of manifestation – in either the "*bottom–up*" manner of the reductionists *or* the manner of the structuralists, who effectively "raise" the level of relevant reference and then inexplicitly "reduce" (in quite a different sense – perhaps epiphenomenally) the individual to the fundamenta of the altered world.

It *is* logically possible (as, in rather different ways, both Wittgenstein and Chomsky concede) that language may be acquired in "some" way that does not involve enculturation; but *there is no plausible ground for supposing that that is so* for any of the known phenomena of natural language. The mere admission that there must be innate structures ingredient in some sense *in* enculturation does not preclude the likelihood of socialized development; and the slim examples of certain creoles (but not others) and certain cases of signing deaf children (but not others) do not actually confirm that the possibility barely mentioned is an actuality. Trevor Pateman, for example, is simply too quick to attribute language to "individuals" (that is, without attention to the symbiosis of self and society), when the evidence he adduces merely shows that language may be idiosyncratically generated or generated even under conditions of individual isolation or limitation *within* the span of a socialized or encultured life.[71] (Wittgenstein's purpose, on the other hand, in the Robinson Crusoe speculation, is essentially to segregate the question of the possible source of language from that of its functioning intelligibly *as* a language. He clearly is not interested in speculating about what might go on within the black box so casually postulated in the marginal, utterly unfamiliar case.) In the sense here intended, the Wittgensteinian "gauge" is the gauge of what has elsewhere been termed "*top–down*" strategies of analysis: factorial rather than compositional, *not* symmetrical with bottom–up strategies,[72] committed to the full reality of the human, and committed as well to the conceptual symbiosis (and mutual irreducibility) of the societal and the psychological.

Nevertheless, Pateman's question invites and demands a measure of care, because it forces an open confrontation between "Chomskyans" and "Wittgensteinians." Summarizing "Chomskyan linguistics" (sympathetically), Pateman offers the following distinction:

language is studied as a property of the individual human mind, both as the innate universal grammar which makes the development of language possible in the individual and as an attained mentally represented grammar, what Chomsky now calls an "I-language," an internalized language as opposed to an externalized language, an "E-language" [the latter being favored by the Wittgensteinians preeminently]. This study is individualistic in the sense that properties are ascribed to individuals independently of any reference to other individuals, reference to other individuals is unnecessary either to the *ontology* of language in the individual or the *epistermology* of coming to know what linguistic properties an individual instantiates. It is not denied that *social* interaction is a necessary condition of the triggering of linguistic development in the child, but it is denied that reference to the language of other individuals is necessary in characterizing that linguistic development; it is also denied that specifically linguistic (as opposed to social) interaction is necessary to linguistic development. . . .

The deepest philosophical challenge to the view that language is an individual property and can be ascribed individualistically comes from a deployment of Wittgenstein's arguments against the possibility of a private language, to develop a "community view" of language.[73]

This is admirably straightforward, and the issue it raises is a most critical one. But it is also defective and not really responsive in a variety of ways. First of all, as we have seen, Wittgenstein does not oppose the possibility of a contingently private language (Robinson Crusoe), only the viability of a logically private language.[74] Secondly, the "Wittgensteinian" line is, therefore, not restricted to or even most characteristically or most viably conveyed by the " 'community view' of language" (Kripke's thesis, for instance).

Thirdly (now, less eristically and more substantively), Pateman (also, Chomsky) fails to address the question of the very formation of an "individual" (a person or self apt for language). Unless we know more about the conditions under which "individuals" are properly formed, neither the conceptual nor the empirical possibilities Pateman advances are entirely serious contenders: the Wittgensteinian thesis about "forms of life" is most perspicuously read in terms of the social formation of selves (as we have been arguing). Fourthly, it is therefore quite unclear what the intended sense is in which "specifically linguistic (as opposed to social) interaction" is not "necessary to linguistic development." *If* linguistic development is entailed in the formation of the self, *if* the social interaction necessary to the formation of the self is itself formed by (*inter alia*) linguistic interaction or is actually structured in ways that profoundly implicate language, then it is not responsible on Pateman's part to disjoin the linguistic and the social. (Permit this issue to remain a little vague for the moment. We shall return to it after tallying the objections promised. In any case, Pateman intends to support both an empirical claim and a realistic conceptual possibility suited to man's actual nature.)

Fifthly, the usual pidgins are clearly second languages; the usual creoles fit the rule that the linguistic aptitude of parents is relatively superior to that of children;[75] the entire issue of pidgins and creoles and its implications for "standard" languages really concern the fixity and the uniqueness of rules for a viable language or language-like "system," not (or at least not in any obvious or inescapable sense) the quarrél between the Chomskyans and the Wittgensteinians (I- and E-theorists). Sixthly, the "first-generation creolization of pidgin languages" (which Pateman reports from Derek Bickerton's studies) is not in principle a problem for the Wittgensteinian who does *not* subscribe to the "community view" any more than it is a problem for the Chomskyan who does *not* subscribe to the view that, at *every* operative level in the analysis of a natural language, the structures of its generative grammar are and must be identical with those of every other language;[76] but the Chomskyan, unlike the Wittgensteinian, does not explain the *social* (not merely the "linguistic") perspicuousness (to employ Pateman's terms here) of the actual categories and predicates of the language thus generated, which may well indicate a deeper socialization *of* the linguistic than the "individualists" acknowledge – very probably linked to the formation of the self.

Seventhly, the nativist about language is a realist; hence, as an individualist (in the sense drawn from Pateman), the nativist is also a "mentalist" – that is, committed to the feasibility and pertinence of studies intermediate "between brain science and social phenomenology," particularly the study of "non-introspectible states and processes";[77] *hence*, the nativist must also be a "cognitivist" – that is, he must be committed to "a theory which makes essential use of the idea of non-introspectible computation operations on objects properly considered to be [linguistic] representations."[78] But the nativist, Chomsky preeminently, requires that, "at the appropriate level of abstraction" (not elsewhere),[79] there is a universal grammar (UG) to be discovered, which must therefore actually be "cognized" (rather than "known," in Chomsky's special sense of that term[80]). As Chomsky summarizes the matter,

Let us recall the basic character of the problem we face. The theory of UG must meet two obvious conditions. On the one hand, it must be compatible with the diversity of existing (indeed, possible) grammars. At the same time, UG must be sufficiently constrained and restricted in the options it permits so as to account for the fact that each of these grammars develops in the mind on the basis of quite limited evidence. In many cases that have been carefully studied in recent work, it is a near certainty that fundamental properties of the attained grammars are radically underdetermined by evidence available to the language learner and must therefore be attributed to UG itself.[81]

It is, however, not clear whether or in what respects "the attained grammars are radically underdetermined": they are certainly underdetermined from the "community view." But the Wittgensteinian can admit, as resources for explaining the convergence of deep grammars, innate, sub-linguistic, biological dispositions and other invariances (even of a socially directed sort);[82] *some* limited language-like invariances (not sufficiently rich to account for UG or even for obviously culturally required aptitudes at levels of lesser generality); as well as socially and linguistically pertinent inferential powers tacitly entailed in the very formation of the self (about which we seem to know very little). Also, he is *not* obliged, as is the Chomskyan, *to postulate any "cognizing" of UG*, for he is not obliged to concede that there *is* "an appropriate level" at which UG actually obtains. Chomsky very clearly holds that "our minds are fixed biological systems with their intrinsic scope and limits."[83] He also holds, therefore, that, in searching for the "mental organ" ("the system of grammatical rules") that forms that part of those "fixed biological systems" that control the development of language, we may suppose our *"idealizations"* of the relevant grammar to constitute approximations to the actual underlying UG of all languages.[84] But that means that the Wittgensteinian has much more flexibility, conceptually, than the Chomskyan, provided either that *there is no actual UG* or that *the reality of language, like the reality of culture, is ontically indeterminate* (in the sense already given) – that is, *real!* – or both of these.[85]

Eighthly and finally, the nativist, construed in the very strong sense that Chomsky favors, nowhere explains or justifies – on either empirical or second-order legitimative grounds – the exclusive force of his own conjecture or its conceptual incongruity with the global trend of philosophical speculation we have been at pains to characterize over the entire course of our gathering argument. If, it seems reasonable, the essential issue is an empirical one, then, on the face of it, the nativist-individualist-mentalist-cognitivist cannot have demonstrated the falsity or even the implausibility of the "Wittgensteinian" thesis and strategy. For example, Chomsky nowhere demonstrates *that* conceptual universals are genetically triggered and nowhere explains *how*, if the universals of language are not instinct-driven (as seems reasonable), they can be innatist in an operative way. If, however, UG (in Chomsky's strong sense) were a fact, the tables would be turned completely.

These considerations constitute the dialectical advantage of Wittgensteinian forms of life. We may also take notice of the fact that "individualists" (not merely Chomskyans) do not ordinarily sort the differences between *language* and *speech*. For example, if the very formation of the self entails internalizing language in some sense and to some extent, then language cannot be confined to overt speech behavior and the underdetermination Chomsky speaks of becomes altogether moot. The general practices of a society are, then, *languaged* or *lingual* in the sense, jointly, that they presuppose linguistic aptitude in the narrow respect speech behavior signifies; and that certain of the actual linguistic structures of speech behavior; or structures on which similar "narrow" linguistic structures analogous to those of actual speech could be generated, may be inferentially recovered from behavior that is *not* itself explicit speech. (This could, for instance, go some distance toward explaining first-generation creolizing and "home-signing" among deaf children.)

Wittgenstein's notion, therefore, offers an ingenious economy. First of all, *our* sharing certain forms of life makes it possible to interpret and comprehend the forms of life of other human communities. This draws attention to the biological, species-wide similarities on which all cultural divergences depend; the inescapable cultural skewing of all such interpretation and comprehension; *and* the possibility of being *culturally* baffled, despite whatever may be the pertinently common biology of the species. (This is the point of Wittgenstein's remark about entering a "strange country with entirely strange traditions."[86]) Second, sharing a form of life essentially entails, and is paradigmatically manifested in, sharing a natural language. Hence, to the extent that we attribute forms of life to animals – or patterns of social existence that favorably resemble human forms of life – we anthropomorphize them; and we are conceptually bound to do so if we suppose we can "understand" them at all. (This is the point of Wittgenstein's remark about our not being able to understand a lion who could speak.[87]) Third, insofar as we understand ourselves – that is, each one himself and his fellows – our ability presupposes and manifests our sharing a form of life, sharing sufficiently resemblant families of practices (however idiosyncratically divergent), to sustain a viable society; nevertheless, that viability entails neither a fixity nor uniformity of rules nor any cognitive mastery of any particular such rules, explicit or implicit.[88] There is, in fact, a consensual tolerance of behavior and activity that is *not* capable, in principle, of being or needing to be independently fixed in cognitive terms; that tolerance ensures no more then a "general" (or holist) effectiveness among cogniscent activities, and entails at every moment of social exchange the potentiality for improvisations both productive and receptive. (This is the point of Wittgenstein's famous remark, "What has to be accepted, the given, is – so one could say – forms of *life*."[89])

IV

Now, Wittgenstein does not adequately explore such issues as we have just tallied, in terms of the details of psychology or the social sciences. In a sense, he makes "implicit" provision for them but he hardly pursues them: in particular, he hardly pursues

1 the import of the historicized variability of human societies – both synchronically divergent and diachronically changing – upon infra-societal understanding, communicative interpretation, psychological development;

2 the analysis of the difference between, and the relationship between, empirical predicates designating individual psychological attributes and

predicates designating attributes of societies considered as ensembles not obviously reducible to mere aggregates (as in speaking of languages, institutions, traditions, and the like);[90] and

3 the analysis of the notion of a human culture itself (qualified as the sharing of forms of life) in contrast with the notion of physical nature *and* of sub-cultural animal sociality.

The most striking thing about Wittgenstein's analyses is that he lacks a developed interest in history – in the dual sense critical to contemporary theory: the detailed study of the import of diachronically changing practice on individual lives and on the social functioning of individual lives thus affected, as well as the hermeneutic significance of the very historicity of human existence (as in the work of Heidegger, Gadamer, Foucault).

Both of these themes bear decisively on the distinctive *realism* suited to the cultural world – *a fortiori*, on the prospects of a realist conception of the human sciences. (Also, there is no reason for supposing that the Wittgensteinian template could not be explicitly historicized.) The realism of human existence, human society, human culture, human history is, we may say, essentially marked by the following features:

(a) that the Intentionality of cultural space is inseparable, causally, ontologically, and hermeneutically, from the Intentionality of the mental states and behavior of the aggregated individuals living within it – although particular ascriptions to the collective and individual or aggregated "parts" of that space need not be, and cannot be, quite the same;

(b) that the structures of that space are sufficiently robust and flexible for it to be the case that cultural variation between and within societies, however collectively, individually, aggregatively construed, and however measured synchronically or diachronically, can actually be identified;

(c) that the dynamics of enculturation can be traced, in terms of differences between the detailed structures assignable within that space, to an ordered sequence of parental and successor generations and to the interacting agencies of both; and

(d) that conditions (a)–(c) constitute a flux that is ontologically indeterminate, in the joint sense that the structures than obtain are and may be affected by reflexive consensual efforts to determine what they are, and that they are inseparable from and implicated in the improvisatory activity of the apt, somewhat idiosyncratically motivated members of any particular society.

(We have of course, already construed the realism due the cultural world in terms of the "real!")

Features (a)–(d) are peculiar to the human world, entirely absent from the usual "objective" accounts of the attributes of the physical world; and they are most handily collected in a historicized reading of Wittgenstein's forms of life. All address the Intentionality of the human world, and each designates a particular constraint on the human sciences. (a) designates the *contextedness* of pertinent properties and structures: that there is no sense in which actual cultural phenomena *have* the (Intentional) properties they possess, independently of the beliefs and concepts and activity of the members of the society in question. This does not preclude objectivity in the human sciences, but it does serve to contrast it with what is usually claimed in the natural sciences.[91] (b) designates the primacy of *agency* in the human world, that the individual and the societal are symbiotized in thought and activity: that there is and can be no ontological priority favoring the rule-like norms of an enveloping society over the improvisatory behavior of its individual members, except, contingently, in terms of intergenerational enculturation. (c) designates the dialectical nature of the abstracted collective dynamics of social history, of what may now be termed *praxis*[92]: that the Intentional structures a society exhibits are always historically, interpretively, retrospectively emergent from the structures of its earlier career but may not be explicable except in terms of its emergent structures.[93] Finally, (d) designates the *hermeneutic indeterminacy* of the structures of that Intentional space: that its properties cannot, in principle, be uniquely fixed; that what they actually are is a function of reflexive and consensual interpretation; that any empirical fixity assigned is assigned under some preformed historical prejudice (in Gadamer's sense); that such assignments are not merely epistemically contingent to their actual features; that there is no principled disjunction between what they "are" and what they "appear" to be;[94] that they themselves are historical or historicized features; and that, therefore, what is intrinsic to the nature of the phenomena that manifest such properties is itself a function of their history.[95]

Having said this much, the supreme advantage of the Wittgensteinian template drifts into view at once. *It is the forms of life themselves that set reasonable constraints on what we may posit as the intrinsic properties of the cultural world*: both in the abstract, generic sense suited to Wittgenstein's *Lebensformen*, Bourdieu's *habitus*, Gadamer's *Wirkungsgeschichte*, Foucault's *normalisations*, and in the sense of the relatively determinate interpretive histories of Hegel's *Weltgeist*, the German Romantic historians' "individualities," the ordered phases of Marxian "historical materialism," Althusser's *problématiques*, Foucault's *généalogies*, Kuhn's "paradigms," and the seemingly infinitely many analogues of both sorts that congeal from time to time. The point is that the *objectivity* of the human sciences lies primarily in the historicized measure of their perceived congruity with what, reflexively, are construed as the prevailing forms of life of one's own society – aided in whatever way (also historically infected) by a society's capacity for critique. This is *not* to say that objectivity *is* consensus; only that claims of objectivity are consensually processed *and* that that process is itself historicized and subject both to historical reinterpretation and to the divergence of a multiplicity of shifting centers of consensus (rather like dialectic and idiolectic variations within a viable linguistic field, or "system" in Bickerton's adjusted sense) that inevitably compete with one another for a measure of hegemony. It is in this sense, of course, that inquiry has a rhetorical cast, though one not without rigor. Objectivity in the human sciences is a function of the tradition of objectivity, constrained by forms of life, interpretive schemata, congruity with physical uniformities, the vagaries of consensus, the divergences of conviction, the contingencies of experience, and the ontology of historicized existence itself.

In a curious way, the description and interpretation of artworks serves as the richest, most variegated, and most instructive model we are likely to have of the work of the human sciences. But, if we admit that, then we must ponder such concessive remarks – now radicalized by the very history of philosophical reflection – as the following (Monroe Beardsley's) extraordinarily candid pronouncement regarding the interpretation of a poem:

> Some things are definitely said in the poem and cannot be overlooked; others are suggested, as we find on careful reading; others are gently hinted, and *whatever methods of literary interpretation we use, we can never establish them decisively as "in" or "out." Therefore whatever comes from without, but yet can be taken as an interesting extension of what is surely in,* may be admissible. It merely makes a larger whole.[96]

Beardsley speaks here as a firm advocate of an objectivism in literary criticism – metonymically, in the human sciences in general – attracted to an enlargement of some version of the unity-of-science program (no longer, of course, bound by the early reductive strains of that movement). But his unaccented acknowledgement of the complexities of Intentionality (which, in much the same spirit as, at least methodologically, may be found in Quine, Beardsley was prepared to dismiss as largely irrelevant to the work of the discipline) forced him to admit the profound lack of fixity in the *nature* – consequently, also, the lack of fixity in the identity, of the *referent* – of critical discourse. The continuity of that identity is a function of the continuity of the tradition of historical and interpretive reflection on the materials of cultural life; it cannot be fixed by any merely causal or formal model.[97] Texts are *not* referents, *if* we insist on the canonical view; or they are not altogether reliable referents, if mention of their intrinsic properties is also a function of their charging histories. The ontic inde-terminancies are themselves intrinsic. Texts *are* referents, *if* we allow (1) that reference is quite effective even if generally story-relative; (2) that referents may be characteristically distinguished in Intentionally complex ways; and (3) that referents may be ontically indeterminate in their intentional features.

Clearly, the admission has the most radical implications – affecting the pretensions of every form of system. We are at home, however, in the flux of things, provided only they appear to us to change at a conservative pace – which is to say, provided also that we ourselves appear to change conformably. *There* is the saving theme of Wittgenstein's insight. It is also the fine theme of

Gadamer's "fusion of horizons" (*Horizontverschmelzung*), of the ontology of historicized understanding, if we may so speak. It is the historicizing of Wittgensteinian *Lebensformen*.

Unfortunately, Gadamer himself is hopelessly caught up in the fear of "method," in the need to contrast the work of historical reconstruction and hermeneutic understanding, in a rearguard action against the incipience of relativism and the fall of universal values.[98] But, if we set all that aside (as we have, already, the cognate worries of objectivists such as Beardsley and E. D. Hirsch – to stay roughly within the same span of criticism or understanding or *Verstehen*), then the puzzle of our time is, precisely, how to recover a sense of reasonable rigor and effective communication within the bounds of changing history. If we accept all the *caveats* indicated, which force Gadamer's perception into an antiseptic tube, then the following is as clear a statement of the ontology of the "fusion" – hence, as clear a challenge to our sense of rigor – as we are likely to find for the foreseeable future:

> the horizon of the present is being continually formed, in that we have continually to test all our prejudices. An important part of this testing is the encounter with the past and the understanding of the tradition from which we come. Hence the horizon of the present cannot be formed without the past. . . . We [may describe] the conscious act of this fusion as the task of the effective-historical consciousness [*wirkungsgeschichtliches Bewusstsein*]. . . . all reading involves application, so that a person reading a text is himself part of the meaning he apprehends. He belongs to the text that he is reading.[99]

We must ponder that still-fresh notion, but we must surely ponder more. We have demonstrated the coherence and viability of the ramified vision entailed. But we have said nothing as yet of how man grasps the direction of, or gives deliberate direction to, his own life and the aggregated and collective life of his society and the entire human race. But that is a tale for another occasion.

We have confined ourselves to enriching a Wittgensteinian template. Its virtue lies in facilitating the finding that the forms of human life at the full level of culturally diverse activity need not be and very probably do not form a closed system of any sort – however much closed systems may be made to simulate finite temporal segments of that open-ended life, and however much modular sub-systems of a species-wide biological or biosocial sort (whether closed or open) may be plausibly assigned to the initial resources that all divergent cultures are embodied in. At the most abstract level of social description (meaning by that to include the cognitive achievements of a reflexive human science), all extensional discourse is a carpentered model of Intentional analysis fitted to itself.[100] In that sense, the *passage* of Wittgenstein's efforts from the *Tractatus* to the *Investigations* is a marvel of economy. Nevertheless, there is, in Wittgenstein, very nearly no mention of the dynamics of human *praxis* and human history. In a large sense, therefore, what we have been exploring is the prospect of embedding Wittgenstein's template in a suitably ample account of the complexities of the actual human world: of the symbiosis of the psychological and the societal, of the dialectic of preformational and critical processes affecting thinking and behavior, of the interconnection between horizonal limit and consensual effectivity, of the profound contingency and diversity of the patterns of human practice, of the ambivalence of interpretive continuities cast upon historical discontinuities, of the search through cognitive saliencies for the certitudes of invariance.

To have provided a conceptual vision within which these themes may be comfortably contained – coherently and effectively against the principal rival proposals of our time – is the master-gift of the praxicalized template we have been pursuing. It confirms, without the silliness of ignoring the enormous differences among the most influential minds of our age, the instructive convergence among the lines of thought of Wittgenstein and Marx and Nietzsche at least. In doing that, it cannot fail to inform what we may understand to be the largest rational measures by which we govern ourselves and give direction to our life – morally, politically, religiously, creatively.

We must, however, stop to catch our breath. For we have sketched the elusive strategies by which, within the flux we honor and inhabit, we still manage to trace the intelligibility of our world and ourselves without betraying at any point presumptions of cognitive privilege or of the determinately structured "presence" of a fixed and independent world.[101]

Notes

1   The opposing view is, of course, the relaxed, *laissez-faire*, libertarian doctrine fashionably championed in recent years by Richard Rorty. See for instance Rorty's *Philosophy and the Mirror of Nature* (Princeton, NJ: Princeton University Press, 1979).

2   See ch. 1, above.

3   Rom Harré, "Social Sources of Mental Content and Order," in Joseph Margolis et al., *Psychology: Designing the Discipline* (Oxford: Basil Blackwell, 1986), p. 92.

4   Rom Harré, *Personal Being: A Theory for Individual Psychology* (Cambridge: Harvard University Press, 1984), p. 145.

5   Cf. ibid., p. 16. See Joseph Margolis, *Science without Unity: Reconciling the Human and Natural Sciences* (Oxford: Basil Blackwell, 1987), ch. 12.

6   Rom Harré, *Social Being: A Theory for Social Psychology* (Totowa, NJ: Rowman and Littlefield, 1979), p. 7; see further ch. 5., for an excellent sketch of institutions.

7   Harré, *Social Being*, p. 91.

8   Harré, *Personal Being*, p. 20.

9   See ch. 8, above. See also Norbert Elias, *The History of Manners*, vol. 1: *The Civilizing Process*, tr. Edmund Jephcott (New York: Pantheon, 1978).

10   Harré, *Personal Being*, pp. 76–7.

11 Harré, *Personal Being*, p. 77.
12 Ibid., p. 26.
13 P. F. Strawson, *Individuals: An Essay in Descriptive Metaphysics* (London: Methuen, 1959), p. 89.
14 Ibid., p. 108.
15 John R. Searle, *Speech Acts: An Essay in the Philosophy of Language* (Cambridge: Cambridge University Press, 1969). Cf. also Searle's, *Expression and Meaning: Studies in the Theory of Speech Acts* (Cambridge: Cambridge University Press, 1979).
16 Searle, *Speech Acts*, pp. 55, 65 (I have italicized "idealization").
17 See J. L. Austin, *How to Do Things with Words*, ed. J. O. Urmson (Oxford: Clarendon Press, 1962), especially Lecture IV.
18 Harré, *Personal Being*, p. 86ff. Harré supplies the relevant references, p. 110.
19 Ibid., p. 26.
20 Here, Harré invokes Hume, Kant, and Husserl. Cf. *Personal Being*, ch. 4. See also Margolis, *Science without Unity*, ch. 3.
21 Harré, *Personal Being*, pp. 38–40.
22 This is a little curious, since Harré mentions Dennett's view with approval. See further Margolis, *Science without Unity*, ch. 5. See also John Shotter, *Social Accountability and Selfhood* (Oxford: Basil Blackwell, 1984), which conforms rather more closely to Harré's view; Jeff Coulter, *The Social Construction of Mind* (London: Macmillan, 1979), which, more enthnomethodologically, strongly converges with Harré's view; and Jeff Coulter, *Rethinking Cognitive Theory* (New York: St Martin's Press 1983).
23 Harré, *Personal Being*, p. 93.
24 Cf. Margolis, *Science without Unity*, ch. 3.
25 This bears particularly on his use of a "dramaturgical model" applied to something quite close to Erving Goffman's notion of a "moral career." See Harré, *Social Being*, chs 10, 14; Erving Goffman, *Asylums* (Harmondsworth: Penguin, 1968).
26 George Herbert Mead, *Mind, Self and Society: From the Standpoint of a Social Behaviorist*, ed. Charles W. Morris (Chicago: University of Chicago Press, 1934), pp. 150–1.
27 See for instance Mead's "The Biologic Individual," a supplementary essay included in *Mind, Self, and Society*; also Lev Vygotsky, *Thought and Language*, tr. and ed. Eugenia Hanfmann and Gertrude Vakar (Cambridge, Mass.: MIT Press, 1962), ch. 2; Alexander R. Luria, *Language and Cognition*, ed. James B. Wertsch (Washington, DC: V. H. Winston, 1981); and Jerome Bruner (with Rita Watson), *Child's Talk: Learning to Use Language* (New York: W. W. Norton, 1983), ch. 2. Cf. Sandra B. Rosenthal, *Speculative Pragmatism* (Amherst: University of Massachusetts Press, 1986), pp. 83–6, for a very brief but focused account of Mead's conception.
28 See Margolis, *Science without Unity*, ch. 12; and ch. 5, above.
29 An extremely clear discussion of the Marxist–structuralist quarrel and the futility of disjoining "materialist" and "idealist" models of social life may be found in Marshall Sahlins, *Culture and Practical Reason* (Chicago: University of Chicago Press, 1976). See also ch. 6, above.
30 For specimen views, see Claude Lévi-Strauss, *Structural Anthropology*, vol. 2, tr.

362 THE REALITY OF THE HUMAN

Monique Layton (Chicago: University of Chicago Press, 1976), pt I: Louis Althusser, "Marxism and Humanism," in For Marx, tr. Ben Brewster (London: New Left Books, 1977); Peter M. Blau, "Objectives of Sociology," in Robert Bierstedt (ed.), A Design for Sociology: Scope, Objectives and Method (Philadelphia: American Academy of Political and Social Science, 1974); Fernand Braudel, On History, tr. Sarah Matthews (Chicago: University of Chicago Press, 1980), pt II; Emmanuel Le Roy Ladurie, "History That Stands Still," The Mind and Method of the Historian, tr. Sian Reynolds and Ben Reynolds (Chicago: University of Chicago Press, 1981); Michel Foucault, "Why Study Power?" in Hubert L. Dreyfus and Paul Rabinow, Michel Foucault: Beyond Structuralism and Hermeneutics (Chicago: University of Chicago Press, 1982).

31 In addition to Vygostky's and Luria's work, mention may be made of Erich Fromm's Escape from Freedom (New York: Farrer and Rinehart, 1941), which offers one of the most convincing examples of how Freudian psychology may be both historicized and encultured along developmental lines – Marxified, in fact. Fromm's account, therefore, offers a fine antidote to the "structuralist" tendencies in Erik H. Erikson, Childhood and Society (New York: H. H. Norton, 1950); and Philip Rieff, Freud: The Mind of the Moralist (New York: Viking, 1969).

32 See Margaret A. Boden, Artificial Intelligence and Natural Man (New York: Basic Books, 1977).

33 See Massimo Piattelli-Palmarini (ed.), Language and Learning: The Debate between Jean Piaget and Noam Chomsky (Cambridge, Mass.: Harvard University Press, 1980); also Margolis, Science without Unity, ch. 12.

34 See for instance Pierre Bourdieu, Outline of a Theory of Practice, tr. Richard Nice (Cambridge: Cambridge University Press, 1977); Pierre Bourdieu and Jean-Claude Passeron, Reproduction in Education, Society and Culture, tr. Richard Nice (London: Sage Publications, 1977); Hans-Georg Gadamer, Truth and Method, tr. Garrétt Barden and John Cumming from 2nd German edn (New York: Seabury Press, 1975); Jürgen Habermas, Communication and the Evolution of Society, tr. Thomas McCarthy (Boston, Mass.: Beacon Press, 1979); Jürgen Habermas, Legitimation Crisis, tr. Thomas McCarthy (Boston, Mass.: Beacon Press, 1975); Mikhail Bakhtin, The Dialogic Imagination, ed. Michael Holquist, tr. Caryl Emerson and Michael Holquist (Austin: University of Texas Press, 1981); and Michel Foucault, Discipline and Punish: The Birth of the Prison, tr. Alan Sheridan (New York: Vintage Books, 1979). These are intended primarily as offering unlikely but essential lines of speculation for developmental psychology.

35 See Meredith Williams, "Wittgenstein's Rejection of Scientific Psychology," Journal for the Theory of Social Behavior, XV (1985).

36 An intriguing specimen demonstration of our theme may be found in Susan M. Easton, Humanist Marxism and Wittgensteinian Social Philosophy (Manchester: University of Manchester Press, 1983), particularly ch. 8. Easton shows a reasonable congruity between Wittgenstein and Marx, despite a fair criticism of Wittgenstein's "apolitical" and "conservative" tendencies and the absence, in Wittgenstein's work, of close attention to empirical history.

37 Ludwig Wittgenstein, Philosophical Investigations, tr. G. E. M. Anscombe (New York: Macmillan, 1954), pt I, section 292.

38 Ibid., sections 201–2.

39 Ibid., section 378.

40 Finch rightly criticizes one of the few earlier analyses of Wittgenstein's notion, in J. F. M. Hunter, "Wittgenstein's *Philosophical Investigations*," *American Philosophical Quarterly*, V (1968).

41 Henry Le Roy Finch, *Wittgenstein – the Later Philosophy: An Exposition of the "Philosophical Investigations"* (Atlantic Highlands, NJ: Humanities Press, 1977), p. 90.

42 Mention should be made, however, of Wittgenstein's speculations about "a" Robinson Crusoe, who not only is shipwrecked but who (somehow) acquires a language – "private" in a merely contingent sense – that "we" nevertheless may fathom as we would any alien language. Here Wittgenstein allows for the possibility that languages need not be acquired in a natural way, by membership and growth within a viable society. The Robinson Crusoe case, therefore, is neither to be assimilated to the issue of the private-language argument nor to the normal case of a natural language or natural culture. *How* Crusoe may have acquired his language is evidently irrelevant to Wittgenstein's concerns at this point. Cf. Ludwig Wittgenstein, *Philosophical Grammar*, tr. Anthony Kenny, ed. Rush Rhees (Berkeley, Calif.: University of California Press, 1974): "It may be all one to us whether someone else has learned the language, or was perhaps from birth constituted to react to sentences in German like a normal person who has learned it" (p. 188). I have found G. P. Baker and P. M. S. Hacker, "On Misunderstanding Wittgenstein: Kripke's Private-Language Argument," *Scepticism, Rules and Language* (Oxford: Basil Blackwell, 1984), helpful. Baker and Hacker have located in Wittgenstein's *Nachlass* a number of references to Robinson Crusoe in the context just supplied, for instance at pp. 41–2 of their essay. It is worth a moment to take note of the larger range of Wittgenstein's speculation here as compared with Marx's famous opening remarks in the *Grundrisse*; but, with respect to the normal case of acquiring a language and a culture, Wittgenstein and Marx are essentially in agreement – except that Wittgenstein always considers the matter in terms of what we are here calling his "template" for cultural or historical analysis and Marx always combines his empirical studies with his own particular form of historical materialism. Cf. Karl Marx, Introduction to *Grundrisse: Foundations to the Critique of Political Economy*, tr. Martin Nicolaus (New York: Vintage Books, 1973), particularly pp. 83–5. It is also worth adding, since the issue arises in theorizing about the relationship between the formation of the self and the mastery of a language, that Gadamer uses the Robinson Crusoe story for his own purpose – congruently with Wittgenstein's and Marx's. For, by its use, he attacks "the alleged primary phenomenon of the solus ipse": "Just as the individual is never simply an individual, but he is always involved with others, so too the closed horizon that is supposed to enclose a culture is an abstraction. The historical movement of human life consists in the fact that it is never utterly bound to any one standpoint, and hence can never have a truly closed horizon. The horizon is, rather, something into which we move and that moves with us. Horizons change for a person who is moving. Thus the horizon of the past, out of which all human life lives and which exists in the form of tradition, is always in motion. It is not historical consciousness that first sets the surrounding horizon in motion. But in it this motion becomes aware of itself" *Truth and Method*, p. 271). Chomsky, for example has never come to terms with the question.

43 See Margolis, *Science without Unity*, ch. 10.

44 See ch. 5, above.

45 See the relaxed but plausible attempt, along the lines of the sociology of knowledge, to historicize Wittgenstein's program in David Bloor, *Wittgenstein: A Social Theory of Knowledge* (London: Macmillan, 1983), particularly ch. 7. (It ignores or is unaware of Wittgenstein's speculation about the Robinson Crusoe case.) But the chief difficulty in Bloor's account rests not so much with the explicit relativism as with the failure to grasp the irreducible conceptual diference between "natural" and epistemological questions. Cf. Joseph Margolis, *Pragmatism without Foundations: Reconciling Realism and Relativism* (Oxford: Basil Blackwell, 1986), ch. 4.

46 Wittgenstein, *Philosophical Investigations*, I, section 240.

47 Ibid., section 241.

48 Cf. Finch, *Wittgenstein – the Later Philosophy*, ch. 6, which is incompatible with the thesis here challenged (and which is closer to Wittgenstein's meaning).

49 Ludwig Wittgenstein, *On Certainty*, tr. Denis Paul and G. E. M. Anscombe, ed. G. E. M. Anscombe and G. H. Von Wright (New York: Harper and Row, 1969), section 559.

50 See Saul A. Kripke, *Wittgenstein on Rules and Private Language: An Elementary Exposition* (Cambridge, Mass.: Harvard University Press, 1982). An earlier version appears, under the same title, in Irving Block (ed.), *Perspectives on the Philosophy of Wittgenstein* (Oxford: Basil Blackwell, 1981). It is subjected to what can only be called a devastating rebuttal by Baker and Hacker, (in "On Misunderstanding Wittgenstein," *Scepticism, Rules and Language*) at least as far as textual accuracy is concerned (that is, with respect to Wittgenstein's meaning). Baker and Hacker, however, also catch Kripke's intended qualification, in the amusingly titled section "Wittgenstein's argument as it struck Kripke." They therefore subject Kripke's so-called "rule-skepticism" and its would-be resolution to a criticism that goes well beyond the textual issue and exposes its inherent untenability quite apart from the Wittgensteinian texts. That view (Kripke's) is extremely fashionable, however, and so needs to be addressed with care. Other versions of the general doctrine Baker and Hacker consider are examined in "The Illusions of Rule-Skepticism," *Scepticism, Rules and Language*. They cite particularly Robert J. Fogelin, *Wittgenstein* (London: Routledge and Kegan Paul, 1976), ch. 12; Crispin Wright, *Wittgenstein on the Foundations of Mathematics* (London: Duckworth, 1980), chs 2, 12; and Christopher Peacocke, "Rule-Following: The Nature of Wittgenstein's Arguments," in S. H. Holtzman and C. M. Leich (eds), *Wittgenstein: To Follow a Rule* (London: Routledge and Kegan Paul, 1981). This is not to say, it must be added, that *this* argument undermines in the least the sort of nativism Chomsky favors. Baker and Hacker oppose Chomsky, of course, but their argument on that score, however ardent, is less than decisive. See G. P. Baker and P. M. S. Hacker, *Language, Sense and Nonsense* (Oxford: Basil Blackwell, 1984), chs. 8–9. In particular, to prefer Chomsky is to abandon altogether Wittgenstein's notion of "forms of life" though not the notion of a natural language. Baker and Hacker argue chiefly *from* or *to* the Wittgensteinian position. One may even say that their thesis represents the polar extreme that concedes no ground at all to the plausibility of Chomsky's line of theorizing. Nevertheless,

within the "Wittgensteinian" camp, Baker and Hacker have identified a number of erroneous (and independently untenable) accounts. By and large, I concur with their objections against those accounts but not quite with the conclusion they draw from them.

51 A convenient account is given in Trevor Pateman, *Language in Mind and Language in Society: Studies in Linguistic Reproduction* (Oxford: Clarendon Press, 1987), pp. 66–72 and ch. 6. See also Derek Bickerton, *Roots of Language* (Ann Arbor, Mich.: Karoma Publishers, 1981), which cites, for instance, the unusual case of creolizing in the Hawaiian Islands; Bickerton's "The Language Bioprogram Hypothesis," *Behavioral and Brain Sciences*, VII (1984), and "Peer Commentaries" section following this paper, ibid.; and Heidi Feldman, Susan Goldin-Meadow, and Lila Gleitman, "Beyond Herodotus: The Creation of Language by Linguistically Deprived Deaf Children," in Andrew Lock (ed.), *Action, Gesture and Symbol: The Emergence of Language* (London: Academic Press, 1978). These materials are cited and discussed by Pateman. Pateman, it may be noted, is particularly exercised by the Wittgensteinians, notably Baker and Hacker, and by Esa Itkoran, *Grammatical Theory and Metascience: A Critical Investigation into the Methodologies and Philosophical Foundations of "Autonomous Linguistics"* (Amsterdam: John Benjamins, 1978). I take the expressions "community agreement ," "truth-conditional rules," "assertability-condition rules" from Kripke's and Baker and Hacker's usage.

52 See Bruner, *Child's Talk*, ch. 2.

53 See for example Rachel Gelman and C. R. Gallistel, *The Childs's Understanding of Number* (Cambridge, Mass.: Harvard University Press, 1986); and Steven Pinker, *Language Learnability and Language Development* (Cambridge, Mass.: Harvard University Press, 1984), particularly ch. 9. Both of these studies are distinctly favorably disposed to nativism or innatism, but both are notably reluctant on the evidence to tip the scales toward an exclusive nativism. *Some* range of nativism seems undeniable or difficult to counter, but how much is really needed is not clear. For example, at one great extreme, recent studies of the distribution of mitochondrial DNA distinctly suggest a unique or nearly unique ancestral genetic source for the entire human race. Precisely how to map a diachronic enculturation thesis for the whole history of language acquisition is admittedly difficult, perhaps really impossible on the evidence; but the biological evidence does provide a basis for species-wide uniformities that could cut both ways. The weakness of Chomsky's position depends largely on the fact that, though he offers very reasonable grounds for admitting a more than negligible contribution of nativist processes, he is inclined to draw an exclusive and unusually strong nativism from the evidence; in fact, he shows that an exclusive enculturation thesis is probably impossible, but he usually draws the conclusion that the whole idea (even non-exclusively pursued) of the social formation and acquisition of natural language is empirically quite impossible. This is the point of his recent strong distinction between E- and I-languages. See Noam Chomsky, *Knowledge of Language: Its Nature, Origin, and Use* (New York: Praeger, 1986), particularly chs 1–2. Cf. also Margolis, *Science without Unity*, ch. 12. Bickerton's notion of the "language bioprogram" is, in this sense, indecisive but not in the least negligible. See Bickerton, "The Language Bioprogram Hypothesis," *Behavioral and Brain Sciences*, VII. In fact, in *Roots of*

Language, Bickerton had distinguished rather pointedly between what he calls the "bioprogram" (an innate predisposition for language) and the specification of "substantive universals" or "universal grammars" (ch. 5, particularly p. 298). In "The Language Bioprogram Hypothesis," Bickerton refines the argument to favor nativism but in a way that "suggests that the biological infrastructure of language may not necessarily be as complex and as extensive as some nativists [particularly Chomsky] have suggested" (p. 188). Bickerton's argument is understandably hedged, but it does suggest the possibility of incorporating an element of an entirely non-nativist cast. How specific the grammar of the "bioprogram" can really be and how fundamental we are justified in supposing its putative structure to be (on the evidence adduced) are, clearly, strenuous questions. See the "Peer Commentaries" section following Bickerton's article.

Meanwhile, biological studies are distinctly more open to the alterability of structure (hence, of function) under a variety of causal conditions (that do not, in fact, preclude the effect of "memory"-like and "learning"-like processes even at the macro-molecular level). If it were not for its bad name, *vitalism* might well be revived as the doctrine that (i) the would-be fundamenta of basic physics and the laws governing them are not demonstrably fundamental though fundamentally relevant, of course, for living processes, proto-life, and processes analogous to those of life (Leibnizianism); (ii) a general self-replicating and self-preservative function is distinctive of living processes and is sustained through open-ended changes affecting organisms, cells, macro-molecules, and populations (homeostasis, open systems, analogous processes); and (iii) emergent sub-functions of (ii) tend to be instantiated among altered or emergent structures of living systems even at the macro-molecular level and appear to involve what, functionally (metaphorically), may be described as intermolecular "recognition" and "cooperation" (allosterism). ("Allosterism" is a term not in general use, coined it seems by Mikhail V. Vol'kenshtein, *Molecules and Life: An Introduction to Molecular Biology*, tr. Serge N. Timasheff [New York: Plenum, 1970], ch. 8.) It is perhaps this combination of elements that wrongly encourages a strong progressivism and a too-sanguine view of "proto-intelligence" in biochemical and cosmic processes; but the essential puzzles clearly elude the correction. See Jacques Monod, *Chance and Necessity*, tr. Austryn Wainhouse (New York: Knopf, 1971); and Gerald M. Edelman, *Neural Darwinism* (New York: Basic Books, 1988). In the context of this larger biological world, it is hard to understand the sheer fixity of Chomsky's claims.

54 Pateman, *Language in Mind and Language in Society*, p. 132.

55 See ch. 5, above.

56 Baker and Hacker are right to press the point. They are also right to contrast Chomskyan "competence" and Wittgensteinian "ability," but their charge of "absurdity" against the former is more tendentious than it need be. Cf. *Language, Sense and Nonsense*, pp. 181–3. The truth is that Wittgenstein's emphasis is praxical, whereas Chomsky's is not. The argument in favor of Wittgenstein's orientation – which need not altogether preclude Chomsky's insistence on nativist "competence," even if it must preclude Chomsky's actual thesis – is, precisely, that it is unlikely that any theory of human cognition and intelligence could fail to be strongly praxical (in both Wittgenstein's sense and in the sense developed by Marx and similar-minded theorists). Cf. ch. 4, above.

57   Wittgenstein, *On Certainty*, sections 141, 144.
58   Ibid., sections 141, 144.
59   See for example the brief account in James M. Edie, *Edmund Husserl's Phenomenology: A Critical Commentary* (Bloomington: Indiana University Press, 1987), ch. 5.
60   For a sense of connectionism's overview, see David E. Rumelhart et al., *Parallel Distributed Processing*, 2 vols (Cambridge, Mass.: MIT Press, 1986), for instance D. E. Rumelhart and J. L. McClelland, "On Learning the Past Tenses of English Verbs," in vol. 2. See also for a more informal overview, Jerome A. Feldman, "Connections"; Carl Hewitt, "The Challenge of Open Systems"; and Geoffrey E. Hinton, "Learning in Parallel Networks" – all in *Byte*, X (April 1985).
61   See Margolis, *Science without Unity*, ch. 5.
62   Wittgenstein, *Philosophical Investigations*, pt I, section 242.
63   Ibid., pt II, p. 223e.
64   Cf. Pateman, *Language in Mind and Language in Society*, p. 139.
65   W. V. Quine, *The Roots of Reference* (LaSalle, III.: Open Court, 1973).
66   Jean Piaget, *The Language and Thought of the Child*, 3rd, rev. and enlarged edn (London: Routledge and Kegan Paul, 1971).
67   See for instance Noam Chomsky, *Rules and Representations* (New York: Columbia University Press, 1980), ch. 1.
68   Cf. Urie Bronfenbrenner, *The Ecology of Human Development: Experiments by Nature and Design* (Cambridge, Mass.: Harvard University Press, 1979); and James J. Gibson, *The Ecological Approach to Visual Perception* (Boston, Mass.: Houghton Mifflin, 1979).
69   Cf. Bronfenbrenner, *The Ecology of Human Development*, ch. 11; and A. R. Luria, *Cognitive Development: Its Cultural and Social Foundations*, tr. Martin Lopez-Morillas and Lynn Solotaroff, ed. Michael Cole (Cambridge, Mass.: Harvard University Press, 1976).
70   See Ernst Tugendhat, *Self-Consciousness and Self-Determination*, tr. Paul Stern (Cambridge, Mass.: MIT Press, 1986).
71   Bickerton, influenced by William Labov's work and Labov's emphasis on the importance of "variations" within fairly standardized languages, had in an early study of the Guyanese Creole, already stressed *individual* variations of rule-like regularities *within* the context of a socially acquired creole. This was partly directed against the "monoglot competence envisaged by Chomsky and other early generationists"; but it was also meant to accommodate idiosyncrasy within a language (or "system," as Bickerton calls the Guyanese family of somewhat improvised idioms, adjusting Labov's notion), that at "one end . . . . is indistinguishable from English." See Derek Bickerton, *Dynamics of a Creole System* (Cambridge: Cambridge University Press, 1975), pp. 166, 180. Very much the same pattern is reported in Beryl Loftman Bailey, Introduction to *Jamaican Creole Syntax: A Transformational Approach* (Cambridge: Cambridge University Press, 1966), See also William Labov, *Language in the Inner City: Studies in the Black English Vernacular* (Oxford: Basil Blackwell, 1977). Mention should also be made of a range of phenomena involving prodigies who have mastered what distinctly appear to be culturally contingent forms – for example, post-Renaissance foreshortening in drawing or particular musical forms. One thinks, here, of such talents as the autistic child artist Nadia or

Mozart or certain idiot savants. See for instance Lorna Selfe, *Nadia: A Case of Extraordinary Drawing in an Autistic Child* (New York : Academic Press, 1978); John A. Sloboda, *The Musical Mind: The Cognitive Psychology of Music* (Oxford: Clarendon Press, 1985), chs 2, 4, 6, 7.

72   See Margolis, *Science without Unity*, ch. 5; cf. in particular, Daniel C. Dennett, *Brainstorms* (Montgomery, Vt: Bradford Books, 1978).

73   Pateman, *Language in Mind and Language in Society*, p. 122.

74   See Wittgenstein, *Philosophical Investigations*, sections 143–242, particularly section 202. Cf. Baker and Hacker, "On Misunderstanding Wittgenstein," *Scepticism, Rules and Language*.

75   See Bickerton, *Dynamics of a Creole System*.

76   See Pateman, *Language in Mind and Language in Society*, pp. 67, 88–9; Bickerton, *Roots of Language*, pp. 5–6; Noam Chomsky, *Lectures on Government and Binding: The Pisa Lectures* (Dordrecht: Foris, 1981), ch. 1.

77   Pateman, *Language in Mind and Language in Society*, p. 133.

78   Ibid., p. 105.

79   Chomsky, *Lectures on Government and Binding*, p. 3.

80   Cf. Chomsky, *Rules and Representations*, ch. 1.

81   Chomsky, *Lectures on Government and Binding*, p. 3.

82   As remarked by Bruner and Mead.

83   Chomsky, *Rules and Representations*, p. 6.

84   Ibid., pp. 188–9.

85   See above, ch. 8.

86   Wittgenstein, *Philosophical Investigations*, pt II, p. 223e.

87   See Joseph Margolis, *Culture and Cultural Entities* (Dordrecht: D. Reidel, 1984), ch. 3.

88   Cf. Chomsky, *Rules and Representations*, ch. 2, particularly the fretting about "cognizing" – which Chomsky's strong nativism requires (p. 70). Chomsky pretty well needs, as already argued, a tacit "cognizing" of a uniquely idealized, uniform, species-wide set of universals. The accommodation of closely related "variations" or "linguistic variables" of a "common" language or language-like "system" (in Bickerton's sense, following Labov) may not (and seems not to) require the "cognizing" *of* an ideal set of rules. But to admit that would entail a significant modification of nativist assumptions. See for instance William Labov, "On the Mechanism of Linguistic Change," in John J. Gumperz and Dell Hymes (eds), *Directions in Sociolinguistics*, corr. with additions (Oxford: Basil Blackwell, 1986). See also the extremely sensible and compelling discussion in Henning Wode, "Some Theoretical Implications of L2 [that is, second-language] Acquisition Research and the Grammar of Interlanguages," in Alan Davies, C. Criper, and A. P. R. Howatt (eds), *Interlanguage* (Edinburgh: Edinburgh University Press, 1984). It may be useful to mention here, also, that the intriguing study (mentioned by Pateman of "linguistically deprived" deaf children, who, in effect, invent their own primitive signing, is hardly decisive. In the study reported in Feldman et al., "Beyond Herodotus" (in Lock (ed.), *Action Gesture and Symbol*), motivated along mildly Chomskyan lines, it is clear that there was, inevitably, a strong interpretive overlay probably impossible to discount; there was some lip-reading; there was some independent signing by parents said to have been opposed to any signing at all; there was

even some instructional signing that the parents used; and there was the difficulty of monitoring the entire sequence of communicatin involving a number of children ranging in age from 17 to 49 months (at the first interview) and 30–54 months (at the last). But it does support an improvisational language-like capacity and a fair basis for some nativism. The authors worry some about the possible structural differences between communication by verbal language and communication by primitive signing.

89 Wittgenstein, *Philosophical Investigations*, pt II, p. 226e.

90 See Margolis, *Science without Unity*, ch. 12.

91 Pateman, following Roy Bhaskar here, fails to come to terms with the problem though he mentions it. Cf. Pateman, *Language in Mind and Language in Society*, ch. 3. See Roy Bhaskar, *The Possibility of Naturalism* (Brighton: Harvester Press, 1979); and Margolis, *Science without Unity*, ch. 10.

92 See ch. 4, above.

93 One of the best versions of this conception of *praxis* – also, a fair candidate for a historicized formulation of Wittgenstein's template – appears in Pierre Bourdieu's notion of *habitus*: "The habitus, the durably installed generative principle of regulated improvisations, produces practices which tend to reproduce the regularities immanent in the objective conditions of the production of their generative principle, while adjusting to the demands inscribed as objective potentialities in the situation, as defined by the cognitive and motivating structures making up the habitus" – *Outline of a Theory of Practice*, p. 78; cf. further pp. 78–95.

94 There is a suggestive anticipation of the point in Isabel C. Hungerland, "Once Again, Aesthetic and Non-Aesthetic," *Journal of Aesthetics and Art Criticism*, XXVI (1968). In a larger sense, it accords with Hegel's notion of *"Erscheinungen"* without the encumbrance of Hegel's particular philosophical system. See for instance G. W. F. Hegel, Introduction to *Phenomenology of Spirit*, tr. A. V. Miller (Oxford: Oxford University Press, 1977).

95 See ch. 8, above.

96 Monroe C. Beardsley, *The Possibility of Criticism* (Detroit: Wayne State University Press, 1970), p. 36 (italics added).

97 See ch. 7, above.

98 See Gadamer, *Truth and Method*, pt II, I, section 2.

99 Ibid., pp. 275, 304. For a recent account, quite sympathetic with the argument here developed – oriented largely in tems of Gadamerian hermeneutics but drawn rather in the Nietzschean direction (against both Husserl and Gadamer) and strongly committed to a *"communicative praxis,"* see Calvin O. Schrag, *Communication, Praxis, and the Space of Subjectivity* (Bloomington: Indiana University Press, 1986), particularly chs 2, 6, 9.

100 This single theme – which amounts to the *realism* of Intentionality, the reality of persons, history, art, human actions and deeds, conscious states, institutions, cultures – is clearly becoming the decisive *champ de bataille* for the whole of Western philosophy. At the point of concluding this volume, there has just appeared a new book by Daniel Dennett, in which , rather too easily in his pleasantly relaxed way, Dennett counts himself among "the most wholehearted Quineians" on the intentionality score: that is, he holds, as he has always held from his very first publications, "one will not be inclined to be a (strict) realist

about attributions of propositional attitude, and hence will not be inclined to be a Realist about psychological content (genuine or intrinsic intentionality)" – Daniel C. Dennett, *The Intentional Stance* (Cambridge, Mass.: MIT Press, 1987), p. 345; cf. also ch. 8. Unfortunately, this is a tired melody that Dennett has never vindicated but that has become familiar merely by being endlessly whistled. See Margolis, *Science without Unity*, ch. 5. I may perhaps be permitted to say that, although there may be no Mozart of intentionality, there are always more than enough dismissive Salieris.

101   On the notion of "the historical determination of the meaning of being in general as *presence*," see Jacques Derrida, *Of Grammatology*, tr. Gayatri Spivak Chakravorty (Baltimore: Johns Hopkins University Press, 1976). "The End of the Book and the Beginning of Writing," particularly p. 12. This suggests the crux of the principal philosophical dispute of the day: whether metaphysics, second-order legitimation, and the like can be pursued without succumbing to the philosophy of presence. Our own effort has been premissed on the belief that we can separate the two. Derrida's view seems to be that we can't but that, since we can't avoid the "phonocentric" or the "logocentric," we must be forever (deconstructively) on guard against its intrusion. Others, the so-called post-modernists, Richard Rorty for instance, claim that we can and should avoid legi-timative philosophy altogether. See for instance Richard Rorty, *Consequences of Pragmatism* (Minneapolis: University of Minnesota, 1982), Introduction: "Pragmatism and Philosophy."

Epilogue

One final, uneasy word.

It is reassuring, writing about what is plainly a fragment of a fragment of a topic, to suppose there is somewhere a totality or at least a conceptual beginning that assembles all relevant contributions. That way one may enjoy the security of one's own splinter of thought. The gathering achievement of human scholarship ensures one one's place in the Great Inquiry. Such a confidence is now utterly lost – on the argument of this trilogy or on other arguments favored in our own time. It is not simply the infinitude of distinctions that could be generated that no one could exhaust, or the possibility that another might discover a principle of order so powerful that one's own small finding would, in time, seem ever smaller and smaller. The innocence of that maneuver is now forever subverted; its calculations make no sense.

We live in a world in which the structures we discern we treat as historical constructions made by entities (ourselves) that are also somehow historically constructed. The fixities we think we have found rest on the slow pace of conceptual change we claim, retrospectively, to have discerned as such. The fortunes and influence of any theory are the sport of that perception – and of fresh possibilities that, at a later time, will seem external to or ignored within the scope of the other. Even what is remembered is remembered in a skewed way we cannot fully monitor, being ourselves creatures of that same process.

Our best thought is transient, risked in the extreme. And yet we press on in the direction of closure and invariance and universality. The effort is not illegitimate, though what it finds is doomed to be replaced – discontinuously and incommensurably. We content ourselves with the saliencies of our perceived world that serve us as the best depictions of what we imagine are the underlying fixities of the real world.

Disputes remain entirely dialectical as before. Ultimately, it is the perceived slowness of conceptual change and the perceived need for slow conceptual change that yield a semblance of the stable order of debate. We work within that semblance, but the entire project threatens to explode at any moment. Our best skill lies in the persuasive recovery of the contours of a moving contest fixed within that flux.

Even so, there are at least two important signs of the inherent insufficiency of what these books have assembled. First of all, there is in them a kind of planetary illiteracy. The work collected ranges only through the English-speaking world and through the fringe of Western Europe. There may in time be a planetary forum, though there is none yet. It would not, of course, ensure totality or originary source, though it would probably appear to. Its virtue would simply be that it would not harbor an incompleteness by exclusion or by sheer ignorance of what others might claim. But it would remain incompletable as before – and for essentially the same reasons.

Secondly, these books have said nothing in the way of an analysis of the deliberate conduct and activity of man: as artist, agent, sexual and political creature, hankerer after local and cosmic meanings, site of inner sensibilities and powers, the mortal source of these and similar reflections. No story could be complete without touching these matters. They would still defy closure and invariant truth, of course, but their incompleteness would have been responsibly earned.

There is a clear need to extend our study to the entire range of practical life. It cannot be done here. It is almost not worth mentioning since it invites an entirely new beginning. But it raises a question that cannot be ignored. It is a question that addresses what is quintessentially human, a question that admits that an inquiry like that of these books must affect in a profound way every account of rational purpose and commitment the least bit attracted to their findings. The irony remains that in bringing our own large effort to a close we have implicitly challenged all the conventional dogmas of what is normative in the human world, we have uncovered what may be the principal conceptual lacuna of our age, and we have simply turned the inquiry off at its most decisive moment. The fact is that there *is* no sustained vision of human life reconciled with the master-themes we have sought to put into coherent order; and yet those same themes are bound to generate the commanding puzzles of our entire future. We can make this second limitation good by a further effort. But the first insufficiency is in the bone, the endless charm of the human condition itself.

Index